MILITARY Living's ™

Temporary Military Lodging

Around the World

by

Lela Ann Crawford
and
William "Roy" Crawford, Sr., Ph.D.

Editor: Marilyn Depew
Cover Design: Russ Brown
Editorial Assistant: Sheryl Usener

Vice President - Marketing: William R. Crawford, Jr.
Sales Manager - Arno "Jack" Frost
Chief of Staff - Anna Bell Causey

Office Staff:
Eula Mae Brownlee, Irene Kearney, Tom Hogan, Tony Hortert,
Rose McLain, Michelle Rasberry,
Nigel Fellers, Lourdes Medina, Kenneth Slater.

Military Living Publications
P. O. Box 2347
Falls Church, Virginia 22042-0347
TEL: (703) 237-0203
FAX: (703) 237-2233

NOTICE

The information in this book has been compiled and edited either from the activity/installation listed, its superior headquarters, or from other sources that may or may not be noted by the authors. Information about the facilities listed, including contact phone numbers and rate structures, could change. This book should be used as a guide to the listed facilities with this understanding. Please forward any corrections or additions to: **Military Living Publications, P. O. Box 2347, Falls Church, Virginia 22042-0347.**

This directory is published by Military Marketing Services, Inc., a private business in no way connected with the U.S. Federal or any other government. This book is copyrighted by Lela Ann and William Roy Crawford, Sr. Opinions expressed by the publisher and authors of this book are their own and are not to be considered an official expression by any government agency or official.

The information and statements contained in this directory have been compiled from sources believed to be reliable and to represent the best current opinion on the subject. No warranty, guarantee, or representation is made by Military Marketing Services, Inc., as to the absolute correctness or sufficiency of any representation contained in this or other publications and we can assume no responsibility.

Library of Congress Cataloging-in-Publication Data

Crawford, Ann Caddell.
    Temporary military lodging around the world / by Lela Ann Crawford
and William 'Roy' Crawford, Sr.
    p. cm.
    Rev. ed. of: Military living's temporary military lodging around
the world / by William 'Roy' Crawford, Sr., and Lela Ann Crawford.
c1990.
    ISBN 0-914862-32-4 : $10.95
    1. United States--Armed Forces--Barracks and quarters-
-Directories. 2. Military bases, American--Directories.
    I. Crawford, William Roy, 1932-   . II. Crawford, William Roy,
1932- Military living's temporary military lodging around the
world. III. Title.
UC403.C72   1992
355.7'025'73--dc20
                                                    92-16055
                                                        CIP

ISBN 0-914-862-32-4

ii

INTRODUCTION

This book will pay for itself many times over. All you have to do is use it! There are places to stay on military installations for as little as $4 or $5 per night. The most common charges we found quoted were in the $25-$35 price range for a family of five sharing one unit in a transient lodging facility, or $30-$35 for a Navy Lodge unit, many of which have sleeping space for five, wall-to-wall carpeting, color TV, kitchenette with all utensils, and more. Since our last edition, inflation has caused some military lodging prices to increase; however, they have not increased to the same degree or at the same rate as prices in the civilian sector. In some large cities, the cost of lodging has risen to $200 per night, or more. Clearly, *Temporary Military Lodging Around the World* can greatly reduce the high cost of travel experienced by military families.

Before the first edition of this book was published in 1971, there was a big "catch" involved in getting to use temporary lodging facilities. The problem was finding out which installation had what. Military Living Publications has solved that problem by doing the leg work for you. Just glance through the hundreds of listings that follow and you will find out why this book is indispensable if you want to "travel on less per day...the military way."

Ann & Roy Crawford

AREA VOICE CODES FOR THE DEFENSE SWITCHED NETWORK (DSN) TELEPHONE SYSTEM

CONUS - 312	ALASKA - 317
EUROPE - 314	PACIFIC - 315

CARIBBEAN - 313

STANDARD EMERGENCY & SERVICE NUMBERS FROM ALL ARMY DIAL TELEPHONES IN GERMANY

EMERGENCY	DDD*	ETS**
Engineer	91	115
Fire	95	117
Ambulance/Hospital/Clinic	97	116
Military Police	98	114

SERVICE		
Operator	0	0 or 1110
European DSN	314 or thru 112	
CONUS DSN	312	
Booking	90	112

Information	92	113
Telephone Repair	96	119
Civilian Access	99	99

Note: * The Direct Distance Dial (DDD) system (also known as the Military system) is being replaced with the new ** European Telephone System (ETS). This replacement has been completed in most military communities.

HOW TO USE THIS DIRECTORY

Each listing has similar information, listed in the following order:

Name of Installation (AL01R2)
Street/PO Box (if required)
City/APO/FPO, State, ZIP Code

TELEPHONE NUMBER INFORMATION: C- This is the commercial telephone service for the installation's main or information/operator assistance number, the designation has also been used for other commercial numbers in this directory, including the number to be called for billeting reservations. Within the U.S. Area Code System, the first three digits are the area code. For foreign country locations, we have provided full telephone numbers from the U.S. and in-country. The first two digits, after direct dial long distance, are the Country Code (consult your local directory or operator for specific dialing instructions). The next three digits are the area telephone exchange/switch number. For foreign countries, the exchange number can be either fewer or more digits than in the U.S. system. The last four digits are usually the information or operator assistance number. In the United Kingdom (UK), dialing instructions are given from the telephone exchange serving the installation. These numbers are different for each location in the UK from which you are dialing. Consult the local directory or operator for specific dialing instructions.

D- This is the Department of Defense, worldwide, Defense Switched Network (DSN). We have, at the request of our readers, included the DSN prefix with most numbers in each listing. In most cases, the number given is for information/operator assistance.

ETS: This is the European Telephone System. ETS prefixes for military communities are the same as DSN prefixes. The ETS system has now largely supplanted the old Direct Distance Dial (DDD) or military system once used throughout Germany (see Mil below).

FTS: This is the Federal Telephone System. The number given is for information/operator assistance. On smaller installations the information/operator assistance number may be the contact number for Temporary Military Lodging.

Location Identifier: Example (AL01R2). The first two characters (letters) are Country/State abbreviations used in Military Living's books (Appendix A). The next two characters are random numbers (00-99) assigned to a specific location. The fifth character is an R indicating region and the sixth character is the region number.

Location: Specific driving instructions to the installation from local major cities, interstate highways and routes are given. More than one routing may be provided. **USM:** is **MILITARY LIVING'S** *"US Military Installation Road Map"* reference to the location. **HE:** is the Hallwag Europe Road Atlas reference to the location. **NMC:** is the nearest major city. The distance in miles and direction from the installation to the NMC are given where possible.

Billeting Office: The attention line (ATTN:), building number, etc., are for your information and can be added to the address when writing to the billeting office. The C-, D-/ETS, and/or FTS telephone numbers of the billeting office are given where provided to us. **We have "bolded" (darkened) reservation numbers for the convenience of our readers - this should help, particularly when making expensive overseas calls.** Hours of operation of the billeting office, main desk, or contact office are listed. Check in/check out points and times are given. Use of Temporary Military Lodging (TML) by government civilian employees on duty is specified. Other helpful general billeting information is detailed.

TML: Each category of TML, i.e., Guest House, Hotel, Army/Navy/Air Force/Marine Corps Lodge, and so on, is listed separately in most cases. The category of occupancy, i.e. all ranks, specific grades, officer, enlisted, male, female, is given. Occupancy by leave or duty status is given. Reservation requirements and some contact telephone numbers are listed. The accommodations (bedroom, two bedroom, three bedroom, separate bedroom, suite), and amount of each category of accomodation is given last in parenthesis. Appointments, services and supporting facilities such as kitchens, utensils, television, air conditioning, maid service, cribs, cots, washer/dryer, ice, vending machines, handicapped facilities, etc., are given where they were provided to us. Where there is a charge for services it is noted, otherwise it is free. Whether the structure is older or modern, its condition, and if renovations or improvements have taken place since 1990 are specified. The per day rates are listed for each category of occupant. Please note that rates can change often. Priorities and restrictions on occupancy are listed. **NOTE:** Pets are not allowed in temporary lodging facilities unless otherwise noted, but for the convenience of our readers we have noted where kennel facilities are available. Also, all facilities are open to men and women unless otherwise noted.

DV/VIP: The contact office or person, building, room and telephone number for DV/VIP lodging and other support is given where available. The grade/status for DV/VIPs at the installation is specified. The use of DV/VIP facilities/services by retirees and lower grades is indicated.

TML Availability: The best and most difficult times for TML are listed as reported. If possible, call or write regarding availability before you travel or take your chances on space-available use.

☞ Points of interest for visitors are indicated. Some listings carry military information of interest to visitors such as famous units stationed, or on post/base military museums.

Post/base/station locator, medical emergency and police telephone numbers are provided where available. Other Military Living publications carry many support facility telephone numbers

☺ ☹ are used on listings that are closing or expanding in some manner, "inside information" may also be included here.

Please review Appendix A, Country and State Abbreviations, and Appendix B, General Abbreviations. Also read the other appendices and the questions and answers about TML that supplement the basic TML listings.

A Few Words About Telephone Systems in Germany

Each of the commercial/civilian telephone numbers at the top of all listings in Germany follow the same pattern. When dialing from the USA, the first set of digits is the international access, 011, the second set of digits is the country code (49 in Germany). The third set of digits is the local area civilian prefix. The next set of digits is the civilian-to-military conversion code. The last set of digits is the line number/extension (or a set of Xs indicating line number/extension). Telephone calls originating on civilian instruments and terminating on military instruments require the conversion code. Telephone calls originating and terminating on civilian instruments do not require the conversion code. Commercial-to-commercial or commercial-to-military telephone calls originating and terminating in the same local area do not generally require the use of the civilian prefix either. Also, local area civilian prefixes all begin with a "0". The "0" is only used in-country. Drop the "0" if dialing from outside the country.

Some Words About Our Changing World

The military is undergoing sweeping changes which have made this book both challenging and interesting to publish. Some installations are closing, and others are realigning. We have included the dates of expected closure as provided to us in the Table of Contents, and in the body of each listing. Installations which will close prior to 30 Sep '92 have been excluded from this book. The information in this book is as accurate as we can make it. It has been provided by billeting facilities worldwide. However, as with all directories, there are changes that happen daily that cause inacuracies. **Military Living Publications** has always relied on its readers to write or call when information has become outdated. It is the secret of our success. Please do not hesitate to let us know when information in incorrect, or if we have missed a lodging opportunity for your fellow travelers. Enjoy.

Our Covers:
Front Cover: Armed Forces Recreation Center (AFRC) Hale Koa Hotel, Honolulu, HI (*photo courtesy Hale Koa Hotel*).
Back Cover: Top right, Navy Lodge Registration Desk, Staten Island, NY; center left, Navy Lodge, Key West, FL; center right, Navy Lodge guest unit, Staten Island, NY (*photos courtesy Navy Lodge Program*); bottom left, Lakeside Hall, Fort Ritchie, MD; bottom right, Terrace Deck, Lakeside Hall, Fort Ritchie, MD (*photos courtesy MWR Fort Ritchie*).

UNITED STATES

California, continued

COLORADO

CONNECTICUT

DELAWARE

DISTRICT OF COLUMBIA

FLORIDA

GEORGIA

Georgia, continued

HAWAII

IDAHO

ILLINOIS

INDIANA

IOWA

NONE

KANSAS

KENTUCKY

LOUISIANA

MAINE

MARYLAND

MASSACHUSETTS

MICHIGAN

MINNESOTA

MISSISSIPPI

MISSOURI

MONTANA

NEBRASKA

NEVADA

NEW HAMPSHIRE

NEW JERSEY

OKLAHOMA

OREGON

PENNSYLVANIA

RHODE ISLAND

SOUTH CAROLINA

SOUTH DAKOTA

TENNESSEE

TEXAS

Texas, continued

UTAH

VERMONT

NONE

VIRGINIA

Virginia, continued

WASHINGTON

WEST VIRGINIA

NONE

WISCONSIN

WYOMING

UNITED STATES POSSESSIONS

GUAM

MIDWAY ISLAND

PUERTO RICO

FOREIGN COUNTRIES

ANTIGUA

AUSTRALIA

BELGIUM

BERMUDA

CANADA

CUBA

GERMANY

Germany, continued

GREECE

HONG KONG

ICELAND

ITALY

JAPAN

KOREA

NETHERLANDS

PANAMA

PORTUGAL

SPAIN

TURKEY

UNITED KINGDOM

APPENDICES

NOTE: Base closures are listed in the President's FY 1992 budget. Some bases scheduled for closure or realignment do not have TML and consequently are not listed in this book. Where available, we have placed a date in parenthesis in the Table of Contents.

INFO ON MILITARY LIVING

MILITARY LIVING PUBLICATIONS
(MILITARY MARKETING SERVICES, INC.)

Military Living was founded in 1969. The company publishes **Military Living**, a 30,000-copy circulation monthly magazine distributed on more than twenty military installations in the Washington, D.C. area.

Our travel newsletter, Military Living's **R&R Space-A Report**, has been published since 1971 and is available worldwide by subscription.

Military Living currently publishes seven travel guides and is researching additional titles to improve the quality of life for military personnel and their families. See Central Order Coupons at the back of this book.

HOW TO RECOGNIZE MILITARY LIVING'S BOOKS

All of Military Living's books carry the famous Military Living logo. Military Living is known as "The Morale Booster Publisher." The slogan, "Travel on Less Per Day...The Military Way," is copyrighted by Military Living. Ann Crawford, the founder of Military Living, is a well-known travel writer whose articles reach military families around the world. The president of the parent company, Military Marketing Services, Inc., is William "Roy" Crawford, Sr., Ph.D.

Corporate offices are located at 137 North Washington Street, Suite 201, Falls Church, Virginia 22046-4515. The corporate mailing address is P. O. Box 2347, Falls Church, Virginia 22042-0347. The telephone number is (703) 237-0203. Our FAX number is (703) 237-2233.

-NOTES-

UNITED STATES

Alabama

Dauphin Island Recreational Complex (AL07R2)
Mobile Coast Guard Base
Mobile, AL 36615-1390

TELEPHONE NUMBER INFORMATION: Main installation numbers: C-205-690-2240, FTS-537-2240.

Location: Off base. On the Gulf of Mexico approximately 40 miles south of Mobile. I-10 to AL-193 (Exit 17). South approximately 35 miles to Dauphin Island. Left at dead end to east end of island. Follow signs to complex. NMI: Mobile CG Base, 40 miles north. USM: J-7. NMC: Mobile, 40 miles north.

Billeting Office: None. Reservations required, by application only, with advance payment. Summer (1 May-30 Sep): up to 60 days in advance for active CG; up to 30 days, all others. Fall/winter (1 Oct-30 Apr): 15-30 days in advance. Address: Dauphin Island Recreational Complex, PO Box 436, Dauphin Island, AL 36528-0436. C-**205-861-7113**.

TML: TLF. Three bedroom cottages, private bath (13). Bedding and linens provided. Seven day maximum stay for cottages during summer. Rates: weekend (F afternoon-Su afternoon) $45-$75; weekly (Su afternoon-F afternoon) $55-$100. Reservations as outlined above.

☞ **Gulf beaches, visits to historic Fort Gaines and Mobile, serious bird watching, wading for flounder and crab at night, or deep sea fishing are all a part of the simple, unhurried relaxation that is Dauphin Island.**

Fort McClellan (AL01R2)
Fort McClellan, AL 36205-5000

TELEPHONE NUMBER INFORMATION: Main installation numbers: C-205-848-4611, D-312-865-1110.

Location: Nine miles north of I-20. Take AL-21 north to fort. Also located 25 miles southeast of I-59. Take US-431 to fort. USM: K-6. NMC: Anniston, 3 miles southeast.

Billeting Office: Building 3295, 14th Street & Summerall Road, 24 hours daily. C-**205-848-4338/3546**, D-314-865-4338/3546. Check in billeting, check out 1000 hours.

TML: Fort McClellan Lodge. Building 3127, all ranks, leave or official duty. Check in at lodge. Handicapped accessible. C-EX-4916. Rooms, two double beds/queen size sofa sleeper, private bath (50). A/C, cribs, essentials, ice vending, kitchenette, complete utensils, maid service, special facilities for DAVs, color TV in room & lounge, coin washer/dryer. New structure. Rates: $31.50 per night. Maximum 6 persons. DAVs (hospital patients) and dependents, and PCS can make reservations, others Space-A.

ALABAMA
Fort McClellan, continued

TML: VEQ. Buildings 269, 937, 938, 940, 941, 943-946, enlisted, all ranks, official duty only. C-EX-4338. Rooms, private and semi-private baths (640); three bedroom cottage, private bath (1). A/C, essentials, ice vending, maid service, refrigerator, color TV, washer/dryer. Modern structures. Rates: $10 per person. Maximum 1 per room.

TML: VOQ. Buildings 2275-2277, 3133, 3134, 3136, 3137, officers all ranks, official duty only, C-EX-4338. Bedroom, private bath (187); bedroom, semi-private bath (80). A/C, community kitchen, essentials, refrigerator, kitchenette (some units), color TV in room & lounge, washer/dryer, ice vending. Older structures. Renovated '90. Rates: $10 per person. Maximum 1 per room.

TML: DV/VIP. Buildings 57, 300, 900, 1026, leave or official duty, officers 06+. Bedroom, private bath (4); two bedroom, private bath (5); three bedroom cottages, private bath (3). A/C, essentials, ice vending, kitchenette, complete utensils, maid service, refrigerator, color TV, washer/dryer. Older structures, remodeled. Rates: sponsor $19, adult $12, child/infant $3. Duty can make reservations. Retirees, lower ranks Space-A.

DV/VIP: Protocol, USACML+MPCEN+FM, C-EX-5616, 06+, GS-13+. Retirees and lower ranks Space-A.

TML Availability: Best Nov-Dec. Difficult, other times.

☞ **For military history buffs, trace the history of women in the Army in building 1077, the role of chemical and biological weapons in building 2299, and the history of the military police corps in building 3182.**

Locator 848-3795   **Medical 848-2345**   **Police 848-5555**

Fort Rucker (AL02R2)
Fort Rucker, AL 36362-5000

TELEPHONE NUMBER INFORMATION: Main installation numbers: C-205-255-6181, D-312-558-1110.

Location: Ninety miles southeast of Montgomery, midway between the capital city and Florida Gulf Coast, and 7 miles south of Ozark, off US-231 on AL-249. Clearly marked. USM: K-7. NMC: Dothan, 22 miles southeast.

Billeting Office: Building 308, 6th Ave, C-205-598-3780, 24 hours daily. Reservations: C-**205-598-5216**. All travelers report to billeting. Check out 1100 hours daily. Government civilian employee billeting in VOQ.

TML: Guest House, building 124, all ranks, leave or official duty, 0600-2200 daily. C-205-598-6352, D-312-558-4432. Two double beds, sofa bed, private bath (36). Kitchen, maid service. Rates: $27 per unit. Official PCS orders, all others Space-A.

TML: VOQ/VEQ/DVQ. Building 308, officer all ranks, enlisted E7-E9. Bedroom, private bath (355); two bedroom cottages, semi-private bath (2); three bedroom cottages (3 are DVQ), semi-private bath (5); four bedroom cottages (1 is DVQ), semi-private bath (3); separate bedroom DVQ suites, private bath (2). Kitchen (50%), refrigerator, A/C, color TV, maid service, washer/dryer, ice vending. Modern structure, renovated. Rates: sponsor $20, others $4. Duty can make reservations. Others Space-A.

ALABAMA

Fort Rucker, continued

DV/VIP: ATTN: Protocol, building 114 (Post Hq). C-EX-3100, D-EX-3400. 06/GS-15+. Retirees and lower ranks one night only.

TML Availability: Best, Oct-Apr. Limited, May-Sep.

☞ **"Dixie's Heartland"** is sprinkled with fine fresh water fishing, Landmark Park has sixty acres of shady nature trails and boardwalks, picnic sites and historic restorations. Waterworld in Dothan is good family entertainment.

Locator 255-6181   Medical 255-7900   Police 255-4175

Gunter Air Force Base (AL04R2)
Gunter AFB, AL 36114-5000

TELEPHONE NUMBER INFORMATION: Main installation numbers: C-205-416-1110, D-312-596-1110.

Location: Take I-65 to Northern bypass, 6 miles to exit on AL-231, continue west 1 mile to AFB. Coming from the opposite direction, from I-85, follow signs and take eastern bypass north 1 mile to AL-231. Then west 1 mile to AFB. USM: J-6. NMC: Montgomery, 2 miles southwest.

Billeting Office: ATTN: Gunter billeting, building 1503, 24 hours daily, C-**205-416-3360/4611.**

TML: VAQ. Buildings 1014-101, enlisted all ranks, leave or official duty. Check in at billeting. Separate bedroom, semi-private bath (247); suites, private bath (4). Refrigerator, A/C, color TV, maid service, washer/dryer. DAV facilities, modern structure. Check out 1200 hours daily. Rates: $6 per person. Duty can make reservations, others Space-A.

TML: VOQ. Buildings 301, 314, 315, 872 & 1503, officers all ranks, leave or official duty. Handicapped accessible. Buildings 301-315: suites with private bath (33). Building 1503: rooms with semi-private bath (Airmen can also use this facility) (69). Building 872: rooms, private bath (40), suites (4). Refrigerator, A/C, color TV, maid service, cribs & cots, washer/dryer, DAV facilities, older buildings. Check out 1200 hours daily. Rates: $5 per person (rooms); $10 per person (suites). Duty can make reservations, others Space-A.

TML: TLF. Building 200, all ranks, leave or official duty. Two bedroom, private bath (3); three bedroom apartment, private bath (1). Kitchen, utensils, A/C, color TV, maid service, cribs & cots, washer/dryer. Modern structure. Check out 1200 hours daily. Rates: $17 per person. Maximum $17 per family. Duty can make reservations, others Space-A.

DV/VIP: See Maxwell AFB listing.

TML Availability: Good, except for enlisted quarters (SNCOA expansion).

ALABAMA
Gunter Air Force Base, continued

☞ Visit Oak Park's W.A. Gayle Planetarium, the Montgomery Zoo, the state capital building, where Jefferson Davis took oath of office as President of the Confederate States of America.

Locator 416-1110   Medical 416-4211   Police 416-4250

Maxwell Air Force Base (AL03R2)
Maxwell AFB, AL 36112-5000

TELEPHONE NUMBER INFORMATION: Main installation numbers: C-205-953-1110, D-312-493-1110.

Location: Take I-85 South to I-65, exit on Day St which leads to main gate of base. USM: J-6,7. NMC: Montgomery, 1.5 miles southeast.

Billeting Office: 3800 ABW/SVH, building 157, West Drive, C-205-953-2401, 24 hours daily. Check in billeting, check out 1200 hours. Government civilian employee billeting.

TML: TLF. Buildings 46-49, all ranks, leave or official duty. Bedroom apartments, private bath (30). Kitchen, limited utensils, A/C, color TV, housekeeping service, cribs/cots, washer/dryer, ice vending. Modern structure. Rates: $20 per apartment. Maximum 5 persons. Duty can make reservations, others Space-A.

TML: VAQ. Building 695, enlisted all ranks, leave or official duty. SNCO suites, private bath (6); single rooms, shared bath (38); double rooms, shared bath (24). Rates: $6-$10 per person, maximum $20.

TML: VOQ. Buildings 1412-1419, 1428, 1429, 1430-1434, 1468, 1470, all ranks, leave or official duty. Bedroom, semi-private bath (816); separate bedroom, private bath (342); Suites with kitchenette, private bath (99). Kitchen, A/C, color TV, housekeeping service, cribs/cots, washer/dryer, ice vending. Modern and older structures. Complete renovations in process 1412-1419, 1430-1434. Rates: sponsor $6, adult $6, maximum charge $12. Maximum 3 persons per unit. Duty can make reservations, others Space-A.

TML: Chief Suites. Building 697, enlisted to E-9, leave or official duty. Separate bedrooms, private bath (5). A/C, essentials, ice vending, housekeeping service, refrigerator, color TV, washer/dryer, wet bar, microwave. Renovated. Rates: sponsor $10, adult $10, maximum charge $20. Maximum 3 persons per unit. Duty can make reservations, others Space-A.

TML: DVQ. Buildings 117, 121, 142, 143, 157. Bedroom, private bath, shared kitchenette (84). Rates: sponsor $10, $10 adult, maximum $20.

DV/VIP: AU Protocol Office, building 800. C-EX-2095. 07+. Retirees Space-A.

TML Availability: Extremely limited year-round.

Maxwell Air Force Base, continued

☞ Nearby Montgomery brings Old-South charm and New-South dazzle to visitors with its history, theater, museums and recreational opportunities.

Locator 953-5027   **Medical 953-2333**   **Police 953-2766**

Redstone Arsenal (AL06R2)
Redstone Arsenal, AL 35809-5099

TELEPHONE NUMBER INFORMATION: Main installation numbers: C-205-876-2151, D-312-746-0011.

Location: Off US-231 South on Martin Rd to main gate with visitor control. For uniformed personnel, Gate 8 is on Drake Ave. Take US-72 East to Jordan Lane, south to Drake. Drake becomes Goss Road at the Arsenal. USM: J-6. NMC: Huntsville, adjacent north and east sides.

Billeting Office: ATTN: AMSMI-RA-EH-HM-BH, building 244, Goss Rd, C-205-876-5713/8028, 24 hours daily. Check in facility, check out 1100 hours daily. Government civilian employee billeting.

TML: The Trail Blazer. Building 244, all ranks, leave or official duty. C-205-837-4130. Bedroom, private bath (17); bedroom, kitchen, private bath (4). Refrigerator, community kitchen, limited utensils, A/C, color TV, maid service, cribs, coin washer/dryer, ice vending. Modern structure, renovated. Rates based on BAQ. Duty can make reservations, others Space-A.

TML: VOQ/VEQ. Buildings 131-136, 55, 60, 62, all ranks, official duty only. Bedrooms, private bath (17); Two bedroom, semi-private bath (74). Three bedroom cottages fully equipped (3). All units have color TV, A/C and maid service, other amenities. Rates: $15 per person. Duty can make reservations. Duty on leave Space-A. Check with billeting for availability.

TML: DVQ. Buildings 56, 58. Field grade and General Officers. Decorated and fully equipped 3 bedroom cottages. Rates: sponsor $15, $5 each additional person, maximum $25 per family. Duty can make reservations, others Space-A.

DV/VIP: Contact billeting office. 06+. Retirees and lower ranks Space-A.

TML Availability: Very good, Nov-Feb. More difficult, other times.

☞ Visit the Alabama Space & Rocket Center, I-565 West of Huntsville.

Locator 876-3331   **Medical 876-5780**   **Police 876-2222**

Alaska

Adak Naval Air Station (AK04R5)
FPO AP 98791-5000

TELEPHONE NUMBER INFORMATION: Main installation numbers: C-907-592-8001, D-317-692-8001.

Location: On Adak Island of the Aleutian Island chain, accessible only by air or ship. USM: A-9. NMC: Anchorage, 1200 air miles northeast. Note: Closed Station, only assigned personnel and cleared/sponsored guests are allowed on base. Write to Commander for clearance.

Billeting Office: Housing Office, C-**907-592-8604, 4226**, D-317-692-8604, FAX-907-592-8604/4134, 0800-1700 hours duty days. Check in facility, check out 1000 hours daily. Government civilian employee billeting.

TML: TLQ. All ranks, leave or official duty. Two bedroom, living room, private bath (14). Kitchen, color TV, coin washer/dryer, vending machine. Modern structure. Rates: BAQ/VHA rates. PCS in/out can make reservations, others Space-A.

TML: Apartments. Officers all ranks, enlisted E4-E9. Duty only. Two bedroom apartments, private bath (6). Houses, various configurations (17). Kitchen, complete utensils, color TV, cribs/cots, washer/dryer. Modern structures. Rates: same as above. PCS can make reservations, others Space-A.

TML Availability: Extremely limited.

☞ The Navy Lodge here is closed, and has become the TLQ. There's not much to see and little opportunity to come here, but for those who need to visit someone stationed here, it may be an opportunity to see a far flung area.

Locator 592-8001   **Medical 592-8201**   **Police-555**

Eielson Air Force Base (AK15R5)
Eielson AFB, AK 99702-5000

TELEPHONE NUMBER INFORMATION: Main installation numbers: C-907-377-1110, D-317-377-1110.

Location: On the Richardson Highway (AK-2), AFB is clearly marked. USM: C-8. NMC: Fairbanks, 20 miles northwest.

Billeting Office: Building 3108, Wabash St, C-**907-377-1844**, 24 hours daily. Check in billeting, check out 1200 hours daily. Government civilian employee billeting.

TML: TLF. Building 3305, all ranks, leave or official duty. Separate bedrooms, private bath (living room has sleeper sofa & chair) (40). Kitchen, complete utensils, color TV, maid service, cribs, washer/dryer, accessible to handicapped. Modern structure. Rates: $25 per room. Maximum 5 per room. Duty can make reservations, others Space-A.

ALASKA
Eielson Air Force Base, continued

TML: VOQ/VAQ. Buildings 5180 & 6 others. All ranks in respective quarters. Leave or official duty. Some buildings accessible to handicapped. One bedroom, semi-private bath (VOQ) (26). Separate bedrooms, private bath (VOQ) (76); One bedroom, shared bath (VAQ)(80). Community kitchen, limited utensils, refrigerator, cribs, essentials, ice vending, color TV in room & lounge, maid service, washer/dryer. Older structure. Rates: $8 per person (VOQ), $8 per person (VAQ). Duty can make reservations, others Space-A.

DV/VIP: Protocol Office, 343Wing/CCE, building 3112, room 5, C-EX-6101. E9/06+. Retirees Space-A.

TML Availability: Good, Sep-Apr. Difficult, other times.

☞ **Enjoy Denali National Park, historical Fairbanks, hunting, fishing and skiing in season. All outdoor activities are available both on and off base.**

Locator-377-1841   Medical-377-2296   Police-377-5130

Elmendorf Air Force Base (AK09R5)
Elmendorf AFB, AK 99506-5000

TELEPHONE NUMBER INFORMATION: Main installation numbers: C-907-552-1110, D-317-552-1110.

Location: Off Glenn Highway. Take Muldoon, Boniface, Post Rd or Government Hill exits. The AFB is next to Ft Richardson. USM: B-9. NMC: Anchorage, 2 miles southwest.

Billeting Office: North Star Inn, building 31-250, Acacia St, C-**907-552-2454**, 24 hours daily. Check in facility, check out 1200 hours daily.

TML: TLF. Building 31-250, all ranks, PCS or official duty. Three bedrooms, private bath (50). Bedroom, private bath, sofa bed, kitchen (46). Refrigerator, color TV, maid service, washer/dryer. Older structure. Rates: $40 per unit. Duty can make reservations, others Space-A.

TML: VOQ. Officer all ranks, TDY or official duty. Bedroom, private bath (96); bedroom, private bath, kitchenette (20). Rates: $8 per person. Duty can make reservations, others Space-A.

TML: VAQ. Enlisted all ranks, TDY or official duty. Bedroom, shared bath (224). Same as VOQ. Rates: $8 per person.

DV/VIP: Protocol Office. Reservations C-EX-3210. 06+.

TML Availability: Fairly good. Best, Nov-Jan.

☞ **Alaska's largest city boasts many cultural events, museums, sporting events (the Anchorage Bowl is a world class ski resort), and restaurants in a spectacular setting. Outdoor activities, of course, abound.**

Locator 552-4860   Medical 552-5555   Police 552-3421

ALASKA

Fort Greely (AK10R5)
Fort Greely, AK 98733-5000

TELEPHONE NUMBER INFORMATION: Main installation numbers: C-907-873-1121, D-317-363-1121.

Location: Off AK-4, 6 miles south of junction of AK-2 & AK-4. Five miles south of Delta Junction. USM: C-8. NMC: Fairbanks, 105 miles northwest.

Billeting Office: ATTN: Billeting. Building 663, First St, C-**907-873-3285**, D-317-363-3285, 0730-1500 hours M-F. Others hours, call, or report to SDO, Building 501, EX-4220. Check in billeting, check out 1100 hours daily. Government civilian employee billeting.

TML: VOQ/VEQ. Building 702, 801, all ranks, leave or official duty. Sitting room, double bed, private bath (14); family quarters, 2 single beds, 1 double, separate bedrooms, private bath (5). Refrigerator, color cable TV, maid service, cribs/cots, washer/dryer. Building 801, double bed, sitting room, telephone, private bath, kitchenette, cable color TV (16). DVQ, same as above, but larger (4). Older structures. Rates: $16 per person VEQ, $7.00 each additional person; $21 per person VOQ, $7 each additional person. DVQ $23 per person, $7 each additional person. TDY or PCS can make reservations 60 days in advance, unofficial, 3 days, others Space-A. **No pets.**

TML Availability: Good. Best, Mar-Apr, Dec. More difficult, Jan-Feb.

☞ **Hunting, fishing, all outdoor summer and winter sports are part of living in Alaska. A visit to nearby Delta Junction and Fairbanks, farther north, will give a visitor a taste of life on "the last frontier."**

Locator 873-3255   **Medical-873-3105**   **Police 873-1202**

Fort Richardson (AK03R5)
Fort Richardson, AK 99505-5000

TELEPHONE NUMBER INFORMATION: Main installation numbers: C-907-384-1110, D-317-864-1110.

Location: Main gate is on Glenn Highway, 5 miles south of Eagle River. USM: B-9. NMC: Anchorage, 8 miles southwest.

Billeting Office: Building 600, Room 105A, 5th St and Richardson Dr, C-**907-384-0436,0421,** D-317-863-8216, 0600-2230, hours M-F, 0900-1645 Sa. Other times SDO, building 1, EX-0104. Check in billeting, check out 1100 hours daily. Reservations check in after 1300. Government civilian employee billeting in VOQ/DV/VIP.

TML: VOQ. Buildings 57, 58, 345, 347, 1107, 1113, 1114, officers and enlisted all ranks, leave or official duty. Separate bedroom, private bath (125). Kitchen (some), refrigerator, central microwave, color TV, maid service, cribs/cots, washer/dryer, ice vending. Older structure, renovated. Rates: $21, others $7 each. Reservation 10 days in advance for official PCS, TDY or ADT, 3 days in advance for other categories if space is available.

Fort Richardson, continued

TML: DV/VIP. **The Igloo,** building 53. Officers 06+, leave or official duty. C-**907-384-1586.** Bedroom, private bath (3); separate bedroom suites, private bath (13); bedroom, kitchen, private bath apartments (2). Refrigerator, limited utensils, color TV, maid service, cribs/cots, washer/dryer, ice vending. Older structure, renovated. Rates: apartments $25, additional person $7 each, suites $23, $7 additional person. Reservation policy same as VOQ.

DV/VIP: ATTN: AFVR-GS, Protocol Office, building 1, Room 111, C-384-0306, 06+. Retirees and lower ranks Space-A 3 days in advance.

TML Availability: Good, Oct-Apr. Difficult, other times.

☞ **Visit the free Fish and Wildlife Museum in Building 600. Earthquake Park in Anchorage commemorates the violence of the far North, while towering mountains, and great downhill skiing welcome visitors nearby.**

Locator 384-0306   Medical 552-5555   Police 384-0823

Fort Wainwright (AK07R5)
Fort Wainwright, AK 99703-5000

TELEPHONE NUMBER INFORMATION: Main installation numbers: C-907-353-6113/7500, D-317-353-6113/7500.

Location: From Fairbanks, take Airport Way East which leads to the main gate of the post. USM: C-8. NMC: Fairbanks, 3.5 miles west.

Billeting Office: Building 1045 (**Murphy Hall**), Gaffney Rd, C-**907-353-7291**, 0630--2230 hours M-F, Sa 1030-1730 hours. Other hours SDO, building 1555, C-EX-7500. Check in billeting, check out 1200 hours daily.

TML: VEQ/VOQ. Building 4056, enlisted and officer all ranks, leave or official duty. Bedroom, private bath (27, 12 suites). Refrigerator, color TV, maid service, cribs/cots, washer/dryer, food/ice vending, microwave available. Older structure. Rates: singles, sponsor, $16, suites - $21, each additional person $7. Duty can make reservations 60 days in advance, others 3 days.

TML: VEQ/VOQ. Building 4063, enlisted and officer all ranks, leave or official duty. Two bedroom, private bath (4); bedroom, private bath (16) (12 suites). Refrigerator, color TV, maid service, cribs/cots, washer/dryer, ice vending, microwave available. Rates: sponsor $16, each additional person $7. Duty can make reservations 60 days in advance, others 3 days.

TML: VEQ/VOQ. Buildings 4064, enlisted and officers all ranks, leave or official duty. Two bedroom, private bath (8); bedroom, private bath (8). Refrigerator, color TV, maid service, essentials, cribs/cots, washer/dryer, food/ice vending. Older structures. Rates: sponsor $21, each additional person $7. Duty can make reservations 60 days in advance, others 3 days.

TML: VEQ/VOQ. Building 1045, enlisted and officers, all ranks. Leave or official duty. Bedroom, private bath (26). Refrigerator, color TV, maid service, cribs/roll away,

ALASKA
Fort Wainwright, continued

washer/dryer, food/ice vending, microwave available. Rates: sponsor $21, each additional person $7. Duty can make reservations 60 days in advance, others 3 days.

DV/VIP: Building 1045. Officers 06+, leave or official duty, C-EX 6671. Bedroom deluxe suite (kitchen in one unit) (4). Duty reservations 60 days in advance, others 3 days.

TML Availability: Difficult year round.

☞ In summer Fairbanks hosts Midnight Sun baseball games, in winter (Feb-Mar) the North American Championship Sled Dog Race (and others), U. of Alaska Eskimo Olympics. New shopping malls belie wilderness nearby.

Locator 353-6586   Medical-353-5110   Police 353-7535

King Salmon Airport (AK17R5)
APO AP 96513-5000

TELEPHONE NUMBER INFORMATION: Main installation numbers: C-907-721-3492, D-317-721-3492.

Location: Accessible only by air and water. USM: B-9. NMC: Anchorage, 300 miles northeast.

Billeting Office: King Salmon Inn. ATTN: Billeting, 643 SPTS/SVH, Unit 12526, APO AP 96513-5000, building 647, C-**907-721-3492**, D-317-721-3492, 0730-1600 M-F. Other hours, call C-EX-3560. Check in billeting 0730-1600 hours, check out 1200. Government civilian employee billeting.

TML: BEQ, BOQ, VOQ, DV/VIP. Building 647, all ranks, leave or official duty. Rooms with shared bath, rooms with private bath. Food vending, maid service, refrigerator in unit, color TV in unit and lounge, washer/dryer. Older structure, remodeled '91. Rates: $8-$10 per person, per night, maximum charge per family $16-$20. No pets. Active duty, reserve, national guard on orders can make reservations, others Space-A.

DV/VIP: Building 647, 06+, SMSgt, AF, others Space-A. Write to: First Sergeant, 643 SPTS, Unit 12526, APO AP 96513-5000, C-907-721-3310, D-317-721-3310.

TML Availability: Good. Best, winter/spring. More difficult, Jun-Aug.

☞ Salmon and trout fishing; bear, moose and caribou hunting; summer and winter sports of all kinds are important to this area in the "Alaskan bush". This is a popular vacation spot for those stationed in Alaska who are "in the know".

Locator 721-3492   Medical 721-3404   Police 721-3569

Kodiak Coast Guard Support Center (AK08R5)
Kodiak CGSC, AK 99619-5000

TELEPHONE NUMBER INFORMATION: Main installation numbers: C-907-487-5267, D-317-487-5267.

ALASKA

Kodiak Coast Guard Support Center, continued

Location: From Kodiak City, take main road southwest for 7 miles. Base is on the left side. USM: B-9. NMC: Kodiak, 7 miles northeast.

Billeting Office: Housing Office, C-**907-487-5446**, 0745-1630 duty days. Other hours, Security, Administration Building, C-EX-5265. Check in facility, check out 1200 hours, check in 1400 hours. Government civilian employee billeting Space-A.

TML: Guest House. Building 301, all ranks, leave or official duty, 0730-2200 hours daily. Bedroom, private bath (3); Bedrooms, shared bath (37), suites, private bath (2), Community kitchen, CATV in lounge, maid service, cribs/cots, washer/dryer, ice vending. Older structure, renovated. Rates: $22 single, $30 double, $35 family suite. All categories can make reservations one week in advance.

TML: BOQ. Officers all ranks, leave or official duty. Bedroom, private bath (19). Some rooms converted to suites. Color TV in room & lounge, maid service, cribs/cots, washer/dryer, ice vending. Older structure, renovated. Rates: suites $50, rooms $30. Duty can make reservations, others Space-A.

TML: BEQ. Units, (200), E1-E6 on duty only, C-**907-487-5260**. Rates: no charge.

TML: DV/VIP. BOQ. Officer 05+. Leave or official duty. Reservations accepted. C-EX-5446, same facilities, rates & occupancy as BOQ above.

DV/VIP: Cmdr,C-EX-5446. 05+. Retirees Space-A.

TML Availability: Good, Oct-May. Difficult, Jun-Aug.

☞ **Kodiak is known for its big bears (the biggest in the world), which are tourist attractions in themselves, and great scenery, and wonderful king crab, which is not so threatening, and more tasty.**

Locator 487-5267   **Medical 487-5227**   **Police 487-5266**

Shemya Air Force Base (AK11R5)
APO AP 96512-5000

TELEPHONE NUMBER INFORMATION: Main installation numbers: C-907-392-1110, D-317-392-1110.

Location: Accessible only by air. USM: A-8. NMC: Anchorage, 1800 miles east.

Billeting Office: Crosswinds Inn, building 600, C-**907-392-3240**, D-317-392-3240, 24 hours daily. Check in facility, check out 1200 hours daily. Government employee billeting.

TML: BOQ, BEQ. Officers and enlisted, all ranks, official duty only. Rooms, refrigerator, maximum capacity, two. Modern structure. Rates: $8 per person per night. Active duty, reservists and national guard on orders. No pets. Reservations only, above numbers.

TML: VIP/DV. Protocol Office. Limited facilities.

ALASKA
Shemya Air Force Base, continued

DV/VIP: Protocol Office. Reservations, above numbers, 06+.

TML Availability: Extremely limited all year.

☞ **Shemya AFB is in the Aleutian Island Chain, between Adak and Attu. Island clearance required from the Base Commander. Vacationing not authorized due to limited facilities.**

Locator 392-1110   **Medical 392-3404**   **Police 392-3404**

Arizona

Davis-Monthan Air Force Base (AZ01R4)
Davis-Monthan AFB, AZ 85707-5000

TELEPHONE NUMBER INFORMATION: Main installation numbers: C-602-750-3900, D-312-361-1110.

Location: Exit I-10 North Palo Verde, circle around to the Golf Links, turn right on Craycroft and proceed to main gate. USM: D-6. NMC: Tucson, 3 miles northwest.

Billeting Office: Building 2350, 10th St, ATTN: Inn on Davis Monthan, P.O. Box 15013. C-602-748-1500, D-312-361-3230, 24 hours daily. Check in billeting, check out 1200 hours daily. Government civilian employee billeting.

TML: TLF. Various buildings, all ranks, leave or official duty, C-EX-3309. Two bedroom, private bath (16); four bedroom, private bath (1). Kitchen, complete utensils, A/C, color TV, maid service, cribs/cots, washer/dryer. Modern structure. Rates: $22 per unit. PCS in/out can make reservations, others Space-A.

TML: VAQ. Buildings 3511, 4210, enlisted all ranks, leave or official duty, C-EX-3309. Bedroom, 2 beds, common bath (207); separate bedroom Senior Non-commissioned Officer suites (8), kitchen, private bath; bedroom, 2 beds, share kitchen, private bath (24); separate bedroom Chief Suites, private bath (E9 only) (4). Refrigerator, A/C, color TV in room & lounge, maid service, washer/dryer. Modern structure. Rates: $6 per person; Senior Non-commissioned Officer suites, $10 per person. Official duty can make reservations, others Space-A.

TML: VOQ. Buildings 2350, 2550, 4065, officer all ranks, leave or official duty, C-EX-3309. Bedroom, share kitchen, private bath (43); separate bedroom, kitchen, bar, private bath (16); Two bedroom, refrigerator, private bath (8). A/C, color TV in room & lounge, maid service, washer/dryer, ice vending. Modern structure. Rates: $8 per person. Maximum $16 per family. Official duty can make reservation, others Space-A.

TML: DV/VIP. Building 4065, officer 06+, leave or official duty, C-EX-3600. Two bedroom suites, 06+, private bath (8) (one special for general/flag officers). Refrigerator, microwave, limited utensils, A/C, color TV, maid service, washer/dryer, ice vending. Modern structure. Rates: $10 per person. Maximum $20 per family. All categories can make reservations. Protocol may cancel reservations for non-AD if AD requires space.

Davis-Monthan Air Force Base, continued

DV/VIP: 836 AD/CCP. EX-3600. 06+. Retirees Space-A.

TML Availability: Difficult. Best, Aug, Dec.

☞ Visit Old Tucson; Reid Park & Zoo; Arizona-Sonora Desert and Pima Air Museum. Nearby Mt Lemmon is the site of local snow sports in winter.

Locator 750-3347   Medical 750-3878   Police 750-3200

Fort Huachuca (AZ02R4)
Fort Huachuca, AZ 85613-6000

TELEPHONE NUMBER INFORMATION: Main installation numbers: C-602-538-7111, D-312-879-0111.

Location: From I-10 take AZ-90 south to Sierra Vista and main gate of fort. USM: D-7. NMC: Tucson 75 miles northwest.

Billeting Office: ATTN: ATZS-EHU, building 43083, Service Road, C-602-533-2222/5361, 24 hours daily. Check in billeting 1400, check out 1100 hours. Government civilian employee billeting.

TML: Guest House. Buildings 42017, 52054, all ranks, leave or official duty. Bedroom, 2 double beds, private bath (21); separate bedroom, double bed, private bath (6); two bedroom, double beds, private bath (3); three bedroom, double beds, private bath (3). Community kitchen, refrigerator, A/C, color TV, maid service, cribs, washer/dryer. Modern structure. Rates: $29.50 per unit. Maximum eight persons in 42017, five persons in 52054. Duty can make reservations, others Space-A. **Pets OK first night only. Must be boarded by second day. On-post kennels available.**

TML: DVQ. Building 22104, officers 06+, leave or official duty. Suites - separate bedroom, private bath (6); two bedroom, private bath (2). Kitchen, A/C, color TV, maid service, cribs $2, washer/dryer. Older structures. Rates: sponsor $37, $2 each additional person. Duty can make reservations, others Space-A.

TML: VOQ/VEQ. Buildings 43083-43086, all ranks. Bedroom, private bath or semi-private bath (185). Kitchen & refrigerator in most units, A/C, color TV, maid service, washer/dryer. Modern structure. Rates: VOQ $15, VEQ $13, $2 for spouse. Restricted to active duty.

DV/VIP: Commander, USAISC, ATTN: AS-SGS-P, Room 3209, C-602-538-6040, 06+. Retirees and lower ranks Space-A.

TML Availability: Best, Dec. Difficult, other times

☞ Visit historic Bisbee and Tombstone, the "Town too tough to die". The ITR office on post is the information office on local activities. Hunting and fishing are good. How about a picnic on Reservoir Hill with a view of 100 miles?

Locator 538-7111   Medical-533-5152   Police-533-2181

ARIZONA

Gila Bend Air Force Auxiliary Field (AZ16R4)
Gila Bend AFAF, AZ 85337-5000

TELEPHONE NUMBER INFORMATION: Main installation numbers: C-602-683-6200, D-312-853-5200 (Security Police).

Location: From Phoenix, take I-10 West to AZ-85 south to Gila Bend. The field is four miles out of town. Also off I-8 between Yuma and Casa Grande. USM: C-6. NMC: Phoenix, 65 miles northeast.

Billeting Office: ATTN: **Desert Hideaway Inn**, PO Box 1086, Gila Bend AFAF, AZ 85337. Building 4250, C-**602-683-6238**, D-312-853-5238, 0700-2000 M-F, by special arrangement on weekends. Check in billeting, check out 1200. Government civilian employee billeting.

TML: Desert Hideaway Inn, all ranks, leave or official duty. Two beds per unit, semi-private bath (22); separate bedrooms, semi-private bath (5); Two bedroom, semi-private bath (4). Three bedroom, private bath (3). A/C, community kitchen, cribs, essentials, maid service, refrigerator, color TV in lounge & room, washer/dryer. Older structure, remodeled. Rates: $5.50 per night, maximum charge $18. Maximum 2 persons. Duty can make reservations, others Space-A.

TML: TLF. Buildings 114, 118, 122, all ranks, leave or official duty. Handicapped accessible. Three bedroom houses, private bath (3). A/C, cribs, essentials, kitchen, complete utensils, maid service, color TV, washer/dryer. Older structures, renovated remodeled. Maximum charge $18. Maximum 5 beds per unit. Duty can make reservations, others Space-A.

TML: VAQ. Building 4250, enlisted, all ranks, leave or official duty. Bedroom, semi-private bath, 2 beds per room (22); separate bedrooms, semi-private bath (5). A/C, community kitchen, essentials, maid service, color TV in lounge & room, washer/dryer. Older structure, renovated, remodeled. Rates: sponsor $5.50, adult $5.50. Maximum 2 persons. Duty can make reservations, others Space-A.

TML: VOQ. Buildings 2358 A, B, C, D, officer, all ranks. Handicapped accessible. Two bedroom, semi-private bath (4). A/C, community kitchen, essentials, kitchen, maid service, refrigerator, color TV in lounge. Older structure. Rates: sponsor $8.50, adult $8.50. Maximum 2 persons. Duty can make reservations, others Space-A.

DV/VIP: Protocol Office, 832 CSG/CC, C-602-683-6262, D-312-853-5262. 06+. Retirees and lower ranks Space-A.

TML Availability: Very good. Difficult Oct-Jan.

☞ **Hunting, fishing, boating, and trips to Tucson, and Old Mexico are favorite activities in this area.**

Locator 683-6200　　　**Medical 853-5270**　　　**Police 853-5220**

ARIZONA

Luke Air Force Base (AZ03R4)
Luke AFB, AZ 85309-1000

TELEPHONE NUMBER INFORMATION: Main installation numbers: C-602-856-7411, D-312-853-0111.

Location: From Phoenix, west on I-10 to Litchfield Rd, north on Litchfield Rd approximately 5 miles. Also, from Phoenix, on I-17 to Glendale Ave, west on Glendale Ave to intersection of Glendale Ave and Litchfield Rd, approximately 16 miles. USM: D-6. NMC: Phoenix, 20 miles southeast.

Billeting Office: ATTN: **Fighter Country Inn**, building 660, 2nd St. C-602-856-3941, D-312-853-3941, 24 hours daily. Check in billeting, check out 1200 hours daily.

TML: VOQ. Six buildings, officers all ranks, leave or official duty. Bedroom, private bath (68); shared suites, private bath (28). Kitchen, refrigerator, A/C, color TV, maid service. Modern structure. Rates: $20 per night.

TML: TLF. Four buildings, all ranks, leave or official duty. Bedroom, private bath (40). Kitchen, utensils, A/C, color TV, maid service, washer/dryer. Modern structure. Rates: $20 per night.

TML: VAQ. Two buildings, enlisted all ranks, leave or official duty. Bedroom, private bath (12); two bedroom, semi-private bath (13). Kitchen, utensils, A/C, color TV, maid service, washer/dryer. Older structure. Rates: Maximum $11 per unit.

TML: DV/VIP. Two buildings, officer 07+, leave or official duty. Two bedroom suites, private bath (2). Kitchen, utensils, A/C, color TV, maid service. Older facility. Rates: $10 per night. Duty can make reservations, others Space-A.

DV/VIP: Protocol Officer, 832AD, C-EX-5840, ranks 07+. Retirees and lower ranks Space-A on a day-by-day basis.

TML Availability: Best, Jun-Aug & Dec. Difficult, other times.

☞ See Phoenix State Capital Building's murals, the Desert Botanical Garden in Papago Park, and Legend City for Disneyland-like family fun. Pioneer Arizona, a living history museum, and the Phoenix Zoo are worth a visit.

Locator 856-7411   Medical-856-7506   Police-856-6349

Williams Air Force Base (AZ09R4)
Williams AFB, AZ 85224-5000

TELEPHONE NUMBER INFORMATION: Main installation numbers: C-602-988-2611, D-312-474-1110.

Location: From I-10 exit go east on Chandler Blvd, 17 miles to AFB. USM: D-6. NMC: Phoenix, 30 miles northwest.

ARIZONA
Williams Air Force Base, continued

Billeting Office: ATTN: 82 ABG/SVH. Building 321, 7th St at O'Club Circle. C-**602-988-5546**, 24 hours daily. Check in billeting, check out 1200 hours daily. Government civilian employee billeting.

TML: TLQ. Buildings 775 through 778, all ranks, leave or official duty. Separate bedrooms, private bath (40). Kitchen, refrigerator, limited utensils, A/C, color TV, maid service, cribs, washer/dryer, ice vending. Modern structure, renovated. Rates: E6 below $14 per family; E7+ $18 per family. Duty can make reservations, others Space-A.

TML: BOQ. Buildings 324, 326. All ranks. Leave or official duty. Bedroom, private bath (70). Kitchen, refrigerator, limited utensils, A/C, maid service, cribs, washer/dryer, ice vending. Modern structure, remodeled. Rates: $17 officers, $6 enlisted. Duty can make reservations, others Space-A.

TML: DV/VIP. Building 324. Officer 07+. Leave or official duty. C-EX-5212. Bedroom suites, private bath (6). Kitchen, utensils, A/C, color TV, maid service, washer/dryer. Modern structure. Rates: $10 per pers. Duty can make reservations, others Space-A.

DV/VIP: 82 FTW/CC, S-1, C-EX-5212. 07+. Retirees and lower ranks Space-A.

TML Availability: Good, Dec-Feb. Difficult, other times.

☞ Phoenix, with its museums, theaters, and symphony provides the culture, while the desert's red cliffs and unusual rock formations fascinate visitors.

⊖This base will close in 1993. Keep updated with Military Living's R&R Space-A Report.

Locator 988-2611   **Medical 988-5452**   **Police 988-6993**

Yuma Army Proving Ground (AZ05R4)
Yuma Army Proving Ground, AZ 85364-0010

TELEPHONE NUMBER INFORMATION: Main installation numbers: C-602-328-2151, D-312-899-2151.

Location: Northeast of I-8 turn right on US-95. Southwest of I-10 turn left on US-95. US-95 is north/south route which bisects APG. USM: C-6. NMC: Yuma, 27 miles southwest.

Billeting Office: ATTN: STEYP-EH-H, building 1000, Seventh St, C-**602-328-2129/2127**, 0700-1530 hours. Other hours, SDO, building 506, C-EX-2020. Check in billeting, check out 1100 hours daily. Government civilian employee billeting.

TML: Guest House. Building 538, all ranks, leave or official duty. Bedroom, private bath (10). Kitchen, utensils, A/C, color TV in room & lounge, maid service, cribs/cots, washer/dryer, ice vending. Modern structure. Rates: sponsor $18, each additional person $3. Maximum 4 per room. Reservations required. One room handicapped accessible.

TML: VOQ. Building 1004, all ranks, official duty only. Bedroom, semi-private bath (16); Two bedroom, kitchen, private bath (5). Community kitchen, A/C, color TV in room &

ARIZONA

Yuma Army Proving Ground, continued

lounge, maid service, washer/dryer, ice vending. Modern structure. Rates: sponsor $21, each additional person $4. All categories can make reservations.

TML: DV/VIP. Building 944 A/B, officer 06+, official duty. Suites, private bath (2). Refrigerator, community kitchen, A/C, color TV, maid service, cribs/cots, washer/dryer, ice vending, coffee machine, beverages. Older structure. Rates: sponsor $25, each additional person $7. 06/GS-15+.

TML Availability: Fairly good, Apr-Sep. More difficult, Oct-Mar.

☞ Visit the Century House Museum for local history, Fort Yuma and the St Thomas Mission, Yuma Territorial Prison and Museum, and the Quechan Indian Museum in Old Fort Yuma to get a taste of this pre-old west town.

Locator 328-2151   **Medical 328-2911**   **Police 328-2720**

Yuma Marine Corps Air Station (AZ04R4)
Yuma MCAS, AZ 85369-5000

TELEPHONE NUMBER INFORMATION: Main installation numbers: C-602-726-2011, D-312-951-2011.

Location: From I-8 take Ave 3E south for 1 mile to MCAS on the right. Adjacent to Yuma IAP. USM: C-6. NMC: Yuma, 3 miles northwest.

Billeting Office: Building 1020, Thomas Ave, C-**602-726-3578**, D-312-951-3578, 24 hours daily. Check in billeting, check out 1000 hours.

TML: TLQ. **Hostess House,** building 1020, all ranks, leave or official duty, C-EX726-2262. Separate bedroom, private bath (13). Refrigerator, community kitchen, A/C, color TV, maid service, cribs/cots, ice vending. Older structure. Rates: station personnel $16 per unit, transient personnel $20. Seven day limit, then daily. All categories can make reservations.

TML: BEQ. Building 1020, E6-E9, leave or official duty. Bedroom, semi-private bath (52); Refrigerator, A/C, color TV in room & lounge, maid service, washer/dryer, microwave in lounge. Older structure. Rates: $6 per pers. All categories can make reservations on Space-A basis.

TML: BOQ. Building 1020, officers all ranks, leave or official duty. Bedroom, semi-private bath (78); separate bedrooms, private bath (4). Refrigerator, A/C, color TV in room and lounge, maid service, washer/dryer, ice vending. Modern structure. Rates: $8 per person. All categories make reservations on a Space-A basis.

DV/VIP: Adjutant, C-EX-2253. 06/GS-15+. Retirees Space-A.

TML Availability: Extremely limited.

ARIZONA
Yuma Marine Corps Air Station, continued

☞ Located on the Colorado River, fine water recreation is available, as well as hunting, golf, and trips to nearby Mexico for shopping, festivals and restaurants.

Locator 726-2011   Medical 726-2772   Police 726-2361

Arkansas

Fort Chaffee (AR04R2)
Fort Chaffee, AR 72905-0099

TELEPHONE NUMBER INFORMATION: Main installation numbers: C-501-484-2141, D-312-962-2111.

Location: From I-40, take the I-540 spur to Fort Smith. From I-540, exit at Ft Chaffee exit sign. Take state highway 59 south across Arkansas River to highway 22. It goes past Ft Chaffee main gate. Five to six miles total. USM: H-6. NMC: Fort Smith, 6 miles southwest.

Billeting Office: Building 1377, Fort Smith Blvd, C-501-484-2252, D-312-962-2252, 0730-2400 seven days a week.

TML: Guest House utilizes converted WWII building. Inadequate. Limited space; priority given to PCS and TDY personnel. A/C, heat, TV, refrigerator. Community kitchen, washer/dryer. Rates $8 per day. No Pets.

TML: VEQ. Inadequate facility rates: $5 day.

TML: VOQ. Adequate facility rates $10 to $15. Inadequate rates: $8 to $10.

TML: DVQ. Nine DVQ's with priority to TDY. Very limited space for retirees. Rates: $22 single; $29 married. No Pets.

TML Availability: More difficult, summer.

☞ Historic Fort Smith, on the Arkansas River, 5 miles. Gateway to the Ozarks. Fayetteville - University of Arkansas is an opportunity for sporting events. Wildlife management area, excellent hunting and fishing.

Little Rock Air Force Base (AR02R2)
Little Rock AFB, AR 72099-0001

TELEPHONE NUMBER INFORMATION: Main installation numbers: C-501-988-3131, D-312-731-1110.

ARKANSAS
Little Rock Air Force Base, continued

Location: Use US-67/167 to Jacksonville, take AFB exit to main gate. USM: I-6. NMC: Little Rock, 18 miles southwest.

Billeting Office: PO Box 1192, building 1024, Cannon Circle, C-**501-988-6753/1141**, 24 hours daily. Check in billeting, check out 1200 hours daily.

TML: VOQ/VAQ. **Razorback Inn**, building 1024, all ranks, official duty, C-EX-6652. Spaces available (290). No TLF. Refrigerator, A/C, color TV, maid service, washer/dryer, ice vending. Modern structure, remodeled. Rates: VAQ/VOQ $8, DV $14. Children not authorized. Duty can make reservations, others Space-A.

DV/VIP: 314 TAW/CCE. C-EX-6828/3588. 06+. Retirees Space-A, limited.

TML Availability: Extremely limited. Best, Dec.

☞ See **War Memorial Park, Arkansas Traveller's Baseball, Burns Park, and Governor's Mansion.**

Locator 988-3131   **Police 988-3221**

Pine Bluff Arsenal (AR03R2)
Pine Bluff Arsenal, AR 71601-9500

TELEPHONE NUMBER INFORMATION: Main installation numbers: C-501-543-3000, D-312-966-3000.

Location: Off US-65 northwest of Pine Bluff. Take AR-256, cross AR-365 into main gate of Arsenal. Or south on US-65 from Little Rock, 35 miles, follow signs. USM: I-6. NMC: Pine Bluff, 8 miles southeast.

Billeting Office: ATTN: SMCPB-EHH, building 34-970, Hoadley Rd, C-**501-543-3008**, 0730-1600 hours daily. Other hours OC, C-EX-2700. Check in billeting, check out 1200 hours daily. Government civilian employee billeting.

TML: TQ & BOQ. Buildings 15-330, 15-350, all ranks, leave or official duty. Bedroom, private bath (6); separate bedroom, private bath (14); two bedroom, private bath (1). Refrigerator, community kitchen, utensils, A/C, color TV, maid service, cribs/cots, washer/dryer. Older structure, Rates: sponsor $15, adults $1, children (13+) $1.00, under 12 free. Duty can make reservations, others Space-A.

TML Availability: Extremely limited.

☞ Some of the finest hunting and fishing available in Arkansas is at **Pine Bluff Arsenal.** The post also has a 9 hole golf course, and a Special Services recreational area, building 16-310.

Locator 543-3000   **Medical 543-3409**   **Police 543-3505/3506**

California

Alameda Coast Guard Support Center (CA28R4)
Alameda, Coast Guard Island, CA 94501-5000

TELEPHONE NUMBER INFORMATION: Main installation numbers: C-510-437-3151, FTS-536-3151.

Location: Take I-880 south to 23rd St exit, right and straight to causeway and Island. Signs posted. USM: A-7. NMC: Oakland, 1 mile east.

Billeting Office: No central billeting office. Housing office in building 21, McCullough Dr, C-510-437-3437, 0700-1530 hours. No government civilian employees billeting.

TML: Guest House transient quarters, building 18, BOQ, 3rd floor, by reservation only, C-510-437-3304. Bedroom, 2 beds (shared rooms), hall bath (6). Refrigerator, TV, washer/dryer. PCS have priority, call for reservations. BEQ buildings 24/26, reservations not taken.

TML Availability: Very limited.

☞ **All Hands Club is downstairs, and the wonderful city of San Francisco is just across the bay.**

Locator 437-3151   **Medical 437-3581**   **Police 437-3151**

Alameda Naval Air Station (CA33R4)
Alameda NAS, CA 94501-5000

TELEPHONE NUMBER INFORMATION: Main installation numbers: C-510-263-0111, D-312-993-0111.

Location: From Nimitz Highway, I-88 south, take the Broadway/Alameda exit. From I-880 north take Broadway exit. Directions to NAS clearly marked. USM: A-7. NMC: Oakland, 2 miles northwest.

Billeting Office: Building 17, B St, C-510-236-3649, **24 hours daily**. Check in at facility, check out 1200 hours daily. Government civilian employee billeting.

TML: Navy Lodge. Building 17, all ranks, leave or official duty. Reservations call **1-800-NAVY-INN**. Check in 0600-2230 hours daily. Bedroom, 2 beds, living room, private bath (70). Kitchen, complete utensils, A/C, color TV room in & lounge, maid service, cribs, coin washer/dryer, ice vending. Modern structure. Rates $32 per unit. Maximum 5 persons. All categories can make reservations.

TML: BOQ: Building 17, officers, all ranks, leave or official duty. Bedroom, semi-private bath (163); separate bedrooms, private bath (9); suites, private bath (30); suites (VIP, 07+), private bath (4). Refrigerator, color TV in room & lounge, washer/dryer, ice vending, telephone in room. Older structure, renovated. Rates: regular room $8, suites $15, VIP suites $20, add $10 for dependents.

CALIFORNIA

Alameda Naval Air Station, continued

DV/VIP: CO, building 1, O7+. Retirees, Space-A.

TML Availability: Good, all year.

☞ **Within easy access of San Francisco, Berkeley, and the California wine country. Visit Lake Merritt in the heart of Oakland, the Oakland Art Museum, and Joseph Knowland Arboretum.**

Locator 263-0111   Medical 263-4420   Police 263-3766

☺**A new Navy Lodge is planned at this location. Keep posted on new developments with Military Living's, *R&R Space-A Report.***

Barstow Marine Corps Logistics Base (CA13R4)
Barstow MCLB, CA 92311-5007

TELEPHONE NUMBER INFORMATION: Main installation numbers: C-619-577-6211, D-312-282-0111

Location: On I-40, 1.5 miles east of Barstow. Take I-15 northeast from San Bernardino, or west from Las Vegas, NV. Signs mark direction to MCLB. USM: B-5. NMC: San Bernardino, 75 miles southwest.

Billeting Office: Building 44. C-**619-577-6896,** 0700-1530 hours daily. Other hours OD, Building 30, Room 8, C-EX-6611. Check in/out at billeting.

TML: TLF. Buildings 114, 187, all ranks, leave or official duty. AD 45 days in advance. Food and Hospitality Building 171, C-EX 6418. Bedroom, private bath (2); two bedroom, private bath (2). Kitchen, utensils, A/C, BW TV. Older structure. Reservations accepted. Rates: Based on rank & 1/30th of BAQ. Check out 1000 hours daily.

TML: VIP. Building 11-A, 06+, leave or official duty. Two bedroom, private bath (1). Kitchen, utensils, A/C, color TV, maid service, washer/dryer. Older structure. Rates: $25 per unit. All categories can make reservations. Check out 1100 hours daily.

DV/VIP: Commanding General, Building 15, C-EX-6555. 06+. Retired & lower ranks Space-A.

TML Availability: Good, Oct-Apr. Difficult, other times.

☞ **Visit Calico Ghost Town, 8 miles east. Lake Delores is 13 miles east for water recreation. Southern California is in easy reach, and Las Vegas not too far east.**

Locator 577-6663   Medical 577-6588   Police 577-6666

CALIFORNIA

Beale Air Force Base (CA47R4)
Beale AFB, CA 95903-5000

TELEPHONE NUMBER INFORMATION: Main installation numbers: C-916-634-3000, D-312-368-3000

Location: From CA-70 North exit south of Marysville, to North Beale Rd, continue for 10 miles to main gate of AFB. USM: B-4. NMC: Sacramento, 40 miles south.

Billeting Office: Gold Country Inn. Building 2156, Warren Shingle Blvd, C-**916-634-2953**, 24 hours daily. Check in billeting, check out 1200 hours daily. Government civilian employee billeting.

TML: TLF. Buildings 5109-5112, all ranks, official duty, Space-A. Two bedroom, private bath (4); three bedroom, private bath (6); four bedroom, private bath (7). Kitchen, complete utensils, A/C, color TV in room & lounge, maid service, cribs/cots, washer/dryer, microwave, dishwasher. Older structure. Rates: $19 two bedroom, $22 three bedroom, $25 four bedroom. All must make reservations.

TML: VOQ. Buildings 2350, 2360, officer all ranks, official duty, Space-A. Bedroom, private bath (47). Kitchen, A/C, limited utensils, color TV in room & lounge, maid service, cribs/cots, washer/dryer, microwave. Older structure. Rates: $9 per person. $13.50 per couple.

TML: VAQ. Building 2156, enlisted all ranks, official duty, Space-A. Bedroom, semi-private bath, (18); Two bedrooms, semi-private bath (29); SNCO suites, private bath (3). Refrigerator, A/C, color TV in room & lounge, maid service, cribs/cots, washer/dryer, ice vending, microwave. Older structure, remodeled. Rates: $9 per person, $13.50 per couple. SNCO rates: $13 per person, $19.50 per couple. Reservations accepted.

DV/VIP: Protocol Office, C-EX-2120, 06+, retirees. Reservations required.

TML Availability: Good, Sep-May. Difficult, other times.

☞ In the center of historic California gold rush country, east of Marysville and north of Sacramento. Outdoor sports are popular.

Locator 634-2960   **Medical 634-4444**   **Police 634-2000**
☻This base is due for realignment, but not closure, in Sep '93.

Camp Pendleton Marine Corps Base (CA30R4)
Camp Pendleton MCB, CA 92055-6092

TELEPHONE NUMBER INFORMATION: Main installation numbers: C-619-725-4111, D-312-365-4111.

Location: On I-5 which is adjacent to main gate. Take Camp Pendleton off ramp from I-5 at Oceanside. USM: B-6. NMC: Oceanside, adjacent to base.

Billeting Office: Building 1341, Mainside. From main gate, Vandergrift Blvd 10 miles to right on Rattlesnake Canyon Rd, right at fire station to Vandergrift Blvd again, 3

Camp Pendleton Marine Corps Base, continued

blocks right at theater, 4 blocks to billeting sign, left to building 1341. C-619-725-3718/3451/3732, 24 hours daily. Check in as indicated, check out 1100 hours daily. Government civilian employee billeting.

TML: TOQ. Buildings 1341, 1342, Mainside, officers all ranks, WO1-O6. Check in at billeting. Bedroom, single occupancy, semi-private bath (20); separate bedrooms, private bath (20). Refrigerator, community kitchen, TV, maid service, cribs ($1), washer/dryer. Older structure, renovated. Rates: $12; TAD/TDY, $14-$14.50, others $5 each additional person. TAD/TDY and PCS in/out can make reservations, others Space-A.

TML: TEQ. Building 16146, enlisted all ranks, leave or official duty. Check out 1200. Bedroom, community bath (42). Refrigerator, color TV, maid service, washer/dryer. Older structure. Rates: sponsor $10 TAD/TDY, $11.50 others, $5 each additional person over 12 years. Duty can make reservations, others Space-A.

TML: DV/VIP. Building 1751. Officer O6+, leave or official duty, C-EX-5810 (CG's secretary). Two bedroom suites (3), living room, dining room, den, private bath. Kitchen, utensils, A/C, color TV, maid service, washer/dryer, dishwasher. Older structure, Rates: $25, $30 others, $5 each additional person over 12 years. Maximum 6 per suite. TAD/TDY can make reservations, others Space-A. General/Flag rank have priority.

DV/VIP: ATTN: Joint Protocol Officer, building 1160, C-EX-5080/5780. O5+. Retirees and lower ranks Space-A.

MWR TML: Guest House. Building 1310, all ranks, leave or official duty. Reservations accepted, C-EX-5194/5304. Check in at facility. Bedroom, private bath (64). Kitchen (36 units), limited utensils, A/C, color TV in room & lounge, maid service, cribs (50¢), cots ($1), coin washer/dryer, ice vending, facilities for DAVs, swimming pool. Modern structure. Rates for PCS/leave personnel: $20 with kitchen, $15 without kitchen. All categories can make reservations.

TML: Club Del Cottages, (Camp Del Mar Beach) mobile homes, reservations by phone or in person, C-619-725-2463. Leave or official duty. Cottages, one bedroom, private bath (48); mobile homes, two bedrooms, 2 sets bunk beds, sleep 6 private bath (14); mobile home, four bedrooms, double wide, sleeps 16, private bath (1). Kitchen, fully equipped, no maid service, bring bed linens, blankets, pillows, towels, etc. Recreation area with many amenities, ITT Office tickets to Southern California attractions available. Rates: cottages $30 daily; 2 bedroom mobile home $30; 4 bedroom mobile home $60. Winter rates available, security deposit required. All categories can make reservations. **Note: More information available in Military RV, Camping & Rec Areas Around the World.**

TML Availability: Fairly good, Oct-Mar. More difficult, other times.

☞ Beaches, all forms of water recreation, Mission San Luis Rey, and 72 golf courses are within easy reach of Camp Pendleton.

Locator 725-4111   **Medical 725-6308**   **Police 911**

CALIFORNIA

Camp San Luis Obispo (CA83R4)
San Luis Obispo, CA 93403-8104

TELEPHONE NUMBER INFORMATION: Main installation numbers: C-805-549-3800, FTS-629-3800.

Location: Take Highway 1 five miles northwest of the city of San Luis Obispo. USM: B-5. NMC: San Luis Obispo, five miles southeast.

Billeting Office: Building 738, San Joaquin Avenue, ATTN: Billeting Manager, PO Box 8104, **C-805-549-3800**, 0800-1630 hours daily. After duty hours C-3806, Operations. Check in during hours, check out 1200 hours. Government civilian employee billeting.

TML: BOQ. Transient housing. Rooms, apartments, cottages, officers all ranks, E-7 thru E-9, leave or official duty. Bedroom, community bath (101); bedroom, hall bath (39); two bedroom, private bath (3); three bedroom, private bath (3); various bedroom/bath combinations (4). Refrigerator, kitchen (some units), limited utensils, color TV, maid service. Older structure, redecorated. Rates: on leave, sponsor, adult, child $12 each. On duty, sponsor, $8.50, adult, child $12 each. Maximum varies with unit. Duty can make reservations, others Space-A. **No pets allowed.**

DV/VIP: No separate office, call billeting, 06+. Retirees, lower ranks Space-A.

TML Availability: Fairly good. Best Sept thru Mar. Difficult other times.

☞ **There is a small aircraft museum on post, and don't miss local state beaches. Visit local wineries, Hearst Castle, San Luis Obispo Mission Plaza and Farmers Market.**

Locator 549-3800   **Police 911**

Castle Air Force Base (CA10R4)
Castle AFB, CA 95342-5000

TELEPHONE NUMBER INFORMATION: Main installation numbers: C-209-726-2011, D-312-347-1110

Location: From Sacramento, take CA-99 south to Atwater, take Buhach exit to AFB. USM: B-4. NMC: Fresno, 60 miles south.

Billeting Office: Building 1108, 4th & C St, **C-209-727-2531**, 24 hours daily. Check in billeting, check out 1200 hours daily. No government civilian employee billeting.

TML: Guest House. Buildings 1109, 1116, 1117, 1118, 1119, all ranks, leave or official duty. Two bedroom apartments, private bath (20). Kitchen, utensils, A/C, color TV, maid service, washer/dryer. Older structure. Rates: $16-$21 per apartment. PCS personnel in/out can make reservations, others Space-A.

TML: VOQ. Building 427, officers all ranks, leave or official duty. Bedroom, private bath (20). Kitchen, utensils, A/C, color TV, maid service, washer/dryer. Modern structure. Rates: $9 per person. Duty can make reservations, others Space-A.

CALIFORNIA

Castle Air Force Base, continued

TML: VAQ. Buildings 1111, 1112, 300, enlisted all ranks, leave or official duty. Two bedroom (88) (8 reserved for MSgt+); building 300 - rooms, no kitchen (57). Kitchen, A/C, color TV, maid service. Modern structure. Rates: $9 per person. Duty can make reservations, others Space-A.

TML: DV/VIP. Building 427, officer 05+, leave or official duty. Bedroom apartments (8). Kitchen, utensils, A/C, color TV, maid service, washer/dryer. Modern structure. Rates: $14-$21 per person. Duty can make reservations, others Space-A.

DV/VIP: Contact billeting, 06+, retirees Space-A.

TML Availability: Limited, all year.

☞ Peaceful picnicking is available along the Stanislaus River, and just north of Merced is Lake Yosemite, for water sports. State highway 49 leads through Mother Lode Country where tales of the Gold Rush can still be heard.

Locator 726-2011   **Medical 726-4123**   **Police 726-2111**

⊗This base is scheduled to close Sep '95. Keep up to date with Military Living's *R&R Space-A Report.*

Centerville Beach Naval Facility (CA71R4)
Ferndale, CA 95536-5000

TELEPHONE NUMBER INFORMATION: Main installation numbers: C-707-786-9531, D-312-896-3381.

Location: Take CA Highway 101, 250 miles north of San Francisco to the Ferndale Exit, then 5 miles through Ferndale on Main Street, then right turn on Ocean Avenue, 5 miles to gate. USM: A-3. NMC: Eureka, 23 miles north.

Billeting Office: Building 23, C-**707-786-9531-EX-216**, D-312-896-3381. Hours 0730 thru 1630. After duty hours contact prior reservation required: CDO, Quarterdeck. Government civilian employee billeting.

TML: BOQ (with accommodations for families). Building 20, officers, all ranks, leave or official duty. Handicapped accessible. Suites: bedroom, private bath (4); half bedroom, private bath (1). Refrigerator, community kitchen, washer/dryer, color satellite TV, maid service, essentials, cribs. Coffee maker, hair dryer, beverage & sundry resale in each room, coffee. Older structure, renovated. BBQ area. Rates: sponsor, $15; adult, $15. All categories can make reservations.

TML: Enlisted Transient Quarters (with accommodations for families). Building 64, enlisted, all ranks. Handicapped accessible. Bedroom, private bath (5). Refrigerator, food vending, color TV, maid service, washer/dryer, essentials, cribs, coffee maker, coffee, hair dryer. Older structure, remodeled. Rates: sponsor, $7; adult, $7. All categories can make reservations.

DV/VIP: No protocol office.

CALIFORNIA
Centerville Beach Naval Facility, continued

TML Availability: Very good. Best in the winter. Difficult in summer.

☞ **Direct coastal access. Visit the Redwood forests, the Victorian village of Ferndale. This area is known for its outdoor recreation.**

China Lake Naval Weapons Center (CA34R4)
China Lake NWC, CA 93555-6100

TELEPHONE NUMBER INFORMATION: Main installation numbers: C-619-939-9011, D-312-437-9011

Location: From US-395 or CA-14, take CA-178 east to Ridgecrest and the main gate. USM: B-5. NMC: Los Angeles, 150 miles southwest.

Billeting Office: Officers, BOQ A, next to O'Club, **C-619-939-2383/2789**, enlisted, BEQ 2, **C-619-939-3146/3039**, 0700-2400 hours daily. Check in facility, check outs 1200 hours daily. Government civilian employee billeting.

TML: Transient House/Transient Rooms. Many buildings, all ranks, leave or official duty. Three bedroom, private bath (Transient House/VIP suites) (12); bedroom, private bath (Transient Rooms) (23). Transient House: kitchen, limited utensils, A/C, color TV, maid service, cribs, ice vending. Transient Rooms: refrigerator, color TV, maid service. Rates: $8 per person. Max $25 per family in house. Duty can make reservations, others Space-A.

TML: BOQ. Buildings 00496, 00499, officers all ranks, leave or official duty. Bedroom, private bath (6); separate bedrooms, private bath (17). Refrigerator, A/C, color TV in room & lounge, washer/dryer, ice vending (building 00496). Older structure. Rates: $8 per person. 1 per room. Unaccompanied persons only. Duty can make reservations, others Space-A.

TML: BEQ. 1915 Mitscher, building 00484, all ranks, leave or official duty. Three bedroom, private bath (4). Kitchen, limited utensils, A/C, color TV, maid service, cribs, washer/dryer. Older structure. Rates: $15 per unit. Reservations PCS in/out only. Duty can make reservations, others Space-A. **Pets allowed.**

TML: BEQ. 1805 Harpoon, building 02340, enlisted all ranks, leave or official duty. Bedroom, private/semi-private baths (39). Kitchen, limited utensils, A/C, color TV in lounge, maid service, washer/dryer, ice vending. Older structure. Rates: $2-$4 per person. Unaccompanied person only. Duty can make reservations, others Space-A.

TML: DV/VIP. Buildings 00662, 00663, officers 06/GS-15+, leave or official duty. Three bedroom suites, private bath (4). Kitchen, limited utensils, A/C, color TV, maid service. Older structure. Rates: $25 accompanied. Maximum 3-4 per unit. Duty can make reservations, others Space-A.

DV/VIP: Protocol Office, C-EX-1365, 06+. Retirees and lower ranks Space-A.

CALIFORNIA

China Lake Naval Weapons Center, continued

TML Availability: Good.

☞ Four wheelers enjoy hundreds of trails nearby, while popular mountain areas (Mammoth and June and the Greenhorn Mountains) draw other enthusiasts year round. Visit Red Rock Canyon, and Fossil Falls.

Locator 939-2303   **Medical 939-2911**   **Police 939-3323**

Coronado Naval Amphibious Base (CA38R4)
Coronada NAB, CA 92155-0001

TELEPHONE NUMBER INFORMATION: Main installation numbers: C-619-437-2011, D-312-577-2011.

Location: From San Diego, I-5 south to Palm Ave (CA-75) west 10 miles. Follow signs to Naval Amphibious Base, Coronado. USM: B,C-7. NMC: San Diego, 5 miles north.

Billeting Office: Building 504, Tulagi St, C-619-437-3860 **(BOQ)**; building 303, C-619-437-3494 **(BEQ)**, 24 hours daily. Check in billeting, check out 1200 hours daily. Government civilian employee billeting with orders.

TML: BOQ. Buildings 500, 504, 505, officers all ranks, leave or official duty. Accessible to handicapped. Bedroom units, private bath (374); separate bedroom, private bath (90). Refrigerator, color TV, maid service, washer/dryer, ice vending. Modern structure. Rates: sponsor $8, adult $6. Duty can make reservations, others Space-A reservations 24 hours in advance.

TML: BEQ. Building 303, enlisted all ranks, leave or official duty. Handicapped accessible. Bedroom, common bath (68); bedroom, private bath (4). Maid service, refrigerator, color TV, washer/dryer. Rates: $3 per person. Duty can make reservations, others Space-A, 24 hours in advance.

TML: DV/VIP. Building 504. Officers 06-10, leave or official duty. Separate bedroom suites, private bath (10). Refrigerator, color TV, maid service, washer/dryer, ice vending. Modern structure. Rates: Moderate. Duty can make reservations, others Space-A 24 hours in advance.

DV/VIP: Reservations: C-619-437-3860, 06/civilian equivalent+. Retirees Space-A.

TML Availability: Good most of the year.

☞ Coronado Bay and the Pacific Ocean offer all water sports; Seaport Village is good family fun. There are a multitude of attractions in San Diego.

Locator 437-2011   **Medical 437-2900**   **Police 437-3432**

CALIFORNIA

Del Mar Recreation Beach (CA03R4)
Camp Pendleton Marine Corps Base
Camp Pendleton, CA 92055-5018

TELEPHONE NUMBER INFORMATION: Main installation numbers: C-619-725-7935, D-312-365-2463.

Location: Exit I-5 on Harbor Drive/Camp Pendleton. Enter either the Del Mar Gate or the Main Gate on Camp Pendleton. Approximately 2.5 miles from either gate. USM: B-5,6. NMC: Oceanside, 1 mile south.

Billeting Office: Building 210595, C-**619-725-2463**. Check in facility 1400-1630 hours daily. Late arrival should be pre-arranged. Check out 1200 hours daily. No government civilian employees billeting.

TML: Club Del, mobile homes, officer, enlisted E6+, leave or official duty. Two bedroom, private bath, beach front, sleeps 6 (1). Four bunkbeds, 1 double, full bath, livingroom, kitchen w/refrigerator, microwave, stove, coffeemaker, cooking utensils, TV. No. 6 is doublewide, 4 bedrooms, sleeps 16 with 8 beds, 4 sleeper couches, 2 baths, fully equipped kitchen. One bedroom, double bed and sleeper couch sleeps 4 (47). Fully equipped kitchen and bath. Housecleaning aids furnished, bring bed linens, pillows, dishsoap, towels, food and firewood. Inspection prior to refund of $50-$100 security deposit. Ice vending, washer/dryer. Rates: $25-$30, winter/summer, 1-2 bedroom units; $55-$60, 4 bedrooms. If checkout occurs during non-working hours, patron forfeits the right to be present for inspection. Visa, Mastercard, Discover cards accepted. Reservations all categories, must be paid 4 weeks prior to occupancy. Duty Camp Pendleton can make reservations 12 weeks in advance, duty (other stations) 10 weeks, retirees, reservists 8 weeks. No bumping, mail in reservations not accepted. Call 619-725-2134 for further information. **Pets allowed but they must remain outside. Not allowed on beach.**

TML Availability: Good, Oct-Apr. Difficult, other times.

☞ **All ocean activities available in the area, a 26 mile Ocean shoreline. The communities of Oceanside, San Clemente, and Carlsbad nearby. Convenience store: 725-6233. See Camp Pendleton listing for other Support Facilities. This facility has 26 miles of Pacific Ocean shoreline.**

Edwards Air Force Base (CA48R4)
Edwards AFB, CA 93523-5000

TELEPHONE NUMBER INFORMATION: Main installation numbers: C-805-277-1110, D-312-527-1110

Location: Off CA-14, 18 miles east of Rosamond and 30 miles northeast of Lancaster. Also, off CA-58, 10 miles southwest of Boron. USM: B-5. NMC: Los Angles, 90 miles southwest.

Billeting Office: Building 5602, C-**805-277-4101/3394**, 24 hours daily. Check in facility, check out 1200 hours daily.

TML: VOQ. Buildings 5601, 5602, officers all ranks, leave or official duty. Bedroom, semi-private bath (81). Fully furnished, A/C, color TV, maid service, washer/dryer, ice

Edwards Air Force Base, continued

vending. Older structure, newly furnished. Rates: $8 per person. Duty can make reservations, others Space-A.

TML: VAQ. Buildings 5604, 2410, all ranks, leave or official duty. Building 5604: One bedroom SNCO suites (5). A/C, color TV, maid service. Older structure. Building 2410: One bedroom SNCO rooms (4); two bedrooms (28). A/C, color TV, maid service, washer/dryer. Older structure. Rates: $8 per person. Duty can make reservations, others Space-A.

TML: TLF. Buildings 7022-7031, all ranks. One bedroom suite/family quarters, private bath (53). Double and single bed, sleeper couch in livingroom, A/C, color TV, washer/dryer, kitchen/microwave. Rates: $16. PCS personnel can make reservations, others Space-A.

TML: DV/VIP. Building 5601, officer 06+. One bedroom suites, private bath (10). A/C, color TV, maid service. Older structure. Rates: $14 per person. Duty can make reservations, others Space-A.

DV/VIP: Protocol Office, ATTN: AFFTC/CCP, building 2650, room 200, C-EX-3326. 07+/SES.

TML Availability: Good, all year.

☞ **Los Angeles, 90 miles, many Southern California attractions are nearby.**

Locator 277-2777   Medical 277-4427   Police 277-3340

El Centro Naval Air Facility (CA09R4)
El Centro NAF, CA 92243-5000

TELEPHONE NUMBER INFORMATION: Main installation numbers: C-619-339-2555, D-312-958-8555

Location: Take I-8, 2 miles west of El Centro, to Forrester Rd exit, 1.5 miles to Evan Hewes Hwy left west for 4 miles, right on Bennet Rd to main gate. USM: C-6. NMC: El Centro, 7 miles east.

Billeting Office: Building 270, B & 2nd St's. C-619-339-2535, D-312-958-8535. 24 hours daily. Check in billeting, check out 1000 hours daily. Government civilian employees billeting.

TML: Navy Lodge. Building 387, all ranks, leave or official duty. Reservations: 1-800-NAVY-INN. Lodge number is 714-339-2478. Two bedroom trailers, private bath (4). Kitchen, utensils, A/C, color TV, maid service, coin washer/dryer. Rates: $24 per unit. All categories can make reservations.

TML: BOQ. Building 270, all ranks, leave or official duty. Bedroom, 2 beds, private bath (36); separate bedrooms, private bath (2); bedroom suite, private bath (DV/VIP) (2). Refrigerator, limited utensils, A/C, color TV room & lounge, maid service, ice vending. Older structure, remodeled. Rates: $4 per person. Duty can make reservations, others Space-A. Also BEQ rooms and houses. Inquire.

CALIFORNIA
El Centro Naval Air Facility, continued

DV/VIP: Contact billeting, O6+, retirees Space-A.

TML Availability: Good. Sep-Dec, more difficult.

☞ Hunting, fishing, golf, tennis, hiking and camping are all available in the Imperial Valley, an agricultural center of California. This is wonderful flying country - this is also the winter home (Jan-Mar) of the "Blue Angels".

Locator 339-2555　　　　Medical 339-2675/2666　　　Police 339-2525

El Toro Marine Corps Air Station (CA22R4)
El Toro MCAS, CA 92709-5001

TELEPHONE NUMBER INFORMATION: Main installation numbers: C-714-726-3011, D-312-997-3011.

Location: Off I-5, take the Sand Canyon Rd exit. Follow the signs to the MCAS. USM: B-6. NMC: Los Angeles, 40 miles northwest.

Billeting Office: Building 58, C-**714-726-2381,** D-312-977-2381, FAX-726-3308, 14 hours daily. Check in facility, check out 1100 hours daily. Government civilian employee billeting.

TML: TLF. Building 823, all ranks, leave or official duty. C-EX-2095, 0700-2000 hours daily. Suites, sitting room, bedroom, queen size bed, sofa bed. Kitchen, complete utensils, A/C, color TV in room & lounge, maid service, coin washer/dryer, ice vending, facility for DAVs. Modern structure. Rates: $25 per unit. Maximum 6 per unit. All categories can make reservations.

TML: VOQ/DV/VIP. Buildings 33, 35, 248, 249, 250, officers all ranks, leave or official duty. C-EX-3001. Bedroom, common bath; separate bedrooms, private bath (17); two bedroom, private bath (VIP) (2); three bedroom, private bath (VIP) (3). Kitchen (5 units), refrigerator, A/C (VIP), color TV in room & lounge, maid service, cots, washer/dryer, ice vending. Older structures, some renovated. Rates: common bath rooms $5.50; private bath rooms, leave $5.50, civilians $7; VIP rooms $20. Additional person $4.00 (VIPs $5).

TML: Big Bear Recreation Area. Write to: The Lodge, building 823, MCAS El Toro, Santa Ana, CA 92709, C-**714-726-2095/2084,** D-312-997-2095/2084. All ranks, leave or official duty. Chalets, one bedroom, sofa bed, livingroom, loft (2 double beds) (8). Kitchen, microwave, utensils, fireplace, color TV, VCR, bring personal items, many recreational facilities. All categories may make reservations, active duty MCAS El Toro and Tustin have priority.

DV/VIP: Building 65, C-EX-3624, O6+. Retirees and lower ranks Space-A.

TML Availability: Good, winter months. Difficult, summer months.

☞ Orange County is one of the largest and most affluent counties in the nations. Mission Viejo, Laguna Hills, Laguna Niguel are all nearby. Don't miss Newport beach for old waterfront charm and San Juan Capistrano Mission.

Locator 726-2100　　　　Medical 911　　　　Police 726-3527/8

CALIFORNIA

Fort Hunter Liggett (CA37R4)
Fort Hunter Liggett, CA 93928-5001

TELEPHONE NUMBER INFORMATION: Main installation numbers: C-408-385-5911, D-312-949-2291.

Location: From US-101 south exit at King City to CA-G-14, south to main gate. USM: B-5. NMC: San Luis Obispo, 60 miles south.

Billeting Office: Building T-105, C-408-385-2511/2108, 0800-1630 hours duty days. Other hours SDO, building 205, C-EX-2503. Check in billeting, check out 1000 hours daily. Government civilian employee billeting.

TML: Hacienda Guest House. Building T-101, all ranks, leave or official duty. Bedroom, private bath (6); bedroom, hall bath (5). Refrigerator, color TV in lounge, maid service. Older structure. Rates: $20 with bath, $12 without bath. Reservations accepted duty only, others Space-A.

TML: VOQ. Building T-105, officers all ranks. Separate bedrooms, private bath (50); bedroom, hall bath (10). Refrigerator, A/C, color TV, maid service. Modern structure. Rates: $20 per room (1 or 2 people). Reservations accepted duty only, others Space-A.

TML: VEQ. Building T-128, enlisted all ranks. Bedroom, semi-private bath (38). Rates: $15 private, $8 each share. Reservations accepted duty only.

TML: DV/VIP. Building T-101, officers 06+, leave or official duty. Two bedroom, 2 bed suites, private bath. Refrigerator, color TV, maid service, cribs. Older structure. Reservations required. Rates: $21 duty, $24 off duty. Duty can make reservations, others Space-A.

DV/VIP: Post Headquarters, building 205, C-EX-2505/06. O6+. Retirees and lower ranks Space-A.

TML Availability: Good, most of the year.

☞ **Famous for the yearly return of the swallows--just like Capistrano. The old California Hacienda formerly belonged to the Hearst family. Nearby is Mission San Antonio de Padua. Hunting and fishing available on post in season.**

Locator 385-2520   **Medical 385-2610**   **Police 385-2513**

Fort Irwin National Training Center (CA01R4)
Fort Irwin, CA 92310-0041

TELEPHONE NUMBER INFORMATION: Main installation numbers: C-619-386-4111, D-312-470-4111.

Location: Take I-15 east from Los Angeles for 125 miles or I-15 west from Las Vegas, NV, for 150 miles. Fort is north of I-15 near Barstow, watch for signs. USM: B-5. NMC: San Bernardino, 60 miles southwest.

Billeting Office: Building 109, Langford Lake Rd, C-619-386-4599/1428, 24 hours daily. Check in 1400-1800 hours, check out 1200 hours daily.

CALIFORNIA
Fort Irwin National Training Center, continued

TML: Guest House. All ranks, leave or official duty. Mobile homes, private bath. Kitchen, utensils, A/C, color TV, maid service, washer/dryer. Reservations accepted. Rates: moderate. Maximum 7 per unit. All categories eligible, early reservations suggested.

TML: DVQ. Building 28, officers O6+, C-EX-3000. Bedroom, private bath (8). Refrigerator, A/C, color TV, maid service. Modern structure. Rates: moderate. Maximum 3-5 per unit. Reservations required.

DV/VIP: Protocol, building 151, C-EX-3000, O6+. Lower ranks Space-A.

TML Availability: Good, winter. Difficult, summer.

☞ Visit NASA's Goldstone Deep Space Tracking Station for a group tour. Rainbow Basin has many interesting fossils (not collectable!), and Park Moabi Marina in a quiet cove off the Colorado river are of interest to visitors.

Locator 386-3369   **Medical 386-3242**   **Police 386-4444**

Fort MacArthur (CA46R4)
Los Angeles Air Force Base Annex
Fort MacArthur, CA 90731-2960

TELEPHONE NUMBER INFORMATION: Main installation numbers: C-310-363-8296, D-312-833-8296.

Location: At the end of Harbor 110 Freeway south, left on Gaffey Ave to 22nd St, left to Pacific Ave, right two blocks, left to gate. USM: B-5. NMC: Los Angeles, 18 miles north.

Billeting Office: ATTN: Billeting Manager, building 37, Patton Quadrangle, San Pedro, CA 90731-5000, **C-310-363-8296**, 24 hours. Check in 1400, check out 1100 hours.

TML: TLF. Building 40, all ranks, leave or official duty. Reservations only for official duty, others Space-A. Separate bedrooms, private bath (22). Sofa becomes double bed, chair single bed. Kitchen, utensils, color TV, HBO, maid service, cribs/cots, washer/dryer, ice vending. Older structure. Renovated '92. Rates: based on rank, $20-$30 per night. Maximum 3-5 per room. DAVs can make reservations if outpatient in local VA hospital & have letter from doctor confirming appointment.

TML: VOQ/VAQ. Building 36, all ranks. Reservations only for official duty, others Space-A. Bedroom, private bath (27). Microwave, complete utensils, color TV, HBO, maid service, cribs/cots, washer/dryer, ice vending. Older structure. Rates: $8 per person, maximum $16.

TML: DV/VIP. Cottages 14-17, officers O6+, enlisted E9, leave or official duty. Two bedroom units, private bath (2); bedroom, private bath (2). Kitchen, utensils, color TV, maid service, cribs/cots, washer/dryer. Older structure, renovated. Rates: sponsor $14, maximum $28 per family. Maximum 1-4 per cottage. Duty can make reservations. Call Protocol **C-310-363-2030**.

TML Availability: Best, Nov-Apr. Difficult, other times.

Fort MacArthur, continued

☞ **Fort MacArthur is a sub-post of the Los Angeles Air Force Base, and is located 20 miles from Los Angeles AFB in San Pedro.**

Locator 363-1876   Medical 363-8301   Police 363-8385

Fort Mason Officers' Club (CA45R4)
San Francisco, CA 94123-5000

TELEPHONE NUMBER INFORMATION: Main installation numbers: C-415--441-7700, D-312-859-0111.

Location: Entrance on Bay and Franklin Sts, 3 blocks north of US-101 (Lombard Street). USM: A-7. NMC: San Francisco, in the city.

Billeting Office: Reservation Office: building #1, Bay and Franklin Sts. San Francisco, CA 94123, **C-415-441-7700,** FAX-415-441-2680. Tu-Sa 0900-1700 hrs. Check in 1200 hrs, checkout 1100 hours daily.

TML: VIP Guest Quarters, historic building, officers all ranks, leave or official duty. Reservations advised up to 30 days in advance. Suites, private bath (2); bedroom, private bath (3); CATV, telephone, refrigerator, bar, maid service, ice available, continental breakfast, morning paper and other amenities. Lunch and dinner available on scheduled days. Older structure, remodeled '90. Rates: Single or double 1 bedroom $55; suites $65. Additional persons $10 extra, deposit required. Active duty, reserves, retirees or GS-7 DOD employees on official business.

TML Availability: Difficult, all year. Reserve early. See listing for Marines' Memorial Club at 609 Sutter Street.

☞ **Fort Mason is a National Park. It offers a magnificent view of Alcatraz and San Francisco Bay. Close to North Beach, Fisherman's Wharf, Chinatown. Convenient location, good public transportation. Superb Officers' Club.**

Fort Ord (CA36R4)
Fort Ord, CA 93941-5000

TELEPHONE NUMBER INFORMATION: Main installation numbers: C-408-242-2211, D-312-929-1110.

Location: From San Francisco, south for 100 miles on US-101, right onto CA-156 for 10 miles to main gate of post. USM: A-4. NMC: Monterey, 7 miles south.

Billeting Office: Building 2798, 11th & 12th Sts, **C-408-242-3181,** 24 hours daily. Check in facility, check out 1000 hours. Government civilian employee billeting.

TML: Guest House, building 2798, all ranks, leave or official duty. Apartments: bedroom, private bath (9); two bedrooms, private bath (4); three bedrooms, private bath (26). (Two apartments located at Presidio of Monterey). Kitchen, refrigerator, limited utensils, color TV, maid service, cribs. Older structure. Rates: $17 first occupant, $2 each additional

CALIFORNIA
Fort Ord, continued

occupant. Presidio of Monterey: $16.50 and $2. Rates apply to PCS & TDY personnel. Duty can make reservations, others Space-A. Also, **Lightfighter Lodge**, 30 hotel-type rooms, sleeps 7. Refrigerator, color TV, maid service, cribs. Rates: $17 and $2 for each additional occupant. Duty can make reservations, others Space-A.

TML: VOQ, buildings 4360-4365, officers all ranks, leave or official duty. Bedroom, single, private bath (150); bedroom, double, private bath (23). Rates: $10.50, first occupant, $2 each additional occupant. VOQ at Presidio of Monterey. Bedroom (90). Rates $16.50, $2 each additional occupant. Duty can make reservations, all others Space-A.

TML: DV/VIP, building 2789, C-EX 4227/4225, officers all ranks, leave or official duty. Three bedroom, private bath cottages (6) (1 located at Presidio of Monterey). Kitchen, refrigerator, limited utensils, color TV, maid service, cribs. Older structure. Rates: $21 first occupant, $3 each additional occupant. Duty can make reservations, others Space-A.

DV/VIP: Protocol Office, building 2879, C-EX-4227/4225, 06+.

TML Availability: Good, most of the year.

☞ **Check out Sitwell Recreation Center, and Recreation Center Number Two. Scheduled entertainment, recreational activities, and individual activities. From Monterey south to Big Sur Country, beaches are spectacular.**

Locator 242-2271   **Medical 242-2020**   **Police 242-7851**

⊗**Fort Ord is due to close in Sep '96.**

Lemoore Naval Air Station (CA06R4)
Lemoore NAS, CA 93245-5000

TELEPHONE NUMBER INFORMATION: Main installation numbers: C-209-998-0100, D-312-949-1110.

Location: On CA-198, 24 miles east of I-5, 30 miles west of CA-99 in the south central part of the state. USM: B-4. NMC: Fresno, 40 miles north northeast.

Billeting Office: Barracks 7, building 852, Hancock Circle, C-**209-998-4783** 24 hours daily.

TML: Navy Lodge. Building 908/909, all ranks, leave or official duty. For reservations call **1-800-NAVY-INN.** Lodge number is 998-5791. D-312-949-4861. Check out 1200 hours daily. Efficiency rooms, private bath, 2 double beds (46). Kitchen, utensils, A/C, CATV, maid service, coin washer/dryer, ice vending. Modern structure. Rates: sponsor $31. Maximum 5 per room. All categories can make reservations. Military member may sponsor guest.

TML: BEQ. Building 852, enlisted all ranks, leave or official duty. Check in and out (1200 hours daily) at billeting office. Rooms (48), 32 male, 16 female, three persons per room. Refrigerator, A/C, 45" CATV in lounge, maid service-5 days, washer/dryer. Modern structure. Rates: Sponsor $4. Duty can make reservations, retirees & DAVs Space-A.

Lemoore Naval Air Station, continued

TML: BOQ. Building 800, officer all ranks, leave or official duty, C-EX-4609. Check in and out (1200 hours daily) front desk of facility. Rooms, private bath (60). Refrigerator, community kitchen, A/C, CATV, maid service, washer/dryer, ice vending, 50" TV in lounge. Modern structure. Rates: On orders $8. Retirees, DAVs, reservists Space-A, others can make reservations.

DV/VIP: Commanding Officer, C-EX-3344, O6+. Retirees Space-A.

TML Availability: Good all year.

☞ In the San Joaquin Valley, near Sequoia and Yosemite National Parks, two hours from the coast or mountains, and three hours from Los Angeles and San Francisco. Excellent base facilities.

Locator 998-4709   **Medical 998-4435**   **Police 998-4749**

Long Beach Naval Station (CA55R4)
Long Beach NS, CA 90822-5000

TELEPHONE NUMBER INFORMATION: Main installation numbers: C-310-547-7924, D-312-360-6202.

Location: Take Long Beach Freeway, CA-710 south, to Terminal Island exit to NS. Clearly marked. USM: B-5. NMC: Long Beach, 2 miles east.

Billeting Office: Building 422, Military Support, C-**310-547-7924,** D-312- 360-7928, 24 hours. 7 days. Check out 1200 hours.

TML: Navy Lodge. All ranks, leave or official duty. Check in 24 hours daily. Check out 1200 hours. For reservations call **1-800-NAVY-INN**. Lodge number is 833-2541. One bedroom, 2 double beds, private bath (50), washer/dryer, ice vending. Rates: $35 per room. All categories can make reservations.

TML: BOQ. Building 257, officers, all ranks, leave or official duty. Check in 24 hours daily. Check out 1200 hours. Handicapped accessible. Bedroom rooms and suites, private and semi-private baths (81). Refrigerator, food vending, ice vending, maid service, color TV, washer/dryer. Older structure. New phone system and CATV. Rates: $8 (room), $12 (suite). Maximum one person. Duty can make reservations, others Space-A.

TML: Enlisted quarters, building 422, all ranks. Bedroom, private and semi-private baths (600). Refrigerator, food vending, maid service, CATV, washer/dryer. Modern structure. Rates: sponsor $4. Maximum 3 per unit. Duty can make reservations, others Space-A.

TML Availability: Extremely limited. Best Nov-Jan. Difficult May-Jul.

☞ The Sailing Marina has boat rentals, sailing lessons and a clubhouse, "Gull Park" is located on the tip of the Mole, and "Marine Park" is used for picnics and has a spectacular view of busy Los Angeles Harbor.

CALIFORNIA
Long Beach Naval Station

Locator 547-6002   Medical 547-7979   Police 547-7731

⊗This base has been scheduled for closure in '96. Keep updated with Military Living's R&R Space-A Report travel newsletter.

Los Alamitos Armed Forces Reserve Center (CA39R4)
Los Alamitos, CA 90720-5001

TELEPHONE NUMBER INFORMATION: Main installation numbers: C-310-795-8000 D-312-972-2000.

Location: Off I-605 east of Long Beach. Clearly marked. USM: B-5. NMC: Los Angeles, 35 miles northwest.

Billeting Office: Hq Armed Forces Reserve Center. Check in facility, check out 1200 hours daily. C-310-795-2124/2125, D-972-2124/2125.

TML: TLF. All ranks, leave or official duty. Two bedroom shared, shared bath (female) (10); Two bedroom shared, hall bath (enlisted (96); two bedroom shared, hall bath (officers) (50); bedroom, private bath (06+) (1); suites, private bath (07+) (5). Amenities. E1-O5 share quarters. Duty can make reservations, others Space-A.

TML Availability: Limited, particularly on weekends, call ahead.

☞ Los Alamitos is used extensively for reserve training, and facilities are spartan, according to billeting personnel. But Anaheim (Disneyland!) and Orange County, including great beach cities are nearby.

March Air Force Base (CA08R4)
March AFB, CA 92508-5000

TELEPHONE NUMBER INFORMATION: Main installation numbers: C-714-655-1110, D-312-947-1110.

Location: Off CA-60 and on I-215 which bisects AFB. USM: B-5. NMC: Riverside, 11 miles southwest.

Billeting Office: Building 100, **The March Inn**, Myers & DeKay, C-714-655-5241, 24 hours daily. Check in billeting office, check out 1100 hours daily.

TML: VOQ/TLQ/TAQ. Buildings 100, 102, 125, 501, 2418, 2419, 2420, 2421, all ranks, leave or official duty. Rooms, apartments, & suites (500+ beds). Refrigerator, kitchen, utensils, A/C, color TV room & lounge, maid service, cots & washer/dryer, ice vending. Modern structure. "McBride Suites" (VOQ) dedicated '90. TLF refurbishing includes new TVs, dishware, cookware and blinds. VAQ refurbishment complete by October 1991. Rates: VOQ, sponsor $11; VAQ, sponsor $9-$11; TLF, sponsor, $23. Duty can make reservations, others Space-A.

DV/VIP: HQ 15th Air Force, Protocol, March AFB, D-EX-4764, 06+. DVQ rate: $13-$14.

CALIFORNIA

March Air Force Base, continued

TML Availability: Good, Oct-Feb. More difficult, May-Sep.

☞ This Inn has more than 500 bedspaces, serving 40,000 visitors a year with a staff of about 65, lots of recent improvements, a good place to stay. See nearby Riverside, the Mission Inn, Castle Park, the Riverside International Raceway.

Locator 655-3192   **Medical 655-4266**   **Police 655-2981**

Mare Island Naval Shipyard (CA56R4)
Mare Island Naval Shipyard, CA 94592-5000

TELEPHONE NUMBER INFORMATION: Main installation numbers: C-707-646-1111, D-none.

Location: Exit I-80 N or S at Tennessee St, on CA-37, follow signs to Mare Island Naval Shipyard. USM: A,B-6. NMC: San Francisco, 45 miles east.

Billeting Office: Building 999, C-**707-646-2138,** D-312-253-2138, 24 hours daily. Check in billeting. Government employee billeting.

TML: BOQ, building 926, all ranks, leave or official duty. Check in 24 hours daily, check out 1200 hours. Rooms, private bath (12). Essentials, food vending, maid service, refrigerator, color TV, washer/dryer. Rates: $8. Active duty on orders can make reservations, all others Space-A.

TML: BEQ. Building 999, enlisted, all ranks, leave or official duty. Check in billeting, check out 1200 hours. Rooms, shared bath (60). Refrigerator, food vending, maid service, color TV, washer/dryer. Rates: $3. Active duty on orders can make reservations, others Space-A. No children. No pets.

TML Availability: Extremely limited, all year.

☞ The proximity of the Naval Shipyard to so many attractive recreational features makes it hard to find lodging here, but give them a call, maybe you'll get in!

Medical 646-4444   **Police 646-2222**

Marines' Memorial Club (CA20R4)
609 Sutter Street
San Francisco, CA 94102-5000

TELEPHONE NUMBER INFORMATION: Main installation numbers: C-415-673-6672. Reservations, **1-800-5-MARINE** or **415-673-6604 (direct).** D-None.

Location: Use CA-101 or CA-580. Take CA-580 north to SF, cross the Bay Bridge. Take 5th St exit, up 5th St to O'Farrell. Turn right and go to Powell St. Turn left, go to Sutter St, turn left. Corner of Sutter and Mason. USM: A-7. **Author's Note:** This is NOT "military lodging" in the sense that we list other military installations in this book. The Marines' Memorial Club is a club/hotel exclusively for uniformed services

CALIFORNIA
Marines' Memorial Club, continued

personnel, active duty & retirees and their guests. The club is not a part of the government but is a private, non-profit organization and is completely self-supporting. This club/hotel is a living memorial to Marines who lost their lives in the Pacific during WWII. It opened on the Marine Corps' Birthday, 10 Nov 1946, and chose as its motto "A tribute to those Marines who have gone before; and a service to those who carry on."

Office: Check in and out at lobby desk. Check out 1200 hours daily. Occupancy limited to two weeks except when vacancies exist, 24 hours daily. For brochure or more info write to the above ATTN: Club Secretary, or call 415-673-6672.

TML: Hotel, all ranks, leave or official duty. Guest rooms (137); deluxe suites (11); family suites (3). Reservations required. Courtesy coffee/tea in room, ice, soft drinks vending, room service, large closets. Rates: average room $55, average suite $125. Rates higher for guests of members. All active duty military services, PHS and NOOA considered as members. Retirees membership fee tax deductible. Club facilities include theater, library/museum, swimming pool, gym, coin-operated launderette, valet, exchange store, package store, rooms for private parties, and a dining room and lounge in the Skyroom on the 12th floor, overlooking San Francisco. Convenience store/news stand and coffee shop outside hotel adjacent to entrance. Hotel discount parking on Sutter St. Ask at desk.

TML Availability: Best, winter months. Make reservations well in advance.

☞ In the heart of San Francisco, within walking distance of Cable Cars, many major attractions.

Mather Air Force Base (CA12R4)
Mather AFB, CA 95655-5000

TELEPHONE NUMBER INFORMATION: Main installation numbers: C-916-364-1110, D-312-674-1110.

Location: In Rancho Cordova, US-50 to Mather Field Rd direct to main gate. USM: B-4. NMC: Sacramento, 12 miles west.

Billeting Office: ATTN: 323 ABG/SVH, building 2750, "A" Ave at Gilbert St, C-916-364-2932, 24 hours daily. Check in at billeting, check out 1200 hours daily. Billeting C-EX 2457.

TML: TLQ/VOQ/VAQ/VOQ/VIP. Building 2750, all ranks, leave or official duty. Rooms and suites. Kitchen, refrigerator, complete utensils, A/C, color TV in room & lounge, maid service, cribs, washer/dryer, ice vending. Rates: Moderate. Duty can make reservations, others Space-A. Advance reservations for TDY/PCS personnel.

TML Availability: Fairly good, Dec-Feb. Difficult, other times.

☞ The Sacramento area is rich in historical, cultural, educational and recreational activities. Lake Tahoe and the Sierra Nevada are 90 miles to the northeast. San Francisco and the Pacific Ocean are 90 miles to the southwest.

CALIFORNIA

Mather Air Force Base, continued

Locator 364-2597   **Medical 364-3213**   **Police 364-2200**

⊗ **This base closes September '93. Billeting operating hours from 0600-2200 hours by year end.**

McClellan Air Force Base (CA35R4)
McClellan AFB, CA 95652-5000

TELEPHONE NUMBER INFORMATION: Main installation numbers: C-916-643-2111, D-312-633-1110.

Location: Off I-80 North. From I-80 take Madison Ave exit. Clearly marked. USM: B-4. NMC: Sacramento, 10 miles southwest.

Billeting Office: Building 89, Palm & 30th St, Gate 3, C-**916-643-6223,** 24 hours daily. Check in billeting, check out 1200 hours daily. Government civilian billeting.

TML: Guest House. Building 1430, all ranks, leave or official duty. Bedroom, private bath (7); Two bedroom, private bath (42). Kitchen, limited utensils, A/C, color TV, maid service, cribs/cots, washer/dryer, ice vending. Modern structure. Rates: $22 per unit. Duty can make reservations, others Space-A. Also, VOQ/VAQ available for single occupancy only. $8.

DV/VIP: Protocol, building 200, C-EX-4311. 06+. Retirees/lower ranks Space-A.

TML Availability: Good, winter months. Difficult, summer months.

☞ **Northern Californian skiing, water sports, and Sacramento cosmopolitan activities make McClellan a good choice for a stopover.**

Locator 643-4113   **Medical 643-4733**   **Police 643-6160**

Miramar Naval Air Station (CA14R4)
Miramar NAS, CA 92145-0001

TELEPHONE NUMBER INFORMATION: Main installation numbers: C-619-537-1011, D-312-577-1011.

Location: Fifteen miles north of San Diego, off I-15. Take Miramar Way exit. USM: B-6. NMC: San Diego, 15 miles southwest.

Billeting Office: No central billeting office. Check in facility, check out 1200 hours daily. C-**619-537-4235,** D-312-577-4235.

TML: Navy Lodge. Building 516, all ranks, leave or official duty. Reservations: 1-800-NAVY-INN. Lodge number is 271-7111, 24 hours daily. Units, private bath (90). Kitchen, A/C, color TV, cribs, coin washer/dryer, maid service. Modern structure. Rates: $34 per unit. All categories can make reservations. Kennels near lodge.

CALIFORNIA
Miramar Naval Air Station, continued

TML: BEQ. Building 638, all ranks, official duty only, C-EX-1174, 24 hours daily. Units, semi-private bath (206). Color TV in lounge, washer/dryer. Older structure. Reservations: call above number. Rates: $4 per person.

TML: BOQ. Building M-312, all ranks, leave or official duty, C-EX-4235, 24 hours daily. Rooms & suites, private bath. Color TV, maid service, washer/dryer. Older structure. Rates: $8 per person. Duty on orders can make reservations, others Space-A.

DV/VIP: C-619-537-1221, 06+. Retirees Space-A.

TML Availability: Very good all year.

☞ San Diego's Old Town, Shelter and Harbor Islands, Sea World, Balboa Park downtown are all not to be missed. Water sports, golf, tennis, and nearby Mexico will keep visitors from ever being bored in this lovely city.

Locator 537-6017   **Medical 537-4656**   **Police 537-4059**

Moffett Field Naval Air Station (CA15R4)
Moffett Field NAS, CA 94035-5000

TELEPHONE NUMBER INFORMATION: Main installation numbers: C-415-404-4000, D-312-494-4000.

Location: On Bayshore Freeway, US-101, 35 miles south of San Francisco, CA. USM: A-4. NMC: San Jose, 7 miles south.

Billeting Office: Building 583, C-415-404-8299, D-312-494-8299, 24 hours daily.

TML: Navy Lodge. All ranks, leave or official duty. For reservations call 1-800-NAVY-INN, Lodge number is 962-1542, 0700-2300 hours daily. Bedroom, 2 double beds, kitchen, private bath (50). Maid service, washer/dryer, ice vending. Modern structure. Rates: $36 per unit. All categories can make reservations.

TML Availability: Limited.

☞ Visit historic Hanger One for a trip into navy history.

Locator 404-4088   **Medical 404-4628**   **Police 404-6603**

⊗Latest information is that Moffett Field will close in Sep '97, the Navy Lodge will close in '93. Keep updated with Military Living's *R&R Space-A Report*.

Monterey Naval Postgraduate School (CA16R4)
Monterey Naval Postgraduate School, CA 93943-5000

TELEPHONE NUMBER INFORMATION: Main installation numbers: C-408-646-2441, D-312-878-0111.

CALIFORNIA

Monterey Naval Postgraduate School, continued

Location: Take CA-1 to central Monterey exit, right at light onto Camino Aguajito. Left at stop sign onto Thomas Dr, left at light onto Sloat Ave and to base entrance. Or north on CA-1, Aguajito Rd exit to Mark Thomas Dr, to left on Sloat Ave, right at 3rd St gate. USM: A-4. NMC: Monterey, in city limits.

Billeting Office: Building 220, **Herrmann Hall**, Middle Rd, C-**408-646-2060**, 24 hours daily. Check in billeting 1500 hours, check out 1100 hours daily. Duty billets available during school vacations.

TML: BOQ. Buildings 220, 221, 222, officers all ranks, official duty only. Bedroom, private bath (154); bedroom, semi-private bath (26). Two room suites (VIP) (4); single room suites (VIP) (4). Microwave/Refrigerator, community kitchen (building 220), color TV in room & lounge, maid service, washer/dryer, food/ice vending. Older, structure. Rates: standard room $8 per day per person; single VIP suite $20, two room suite ($25), each additional person $8 per day. Duty can make reservations.

TML: BEQ. Building 259, enlisted E1-E6. Check out anytime. Two rooms, three beds each. Hall baths. Refrigerator, community kitchen, limited utensils, color TV in lounge, washer/dryer. Rates: no charge. Orders only.

DV/VIP: Building 220, officers 06+, leave or official duty, Space-A. Duty can make reservations, others Space-A. C-EX-2513/2514.

TML Availability: Best, Christmas during school vacation and Jun. Other times, extremely limited.

☞ **In the heart of one of the most prestigious areas of California, Herrmann Hall began life as the Hotel Del Monte. Nearby are Pebble Beach, 17 mile drive, Steinbeck's Cannery Row, Fisherman's Wharf and Carmel Mission.**

Locator 646-2441   **Medical 911**   **Police 646-2555**

North Island Naval Air Station (CA43R4)
North Island NAS, CA 92135-0001

TELEPHONE NUMBER INFORMATION: Main installation numbers: C-619-545-8123, D-312-735-0444.

Location: From I-5 north or south exit at Coronado Bridge (toll). Also, from CA-75 north to CA-282 to Base. In Coronado. USM: B-7. NMC: San Diego, 4 miles northeast.

Billeting Office: Building 1 for officers, C-**619-545-7545**. Building 773 for enlisted, C-**619-545-9551**, 24 hours daily. Check in facility (between 1500-1800 for confirmed reservations), check out 1200 hours daily. Government civilian employee billeting available at BOQ.

TML: Navy Lodge. Building 1402, all ranks, leave or official duty. Reservations call **1-800-NAVY-INN**. Lodge number is 545-6940. Bedroom, 2 double beds, studio couch, private bath (90). Kitchen, limited utensils, A/C, color TV, maid service, cribs, coin washer/dryer, ice vending. Modern structure, renovated. Rates: $34. Maximum 5 per room. All categories can make reservations.

CALIFORNIA
North Island Naval Air Station, continued

DV/VIP: PAO. C-EX-8167, 06+, retirees and lower ranks if approved by commander.

TML Availability: Good, except Oct-Mar.

☞ North Island is the birthplace of Naval aviation. The San Diego Trolley connects to downtown and bus routes. San Diego is filled with things to see and do; Mission Valley, the zoo and Balboa Park are only a few.

Locator 694-3155   Medical 545-4306   Police 545-7423

Norton Air Force Base (CA17R4)
Norton AFB, CA 92409-5000

TELEPHONE NUMBER INFORMATION: Main installation numbers: C-714-382-1110, D-312-876-1110.

Location: From I-10 in Loma Linda take Tippecanoe exit north to Base, approximately 1.5 miles. USM: B-5. NMC: San Bernardino, 3 miles northwest.

Billeting Office: Building 512, 3rd St. C-714-382-5531. For reservations call C-**714-382-4855**. 24 hours daily. Check in billeting, check out 1200 hours daily.

TML: TLF. Buildings 901-904, all ranks, leave or official duty. Separate bedrooms, private bath, sleeps 4 persons (39). Kitchen, A/C, color TV, maid service, cribs, washer/dryer. Older structure. Rates: $26 per unit. Maximum 4 per unit. Duty can make reservations, others Space-A.

TML: VAQ. Buildings 512, 515, enlisted all ranks, leave or official duty. Bedroom, semi-private bath (162); separate bedroom suites, private bath (5). Refrigerator, A/C, color TV, maid service, washer/dryer. Older structure. Rates: $8 per person. Maximum 1 per room. Duty can make reservations, others Space-A.

TML: VOQ. Buildings 503, 517, 561-563, officer 01-05, leave or official duty. Bedroom, private and semi-private baths (162); separate bedrooms, private bath (5). Kitchen (some), refrigerator, A/C, color TV, maid service, washer/dryer. Older structure. Rates: $10 per person. Duty can make reservations, others Space-A.

TML: DV/VIP. Building 504, 06+, leave or official duty, C-EX-7615. Separate bedroom suites, private bath. Kitchen, A/C, color TV, maid service, washer/dryer. Older structure. Rates: $14 per person. Duty can make reservations, others Space-A.

DV/VIP: Building 673, 63 MAW/CCP, 06+, C-EX-7616. Retirees & lower ranks Space-A.

TML Availability: Good, Oct-Apr. Difficult, other times.

☞ Visit Big Bear Lake; see the desert wildflowers in spring; Colorado River waterskiing; free concerts at the Redlands Bowl; shop 'til you drop in Lake Arrowhead village.

Locator-382-5381   Medical-382-7818

⊗Norton is tentatively scheduled to close in Aug '94.

CALIFORNIA

Oakland Army Base (CA18R4)
Oakland Army Base, CA 94626-5000

TELEPHONE NUMBER INFORMATION: Main installation numbers: C-510-466-9111, D-312-859-9111.

Location: Near junction of I-80, I-580, and CA-880, south of the San Francisco-Oakland Bay Bridge. USM: A-7. NMC: Oakland, 2 miles southeast.

Billeting Office: Building 650, C-510-444-8107, D-312-859-3113, 24 hours daily. Check in front desk, check out 1100 hours daily. Government civilian employee billeting.

TML: Guest House, Building 650, all ranks, leave or official duty. Bedroom, double beds, private bath (23); two room suites, queen-size bed, living room, sofa bed, private bath (25); three room suites with bedroom, living room, den with sofa bed, private bath (4). All have refrigerator, cable color TV w/HBO. Video movie rentals, ice vending, maid service, irons and ironing boards, complimentary coffee, some non-smoking rooms. Modern structure. Rates: Standard $25-$35, two room suite $35-$45, three room suites $45-$55. All categories can make reservations.

TML Availability: Good.

☞ **Lake Merritt, Lakeside Park, the Oakland Museum, Jack London Square in Oakland are of interest to visitors. Across the bay is San Francisco itself; just north is the wine country and the Redwoods, both treasures.**

Medical 466-2918   **Police 466-3333**

Oakland Naval Hospital (CA41R4)
8750 Mountain Blvd
Oakland NMC, CA 94627-5025

TELEPHONE NUMBER INFORMATION: Main installation numbers: C-510-633-5000 (After duty hours EX-6200), D-312-855-6200.

Location: Off I-580 south from San Francisco-Oakland Bridge, take either Keller Ave or Golf Links Rd exit. Clearly marked. USM: B-7. NMC: Oakland, 38 miles northwest.

Billeting Office: Billeting reserved for patients and permanent party PCS in/out only.

☺**This Navy Lodge has been closed, but a new lodge may be built. Keep posted by reading Military Living's *R&R Space-A Report* travel newsletter.**

TML Availability: Limited.

Locator 633-5000   **Medical 433-5440**

CALIFORNIA

Petaluma Coast Guard Training Center (CA23R4)
Petaluma, CA 94952-5000

TELEPHONE NUMBER INFORMATION: Main installation numbers: C-707-765-7211, FTS-623-7211.

Location: Exit US-101 north to East Washington Ave West. Follow Washington Ave 9 miles west to Coast Guard Training Center. USM: A-4. NMC: San Francisco, 49 miles south.

Billeting Office: Building T-134, Nevada Ave, C-**707-765-7247**, 0730-1600 hours daily. Other hours Security, C-EX-7211. Check in at facility, check out time discussed with manager. Government civilian employee billeting, maximum stay 2 weeks.

TML: TLQ. Building 134, all ranks, leave or official duty. Bedroom, private bath (8); Four person unit, semi-private bath (1). Refrigerator, color TV, cribs, washer/dryer, ice vending, microwave. Older structure. Rates: $16-$19 per room. Maximum $16 per family. All categories can make reservations. PCS have priority.

DV/VIP: One VIP suite in Harrison Hall (06+), leave or official duty. Private bath, refrigerator, color TV, maid service. Rate: $25 per night. Retirees Space-A. Call CO's office for reservations, C-EX-7320.

TML Availability: Generally good. Difficult, summer months.

☞ **The Petaluma area is saturated with historical lore and legend. Early California missions, a Russian fort (Fort Ross), Sonoma County wineries, and Russian River swimming, fishing and canoeing will all draw visitors.**

Locator 554-4020   Medical 765-7200   Police 765-7215

Point Mugu Naval Air Weapons Station (CA40R4)
Point Mugu NAWS, CA 93042-5000

TELEPHONE NUMBER INFORMATION: Main installation numbers: C-805-989-1110, D-312-351-1110.

Location: Eight miles south of Oxnard and 40 miles north of Santa Monica, on Coast Highway, CA-1. USM: B-5. NMC: Los Angeles, 50 miles southeast.

Billeting Office: Building 27, D Street, between Sixth and Seventh Streets. C-**805-989-7510/8235**, 24 hours daily. Check in facility, check out 1000 hours daily. Government civilian employee billeting.

TML: BOQ. Various buildings, some cottages. Officers all ranks, leave or official duty. Bedroom, two beds, private bath, (35). Refrigerator, color TV, VCR, maid service, roll-away cots, washer/dryer, essentials, food and ice vending. Older structure, renovated. Rates: $8 per person. Maximum charge $25. Duty and civilians on orders can make reservations, all others Space-A.

CALIFORNIA

Point Mugu Naval Air Weapons Station, continued

TML: BEQ. Enlisted E1-E6, leave or official duty. Bedrooms, common bath. Refrigerator, color TV, VCR, maid service, essentials, food vending, washer/dryer. Older structure, renovated. Rates: $4 per person. Duty only can make reservations, unaccompanied retirees Space-A. No dependents.

TML: TVEQ. Enlisted E7-E9, leave or official duty. Suites, private bath (9). Refrigerator, color TV, VCR, maid service, essentials, food and ice vending, washer/dryer. Older structure, renovated. Rates: $8 per person. Eligibility same as BEQ.

TML: DV/VIP. Building 170, officers 06+, leave or official duty. Bedroom suites, private bath (8). Kitchenette, above amenities. Older structure, renovated. Rates: $25 per person. Duty can make reservations, others Space-A.

TML: Recreation area has 5 cabins and 11 motel-type rooms with kitchenette, which will be closed on opening a new beach Recreation Lodge, which is on one of the finest surfing and swimming beaches in California, C-805-989-7509. Bedrooms, two beds, private bath (22); family bedrooms, six persons, private bath (2). Kitchenette, refrigerator, microwave, basic utensils, color TV, lounge telephones vending machines. Rates: $38-$43. All categories may make reservations. **To open in August or September '92.**

DV/VIP: Command Protocol, building 36, C-EX-8672, 06+.

TML: Availability: Fair. Difficult, Mar-Sep.

☞ **This facility is on the Pacific Ocean, close to the great shopping in Santa Monica, and within reach of coastal range recreation as well as the famous beaches of Southern California. Full range of support facilities on base.**

Locator 989-1110   **Medical 911**   **Police 911**

Port Hueneme Naval Construction Battalion Center (CA32R4)
Port Hueneme NCBC, CA 93043-5000

TELEPHONE NUMBER INFORMATION: Main installation numbers: C-805-982-4711, D-312-360-4711.

Location: Seven miles west of US-101. Take Victoria Ave exit in Ventura to Channel Islands Blvd (turn left), to Ventura Road (turn right), to Pleasant Valley Road (turn right). Enter at Pleasant Valley Gate. USM: B-5. NMC: Los Angeles, 40 miles southeast.

Billeting Office: ATTN: Code 61, building 1435, Pacific Road. C-805-982-4497, 24 hours daily. Check in at facility. Government civilian employee no billeting.

TML: Navy Lodge. Building 1172, all ranks, leave or official duty. Reservations required. For reservations call **1-800-NAVY-INN**. Lodge number is 985-2624. Bedroom studio efficiency, private bath (22). Kitchen, utensils, color TV, maid service, cribs, coin washer/dryer, ice vending, accessible to handicapped. Modern structure, remodeled. Rates: $33 per unit. Maximum 4 persons. Duty and retirees can make reservations, others Space-A.

CALIFORNIA
Port Hueneme Naval Construction Battalion Center, continued

TML: BEQ: Duty only, C-EX-4497. BOQ: Duty only, C-EX-5785. Female enlisted quarters: Duty only, C-EX-4497. May have TML Space-A.

TML: DV/VIP. Guest House, buildings 39, 1435, officers 06+, leave or official duty. Reservations required, call protocol C-EX-4741, check in Building 1164. Building 39, 1 cottage (Doll House), private bath. Kitchen, utensils, color TV, maid service. Older structure (1925), patio back yard. Duty can make reservations, others Space-A.

DV/VIP: Plan & Mob Office. Building 14, Room 204, C-EX-4401, 07/GS-16+.

TML Availability: Good, winter months. Difficult, summer months.

☞ **In easy access of metropolitan Los Angeles, coastal Ventura County boasts wonderful weather. This is the home of the famous Seebees, a bustling complex of 10,000 military and civilians, and more than 1600 acres.**

Locator 982-4711   **Medical 982-6301**   **Police 982-4591**

☺**A new Navy Lodge is planned at this location. Keep posted on new developments with Military Living's *R&R Space-A Report.***

Presidio of San Francisco (CA19R4)
Presidio of San Francisco, CA 94129-5000

TELEPHONE NUMBER INFORMATION: Main installation numbers: C-415-561-2211, D-312-586-1110.

Location: At the South end of the Golden Gate Bridge. From US-101 North exit onto Lombard St. From US-101 South exit onto Merchant Rd, follow signs to Lombard St and Presidio. USM: A-7. NMC: San Francisco, south & east in city limits.

Billeting Office: Building 42, Lincoln Blvd, ATTN: AFZM-DEH-HB, C-415-561-4757, 0730-1615 hours daily. Check in at desk of facility, 24 hours daily. Check out 1100 hours daily.

TML: Guest House. Building 42, **Pershing Hall**, building 951, Scott Hall, C-415-561-3411, D-312-561-2096, all ranks, leave or official duty. Pershing: two bedroom apartments, private bath (2); bedroom apartments, private bath (12); Scott: two bedroom, semi-private bath (16); bedroom, private bath (1). Kitchen in some, limited utensils, CATV, TV in room & lounge, maid service, cribs, free & coin washer/dryer, ice vending. Older structures. Rates: Pershing: single w/o bath $13, w/bath $17, two bedroom for two $36, one bedroom for two $31, each additional person $4; Scott: 1 bedroom $22, suites for two $27, each additional person $3. Furnished kitchens available $3 daily. PCS & medical outpatient can make reservations 30 days in advance, retirees, military widows, and dependents Space-A.

TML: Lake Tahoe/Heavenly Valley Cabins. West shore, south shore. Community Recreation Division, Presidio of San Francisco, CA, 42129-5206, C-415-561-4356. All ranks, leave or official duty, retirees. Two bedroom A-frame (sleeps 8) (1); two bedroom condominium (1). Kitchen, utensils, TV, no maid service, bring linens, deck, barbecue (W shore), same amenities, plus pool, hot tub, game room (S shore). No pets. Rates: $60 daily Su -Th, $85 F, Sa and any night preceding holiday. All categories may make

CALIFORNIA

Presidio of San Francisco, continued

reservations, 1 year in advance Presidio assigned personnel, 6 months others, 4 months retirees, 90 days reservists, federal employees in SF. **Note:** more information in Military RV, Camping and Rec Areas Around the World.

DV/VIP: Protocol Office, building 38, C-EX-3950/2540, 06+, retirees & lower ranks Space-A at discretion of Protocol. Rates: $29.50 each additional person $6.50.

TML Availability: Good.

☞ Located in the shadow of the Golden Gate Bridge, the Presidio is strategically located close to the Marina District, excellent shopping and dining, Fisherman's Wharf, China Town, Nob Hill, and scenic Lincoln and Golden Gate Parks. If you can land lodging here, it's well worth it!

Locator 561-4431   **Medical 561-5656**   **Police 561-2251/2252**

⊗The Presidio is scheduled to close the 4th quarter of '94. Keep posted on latest developments with Military Livings' *R&R Space-A Report.*

San Diego Marine Corps Recruit Depot (CA57R4)
San Diego MCRD, CA 92140-5012

TELEPHONE NUMBER INFORMATION: Main installation numbers: C-619-524-1011, D-none.

Location: From airport, Pacific Coast Highway to MCRC exit. From Interstate 5 S and 8 W take Rosecrans exit, turn left on Midway, and right on Barnett Ave. USM: B-7. In the city.

Billeting Office: Building 13, C-619-524-4401. D-none, 0700-2300, daily. After duty hours, DOOD, Building 31, C-619-524-1276. Lodging available for DoD civilians on official duty.

TML: Transient Officers Quarters. Building 312, officers, all ranks, leave or official duty. Check in billeting 0700-2300 hours daily. Check out 1200 hours. Rooms with shared bath (8); rooms with private bath (2); suites with separate bedroom, private bath (8). Kitchenettes in suites, others common kitchen, refrigerators, coffee pots and essentials, color TV, telephones, maid service, washer/dryer, pool table in lounge, cribs, new carpeting, on going remodeling, modern structure. Handicapped accessible. Rates: sponsor $12-$15, additional adult $18-$22. Maximum $22 per family. Maximum 3 persons per room. Pets OK. Military on orders have priority, all categories can make reservations.

TML: Transient Enlisted Quarters. Buildings 619, 625, enlisted all ranks, leave or official duty. Check in billeting 0700-2300 hours daily, check out 1200 hours. Room with two beds, private bath (77); suites, separate bedroom, private bath (2); units with shared bath (88). Refrigerator, coffee pots, essentials, maid service, color TV, washer/dryer, cribs. Modern structure, new carpeting, satellite service under constructions, telephones mid Jan '92. Handicapped accessible. Pets allowed. Rates: sponsor $13, additional adult $15. Maximum $15 per family. Maximum 2 per room. All categories can make reservations, military on orders have priority, others Space-A.

CALIFORNIA
San Diego Marine Corps Recruiting Center, continued

TML: DV/VIP. MCRC building 31, rm 238. Protocol officer, D-619-524-1275, O6+. Active duty and retirees, DoD civilians: TOQ & TEQ available. Others Space-A.

TML Availability: Good to very good. Best Jan-May, Sep-Dec. Difficult Jun-Aug.

☞ This is the Marine Corps oldest operating installation on the West coast, and is a short distance from downtown San Diego. Check out San Diego Zoo, Seaworld, beaches, fishing, and bargain shopping in nearby Tijuana, Mexico.

Locator 524-1728　　　　**Medical 524-4079**　　　　**Police 524-4202**

San Diego Naval Station (CA26R4)
San Diego NS, CA 92136-0001

TELEPHONE NUMBER INFORMATION: Main installation numbers: C-619-556-1011, D-312-526-1011.

Location: Off I-5, 7 miles south of San Diego. Take 28th St exit. NS is at 28th & Main St's. USM: C-7. NMC: San Diego, 7 miles south.

Billeting Office: Building 3362 (BEQ), Building 254 (BOQ). C-619-556-2745 (BEQ). C-619-556-6134 (BOQ) 0730-1630 hours daily. Other hours, Watch Section/Central Assignments, Building 3362. Check in facility, check out 1200 hours daily. Government civilian employees billeting.

TML: Navy Lodge. Building 3191, all ranks, leave or official duty. For reservations call 1-800-NAVY-INN. Lodge number is 234-6142, 24 hours daily. Check in 1500-1800 hours. Check out 1200 hours. Bedroom units, private bath (45). Each room has 2 double beds, couch, sleeps 5. Kitchen, utensils, A/C, color TV, telephone, coin washer/dryer, ice vending, vending machine, playground, maid service, cribs. Facilities for DAVs. Rates: $34. Government civilian employees billeting only if 02+ equivalent with ID and orders. All categories can make reservations. Note: Two rooms handicapped accessible.

TML: BEQ. Building 8, enlisted all ranks, official duty only. Beds, semi-private bath (E7+ private bath) (3500). TV lounge, maid service, washer/dryer, ice vending. Rates: $2 per person. Dependents not authorized. Reservations required.

TML: BOQ. Building 254, officers all ranks, official duty only. Bedroom, private bath (75); separate bedrooms, private bath (57). Refrigerator, color TV, maid service, washer/dryer, ice vending. Rates: $4 per person. Maximum 2 per room. Children not authorized. Duty can make reservations, others Space-A.

TML Availability: Good except PCS rotations, summer months.

☞ Aside from the wonderful weather, beaches, etc, visitors shouldn't miss Sea World, the world famous San Diego Zoo, Balboa Park and Sea Port Village.

Locator 556-1011　　　　**Medical 556-1801**　　　　**Police 556-1526**

☺ This Navy Lodge is scheduled for a 98 unit addition in late '93. Watch for updates in Military Living's *R&R Space-A Report.*

CALIFORNIA

San Diego Naval Submarine Base (CA79R4)
San Diego NSB, CA 92106-3521

TELEPHONE NUMBER INFORMATION: Main installation numbers: C-619-553-1011, D-312-933-1011.

Location: From I-5 take Rosecrans west onto base. USM: B-7. NMC: In the city, San Diego.

Billeting Office: BOQ. Building 601, C-619-553-9381. Check in facility. Check out 1200 hours.

TML: BOQ. Building 601. Officers, all ranks, leave or official duty. Enlisted E7-E9, official duty only. Bedroom, private bath (75); separate bedrooms, private bath (55); VIP suites, private bath (6). Cots, essentials, food/ice vending, kitchenette (suites), limited utensils, maid service, refrigerator, color TV, washer/dryer. Modern structure. Rates: sponsor $8, VIP suites $25. Maximum 2 persons. Duty can make reservations, others Space-A.

TML: BEQ. Building 300, enlisted, E1-E6, official duty only, C-EX-7535. Rooms with various bath combinations. Food/ice vending, maid service, refrigerator, color TV lounge, washer/dryer. Modern structure. Rates: sponsor $4.

TML Availability: Fairly good. Best Dec. Difficult May-Aug.

☞ **Located on beautiful Point Loma, with a spectacular view of San Diego Harbor, and the city, this facility is also close to beaches, Old Town, the San Diego Zoo, and many other recreational delights.**

Locator 553-1011   Police 553-7070

San Pedro Coast Guard Personnel Support Center (CA25R4)
San Pedro, CA 90731-0208

TELEPHONE NUMBER INFORMATION: Main installation numbers: C-310-514-6450, FTS-795-6450.

Location: On Coast Guard Base, Terminal Island, San Pedro, CA, 6 miles west of Long Beach. USM: B-5. NMC: Long Beach, 2 miles east.

Billeting Office: Local Housing Authority, Long Beach, P. O. Box 8, Terminal Island Station, San Pedro, CA 90731-0208, C-310-514-6450, 0700-1600 M-F, check in facility, check out 1400 hours daily. No government civilian employee billeting.

TML: Guest House. All ranks, leave or official duty. Two bedroom, private bath (2). Kitchen, complete utensils, color TV, washer/dryer. Modern structure. Rates: vary by rank. Duty and retired can make reservations.

CALIFORNIA
San Pedro Coast Guard Personnel Support Center, continued

TML Availability: Good year round.

☞ Close to beach cities, Los Angeles harbor, and all that Southern California has to offer.

Sierra Army Depot (CA44R4)
Herlong, CA 96113-9999

TELEPHONE NUMBER INFORMATION: Main installation numbers: C-916-827-2111, D-312-855-4910.

Location: 55 miles north of Reno, NV, off US-395. Right on CA-A26 from Reno. When traveling south on US-395, left on CA-A25. USM: B-3. NMC: Reno, 55 miles southeast.

Billeting Office: Building T-26, **C-916-827-4544** duty hours. Other hours, Sec Radio Room, Building P-100, C-916-827-4345. Check in facility, check out 1100 hours daily. Government civilian employee billeting.

TML: Guest House. Building T-26 (O'Club), all ranks, leave or official duty. Bedroom, semi-private bath (2); Two bedroom apartments, private bath (DV/VIP)(2); bedroom (VOQ/VEQ), semi-private bath (8). Kitchen in apartments, refrigerator, community kitchen, limited utensils, maid service, cribs/cots $1, washer/dryer. Older structure. Rates: Private Bath $14, plus $4 for each additional person, and $16 plus $5 for each additional person. PCS rate determined by rank, all rooms. Semi-private bath $12 plus $3 each additional person. Duty can make reservations, others Space-A.

DV/VIP: PAO, C-EX-4544. Determined by Commander.

TML Availability: Good, winter. Difficult, summer.

☞ Water sports, hiking, skiing, and most outdoor activities are popular in this Northern California paradise. Lassen Volcanic National Park, the Eagle Lake Marina, and the Reno/Tahoe areas have rich recreational opportunities.

Locator 827-4328   Medical 827-4141/4575   Police 827-4345

✪The Armed Services Committee has approved MWR funds for a guest house for this facility. Keep updated with Military Living's travel newsletter, *R&R Space-A Report.*

Stockton Naval Communications Station (CA51R4)
Stockton, CA 95203-5000

TELEPHONE NUMBER INFORMATION: Main installation numbers: C-209-944-0284/0343, D-312-466-7284/7343.

Location: From I-5 north exit at Rough & Ready Island, right at Fresno St to Washington St to Station. USM: B-4. NMC: Stockton, in the city.

CALIFORNIA
Stockton Naval Communications Station, continued

Billeting Office: Building 128, Hooper Dr & McCloy Ave, C-**209-944-0284/0343**, 0730-1600 M-F. Other hours. DMAA Office, building 128. Check in facility, check out 1200 hours daily.

TML: TLQ/BOQ/BEQ. Buildings 24, 128, 129, all ranks, leave or official duty. E7+ and civilian equivalents, suites (4). Rates: $8 per person. E5, E6 unaccompanied males, two persons per room. E4 and below male, four man rooms. E6 and below female, 2 women per room (1). Rates $2. For O3+ VIP suite (1). Rate: $15 per person. Refrigerator, A/C, Cable TV, maid service (M-F), washer/dryer. Under 12 free. Maximum 4 per room. Duty can make reservations, others Space-A.

TML Availability: Fairly good, winter months and holidays. Difficult, summer.

☞ Situated between San Francisco, Sacramento and near Yosemite, Stockton is within reach of many California landmarks.

Locator 944-0284/0343   Medical 944-0445   Police 944-0451

Travis Air Force Base (CA50R4)
Travis AFB, CA 94535-5000

TELEPHONE NUMBER INFORMATION: Main installation numbers: C-707-424-5000, D-312-837-1110.

Location: Off I-80 North, take Travis AFB Parkway exit. USM: B-4. NMC: San Francisco, 45 miles southwest.

Billeting Office: Building 404, Sevedge Dr. C-**707-424-2987**, D-312-837-2987, 24 hours daily. Check in facility, check out 1200 hours daily. Government civilian employee billeting.

TML: TLQ. Building 404, all ranks, leave or official duty. Studio apartments, private bath (40). Kitchen, color TV, A/C, maid service, telephone. Modern structure. Rates: $21 per unit. Duty can make reservations, others Space-A.

TML: VOQ. Building 404, officers all ranks, leave or official duty. Bedroom, semi-private bath (231). Refrigerator, A/C, TV, maid service. Older structure. Rates: $6 per person. Duty can make reservations, others Space-A.

TML: VAQ. Building 404, enlisted all ranks, leave or official duty. Reservations accepted. Bedroom, semi-private bath (667). Same as VOQ above.

TML: DV/VIP. Building 404, officer 06+, leave or official duty. D-EX-3185. Suites, private bath (23). A/C, color TV, maid service. Older structure. Rates: $10 per person. Duty can make reservations, others Space-A.

DV/VIP: DV lounge at Air Term, D-EX-3185, 06+. Retirees Space-A.

TML Availability: Very limited, summer. Good, other times.

CALIFORNIA
Travis Air Force Base, continued

☞ **San Francisco, almost unlimited cultural and recreational opportunities. California beach towns and wine country, the capital city of Sacramento, and the Sierra Nevada mountains are all within reach of Travis.**

Locator 424-2026   Medical 423-3462   Police 438-2011

Treasure Island Naval Station (CA21R4)
Treasur Island NS, CA 94130-5004

TELEPHONE NUMBER INFORMATION: Main installation number: C-415-395-1000; D-312-475-1000.

Location: On Treasure Island in San Francisco Bay off Hwy I-80 (Oakland Bay Bridge), take exit from left lane. USM: A-7. NMC: San Francisco, 3 miles southwest.

Billeting Office: BOQ. Building 369, California Ave, C-415-395-5274, D-312-475-5274, 24 hours. Reservations: **C-415-395-5273 (BOQ)**, D-312-475-5273; **C-415-395-5412 (BEQ)**, D-312-475-5412. Check in facility, check out 1100 hours daily. Space-A call after 1800 hours.

TML: BOQ/BEQ. All ranks, leave or official duty. BOQ rooms, private and semi-private baths (285). Refrigerator, color TV, maid service, washer/dryer, hot tub, sauna, mini weight room. Older structure, renovated. Rates: sponsor $25, each additional person $8. Duty can make reservations, others Space-A.

DV/VIP: Protocol Office, Code 120, building 369, C-EX-5274, D-EX-5274. 07+, retirees Space-A.

TML Availability: Good, Dec. Other times, limited.

☞ **Boat rentals at the base marina (395-3396), miniature golf, theater, bowling and a fitness center are available on base; Golden Gate bridge, Fisherman's Wharf, Coit Tower, China Town and wonderful dining and entertainment in S.F.**

Locator-395-6433   Medical-395-3649

⊗**This Station will close in '97.**

Tustin Marine Corps Air Station (CA86R4)
Tustin MCAS, CA 92710-5001

TELEPHONE NUMBER INFORMATION: Main installation numbers: C-714-726-3011, D-312-977-3011.

Location: Near the I-5 and 55 interchange, take Red Hill Ave exit. West 1 1/2 miles to main gate (Valencia is the cross street). USM: B-5,6. NMC: Irvine/Tustin, Los Angeles, 45 miles NW.

CALIFORNIA

Tustin Marine Corps Air Station, continued

Billeting Office: Billeting Office, building 20A, Moffett/Cross Sts, C-**714-726-7983/4,** 0700-1530 daily. After duty hours SDO, building 4, C-714-726-7324. Check in, check out at billeting.

TML: BOQ. Building 93, officers, W-1 to O5, official duty, only. Bedooms, private bath, (16). Kitchenette, maid service, washer/dryer. Modern structure. Rates: inquire. Maximum 2 persons per room. No pets. Active duty, reservists and national guard on orders Space-A. Reservations accepted.

TML: BEQ. Building 245, enlisted, E6-E9, official duty only. Rooms, private bath (67). Refrigerator, color TV in lounge, washer/dryer. Modern structure. No pets. Rates: inquire. Two persons maximum per rooms. Active duty, reservists and national guard. Reservations accepted.

TML: DV/VIP "Quarters C" **(Hideaway).** 06+, leave or official duty. Commanding Officer, MCAS Tustin. C-EX-7301, D-EX-7301.

TML Availability: Difficult to extremely limited.

☞ **Located near Disneyland, Newport Beach, and Laguna, there is no shortage of entertainment nearby, if you can stay here.**

⊖**This station will close in Sep '97.**

Locator 726-3736   **Medical 726-9911**   **Police 726-9911**

Twentynine Palms Marine Corps Air/Ground Combat Center (CA27R4)
Twentynine Palms MCA/GCC, CA 92278-5000

TELEPHONE NUMBER INFORMATION: Main installation numbers: C-619-368-6000, D-312-952-6000.

Location: From west on I-10 exit on CA-62 NE to Base. From east on I-40 exit south at Amboy. USM: B,C-5. NMC: Palm Springs, 60 miles southwest.

Billeting Office: Building 1565, 5th St near O'Club, C-**619-368-7375/6642,** FAX C-619-368-5980, D-312-957-5980, 24 hours daily. Check in facility 1400, check out 1100 hours daily. Government civilian employee billeting.

TML: BOQ/BEQ, all ranks, leave or official duty. VIP Quarters 04/GS-10+ (4); three CG guest house rooms; 16 rooms (04+); 69 rooms (03-); 40 SNCO rooms. Community kitchen, A/C, color TV in room & lounge, maid service, washer/dryer, ice vending. Older structure. Rates: Adults $9, $12, $19.50, $35. Maximum $30 per family. Duty can make reservations, except in guest house, others Space-A. No pets.

TML: TLF. Building 690, C-EX-6573/6583. One bedroom family units, trundle beds, private bath. Kitchen, washer/dryer, BBQ, playground. Rates: $17.50-$31 per unit. Call for reservations information. No pets.

DV/VIP: Protocol Office, C-EX-6109, 04+. Retirees and lower ranks Space-A.

CALIFORNIA
Twentynine Palms Marine Corps Center, continued

TML Availability: Good, winter months. Difficult, summer months.

☞ **Five miles from Joshua Tree national monument where the low Colorado and the high Mojave deserts come together. Many come from miles around to see the desert blooming with wildflowers.**

Locator 368-6853   **Medical 368-7254**   **Police 368-6800**

Vandenberg Air Force Base (CA29R4)
Vandenberg AFB, CA 93437-5000

TELEPHONE NUMBER INFORMATION: Main installation numbers: C-805-866-1110, D-312-276-1110.

Location: From south on US-101, west on CA-246, north on CA-S20 to AFB. From north on US-101, west on US-1 from Gaviota, north on CA-S20 to AFB. USM: B-5. NMC: Santa Maria, 22 miles north.

Billeting Office: ATTN: Vandenberg Billeting, Box 5579. Building 13005, Oregon at L St. C-805-866-1844, 24 hours daily. Check in billeting, check out 1200 hours daily. Government civilian employee billeting.

TML: TLF. Building 13007, all ranks, leave or official duty. Handicapped accessible. Bedroom, private bath (15). Kitchen, complete utensils, CATV, maid service, cribs/cots, washer/dryer, essentials. Older structure, renovated. Rates: $25 per room. Maximum 5 per room. Duty can make reservations. Retirees can make reservations for medical appointments only, others Space-A.

TML: VAQ. Building 13140, enlisted all ranks, leave or official duty. Separate bedrooms, semi-private baths (E1-E8) (76); bedroom, private bath (E9 only)(4). Color TV, maid service, washer/dryer, vending machines, essentials. Older structure, remodeled. Rates: $9 per person. Maximum 2 persons in E9 rooms. Duty can make reservations, others Space-A.

TML: VOQ. 11000 area. Officers all ranks, leave or official duty. Handicapped accessible. Bedroom, private bath (78); bedroom, private bath (4); two bedroom, semi-private bath (224). Color TV, maid service, washer/dryer, essentials, ice vending, special facilities DAVs. Modern structure. Rates: $9 per person. Maximum 2 persons per unit. Duty can make reservations, others Space-A.

TML: VOQ. Building 13000 area. Officers all ranks, leave or official duty. One bedroom suites, private bath (16); Two bedroom, semi-private bath (224). Refrigerator, community kitchen, color TV, maid service, cots, washer/dryer, special facilities DAVs. Older structure. Rates: $9 per person. Duty can make reservations, others Space-A.

TML: BOQ. Building 13800, officers all ranks, official duty only. Reservations not taken. Two bedroom apartments, private bath (10). All other same as VOQ above. Maid service optional.

TML: DV/VIP. **Marshallia Ranch**, building 1338, officers O6/GS-17+, leave or official duty, C-EX-3711. Bedroom, private bath, suites (5). Kitchen, utensils, A/C, color TV,

CALIFORNIA

Vandenberg Air Force Base, continued

maid service, washer/dryer, ice vending. Older structure. Rates: $14 per person. All categories can make reservations.

DV/VIP: 1 STRAD/CSP, building 10577. C-EX-3711. 06+.

TML Availability: Best, Nov-Jan. Difficult Apr-Oct.

☞ Central Coastal California is a treasure trove for visitors. Visitors should see Solvang ("little Denmark"), Gaviota Beach, Santa Barbara and the Hearst Castle, (San Simeon), to name only a few attractions within reach of Vandenberg.

Locator 866-1841   Medical 866-1847   Police 866-3911

Colorado

Fitzsimons Army Medical Center (CO10R3)
Aurora FAMC, CO 80045-0501

TELEPHONE NUMBER INFORMATION: Main installation numbers: C-303-361-8241, D-312-943-8241, FTS-337-8241.

Location: From I-70 take Peoria Ave (281), exit south on Peoria Ave, about 1 mile to Colfax Ave, Turn left (east) to first traffic light. Left again to enter main gate. From I-25 take I-225 north to Colfax Ave, west on Colfax Ave to third traffic light. Right at light to enter main gate. USM: F-4. NMC: Denver 8 miles east.

Billeting Office: Building 400, Charlie Kelly Blvd, C-**303-361-8903**, D-312-943-8903, 24 hrs daily. Reservations accepted Mon-Fri 0800-1500. Check in/out at facility.

TML: VOQ/VEQ: Building 400, all ranks, leave or official duty. Check out 1100 hours daily. Rooms, private bath, 1 person (115); rooms, private bath, 2 persons (75). CATV, refrigerator, telephone w/wake-up service/private voice mail, coffee makers, cribs, rollaways, maid service, washer/dryer, ice machine. No pets, kennels near installation. Rates: $13 - $18. TDY military and DOD civilian, PCS military, reservists on individual orders, military family members on medical TDY orders and attendants to patients in hospital can make confirmed reservations, others Space-A.

DV/VIP: Commander's office, C-303-361-8824, D-312-942-8824, 06+. Retirees Space-A.

TML Availability: Good, Oct-Dec. More difficult, other times.

☞ Outdoor activities abound in two national parks, four national monuments, and eleven national forests. Denver visitors "musts" are the state capital complex, US Mint, Larimer Square, and the Denver Museum of Art.

Locator 361-8223   Medical 361-8350   Police 361-3791

COLORADO

Fort Carson (CO02R3)
Fort Carson, CO 80913-1003

TELEPHONE NUMBER INFORMATION: Main installation numbers: C-719-579-3431, D-312-619-3431

Location: From Colorado Springs, take I-25 or CO-115 south. Clearly marked. USM: F-5. NMC: Colorado Springs, 6 miles north.

Billeting Office: Ivy Inn, building 6227, Prussman St, C-**719-579-4832**, 24 hours daily. Check in facility, check out 1100 hours daily. Government civilian employee billeting.

TML: BOQ. Building 7305, officers, all ranks, leave or official duty. Bedroom, private bath (6). A/C, cribs/cots, essentials, kitchen, maid service, color TV, washer/dryer. Older structure. New carpets/paint '90. Rates: sponsor, $17.50, adult $7, child $1. Maximum charge $45. Maximum 4 persons. Duty can make reservations, others Space-A.

TML: VOQ. Buildings 7303, 7305, officers, all ranks, leave or official duty. Bedroom, private bath (48). Description as above.

TML: VEQ. Buildings 6227, 6228, 7301,7302, enlisted, all ranks, leave or official duty. Bedroom, private bath (135). Bedrooms, single bed, shared bath (33). A/C, community kitchen, cribs/cots, essentials, kitchen, maid service, refrigerator, color TV, washer/dryer. Older structure. New carpets/paint '90. Rates: sponsor $21.50, adult $10.50, child $6. Maximum charge $45. Maximum 8 persons. All categories can make reservations, others Space-A.

TML: DV/VIP. Buildings 6227, 6215, officer 04+, enlisted E9, leave or official duty. Two bedroom, private bath (3); three bedroom, private bath (2). A/C, cribs/cots, essentials, maid service, color TV, washer/dryer. Older structures, painted '90. Rates: sponsor $21.50, adult $10.50, child $6. Maximum charge $45. Maximum 8 persons. All categories can make reservations.

DV/VIP: Protocol Office, building 1430, C-EX-4601, 05+. Retirees, lower ranks Space-A.

TML Availability: Difficult. Best Nov-Apr.

☞ **Visit historic Pikes Peak, the Royal Gorge and early mining town, Cripple Creek.**

Locator 579-3341/4275   Medical 9-911   Police 579-2333

Lowry Air Force Base (CO05R3)
Lowry AFB, CO 80230-1101

TELEPHONE NUMBER INFORMATION: Main installation numbers: C-303-676-1110, D-312-926-1110.

Location: From West to Denver, I-70 to Quebec Exit, south past Stapleton IAP to Sixth and Quebec Street Gate. From North to Denver I-25 north to I-225, exit Sixth Ave exit. USM: F-4. NMC: Denver, 6 miles west.

Billeting Office: 3415 ABG/SVH, ATTN: Reservation Clerk, building 1400, Lowry Dr, C-**303-676-5532**, 24 hours daily. Check in billeting, Check out 1200 hours daily.

COLORADO

Lowry Air Force Base, continued

TML: TLF. Buildings 572, 574, 576, 578, all ranks, leave or official duty. Bedroom, apartments, private bath (40). Kitchen, complete utensils, A/C, color TV, maid service, cribs, washer/dryer, ice vending. Modern structures. Rates: $16 per room E1-E6, $20 per room E7+. Maximum 5 per room. Duty can make reservations, others Space-A.

TML: VOQ. Buildings 1111, 1112, 1113, 1119, officers 01-03, leave or official duty. Bedroom, semi-private bath (8 units private bath) (216). Refrigerator, A/C, color TV, maid service, washer/dryer, ice vending. Modern structures. Rates: $6 per person. Maximum 2 per room. Duty can make reservations, others Space-A.

TML: VOQ. Buildings 397, 405, 406, officers 04-06, leave or official duty. Bedroom, private bath (100). Kitchen, A/C, color TV, maid service, washer/dryer, ice vending, microwave. Modern structures. Rates: $6 per person. Maximum 2 per room. Duty can make reservations, others Space-A.

TML: VAQ. Building 963, enlisted E6, leave or official duty. Bedroom, semi-private bath, (87). Refrigerator, A/C, color TV, maid service, washer/dryer, ice vending, microwave in lounge. Modern structures. Rates: $5 per person. Maximum 2 per room. Duty can make reservations, others Space-A.

TML: VAQ. Building 1400, enlisted E7-E9, E1-E5, leave or official duty. Bedroom, semi-private bath (873). Refrigerator, A/C, color TV, maid service, washer/dryer, ice vending, microwave in lounges. Modern structure. Rates: $5 per person. Maximum 2 per room. Duty can make reservations, others Space-A.

DV/VIP: Protocol Office, building 349, C-EX-2261, 06/GS-15+. Retirees and lower ranks Space-A.

TML Availability: Good, Nov-Jan. More difficult, other times.

Locator 676-4171　　　　**Medical 676-2193**　　　　**Police 676-2000**

⊗**This base will close in Sep '94.**

Peterson Air Force Base(CO06R3)
Peterson AFB, CO 80914-5000

TELEPHONE NUMBER INFORMATION: Main installation numbers: C-719-554-7321, D-312-692-7321.

Location: Off US-24 (Platte Ave) east of Colorado Springs. Clearly marked. USM: F-4. NMC: Colorado Springs, 4 miles west.

Billeting Office: Building 1042, Stewart Ave, C-719-554-7851, D-312-692-7851. Reservations: **719-554-6293**, 24 hours daily. Check in facility, check out 1200 hours daily. Government civilian employee billeting.

TML: TLQ. Buildings 1091-1094, all ranks, leave or official duty. Handicapped accessible. Bedroom, private bath (40). Refrigerator, kitchen, complete utensils, color TV, A/C, maid service, cribs, washer/dryer, ice vending. Older structure, redecorated.

COLORADO
Peterson Air Force Base, continued

Rates: $20 per unit, sleeps 5 persons. Duty can make reservations, others Space-A. Space-A policies same as VOQ below.

TML: VOQ. Buildings 1026, 1030. Officers all ranks, leave or official duty. Handicapped accessible. Bedroom, private bath (32); bedroom suites, private bath (DV/VIP) (33). Kitchen, cots, essentials, ice vending, refrigerator, A/C, color TV, maid service, washer/dryer. Modern structures. Rates: sponsor/adult, building 1026 $8 per person, building 1030 $14 per night. Maximum 2 persons per unit. Maximum charge $16 (building 1026), $28 (building 1030). No children, no infants. Duty can make reservations, others Space-A. Space-A released at 1700 hours Sat-Thurs, Fridays at 2000 hours. First come, first served. Unaccompanied dependents may be Space-A with active duty or retired sign in.

TML: VAQ. Building 1143, enlisted E1 to E6, leave or official duty. Bedroom, double occupancy, semi-private bath, (64); bedroom, double occupancy, private bath (18); senior NCO suites, private bath (7). A/C, color TV in room & lounge, refrigerator, maid service, washer/dryer, ice/food vending, essentials. Modern structure. Rates: VAQ, sponsor/adult, $5 per person. No children, no infants. Maximum 2 persons per unit. Maximum charge $10. Rates: SNCO suites, sponsor/adult, $14 per person. Maximum 2 persons per unit. Maximum charge $28. No children, no infants. Duty can make reservations, others Space-A. Space-A policies same as VOQ above.

TML: DV/VIP. Buildings 999, 1026, 1030, officer O7+. Bedroom, private bath (10). A/C, cots, essentials, ice vending, kitchen w/complete utensils, maid service, refrigerator, color TV, washer/dryer. Buildings 999 and 1030 upgraded. Rates: sponsor/adult, $14 per person. Maximum 2 persons per unit. Maximum charge $28 on leave, $14 active duty. No children, no infants. Rooms only for protocol reservations.

DV/VIP: Protocol, building 1, 554-5007, O7+. Retirees Space-A. VOQ Space-A policies.

TML Availability: Difficult. Best Dec-Feb.

☞ **Area skiing and camping are some of the finest in the US; this is the home of NORAD, Space Command HQ. Visit historic Pikes Peak and USAF Academy.**

Locator 554-4020   Medical 554-4333   Police 554-4000

United States Air Force Academy (CO07R3)
Colorado Springs, CO 80840-5231

TELEPHONE NUMBER INFORMATION: Main installation numbers: C-719-472-1818, D-312-259-3110.

Location: West of I-25 north from Colorado Springs. Two gates, about 5 miles apart, provide access from I-25 and are clearly marked. USM: F-4. NMC: Colorado Springs, 5 miles south.

Billeting Office: ATTN: Reservations, building 3130, Academy Dr., C-719-472-3060, 24 hours daily. Check in facility, check out 1100 hours daily. Government civilian employee billeting.

TML: DVQ. Building 3130, officers O7+, leave or official duty. Bedroom, private bath (8).

COLORADO
United States Air Force Academy, continued

Kitchen, study, living room, refrigerator, utensils, color TV, maid service, washer/dryer, cribs/cots, ice vending, handicapped accessible. Modern structure, renovated. Rates: sponsor $10, adult $10. Maximum 2 per family. Most reservations handled through protocol office for 07+ and equivalent.

TML: VOQ. Building 3130/3134, officers all ranks, leave or official duty. Bedroom, private bath (10); separate bedrooms, semi-private bath (14); two bedroom, semi-private bath (16). Refrigerator, color TV in lounge, maid service, cribs/cots, washer/dryer, ice vending, handicapped accessible. Modern structures. Rates: sponsor $6, adult $6, child $6, infant up to 2 years free. Maximum capacity depends on type of room. Duty can make reservations, others Space-A.

TML: TLF. Building 4700/02, all ranks, official duty or leave. Three bedroom houses (26). Kitchen, complete utensils, color TV, maid service, cribs/cots, washer/dryer. Modern structures. Rates: E1-E5 $15 per night, E6+ $22 per night. Family quarters intended primarily for use by PCS personnel in/out. Others Space-A on day-to-day basis.

DV/VIP: Protocol Office, Harmon Hall, Building 2304, Room 328, C-EX-3540, 07+.

TML Availability: Best, Jan-Apr. Difficult, other times.

☞ At the foot of the Rocky Mountains, near skiing and mountain resorts. New visitor's center, gift shop and exhibits. Guided tours, 18 hole golf courses. Cadet Wing holds 1300 hrs formation, visitors watch from the chapel wall.

Locator 472-4262   Medical 472-5000   Police 472-2000

Connecticut

New London Naval Submarine Base (CT01R1)
Groton, CT 06349-5000

TELEPHONE NUMBER INFORMATION: Main installation numbers: C-203--449-3011, D-312-241-3011, FTS-648-3011.

Location: From I-95 north take exit 86 to CT-12. Go left on Pleasant Valley Rd, then right on Lestertown Rd. Base clearly marked. USM: M-3. NMC: Hartford, 50 miles northwest.

Billeting Office: None.

TML: Navy Lodge, 77 Dewey Ave, Groton, CT 06340, all ranks, leave or official duty. Check in 1500-1800 daily, check out 1200 hours daily. For reservations call **1-800-NAVY-INN.** Lodge number is 446-1160. Bedroom, 2 double beds, private bath (67). Kitchen, refrigerator, limited utensils, A/C, color TV in room & lounge, maid service, cribs, coin washer/dryer. Modern structure, renovated. Rates: $34 per unit. Maximum 5 persons. All categories can make reservations.

TML: BOQ. Buildings D, 379, M, L, all ranks, leave or official duty. C-203-449-3416.

CONNECTICUT
New London Naval Submarine Base, continued

Check in 24 hours daily, check out 1100 hours daily. Bedroom, private bath (67); bedroom suites, private bath (21); bedroom, semi-private bath (106); bedroom, hall bath (54). Refrigerator, community kitchen, A/C (suites only), color TV (suites only), color TV lounge, maid service. Older structure. Rates: $7 per person. Duty can make reservations, others Space-A.

DV/VIP: No office. C-EX-3416. 07+.

TML Availability: Fairly good, Navy Lodge, all year.

 Visit Mystic seaport for history, USCG Academy, USS Nautilus Memorial/Submarine Force Library and Museum for a view of the modern Navy.

Locator 449-4761   **Medical 449-3666**   **Police 449-3222**

Delaware

Dover Air Force Base (DE01R1)
Dover AFB, DE 19902-5000

TELEPHONE NUMBER INFORMATION: Main installation numbers: C-302-677-3000, D-312-445-3000.

Location: Off US-113. Clearly marked. USM: M-4. Dover, 5 miles northwest.

Billeting Office: Building 805, 14th St (across from O'Club), C-302-677-5981, 24 hours daily. Check out 1200 hours daily. Space-A billeting roll call at 1700 hours daily.

TML: VOQ/TLF. Building 803, all ranks, leave or official duty. TLF: bedroom family suites, private bath (14); VOQ: bedroom, double beds, shared bath (27). Kitchenette, sofa sleeper (TLF) refrigerator, A/C, color TV, maid service, cribs/cots, washer/dryer, ice vending. Older structure. Rates: maximum $20 per family. PCS/TDY can make reservations, others Space-A.

TML: VOQ/DV. Building 806, officers 06+, enlisted SNCOs, leave or official duty. Suites, private bath (DV) (10); suites, private bath (SNCO) (5). Refrigerator, A/C, color TV, maid service, washer/dryer. Modern structure. Rates: $14 per person. Maximum 4 per room. (Arnold Suite - 24 rooms controlled by Protocol).

TML: VAQ. Buildings 472, 481, 482, enlisted E1-E4, leave or official duty. Bedrooms, single beds, common bath (141). A/C, color TV, refrigerator, maid service, clock radio, coffee makers. Rates: $8. No children.

TML: VAQ. Building 801, all ranks, leave or official duty. Bedrooms, single beds, shared bath (55). A/C, refrigerator, color TV, maid service, telephones, clock radio, coffeemaker. Rates: $8. No children.

Dover Air Force Base, continued

TML: VAQ. Building 802, enlisted aircrew members, TDY, SNCOs. Bedrooms, single beds, shared bath (55). A/C, refrigerator, color TV, maid service, telephones, clock radio, coffeemaker. Rates $8. No children.

TML: VOQ. Buildings 804, 805, 804 all ranks, leave or official duty. 805, official aircrew members. Bedrooms, single bed, shared bath (18); bedrooms, single beds, shared bath (Alpha Alert) (9); bedrooms, double beds, kitchenette, private bath (12); UOQ, double beds, kitchenette, private bath (2). 805 bedrooms, double and single beds, shared bath (54). Rates: $16, (805)$8, UOQ $50/mo.

DV/VIP: Building 201, room 101, C-EX-6649/6610, O6+. Retirees, lower ranks Space-A.

TML Availability: Very good, Oct-Apr. Limited, other times.

☞ **Dover is the jumping off point for many Space-A flights to Europe and beyond. See Military *Space-A Opportunities Around the World*, and *Military Space-A Air Basic Training* for information on this money saver for the military.**

Locator 677-2841   **Medical 735-2600**   **Police 677-6664**

District of Columbia

Bolling Air Force Base (DC01R1)
1100 Air Base Wing
Bolling AFB, DC 20332-5000

TELEPHONE NUMBER INFORMATION: Main installation numbers: C-202-545-6700, D-312-297-0101.

Location: Take I-95 (east portion of Capital Beltway, I-495) north or south, exit to I-295 north, exit 1, right onto Overlook Ave at the light, and continue to South Gate. I-295 south, exit 1 to first light. Right at the light to the South Gate. From South Capitol St, south past Main Gate and bear right onto Overlook Ave to South Gate. Clearly marked. USM: N-7. NMC: Washington, in southeast section of the city.

Billeting Office: Bolling Inn. Building 602, Theisen St. C-202-545-5316/5741, 24 hours daily. Check in billeting, check out 1000 hours daily.

TML: TLQ. Apartments, all ranks, leave or official duty. Separate bedrooms, private bath (49). Kitchen, A/C, color TV in room & lounge, housekeeping service, washer/dryer, ice vending. Older structure. Rates: $25 per room. Maximum 4 persons. Unaccompanied dependents not authorized. Reservations TDY, others Space-A.

TML: VOQ. Officer 01-06, leave or official duty. Suites, private bath (8); bedroom, semi-private bath (52). Refrigerator, A/C, color TV in room & lounge, housekeeping service, washer/dryer, ice vending. Older structure. Rates: $10.50-$14 per person. Reservations TDY personnel only, others Space-A.

DISTRICT OF COLOMBIA
Bolling Air Force Base, continued

TML: TAQ. **Mathies Manor,** building 3621. Enlisted E1-E6. Bedroom, shared bath (13); Refrigerator, CATV, housekeeping service, washer/dryer. Older structure. Rates: $6 per person. Reservations TDY, others Space-A.

TML: VIP. 07+. Suites, private bath (23). Refrigerator, A/C, color TV, housekeeping service, washer/dryer. Older structure. Rates: $14 per person. Duty can make reservations. Also senior noncommissioned officers' quarters, $14 per person, reservations via Protocol. Others Space-A.

DV/VIP: Protocol Office, building P-20, C-EX-5584, 07+. Retirees Space-A.

TML Availability: Difficult. Better during winter months.

☞ On the Potomac, across from historic Alexandria, and in sight of the Capitol, and famous monuments, Bolling is headquarters for the Air Force District of Washington.

Locator 767-4522 **Medical 767-5233**

Walter Reed Army Medical Center (DC03R1)
Washington, DC 20307-5000

TELEPHONE NUMBER INFORMATION: Main installation numbers: C-202-576-3501/02, D-312-291-3501/02.

Location: 6900 Georgia Ave, NW. From I-495 (Capital Beltway) take Georgia Ave/Silver Spring exit south to Center, enter first or second gate. To reach the Forest Glen support facilities from Georgia Ave, south, right turn on to Linden Lane, cross over B&O railroad bridge, support facility on left (.75 miles from Georgia Ave). USM: N-6. NMC: Washington, DC, in the city.

Billeting Office: ATTN: Housing Referral, Main Dr, building 1, room G-01, **C-202-576-3117/18/19,** 0800-1530 daily. Check in facility, check out 1100 hours daily. No government civilian employee billeting.

TML: Guest House. Building 17, all ranks, leave or official duty, C-EX-3044 or 882-1000. Rooms, common baths, semi-private bath, private bath (62). A/C, CATV, maid service, cribs/cots, coin washer/dryer, ice vending, facilities for DAVs. Older structure. Rates: $28-$32/night. Maximum 3 per unit. Priority to PCS, E-7+ on TDY, members of immediate family of seriously ill patients and MEDEVAC/AIRVAC personnel. Out-patients, others Space-A.

TML: VOQ. Building 18, all ranks, leave or official duty, C-EX-2076/2096. Check out 1100 hours daily. Bedroom, private bath (54)(3 with kitchen); separate bedrooms, private bath (5). Kitchen, complete utensils, A/C, CATV, maid service, cots, coin washer/dryer, ice vending. Modern structure, remodeled '92. Rates: $32, $37 suites w/kitchen (funded TDY personnel). Maximum 3 per room. Duty can make reservations, others Space-A.

DV/VIP: Chief of Staff, C-EX-4949.

Walter Reed Army Medical Center, continued   DISTRICT OF COLUMBIA

TML Availability: Best, Mar-Apr & Sep-Oct. Difficult, others times.

☞ Walter Reed is in D.C. near the National Zoo and National Cathedral, both star attractions for visitors. Other monuments are within 1/2 hour's drive.

Locator 576-3501/02   **Medical 576-3317**   **Police-576-2511**

Washington Navy Yard (DC04R1)
Washington, DC 20374-5000

TELEPHONE NUMBER INFORMATION: Main installation numbers: C-202-545-6700, D-312-222-6700.

Location: The Hq is in the Washington Navy Yard, 9th & M Sts SE. The TML is adjacent to Bolling AFB. From I-95 (beltway) take I-295 north, exit at Naval Research Laboratory onto Overlook Ave. Left at first light into Bellevue Housing, building 12, Bowling Green S.W. USM: N-7. NMC: Washington, DC, in the city.

Billeting Office: ATTN: Anacostia CMAA: NAVSTA, C-433-3232, 0730-1600 hours daily, other hours, 433-2193. Check in 1500-1800, check out 1200 hours daily. No government civilian employees billeting. This office is for permanent party only.

TML: Navy Lodge. Located Bellevue Navy Housing Community, Bolling AFB, all ranks, leave or official duty. For reservations call **1-800-NAVY-INN** (1-800-628-9466). Lodge number is 563-6950. Bedroom, private bath (50). Kitchen, utensils, A/C, color TV, cribs, high chairs, ironing boards, dining/living room areas, sleeps up to 5 persons (2 double beds, 1 converted sofa). Modern structure. Rates: $37 per unit. Active duty may make reservations 60 days in advance, others 5 days in advance.

TML Availability: Good, Dec-Apr. Difficult, other times.

☞ For military history buffs, visit the Navy Memorial Museum, the Display Ship Barry (DD-933), the Marine Corps Museum (with famous flags raised over Mt. Suribachi and Iwo Jima), and the Combat Art Gallery.

Locator 694-3155   **Medical 433-2204**   **Police 433-2411**

Avon Park Air Force Range (FL16R1)
Avon Park AFR, FL 33825-5000

TELEPHONE NUMBER INFORMATION: Main installation numbers: C-813-452-4191, D-312-968-1110-EX-191.

Location: Off FL-64, 10.5 miles east of Avon Park, 15.5 miles northeast of Sebring. USM: L-8. NMC: Orlando, 60 miles north.

FLORIDA
Avon Park Air Force Range, continued

Billeting Office: Building 475, C-813-452-4114, 0800-1600 hours duty days. Other hours contact Security Police Desk Sgt, building 424. Check in facility, check out 1100 hours daily. Government civilian employee billeting.

TML: Mobile Homes, all ranks, leave or official duty. Thirty days advance reservations. C-EX-4251. Two bedroom, private bath mobile homes, fully furnished (5). Kitchen, complete utensils, A/C. Rates: $20 per unit. TML for single enlisted, building 240. Duty can make reservations, others Space-A.

TML: VOQ. Building 447, officers all ranks, leave or official duty. Handicapped accessible. Bedroom apartments, private bath (4). A/C, kitchen, limited utensils, maid service, color TV. Modern structure. Rates: sponsor, $8. Maximum 2 persons. Maximum charge $16. Duty can make reservations, others Space-A.

TML: VAQ. Building 240, enlisted all ranks, leave or official duty. Bedroom, private and semi-private bath (12). A/C, ice/food vending, maid service, refrigerator, color TV in lounge & room, washer/dryer. Older structure. Rates: sponsor, $8. Duty can make reservations, others Space-A.

DV/VIP: Protocol, Building 236, 56CSS/CCE, C-EX-191, 06+. No DV or VIP suites.

TML Availability: Fairly good. Best May-Nov. Difficult other times.

☞ Nature activities, call Natural Resources 452-4119. Boat rentals and camping sites. Call MWR 452-4251.

Locator 452-4120   **Medical 452-4140**   **Police 454-4194**

Cecil Field Naval Air Station (FL06R1)
Cecil Field NAS, FL 32215-5000

TELEPHONE NUMBER INFORMATION: Main installation numbers: C-904-778-5626, D-312-860-5626.

Location: Take Normandy exit west off I-295 and follow Normandy (FL-228) to main gate. USM: L-7. NMC: Jacksonville, 20 miles east.

Billeting Office: Building 331, D Ave & 4th St. C-904-778-0641. D-860-5255/5258, 24 hours daily M-F. Check in facility, check out 1400 hours daily.

TML: BOQ. Building 331, officers all ranks, leave or official duty. Bedroom, private bath (45); separate bedroom, private bath (86). Refrigerator, A/C, essentials, color TV, maid service, cribs/cots, washer/dryer, food/ice vending. Modern structure. New AC/carpets/TVs '89. Rates: sponsor on leave $8, sponsor on duty $4, adult $4, child $4, under 3 years no charge. Maximum charge $16 on leave, $12 on duty. Duty can make reservations, others Space-A.

TML: BEQ. Building 92, enlisted, all ranks, leave or official duty. Check out 1200 hours. C-EX-6191/92. Bedroom, private bath (10). Two (or more) beds in room (28). A/C, essentials, food vending, maid service, color TV in lounge, washer/dryer. Older structure. Renovated, remodeled. Rates: sponsor $4. Duty can make reservations, others Space-A.

FLORIDA

Cecil Field Naval Air Station, continued

DV/VIP: BOQ, building 331. C-EX-5255. 06+. Retirees and lower ranks Space-A. BEQ, building 902. E7+.

TML Availability: Good, Dec-Feb, Sep-Oct. More difficult at other times.

☞ **St Augustine is 45 miles south. Beaches, and the Jacksonville seaport.**

Locator 778-5240   Medical 778-5508/5378   Police 778-5381

Eglin Air Force Base (FL27R1)
Eglin AFB, FL 32542-5000

TELEPHONE NUMBER INFORMATION: Main installation numbers: C-904-882-6668, D-312-872-1110.

Location: Exit I-10 at Crestview, & follow posted signs to Niceville and Valparaiso, (Eglin AFB). USM: J,K-7. NMC: Fort Walton Beach, 14 miles west.

Billeting Office: Building 11001, Boatner Rd, C-**904-882-8761**, D-312-872-8761, 24 hours daily. Check in billeting 1500, check out 1100 hours daily. Government civilian employee billeting.

TML: VAQ. All ranks, leave or official duty. Bedroom, private bath (VSNCOQ) (6); bedroom, private bath (83); bedroom, shared bath (72). Rates: $8 per person. TLF. Bedroom, private bath (52); two bedroom, private bath (32); three bedroom, private bath (1); separate bedroom, private bath (1). Rates: $14-$18. VOQ. Bedrooms, private bath (112); suites (several). Rates: $8, $10, $14 per person. Refrigerator, microwave, A/C, color TV, housekeeping service, ice and food vending. Duty can make reservations, others Space-A.

DV/VIP: HQ MSD/CSP, building 1 (Command Section). C-EX-3011.

TML Availability: Very good, Nov-Jan. Difficult, other times.

☞ **Phone Natural Resources on Eglin for information on the wonderful outdoor activities on Eglin Reserve. Don't miss Fort Walton Beach's Miracle Strip, deep sea fishing off Destin, and visit Pensacola, 50 miles west.**

Locator 882-4478   Medical 882-7227   Police 882-2502

Homestead Air Force Base (FL17R1)
Homestead AFB, FL 33039-5000

TELEPHONE NUMBER INFORMATION: Main installation numbers: C-305-257-8011, D-312-791-0111.

Location: Off Florida Turnpike, US-1, take Homestead exit, clearly marked. USM: M-8. NMC: Miami, 25 miles north.

FLORIDA
Homestead Air Force Base, continued

Billeting Office: Building 945, Saint Nazair St, C-**305-257-5831**, D-312-791-8224, 24 hours daily. Check in facility, check out 1200 hours daily. Government civilian employee billeting.

TML: TLF. **Mango Way Apartments** (located off-base), all ranks, leave or official duty. Bedroom, private bath (19). Kitchen, utensils, A/C, color TV, housekeeping, washer/dryer. Older structures. Rates: $21 per unit, with $40 deposit for Space-A, PCS out, separations (refundable upon checkout if there is no damage and appliances are clean). Reservations for PCS in/out, others Space-A.

TML: VOQ. Buildings 434, 938, 945, 951, officers, all ranks, leave or official duty. Bedroom, semi-private bath (57); bedroom, private bath (80). Refrigerator, community kitchen, A/C, color TV, housekeeping, washer/dryer, ice vending. Older structures. Rates: $8 per person. Building 938 is $10 per person. Maximum 1 per unit. Duty, retired, DAVs, Reservists on orders can make reservations. Reservations for official TDY or PCS in/out have priority, all others Space-A.

TML: VAQ. Buildings 434, 435, enlisted all ranks, leave or official duty. Bedroom, 2 beds, semi-private bath (64); bedroom SNCO suites (1 bed, living room, private bath-E7-E9) (6); bedroom Chief suites, 1 bed, living room, private bath (E9) (3). Refrigerator, A/C, color TV, housekeeping, washer/dryer. Older structures. Rates: $5.50 per person, Chief suites $10. Maximum 2 per unit. Reservations for PCS in/out and official TDY only, others Space-A.

TML: DV/VIP. Buildings 963, 938, officers all ranks, leave or official duty, C-EX-7212. Bedroom suites, private bath (40); two bedroom suites, private bath (10); Kitchen, utensils, A/C, color TV, maid service, washer/dryer. Older structures. Rates: $10 per person. Reservations for PCS in/out or official TDY only, others Space-A.

DV/VIP: Protocol Office, building 931, Conference Center, C-EX-7212, 06+. Retirees Space-A.

TML Availability: Limited. Best, May-Nov. Difficult, Dec-Apr.

☞ **The Homestead Bayfront has picnic, swimming, a marina and boat launch. Don't forget Miami, and the fabulous Everglades National Park and the Florida Keys, which are all within reach of this popular base.**

Locator 257-7621   Medical 257-7233/7668   Police 257-7867

Hurlburt Field (FL18R1)
Hurlburt Field, FL 32544-5000

TELEPHONE NUMBER INFORMATION: Main installation numbers: C-904-882-1110, (Eglin Base Info) D-312-579-1110.

Location: Off US-98, 5 miles west of Fort Walton Beach. Clearly marked. USM: J-7. NMC: Pensacola, 40 miles west.

FLORIDA

Hurlburt Field, continued

Billeting Office: Building 90509, Simpson St, C-**904-884-6245 & 581-1627**, D-312-579-6245, 24 hours daily. Check in billeting, check out 1200 hours daily. Government civilian employee billeting.

TML: VAQ/VOQ. Buildings 90344-90346, 90507, 90508, all ranks, leave or official duty. Handicapped accessible. Bedroom, private and semi-private bath (179); separate bedrooms, private bath (29). Kitchen, limited utensils, A/C, color TV, maid service, cribs/cots, essentials, washer/dryer, ice vending, VOQ stocked wet bar. Older structure. Rates: sponsor, $8; DVs, $14. Maximum 2 persons per unit. Duty can make reservations, others Space-A. See Eglin AFB listing for other TML.

TML: TLF. Units (24). $18 per night.

DV/VIP: Protocol Office, building 1, C-EX-2308. 06+. Retirees and lower ranks Space-A.

TML Availability: Difficult. Best, Dec-Mar.

☞ **The catching and eating of fish is a big deal here! "The World's Luckiest Fishing Village" caters to all fishing needs. Numerous fine restaurants.**

Locator 884-6333   **Medical 884-7882**   **Police 884-6423**

Jacksonville Naval Air Station (FL08R1)
Jacksonville NAS, FL 32212-5000

TELEPHONE NUMBER INFORMATION: Main installation numbers: C-904-772-2345, D-312-942-2345.

Location: Access from US-17 south (Roosevelt Blvd). On the St Johns River. USM: L-7. NMC: Jacksonville, 9 miles northeast.

Billeting Office: Building 11, ATTN: Box 27, C-**904-772-4050/51/52**, 24 hours daily. Check in facility, check out 1200 hours daily. Government civilian employee billeting.

TML: Navy Lodge. All ranks, leave or official duty. For reservations call **1-800-NAVY-INN**. Lodge number is 772-6000, 0700-2300 daily. Bedroom, 2 double beds, studio couch, private bath (50). Kitchen, A/C, color TV, maid service, coin washer/dryer, food/ice vending. Modern structure. Rates: $33 per unit. Duty can make reservations, others Space-A. **Note:** This lodge won the Edward E. Carlson Award for excellence, '92.

TML: BOQ. Buildings 11, 845, officers all ranks, leave or official duty, C-EX-3147/3138. Bedroom, private bath (110); bedroom, shared bath (8); separate bedroom, private bath (96). Refrigerator, telephones, TV in lobby, one large, two small conference rooms, maid service, cribs/cots, washer/dryer, food/ice vending, sauna, fishing dock, dock. Building 11, older structure. Rates: TAD $8 per person, dependents 7 years+ $8 (one charge). Reservations taken 3 months in advance for transient personnel. No pets. Call billeting for more information. Geographical bachelors berthed on Space-A basis in inadequate quarters.

DV/VIP: PAO, C-3147/3138, 06/GS-15+. Retirees Space-A.

FLORIDA
Jacksonville Naval Air Station, continued

TML Availability: Fair. Difficult, summer months.

☞ Don't miss boating and water sports on over 74 square miles of inland waters, golf courses, wonderful beaches that are among Florida's finest. Also visit museums, symphony, St Augustine, and Cypress Gardens.

Locator 772-2340   Police 772-2662

Key West Naval Air Station (FL15R1)
Key West NAS, FL 33040-5000

TELEPHONE NUMBER INFORMATION: Main installation numbers: C-305-296-3561, D-312-483-3561.

Location: For Trumbo Point Annex, take Florida Turnpike, US-1 south, turn right at Key West. At intersection of Palm turn right. Next traffic light, look for 6 story white building. Boca Chica Key is 7 miles north of Key West. USM: L-9. NMC: Miami, 150 miles north.

Billeting Office: No central billeting office. BOQ at Trumbo Point Annex, building 2076. C-305-294-5571, 24 hours daily. Check in facility, check out 1200 hours daily. Government civilian employee billeting, GS 7+. **Note: at press time we heard the prefix for this base will change in August '92 to from 296 to 293 prefix, it is unknown if switch or line numbers in this listing will change.**

TML: BOQ/BEQ. Officer and enlisted. All ranks, leave or official duty. Handicapped accessible. Reservations required. BOQ: bedroom, private bath (8); suites, separate bedroom, private bath (10); rooms to share (50); VIP suite, hall bath (1). Community kitchen, ice/food vending, maid service, refrigerator, color TV in rooms and lounge, washer/dryer. Older structure, under renovation at press time. Target completion is Dec '92. More rooms in future, but O3 and under will continue to share rooms. Rates: single rooms $8, suites $10, guests $8. Maximum 3 persons per unit.

TML: BEQ Boca Chica, E1-E6, C-305-292-2488. Substandard rooms, barracks type, common bath (600); VIP suite, private bath (1). Community kitchen, ice/food vending, washer/dryer. Rates: barracks $4, VIP $15.

TML: Navy Lodge. Sigsbee Park, 6 miles south of NAS in Key West, on the bay. Reservations call **1-800-NAVY-INN.** Lodge number is 296-7556. All ranks, leave or official duty. Bedrooms, 2 double beds, private bath (26). Two units handicapped accessible. Kitchen, microwave, all utensils, hair dryer, iron, board, A/C, cribs/cots, coin operated washer/dryer, ice vending, complimentary coffee in lobby. Marina boat and snorkel rental gear. MWR Sunset Lounge, community center with tickets, commissary and exchange across the road. Modern structure, new June '91. All categories may make reservations.

TML: MWR Trailers. Near Old Town Key West. C-305-292-3144, D-312-483-3144, duty or retired, DOD civilians, dependents. Two bedroom, double beds, private bath (12). A/C, kitchen, complete utensils, dining room, microwave, linens provided, limited maid service, within walking distance of Old Key West. Rates: $40 per night. All categories can make reservations 3 - 4 months in advance.

Key West Naval Air Station, continued

TML: DV/VIP. Quarters FF Guesthouse, Trumbo Point Annex, 06+. Three bedroom beachhouse (1). A/C, kitchen, all amenities. Rates: $25, guests $10. Call CO Secretary, NAS Key West, Fl 33040. Reservations required, others Space-A.

TML Availability: Extremely limited. Best in summer.

☞ Here is the place to kick back and relax by the ocean. Although TML has been limited at Key West due to heavy flight school classes, at press time it was not. Don't miss the picture of this beautiful new Navy Lodge on the back cover!

Locator 292-2256   **Medical 292-4444**   **Police-292-2531**

MacDill Air Force Base (FL02R1)
MacDill AFB, FL 33608-5000

TELEPHONE NUMBER INFORMATION: Main installation numbers: C-813-830-1110, D-312-968-1110.

Location: Take I-75 south to I-275 south. Exit at Dale Mabry west, 5 miles south to MacDill AFB main gate. USM: L-8. NMC: Tampa, 5 miles north.

Billeting Office: MacDill Inn, 56 CSG/SVH/Billeting, PO Box 6826, building 411, corner Garden Dr & Tampa Blvd, C-813-830-4259, 24 hours daily. Check in billeting, check out 1200 (TLQ 1100) hours daily. No government civilian employee billeting.

TML: TLQ. Buildings 890-893, 905-906, all ranks, leave or official duty. Handicapped accessible. Bedroom, private bath (24). Kitchen, refrigerator, utensils, A/C, color TV, cots/cribs, maid service, essentials, washer/dryer, food/ice vending. Rates: $18 per family. Maximum 5 persons. Duty can make reservations, others Space-A.

TML: VAQ. Building 372, enlisted E1-E9, leave or official duty. Bedroom, common bath (60). Refrigerator, A/C, color TV in room & lounge, maid service, washer/dryer. Older structure. Rates: $8 per person. Maximum 2 persons. Duty can make reservations, others Space-A.

TML: VOQ. Buildings 312, 366, 390, 411, officers all ranks, leave or official duty. Bedroom, private bath (56); bedroom, semi-private bath (44); separate bedroom, private bath (28). Kitchen (85), refrigerator (44), A/C, color TV, maid service, washer/dryer, ice vending. Modern structure. Rates: sponsor $8 per person. Maximum 2 persons. No children. Duty can make reservations, others Space-A.

DV/VIP: 56th TTW/CCP, Building P-9, C-EX-2056. 06+.

TML Availability: Extremely limited. Best Oct-Jan.

☞ Local attractions include Busch Gardens, Epcot Center, Disney World, Sea World, Circus World - this is an area with lots of interesting things to see.

Locator 830-2444   **Medical 830-3334**   **Police 830-3322**

FLORIDA

Mayport Naval Station (FL13R1)
Mayport NS, FL 32228-5000

TELEPHONE NUMBER INFORMATION: Main installation numbers: C-904-270-5011, D-312-960-5011.

Location: From Jacksonville, FL on Atlantic Blvd (FL-10) east to Mayport Rd (FL-A1A) left (north) to Naval Station. USM: L-7. NMC: Jacksonville, 10 miles west.

Billeting Office: No central billeting office. Check in facility, check out 1200 hours daily. Government civilian employee billeting.

TML: BOQ. Building 425, officers all ranks, leave or official duty, C-**904-270-5423**. Kitchen (DV/VIP), refrigerator, A/C, color TV in lounge, maid service, washer/dryer, ice vending. Modern structure. Rates: $5 per person. Duty on orders can make reservations, others Space-A.

TML: BEQ. Building 1586, enlisted all ranks, leave or official duty, C-**904-270-5575**. Bedroom, hall and private baths (244); separate bedroom (1). DV/VIP with kitchen. Rates: $4 per person. Duty on orders can make reservations, others Space-A.

TML: Navy Lodge. All ranks, leave or official duty. For reservations call **1-800-NAVY-INN.** Lodge number is 270-5554. Check in duty hours. Check out 1200 hours daily. Two and three bedroom mobile homes, private bath (19), kitchen, complete utensils, A/C, color TV, cribs/cots, maid service, coin washer/dryer. Rates: $15 per unit. All categories can make reservations.

DV/VIP: Cmdr/DO, C-904-270-4501, E9, 06+.

TML Availability: Very good, Nov-Mar. Difficult, other times.

☞ **Near Jacksonville, historic St. Augustine. Deep sea fishing, and famous Florida beaches - shark's teeth are picked up on local beaches.**

Locator 270-5401   Medical 270-5631   Police 270-5583

☏**This facility is scheduled for a new Navy Lodge in '93. Keep posted with Military Living's R&R Space-A Report.**

Oak Grove Park (FL09R1)
Pensacola, FL 32508-5000

TELEPHONE NUMBER INFORMATION: Main installation numbers: C-904-452-0111, D-312-922-0111.

Location: From I-10, south on I-110, Garden Street Exit to Navy Blvd to front gate. USM: J-7. NMC: Pensacola, 2 miles northeast.

Billeting Office: None.

Oak Grove Park, continued

TML: Recreational Cabins, officer and enlisted, all ranks, leave or official duty. C-904-452-2535, check in 1200-1530 hours. Check out 0730-1000 hours. Handicapped accessible. One bedroom cabins, private bath (12). A/C, cots/cribs ($2 daily), kitchen, complete utensils, refrigerator. Modern structures built Apr '89. All categories can make reservations. Rates: $30. Maximum 5 persons per unit.

DV/VIP: No Protocol Office.

TML Availability: Best, Oct-Apr. Difficult other times.

☞ **On the coast of Florida, near Pensacola. This area is known for its water recreation, sports, fishing. Visit the Naval Aviation Museum.**

Locator 452-0111   Medical 452-4256   Police 452-2353

Orlando Naval Training Center (FL11R1)
Orlando NTC, FL 32813-5005

TELEPHONE NUMBER INFORMATION: Main installation numbers: C-407-646-4111, D-312-791-4111.

Location: On Bennet Rd, .5 miles north of FL-50 (Colonial Dr). Bennet Rd is about 3 miles from I-4 on FL-50. USM: L-7. NMC: Orlando, in the city.

Billeting Office: Building 2010, Hibiscus St, C-407-646-5163/5722, 0730-1600 hours duty days. Other hours, SDO, building 2702, C-EX-4501. Check in facility. Government civilian employee billeting (GS-7+).

TML: BEQ/BOQ. Building 375, officer and enlisted all ranks, official duty only, C-EX-5614. Check out 1000 daily. Bedroom, 3 beds, private bath (130). A/C, color TV in lounge, washer/dryer. Modern structure. Rates: $4 per person. Duty on official orders Space-A. Bedroom, semi-private bath (28); bedroom, private bath (22); two bedroom cottage, private bath (senior VIPs/Flag Officers). Refrigerator (12) units, A/C, color TV, maid service, cots, washer/dryer. Older structure, renovated. Rates $8-$25. Duty can make reservations, others Space-A.

TML Availability: Best, Aug-Nov, Jan-Apr.

☞ **Don't miss these local attractions: Disney World, Cypress Gardens, Universal Studios, Sea World.**

Locator 646-4501   Medical 646-4911   Police 646-5380

☺**While the navy lodge at this facility has closed, a new one is slated for the future. Keep updated with Military Living's *R&R Space-A Report*.**

Panama City Naval Coastal Systems Station (FL35R1)
Panama City NCSS, FL 32407-5000

TELEPHONE NUMBER INFORMATION: Main installation numbers: C-904-234-4011, D-312-436-4011.

FLORIDA
Panama City Naval Coastal Systems Station, continued

Location: In the Northwest section of Florida. Exit I-10 (N&S) to Hwy 231 (N&S) to Florida Hwy 98 (N&S). The facility is located off Hwy 98. USM: K-7, NMC: Pensacola and Tallahassee, 100 miles west and east.

Billeting Office: Building 126, NCSC Crag Rd. C-**904-234-4425/4248**. D-312-436-4425/4248. Open 24 hours daily. Housing referral office open 0800 to 1600 M-F.

TML: BOQ. Building 349, all ranks, leave or official duty. Bedrooms, bath configuration unknown (47), includes female military personnel, DV suites, junior rooms. Handicapped accessible. A/C, cots (6), cribs, essentials, food and ice vending, kitchenettes and utensils, maid service, color TV, washer/dryers, jacuzzi. Modern structure with recent and planned remodeling. Rates: DV suites $16 (member), $4 (guest). Suites $12 (member) $4 (guest). Junior Rooms $8 (member), $4 (guest)Limit 2 to 3 persons per room. Reservations required for official duty, all others Space-A) C-**904-234-4631/4278**, D-312-436-4631/4278. Check in at front desk 24 hrs daily. Check out time 1100. Additional daily rate charged for late checkout. No pets allowed.

TML: All ranks. BEQ Building 304. 89 units: bedrooms, private bath (30), with communal bath (29); separate bedroom, private bath (17); bedrooms, private baths (59). A/C, cots ($6), cribs, essentials, food and ice vending, maid service, refrigerators, color TV in lounge & some rooms, washer and dryer. Modern building with recent remodeling, and more anticipated. **A new BEQ is planned for FY 93.** All rooms $4.

DV/VIP: Bedrooms, bath configuration unknown (2). O6+, GM/GS 15 & above, others Space-A. Call PA Officer, building 110, C-EX-5464, D-EX-5467.

TML Availability: Good, Dec, Jan difficult, Mar to Sept. BOQ can be extremely limited. For DoD civilians on official duty, if space is not available member is issued a certificate of non-availability.

☞ Visit the Armament Museum, beautiful beaches, and enjoy Florida sport fishing. The dog races are a local attraction also.

Locator 234-4378/4379   Medical 234-4316   Police 234-4332

Patrick Air Force Base (FL03R1)
Patrick AFB, FL 32935-5152

TELEPHONE NUMBER INFORMATION: Main installation numbers: C-407-494-1110, D-312-854-1110.

Location: Take I-95 south to exit 73 (Wickham Rd), 3 miles to FL 404 (Pineda Causeway), left on South Patrick Dr to Patrick AFB. USM: L-7,8. NMC: Cocoa Beach, 2 miles north.

Billeting Office: Space Coast Inn, ATTN: 1040 SSG/SVH, building 400, C St between 1st & 2nd Sts, C-**407-494-2075,** 24 hours. Check in billeting, check out 1100 hours daily. Government civilian employee billeting.

TML: TLF. Buildings 1030, 1034, 1036, 1042, 1058, 1060, 1062, all ranks, leave or official duty. Bedroom, private bath (32); three bedroom, private bath (20). Kitchen,

FLORIDA

Patrick Air Force Base, continued

utensils, A/C, color TV, maid service, cribs/cots, washer/dryer. Older structure, renovated. Rates: $25 per unit. Duty can make reservations, others Space-A. Used primarily for PCS families.

TML: VAQ. Buildings 255, 556, 557, 727, 734, enlisted E1-E4, leave or official duty. Bedroom, hall bath (195). Refrigerator, A/C, color TV in room & lounge, maid service, washer/dryer, ice vending, microwave. Older structure, renovated. Rates: $8, $10 and $12 per person. Maximum 2 persons. Duty can make reservations, others Space-A.

TML: VOQ. Buildings 250, 251, 253, 264, 265, 400, 404, officers all ranks, leave or official duty. Bedroom, semi-private bath (71); two bedroom, mixed private and semi-private baths (182). Kitchen, utensils, A/C, color TV, maid service, cribs/cots, washer/dryer, ice vending. Older structure, renovated. Rates: $10, $12 and $14 per person. Duty can make reservations, others Space-A.

DV/VIP: ESMC/CEP, building 423, C-EX-4506, 07+. Retirees Space-A.

☞ Florida's "Space Coast" includes **US Air Force Space Museum, Kennedy Center, Disney World, Sea World, Epcot Center.**

TML Availability: Good, Nov-Jan. Limited, other times.

Locator 494-4542   **Medical 494-8133**   **Police 494-7777**

Pensacola Naval Air Station (FL14R1)
Pensacola NAS, FL 32508-5000

TELEPHONE NUMBER INFORMATION: Main installation numbers: C-904-452-0111, D-312-922-0111.

Location: Off US-98, 4 miles south of I-10. Take Navy Blvd from US-98 or US-29 directly to NAS. USM: J-7. NMC: Pensacola, 8 miles north.

Billeting Office: No central billeting office.

TML: Navy Lodge. Buildings 221 & 3448, all ranks, leave or official duty. For reservations call **1-800-NAVY-INN.** Lodge number is 456-8676, 0800-2000 daily. After duty hours, OD, C-EX-2353. Efficiency apartments, private bath (38). Kitchen, complete utensils, A/C, color TV in room & lounge, maid service, cribs/cots, coin washer/dryer, ice vending, handicapped accessible. Modern structure. Lodge 221 renovated. Rates: $27-$31 per unit. No maximum per unit. All categories can make reservations.

TML: BOQ. Building 600, officers all ranks, leave or official duty, C-904-452-2755, 24 hours daily. No stated check-out time. Approximately 780 one bedroom, private bath; some have 2 bedrooms. Refrigerator, A/C, color TV in lounge, cots, washer/dryer. Building renovated. Older structure. Rates: $6 per room, VIP $10. Active duty, retired, Reservists can make reservations, others Space-A.

TML: BEQ. Buildings 3468-3475 (3474/5 female). Enlisted E1-E6. C-904-542-4609, 24 hours daily. males, 513 beds; female, 189 beds, transient beds, 969. Two to 3 beds per room, 4 rooms per suite. Refrigerator, A/C, color TV in lounge, washer/dryer, ice vending,

FLORIDA
Pensacola Naval Air Station, continued

microwave. Modern structure. Rates: $2 for temporary attached duty, leave, retired. Student and staff personnel free. Maximum 11 per suite. Active duty, retired, reservists can make reservations, others Space-A.

DV/VIP: Protocol, building 45-M, room M-7. C-EX-2311. 08+. Retirees Space-A.

TML Availability: Good, all year. Best, during winter.

☞ Miles of sugar-white sand and beaches, excellent fishing and outdoor activities, Saenger Theater performing arts in Pensacola, historical and other museums, and the Blue Angels, the Aviation Museum and the USS Lexington, make this area important.

Locator 452-4693   Medical 452-2492   Police 452-2653

☺This navy lodge will expand to 50 rooms in '93. Watch Military Living's *R&R Space-A Report* for a picture of the spectacular building.

Tyndall Air Force Base (FL04R1)
Tyndall AFB, FL 32403-5000

TELEPHONE NUMBER INFORMATION: Main installation numbers: C-904-283-1110, D-312-523-1110.

Location: Take I-10, exit US-231 south to US-98 east, signs mark the AFB. USM: K-7. NMC: Panama City, 10 miles northwest.

Billeting Office: PO Box 40040, building 1332, Suwannee & Oak Dr, C-**904-286-6200,** D-312-523-4211, 24 hours daily. Check in billeting, check out 1200 hours daily. Government civilian employee billeting.

TML: VAQ/VOQ/DV/TLF. **Sand Dollar Inn,** all ranks, leave or official duty, C-EX-2394. Separate bedrooms, kitchen, private bath (VOQ) (240); bedroom, semi-private bath (VAQ) (460); efficiency apartments, private bath (40), sleeps 5, cribs/roll-away available (TLF). A/C, color TV in room and lounge, maid service, washer/dryer, ice vending. Modern structure. Rates: $20 per unit TLF, $6 per person VOQ & VAQ. $10 per person VIP. Official duty should make reservations, others Space-A.

Note: Tyndall Fam-Camp has two bedroom cottages (3). Rates: $32 sponsor, $2 each additional person. Call 904-283-2798 for more information and reservations.

DV/VIP: Hq, Building 647. C-EX-2232. 06+. Retirees and lower ranks Space-A.

TML Availability: Very good, Jan & Dec. Fair, other times.

☞ Beautiful white sand beaches, water sports, fishing, and small communities.

Locator 283-2138/4210   Medical 283-7523   Police 283-4124

FLORIDA
Whiting Field Naval Air Station (FL05R1)
Whiting Field NAS, FL 32570-5000

TELEPHONE NUMBER INFORMATION: Main installation numbers: C-904-623-7011, D-312-868-7011.

Location: From US-90 east exit, FL-87 north 7 miles to NAS. USM: J-7. NMC: Pensacola, 40 miles southwest.

Billeting Office: Building 2942, Lexington Circle, C-**904-623-0354,** D-312-868-7606, 24 hours daily. Check in facility, check out 1200 hours daily. Government civilian employee billeting.

TML: BOQ. Building 2942. Two-bedroom suites (123). Officers assigned bedrooms and share living room/lounge with one other person. BOQ houses barber shop, pool table, lounge w/large screen TV, physical fitness, sauna and laundry facilities. O'Club, swimming pool and academic training buildings within walking distance of BOQ.

TML: BEQ. Building 2942, all ranks, leave or official duty. Rooms suites, private bath (52). Refrigerator, A/C, color TV in lounge, maid service, cribs, washer/dryer, ice vending. Modern structure, renovated. Rates: $8 per room single, $12 per room double, $16 suite. No children. Duty can make reservations, others Space-A.

DV/VIP: Admiral's Office, building 1401. C-EX-7201. 06+. Retirees Space-A.

TML Availability: Good, Dec-Feb. Limited, other times.

☞ **Within walking distance are national parks, historic sites and the sugar-white beaches along Florida's famous miracle strip on the Gulf of Mexico.**

Locator 623-7011   **Medical 623-7584**   **Police 623-7387**

Georgia

Albany Marine Corps Logistics Base (GA17R1)
Albany MCLB, GA 31704-5000

TELEPHONE NUMBER INFORMATION: Main installation numbers: C-912-439-5000, D-312-567-5000.

Location: Approximately 3 miles SE of Albany. Accessible from US-82, US-300, and US-19. Follow the signs. USM: K-7.

Billeting Office: Housing Office, building 3600, C-**912-439-5614,** 0730-1700 M-F. After hours, contact Base Duty Officer, building 3500. Check out time 1130. Live Oak Lodge.

TML: Family Transient Quarters. Buildings 9257, 9259. Separate houses, 3 bedrooms, 1 1/2 baths, recently upgraded. All facilities and amenities. All ranks, primarily for active duty military on PCS. Rates: equivalent to 1/30th BAQ (w/dependents rate), retirees $20 per night. Maximum 6 adults or children per unit. Maid service not available during occupancy. Military on leave, retirees, Space-A.

GEORGIA
Albany Marine Corps Logistics Base, continued

TML: TEQ. Building 7966. One bedroom, private bath units for E6 and above, equivalent graded government employees on official orders. Rate: $7 per night. Maximum 2 adults, 2 children per unit. Retired military, Space-A.

TML: Enlisted quarters available for E5 and below. No charge, call for information. No maid service.

TML: TOQ. Buildings 10201, 10202, officers all ranks on leave/official duty. Equivalent government employees on official duty. One, three, and four-bedroom suites with kitchenettes. Handicapped suite available. Renovated. Rates: $10 to $20 per unit. Retired military, Space-A.

TML: DV/VIP. Building 10300, officer 06+, leave or official duty. Two bedroom, completely furnished detached house, private bath. All facilities and amenities. Maid service, color TV, washer/dryer. Modern structure. Rates: $25. Official duty, leave/retirees, Space-A.

DV/VIP: Protocol Office, building 3600, C-EX-5204, 05+. Retirees and lower ranks Space-A.

TML Availability: Fairly good. Best Nov-Mar.

☞ **Swimming at beautiful Radium Springs, south of Albany, outdoor sports, local Concert Association, Little Theater. Albany is a trade and distribution center for Southwest Georgia.**

Locator-439-5000/5103   **Medical-435-0806**   **Police-439-5181**

Athens Navy Supply Corps School (GA12R1)
Athens NSCS, GA 30606-5000

TELEPHONE NUMBER INFORMATION: Main installation numbers: C-404-354-1500, D-312-588-1500.

Location: From Athens take bypass, exit to Prince Ave, continue 1 mile to Base at intersection of Prince & Oglethorpe Avenues. USM: K-6. NMC: Atlanta, 70 miles west.

Billeting Office: Brown Hall. C-404-354-7360, D-312-588-7360, 24 hours daily. Check out 1300 hours daily. Government civilian employee Space-A, on orders.

TML: VQ. 05+, leave or official duty. Two bedroom suites, private bath (5); family quarters two bedroom suites, private bath (8) (all ranks/active duty). Refrigerator, A/C, color TV in room & lounge, maid service, washer/dryer, ice vending, microwave. Older structure. Rates: $20, suites, $8 rooms. Active duty can make reservations, others Space-A unless on orders for duty.

TML Availability: Dependent on student/class loading.

Athens Naval Supply Corps School, continued

☞ Athens packs a whollop, museums, restaurants, shopping, and the University of Georgia; the state botanical garden, and the Chattahoochee National Forest nearby. And then there's Atlanta 70 miles away...lots to do and see.

Locator 354-1500   Medical 354-7321

Atlanta Naval Air Station (GA16R1)
Marietta, GA. 30060-5099

TELEPHONE NUMBER INFORMATION: Main installation numbers: C-404-421-5392, D-312-925-5392.

Location: From I-75, exit to GA-280, W to GA-3, S to main gate, adjacent to Dobbins AFB on the W. USM: K-6. NMC: Atlanta, 15 miles SE.

Billeting Office: Building 54. C-404-421-5393, D-312-925-5393, 24 hours daily. Check at billeting, check out 1300 hours daily. Government civilian employees billeting on orders.

TML: BOQ. Building 53, officers, all ranks, on orders. Suites, private bath (4). Leave or official duty. Maid service, washer and dryer in building, long distance phone. Color TV. Modern structure. No pets. Rates: $6 per night. Others Space-A. Reservations required.

TML: BEQ. Building 54, 63, enlisted, all ranks, no females, on orders. Bedroom, shared bath (23). Bedroom, private bath (1). Maid service, color TV in lounge. Modern structure. No pets. Rates: $6 per night. Reservations required. Call above number.

TML Availability: Very good during the week, weekends very difficult.

☞ Stone Mountain State Park, with hiking, fishing and other outdoor activities, Six Flags over Georgia, and the vibrant city of Atlanta are visitors' attractions.

Locator 421-5392   Medical 421-5304/5

Dobbins Air Force Base (GA13R1)
Dobbins AFB, GA 30069-5000

TELEPHONE NUMBER INFORMATION: Main installation numbers: C-404-421-5000, D-312-925-1110.

Location: From I-75 north exit to GA-280 west to AFB. Clearly marked. USM: K-6. NMC: Atlanta, 17 miles northwest.

Billeting Office: Dobbins Inn. ATTN: SVH, building 800, Atlantic St, C-404-421-4745, 24 hours daily. Check in facility, check out 1200 hours daily. Government civilian employee billeting.

GEORGIA
Dobbins Air Force Base, continued

TML: VAQ. Building 801, enlisted, E1-E6, leave or official duty. Bedroom, semi-private bath (75). Refrigerator, A/C, cribs, essentials, color TV, washer/dryer, ice vending. Older structure, renovated '90. Rates: $6 per person. Maximum 2 persons. Duty can make reservations, others Space-A.

TML: DV/VIP. Building 401, officer 06+, available to lower ranks Space-A. Leave or official duty. Bedroom suites, private bath and sitting room (4). Bedrooms (42). Refrigerator, A/C, cribs, essentials, ice vending, maid service, color TV, washer/dryer. Billets renovated '92. Rates: $10 per person, maximum charge $20. Maximum 4 persons. Duty can reserve rooms, others Space-A.

TML: Senior NCO Quarters. Building 800. Two room suites (4). Rate: $10 per person per night. Other SNCO rooms (25) single occupancy, share bath. SNCO billets renovated '92. Rate: $6 per person per night.

DV/VIP: PAO, C-EX-5055/1110. 06+. Retirees and lower ranks Space-A.

TML Availability: Good, Nov-Mar. More difficult, Apr-Oct.

☞ **Excellent fishing and boating in the Metro Atlanta area at Lake Altoona and Lake Lanier. Visit underground Atlanta, the Cyclorama, Stone Mountain Park and the Jimmy Carter Presidential Library.**

Locator 421-5000   **Medical 421-5302**   **Police 421-4907**

Fort Benning (GA11R1)
Fort Benning, GA 31905-5065

TELEPHONE NUMBER INFORMATION: Main installation numbers: C-404-545-0110, D-312-835-0110.

Location: 12 miles South of Columbus off I-185. Can be reached from US-80 and US-280. USM: K-6.

Billeting Office: Building 399, C-404-689-0067 (Auto Attendant), D-312-835-3145/46, 24 hours. Check in facility, check out 1200 hours. All ranks, dependents (Space-A), reservists, and government civilian employees on TDY orders. Fee charged for late checkouts.

TML: Guest House. Buildings 36-38, C-EX-4101, all ranks. Priority PCS personnel, all others Space-A. Bedrooms, private bath (62), refrigerator, AC, color TV, maid service (M-F), living room 2 sofa beds. Older structure. Rates $16 per unit. Check out time: 1100. (Fee equal to room).

TML: VOQ/VEQ. Buildings 73, 75, 83, 399, all ranks, primarily for TDY students, may have Space-A for transients. C-EX-2505. Children not authorized. Check out time 1200. (Fee equal to room).

TML: MWR Destin Army Recreation Area, 557 Calhoun Ave, Destin, Fl 32541, C-1-800-642-0466, 904-837-2725. All ranks, leave or official duty, retirees, Fort Benning personnel. Motel: bedrooms, two double beds, private bath (34); cottages, two bedroom, private bath (20); three bedroom, private bath (4). Refrigerator, CATV, coffee pot,

Fort Benning, continued

towels/linens, recreation rental equipment (large fishing and party vessels), close to Hurlburt field support. Rates: based on rank, motel $30-36 daily; cottages $37-$47 daily. Additional fee for non ID card holders. Cabin #1 06+, call SGS 404-1545-3946/4411 for reservations. New motel and renovation project at press time. No pets. **Note:** see **Military RV, Camping & Rec Areas Around the World** for additional information.

TML: DV/VIP. McIver St. Officer 06+. Protocol RSVP C-404-545-5724, D-312-835-5724, private bath suite. Refrigerator, A/C, color TV, maid service (M-F). Older structure. Rates $23, $10 for additional occupant. Retired and lower ranks Space-A. Check out 1100 (fee of $15 for late check out).

TML Availability: Best: Dec, worst: Jun-Sep.

☞ **For those interested in military history, visit the Infantry museum and a number of other Fort Benning points of interest.**

Locator 545-5216   **Medical 544-2041**   **Police 544-3911**

☺A **$3 million guest house will be built on this facility. Check Military Living's** *R&R Space-A Report travel newsletter for updates.*

Fort Gillem (GA21R1)
Fort Gillem, GA 30050-5000

TELEPHONE NUMBER INFORMATION: Main installation numbers: C-404-363-5000, D-312-797-1001.

Location: From I-75, east on I-285 to US-54 (Jonesboro Road), S for 3 miles to the main gate. Fort is 5 miles from Hartsfield IAP. USM: K-6. NMC: Atlanta, 10 miles northwest.

Billeting Office: Building 817, Hood Ave, C-**404-363-5431,** 0730-1600 hours duty days. Check in facility, check out 1000 hours daily. Government civilian employee no billeting. This is a sub-post of Fort McPherson.

TML: VOQ/VEQ. Buildings 131, 134, all ranks, leave or official duty. Bedrooms, private bath (7); bedroom, private bath, (2). Kitchen, utensils, A/C, color TV, maid service, washer/dryer, ice vending. Older structure. Rates: $23/$25 per apartment. Duty can make reservations, others Space-A.

DV/VIP: Billeting Office, C-EX-5431, 06/GS-15+. Retirees and lower ranks Space-A.

TML Availability: Extremely limited.

☞ **"Gone with the Wind" country, and historic Atlanta attractions, combine with seashore, flatlands and mountains to make this area a joy to visit.**

Locator 363-5000   **Police 363-5582**

Fort Gordon (GA09R1)
Fort Gordon, GA 30905-5000

TELEPHONE NUMBER INFORMATION: Main installation numbers: C-706-791-0110, D-312-780-0110.

Location: Between US-78/278 and US-1. Gates are on both US-78 & US-1. USM: K,L-6. NMC: Augusta, 12 miles northeast.

Billeting Office: Griffith Hall, building 250, Chamberlain Ave, 0730-2400 hours daily. Reservations: C-**706-791-2277,** check in facility, check out 1100 hours daily. Government civilian employee billeting.

TML: Guest House (**Stinson**). Guest House Annex, all ranks, leave or official duty, C-EX-7160/9029, 24 hours daily. Bedroom suites, private bath (9); handicapped accessible room, private bath (1); rooms with kitchenettes (12); bedroom, 2-double beds, private bath (75). Refrigerator, A/C, color TV, maid service, cribs/cots ($2), coin washer/dryer, ice vending, facilities for DAVs. Modern structure. Rates: $24 per room; Guest House Annex: $28 per room. PCS and hospital visitors can make reservations 60 days in advance, others Space-A, reservations 2 days in advance.

TML: Guest House. Building 34602, enlisted E1-E4, check in billeting. Bedroom, common bath (4); separate bedroom, private bath (15). Refrigerator, A/C, color TV in room & lounge, maid service, washer/dryer. Older structure. Rates: $5 single, $8 double, children free. Maximum 2-3 per room. PCS and hospital visitors can make reservations, others Space-A.

TML: Guest House. Building 18404, enlisted E7-E9, check in billeting. Two bedroom apartments, private bath (2). Kitchen, utensils, A/C, color TV, maid service. Modern structure. Rates: $20 per room. PCS and hospital visitors can make reservations, others Space-A.

TML: VOQ. Buildings 250, 36700, officers all ranks, leave or official duty. Check in billeting. Bedroom, private bath (438). Kitchen, A/C, color TV in room & lounge, maid service, washer/dryer, ice vending. Modern structure. Rates: $16 single, $2 each additional person. Maximum 2 per room. Duty can make reservations, others Space-A.

TML: VEQ. Buildings 28410, 28411, enlisted all ranks, leave or official duty. Bedroom, 2 beds, private bath (68). Refrigerator, A/C, color TV, maid service, washer/dryer. Duty can make reservations, others Space-A.

TML: DVQ. Buildings 34503/04/06, 3460, 34605, officers 06+. Separate bedrooms, private bath (5). Kitchen, complete utensils, A/C, color TV, maid service, cots. Older structure. Rates: $24 single, $2 each additional person. Duty can make reservations, others, including lesser ranks, Space-A.

DV/VIP: Protocol Office, 10th floor, Signal Towers, C-EX-5376/5138, 06+. Retirees and lower ranks (03+) Space-A.

TML Availability: Good.

Locator 791-4675   **Medical 911**   **Police 791-4380**

Fort McPherson (GA08R1)
Fort McPherson, GA 30330-5000

TELEPHONE NUMBER INFORMATION: Main installation numbers: C-404-752-3113, D-312-572-1110.

Location: Off I-75 take Lakewood Freeway (GA-166), exit to US-29 (Main St exit). Main gate is at Main St exit. USM: K-6. NMC: Atlanta, in city limits.

Billeting Office: Building T-22. C-404-752-3833, 0630-2200 hours duty days. Other hours, SDO, building 65, EX-2980. Check in facility, check out 1000 hours daily. Government civilian employee billeting.

TML: Transient Quarters. Building T-109 (**Chalet**), all ranks, leave or official duty. One bedroom, semi-private bath (8). Community kitchen, complete utensils, A/C, color TV lounge, maid service, washer/dryer. Older structure. Rates: $22 officer, $20 enlisted, $20 TDY. Duty can make reservations, others Space-A.

TML: VOQ/VEQ. Building T-22 (**Chateau**), all ranks, leave or official duty. One bedroom, private bath (22). Community kitchen, A/C, color TV in room & lounge, maid service, washer/dryer, ice vending. Older structure. Same rates and occupancy as above. Building 168. Three bedrooms, private bath (10); Two bedrooms, private bath (2); A/C, cots/cribs, food/ice vending, kitchen, maid service, handicapped accessible, color TV in room, telephone in room, washer/dryer. Modern structure. Same rates as above. Duty can make reservations.

TML: DV/VIP. Lee Hall, officer 06+, leave or official duty, C-EX-4145. Various size suites, private bath (8). Refrigerator, community kitchen, A/C, color TV in room & lounge, maid service, ice vending. Older structure. Call for rates. Duty can make reservations, others Space-A.

DV/VIP: Protocol Office, building 200, C-EX-5388/5398, 06+. Retirees and lower ranks Space-A.

TML Availability: Good. Best Dec-Feb.

☞ Fort McPherson is steeped in history, and surrounded by the vibrant city of Atlanta. Visit the Atlanta Historical Society, Fox Theater, Governor's Mansion, Martin Luther King Jr Historic District, Inman Park, Six Flags over Georgia.

Locator-752-2743/4174   Medical-752-3139   Police-752-3050

Fort Stewart (GA15R1)
Fort Stewart, GA 31314-5000

TELEPHONE NUMBER INFORMATION: Main installation numbers: C-912-767-1110, D-312-870-1110.

Location: Accessible from US-17 or I-95. Also GA-119 or GA-144 crosses the Post. USM: L-6. NMC: Savannah, 35 miles northeast.

GEORGIA
Fort Stewart, continued

Billeting Office: ATTN: AFZP-DEH-B. Building 4951. C-**912-368-4184,** D-312-870-8384, 0730-2345 hours daily. Other hours, SDO, building 01, C-EX-8666. Check in billeting, check out 1100 hours daily. Government civilian employees billeting.

TML: Guest House. Building 4951, all ranks, leave or official duty, C-EX-8384. Bedroom, dining room, private bath (sleeps 6) (70). Kitchen, A/C, CATV, maid service, cribs/cots, essentials, handicapped accessible, coin washer/dryer, ice vending. Modern structure. Rates: $20 per room per night. Duty and DAVs can make reservations, others Space-A.

TML: BOQ/VOQ. Building 4950, C-EX-8384, officers all ranks, official duty only. Reservations accepted (VOQ), not taken (BOQ). Bedroom, private bath (30). Kitchen, A/C, color TV, maid service, washer/dryer, ice vending. Modern structure. Rates: $19 per room per night. BOQ rooms, rates not available. Inquire at above number. Maximum 1 per room.

TML: DVQ. Officer 06+, leave or official duty, C-EX-8610. Two bedroom cottages, private bath (2). A/C, cots/cribs, essentials, ice vending, kitchen, complete utensils, maid service, handicapped accessible, color TV, washer/dryer. Rate: $20. Active and retirees can make reservations, others Space-A.

TML: TLQ. Building 4950, all ranks, leave or official duty. C-EX-8384. Handicapped accessible. Bedroom, private bath (35). A/C, essentials, ice vending, kitchen, maid service, color TV, washer/dryer. Being remodeled. Rate: $19. Maximum 2 per unit. Duty can make reservations, others Space-A.

DV/VIP: Protocol, building 01, C-EX-8610. 06+. Retirees and lower ranks Space-A.

TML Availability: Fairly good. Best Nov-Apr. More difficult, other times.

☞ **Local recreational activities are hunting, fishing, tennis and golf. Ocean beaches are within driving distance, and historic Savannah is 40 miles northeast with many attractions.**

Locator 767-2862   **Medical 767-6666**   **Police 767-2822**

Hunter Army Airfield (GA10R1)
Hunter Army Airfield, GA 31409-5023

TELEPHONE NUMBER INFORMATION: Main installation numbers: C-912-352-6521, D-312-971-1110.

Location: From I-95 to GA-204 east for 13 miles to Savannah. Turn left onto Stephenson Ave, proceed straight into Wilson Ave Gate to Installation. USM: L-6. NMC: Savannah, in southwest part of city.

Billeting Office: ATTN: AFZP-DEH-B(H). Building 6010, Duncan and Leonard Sts. C-**912-352-5910/5834** or 355-1060 (reservations), 0700-2400 hours M-F, 0800-1700 hours Sa-Su, holidays. After hours, SDO, building 1201, C-EX-5140. Check in time 1400, check out 1100 hours daily. Government civilian employee billeting.

TML: Guest House/VOQ/VEQ. Buildings 6005, 6010, all ranks, leave or official duty. Two bedroom suites, private bath (32); bedroom, semi-private bath (9). Kitchen, complete

GEORGIA

Hunter Army Airfield, continued

utensils, essentials, A/C, color TV in room & lounge, maid service, cribs/cots, washer/dryer, food/ice vending, handicapped accessible. Older structures. Renovated and remodeled. Rates: $20 per family. All categories can make reservations. PCS have priority.

DV/VIP: Cmdr, 24th Inf Div, ATTN: AFZP-CS-P, building 1. C-912-767-8610, D-EX-8610. 05+. Retirees Space-A.

TML Availability: Very good, all times.

☞ **Near historic Savannah. Hunting, fishing, coastal Georgian beaches.**

Locator 767-2862   **Medical 352-5551**   **Police 352-6133**

Kings Bay Naval Submarine Base (GA03R1)
Kings Bay NSB, GA 31547-5015

TELEPHONE NUMBER INFORMATION: Main installation numbers: C-912-673-2000, D-312-860-2000.

Location: Off I-95 north of GA/FL border. Take exit 1 which leads right into base, or exits 2A or 2B, east to Kings Bay and follow road north to base. USM: L-7. NMC: Jacksonville, 40 miles south.

Billeting Office: ATTN: Housing Office N53, building 1051-N, James Madison Rd, C-912-673-2056, 0800-1630 hours M-F. Check in billeting, check out 1200 hours daily.

TML: Navy Lodge. Building 0158, all ranks, leave or official duty. For reservations call 1-800-NAVY-INN, lodge number is 882-6868. Check in facility, 0700-2000 hours daily. Bedroom, 2 beds, private bath (26). Kitchen, complete utensils, A/C, color TV, maid service, cribs, coin washer/dryer, ice vending, handicapped accessible, cable HBO. Modern structure. Rates: $34 per room. Maximum 5 per room. Duty and retirees can make reservations.

TML: BEQ. Building 1041, enlisted all ranks, leave or official duty, C-EX-2163/2164. Bedroom, private bath (142). Refrigerator, A/C, cots, essentials, food/ice vending, maid service, washer/dryer, (microwave and coffee pot, color TV in lounge & room CPO & VIP). Modern structure. Rates: VIP $10 for one person, $15 for two or more; all others $4 for one person, $10 for two or more. Maximum charge VIP & family suite $15, maximum charge for rooms $10. Maximum 4 persons. Duty can make reservations, others Space-A.

TML: BOQ. Building 1056, officers, all ranks, leave or official duty, C-EX-2165/2169. Handicapped accessible. Bedroom, private bath (38); separate bedroom, private bath (98). A/C, cots, essentials, food/ice vending, maid service, color TV in room, washer/dryer. Modern structure. Rates: $8-$15 per person, maximum charge $16-$20. Maximum 4 persons. Duty can make reservations, others Space-A.

TML Availability: Good. Best Oct-Dec. Difficult Jun-Sep.

GEORGIA
Kings Bay Naval Submarine Base, continued

☞ From the beauty and history of old Savannah to the beaches of the Golden Isles near Brunswick and the Cumberland Island National Seashore, coastal Georgia offers everything from sightseeing to fishing and hunting.

Locator 673-2000   Medical 882-5109   Police 882-2265

Moody Air Force Base (GA02R1)
Moody AFB, GA 31699-5000

TELEPHONE NUMBER INFORMATION: Main installation numbers: C-912-333-4211, D-312-460-1110.

Location: On GA 125, 10 miles north of Valdosta. Also can be reached from I-75 via GA-122. USM: K-7. NMC: Valdosta, 10 miles south.

Billeting Office: Building 320, Cooney St, C-**912-333-3893**, 24 hours daily. Check in billeting, check out 1200 hours. Government employee off base contract quarters. **Note: this facility won the Air Force Inn-keeper Award for 1992.**

TML: TLF. Building 325, all ranks, leave or official duty. Two bedroom, private bath (12). Kitchen, A/C, color TV, maid service, cribs/cots, washer/dryer. Community motel design. Rates: $16 - 2 bedroom. PCS in/out, TDY can make reservations, others Space-A.

TML: VAQ. Building 325, enlisted all ranks, leave or official duty. Units, private bath (29). Refrigerator, A/C, color TV, maid service, washer/dryer. Community motel design. Rates: $6 per person. PCS in/out, TDY can make reservations, others Space-A.

TML: VOQ. Building 213, officers all ranks, leave or official duty. Bedroom, private bath (23). Kitchen, refrigerator, A/C, color TV, maid service, washer/dryer. Community motel design. Rates: $6 per person. PCS in/out, TDY can make reservations, others Space-A.

TML: DV. Buildings 213/325, officers 06+, E8-E9, leave or official duty. Bedroom suites, private bath (officer) (5); two bedroom suite, private bath (Officer) (1); bedroom suites, private bath (E8-E9) (2). Kitchen, A/C, color TV, maid service, washer/dryer. Community motel design. Rates: $10 per person. PCS in/out, TDY can make reservations, others Space-A.

DV/VIP: Protocol Office, 347 CSG/CCE, building 101, C-EX-3480, 06+, E9, retirees and lower ranks Space-A.

TML Availability: Good, May, Sep, Dec. Difficult, Jun-Aug.

☞ Visit the mansion Crescent, in Valdosta, for tours, particularly at Azalea season. There are many freshwater lakes for fishing and water sports. Dove, quail, turkey and other wild game hunting in season is also popular.

Locator 333-3585   Medical 333-3232   Police 333-3108

Robins Air Force Base (GA14R1)
Robins AFB, GA 31098-5000

TELEPHONE NUMBER INFORMATION: Main installation numbers: C-912-926-1110, D-312-468-1001.

Location: Off US-129 on GA-247 at Warner Robins. Access from I-75 south. USM: K-6. NMC: Macon, 18 miles northwest.

Billeting Office: Pine Oaks Lodge, building 557, Club Dr, C-912-926-2100, 24 hours daily. Check in facility. Government civilian employee billeting.

TML: TLF. Building 1180-1183, all ranks, leave or official duty. Check out 1000 hours. Bedroom, private bath (40). Kitchen, complete utensils, A/C, color TVs, maid service, cots/cribs, ice vending, washer/dryer. Older structure. Rates: E4- $14, E5+ $18, maximum family rate $14-$18. Maximum 5 per unit. Duty and retired can make reservations, others Space-A.

TML: VOQ. Buildings 551/2/3/7, officers all ranks, leave or official duty. Handicapped accessible. Check out 1200 hours. Bedroom, private bath (51); Two bedroom, semi-private bath (47). Kitchen, complete utensils, A/C, refrigerator, color TV, maid service, cribs/cots, washer/dryer. Older structure, renovation on-going. Rates: $8 per person, maximum family rate $16. Maximum 4 per unit. If more than one unit needed, 2nd unit is free. Duty and retired can make reservations, others Space-A.

TML: VAQ. Building 755, enlisted all ranks, leave or official duty. Check out 1200 hours. Bedroom, shared bath (28); Bedroom, shared bath (39); seven separate bedroom, private bath. Refrigerator, A/C, color TV, maid service, washer/dryer, ice vending. Older structure. Rates: $8 per person. Duty and retired can make reservations, others Space-A. Chief suites $10.

DV/VIP: Building 215, C-EX-2761. 06+.

TML Availability: Good, Oct-May. Difficult, other times.

☞ **Macon, 18 miles northwest, is the geographic center of Georgia, where shopping, parks (this is the Cherry Blossom Capital of the World) welcome visitors with true Southern hospitality.**

Locator 926-6027   Medical 926-3845   Police 926-2187

Hawaii

Barbers Point Naval Air Station (HI10R6)
Barbers Point NAS, HI 96862-5050

TELEPHONE NUMBER INFORMATION: Main installation numbers: C-808-684-6266, D-312-484-6266.

Location: Take HI-1 West (toward Waianee) to Barbers Point NAS/Makakilo exit, south for 2.5 miles to main gate. USM: D-9. NMC: Honolulu, 12 miles east.

HAWAII
Barbers Point Naval Air Station, continued

Billeting Office: Building 1788, **Bealleau Woods**, off Enterprise, BOQ C-**808-684-3191**, BEQ C-**808-684-9146**, 24 hours daily. Active duty check in 0800, check out 1200, Space-A check in 1600, check out 1000 hours. Government civilian employee billeting.

TML: BOQ. Building 77, officers all ranks, leave or official duty. Bedroom, shared bathroom (80); separate bedroom, private bath (28). Refrigerator, A/C, color TV in room & lounge, maid service, washer/dryer, ice vending. Modern structure. Rates: sponsor $8, adult $8. No children. Maximum 2 persons per room. Duty can make reservations, others Space-A.

TML: BEQ. Building 37, enlisted all ranks, leave or official duty. Bedroom, separate, private bath (hall) (60). Refrigerator, A/C, color TV in room & lounge, maid service, washer/dryer, vending machine. Modern structure, renovated '92. Rates: $4 per person. No children. Duty can make reservations, others Space-A.

DV/VIP: C-**808-684-3191**, O6+. Rates $12.

TML Availability: Good, winter months. Difficult, summer months.

☞ **Easy access to commissary and exchange facilities. The southwestern coast of Oahu, known for its beautiful beaches. Check Barber's Point Rec Area listing for more lodging.**

Locator 684-6266   **Medical 684-8245**   **Police 684-6222**

Barbers Point Recreation Area (HI01R6)
Barbers Point Naval Air Station, HI 96862-5050

TELEPHONE NUMBER INFORMATION: Main installation numbers: C-808-684-6266, D-315-484-6266.

Location: Take HI-1 West to Barbers Point/Makakilo exit. Left at sign then go through main gate. Turn right on Shangrila, then turn into the parking lot on the left. Reservations office is in building 19 (Fitness Center). USM: D-9. NMC: Pearl Harbor, 10 miles northeast.

Billeting Office: Morale, Welfare, Recreation Dept, Beach Cottages, Barbers Point NAS, HI 96862-5050, C-**808-682-2019**, D-315-430-0111/2019, 0800-1700 hours M-F. Reservations 60 days in advance. Priority system in effect. Call for information. Confirmation 4 weeks in advance. Mail applications to RSD Cottage Reservations, Naval Air Station, Barbers Point, HI 96862-5050. Reservations for 3 days F-M, 4 days M-F, 7 days M-M or F-F. Check in at area 1400 hours daily, check out 0900 hours daily. Cottages cannot be used as party facility. Operates year round.

TML: Rec Cottages, all ranks, leave only. Handicapped accessible. Enlisted cottages (14); officer cottages (6), VIP cottages (06+) (2). Two Bedroom and three bedroom cottages available at Cedar Beach. Kitchen, complete utensils, color TV (VIP only), cribs/cots, BBQ grills. Rates: enlisted $30 per unit, ($35 for 1778, 1777); officer $35 per unit, VIP

Barbers Point Recreation Area, continued

$40 per unit, two bedroom Cedar Beach unit $40, three bedroom, $45. Maximum 6 persons. All categories can make reservations by written application, see information above.

DV/VIP: Administration Office, building 1, C-EX-4103, 07/GS-16+. Retirees and lower ranks Space-A. Flag Officer Cottages 1760 and 1775 (Space-A to O-6+), Reservations: C-808-474-0111/1181, D-315-430-0111, 315-474/1181.

TML Availability: Good, Jan-Apr & Oct-Nov. Difficult, other times.

☞ Complete beach rec area. Check with Special Services, Ticket Office for tourist/island activities. Complete support facility at NAS. For full details see Military Living's *Military RV, Camping & Rec Areas Around The World.*

Barking Sands Pacific Missile Range Facility (HI04R6)
Kehaha, Kauai, HI 96752-0128

TELEPHONE NUMBER INFORMATION: Main installation numbers: C-808-335-4111, D-315-471-6249.

Location: From the airport, take Highway 50 west about 30 miles. USM: C-8. NMC: Waimea, 8 miles south.

Billeting Office: Building 1261, C-808-335-4383, D-315-471-6383, 24 hours daily. Information, C-MWR 808-335-4446/4753. Make reservations by written application: write Beach Cottages, Reservations MWR PMRF, Barking Sands, Kehaha, Kauai, HI 96752. Must mail application 60 days in advance. Check in MWR Office, 0800-1700, check out 1200, late checkout by appointment.

TML: Beach Cottages. All ranks, leave or official duty. Cottages, two bedrooms, private bath, sofabed, sleep 6 (6). Accessible to handicapped. Kitchenette, utensils, microwave, refrigerator, color TV, washer/dryer, iron and board. Rates: $40/2 persons, $4 each additional person. Two more units planned in near future. All categories can make reservations. All Hands Club, Shenanigans, galley/mess hall Menehune Inn. Camping, fishing snorkeling equipment, tennis, handball, gym, craft center.

DV/VIP: One cottage set aside for 06+. Write above address for information.

TML Availability: Very good, Sep thru Feb. Difficult, Mar thru Aug.

☞ This is truly "Paradise"! Captain Cook's historic landing place, and Waimea Canyon, "the Grand Canyon of Hawaii" are nearby. Seven-mile strip of beach, where hollow sand grains make a popping sound when rubbed together.

Locator 335-4111   **Medical 335-4203**   **Police 335-4356**

HAWAII

Bellows Recreation Area (HI02R6)
Bellows AFS, HI 96853-5000

TELEPHONE NUMBER INFORMATION: Main installation numbers: C-808-259-8841, D-315-259-8841.

Location: From Honolulu Airport or Hickam AFB, take I-HI1 east to exit 21A (Pali Highway); north to HI72 to Waimanalo Town. AFS is on L. Clearly marked. USM: D-9. NMC: Kailua, 9 miles northwest.

Billeting Office: Write to: Bellows Reservation Office, 220 Tinker Rd, Waimanalo, HI 96795-5000. **C-808-259-8841.** Priorities: 90 days in advance, active duty AF and Reserve (in excess of 72 hours), active duty other services and Coast Guard assigned Hickam or Bellows (call for details); 75 days in advance, active duty other services and Coast Guard stationed elsewhere; 60 days in advance, military retired with pay, medal of honor recipients and surviving spouses, DAV's (100 %), reservists at Bellows or Hickam, surviving spouses and former spouses, Naval Academy midshipmen, Army and AF cadets, officer candidates, ROTC cadets and midshipmen on vacation; 45 days in advance, DOD and NAF civilian employees, foreign nation military, other services personnel, retired with pay and reservists, Red Cross employees, contract surgeons, others authorized by base commander. Only registered guests after 2300 hours (Off island relatives guests may stay overnight). Call for further details. Maximum 14 day occupancy, sponsor or spouse must register. Deposit required 15 days before occupancy (one day's rent, MC, Visa, checks accepted). Cancellations up to 7 days without penalty. Reservations 0930-1730 daily. Check in 1400 hours, check out 0900-1200 hours.

TML: Cottages and studios. All ranks, leave only. See above. Cottages, studios, private bath (105) (single & duplex units), 50 for officers, 55 for enlisted. Kitchen, complete utensils, CATV, ceiling fans, cots/cribs $1, dishes, linens, towels, bedding all furniture. Renovated. Rates: studio $40, backrow $45, oceanview $50.

TML Availability: Good, Oct-Apr. Difficult, other times.

☞ On Oahu's northwest coast, about 16 miles from downtown Waikiki, turquoise waters and gorgeous beaches await your arrival! Beach front rec center. For camping see Military RV, Camping & Rec Areas Around The World.

Locator (Mgr) 259-5428   Police-259-5955

Fort Shafter (HI09R6)
Fort Shafter, HI 96858-5000

TELEPHONE NUMBER INFORMATION: Main installation numbers: C-808-471-7110, D-315-430-0111.

Location: Take HI-1 West exit at Fort Shafter, clearly marked. USM: D-9. NMC: Honolulu, 7 miles east.

Billeting: 453B, Burr Rd, **C-808-848-1774,** 0745-1545 hours daily. Write to: USASCH Billeting Fund, 692 McCornack Rd, Wahiawa, HI 96786. Check in billeting or facility, check out 1100 hours daily.

Fort Shafter, continued

TML: Guest House. Building 453B, Burr Rd, all ranks, leave or official duty. Two bedroom (4 units no kitchen) private bath (8); Three bedroom, private bath (4). Kitchen, complete utensils, color TV, maid service, cribs/cots, washer/dryer. Older structure. Rates: sponsor $29 with kitchen, $20 without kitchen, $5 each additional person. Children under 2, free. Maximum 7 per unit. PCS can make reservations and have priority; PCS out 7 days maximum, reservation in advance, PCS in 10 days. Others Space-A.

TML Availability: Fair, most of the year.

☞ **The oldest army post in Hawaii, part of the post is a National Historic Place. Visit the Bishop Museum in Honolulu, the Honolulu Academy of Arts, Mission Houses Museum, and don't miss the beach!**

Locator 438-1904   **Medical 433-6620**   **Police 438-2885**

Hale Koa Hotel AFRC (HI08R6)
2055 Kalia Road
Honolulu, HI 96815-1998

TELEPHONE NUMBER INFORMATION: Main installation numbers: C-808-955-0555 (24 hours), 1-800-367-6027 (0800-1600 hours daily HI time, except holidays).

Location: At 2055 Kalia Road, Waikiki Beach, Honolulu, HI. Fort De Russy, is on Waikiki Beach, between the Ala Moana Blvd, Kalakaua Ave and Saratoga Road, about 9 miles east of Honolulu International Airport. USM: D-8. NMC: Honolulu, in the city.

Description of Area: This morale-boosting, all ranks hotel, was opened in October 1975. Fourteen stories with 420 air-conditioned guest rooms with views of the Pacific Ocean and Koolau Mountains. All rooms identical in size, each with its private lanai, color TVs, room-controlled air-conditioning; most have two double beds. Some rooms handicapped accessible. Coin-operated washers & dryers available. Swimming pool, fitness center, landscaped gardens, and indoor and outdoor sports activities on a beautiful golden sand beach. Also available: cocktail lounges, snack bar, Post Exchange, Show Room, Hale Koa fine dining room, meeting rooms and conference facilities, sauna & locker rooms, coffee house, flower and jewelry shops, barber & beauty shops, and rental cars. Nine magnificent dining, cocktail, and entertainment rooms. The **Hale Koa** is a complete resort. Ocean and pool swimming, snorkeling, tennis, volleyball, sail boats, racquet ball, and paddle tennis available at your door, and one of the world's largest shopping centers. Dress: aloha-wear at all times. The 1991-92 double rates quoted below.

Season of Operation: Year round.

Reservations: Required. Write for reservation and information packet: 2055 Kalia Road, Honolulu, HI 96815-1998.

Eligibility: Active duty, retired, DoD civilian on official business, reserve and National Guard.

HAWAII
Hale Koa Hotel AFRC, continued

1991-92 double rates are quoted below:

Categories* for both Active and Retired	I Active/Retired E1 to E5	II Active/Retired E6 to E9 WO1 to CW3 01 to 03 all TDY, TLA DAV**, Widow(s)	III Active/Retired CW4 04 to 010 Foreign Others
Standard	$37	$47	$61
Superior	$44	$54	$72
Partial Oceanview	$49	$64	$83
Oceanview	$56	$70	$89
Ocean Front	$67	$82	$96

Ocean front rooms have king beds only. Daily rates based on room location (generally the higher floors reflect increased rate) and the number of occupants (maximum of 4 persons permitted per room). Add $10 for each additional person over age 2. Cribs are available at $4 per night. Most rooms are furnished with two double beds. Reservations may be made for a maximum stay of 30 days. Extensions permitted on a space available basis.

* Active and Retired (DD form 2 Retired-Gray or Blue) and dependents (DD1173), all services, all ranks, family & guests meeting eligibility requirements.

** Must have DD1173. Note: Widows(ers) can take guest. Write or call Hotel for more information. The Luau at the Hale Koa is every Thursday evening on the beach (Monday and Thursday June-August). Polynesian Review Dinner Show twice weekly. Magic Show and Italian buffet Tuesday. Adult $22.95, children under 12 $12.95. ID cardholders can sponsor guests.

☞ **If for some reason you get bored with Waikiki, check out the Army Museum, Diamond Head, Honolulu Zoo, Waikiki Aquarium, and Moana Center, not to mention Downtown Honolulu.**

☺**In 1994 a 13-story tower addition to the Hale Koa Hotel with 396 rooms is scheduled to open. Notice our front cover, the Hale Koa AFRC at twilight!**

Hickam Air Force Base (HI11R6)
Hickam AFB, HI 96853-5000

TELEPHONE NUMBER INFORMATION: Main installation numbers: C-808-471-7110, D-315-471-7110.

Location: Adjacent to the Honolulu IAP. Accessible from HI-1 or HI-92. Clearly marked. USM: D-9. NMC: Honolulu, 6 miles east.

Billeting Office: ATTN: 15 ABW/SVH, building 1153, C-808-471-2603, D-315-449-2603, 24 hours daily. Check in facility, check out 1200 hours daily. Government civilian employee billeting.

TML: VOQ. Eight buildings adjacent to O'Club. Officers all ranks, leave or official duty. Bedroom, private bath (34); two bedroom apartments, living room, private bath (88).

Hickam Air Force Base, continued

Kitchen, microwave TV, maid service. Older structure. Rates: $11.50 per person, maximum $46 per family. Duty can make reservations, others Space-A.

TML: VAQ. Buildings 470, 471, 920, senior enlisted E7+, leave or official duty. Two bedroom apartments, private bath (16) (kitchen, microwave, TV); single rooms, private bath (24). Maid service. Older structure. Rates: $9.50 per person. Maximum $38 per family. Duty can make reservations, others Space-A.

TML: VAQ. Building 1153 (female); Buildings 1166, 1168 (male), enlisted E1-E6, leave or official duty. Two bedroom, 2 persons per room, communal bath (33). Maid service. Older structure. Rates: $9.50 per person. Duty can make reservations, others Space-A.

TML: DV/VIP. Building 728, officers 07+, leave or official duty. Two bedroom apartments, living room, private bath (33). Kitchen, microwave, TV, maid service. Older structure. Rates: $11.50 per person, maximum $46 per family. Duty can make reservations, others Space-A.

DV/VIP: PACAF Protocol Office, 07+, C-EX-1781. Building 1153, C-EX-2603.

TML Availability: Difficult, most of the year.

☞ **Waikiki, Pearl Harbor's historic war memorial, shopping and sightseeing in Honolulu, hikes in local parks that put you in touch with Oahu's natural wonders. Whether you want relaxation or excitement, it's all here.**

Locator 449-9480   **Medical 449-6333**   **Police 449-6373**

Kaneohe Bay Beach Cottages (HI06R6)
Kaneohe Bay MCAS, HI 96863-5001

TELEPHONE NUMBER INFORMATION: Main installation numbers: C-808-471-1110, D-315-430-0111.

Location: Take H-3 to MCAS. Cottages are across from the airstrip along the coast line, near Pyramid Rock overlooking Kaneohe Bay. USM: D-9. NMC: Honolulu, 14 miles southwest.

Billeting Office: Temporary Lodging Facility, building 3038, MCAS Kaneohe Bay, HI 96863-5018. Assignment priority list available on request. For reservations for cottages call C-**808-254-2716/2806**.

TML: Beach Cottages, all ranks. Two bedroom, living room, dining areas, private bath (12); CB cottage, private bath (1). Kitchen, complete utensils, color TV, lanai. Completely furnished. Rates: $30 per day. All categories can make reservations.

TML Availability: Fairly good.

☞ **MCAS full support facilities. (For details see Military Living's Military RV, Camping & Rec Areas Around The World). Beaches, boating, or just plain relaxing. You won't regret your stay at Kaneohe.**

HAWAII

Kaneohe Marine Corps Air Station (HI12R6)
Kaneohe MCAS, HI 96863-5001

TELEPHONE NUMBER INFORMATION: Main installation numbers: C-808-471-7110, D-315-430-0110.

Location: At end of H-3 on the windward side of Oahu. Off Mokapu Blvd and Kaneohe Bay Dr. Clearly marked. USM: E-9. NMC: Honolulu, 14 miles southwest.

Billeting Office: Hostess House, building 3038, 0630-1800 hours M-F, 0900-1800 hours Sa-Su, holidays, C-**808-254-2716,** D-315-457-2808, other hours, OD, Building 215, C-808-254-1829. After hours Station Officer of the Day 257-1823. Check in facility, check out 1000 hours daily. Government civilian employee billeting.

TML: Hostess House, building 3038, all ranks, leave or official duty. Two, three, four bedroom, private bath (24). One bedroom SNCO suites, private bath (45). Older structure. Rates: $24 per unit. Duty can make reservations, others Space-A.

TML: BOQ. Building 503, officers all ranks, leave or official duty, C-808-257-2409, D-315-457-2409. Suites, private bath (37). Refrigerator, community kitchen, utensils, color TV in room & lounge, maid service, cots, washer/dryer, ice vending, spa/jacuzzi. Older structure. Rates: sponsor $13, maximum $17 per family. No children under age 10. Maximum 5 per room. Duty can make reservations, others Space-A.

TML: Studios. All ranks. Leave or official duty. Studios, living/dining areas, kitchen, private bath (24). Rates: $25 per day.

DV/VIP: FMF PAC Protocol, Camp H.M. Smith, HI 96861. Building 1, Room 200. C-808-477- 6891, 06+, retirees Space-A.

TML Availability: Good. Best, Mar-Apr. More difficult, May-Jun.

☞ **See Kaneohe Bay Beach Cottages listing.**

Locator 257-2008　　　　**Medical 257-2505**　　　　**Police 257-2123**

Kilauea Military Camp AFRC (HI17R6)
Hawaii National Park, HI 96718-5000

TELEPHONE NUMBER INFORMATION: Main installation numbers: C-808-967-7315, D-None.

Location: On island of Hawaii, 216 air miles southeast of Honolulu, 32 miles from Hilo IAP. Scheduled bus transport to Camp, reservations required Hilo to KMC. USM: E-9. NMC: Hilo, 32 miles northwest.

Billeting Office: ATTN: Reservations Office, Hawaii Volcanoes National Park, HI 96718. C-**808-967-8333,** reservations required. FCFS basis regardless of rank. Include name, rank, service, status & list children & guest(s) when applying for reservation. Priority I, AD, call 90 days in advance; or write 120 days in advance; priority II, retirees, 60 days in advance; priority III, DOD civilian and other authorized personnel, 45 days.

HAWAII

Kilauea Military Camp AFRC, continued

Reservations Office, 0800-1600 daily. Located at 4000 feet, temperature 50-65 degrees F. Check in 1400, check out 1100 hours daily. From Oahu, call toll free C-438-6707 (0800-1600 daily). Others call direct: KMC-808-967-8333.

TML: Apartments & Cabins (all with fireplaces). One bedroom, private bath (33); Two bedroom w/kitchen, private bath (12); two bedroom, private bath (10); three bedroom, private bath (1); four bedroom cabin, private bath (1); two dormitories w/common baths and showers for large groups. Refrigerator or kitchen, CATV, maid service, cribs ($1/night), rollaways ($1), coin laundry. Rec lodge, 18 hole golf course, deep sea fishing and helicopter charters, bus tours. Rates: E1-E5, $23-$33; E6-E9, W1-3, O1-3 $31-$41; W4, O4, DOD Civilian, $39-$49, up to two person occupancy. $5 each additional person. No charge under age 3. Kitchen $10 per night. Dormitories $5-$7.50 per night.

TML Availability: Good, fall, winter, spring. More difficult, summer.

☞ On the rim of Kilauea Crater at 4,000 feet, quiet guest cottages, hiking, lectures, movies, support facilities, this is the place to get away from it all. For more details see Military Living's Military RV Camping & Rec Areas Around the World.

Locator 967-7315   **Medical 967-8367**

Pearl Harbor Naval Station (HI20R6)
Pearl Harbor NS, HI 96860-6000

TELEPHONE NUMBER INFORMATION: Main installation numbers: C-808-474-8053, D-315-471-5210.

Location: Off H-1 adjacent to Honolulu International Airport. Clearly marked. USM: D-9. NMC: Honolulu, 10 miles east.

Billeting Office: Building 1315, B Ave, C-808-474-5210, 24 hours daily. Check in at facility, check out 1300 hours daily. Government civilian employee billeting BOQ.

TML: BOQ. Buildings 372, 1315, officers all ranks, leave or official duty. Handicapped accessible. Bedroom, private bath (72). A/C, refrigerator, color TV, maid service, washer/dryer, food/ice vending, room telephones. Modern structure. Rates: sponsor $8, adult $3. Maximum 2 persons. Duty can make reservations, others Space-A. No children.

TML: BEQ. Buildings 1623, 1507, enlisted all ranks, leave or official duty. Handicapped accessible, singles only. Bedroom, private bath (84). Refrigerator, color TV, maid service, washer/dryer, food/ice vending, telephones in room. Modern structure. Rates: $4 per person. Duty can make reservations, others Space-A. No dependents.

DV/VIP: CINCPAC FIT Protocol, C-EX-7256, 07+. Only 06 Space-A.

TML Availability: Difficult. Best Dec-Jan.

HAWAII
Pearl Harbor Naval Station, continued

☞ Visit the Bishop Museum and Planetarium to see what old Hawaii was like, Pier 9 at the foot of Fort Street Mall has spectacular views of Honolulu and the harbor from the Aloha Tower. Don't forget the Arizona Memorial, USS Bowfin.

Locator 474-6249　　　　Medical 471-9541　　　　Police 474-1237

Schofield Barracks (HI13R6)
Schofield Barracks, HI 96786-5000

TELEPHONE NUMBER INFORMATION: Main installation numbers: C-808-655-4930, D-315-455-4930.

Location: Off H-2 or HI-99 in the center of the Island of Oahu. Clearly marked. USM: D-9. NMC: Honolulu, 20 miles southeast.

Billeting Office: Building 692, McCornack Rd. C-**808-624-9877**, 0730-1600 hours daily. Check in facility, 1500 hours, check out 1200 hours daily. Government civilian employee billeting.

TML: Guest House. **Grant Hall**, all ranks, leave or official duty. Separate bedrooms (55), shared bath (30), or private bath (15); two bedroom suite, private bath (1). Refrigerator, community kitchen, color TV in room & lounge, maid service, cribs/cots, washer/dryer, ice vending, playground, game room, snack vending. Older structure. Rates: sponsor $17-$32, adult $5, child $5, infant under two free. Maximum 3 per room. Reservations from PCS, TDY only, others Space-A.

DV/VIP: Protocol Office, Fort Shafter, building T-100, C-808-438-1577, 06+. Retirees and lower ranks Space-A. Primarily for TDY personnel.

TML Availability: Good, most of the year.

☞ In winter don't miss Major surfing meets held in Haleiwa on the north shore, just nine miles away, golf at Kalakaua, (655-9833), the post museum, and recreation equipment rental (655-0143).

Locator 471-7411　　　Medical 655-4747/48/49　　Police 655-5116

Tripler Army Medical Center (HI03R6)
Tripler AMC, HI 96859-5000

TELEPHONE NUMBER INFORMATION: Main installation numbers: C-808-433-6661, D-312-433-6661.

Location: Take H-1 West from Honolulu to Tripler exit. Turn right on Jarrett White Rd to Tripler AMC. USM: D-9. NMC: Honolulu, 3 miles southeast.

Billeting Office: Building 228B, Jarrett White Rd, C-**808-433-6963**, D-312-600-2200 M-F, 0800-1600 Sa-Su. Other hours, info desk in hospital lobby, EX-6661. Check in billeting, check out 1100 hours daily. Government civilian employee billeting.

HAWAII
Tripler Army Medical Center, continued

TML: Guest House. Building 228B, 226E, 222C, 220D, all ranks, leave or official duty. Bedroom, 2 beds, shared bath (53); separate bedroom, 2 beds, living room, private bath (42). Refrigerator, community kitchen, microwave, color TV, maid service, cribs/cots, washer/dryer, food/ice vending, playground. Older structure, renovated. Rates: $25 with private bath, $18 without private bath, $5 each additional person. Maximum 5 persons with private bath, 3 without. Child under 1 no charge. All categories Space-A.

TML Availability: Difficult. Best, winter.

☞ **Hawaii's rare and endangered plant life may be better appreciated at: Haiku Gardens, Kaneohe, Foster Garden botanical park, and Paradise Park in Manoa Valley. Don't forget the Honolulu Zoo, in Kapiolani Park.**

Locator 433-6661   **Medical 433-6620**   **Police 438-7116**

Waianae Army Recreation Center (HI05R6)
Waianae, HI 96792-5000

TELEPHONE NUMBER INFORMATION: Main installation numbers: C-808-668-3636, D-None.

Location: Located on west coast of Oahu. Take I-H1 West to HI-93 (Farrington Hwy) West to Waianae. USM: D-8. NMC: Honolulu, 35 miles southeast.

Billeting Office: Rest Camp, Waianae Army Recreation Center, building 4070, 85-010 Army St, Waianae, HI 96792, C-**808-668-3636**, 0900-1600 M-F. AD Army 90 days in advance. Other military personnel/retirees 60 days in advance. Reservist/DoD civilian 30 days in advance. Deposit required. Fourteen day occupancy limit in a 60 day period. Year round operation.

TML: Cabins. Leave, official duty, retirees. Deluxe 2 and 3 bedroom cabins with kitchen (25); standard cabins without kitchen (10); deluxe cabins (6). Ceiling fans, refrigerator, color TV, deck, BBQ and picnic facilities. Standard rooms have twin beds. Deluxe rooms have air conditioning, carpeting and VCR's. Utensils, dishes, bedding, tableware all furnished. Bring personal items and beach towels. Cribs/rollaways ($5). No pets. Rates: deluxe 2 bedroom $45-$60 daily, 3 bedroom $50-$65 daily; standard 2 bedroom, kitchen $25-$31 daily, 1 large room, no kitchen $$13-$15. Reservations up to 90 days in advance, duty Army, 80 days other duty and retired, 60 days all others. **Note:** at press time we heard 45 cabins have been rebuilt with sliding glass doors and beach front lanais.

TML Availability: Good all year.

☞ **On the "Leeward", western side of Oahu, with the look of old Hawaii, and Waianae Mountain Range at 4,000 feet to look at. The heart of "Pokai Bay" has one of the best beaches. Rentals, catering and meeting facilities. See Military Living's** *Military RV, Camping and Rec Areas Around the World.*

Locator 668-3636   *Police-696-2811*

Idaho

Mountain Home Air Force Base (ID01R4)
Mountain Home AFB, ID 83648-5000

TELEPHONE NUMBER INFORMATION: Main installation numbers: C-208-828-2111, D-312-857-1110.

Location: From Boise, take I-84 southeast, 39 miles to Mountain Home exit, follow road through town to Airbase Rd, 10 miles to main gate. USM: C-3. NMC: Boise, 51 miles northwest.

Billeting Office: Building 2604, F St, C-**208-828-4661**, D-312-857-6451, 24 hours daily. Check in facility, check out 1100 hours daily. No government civilian employees billeting.

TML: Motel. Building 2640, all ranks, leave or official duty. Bedroom, semi-private bath (105); two bedroom, private bath (11); three bedroom, private bath (4); four bedroom, private bath (1). Units designated DV/VIP (15). Refrigerator, community kitchen, limited utensils, A/C, color TV in room & lounge, maid service, cribs/cots, washer/dryer, ice vending, CATV. Older structure. Rates: $6 per person. Maximum 12-18 per family. Duty can make reservations, others Space-A.

DV/VIP: 366 WG/CCP, building 1506, C-EX-4536, 06+. Retirees Space-A.

TML Availability: Very good, winter. Difficult, Jun-Aug.

Locator 828-2111   **Medical 828-2319**   **Police 828-2256**

Illinois

Chanute Air Force Base (IL06R2)
Chanute AFB, IL 61868-5225

TELEPHONE NUMBER INFORMATION: Main installation numbers: C-217-495-1110, D-312-862-1110.

Location: North of Champaign (14 miles) at Rantoul. Access from I-57 and US-45. USM: J-4. NMC: Chicago, 120 miles north.

Billeting Office: Building 200, 24 hours daily, C-**217-495-2277**. Check in facility, check out, 1200 hours daily. Government civilian employee billeting.

TML: TLQ. Buildings 593, 594, all ranks, leave or official duty. Two bedroom, private bath apartments (24); separate bedrooms, private bath apartments (8). Kitchen, A/C, limited utensils, color TV, maid service, handicapped accessible. Older structures, renovated. Rates: $16 E1-E6, $20 E7+. Maximum 4 per family. Duty can make reservations, others Space-A.

Chanute Air Force Base, continued

TML: VOQ. Buildings 581, 583, 596-599, officers, all ranks, leave or official duty. One bedroom, private bath (240). Kitchen, A/C, color TV, maid service, washer/dryer, ice vending. Modern structures. Rates: $6 per person. Duty, DAVs, dependents of DAVs may make reservations, others Space-A.

TML: VAQ. Building 200, enlisted all ranks, leave or official duty. One bedroom, semi-private bath (846). Refrigerator, A/C, color TV, maid service, washer/dryer, ice vending. Modern structure. Rates: $5 per person. Duty can make reservations, others Space-A.

TML: DV/VIP. Cottages, officer 06+, leave or official duty, C-EX-2277. One bedroom, private bath (2). A/C, color TV, maid service, washer/dryer. Older structure. Rates: $10 per person. Duty can make reservations, others Space-A.

DV/VIP: PAO. C-EX-2400. 06+. Retirees and lower ranks Space-A.

TML Availability: Good, Oct-Jan. Difficult, Jun-Sep.

☞ **Visitors will enjoy big ten football and concerts at nearby University of Illinois, the shrines and memorials to Abraham Lincoln, and the metropolis of Chicago, 120 miles north.**

Locator 495-3545   **Medical 495-3133**   **Police 495-3100**

⊗**This base will close in October 1993.**

Charles Melvin Price
Support Center (IL04R2)
Granite City, IL 62040-1801

TELEPHONE NUMBER INFORMATION: Main installation numbers: C-618-452-4211, D-312-892-4211.

Location: From I-70 take McKinley Bridge exit, cross Mississippi River, follow signs to Center. From I-270, cross river bridges and take first Granite City exit (IL-3) south to Center. USM: I-5. NMC: St. Louis, 7 miles west.

Billeting Office: Building 102, Niedringhaus St, C-**618-452-4287**, 0730-1615 hours daily. Other hours, Security Office, building 221, C-EX-4224. Check in facility, check out 1000 hours daily. No government civilian employee billeting.

TML: Guest House. Buildings 101, 116, all ranks, leave or official duty, C-EX-4287. Separate bedrooms, private bath (5); two bedroom, private bath (2). Microwave in 5 rooms, refrigerator, limited utensils, A/C, color TV, maid service, cribs/cots, washer/dryer. Older structure. New furniture, drapes, bedspreads. Rates: sponsor $15, maximum $17 per family. Maximum 3-5 persons. PCS reservations 90 days in advance, 30 days TDY, others 15 days in advance.

TML Availability: Good, Nov-Mar. Difficult, May-Aug.

ILLINOIS
Charles Melvin Price Support Center, continued

☞ Nearby St Louis, with its cultural offerings, provides the excitement while small middle American communities make visitors feel right at home.

Locator 452-4211   Police 452-4224

Fort Sheridan (IL01R2)
Fort Sheridan, IL 60037-5000

TELEPHONE NUMBER INFORMATION: Main installation numbers: C-708-926-4111, D-312-459-4111.

Location: Take US-41 to Old Elm Rd (Lake Forest) exit, east 1.5 miles to main gate of Post. Or I-294 to Half-Day Rd exit, east to US-41 and proceed north as above. USM: J-4. NMC: Chicago, 28 miles south.

Billeting Office: ATTN: AFKE-ZO-DE-H, building 205, C-**708-926-5506/2735,** 0730-1900 hours M-F, 0730-1600 Sa-Su. Other hours SDO, building 140, C-EX-3098. Check in billeting, check out 1100 hours daily. Government civilian employee billeting at Guest House.

TML: Guest House. Buildings 31, 32, all ranks, leave or official duty. Separate bedrooms, private bath (12); two-bedroom, private bath (3); four-bedroom, private bath (1). Kitchen (4 units), refrigerator, microwave, limited utensils, A/C, CATV, maid service, cribs/cots, washer/dryer. Older structures. Rates: $24 per night in building 31, $32 per night in building 32. Maximum of 5 persons. Barracks, 20 units, $10/night. All categories can make reservations.

TML: VOQ/VEQ. Several buildings, officers & E7-E9, leave or official duty. Separate bedrooms, semi-private bath. Community kitchen, color TV in lounge, maid service, washer/ dryer. Older structures. Rates: sponsor $8.

DV/VIP: Army Protocol, building 140, C-EX-3095. 07+. Retirees and lower ranks Space-A.

TML Availability: Good, Oct-Mar. Difficult, other times.

☞ Two golf courses on post, Great America 12 miles from post. City of Chicago and all it has to offer culturally nearby.

Locator 926-2274   Medical 926-3861   Police 926-2112

⊗This post will close in '94.

Glenview Naval Air Station (IL03R2)
Glenview NAS, IL 60026-5000

TELEPHONE NUMBER INFORMATION: Main installation numbers: C-708-657-1000, D-312-932-0111.

ILLINOIS

Glenview Naval Air Station, continued

Location: From I-294 north, exit Willow Rd, east two traffic lights, right on Phingston Rd to West Lake Ave, left to NAS main gate. USM: J-3. NMC: Chicago, 10 miles southeast.

Billeting Office: BOQ, building 45, C-**708-657-2275**, enlisted in Barracks 55, Ave B, C-**708-657-2453**, both 24 hours daily. Check in facility, check out 1300 hours daily. No government civilian employee billeting. NOTE: These phone numbers may change in the future.

TML: BOQ/BEQ. BOQ, all ranks, leave or official duty. Bedrooms, kitchenette, private bath (PCS in/out) (5); shared bedrooms, shared bath (58); Bedrooms, private bath (16); suites, private bath (DV/VIP) (5). BEQ, rooms (60) - no adequate transient quarters. Refrigerator, utensils, A/C, color TV in room & lounge, maid service, cribs/cots, washer/dryer, ice vending. Older structures, remodeled '92. Rates: single $8, shared bath $6, suites $25, maximum $25 per family. PCS in and reservists on orders can make reservations, others Space-A.

DV/VIP: CO, building 41, C-EX-2136, 06+. Retirees Space-A.

TML Availability: Limited. Best, winter. No TML for enlisted dependents.

☞ **Only 45 minutes from toddlin' downtown Chicago.**

Locator 657-1000 **Medical 657-2222** **Police 657-2311**

Great Lakes Naval Training Center (IL07R2)
Great Lakes NTC, IL 60088-5000

TELEPHONE NUMBER INFORMATION: Main installation numbers: C-708-688-3500, D-312-792-2002.

Location: From I-94 north or US-41 north of Chicago, exit to IL-137 east to NTC. Clearly marked. USM: J-3. NMC: Chicago, 30 miles south.

Billeting Office: BOQ. Building 62, C-**708-688-3777**, D-312-792-3777. BEQ. Building 178, C-**688-2170/6983**, 24 hours, daily. Check in facility, check out 1300 hours. Government civilian employee billeting.

TML: Navy Lodge. Building 2500, C-**1-800-NAVY-INN**. Lodge number is 689-1485, all ranks, leave or official duty. Bedroom, 2 double beds, private bath (50). Kitchen, complete utensils, A/C, color TV, maid service, cribs/cots, coin washer/dryer, food/ice vending. Modern structure. Rates: $36 per room. Maximum 5 per room. No pets. All categories can make reservations.

TML: BEQ. Building 178, enlisted all ranks, leave or official duty. E1 to E6: rooms with 2-3 occupancy, shared bath (101); E7 to E9: bedroom, double bed, private bath (55). Community kitchen, CATV, refrigerator, microwave, A/C, maid service, washer/dryer, food vending. Rates: sponsor $4 (increase to $10 expected). Duty can make reservations, all others Space-A.

TML: BOQ/TVOQ. Building 62, officers all ranks, leave or official duty. Government civilians, all grades, official duty. Bedroom/sitting room, semi-private bath (57); suites,

ILLINOIS
Great Lakes Naval Training Center, continued

separate bedroom/ sitting room, private bath (112). Community kitchen, TV lounges, game room, exercise room, washers/dryers, cribs/cots, snack/drink/ice vending, A/C, color TV, refrigerators, maid service. Older Structure. No pets. Rates: single bedroom/sitting room, sponsor $6 (will increase to $12); suite bedroom, sponsor $14. Additional occupants over 6 $3. Maximum 5 per unit. Duty can make reservations, others Space-A.

DV/VIP: Cmdr, building 1. C-708-688-3400. 06+. Retirees and lower ranks Space-A. Check with commander, building 1. Rates: sponsor $25, additional occupants over 6, $3. Maximum 5.

TML Availability: Fairly good. Best, winter months.

☞ **Boating, swimming and all water sports are available through the marina Beach House. An 18 hole golf course, bowling center, and extensive other support facilities are available on base.**

Locators 688-2014   Medical 688-5618   Police 688-3333

Scott Air Force Base (IL02R2)
Scott AFB, IL 62225-5000

TELEPHONE NUMBER INFORMATION: Main installation numbers: C-618-256-1110, D-312-576-1110.

Location: Off I-64 east or west, exit 19E or 19A west to Il-158 south, 2 miles and watch for signs to AFB entry. USM: I-4,5. NMC: St Louis, 25 miles west.

Billeting Office: Building 1510, Scott Dr, C-**618-256-2045**, C-EX-1200/1844 (front desk), 24 hours daily. Check in billeting, check out 1200 hours daily. Government civilian employee billeting in VOQ.

TML: TLF/VOQ/VAQ. Buildings 1508-1551, all ranks, leave or official duty. Bedroom, semi-private bath (64); bedroom, private bath (176); two-bedroom, private bath (70); double rooms, private bath, two rooms handicapped accessible (3). Family units, private bath (36). Refrigerator, A/C, color TV, maid service, washer/dryer, ice vending. Rates: TLF $20, VOQ $8, VAQ $8, DV suites $14. TDY can make reservations, others Space-A.

DV/VIP: AMC protocol, C-EX-5555, 06+. Retirees Space-A.

TML Availability: Fairly Good, Nov-Jan. Difficult, other times.

☞ Near the "Gateway to the West", visitors enjoy the cultural, sporting, and outdoor activities St Louis affords. Nearby small communities reflect the stability and warmth of middle America.

Locator 256-1841   Medical 256-1847   Police 256-2223

Indiana

Crane Naval Surface Warfare Center (IN03R2)
Crane NSWC, IN 47522-5000

TELEPHONE NUMBER INFORMATION: Main installation numbers: C-812-854-2511, D-312-482-1110.

Location: From US-231 north or south exit to IN-45 or IN-645 to enter the center from the west. USM: J-4. NMC: Bloomington, 22 miles northeast.

Billeting Office: Building 2682, **C-812-854-1176**, 0730-1530. After duty hours, C-812-854-1225/1222, building 1. Check in billeting.

TML: BOQ/VIP. Building 2681, officers, all ranks, leave or official duty. Bedroom, private bath (11); Separate bedrooms, private bath, kitchen, living room (VIP) (2). A/C, essentials, food vending, refrigerator, maid service, CATV in room & lounge, washer/dryer. Handicapped accessible. Modern structure. Older structure, remodeled. Rates: $12 per night, VIP suites $25 per night. Maximum 2 persons. All categories can make reservations.

TML: BEQ. Building 2682, enlisted, all ranks, leave or official duty. Bedrooms, semi-private bath. A/C, essentials, food vending, maid service, refrigerator, CATV in room/lounge, washer/dryer. Handicapped accessible except for wheelchair. Modern structure, renovated. All categories can make reservations. Rates: $7.

DV/VIP: Building 1, C-EX-1210, 06+. Retirees Space-A.

TML Availability: Very good, all year.

Locator 854-2511   **Medical 854-1220**   **Police 854-3300**

Fort Benjamin Harrison (IN02R2)
Fort Benjamin Harrison, IN 46216-5450

TELEPHONE NUMBER INFORMATION: Main installation numbers: C-317-546-9211, D-312-699-1110.

Location: Take I-465 east to Fort Harrison exit 40, east on 56th St, or take Pendleton Pike (IN-67/US-36) exit 42 to Post Rd and North Fort Harrison. USM: J-4. NMC: Indianapolis, 8 miles southwest.

Billeting Office: Building T-609, Green Ave (Post Rd), **C-317-549-5455**, 24 hours daily. Check in facility, check out 1200 hours daily. Government civilian employee billeting. Contract motels available through billeting.

TML: Guest House. Building T-51, all ranks, leave or official duty. Bedroom, 2 full-size beds, private bath (14); bedroom, 1 bed, private bath (2). Handicapped accessible facilities. All have sleeper sofas. Kitchen, complete utensils, A/C, color TV, maid service, cribs/cots, washer/dryer, ice vending. Modern structure. Rates: $25-$30 per room per night. PCS in/out have priority, others Space-A.

INDIANA
Fort Benjamin Harrison, continued

DV/VIP: Protocol Office. Building 600, D-312-542-4186, 06/GS-15+. Retirees Space-A with approval of Protocol Office.

TML Availability: Extremely limited. Best, end of Dec.

☞ See Indianapolis sports events, including the Indianapolis 500; also a world class symphony, two dance troupes and a repertory theater of national note. Parks, museums and a Zoo also will keep you busy here.

Locator 542-4537   Medical 549-5194/5

⊗This post will close in '97. Update with Military Living's *R&R Space-A Report.*

Grissom Air Force Base (IN01R2)
Grissom AFB, IN 46971-5000

TELEPHONE NUMBER INFORMATION: Main installation numbers: C-317-688-2844, D-312-928-2844, FAX C-317-688-2844, FAX D-312-928-8751.

Location: Off US-31, 7 miles southeast of Peru, 65 miles north of Indianapolis. USM: J-4. NMC: Indianapolis, 72 miles north.

Billeting Office: Grissom Inn, building 550, Lancer St, C-**317-688-2596**, 24 hours daily. Check in facility, check out 1200 hours daily.

TML: TLF. All ranks, leave or official duty Two bedroom units, private bath (12); Kitchen, utensils, A/C, color TV, maid service, cribs, washer/dryer, ice vending. Modern structure. Rates: $24 per unit. Duty can make reservations, others Space-A. No pets.

TML: VAQ. Building 550, enlisted all ranks, leave or official duty. Bed spaces (89). Refrigerator, A/C, color TV in room & lounge, maid service, washer/dryer, ice vending. Modern structure. Rates: $9. Duty can make reservations, others Space-A. No pets.

TML: VOQ. Officers all ranks, 62 rooms. Rate: $14. No pets.

DV/VIP: CSG/ESO, building S-1, C-EX-3144. O6+. Retirees Space-A. VOQ suites (4) VAQ suites (2). No pets.

TML Availability: Good, Oct-May. Difficult, summer months.

☞ If the Indianapolis 500 isn't excitement enough, try the historic Union Railroad Station, the Indianan Repertory Theater, the Bluegrass Music Festival, walking tours of Victorian Mansions, and Independence Day in Evansville.

Locator 688-2841   Medical 688-3303   Police 688-3385

⊗This base will close in '94. Update with Military Living's *R&R Space-A Report.*

Iowa

NONE

Kansas

Fort Leavenworth (KS04R3)
Fort Leavenworth, KS 66027-5000

TELEPHONE NUMBER INFORMATION: Main installation numbers: C-913-684-4021, D-312-552-4021.

Location: From I-70 take US-73 north to Leavenworth. Fort is adjacent to city of Leavenworth. USM: H-4. NMC: Kansas City, 30 miles southeast.

Billeting Office: Lodging building 695, Grant Ave, C-**913-684-4091**, 24 hours daily. Check in billeting after 1400 hours, check out 1000 hours daily. Government civilian employee lodging.

TML: Guest House. Building 427, all ranks, leave or official duty, C-651-9522. D-EX-4091. Two and three bedroom, private bath (12). Kitchen, complete utensils, A/C, color TV, maid service, cribs/cots, room telephones, ice vending, washer/dryer. Older structure, renovated. Rates: sponsor $25, flat rate. Duty can make reservations, others Space-A.

TML: VOQ. **Hoge Barracks**, Truesdell Hall, Root & Schofield Hall. Officers all ranks, leave or official duty. Units (750), private and semi-private bath. Kitchen (some), A/C, color TV, maid service, room telephones, ice vending, washer/dryer. Rates: sponsor $12-$16, each additional person $5. TDY can make reservations, others Space-A.

TML: DV/VIP. Building 22 (**Cooke Hall**), building 3 (**Thomas Custer House**), building 213 (**Otis Hall**). Officers O6+, leave or official duty, C-EX-4064. Bedroom, private bath (8); separate bedrooms, private bath (14). Kitchen (some), refrigerator (some), utensils, A/C, TV, maid service, room telephones, ice vending, washer/dryer. Older structure. Rates: sponsor $20, each additional person $5. Duty can make reservations, others Space-A.

DV/VIP: Executive Services, C-EX-4064, O6+. Retirees and others Space-A.

TML Availability: Difficult. Best Jan. & Dec. Limited, other times.

☞ Sample Leavenworth's local performing arts, **Buffalo Bill Days**, and **Kansas City**, where everything is "up to date". Visit the Crown Center, and The Plaza for wall to wall shopping.

Locator 684-3651/4021   Medical 684-6100   Police 684-3456

KANSAS

Fort Riley (KS02R3)
Fort Riley, KS 66442-5000

TELEPHONE NUMBER INFORMATION: Main installation numbers: C-913-239-3911, D-312-856-1110.

Location: On KS-18 and off I-70 in the central part of the state. Junction City, 5 miles southwest and Manhattan, 10 miles northeast. USM: H-5. NMC: Topeka, 64 miles east.

Billeting Office: Building 45, Barry Ave, C-**913-239-2830/6903,** 24 hours daily. Check in facility, check out 1100 hours daily. Government civilian employee billeting on official duty.

TML: Guest House. Building 170, all ranks, leave or official duty. Bedroom, living room, kitchen, private bath (6); two bedroom, livingroom, kitchen, private bath (2). Older structure. Rates: $25-$30 per unit. Duty on PCS orders can make reservations, others Space-A.

TML: Guest House. Building 5309, all ranks, leave or official duty. Two room suites, private bath (27); single rooms, private bath (3). Community kitchen, cribs, washer/dryer. Older structure. Rates: suites $18; rooms $15. PCS can make reservations, others Space-A.

TML: VOQ/VEQ. **Carr Hall,** buildings 620, 621, 541, all ranks, leave or official duty. Two bedroom suites (33); bedroom, living room, private bath suites (2); single rooms, kitchenette (37). Color TV, cribs, washer/dryer. Older structures. Rates: $18-$30 per unit. Pet fee (building 620 only), $5 per night. Duty on PCS/TDY can make reservations, others Space-A.

TML: DV/VIP. **Grimes Hall,** building 510. **Bacon Hall,** building 28. Officer 04+. Leave or official duty. **Bacon Hall** is a 3-bedroom house for $40 per night; **Grimes Hall** offers Custer Suite for $30 per night; Stuart Suite for $25 per night; one bedroom suites for $20 per night (5); a two room suite in the basement for $10 per night. Kitchen, washer/dryer. Older structure, all categories can make reservations.

TML Availability: Limited.

☞ Don't miss the US Cavalry Museum, in building 30, which traces the history of this illustrious post, the battle of the Little Big Horn, Wounded Knee, and then tour the Custer House.

Locator 239-9867   **Medical 239-7777**   **Police 239-3053/MPMP**

McConnell Air Force Base (KS03R3)
McConnell AFB, KS 67221-5000

TELEPHONE NUMBER INFORMATION: Main installation numbers: C-316-652-3840, D-312-743-3840.

Location: Take I-35 south to Wichita, exit at Kellogg St (US-54) east to Rock Rd South and McConnell AFB. USM: G,H-5. NMC: Wichita, 6 miles northwest.

KANSAS

McConnell Air Force Base, continued

Billeting Office: Building 193, Manhatten St, C-**316-683-7711**, D-312-743-6500, 24 hours daily. Check in billeting, check out 1200 hours daily.

TML: TLF. Building 193, all ranks, leave or official duty. Bedroom, private bath (3); separate bedroom, private bath (21). Community kitchen, A/C, CATV, telephones, children's playroom and recreation room w/color TV, housekeeping, washer/dryer, ice vending, microwave ovens. Sundries available at front desk. Rates: 1 bedroom $19. All categories Space-A.

TML: VOQ. Buildings 202, civilians and officers, leave or official duty. Rooms, private bath (8). A/C, CATV, telephones, housekeeping, washer/dryer, ice vending, sundry items on sale in room. Rates: $9 per person, guests, $4.50. Maximum charge $18. Official duty may make reservations, others Space-A. Chief suites (4) will open April '92.

TML:VAQ. Building 317. Enlisted personnel, leave or official duty. Rooms, shared bath (20); SNCO rooms, private bath (6). Dayrooms with pool tables, ice machines, (vending, pinball, video games), A/C, CATV, telephones, washer/dryer, housekeeping, microwaves. Rates: $9/singles, $13.50/suites w/guest. Duty can make reservations, others Space-A.

TML: DV/VIP. Building 202, officer 06+, leave or official duty. Bedroom suites, private bath (4). Kitchen, limited utensils, A/C, CATV, telephones, housekeeping, washer/dryer, ice vending, sundrys on sale in suites. Rates: $13 per person. Maximum $26. Duty can make reservations, others Space-A.

TML: DV/VIP. Building 185, officers 07+, leave or official duty. Two bedroom house, fully furnished, private bath, kitchen (and utensils), washer/dryer, sundries, microwave, CATV, housekeeping, telephones. Rates $14. Maximum $28. Duty can make reservations, others Space-A.

DV/VIP: Hq, C-EX-3107, 06+. Retirees & lower ranks Space-A.

TML Availability: Good, Nov-Feb. Difficult, other times.

☞ Visit Charles Russell, and others in the Wichita Art Museum, and Wyatt Earp in the Old Cowtown Museum. Stroll through one of the 80 municipal parks available to you, still restless? There are more than 600 nightclubs in Wichita.

Locator 652-3555   **Medical 652-3555**   **Police 652-3975**

Kentucky

Fort Campbell (KY02R2)
Fort Campbell, KY 42223-1291

TELEPHONE NUMBER INFORMATION: Main installation numbers: C-502-798-2151, D-312-635-1110.

Location: In the southwest part of KY, 4 miles south of intersection of US-41A and I-24. 10 miles northwest of Clarksville, TN. USM: J-5. NMC: Hopkinsville, 15 miles north.

KENTUCKY
Fort Cambell, continued

Billeting Office: Building 2601, 1581 Lee Rd, C-**502-798-5281/5618**, D-312-635-5281/5618, 24 hours. Check in facility, check out 1000 hours daily. Government civilian employee billeting.

TML: Guest House. **Clifford C. Sims**, building 2601, C-EX-2865, all ranks, leave or official duty. Handicapped accessible. Bedroom, 2 double beds, private bath (74). Community kitchen, refrigerator, A/C, color TV in room & lounge, maid service, cribs/cots, washer/dryer, food/ice vending. Modern structure. Rates: sponsor $16, each additional person $2. Maximum 6 per unit. All categories can make reservations.

TML: Guest House Annex. Buildings 109 & 111, enlisted all ranks. Families only. Reservations accepted. Separate bedrooms, private bath (68). Community kitchen, refrigerator, A/C, color TV, maid service, cribs/cots, washer/dryer, ice vending. Older structure. Rates: sponsor $8, each additional person $2. Maximum $14 per family.

DV/VIP: Protocol Office, building T-39, C-EX-9913, 06+.

TML Availability: Difficult.

☞ Visit Clarksville's Public Square and architectural district for turn-of-the-century architecture. In Nearby Hopkinsville golf, museums and monuments are available. Visit local watershed lakes for fishing and picnicking.

Locator 798-7196   **Medical 798-8388**   **Police 798-2677**

Fort Knox (KY01R2)
Fort Knox, KY 40121-5000

TELEPHONE NUMBER INFORMATION: Main installation numbers: C-502-624-1181, D-312-464-0111.

Location: From I-65 north in Louisville, exit Jefferson Freeway, 841W to 31W. Go south to Fort Knox. From I-64, exit I-264 west (Waterson) to I-65 south, to Jefferson Fort Knox to US-31W south to Fort Knox. From I-71, exit I-65 south to exit Jefferson Freeway 841, west to 31W then south to Fort Knox. Four entrances, look for main gate. USM: J-5. NMC: Louisville, 25 miles north.

Billeting Office: ATTN: ATZK-EH-H, building 4770 (**Newgarden Tower**), Dixie Highway 31W, C-**502-624-3138**, D-312-464-3138, 24 hours daily. Check in/out as indicated. Government civilian employee billeting.

TML: Wickam Guest House. Building 6597, all ranks, leave or official duty, C-EX-0490. Check out 1200 hours daily. Bedroom, 2 beds, private bath (50); bedroom, 3 beds, private bath (24). A/C, telephones, refrigerator/refreshment center, color TV, cribs and microwaves available, washer/dryer, ice machines, vending. Modern structure. Rates: from $11.50. All categories can make reservations.

TML: Guest House. **Loriann Annex**, building 6625. Bedroom, private bath (1); two bedroom, private bath (4); bedroom, 2 double beds, private bath (12). Refrigerator, community kitchen, color TV in lounge, maid service, coin washer/dryer. Older structure. Rates: $5.50 1-2 person, $6.50 for 3 or more. Maximum 6 persons. All categories can make reservations.

Fort Knox, continued

TML: VOQ. Apartments, officers 01-06, leave or official duty. Check out 1200 hours daily. Kitchen, A/C, color TV, maid service, washer/dryer, ice vending, clock/radio. Modern structure. Rates: sponsor $16, each additional person $5. Maximum based on beds available. Duty can make reservations, others Space-A.

TML: VEQ. Apartments, building 4770, enlisted, all ranks, leave or official duty. Check out 1200 hours daily. Kitchen, color TV in room & lounge, maid service, washer/dryer, ice vending, elevator, clock/radio. Modern structure. Rates: sponsor $16, each additional person $5. Duty can make reservations, others Space-A.

TML: DV/VIP. Building 1102, **Henry House**, officers 07+, leave or official duty. C-EX-2744, D-EX-2744. Check out 1100 hours daily. Three bedroom house, private bath (1). Kitchen, color TV, maid service, washer/dryer. Older structure. Rates: sponsor $20, adult $5 each. Duty can make reservations, others Space-A.

TML: DV/VIP. Building 1117, **Yeomans Hall**, enlisted E9, leave or official duty, C-EX-5240/6540/6951. D-EX-2744. Check out 1000 hours daily. Bedroom, queen beds, private bath (2); bedroom, twin beds, private bath (8). Sitting room, refrigerator, A/C, color TV in room & lounge, maid service, cots, washer/dryer. Older structure. Rates: sponsor $20, $5 each additional person. Two military persons $5 each. Duty can make reservations, others Space-A.

DV/VIP: Protocol Office, building 1102, **Henry House**, room 104, C-EX-2744, 06+. Retirees and lower ranks Space-A at discretion of Protocol.

TML Availability: Good. Best, Nov-Mar. More difficult, other times.

☞ Visit the Patton Museum of Calvary and Armor, the US Bullion Depository, and Louisville, home of the Kentucky Derby and historic points of interest.

Locator 624-1141/1336   Medical 624-9999/6450   Police 624-2111

Louisiana

Barksdale Air Force Base (LA01R2)
Barksdale AFB, LA 71110-5000

TELEPHONE NUMBER INFORMATION: Main installation numbers: C-318-456-2252, D-312-781-1000.

Location: Exit I-20 at Airline Dr, go south to Old Minden Rd (.25 mile), left on Old Minden Rd (1 block), then right on North Gate Dr (1 mile) to North Gate of AFB. USM: H,I-7. NMC: Shreveport, 1 mile west. Co-located with Bossier City and Shreveport.

Billeting Office: Building 5155, second building on left after entering North Gate on Davis Ave. C-**318-747-4708**, D-312-781-3091, 24 hours daily. Check in facility, check out 1200 hours daily. Government civilian employee billeting.

LOUISIANA
Barksdale Air Force Base, continued

TML: VAQ. Barksdale Inn, building 5155, 5123, 4359, enlisted, leave or official duty. Handicapped accessible. Separate bedroom, private bath (SNCO)(36); non-smoking, separate bedroom, private bath (SNCO) (3); separate bedroom shared bath (E-1 to E-6)(76). Refrigerator, A/C, black/white TV, color TV lounge, maid service, cribs, washer/dryer, ice vending. Older structure, renovated. Rates: $9 per adult, $4.50 per dependent. Maximum $13.50 per unit. Duty can make reservations, others Space-A.

TML: VOQ. Buildings 5167, 5224 (SAC Inn) officers all ranks, leave or official duty. Separate bedroom private bath (56); building 5224, separate bedroom, private bath (04+)(8); Refrigerator, A/C, color TV in room and lounge, maid service, washer/dryer, ice vending. Older structure, renovated. Rates: building 5167, $9 per adult, $4.50 dependent. Maximum $13.50 per unit; building 5224, $13 per adult, $6.50 per dependent. Maximum $19.50 per unit. Duty can make reservations, others Space-A. Space-A can make reservations for 1 day if available.

TML: TLF. Building 5243, all ranks, leave or official duty. Handicapped accessible. Large family units (sleep 5) (13); small units (sleep 4) (7). One large and 1 small non-smoking unit. Kitchen, complete utensils, refrigerator, A/C, color TV, cribs, maid service, washer/dryer, ice vending. Older structure, renovated. Rates: $26 large units, $22 small units, maximum. Duty can make reservations, others Space-A.

TML: AIRCREW. Building 5123, all ranks, official duty. Quarters (officer) (10); quarters (enlisted) (6). Refrigerator, A/C, color TV, maid service, washer/dryer, ice vending. Older structure, renovated. Rates: $9 per adult per unit. Duty can make reservations.

TML: DV/VIP. Officer 06+, leave or official duty. Three bedroom house, fully furnished, duty 07+ only, no retirees; bedroom suites, private bath (12); two bedroom, private bath (4). Refrigerator, kitchen, complete utensils, A/C, color TV, maid service, washer/dryer, ice vending. Older structure, renovated. Rates: $13 per adult, $6.50 per dependent, maximum $26; house: $14 per adult, $7 per dependent, maximum $26. Duty can make reservations, others Space-A.

DV/VIP: PAO, 2nd Wing, C-EX-4447, 06+. Retirees Space-A.

TML Availability: Good, all year.

☞ **Visit Barnwell Garden and Art Center, and the Shreveport-Bossier City American Rose Center, located in a 118 acre wooded park. Hunting and fishing in season on Barksdale East Reservation, call Base Forestry C-EX-2231/3353.**

Locator 456-2252   **Medical 456-4051**   **Police 456-2551**

Fort Polk (LA07R2)
Fort Polk, LA 71459-5000

TELEPHONE NUMBER INFORMATION: Main installation numbers: C-318-531-2911, D-312-863-1110.

Location: Off US-171, at LA-10, 9 miles south Leesville. USM: I-7. G/4. NMC: Alexandria, 45 miles northeast.

Fort Polk, continued

Billeting Office: Magnolia House, building 522, Utah Ave, **C-318-531-2941** or 318-537-9591, D-312-863-2941/4822, 24 hours daily. Check in Magnolia House, check out 1100 hours daily. Government civilian employee billeting.

TML: Guest House. Building 522, Magnolia House. All ranks, leave or official duty. Bedroom, sleep sofa, private bath (70). Kitchen, color TV, maid service, washer/dryer, vending machine. Rates: $22 for military personnel, $25 non-military per unit. Active duty on PCS, visiting relatives and guests of patients in the hospital, and active and retired military receiving outpatient care can make reservations, others Space-A. No pets.

TML: VOQ. Building 350, Woodfill Hall. Rooms (22); building 331, Cypress Inn. Rooms (28); cottages, North Fort Polk (8). Rates: $17 first person, $2 each additional person; cottages $12 first person, $2 each additional person. Inquire about reservations. No pets.

TML: DV/VIP. Buildings 8-10, 15, 17, 18, 5674, officers 06+, DOD civilian GS-15+, and Sergeant Major of the Army. Official duty only. One and two bedrooms, private bath. Kitchen, complete utensils, A/C, color TV, maid service. Older structure, renovated. Rates: $17 first person, $5 each additional person. Upon request, personnel in grades 05+, on PCS in/out, may be given tentative, unconfirmed reservations. No pets.

TML Availability: Good, Oct-Mar. More difficult, other times.

☞ **Best known for its outdoor recreation, the area is a paradise for hunters, and fishermen. Early Indian sites, a history that reads like a who's who of American legendary characters, and Lake Charles festivals are all of interest.**

Locator 531-6622   **Medical 531-3368/9**   **Police 531-2677**

New Orleans Naval Air Station (LA11R2)
New Orleans NAS, LA 70143-5000

TELEPHONE NUMBER INFORMATION: Main installation numbers: C-504-393-3011, D-312-363-3011.

Location: Off LA-23 in Belle Chase. Clearly marked. USM: J-7,8. NMC: New Orleans, 13 miles north.

Billeting Office: BOQ, building 22, 2nd St, **C-504-393-3841**. BEQ, building 40, 4th St, **C-504-393-3419**, 24 hours daily. Check in facility, check out 1300 hours daily. Government civilian employee billeting.

TML: BOQ. Building 22, all ranks, leave or official duty. Bedrooms, 2 beds, hall bath (42); separate bedroom suites, queen bed, fold out couch, private bath (8). Handicapped accessible (2). Refrigerator, A/C, color TV in room & lounge, maid service, cots, washer/

LOUISIANA
New Orleans Naval Air Station, continued

dryer, ice vending. Older structures, renovated '92. Rates: $8 per person, guests $5. Military widows and unaccompanied dependents of active duty on leave Space-A. Others can make reservations. **Note:** no reservations on drill weekends except command officers and 05+.

TML: BEQ. Building 40, all ranks, leave or official duty. Bedrooms, (2, 3, 4 man rooms), common bath (73). Refrigerator, A/C, color TV in room & lounge, maid service, cots, washer/dryer, ice vending. Older structures, renovated. Rates: $4. Duty may make reservations, others Space-A. No dependents.

DV/VIP: CO, building 46, C-EX-3202, 06+. Retirees Space-A.

TML Availability: Good, except on drill weekends.

☞ **Should you be unable to get lodging here, don't forget there is a Navy Lodge at the Naval Support Activity nearby, call 1-800-NAVY-INN.**

Locator 393-3253   **Medical 393-3663**   **Police-393-3265**

New Orleans Naval Support Activity (LA06R2)
New Orleans, LA 70142-5000-5010

TELEPHONE NUMBER INFORMATION: Main installation numbers: C-504-366-3266, D-312-485-2700.

Location: On the west bank of Mississippi River. From I-10 east, take exit 235 B (right) to Cleveland Ave, to Claiborne Ave, right to Claiborne Center Lane back to I-10, first right. Follow Westbank, Gretna signs (90W) across Mississippi River, take first exit (right) off bridge and follow Gen DeGaulle signs to left. Left turn on Shirley Drive and follow to end. Base is on Gen Meyer Ave at foot of Shirley Drive. Take Gen DeGaulle east exit after passing over bridge and turn left at Shirley Dr which leads to NSA. USM: J-7. NMC: New Orleans, 5 miles east.

Billeting Office: Navy Lodge. Building 702, Hebert Dr, 0700-2000 hours daily. Check in Lodge, check out 1200 hours. All ranks, leave or official duty. For reservations call **1-800-NAVY-INN.** Lodge number is 366-3266. Bedroom, private bath (22). Kitchen, microwave, utensils, A/C, CATV, maid service, cribs, coin washer/dryer, ice vending, ramps for DAVs, irons/ironing boards, clocks. Modern structure, remodeled. Rates: $34 per unit. Maximum 4 persons. All categories can make reservations.

TML Availability: Good, Nov-Jan. Difficult, Apr-Sep.

☞ **Visit stately old homes, take a paddlewheel boat dinner cruise, visit the new zoo, and the Aquarium of the Americas. The French Quarter is made for strolling. One half block to Special Services and tickets!**

Locator 504-393-3011   **Medical 911**   **Police 361-2570**

Maine

Bangor Air National Guard Base (ME10R1)
Bangor ANGB, ME 04401-3099

TELEPHONE NUMBER INFORMATION: Main installation numbers: C-207-990-7700, D-312-698-7700.

Location: Located in Bangor city limits. Northbound on I-95 take exit 45B (West on Route 2). Turn right at Odlin Road (first set traffic lights). One mile, Cleveland St on the right. Up the hill, Pine Tree Inn is located in building 346, 22 Cleveland St.

TML: The Army National Guard operates "**Pine Tree Inn**" for military members, retirees, and their families, **C-207-942-2081**. Check out 1200 hours. Bedroom, semi-private bath (46). Community kitchen, essentials, maid service, refrigerator, color TV lounge, washer/dryer. Rates: official users $5 per night, non-official $10. Duty can make reservations, others Space-A.

DV/VIP: No Protocol Office.

TML Availability: Fairly good any time.

☞ 45 miles east **Dow Pines Air Force Recreation Area offers fishing, camping, hiking and scenic vistas. Call 207-584-3101.**

-NOTES-

MAINE

Brunswick Naval Air Station (ME07R1)
Brunswick NAS, ME 04011-5000

TELEPHONE NUMBER INFORMATION: Main installation numbers: C-207-921-1110, D-312-476-1110.

Location: From I-95 north exit US-1 north to Brunswick, Old Bath Rd (Route 24) to main gate of NAS. USM: M,N-2. NMC: Portland, 30 miles southwest.

Billeting Office: Building 220, ATTN: MSCS(SS), Spanswick, C-**207-931-2245**, 24 hours daily. Check in facility, check out 1100 hours (Navy Lodge 1000 hours). No government civilian employee billeting.

TML: Navy Lodge. **Topsham Annex**, all ranks, leave or official duty. Reservations call **1-800-NAVY-INN**. Lodge C-207-921-2206, 0730-2200 hours, other hours check with OD, C-EX-2214. Bedroom, private bath, singles (2), doubles (12). Cooking facilities in rooms, complete utensils, color TV in lounge, maid service, coin washer/dryer. Older structure. Rates: $31 per unit. All categories can make reservations.

TML: BOQ/BEQ. All ranks, leave or official duty. Bedroom, private bath (10); separate bedroom, private bath (24). Refrigerator, community kitchen, limited utensils, color TV in room & lounge, maid service, cots, washer/dryer, ice vending, picnic tables, tennis courts, sauna, gym. Older structure. Rates: BEQ, PCS $5, VIP suites $12 per night, additional person, $5, Space-A surcharge $10. Maximum 3 per room. Duty can make reservations, others Space-A. Kennels in town.

TML: Transient BOQ/BEQ. Buildings 220, 512, official duty only, officers 06+, enlisted E-8 to E-9. Rooms, private bath (5); two bedroom, private bath (3); three bedroom, private bath (28). Essentials, food vending, maid service, refrigerator, color TV, washer/dryer. VIP suites have VCR, water beds, bar, hair dryers, clock radios. Older and modern structures. Older structure, renovated and remodeled. Rates: BOQ, PCS $8 per night, $2 additional person, VIP suites $20 per night, $5 additional person, Space-A surcharge $10. Families not authorized. Maximum 3 persons. Duty can make reservations.

DV/VIP: Brunswick NAS, building 512, C-EX-2214, 05+, retirees Space-A.

TML Availability: Good, Sep-Jan. Difficult, Apr-Aug.

☞ Fishing and hunting are considered "tops" here, 60 ski areas, including Sugarloaf (it has a 9,000 foot gondola line) make winter skiing here a favorite. But if you've never tasted shrimp and lobster, do it here!

Locator 921-1110   Medical 921-2610   Police 921-2585

Cutler Naval Computer and Telecommunications Station (ME08R1)
East Machias, ME 04630-1000

TELEPHONE NUMBER INFORMATION: Main installation numbers: C-207-259-8226, D-312-476-7226.

Cutler Naval C & T Station, continued

Location: Take Hwy. 95 to Bangor; 395 around Bangor; Routes 1A and 1 to East Machias; 191 to base (7 miles off route 1). USM: N-1. NMC: Bangor, 90 miles west.

Billeting Office: None. C-207-259-8284, or write to: MWR Dept, NAVCOMTELSTA Cutler, E. Machias, ME 04630-1000. Check in MWR Hobby Shop, 0730-1600 hours daily. Check out 1200. After duty hours, Quarterdeck, building 500.

TML: Rustic cabins (2), at Sprague's Neck and Rocky Lake, all ranks, leave or official duty. No electricity. Gas lights, wood stove, running water and indoor toilet at Sprague's Neck (during summer months). Rocky Lake, same facilities, but no running water or indoor toilet. Kitchenette and utensils. Pets allowed. Call for further information and rates. All categories can make reservations.

TML Availability: Extremely limited, best Apr to Sep.

☞ A real rustic get away for hunting, fishing, swimming, skiing, snowmobiling, or enjoying friendly "down east folks". Local festivals in summer are said to have beautiful hand crafted items.

Locator 259-8229   **Medical 259-8209**   **Police 259-8226**

Loring Air Force Base (ME06R1)
Loring AFB, ME 04751-5000

TELEPHONE NUMBER INFORMATION: Main installation numbers: C-207-999-1110, D-312-920-1110.

Location: Take I-95 to Houlton, exit to US-1 north to Caribou (50 miles). The AFB is 1 mile north of ME-89 & ME-223 intersection. Clearly marked. USM: M-1. NMC: Caribou, 3 miles southwest.

Billeting Office: Building 2501, Virginia Place, C-207-999-2227/8, D-312-920-7180, FAX-207-999-7180, 24 hours daily. Check in billeting, check out 1200 hours daily. Government civilian employee billeting.

TML: TLF. Buildings 2101, 2103, 2105, 2107, 2109, 4100, 4116, all ranks, leave or official duty. Separate bedrooms, private bath (7); two bedroom, private bath (20). Kitchen, limited utensils, color TV, maid service, cribs/cots, washer/dryer, microwave. Older structures, remodeled. New TVs/carpets '91. Rates: $20-$24 per family. Duty can make reservations, others Space-A.

TML: VAQ. Building 6550, enlisted all ranks, leave or official duty. Bedroom, 2 beds, semi-private bath (17); separate bedroom suites, private bath (E9)(2). Refrigerator, color TV room & lounge, maid service, cribs/cots, washer/dryer, food/ice vending. Rates: $9 per person. Maximum $13.50 per room. Maximum 2 persons. Duty can make reservations, others Space-A.

TML: VOQ. Building 2501, officers all ranks, leave or official duty. Bedroom, semi-private bath (40); separate bedroom, private bath (05+) (3). Kitchen, essentials, refrigerator, color TV in room & lounge, maid service, washer/dryer, food/ice vending. Modern structure, remodeled lounge, new TVs/carpets '91. Rates for private rooms:

MAINE
Loring Air Force Base, continued

sponsor $13. Maximum $19.50 per room. Maximum 2 persons. Rates for semi-private rooms: sponsor $10. Maximum $15 per room. Maximum 2 person. Duty can make reservations, others Space-A.

TML: DV/VIP. Building 2112, officer 06+, leave or official duty, separate bedrooms, private bath (4). Kitchen, complete utensils, color TV, maid service, cribs/cots, washer/dryer, ice vending, microwave. Older structure. Rates: $14 per room. Maximum $21 per family. Occupancy subject to CO's approval. Duty can make reservations.

DV/VIP: Wing XO, 42 BMW/CCE. Building 6000, C-EX-2275, 06+.

TML Availability: Difficult. Best, winter. Limited, other times.

☞ **Picture-book lakes, snow covered mountains, a coastline notched with bays and coves, and nearby Canada, all make this area interesting for the visitor.**

Locator 999-2100   **Medical 999-5316**   **Police 999-7155**

⊗**This base is scheduled to close in October '94. It will revert to civilian use. For updates read Military Living's *R&R Space-A Report*.**

Winter Harbor Naval Security Group Activity (ME09R1)
Winter Harbor, ME 04693-0900

TELEPHONE NUMBER INFORMATION: Main installation numbers: C-207-963-5534, D-312-476-9011.

Location: From Ellsworth, take US-1 north to ME-186 east to Acadia National Park. Naval Security Station is on Schoodic Point in the park. USM: N-2. NMC: Bangor, 45 miles northwest.

Billeting Office: No central billeting office. Building 84, C-**963-5534/35-EX-223**, D-312-476-9223, 0730-2230 daily. Check in billeting, check out 1200 hours daily. Government civilian employee billeting.

TML: BEQ. Building 84, enlisted all ranks, official duty only. Bedroom, hall bath (E1-E4) (37); bedroom, hall bath (E5-E6)(28); bedroom, semi-private bath (E7-E9) (6). Refrigerator, community kitchen, CATV in room & lounge, washer/dryer. Modern structure, new '91. Rates: $4.

TML: BOQ. Building 192, officers all ranks, leave or official duty. Bedroom, private bath (4). Kitchen, limited utensils, CATV, maid service, washer/dryer. Modern structure. Rates: $8 per person. Maximum 2 per room. Duty can make reservations, others Space-A.

TML: MWR cabins and mobile homes, **Winter Harbor Recreation Area**. All ranks, leave or official duty, retirees, family members, C-**207-963-5537**. Cabins, 3 bedroom, private bath, fully furnished, sleep 6 (6); mobile homes, 2 bedroom, private bath, fully furnished, sleep 5 (5). Fully equipped kitchen, all linens, TV, 1 cabin handicapped

Winter Harbor NSG Activity, continued

accessible, pets allowed for additional fee. Full range of recreational opportunities, both summer and winter available. Close to base support activities. Rates: $45 (seasonal, check prices when calling for reservations. All categories may make reservations 90 days in advance.

TML Availability: Good, Nov-Mar. Difficult, May-Sep.

☞ Located in Schoodic Point section of Acadia National Park, this is a favorite with hunters, fishermen, snow and water skiers. For additional information on the rec area, read *Military RV, Camping & Rec Areas Around the World.*

Locator 963-5534/5535   Medical EX-297   Police EX-202

Maryland

Aberdeen Proving Ground (MD11R1)
Aberdeen PG, MD 21005-5001

TELEPHONE NUMBER INFORMATION: Main installation numbers: (Aberdeen Area) C-410-278-5201,(Aberdeen Area) D-312-298-1110, (Edgewood Area) C-410-671-5201, (Edgewood Area) D-312-584-1110.

Location: Aberdeen Area: take exit 85 east from I-95 north on MD-22 east for 2 miles to main gate. Also, from US-40 north to right on Maryland Blvd, entrance to main gate. NMC: Baltimore, 23 miles southwest. Edgewood Area: take exit 77 from I-95 north on MD-24 east for 2 miles to main gate. Also, from US-40 right on MD-24 to main gate. USM: L-4. NMC: Baltimore, 13 miles southwest.

Billeting Office: Building 2207, ATTN: STEAP-FE-HU, Bel Air St, 24 hours daily. C-410-278-5148/5149. Check in billeting (except TLF), check out 1100 hours. Government civilian employee billeting.

TML: Guest House, check in at front desk, building 3322, all ranks, leave or official duty, C-410-278-3856, D-312-298-3856. Bedroom, 2 double beds, private bath (37); one to four bedroom apartments, private bath (18). Refrigerator, microwave, A/C, color TV in room & lounge, maid service, cribs, cots, washer/dryer, ice vending. Modern structure. Rates: sponsor $20, each additional person $3, child $2, infant no charge. Maximum per family $26, maximum persons per unit: 5 in rooms, 8 in apartments. TDY and active duty, reservists, national guard can make reservations, others Space-A. No pets allowed. Additional units in contracted off-post motel (35).

TML: VOQ. Several buildings, officers all ranks, official duty, C-410-278-5148/49. Check out 1300 hours. Bedroom, private bath (219); separate bedroom, semi-private bath (68). Essentials, kitchenette, A/C, color TV in room & lounge, maid service, washer/dryer. Older structure, recently remodeled. Rates: $26.75 per room. Maximum 1 per room. No pets allowed. Active duty, reservists and national guard can make reservations.

TML: VEQ. Several buildings, enlisted all ranks, official duty, C-410-278-5148/49, check out 1300 hours. Bedroom, private bath (55). Essentials, food vending, refrigerator, A/C,

MARYLAND
Aberdeen Proving Ground, continued

color TV, maid service, washer/dryer. Older structure, remodeled. Rates: $26.75 per room. Maximum 1 per room. Active duty, reservists, national guard can make reservations.

TML: DV/VIP. **Ryan Building,** officers 06+, GS-15 and above, leave or official duty, C-410-278-5156/57. Two separate bedrooms, private bath (1); two bedroom, private bath (4); three bedrooms, private bath (3). Kitchen, complete utensils, A/C, color TV, maid service, cribs/cots. Check out 1300 hours daily. Older structure. Rates: sponsor $32, each additional person $5, infant no charge. Duty can make reservations, others Space-A.

DV/VIP: TECOM Protocol, Ryan Building, C-EX-5156. Or USAOC&S Protocol, building 3071, C-EX-5595, 06+, retirees Space-A.

TML Availability: Good, Nov-Jan. Difficult, other times.

☞ **On the Chesapeake Bay. Hunting, fishing, boating, 3 golf courses, 5 swimming pools, theater, bowling alley, fitness center, Marylander restaurant. Baltimore is 30 miles away, DC 75, and Philadelphia 92. Lots to do here.**

Locator 278-5201   **Medical 272-2557**   **Police 278-5291**

Andrews Air Force Base (MD02R1)
Andrews AFB, MD 20331-5000

TELEPHONE NUMBER INFORMATION: Main installation numbers: C-301-981-1110, D-312-858-1110.

Location: From I-95 (east portion of Capital Beltway, I-495) north or south, exit 9, first traffic light after leaving exit ramp turn right into main gate of AFB. Also, from I-395 north, exit South Capitol St, cross Anacostia River on S Capitol St, bear left to Suitland Parkway east, exit Parkway at Morningside on Suitland Rd east to main gate of AFB. Clearly marked. USM: N-7. NMC: Washington, DC 6 miles northwest.

Billing Office: ATTN: **Gateway Inn,** building 1374, Arkansas Rd, C-301-981-4614, D-312-858-4614, 24 hours daily. Check in billeting, check out 1200 hours daily. Government civilian employee billeting.

TML: TLF. Buildings 1801-1804, 1328, 1330, all ranks, leave or official duty. Separate bedrooms, private bath (60); two bedroom, private bath (8). Kitchen, limited utensils, A/C, color TV, maid service, cribs, washer/dryer, ice vending. Modern structure. Rates: $24. Maximum 5 per room. Duty can make reservation, others Space-A.

TML: DV/VIP. Building 1349. Officers 06+, leave or official duty. DV rooms, private bath (31), DV suites, private bath (18). Kitchen, A/C, color TV, maid service, washer/dryer. Older structure. Rates: $8 rooms, $14 suites per person, per night. Official travellers can make reservations, others Space-A.

TML: VOQ, VEQ. Buildings 1376, 1373, C-2606/7. VOQ units (1373) under construction at press time. VEQ (1376) separate bedroom Chief Suites E8-E9 (5), bedroom Chief suites, private bath (8). A/C, color T.V. Rates: $14 and $8 per person. Reservations required. For duty personnel.

MARYLAND

Andrews Air Force Base, continued

DV/VIP: Protocol, 89 AW/CCP, C-EX-4525, 07+. Retirees Space-A.

TML Availability: Best, Dec. Difficult, Jun-Aug.

☞ **Andrews is the military aerial gateway to Washington, DC for most overseas VIP's, and the home of "Air Force One", the President's aircraft. If you're lucky you can witness "important people" coming and going here.**

Locator 981-6161   Medical 981-6250   Police-981-2000/01

Bethesda National Naval Medical Center (MD06R1)
8901 Wisconsin Avenue
Bethesda, MD 20814-5000

TELEPHONE NUMBER INFORMATION: Main installation numbers: C-301-295-5960, D-312-295-5960/2075.

Location: From I-495 (Capital Beltway) take exit 34, Wisconsin Ave (Md-355, Rockville Pike) south for 1 mile to Naval Medical Center on left. Enter first gate, Wood Rd S, for support facility. Also, can enter the center from Jones Bridge Rd, off Wisconsin Ave. USM: M-6. NMC: Washington, DC 1 mile southeast.

Billeting Office: ATTN: Manager, Housing Referral Office, building 6, C-301-295-1138, 0800-1630 hours daily. Check in facility, check out 1200 hours daily. No government civilian employee billeting. Billeting Office for BOQ/BEQ, building 60, C-301-295-5855/56. Duty Office - main hospital (central figure for problems) C-301-295-4611.

TML: Navy Lodge, building 52, all ranks, leave or official duty. For reservations call 1-800-NAVY-INN. Lodge number is 654-1795, 0800-2200 hours daily. Only for family members of in-patients. Bedroom, private bath (22). Kitchen, A/C, color TV in room & lounge, maid service, cribs, coin washer/dryer, ice vending. Modern structure. Rates: $37 per unit. Maximum 5 per unit. Guest must live in excess of 50 miles from hospital. Family members of in-patients can make reservations.

TML: BOQ. Building 11, officers, all ranks, official duty. Reservations required, C-301-295-1110/1. Bedroom, common bath (89); separate bedrooms, private bath, kitchen (4) (DV/VIP); family rooms, kitchen, private bath (2) maximum 2 persons, rates: $8, $12 and $15. Refrigerator, community kitchen, utensils, A/C, color TV in lounge, maid service, cots, washer/dryer, ice vending. Older structure. Quarters are inadequate & substandard.

DV/VIP: Cmdr, NATNAVMEDCEN, building 1, room 5156A, C-EX-5800, 06+. Retirees Space-A.

TML Availability: Very limited.

☞ **Bethesda is located just north of Washington DC, shopping, and the Metro are closeby.**

Locator 295-5385   Medical 666   Police 295-5960

☺This Navy Lodge is scheduled for an addition of 50 rooms in late '94 -'95.

MARYLAND

Curtis Bay Coast Guard Yard (MD01R1)
Curtis Bay, MD 21226-1797

TELEPHONE NUMBER INFORMATION: Main installation numbers: C-410-636-4194/4188, D-none, FTS-935-4194/4188.

Location: Take I-695 to exit 1, bear to your right, right on Hawkins Point Rd, left into Coast Guard Yard. USM: L,M-4. NMC: Baltimore, 5 miles northwest.

Billeting Office: No central billeting office. ATTN: BOQ Manager, building 28A (BOQ), C-410-636-7356, building 33 (Transient Family Lodge), C-EX-4194, 0700-2300 M-F. After duty hours, OD, building 33, C-EX-7356 (if reservations already made). Check in facility, check out 1000 hours daily. No government civilian employee billeting.

TML: TFL. Building 84. All ranks, leave or official duty. Three bedroom suites, private bath (5). Kitchen, complete utensils, A/C, color TV, cribs, washer/dryer, playground. Handicapped accessible. Older structure. Rates: 1 bedroom $15, 2 bedroom $20, 3 bedroom $25 per night. Sofa bed available. Maximum 8 per family. All categories except widows and unaccompanied dependents can make reservations. PCS in/out have priority.

TML: BOQ. Building 28A, officer all ranks, official duty only. Reservations required. C-EX-7373, 0830-1500. After duty hours, OD, building 33, C-EX-4166. Bedroom, 2 beds, private bath (5). A/C, color in TV lounge, microwave, refrigerator, pool table and VCR in lounge, washer/dryer. Modern structure. Rates: sponsor $5. Maximum 2 persons per unit.

TML Availability: Good, Oct-Apr. More difficult, other times.

☞ **Southeast of Baltimore, a city rich in history and entertainment, where a virtually new harbor buzzes with shopping, dining and recreational opportunities. A convenience store is located at the entrance to the yard.**

Locator 636-4147   Medical 636-3144   Police 636-7476

Fort Detrick (MD07R1)
Fort Detrick, MD 21701-5000

TELEPHONE NUMBER INFORMATION: Main installation numbers: C-301-619-8000, D-312-343-1110.

Location: From Washington, DC, take I-270 north to US-15 north. From Baltimore, take I-70 west to US-15 north. From US-15 north, in Frederick, exit Seventh St. Clearly marked to post. USM: L-4. NMC: Baltimore, 50 miles east and Washington, DC, 50 miles southeast.

Billeting Office: Building 901, Sultan St & Doughten Dr, C-301-619-2154, 0745-1630 hours M-F. Check out 1000 hours daily. No government civilian employee billeting.

TML: Guest House. Buildings 800-801, all ranks, leave or official duty. Two bedroom, private bath (1); three bedroom, private bath (3). Kitchen, limited utensils, A/C, color TV, cribs/cots, washer/dryer. Older structure. New carpet '87. Rates: $24 per roon.. PCS can make reservations, others Space-A. No pets.

Fort Detrick, continued

TML: VOQ. Building 660, all ranks, leave or official duty. Bedroom suites, private bath. Kitchen, limited utensils, A/C, color TV, maid service, washer/dryer, soda machine, pay telephone. Older structure, remodeled. Rates: $13 per room. TDY can make reservations, others Space-A. No pets.

TML: DVQ. Building 715, officers, all ranks, leave or official duty. Suite, private bath (1). Kitchen, limited utensils, A/C, color TV, maid service. Older structure. Rates: $18 per night. TDY can make reservations, others Space-A.

DV/VIP: Hq Ft Detrick. C-EX-7114. 06+. Retirees and lower ranks Space-A.

TML Availability: Good, Oct-Mar. Difficult, Jun-Aug.

☞ **Historic Frederick County offers visitors a variety of cultural, sports and recreational options. Both Baltimore and Washington DC are nearby.**

Locator 663-2061   **Medical 663-2200**   **Police 663-7114**

Fort George G. Meade (MD08R1)
Fort George G. Meade, MD 20755-5115

TELEPHONE NUMBER INFORMATION: Main installation numbers: C-401-677-6261, D-312-923-6261.

Location: Off Baltimore-Washington Parkway, I-295, exit MD-198 east which is Fort Meade Rd. Clearly marked. USM: L-4. NMC: Baltimore and Washington, DC, 30 miles from each city.

Billeting Office: Brett Hall, ATTN: AFKA-ZI-EH-HB, Building 4707, Ruffner Rd, C-**401-677-6529/5884,** 24 hours daily. Check in billeting, check out 1200 hours daily. Government civilian employee billeting.

TML: Guest House. Building 2793, **Abrams Hall,** all ranks, leave or official duty. Handicapped accessible, C-EX-2045. Check in 24 hours daily. Bedrooms with 2 beds, private bath (54). Refrigerator, community kitchen, A/C, essentials, color TV room & lounge, maid service, cribs, washer/dryer, food/ice vending, CATV, in-room telephone, microwaves. Older structure, renovated. Rates: PCS in/out $20-$24 per room. Priorities: PCS, hospital visitors, visitors active duty assigned, TDY. All others Space-A.

TML: VOQ. Buildings 4703, 4704, 4707, 4709, officers all ranks, leave or official duty. Bedroom, semi-private bath (142); one bedroom, private bath (4); separate bedroom suites, private bath (16). Kitchen (8 units), refrigerator, A/C, CATV, maid service, washer/dryer, ice vending. Older structures, bathrooms renovated. Rates: $22.50 per room. Maximum 1 per room. TDY can make reservations, others Space-A.

TML: SEBQ. Building 4705, enlisted E7-E9, official duty. Separate bedroom, private bath (30). Modern structure. Rates: No charge. For SNCO on PCS to Ft Meade only.

TML: BOQ. Buildings 4717, 4720, 4721, officers all ranks, official duty. Separate bedrooms, private bath (62). Modern structure. Rates: No charge. PCS to Ft Meade only.

MARYLAND
Fort George G. Meade, continued

TML: DVQ. Building 4415, officer 05+, leave or official duty. Check in 0800-1600. After hours SDO, building 4420. Separate bedrooms, private bath (5); two bedroom, private bath (2). Kitchen, limited utensils, A/C, color TV, maid service, washer/dryer. Older structure, renovated. Rates: $22.50-$26.50 per room. Duty can make reservations, others Space-A.

DV/VIP: 1st US Army/SGS, Pershing Hall, building 4550, C-EX-3420, 05+ and GS-14+, retirees Space-A.

TML Availability: Good. Best months, Oct-Mar.

☞ **Visit Baltimore's Fort McHenry National Monument, and new Inner Harbor, or visit Annapolis' quaint shopping areas. Maryland's 30 miles of Atlantic Ocean seashore, and Washington DC are all available to Fort Meade visitors.**

Locator 677-6261   Medical 677-2570   Police 677-6622

Fort Ritchie (MD13R1)
Fort Ritchie, MD 21719-5010

TELEPHONE NUMBER INFORMATION: Main installation numbers: C-301--878-1300, D-312-988-1300.

Location: From US-15 north exit at Thurmont, to MD-550 north for 7 miles to Cascade and main gate. From Hagerstown, take MD-64 east to MD-491, north to MD-550 and north to Cascade and main gate. USM: L-4. NMC: Hagerstown, 16 miles southwest, Baltimore, 50 miles southeast, Washington, DC, 55 miles southeast.

Billeting Office: Building 520, West Banfill & Cushman, C-301-241-4445 or 878-5171, D-312-277-5171, 0800-1845 M-F, 0800-1645 Sa-Su, holidays. Other hours, SDO in basement of building 200. Check in facility, check out before 1130 hours daily. Government civilian employee billeting.

TML: Guest House. Building 520, all ranks, leave or official duty. Bedroom, private bath (21). Kitchen (9 units), refrigerator (12 units), complete utensils, color TV, maid service, cribs/cots, coin washer/dryer, ice vending. Modern structure. Rates: PCS without kitchen $24, with kitchen $26. Maximum 5 per room. PCS can make reservations, others Space-A.

TML: VOQ/VEQ. Building 800, officers all ranks, enlisted E7-E9, leave or official duty. Bedroom, private bath (11); bedroom suite (DV)(1). (VQ) refrigerator, community kitchen, color TV room & lounge, maid service, washer/dryer. Rates: VQ $15, DVQ $24, $6 each additional person. TDY can make reservations, others Space-A.

TML: Lakeside Hall. Building 11, C-301-878-4361, all ranks, leave or official duty. Bedroom, private bath, small living area w/pull-out couch (6); apartments with kitchenettes (2); Ritchie Suite (VIP)(1). Rates: non-members: rooms $35, apartments $40. Military Club members take off $5. Refrigerator, microwave, coffee pot, color TV, in room phones, FAX machine, laundry service available, meal service in diningroom, disco on weekends. T-F lunch 11-1, T-F dinner, Sunday brunch. Activities for guests. Overlooking lake, lakeside activities include swimming, paddle boating, fishing, newly renovated, color TV, telephones in room, FAX machine. Laundry service available.

Fort Richie, continued

DV/VIP: HQ 7th SIG, building 307, C-EX-5754, 06+. Retirees, Space-A.

TML Availability: Good, most of the year. Best, Mar-Jun.

☞ **Beautiful scenic small post. Great location for ski resorts in the area, swimming, fishing, golf.**

Locator 878-5685   Medical 878-4132   Police 878-4228

Indian Head Naval Ordnance Station (MD04R1)
Indian Head NOS, MD 20640-5000

TELEPHONE NUMBER INFORMATION: Main installation numbers: C-301-743-4000, D-312-364-4000.

Location: Take I-495 (Capital Beltway) east, exit to MD-210 south for 25 miles to station. USM: L-4. NMC: Washington, DC 25 miles north.

Billeting Office: Central Lodging Office, C-**301-743-4845**, D-312-364-4845.

TML: BOQ. Building 969, all ranks, leave or official duty, 24 hours daily. Officer/enlisted rooms, semi-private baths, most 2 bedroom. Kitchen, limited utensils, A/C, color TV lounge, maid service, washer/dryer, food vending. Older structure, renovated. Rates: $6 permanent/students (longer 21 weeks) $8 transient. Duty can make reservations, others Space-A.

TML: BEQ. Building 902, all ranks, leave or official duty, C-EX-4845, 24 hours. Bedrooms with 2 beds, semi-private bath (108). A/C, color TV in lounge, maid service, washer/dryer, food vending. Rates: $4 per day. Duty can make reservations, others Space-A.

DV/VIP: PAO. Building 20, C-EX-4627. Inquire about qualifying rank. Retirees Space-A.

TML Availability: Fair, Jan-May, Sept-Dec. Difficult, other times.

☞ **Only 22 miles from Washington D.C. makes this place within "shouting distance" of the many cultural and sporting events available to the area. The nearby Potomac River also provides recreational opportunities.**

Locator 743-4303   Medical 743-4601   Police 743-4381

Patuxent River Naval Air Warfare Center (MD09R1)
Patuxent River NAWC, MD 20670-5000

TELEPHONE NUMBER INFORMATION: Main installation numbers: C-301-863-3000, D-312-356-3000.

Location: From I-95 (east portion of Capital Beltway, I-495) exit 7A to Branch Ave (MD-5) south. Follow MD-5 until it turns into MD-235 near Oraville, on to Lexington Park, and the NAS. Main gate is on MD-235 and MD-246 (Cedar Point Rd). USM: M-4. NMC: Washington, DC, 65 miles west.

MARYLAND
Patuxent River NAWC, continued

Billeting Office: No central billeting office. Check in facility, check out 1200 hours daily. No government civilian employee billeting.

TML: Navy Lodge. Building 2119, **1-800-NAVY-INN**. Lodge number is 737-2400. Bedrooms, all ranks leave or official duty, private bath (50). A/C, cots/cribs, ice vending, kitchen, maid service, color TV, utensils, washer/dryer. Rates: $37 per unit. Maximum 2 adults. All categories can make reservations.

TML: BOQ. Building 406, officers all ranks, leave or official duty, C-EX-3601. Rooms/suites, private, semi-private baths (45). Refrigerator, A/C, color TV, maid service, cots, washer/dryer, ice vending, telephone. Rates: $6 per person, child up to 12 free. Reservations only from persons on TAD orders.

TML: DV/VIP. C-EX-7503, one bedroom, king-size bed suites, dining room, living room, private bath, kitchen (3).

TML: DV/VIP. **Crowe's Nest** (located at Officers' Club). 1 suite, private bath. For reservations contact Cmdr, ATTN: Code CT001, C-EX-3601, 06+.

DV/VIP: PAO. C-EX-7503, 07+, retirees Space-A.

TML Availability: Fairly good, winter. More difficult, Jun-Aug.

☞ Discount tickets to **Kings Dominion, Wild World, Busch Gardens, Hershey Park, local ski resorts, Colonial Williamsburg, sporting events are available through the Special Interest Coordinator's office in building 423 (863-3510).**

Locator 863-1036   **Medical 863-3353**   **Police 863-3911**

Solomons Navy Recreation Center (MD05R1)
Solomons, MD 20688-0147

TELEPHONE NUMBER INFORMATION: Main installation numbers: C-410-326-3566, DC area 410-326-4216.

Location: Off base, on Patuxent River. From US-301, take MD-4 southeast to Solomons; or take MD-5 southeast to MD-235, then MD-4 northeast to Solomons. USM: L,M-4. NMC: Washington, DC, 65 miles northwest.

Billeting Office: Building 411, C-**1-800-628-9230,** 0800-2200 Sa-Th, 0800-2400 F, May 1 to Oct 15; 0800-2000 Sa-Th, 0800-2200 F, Oct 16 to April 30. Late check-in if arranged in advance. All ranks, leave or official duty. Check in billeting, check out 1100 hours daily.

TML: Units are bungalows, & cottages. Bedroom, private bath (4); two bedroom, private bath (6); three bedroom, private bath (14); four and five bedroom, private bath (13 & 2); Kitchen, limited utensils, A/C, color TV in lounge (building 6), pay cribs/cots, coin washer/dryer, food/ice vending. Older structures, some renovated. Rates: **renovated bungalows,** E1-E5 $26-$28.50, 3-4 bedrooms, officer $28-$42.50; **economy brick bungalows,** E1-E5 $23-$24, 3-4 bedrooms; **cottages,** E6-E9 $34-$44, 1-5 bedrooms,

MARYLAND
Solomons Navy Recreation Center, continued

officer $41-50. All rates per night. Maximum 3 persons per bedroom. All categories except unaccompanied dependents can make reservations. Call for information about when reservations will be accepted for summer months.

TML Availability: Good, Oct-Apr. Difficult, other times.

☞ **Complete river recreational area. Full support facility available at nearby Patuxent River NAWC. St Maries City, Calvert Cliffs, Calvert Marine Museum, Farmers' Market, charter fishing, Point Lookout State Park. For complete details see *Military RV, Camping & Rec Areas Around The World*.**

Locator 326-3566   Medical 911   Police 301-2436

United States Naval Academy/
Annapolis Naval Station (MD10R1)
Annapolis, MD 21402-5054

TELEPHONE NUMBER INFORMATION: Main installation numbers: C-410-267-6100, D-312-281-0111.

Location: Two miles off US-50/301. Two exits to the Academy, clearly marked. Main gate is on King George St, in Annapolis. Naval Station is across Severn River off US-50/301 east, first exit. Clearly marked. USM: M-4. NMC: Annapolis, in city.

Billeting Office: Billeting Office, 2nd floor, **Officers' and Faculty Club,** C-410-267-3906, 0800-1800 hours M-Th, 0800-1600 F, weekends call base operator. Check in, out at billeting. Government civilian employee billeting.

TML: O & F Club, second & third deck, officers all ranks, equivalent government employees, leave or official duty. Suites, private bath, sleeps to 5 persons (16). A/C, color TV, maid service, washer/dryer. Older historic structure, remodeled. Rates: 1st person $8; 2 persons $16, plus $1 for extra person. PCS, TAD/TDY have priority, others Space-A.

DV/VIP: Superintendents Building, C-EX-2403, 06+. VIP suites, private bath, with kitchen (06+); guest suite, private bath (1). Kitchenette (2), coffee bar. Rates: suites w/ kitchenette $20, plus $1 extra person, guest suite $10, plus $10 second person. Retirees Space-A.

TML Availability: Best, Sep-Apr. Difficult, summer months.

☞ **Don't miss a visit to the waterfront shopping and restaurant area, where dreaming over yachts is "SOP". Visit the Naval Academy Chapel and historic buildings, and walk around historic Maryland's capital.**

Locator 267-6100   Medical 267-3333   Police 267-4444

Massachusetts

Cape Cod Coast Guard Air Station (MA10R1)
Otis ANGB, MA 02542-5003

TELEPHONE NUMBER INFORMATION: Main installation numbers: C-508-968-1000, D-312-557-4401, National Guard Base. Coast Guard Air Station, C-508-968-6300, D-312-557-6300. FTS-642-1000.

Location: Take MA Military Reservation exit off MA-28, south on Connley Ave approximately 2 miles to Bourne Gate. USM: M,N-3. NMC: Boston, 50 miles northwest.

Billeting Office: ATTN: Temporary Quarters, building 5204, C-**508-968-5636**, 0800-1600 hours M-F. 1200-1600 hours Sa & Su. Check in billeting. Check out 1100 hours.

TML: TLF/BOQ. All ranks. Leave or official duty. Accessible to handicapped. Advance payment required. Bedrooms with kitchen, private bath (4); two bedroom townhouses, private bath (6); bedroom, private bath (BOQ) (3); bedroom efficiency apartments, private bath (16). Cots/cribs, essentials, food vending, maid service, refrigerator, color TV in lounge & room, utensils, coin washer/dryer, small child's playroom. Older structure, remodeled. Rates: moderate, determined by rank. Reservations: PCS 90 days in advance, TDY 60 days in advance, others 30 days. In summer vacationers 2 weeks in advance.

TML Availability: Good. Best Oct-Apr.

☞ **Otis has 9-hole golf course and driving range. Newport mansions, beaches, Martha's Vineyard, and Nantucket Islands nearby make this a special place to visit.**

Locator 968-1000　　　**Medical 968-5570**　　　**Police 968-5208**

Fort Devens (MA09R1)
Fort Devens, MA 01433-5000

TELEPHONE NUMBER INFORMATION: Main installation numbers: C-508-796-3911, D-312-256-3911.

Location: From Boston follow MA-2 west and exit at Fort Devens, about 5 miles west of I-495. In Ayer. USM: M-2. NMC: Boston, 35 miles southeast.

Billeting Office: ATTN: AFZD-DEH-B, building P-22, Sherman Ave, C-**508-796-3354**, 0500-2400 hours daily. Other hours, Duty Officer, building P-1, C-508-796-3711. Check in billeting, check out 1100 hours daily. Government civilian employee billeting.

TML: Guest House. Buildings T-3595-3597, T-150, all ranks, leave or official duty. Separate bedrooms, private bath (24); separate bedrooms, semi-private bath (12).

Refrigerator, color TV, maid service, cribs/cots, washer/dryer. Older structure. Rates: E1-E5 $13; E6-E8, W1, 01-02 $17; E9, W2-W4, 03-04 $20; 05-010 $22. Duty can make reservations, others Space-A.

Fort Devens, continued

TML: VEQ. Building P-22, **Washington Hall**, all ranks, leave or official duty. Bedrooms, semi-private bath (55); suites (4). Some amenities. Rates: $12 single rooms, $15 suites. All categories can make reservations.

TML: VOQ. Building P-19, **Rogers Hall**, WO1+, leave or official duty. Bedrooms (14); suites (6). Kitchen (12), some other amenities. Rates: $18 rooms with kitchen, $16 rooms without kitchen; $18 suites 2 & 8; $20 suites 1, 10, 11, 12, $5 each additional person. Maximum $30 per family. All categories can make reservations.

TML: DVQ. Building 314, **Prescott House**, O6+, leave or official duty. Suites, private bath (6). Some amenities. Rates: sponsor $22, each additional person $5, maximum $32 per family. Per diem occupants $22. Reservations accepted through Protocol.

DV/VIP: Protocol Office, building P-1, C-EX-3711, 05+. Retirees Space-A.

TML Availability: Good, Dec-Mar. Difficult, summer.

Locator 796-2748   Medical 796-6816   Police 796-3333

✪**This facility is scheduled to close in '95, a small reserve/national guard enclave will be retained. Status of billeting was not known at press time.**

Fourth Cliff Recreation Area (MA02R1)
Hanscom Air Force Base, MA 01731-5001

TELEPHONE NUMBER INFORMATION: Main installation numbers: C-617-377-4441, D-312-478-4441.

LOCATION: Off base. I-95 or I-93 to MA-3, approximately 30 miles south of Boston; south to exit 12; MA-139 east to Marshfield. 1.5 miles to Furnace St; turn left. Continue to "T" intersection; turn left on Ferry St. Stay on Ferry St to Sea St; right over South River Bridge; left on Central Ave and proceed to gate. Check in at Building 7. NMI: South Weymouth NAS, 15 miles northwest. USM: M-2. NMC: Boston, 30 miles north.

Billeting Office: None. Reservations are required with payment in full (ask for map). Address: Fourth Cliff Recreation Area, PO Box O, Humarock, MA 02047. C-**617-837-9269 (0800-1630 M-F) or 1-800-468-9547**. Rec area operates Memorial Day through Columbus Day. Cabins operate year round.

TML: One to three bedroom cabins (18), all ranks, leave or official duty. Rates: $30-$70 daily. All categories can make reservations. **Pets not allowed in cabins but may be leashed in other areas.**

TML Availability: Limited. Book early.

☞ **Easy access to Boston, Cape Cod, Martha's Vineyard and Nantucket Islands, and located high on a cliff overlooking the Atlantic and scenic North River, this is a superb location for a summer or winter vacation.**

MASSACHUSETTS

Hanscom Air Force Base (MA06R1)
Hanscom AFB, MA 01731-5001

TELEPHONE NUMBER INFORMATION: Main installation numbers: C-617-377-4441, D-312-478-4441.

Location: From I-95 north take exit 31A, MA-2A west for 2 miles to right on Hartwell Rd which bisects the AFB. USM: M-2. NMC: Boston, 17 miles southeast.

Billeting Office: Building 1427, C-617-377-2112, 24 hours daily. Check in facility, 1400 check out 1200 hours daily. Government civilian employee billeting.

TML: TLF. Buildings 1412, 1423, 1426, officers all ranks, leave or official duty. C-EX-2044. Handicapped accessible. Building 1423, single bedroom, sofa bed, private bath (17); double room, private bath (6). Building 1412, single bedrooms, private bath (22) (10 TLF units); building 1426 single bedrooms, semi-private bath (52). Kitchen, complete utensils, A/C, maid service, cribs, washer/dryer. Modern structures, renovated '92. Rates: building 1423, single $24 per person, per night, double $32; buildings 1412, 1426 $10 per person per night. TLF is used for PCS in/out only, 30 days PCS in, 7 days PCS out. VOQ for TDY personnel only. Space-A guests put names on waiting list after 2400 hours, first come first served. Call for details.

DV/VIP: Protocol Office, building 1606, C-EX-5151. 07+, retirees Space-A.

TML Availability: Fair. Best in Oct, Nov, Feb, Mar.

☞ **Delve into U.S. history by visiting Minute Man National Historical Park, Battle Road near Fiske Hill in Lexington, the Wayside Unit, home of the Alcotts, Nathaniel Hawthorne and others, and Lexington Green.**

Locator 377-5111   **Medical 377-2333**   **Police 377-2315**

South Weymouth Naval Air Station (MA05R1)
South Weymouth NAS, MA 02190-5000

TELEPHONE NUMBER INFORMATION: Main installation numbers: C-617-786-2500, D-312-478-5980.

Location: From MA-3 (Pilgrims Highway) exit 16 to MA-18 (Main St). Base is approximately two miles ahead. Main gate is on left side of MA-18. USM: M-2,3. NMC: Boston, 15 miles northwest.

Billeting Office: Building 31, Shea Memorial Dr, C-617-786-2928, 24 hours daily. Check in facility, check out 1000 hours daily. Confirmation numbers given out 24 hours daily.

TML: TLQ. Building 31 and O'Club, all ranks, leave or official duty for officers. Double rooms (2 people), shared bath (3); family suites, living room, bedroom, private bath (O'Club) (9) (4 persons, under 6 free). Rates: $4, doubles; $6, suites. Kitchen, refrigerator (suites), complete utensils, color TV, maid service, microwaves, cribs, washer/dryer, ice vending. Older structures, renovated. All categories can make reservations.

DV/VIP: Executive Officer Secretary, Administration Building, C-EX-2600.

MASSACHUSETTS

South Weymouth Naval Air Station, continued

TML Availability: Space limited F-Sa. Available Su-Th.

☞ **Twenty minutes from historic Boston, Cape Cod, beaches, coastal recreation, and many other exciting attractions.**

Locator 786-2800   Medical 786-2674   Police 786-2610

Westover Air Force Base (MA03R1)
Westover AFB, MA 01022-1309

TELEPHONE NUMBER INFORMATION: Main installation numbers: C-413-557-1110, D-312-589-1110.

Location: Take exit 5 off I-90 (MA Turnpike) in Chicopee. Westover is on MA-33, north of I-90. Signs mark way to base. USM: M-3. NMC: Springfield, 8 miles south.

Billeting Office: Building 2201, Outer Drive. VOQ/TAQ: **C-413-593-5421, EX-3006,** D-312-589-2700, C-EX-3006 weekends only. Space Available check in 1700, check out 1200 hours daily. Government civilian employee billeting.

TML: VOQ. Buildings 2700, 2201. Officers, all ranks, leave or official duty. Bedroom, semi-private bath (10); two bedroom suites, semi-private bath (29). A/C, essentials, color TV in lounge & room, maid service, washer/dryer, ice vending. Older structure, remodeled. Rates: $6 per person. Maximum 4 persons. Maximum depends on number per family. Duty can make reservations, others Space-A.

TML: TAQ. Buildings 5101-5105, enlisted, E-1 thru E-7, leave or official duty. Rooms (400). Food/ice vending, maid service, refrigerator, color TV, washer/dryer. Older structure. Rates: $6 per person. Maximum 2 persons. Duty can make reservations.

DV/VIP: Building 2200. C-593-5421, 05+ or unit commander. Retirees and lower ranks Space-A.

TML Availability: Good, except Jun-Sep.

☞ **Museums, parks, ski areas, professional stage and Symphony Hall in Springfield, are of interest to visitors. Several golf courses. Visit Forest Park Zoo, and the Naismith Memorial Hall of Fame.**

Locator 557-1110   Medical 557-3565   Police 557-3557

Michigan

Camp Grayling (MI10R2)
Grayling, MI 49739-0001

TELEPHONE NUMBER INFORMATION: Main installation numbers: C-517-348-7621, D-312-722-8621.

MICHIGAN
Camp Grayling, continued

Location: On I-75 take Grayling exit. Camp Grayling is 4 miles west of Grayling. USM: J-3. NMC: Traverse City, 60 miles west.

Billeting Office: Officers' Club, C-**517-348-9033**, D-312-722-8621 EX-3225. Building 311, 0900-1600 hours. Check out 1000 hours.

TML: Lakefront Cottages (4) and Mobile Homes (2), buildings 177-182, officer, all ranks. leave or official duty. Handicapped accessible. Two bedroom, private bath (6). Kitchen, complete utensils, maid service. Modern structure, remodeled. Rates: cottages $35, mobile homes $20. Maximum 6 persons. Duty can make reservations, others Space-A.

TML: VOQ. Building 311, officers, all ranks, leave or official duty. Bedrooms, 2 beds, hall bath (10). Maid service, color TV in lounge. Older structure, remodeled. Rates: $7 per person. Maximum 4 persons. Duty, retirees, DAVs, and accompanied dependents of duty persons can make reservations, others Space-A.

TML: Sergeants Major Quarters. No family housing available. Quarters are open bay and mostly unheated. Designated male or female at time of issue. Exception made for PCS orders at no charge, Space-A only.

TML Availability: Limited. Closed Nov-Mar.

☞ Hunting, camping, fishing and winter sports are available on this Limited on post support facilities, but Wurtsmith AFB is 80 miles east. Commercial airlines available in Traverse City.

Locator 348-3611   **Medical 348-3621/2**   **Police 348-3428**

K.I. Sawyer Air Force Base (MI02R2)
K.I. Sawyer AFB, MI 49843-5000

TELEPHONE NUMBER INFORMATION: Main installation numbers: C-906-346-1110, D-312-472-1110.

Location: In the MI upper peninsula. From US-41 south of Marquette, take MI-460 west to gate 2. USM: J-2. NMC: Marquette, 23 miles northwest.

Billeting Office: Sawyer Inn, building 46, A St, C-**906-346-2145**, FAX C-906-346-2062, D-312-472-2062, 24 hours daily. Check in facility, check out 1200 hours daily. Government civilian employee billeting.

TML: VAQ. Building 801, enlisted all ranks, leave or official duty. Bedrooms, 2 beds, private bath (36); two separate bedrooms, semi-private bath (2); bedroom, private bath (2). Refrigerator, essentials, color TV in room & lounge, maid service, washer/dryer, ice vending, microwave. Older structure, renovated. Rates: $9 per person. Maximum 2 per room. Duty can make reservations, others Space-A.

TML: VOQ. Building 802, 806, officer 02-05, leave or official duty. Bedroom suites (6) private bath (6); separate bedrooms, semi-private bath (20); four bedroom, semi-private bath (2). Kitchen, color TV, maid service, washer/dryer, ice vending. Older structure, renovated. Rates: $9 to $13 per unit. Duty can make reservations, others Space-A.

MICHIGAN

K. I.Sawyer Air Force Base, continued

TML: TLF. Buildings 1200-1203, 1244-1245, all ranks, leave or official duty. Bedroom, private bath (20); two bedroom, private bath (3); three bedroom, private bath (12). Cribs/cots, essentials, ice vending, kitchen, complete utensils, maid service, handicapped accessible, color TV, washer/dryer. Older structures. Renovation '90. Rates: $19-$21 per family. All categories except duty Reservists and National Guard personnel can make reservations.

TML: DV/VIP House. Building 807-808, officer 06+, leave or official duty. Two bedroom, private bath. Kitchen, color TV, maid service, washer/dryer. Older structure. Rates: $14 per person. Duty can make reservations, others Space-A.

DV/VIP: C-EX-2763.

TML Availability: Fairly good, fall, winter. Difficult, summer.

Locator 346-2605   **Medical 346-2233**   **Police 346-2131**

☞ See historic Fort Wilkins on the Keweenaw Peninsula, and the National Ski Hall of Fame in Ishpeming. The world's busiest locks at Sault Ste. Marie, and close-to-nature cruises on the Tahquamenon River where you'll see golden-tinted waterfalls.

Selfridge Air National Guard Base (MI01R2)
Selfridge ANGB, MI 48045-5004

TELEPHONE NUMBER INFORMATION: Main installation numbers: C-313-466-4011, D-312-273-4011.

Location: Take I-94 north from Detroit, to Selfridge exit, then east on MI-59 to main gate of base. USM: K-3. NMC: Detroit, 25 miles southwest.

Billeting Office: Building 410, ATTN: AMSTA-CYACH, George Ave. Operated by U.S. Army MWR, C-**313-466-4062**, 24 hours, 7 days. Check in billeting, check out 1200 hours daily. Government civilian employee billeting.

TML: Guest House. Building 916, all ranks, leave or official duty. Two bedroom, living room, dining room, private bath (7); bedroom, living room, dining room, private bath (8). Kitchen, complete utensils, color TV, cribs, washer/dryer. Older structure. Rates: $16 1 bedroom, 2 bedroom $19. Maximum 3 in 1 bedroom, 5 in 2 bedroom. Duty can make reservations, others Space-A. **Pets OK, $3 per day.**

TML: VOQ/VEQ. Building 410, all ranks, leave or official duty. Separate bedrooms, private bath (23). Community kitchen, color TV, maid service, food/ice vending, washer/dryer. Older structure. Older structure, remodeled. Rates for leave status: sponsor $19, adult $7, under 18 free. Rates for duty status: sponsor $21.50, adult $7, under 18 free. Rates for 2 bedroom VIP suites: $32-$37 up to four persons. Duty can make reservations, others Space-A.

TML: DV/VIP. Suites. Controlled by base IO, building 304, room 101, C-EX-5576/4735, 06+. Retirees and lower ranks Space-A.

TML Availability: Fairly good.

MICHIGAN
Selfridge Air National Guard Base, continued

☞ Camping, hunting, fishing, boating, golfing and water sports are available in the many parks and recreational areas. Visit Museums, the Detroit Zoo, and don't forget Canada across Lake St. Clair or cross the border at Port Huron.

Locator 466-4011   Medical 466-4650   Police 466-4673

Wurtsmith Air Force Base (MI03R2)
Wurtsmith AFB, MI 48753-5360

TELEPHONE NUMBER INFORMATION: Main installation numbers: C-517-739-2011, D-312-623-1110.

Location: Off US-23, 2 miles northwest of Oscoda, on F-41. Clearly marked. USM: J,K-3. NMC: Bay City, 65 miles southwest.

Billeting Office: Building 1600, Skeel Ave, C-517-739-6033/6692, 24 hours daily. Check in billeting, check out 1200 hours daily. Government civilian employee billeting.

TML: TLF. Building 1750, all ranks, leave or official duty. Two bedroom, private bath (3); three bedroom, private bath (4); four bedroom, private bath (6). Kitchen, complete utensils, color TV, maid service, cribs, washer/dryer. Older structure, remodeled. Rates: $20 per unit. Duty can make reservations, others Space-A.

TML: VAQ. Building 1600, all ranks, leave or official duty. One bedroom, 2 beds, semi-private bath (16). Refrigerator, color TV in room & lounge, maid service, washer/dryer, ice vending, facilities for DAVs, microwave in lounge. Older structure, renovated. Rates: $9 per person.

TML: VOQ. Building 1602, all ranks, leave or official duty. One bedroom, semi-private bath (16); two bedrooms, private bath (1). Kitchen, color TV, maid service, washer/dryer, facilities for DAVs. Older structure, renovated. Rates: $9 per person. Maximum 2 per room. Children not authorized. Duty can make reservations, others Space-A.

TML: DV/VIP. Buildings 1600, 1602, officer 06+, enlisted E8-E9, leave or official duty. separate bedroom suites, private bath (4). Kitchen, complete utensils, color TV, maid service, ice vending, facilities for DAVs. Older structure, renovated. Rates: $14 per person. Maximum 2 per room. Children not authorized. Duty can make reservations, others Space-A.

DV/VIP: Protocol Office, building 5006, C-EX-6416, 06/GS-15+. Retirees, Space-A.

TML Availability: Fair. Limited from Memorial Day through Labor Day and from 1 Nov-10 Dec because of hunting season.

☞ Vacationer's paradise. Lake Huron, Van Etten Lake, and historic Au Sable River for swimming, boating and excellent fishing. In winter ice fishing, cross country skiing and snowmobile trails.

Locator 739-2011   Medical 747-6333   Police 747-6023

⊗This base will close in '93. Keep updated with Military Living's *R&R Space-A Report.*

Minnesota

Minneapolis-St. Paul IAP (MN01R2)
Minneapolis, MN 55417-5000

TELEPHONE NUMBER INFORMATION: Main installation numbers: C-612-725-5011, D-312-825-5100.

Location: From I-35 west to crosstown MN-62 to 34th Ave and entrance. Follow signs to AFB. USM: H-3. NMC: Minneapolis-St Paul, in the city.

Billeting Office: ATTN: 934 MSS/SVH, building 711, C-**612-725-5320**, 0700-2400 hours. Check in billeting, check out 1200 hours. Government civilian employee billeting.

TML: VOQ/TAQ. Building 711, all ranks, leave or official duty. Bedroom, private, semi-private, hall, and common baths (180); SNCO/DV suites, private bath (8). Refrigerator, A/C, color TV in room & lounge, maid service, washer/dryer, ice vending. Older structure, renovated. Rates: $6 per person, suites $8. Maximum 2 per room. Duty can make reservations, others Space-A.

TML Availability: Good, Oct-Jan. Difficult, May-Sep.

Locator 725-5011   **Medical 725-5402**   **Police 725-5402**

Mississippi

Columbus Air Force Base (MS01R2)
Columbus AFB, MS 39701-5000

TELEPHONE NUMBER INFORMATION: Main installation numbers: C-601-434-7322, D-312-742-7322.

Location: Off US-45 north, 60 miles west of Tuscaloosa, via US-82. USM: J-6. NMC: Columbus, 10 miles south.

Billeting Office: ATTN: 14th ABG/SVH, building 956, B St, C-**601-434-2549**, 24 hours daily. Check in billeting, check out 1200 hours daily. Government civilian employee billeting.

TML: TLF. Building 955, all ranks, leave or official duty. Bedrooms, private bath (20). Kitchen, utensils, A/C, color TV, maid service, cribs/cots, washer/dryer, ice vending, facilities for DAVs. Modern structure. Rate: $14 per unit E1-E6, $18, E7+. Duty can make reservations, others Space-A.

MISSISSIPPI
Columbus Air Force Base, continued

TML: VOQ. Building 954, officers all ranks, leave or official duty. One bedroom (2 DV/VIP rooms), private bath (18). Color TV, maid service, washer/dryer, ice vending. Older structure. Rates: $7 per person, $10 per person DV/VIP. Maximum $30 per room. Duty can make reservations, others Space-A.

TML: VAQ. Building 956, enlisted all ranks, leave or official duty. Spaces, semi-private bath (42); SNCO suites, private bath (3). Color TV, maid service, washer/dryer, ice vending. Older structure. Rates: $6 per person, $10 SNCO. Maximum $30 per room. Duty can make reservations, others Space-A.

DV/VIP: WG Exec, building 724, C-Ex 7001 (active duty 06+ only).

TML Availability: Very good. Best, Nov-Jan. More difficult, other times.

☞ **Columbus, with many antebellum structures never destroyed during the Civil War, is of interest to visitors. The area also hosts excellent fishing, boating and hunting along the Tennessee Tombigbee Waterway.**

Locator 434-2841   **Medical 434-2244**   **Police 434-7129**

Gulfport Naval Construction Battalion
Center (MS03R2)
Gulfport NCBC, MS 39501-5000

TELEPHONE NUMBER INFORMATION: Main installation numbers: C-601-871-2586, D-312-868-2586.

Location: Take US-49 south to Gulfport, follow signs to Center, from US-90 exit to US-49 (Broad Ave), from I-10 exit to US-49. USM: J-7. NMC: New Orleans, LA, 70 miles west.

Billeting Office: ATTN: Code 450, building 85, 2nd St, C-**601-871-2586**, 0700-1630 hours daily, other hours, SDO, building 1, C-EX-2555. Check in facility, check out 1200 hours daily. Government civilian employee billeting.

TML: Navy Lodge. All ranks, leave or official duty. Reservations call **1-800-NAVY-INN**. Lodge number is 864-3101, 0800-1830 hours daily, other hours SDO, building 1. Bedroom, private bath (15). Kitchen, utensils, A/C, color TV, maid service, coin washer/dryer. Modern structure. Rates: $32 per unit. Maximum 5 per room. All categories can make reservations.

TML: BOQ. Building 301, officers all ranks, leave or official duty, C-EX-2226. Bedroom, private bath (36), (2 VIP rooms). Kitchen, A/C, color TV in room & lounge, maid service, cribs/cots, washer/dryer, ice vending. Modern structure. Rates: $8 per person. Maximum 3 persons. Duty can make reservations.

TML: BEQ. Building 317, enlisted all ranks, leave or official duty, C-EX-2506. Bedroom (4 beds), common bath (90); three bedroom (female only), common bath (1). A/C, color TV in lounge, washer/dryer. Modern structure. Rates: $4 per person. Duty can make reservations, others Space-A.

DV/VIP: BOQ. Building 301, C-EX-2226, 06+, retirees and lower ranks Space-A.

Gulfport Naval CBC, continued

TML Availability: Good, Sep-Mar. Difficult, other times.

☞ **Swimming, fishing, sailing, windsurfing, sunning and beachcombing in summer are popular. Visit Beauvoir (Confederate President Jefferson Davis' home), Gulf Islands National Seashore, Shearwater Pottery showroom.**

Locator 871-2286   Medical 871-2809   Police 871-2361

Keesler Air Force Base (MS02R2)
Keesler AFB, MS 39534-5000

TELEPHONE NUMBER INFORMATION: Main installation numbers: C-601-377-1110, D-312-597-1110.

Location: From I-10 exit 46, follow signs to base. From US-90, north on White Ave to main gate. USM: J-7. NMC: Biloxi, in the city.

Billeting Office: Consolidated Front Desk for the **Inns of Keesler:** building 2101, **Muse Manor,** C-601-377-3663/3774, 24 hours. Check in facility, check out 1200 hours. Government civilian employee billeting.

TML: Guest House. Building 0470, all ranks, leave or official duty. Two bedroom, living room, dining room, semi-private bath (21). Refrigerator, maid service, cribs, washer/dryer, ice vending. Rates: $20 per two bedroom unit or $10 per bedroom. Primarily for hospital patients and families of patients.

TML: VAQ. Buildings 2101, 2002, 5025, enlisted all ranks, leave or official duty, C-EX-2631/3244. Bedroom, 2 beds, semi-private bath (638); separate bedrooms, semi-private bath for E7+ (8); bedroom, 1 bed, semi-private bath for E7+ (112). Refrigerator, A/C, color TV, maid service, washer/dryer, food/ice vending. Modern structure, renovated. Rates: $5 per person. Maximum 3 per room. Duty can make reservations, others Space-A.

TML: TLF. 0300 block, all ranks, leave or official duty. Separate bedrooms, private bath (40). Kitchen, utensils, A/C, color TV in room & lounge, maid service, essentials, washer/dryer, food/ice vending, playground rear of facility. Modern structure, renovated. Rates: $16 E1-E6, $20 E7+. Maximum 5 persons. Duty can make reservations, others Space-A.

TML: VOQ. Building 3821, 3823, 0470, 2004, officers all ranks, leave or official duty. Bedroom, private bath (224); bedroom, semi-private bath (328); two bedroom, semi-private bath (12); DV suites, private bath (6). Kitchen (98 rooms), A/C, color TV, maid service, washer/dryer, ice vending. Modern structure. Rates: $6 per person rooms; maximum $18 per room; $10 per person suites, maximum $20 per suite. Duty can make reservations, others Space-A.

DV/VIP: KTTC/CCP, C-EX-3359, E9+ & 06+, retirees and lower ranks Space-A.

TML Availability: Fairly good, all year. Best, Dec-Jan.

MISSISSIPPI
Keesler Air Force Base, continued

☞ Biloxi is rich in history: eight flags have flown over the city. Visit the Old French House off Hwy 90, Ship Island, 12 miles offshore, the Jefferson Davis Shrine. White sand beaches, golf, fishing, boating and sailing are available.

Locator 377-2798   Medical 377-6555   Police 377-3720

Meridian Naval Air Station (MS04R2)
Meridian NAS, MS 39309-5000

TELEPHONE NUMBER INFORMATION: Main installation numbers: C-601-679-2211, D-312-446-2211.

Location: Take Hwy 39 north from Meridian for 12 miles to 4-lane access road, clearly marked. Right for 3 miles to NAS main gate. USM: J-6,7. NMC: Meridian, 15 miles southwest.

Billeting Office: Building 218 (CBQ), Fuller Rd, C-601-679-2186, 24 hours daily. Check in facility, check out 1300 hours daily. Government civilian employee billeting.

TML: Family Quarters. Building 208, enlisted all ranks, leave or official duty. Separate bedrooms, private bath (25). Refrigerator, community kitchen, A/C, color TV, maid service, cribs/rollaways $1, washer/dryer. Older structure, renovated in '88. Rates: $13 per room per night first 3 persons, $1 each additional person. Maximum 5 per room. Duty can make reservations, others Space-A.

TML: BEQ. Buildings 218, enlisted all ranks, leave or official duty, handicapped accessible. Bedroom, semi-private bath (12); bedroom, private bath (18). Refrigerator, community kitchen, A/C, color TV, maid service, washer/dryer, food/ice vending. Older structure, remodeled. Rates: E1-E9 $6. Maximum 2 per room. Duty can make reservations, others Space-A.

TML: VOQ. Building 218, officers all ranks, leave or official duty. Handicapped accessible. Separate bedrooms, private bath (40). Community kitchen, A/C, color TV, maid service, cribs/rollaways $1, washer/dryer, ice vending. Older structure, remodeled. Rates: $10 per night single, $15 per night up to three persons, $1 each additional occupant. Maximum 5 per room.

TML: DV/VIP. Building 218, officer 06+, leave or official duty, handicapped accessible. Two bedroom, private bath (6). Two units have kitchen, all have refrigerators. Community kitchen, limited utensils, A/C, color TV & VCR, maid service, cribs/rollaways $1, washer/dryer, ice vending. Older structure, remodeled. Rates: $18 per room. Maximum charge $18. Maximum 3 per room. Duty can make reservations, others Space-A.

TML Availability: Good, Oct-Dec. Difficult, other times.

☞ Take a driving tour of the historic Natchez Trace, a local flea market, nearby Flora's Petrified Forest, and the Choctaw Fair for American Indian life and lore. ITT (in MWR) has information on theatrical, sports, special events tickets.

Locator 679-2301   Medical 679-2683   Police 679-2528

Missouri

Fort Leonard Wood (MO03R2)
Fort Leonard Wood, MO 65473-5000

TELEPHONE NUMBER INFORMATION: Main installation numbers: C-314-596-0131, D-312-581-0110.

Location: Two miles south of I-44, adjacent to St Robert & Waynesville, at Ft Leonard Wood exit. USM: I-5. NMC: Springfield, 85 miles southwest.

Billeting Office: Building 315, room 126, MO Ave, C-314-596-6169/1635, 24 hours daily. Check in billeting, check out 1200 hours daily. Government civilian employee billeting.

TML: Guest House. Twelve buildings, office building 315, all ranks, leave or official duty. Handicapped accessible. Bedroom, private bath (10), separate bedrooms, private bath (8); two bedroom (43), private bath (19), semi-private bath (24). Kitchen (9 units), refrigerator, utensils (9 units), A/C (51 units), color TV, maid service, essentials, cribs/cots, facilities for DAVs. Older structure. Rates: sponsor $12, each additional person $1. Reservations accepted from PCS in/out, persons with hospital appointments, and families of graduating soldiers, others Space-A. **Pets allowed in 26 units at $3 per day. Note: 70 new units will be added in the Spring of 1992.**

TML: TDY. Fourteen buildings, all ranks, official duty only. Bedroom, private bath (500). A/C, essentials, food/ice vending, kitchen, limited utensils, maid service, refrigerator, color TV, washer/dryer. Modern structure. Rates: sponsor $12, each additional person $3.50. Maximum 2 persons. Duty can make reservations, others Space-A.

TML: VOQ. Buildings 4102, 4104, officers all ranks. TDY only. Bedroom, private bath (74); separate bedroom suites, private bath (8). Kitchen (8 units), refrigerator (74 units), A/C, color TV, maid service, washer/dryer, ice vending, coffee makers, irons/ironing boards. Modern structure, remodeled. Rates: sponsor $12, each additional person $3.50. Maximum 2 per room. Duty can make reservations, others Space-A.

TML: DV/VIP. Building 315, officer 06+, leave or official duty. Separate bedroom suites, private bath (8); three bedroom suite, private bath (1). Kitchen, utensils, A/C, color TV, maid service. Modern structure. Rates: sponsor $13.25, each additional person $3.50. Maximum 2 per room. Duty can make reservations, others Space-A.

DV/VIP: Protocol Office, C-EX-5161, 06/GS-15+. Retirees and lower ranks Space-A.

TML Availability: Good. Best Dec. Difficult May-Oct.

☞ **Crystal clear rivers and streams provide fishing, float trips, canoeing. Campers, hikers, hunters and horseback riders find the Ozarks a paradise. Guided tours through caves, and all levels of spelunking are available.**

Locator 596-2151   **Medical 596-9741**   **Police 596-6141**

MISSOURI

Lake of the Ozarks Recreation Area (MO01R2)
Fort Leonard Wood, MO 65473-5000

TELEPHONE NUMBER INFORMATION: Main installation numbers: C-314-596-0131, D-312-581-0110.

Location: From I-70 at Columbia, take US-54 southwest to Linn Creek area, left at County Rd A for 6 miles to Freedom, left on Lake Rd A-5 for 4.7 miles to travel camp. From I-44 northeast of Springfield, MO-7 northwest to Richland, right on County Rd A and travel 19.8 miles to Freedom, right on Lake Road A-5 4.7 miles to travel camp. USM: I-5. NMC: Jefferson City, 40 miles northeast.

Billeting Office: Fort Leonard Wood LORA, Rt 1, Box 380, Linn Creek, MO 65052, all ranks, reservations required, **C-314-346-5640**. Call 30-45 days in advance, Apr-Oct. Reservations accepted starting 2nd week in March. Full service members weekend-Labor Day weekend. Check in facility, check out 1100 hours day of departure.

TML: Mobile Homes. Two and three bedroom, fully equipped, A/C. Rates: $22-$45 (E-6 & below), $26-$49 (E-7+ DA Civilians) per unit. A/C, kitchen, dishes and utensils, some cleaning supplies, color TV, no linens provided (except lakeview mobile homes). Rates applicable for active and retired personnel. A 10% discount is offered during pre and post seasons. Pets allowed.

TML Availability: Fairly good, in season. Very good, off season.

New lakefront trailers, horseback riding, new rental office, and a 20 bay berthing dock for private boat storage. This is a large and fully equipped recreational area, see Military Living's *Military RV, Camping and Rec Areas Around the World.*

Locator 596-0131   Police 346-3693

Richards-Gebaur Air Force Base (MO02R2)
Richards-Gebaur AFB, MO 64147-5000

TELEPHONE NUMBER INFORMATION: Main installation numbers: C-816-348-2000, D-312-463-1110.

Location: 17 Miles south of Kansas City. From Beltway (Interstate I-435), take US-71 South; 4 miles to 155th St exit, 1 mile west to base. USM: H-5. NMC: Kansas City, 17 miles north.

Billeting Office: ATTN: 442 CSG/SVH, building 250, Kensington Ave, **C-816-348-2125**, 0630-2400 M-F; 0730-2400 weekends. After hours reservations pick up at Security Police, building 602, C-EX-2118. Check in desk building 250. Check out time 1200 daily.

TML: VOQ/VAQ/VIP. Buildings 250/252/243, all ranks, official duty reservations accepted, Space-A welcome - no reservations. Bedrooms, queen bed, semi-private bath (52); bedroom, 2 single beds, semi-private bath (80); private bath (7); VIP suites (06+) (4) - require advance approval. Refrigerator, A/C, CATV, housekeeper service, cribs, washer/dryer, irons and boards, microwave. Older structures. Rates: $6 per person; $8

Richards-Gebauer Air Force Base, continued

for private bath; $10 VIP. No TLA facilities; limited family availability in standard VAQ rooms.

TML Availability: Best M-Th. US AFRES base, units train weekends. Limited space- during summer months.

☞ **Kansas City fun - sporting events (Royals, Chiefs) - shopping at Crown Center, The Plaza. At Westport, visit the Harry S. Truman library and home.**

Locator 348-2000   Medical 348-2114   Police 348-2118

⊗**This base is scheduled to close in mid FY94.**

Whiteman Air Force Base (MO04R2)
Whiteman AFB, MO 65305-5000

TELEPHONE NUMBER INFORMATION: Main installation numbers: C-816-687-1110, D-312-975-1110.

Location: From I-70 east exit to US-13 south to US-50 east for 10 miles, then left on Route J which leads to AFB. USM: I-5. NMC: Kansas City, MO 60 miles west.

Billeting Office: Building 3006, Mitchell Ave, C-**816-687-1844**, 24 hours daily. Check in billeting, check out 1200 hours daily. Government civilian employee billeting.

TML: TLF. Buildings 3003, 3005, all ranks, leave or official duty. Three bedroom apartments, private bath (4). Kitchen, complete utensils, A/C, essentials, refrigerator, color TV, maid service, cribs/cots, washer/dryer, ice vending. Handicapped accessible. Older structure, renovated. Rates: $21 per family. PCS in/out can make reservations (60 days in advance recommended), others Space-A.

TML: Military Hospital. All ranks, leave or official duty, check in facility. Bedroom, semi-private bath (25). A/C, black/white TV, facilities for DAVs. Modern structure. Rates: $6.50 per person. Duty can make reservations, others Space-A.

TML: VOQ. Building 3006, officers all ranks, leave or official duty. Bedroom, living room, private bath (18). Refrigerator, A/C, essentials, color TV, maid service, cribs/cots, special facilities for DAVs. Older structure, renovated. Rates: 1 person $8, 2 persons $12, 3 or more persons $16. Duty can make reservations, others Space-A.

TML: TAQ/VAQ. Building 1551, enlisted all ranks, leave or official duty. Bedroom, semi-private bath (11); separate bedrooms, semi-private bath (12); suites, private bath (5). Refrigerator, A/C, essentials, color TV in room & lounge, maid service, cots/cribs, ice vending, washer/dryer. Handicapped accessible. Modern structure. Rates: sponsor $7.50-$8 for suites, adult $4, maximum charge $16. Maximum 5 persons in suites. Duty can make reservations, others Space-A.

TML: DV/VIP. Building 3006, officers 06+, leave or official duty. Three bedroom house (**Truman House**), 2 baths, (1); bedroom suite (**Chadwell Suite**), private bath (1). Kitchen, all amenities. Rates: $10 1 person, $15 2 persons, $20 3 or more persons

MISSOURI
Whiteman Air Force Base, continued

(Truman House), $8 1 person, $12 2 persons, $16 3 or more persons (Chadwell Suite). Duty can make reservations, others Space-A.

DV/VIP: 351 SMW/CCP, C-EX-6543, 06+. Retirees and lower ranks if other quarters are full.

TML Availability: Good all year except late July/early Aug because of State Fair. Best, winter.

Locator 687-5098   **Medical 687-2186**   **Police 687-3700**

⊗**This facility did not respond to our inquiries, information may be outdated.**

Montana

Malmstrom Air Force Base (MT03R3)
Malmstrom AFB, MT 59402-5000

TELEPHONE NUMBER INFORMATION: Main installation numbers: C-406-731-1110, D-312-632-1110.

Location: From I-15 north or south take 10th Ave south exit to AFB. From east take Malmstrom exit off US-87/89 to AFB. Clearly marked. USM: E-2. NMC: Great Falls, 1 mile west.

Billeting Office: Malmstrom Inn. ATTN: 43rd MWRS/MWMB, building 1680, 5th St, C-406-727-8600/3394, D-312-632-3394, FAX C-406-731-3848, FAX D-312-632-3848, 24 hours daily. Check in billeting, check out 1200 hours daily. Government civilian employee billeting.

TML: TLF. Buildings 1210, 1212, 1214, 1216. One mile from billeting office. All ranks, leave or official duty. Separate bedrooms, private bath (40). Kitchen, utensils, A/C, color TV, housekeeping service, cribs/cots, washer/dryer, ice vending. Older structure, renovated. Rates: E1-E4 $16; E5-O2 $20; O3+ $24; Space-A $24 per unit. Maximum 5 per unit. Duty can make reservations, others Space-A.

TML: VOQ. Building 1680, officers all ranks, leave or official duty. Bedroom, semi-private bath (30); bedroom, private bath (2); separate bedroom suites, private bath (DV/VIP) (8). Refrigerator, color TV, housekeeping service, washer/dryer, ice vending. Older structure, renovated. Rates for leave/duty status: $8 per room, $8 additional person; suites $12, double occupancy $24. Children not authorized. Duty can make reservations, others Space-A.

TML: VAQ. Building 737, enlisted all ranks, leave or official duty. Bedroom, semi-private bath (23). Separate bedroom suites (2). Kitchen, refrigerator, microwave in lounge, essentials, color TV, ice vending, full galley in lounge area, washer/dryer. Rates: $8 single, $16 double, $12 suite, $24 double suite. Maximum 2 persons. No children. Duty can make reservations, others Space-A.

DV/VIP: Protocol Office. 44rd ARQ/CSP, building 500, C-EX-3086, 06+. Retirees Space-A.

Malmstrom Air Force Base, continued

MONTANA

TML Availability: Good, winter. Difficult, Jul-Sep.

☞ **This facility won the SAC Innkeeper Award for 1987 and 1991, and was Air Force runner up in 1992. It is one of four SAC-certified (four star) facilities in the command. Visit the Malmstrom Museum on Base.**

Locator 731-4121   Medical 731-3483   Police 731-4860

Nebraska

Offutt Air Force Base (NE02R3)
Offutt AFB, NE 68113-5000

TELEPHONE NUMBER INFORMATION: Main installation numbers: C-402-294-1110, D-312-271-1110.

Location: From I-80 exit to US-73/75 south to AFB exit, 6.5 miles south of I-80/US-73/75 interchange. USM: H-4. NMC: Omaha, 8 miles north.

Billeting Office: Building 44, Grants Pass St, C-402-294-3671, 24 hours daily. Check in 1400 hours, check out 1200 hours daily. Government civilian employee billeting.

TML: TLF. **Platte River Lodge,** buildings 5089-5093, all ranks, leave or official duty. Two or 3-room cottages (60). Kitchen, utensils, A/C, color TV, maid service, cribs, washer/ dryer, ice vending. Older structure, renovated. Rates: $22.50 per family. Maximum 5 per unit. Reservations accepted on first call, first served basis. Duty personnel encouraged to re-confirm 3 days prior to arrival. Space-A confirmed/non-confirmed 3 duty days prior to arrival.

TML: VOQ. **Offutt Inn,** building 479, officers all ranks, leave or official duty. Bedroom, private bath (40); separate bedroom suites, private bath (5) (VIP). Refrigerator, A/C, color TV, maid service, washer/dryer, ice vending. Rates: $11 per person, $16.50 2 persons. Maximum 2 per unit.

TML: VOQ. Building 432, officers all ranks, leave or official duty. Separate bedroom suites, private bath (36). Refrigerator, A/C, color TV, maid service, washer/dryer, ice vending. Older structure. Rates: $13 per person, $19.50 2 persons. Maximum 2 per unit.

TML: VOQ. **O'Malley Inn,** building 436, officers, all ranks, leave or official duty. Bedroom, private bath (79). Refrigerator, A/C, color TV, maid service, washer/dryer, ice vending, facilities for DAVs. Modern structure. Rates: $11 per person, $16.50 2 persons. Maximum 2 per unit.

TML: VAQ. **McCoy Inn,** building 402, enlisted all ranks, leave or official duty. Bedroom, semi-private bath (57). Rates: $9 per person, $13.50 2 persons. Bedroom, private bath (1); separate bedrooms, private bath (E9 suites)(5). Rates:$13 per person, $19.50 2 persons. Bedroom, 2 beds, semi-private bath (18). Rates: $8 per person, $12 2 persons.

NEBRASKA
Offutt Air Force Base, continued

Refrigerator, A/C, color TV in room & lounge, maid service, washer/dryer, ice vending, microwave each floor. Older structure. Maximum 2 per unit. Reservations first call, first served. Duty re-confirm 3 duty days prior to arrival. Space-A confirmed 3 duty days prior to arrival.
TML: DVQ. Fort Crook House, officers 06+, leave or official duty. Two bedroom, private bath (2). Kitchen, A/C, color TV, maid service. Historic building - 1900. Rates: $15 per person, $22.50 2 persons. Maximum 2 persons per unit.

TML: DVQ. Quarters 13, officers 06+, leave or official duty. Separate bedroom suites, private bath (6). Separate bedroom suites, shared bath (2). Refrigerator, utensils, A/C, color TV, maid service, washer/dryer, microwave. Historic building - 1900. Rates: $14 per person, $21 2 persons. Maximum 2 per unit. Protocol VIP quarters.

DV/VIP: USSTRATCOM Protocol, building 500, C-EX-4212, 07+. Retirees, Space-A.

TML Availability: Good. Best, Dec-Jan. More difficult, other times.

☞ **Try nearby Omaha's Old Town for shopping and dining, Fontenelle Park for hiking and the historic Southern Railroad Depot for getting in touch with this interesting area. Also, the Strategic Air Command Museum is next to the base.**

Locator 294-5125   **Medical 294-3000**   **Police 294-3000**

Fallon Naval Air Station (NV02R4)
Fallon NAS, NV 89496-5000

TELEPHONE NUMBER INFORMATION: Main installation numbers: C-702-426-5161, D-312-830-2110.

Location: From US-50 exit to US-95 south at Fallon, for 5 miles to left on Union St to NAS. USM: B-4. NMC: Reno, 72 miles west.

Billeting Office: BEQ, BOQ C-702-423-6671, open 24 hours daily. BOQ check in facility, check out 1000 hours. Government civilian employee billeting.

TML: BEQ. Barracks 5, 6, 7, 10, 11, enlisted all ranks, leave or official duty. Bedroom, shared bath (100); bedroom, 2 beds, shared bath (306); bedroom, 2 beds, hall bath (366); VIP rooms (8). Refrigerator, A/C, color TV in lounge, maid service, washer/dryer, ice vending. Modern structure. Rates: $3.50 per person. Rates to go up 1 Jan 92. Duty can make reservations, retired and leave, Space-A.

TML: BOQ. Building 468, officers all ranks, leave or official duty. Bedroom, semi-private bath (96); separate bedrooms, private bath (190); 8 DV/VIP suites, private bath. Kitchen (114 units), refrigerator, A/C, color TV, maid service, washer/dryer, ice vending. Modern structure. Rates: sponsor $6.50, each additional person $3.50. Rates to go up 1 Jan 92. Duty can make reservations, others Space-A.

DV/VIP: BOQ billeting C-702-423-6671.

NEVADA

Fallon Naval Air Station, continued

TML Availability: Difficult.

☞ **The Carson River and Lake Lahontan** fishing, boating, swimming, water skiing and local rock collecting are of interest. Call MWR for special rates to Reno, ghost towns, Virginia City, and other points of interest.

Locator 426-5161   Medical 426-3100   Police 426-2803

☺While the 6 room Navy Lodge at this facility has been closed, there are plans to rebuild it in '93. Keep posted with *Military Living's R&R Space-A Report.*

Nellis Air Force Base (NV01R4)
Nellis AFB, NV 89191-5000

TELEPHONE NUMBER INFORMATION: Main installation numbers: C-702-652-1110, D-312-682-1110.

Location: Off I-15 north of Las Vegas. Also accessible from US-91/93. Clearly marked. USM: C-5. NMC: Las Vegas, 8 miles southwest.

Billeting Office: Building 780, Fitzgerald St, C-**702-643-2710**, D-312-682-9174, 24 hours daily. Check in billeting, check out 1200 hours daily. Government civilian employee billeting.

TML: TLF. 2900's (9 buildings). All ranks, leave or official duty. Handicapped accessible. Bedroom, private bath (60). Queen Sofa couch in living room. A/C, refrigerator, kitchen, complete utensils, color TV, maid service, cribs/cots, playground for children, washer/dryer, food/ice vending. Modern structure, remodeled. Rates: $22. Maximum 5 persons per unit. Duty can make reservations, others Space-A.

TML: VAQ. Buildings 536 and 552, enlisted, all ranks. Bedroom, semi-private bath (258). SNCO rooms, private bath (5). Chief's suite, private bath (1). Single rooms (1 double bed), private bath (8). Refrigerator, A/C, color TV, maid service, washer/dryer, essentials, food/ice vending, microwave, room telephone, clock radio. Modern structure, remodeled. Rates: $6 per person. Chief's suite $8.00, $16 2 persons. Maximum 2 persons per unit. Children not allowed during deployments. Duty can make reservations, others Space-A.

TML: VOQ. Buildings 523, 538, 540, 545, officers all ranks, leave or official duty. Bedroom, private bath (153). VIP suites, private bath (5). Kitchen, utensils only in suites, essentials, refrigerator, A/C, color TV, maid service, washer/dryer, microwave, room telephone, clock radio, iron/ironing boards. Modern structures, building 545 updated '89. Rates: $9 per person, $10 per person VIP suites. Maximum charge $18. Maximum 2 persons per unit. No children. Duty can make reservations, others Space-A.

DV/VIP: Protocol Office, building 620, room 112, C-EX-2987, 06+.

TML Availability: Extremely limited. Best, spring & Nov-Dec. Difficult other times.

NEVADA
Nellis Air Force Base, continued

☞ The Las Vegas area offers Lake Mead for boating and swimming, Mt Charleston for skiing, Red Rock Canyon for scenic hiking, and Hoover Dam for sheer wonderment. Of course, Las Vegas is noted for night life and gaming!

Locator 652-1841   **Medical 652-2343**   **Police 652-2311**

New Hampshire

Portsmouth Naval Shipyard (NH02R1)
Portsmouth Naval Shipyard, NH 03801-5000

TELEPHONE NUMBER INFORMATION: Main installation numbers: C-207-438-1000, D-312-684-0111.

Location: From I-95 north exit 2 to US-1 to NH-103 to gate 1. Located on an island on Piscataqua River between Portsmouth and Kittery, ME. USM: M-2. NMC: Boston, 60 miles south.

Billeting Office: Building H-23, C-207-438-1513/2015, FAX-207-438-3580, 24 hours. Check in after 1400, check out 1200 hours. Government civilian employee billeting.

TML: BOQ/BEQ/CPOQ. All ranks, leave or official duty, handicapped accessible. Hot tub with sauna, VCR in rooms with tape rental machine in lobby. Maid service daily. Hairdryer, amenities basket, USA Newspaper, refrigerator/microwave, color TV, large screen TV in lounge, washer/dryer. Rates: officer $8/$4 spouse, $4 additional person. Enlisted E7+ $5 per person. **No pets.** Duty can make reservations, others Space-A.

TML: Enlisted family suites. Six rooms with the above amenities. Rates: $10 per couple and $5 for each additional person. Maximum charge $15 per day. **No Pets.**

DV/VIP: Protocol Office, building 86, C-EX-3800. Commanders+, retirees and other ranks Space-A.

TML Availability: Fairly good. Depends on number of boats in overhaul.

☞ Local skiing at White Mountain, outlet shopping in nearby Kittery, and trips to Boston are some of the favorite pursuits in this area.

Locator 438-1000   **Medical 438-2444**   **Police 438-2351**

New Jersey

Armament Research, Development and Engineering Center (NJ01R1)
Picatinny Arsenal, NJ 07806-5000

TELEPHONE NUMBER INFORMATION: Main installation numbers: C-201-724-4021, D-312-880-4021.

Location: Take I-80 west, exit 34B, follow signs to Center, 1 mile N. From I-80 east, exit 33 follow signs to Center. USM: M-4. NMC: Newark, 30 miles east.

Billeting Office: ATTN: SMCAR-ISE-H, building 3359, Belt Rd, C-**201-724-2633/3506**, 0800-1630 M-F. Check in billeting, check out 1100 hours daily. After hours, persons with reservations may check in with Desk Sgt, building 173, C-EX-6666. Government civilian employee billeting.

TML: Guest House/DVQ. Building 110, all ranks, leave or official duty. Four room, 3 bed DVQ suite, kitchen, living room, dining area, private bath (1); two room apartments, private bath (2); one room apartment, private bath (1). Community kitchen, refrigerator, A/C, color TV in room & lounge, maid service, cribs/cots, washer/dryer. Older structure, renovated. Rates: sponsor Guest House single $15, double $20; child, 2-12 years $1, 13+ $5, N/C under 2; DVQ single $25, double $32, children 2-12 $2, 12+ $7, under 2 N/C. Duty can make reservations, others Space-A.

DV/VIP: Protocol Office, SMCAR-GSP, building 1, 4th fl, C-EX-7026/27, 06+. Retirees and lower ranks Space-A.

TML Availability: Fairly good, Oct-Apr. More difficult, other times.

☞ **Visit the Village Green in Morristown for shopping, enjoy local restaurants specializing in German, French, Italian, Spanish and Greek food. Don't miss the New Jersey Shakespeare Festival at Drew University.**

Locator 724-2852   **Medical 724-2113**   **Police 724-6666**

Bayonne Military Ocean Terminal (NJ10R1)
Bayonne, NJ 07002-5302

TELEPHONE NUMBER INFORMATION: Main installation numbers: C-201-823-5111, D-312-247-0111.

Location: From New Jersey Turnpike, exit 14A to NJ-169 east to main gate. Follow green and white signs. USM: N-4. NMC New York City, 10 miles northeast.

Billeting Office: None.

Guest House: Liberty Lodge. Bedrooms, with two double beds, private bath (40). TV, telephone, individually controlled heating and A/C. Rates: $40 per night. All ranks, retirees Space-A basis. C-**201-823-5666 or 823-8700** for reservations and information. This facility was new in '90.

NEW JERSEY
Bayonne Military Ocean Terminal, continued

TML: VOQ/VEQ. Several buildings. All ranks, leave or official duty. Call for rates and additional information, C-EX-7202.

TML Availability: Fair.

☞ Inexpensive day: take the ferry from Staten Island to Battery Park. From there you can visit the Statue of Liberty, on another ferry, or walk to the World Trade Center, Wall Street, or Chinatown, (Canal St, from the Park subway).

Locator 823-5111/0111   Medical 823-7371   Police 823-6666/6000

Earle Naval Weapons Station (NJ11R1)
Colts Neck, NJ 07722-5000

TELEPHONE NUMBER INFORMATION: Main installation numbers: C-908-577-2000, D-none.

Location: From Golden State Parkway, south, exit 100B, Rt 33 west to Rt 34N. Installation 7 miles from beachfront. USM: M-3. NMC: Newark, 50 miles north.

Billeting Office: MWR Office. Building C-29, C-908-577-2493, 0800-1600 M-F. Check in facility, check out 1100 hours daily. No civilian employee billeting.

TML: BEQ, BOQ, TLQ. Active duty, PCS or active assigned at Earle only. Mobile homes, private bath (8). Maximum 6 per unit. No pets. Refrigerator, color TV, kitchen with utensils. Rates $19.50-$27 per night, depending on rank.

TML Availability: Difficult. Best winter, difficult other times.

☞ Seven miles from the New Jersey shore, where sport fishing, swimming and boating are available. One hour from New York City.

Locator 724-2345   Medical 724-3615   Police 724-2001

☺While this station has little to offer retirees at press time, a new Navy Lodge will open at this facility in '94 - '95. Keep updated with Military Living's R&R Space-A Report.

Fort Dix Army Training Center (NJ03R1)
Fort Dix, NJ 08640-5523

TELEPHONE NUMBER INFORMATION: Main installation numbers: C-609-562-1011, D-312-944-1110.

Location: From NJ Turnpike (I-95), exit 7, right onto NJ-206, short distance left on NJ-68 and continue to General Circle and main gate. USM: L,M-3,4. NMC: Trenton, 17 miles northwest.

Billeting Office: ATTN: ATZD-EH-H, building 5255, Maryland Ave & First St, C-609-562-3188, 24 hours daily. Check in facility, check out 1100 hours daily. No government civilian employee billeting.

NEW JERSEY

Fort Dix Army Training Center, continued

TML: Doughboy Inn. Guest House, building 5997, all ranks, leave or official duty, C-**609-562-6663**. Bedroom, 2 double beds, private bath (76). Community kitchen, A/C, color TV, telephone, maid service, cribs/cots ($2.50 per night), coin washer/dryer, ice vending. Modern structure. Rates: TDY $30, double, $35, three persons, $40 four or more. All categories can make reservations.

TML: VOQ/VEQ. Building 5255, all ranks, leave or official duty. Bedroom, semi-private bath (VEQ) (65); separate bedrooms, private bath (VOQ) (10). Refrigerator, A/C, color TV in room & lounge, maid service, cribs/cots, washer/dryer, ice vending. Older structure, renovated. Rates: TDY $22 per night, $5 each additional person; leave $20. All categories can make reservations.

TML: DVQ. Building 5256, officers 06+, leave or official duty. Bedroom suites, private bath (4); two bedroom apartments, private bath (4). Kitchen (apartments), refrigerator (suites), utensils, A/C, color TV in room & lounge, maid service, cribs/cots, washer/dryer, ice vending. Modern structure. Rates: $22, leave $25, $5 each additional person. All categories can make reservations.

DV/VIP: HQ USATC & Ft Dix, ATTN: Office of The Secretary General Staff, C-EX-5059/6293, 06/civilian equivalent +. Retirees Space-A.

TML Availability: Good, Oct-Mar. Difficult, other times.

☞ **Nearby Brindle Lake, a 30 acre lake surrounded by about 2,000 acres of pine forest provides rental boats (no power boats), camping, picnic and barbecue facilities. Visit Trenton and its historic sites 17 miles northwest.**

Locator 562-1011   **Medical 562-2695**   **Police 562-6001**

Fort Monmouth (NJ05R1)
Fort Monmouth, NJ 07703-5000

TELEPHONE NUMBER INFORMATION: Main installation numbers: C-908-532-9000, D-312-992-9000.

Location: Take NJ Turnpike to I-95, exit 7A (Shore Points); east to Garden State Parkway; north to exit 105 for Eatontown and Fort Monmouth. USM: M-3. NMC: New Brunswick, 23 miles northwest.

Billeting Office: Lodging: ATTN: SELFM-EH-H, building 270, Allen & Barton Ave, C-**908-532-1635/1092/5510**, 0745-2400 hours daily. Other hours, SDO, building 1209, C-EX-1100. Check in billeting office, check out 1000 hours daily. Government civilian employee billeting on official business.

TML: Guest House. Buildings 360, 365, all ranks, leave, or official duty. Suites bedroom/sitting room, private bath (60). All have kitchen, microwave, color TV, maid service, sleeper couch, cots, washer/dryer and ice vending. Three units handicapped accessible. Rates: $17 single, $23 double. PCS can make reservations, others Space-A.

TML: VOQ. Buildings 270, 363, 364, 1202, officers, TDY civilians, senior NCO's on official duty. Inquire about rooms and services. Modern structure, renovated. $20 per night, 2/$15 per person. No children. Duty can make reservations, others Space-A.

NEW JERSEY
Fort Monmouth, continued

TML: DVQ. Building 259, **Blair Hall**, officers 06+, leave or official duty. Inquire about rooms and services available. Modern structure, renovated. Rates: $20 per night, 2/$15 per person. Duty can make reservations, others Space-A.

TML Availability: Difficult, all year.

☞ Within 5 miles of the ocean, the area also has two race tracks for thoroughbreds and trotters. Atlantic City 1 1/2 hours south, New York City, 1 hour north. Nearby Garden State Art Center for ballet has concerts year round.

☺At press time building 365, and existing facilities in building 360, under renovation, opened to raise capacity to 90. Two-room suites with kitchenette, are primarily for PCS or ETS personnel, but others are Space-A.

Locator 532-1492/2540   Medical 532-2789   Police 532-1112

Lakehurst Naval Air Warfare Center (NJ08R1)
Lakehurst, NJ 08733-5085

TELEPHONE NUMBER INFORMATION: Main installation numbers: C-908-323-2011, D-312-624-1110.

Location: Take Garden State Parkway south to NJ-70 west to junction of NJ-547 right and proceed 1 mile to base. USM: M-3. NMC: Trenton, 30 miles northwest.

Billeting Office: Building 481, C-**908-323-2266**, D-312-624-2266, 24 hours daily. Check in facility, check out 1200 hours daily. Government civilian employee billeting.

TML: BOQ. Building 481, **Maloney Hall**, officers, all ranks, official duty. Bedroom suites, private bath (27). A/C, microfridge, essentials, ice vending, maid service, color TV, washer/dryer. Rates: $8/night. Older structure. Active duty, retirees may make reservations at above number, or write to: CBQ, NAWC Lakehurst, NJ, 08733.

TML: BEQ. Building 480, **Casey Hall**, enlisted, all ranks, official duty. Bedrooms, hall bath (62); VIP bedrooms (E-7+), private bath (3). Essentials, ice vending, maid service, color TV, washer/dryer. Rates $4 and $15/night. Older structure. Active duty, retirees may make reservations at above number, or write to: CBQ, NAWC Lakehurst, NJ, 08733.

TML: DV Quarters. Cottages, private bath (6). Kitchenette, complete utensils, essentials, maid service, color TV, washer/dryer. Older structure, renovated '91. Rates $25/night. Maximum 4 per unit. No pets. All categories may make reservations at above number and address.

TML: Guest House, 06+. Contact Exec's Office, C-**323-2369**.

TML Availability: Very good, all year.

NEW JERSEY

Lakehurst Naval Air Warfare Center, continued

☞ This is the site of the crash of the Airship Hindenburg. On base golf course and driving range and club house, biking, boating, fishing and hunting in season. There is a nearby Lakehurst conservation area.

Locator 323-2582   Medical 323-2231   Police 323-2332

McGuire Air Force Base (NJ09R1)
McGuire AFB, NJ 08641-7999

TELEPHONE NUMBER INFORMATION: Main installation numbers: C-609-724-1110, D-312-440-1110.

Location: From New Jersey Turnpike, exit 7 to NJ-68 southeast to AFB. Adjacent to Fort Dix. Clearly marked. USM: M-3. NMC: Trenton, 18 miles northwest.

Billeting Office: All-American Inn/SVH, building 2717, C-609-724-2954, 24 hours daily. Check in facility, check out 1100 hours daily. Government civilian employee billeting.

TML: TLQ. Buildings 2418/19, all ranks, leave or official duty, C-EX-3336/37 0745-1600 hours M-F. Other hours, C-EX-2954. Two bedroom, private bath (30). Kitchen, A/C, maid service, washer/dryer. Older structure. Rates: $26 per unit. PCS have priority, others Space-A.

TML: VOQ/VAQ. Buildings 1903 (VAQ), 2704/07 (VOQ), all ranks, leave or official duty. Bedroom, semi-private bath (VOQ) (186); bedroom, semi-private bath (VAQ) (244). A/C, color TV, maid service. Older structure. Rates: $8 officers, $8 enlisted. All categories can make reservations.

TML: DV/VIP. Building 2706, officers 06+, leave or official duty, C-EX-2954. Bedroom suites, private bath (13). Kitchen in 1 unit. A/C, color TV, maid service. Older structure. Rates: $8 per person. All categories can make reservations.

DV/VIP: Protocol Office, C-EX-2405, 06+.

TML Availability: Good, Oct-Apr. Difficult, other times.

☞ New Jersey coastal fishing is popular here. Trenton, the state capital, has many historic sites and an excellent Cultural Center. Miles of roads and trails show off a number of well kept state forests.

Locator 724-1100   Medical 724-2856   Police 724-2001

New Mexico

Cannon Air Force Base (NM02R3)
Cannon AFB, NM 88103-5361

TELEPHONE NUMBER INFORMATION: Main installation numbers: C-505-784-3311, D-312-681-1110.

Location: From Clovis west on US-60/84 to AFB. From NM-467 enter the Portales Gate. USM: F-6. NMC: Clovis, 7 miles east.

Billeting Office: Caprock Inn. ATTN: 27SVS/SVH, building 1801B, Olympic St, C-**505-784-2918/2919**, D-213-681-2918/2919, 24 hours daily. Check in billeting, check out 1200 hours daily. Government civilian employee billeting.

TML: TLF. Buildings 1812, 1818. All ranks. Leave or official duty. Family units (42); Kitchen, utensils, A/C, color TV, housekeeping service, washer/dryer, ice vending. Older structure. Rates: $18 per room. PCS in/out can make reservations, others Space-A. List of kennels available.

TML: VOQ, VAQ. Building 1800B. Officer all ranks, DOD civilians. Leave or official duty. VOQ units (24). Rate: $8. VAQ units (24). Rate $8. Rooms share community living area & kitchen. A/C, color TV in room and lounge, housekeeping service, washer/dryer, ice vending. Older structure. Maximum $16 per family. Duty can make reservations, others Space-A.

TML: DV/VIP. Buildings 1800A and 1812. C-EX-2727. E-9 and officer O6+. Leave or official duty. Separate bedroom suites, private bath (6). Kitchen, complete utensils, color TV, housekeeping service, washer/dryer, ice vending. Older structure. Rates: $10 per person, maximum charge $20. Duty can make reservations, others Space-A.

DV/VIP: Protocol Office, 27TFW/CCEP, building 1, C-EX-2727, O6+. Retirees Space-A.

TML Availability: Good, Nov-Feb. Difficult, other times.

☞ Visit the Blackwater Draw Museum, Roosevelt County Museum, or the Oasis State Park outside Portales for fishing, hiking, picnics and camping. Local lakes offer good fishing.

Locator 784-2424   **Medical 784-4033**   **Police 784-4111**

Holloman Air Force Base (NM05R3)
Holloman AFB, NM 88330-9999

TELEPHONE NUMBER INFORMATION: Main installation numbers: C-505-479-6511, D-312-867-1110.

Location: Exit US-70/82, 8 miles southwest of Alamogordo NM. Clearly marked. USM: E-6. NMC: La Cruces, 50 miles southwest.

NEW MEXICO

Holloman Air Force Base, continued

Billeting Office: Building 583, west New Mexico Ave, C-505-479-6123, D-312-867-3311/3468, 24 hours daily. Check in facility, check out 1200 hours daily. Government civilian employee billeting.

TML: TLF. Buildings 17, 583, all ranks, leave or official duty. Two bedroom, private bath (14); separate bedrooms, private bath (10). Kitchen, complete utensils, A/C, color TV in room, maid service, cribs/cots, washer/dryer, ice vending. Older structure. Rates: $14 per unit. PCS in/out can make reservation, others Space-A.

TML: VAQ. Buildings 342, 518, enlisted all ranks, leave or official duty. Bedroom, semi-private bath (100); separate bedrooms, private bath (4). Refrigerator, A/C, color TV, maid service, cribs/cots, washer/dryer, ice vending. Modern structure. Rates: $8 per person. Maximum 2 per room. TDY, PCS in/out can make reservations, others Space-A.

TML: VOQ. Buildings 582, 584-587, officers all ranks, leave or official duty. Bedroom, private bath (40); separate bedrooms, private bath (120); two bedroom, semi-private bath (20). Kitchen, A/C, color TV, maid service, cribs/cots, washer/dryer, ice vending. Modern structure. Rates: $8 per person. TDY, PCS in/out can make reservations, others Space-A.

DV/VIP: CSG/CC, building 29, D-EX-5573/74, E9/06+/GS-15+.

TML Availability: Good, Dec-Jan. Difficult, other times.

Locator 479-7510   **Medical 479-3268**   **Police 479-7397**

⊗**This facility did not respond to our inquiries, information may be outdated.**

Kirtland Air Force Base (NM03R3)
Kirtland AFB, NM 87117-0001

TELEPHONE NUMBER INFORMATION: Main installation numbers: C-505-844-0011, D-312-244-0011.

Location: From I-40 east, exit on Wyoming Blvd, south for 2 miles to Wyoming gate to AFB. USM: E-6. NMC: Albuquerque, NM, 1 mile southeast.

Billeting Office: Kirtland Inn, Box 5418, Kirtland AFB, NM 87185, building 22016, Club Dr, C-505-846-1952, D-312-246-1952, 24 hours daily. Check in billeting, check out 1200 hours daily. Government civilian employee billeting.

TML: TLF. All ranks, leave or official duty. Separate bedroom suites, private bath (24). Kitchen, A/C, color TV, maid service, cots, ice vending, washer/dryer. Renovated '90. Rates: $15 per suite, per day. PCS in/out can make reservations, others Space-A.

TML: Cottages. All ranks, leave or official duty. Two bedroom, private bath (15); four bedroom, private bath (1); Kitchen, A/C, color TV, maid service, cots, washer/dryer. Older structure, renovated. Rates: $18 per cottage, per day. PCS in/out can make reservations, others Space-A.

NEW MEXICO
Kirtland Air Force Base, continued

TML: VOQ. Buildings 1911, 22003, 23225, 22011,22012, officers all ranks, official duty and Space-A. Suites, living room, bedroom, private bath (140). Refrigerator, A/C, color TV, maid service, washer/dryer, ice vending. Older structure. Rates: $8 per person, per night. Duty can make reservations, others Space-A.

TML: VAQ. Buildings 22001,22002, 23226 (SNCO, 20 suites), enlisted all ranks, leave or official duty. Beds, semi-private bath (E1-E5) (144). Refrigerator, A/C, color TV, maid service, washer/dryer, ice vending. Older structure, SNCO recently renovated with two Super Chief Suites (reserve through protocol). Rates: $8 per person, per night, Chief Suites $14 per person, per night. Duty can make reservations, others Space-A.

TML: DV/VIP. Buildings 22010, 22000. Suites "top of the line" (25). Rates: $14 per person, per night, leave or official duty.

DV/VIP: 542dCTW/Protocol Office, reservations C-**505-846-4119**, D-312-246-4119, O6+, civilian equivalents.

TML Availability: Best, late fall and winter. F & Sa nights always better than during the week.

☞ Take the tram to the Sandia Mountains, investigate the National Atomic Museum, and Old Town Albuquerque, founded in 1706. Enjoy local skiing, the State Fair in September, the International Hot Air Balloon Fiesta each October.

Locator 844-0011   **Medical 844-4611**   **Police 844-4618**

White Sands Missile Range (NM04R3)
White Sands Missile Range, NM 88002-5076

TELEPHONE NUMBER INFORMATION: Main installation numbers: C-505-678-2121, D-312-258-2121.

Location: From Las Cruces, east on US-70, 30 miles to WSMR. From Alamogordo west on US-70, 45 miles to WSMR. USM: E-6. NMC: El Paso, 45 miles south.

Billeting Office: ATTN: STEWS-EL-H, building 501, Aberdeen Ave, C-**505-678-4559**, 0745-1545 hours daily. Other hours SDO, building 100, C-505-678-2031. Check out 1200 hours daily. Charge for late checkouts.

TML: VOQ/DVQ. Buildings 501, 502. All military and DOD civilians on official duty. Bedroom, private bath (1); suites, private bath (46); three bedroom houses, private bath (8). Refrigerator, community kitchen, complete utensils, A/C, color TV, maid service, cribs, washer/dryer. Rates: TDY $21.50, spouse $6 additional. Reservations confirmed only for TDY or PCS military families in/out. No pets.

TML: Guest House. Building 506. All ranks, PCS, official duty, leave and retired military. Bedroom, 2 beds, sofa bed, private bath (15). Kitchen, complete utensils, A/C, color TV, cribs, washer/dryer, ice vending (in 501, 502), special facilities for DAVs (2 units). Modern structure. PCS rates $21.50 per night first four nights for all ranks, after four nights $21.50 per unit for 04+ and W3, W4, $18 per unit 01-03, W1, W2 and E7-E9, $15 per unit E5-E6, and $13 E1-E4; all others, Space-A and TDY personnel $21.50 per unit. Maximum 6 per room. PCS in/out may confirm reservations.

NEW MEXICO

White Sands Missile Range, continued

DV/VIP: CG, WSMR, ATTN: STEWS-PC, building 100, room 227, C-EX-1028, 06/GS-15+. Retirees and lower ranks Space-A.

TML Availability: Very good.

 **Las Cruces' blending of three cultures, and New Mexico State University supply much entertainment locally. Visit the International Space Hall of Fame in Alamogordo, White Sands National Monument, and El Paso, gateway to the Southwest and Mexico.**

Locator 678-1630   **Medical 678-2882**   **Police 678-1234**

New York

Fort Drum (NY06R1)
Fort Drum, NY 13602-5097

TELEPHONE NUMBER INFORMATION: Main installation numbers: C-315-772-6900, D-312-341-6011.

Location: From Syracuse, take I-81 north to exit 48, past Watertown, and follow signs to Fort Drum. USM: L-2. NMC: Watertown, 8 miles southwest.

Billeting Office: ATTN: Building T-2227, Officers' Loop, 24 hours daily, C-**315-772-5435**. Check in billeting, check out 1100 hours daily. Government civilian employee billeting.

TML: Guest House. Building 2340, all ranks, leave or official duty. Separate bedrooms, private bath (9); two bedroom, private bath (5). Kitchen, complete utensils, color TV, maid service, cribs/cots, washer/dryer. Older structure. Rates: based on BAQ/VHA ranging from $12 -$28, (example: PCS, TDY, leave, or retired E-1 + 1 person, $14). All categories may make reservations.

TML: VOQ. Cottages (9), 1 and 2 bedroom (2), private bath. All ranks, leave or official duty. Kitchens, complete utensils, color TV, maid service, cribs/cots, washer/dryer. Rates $15 plus $5 for additional person per night.

TML: TLF. **The Inn.** Civilian funded motel operated by the Army, all ranks, leave or official duty, C-**315-773-7777**. Rooms (111), 64 with kitchenettes and microwaves. Queen size beds, remote control CATV, room telephones, individual A/C/heating. Rates: **Note: 1 April '92 this facility was included under Guest House rates, as above.**

DV/VIP: Protocol Office, building P-10000, C-EX-5010, 06+. Retirees and lower ranks Space-A.

TML Availability: Good, Oct-Apr. Difficult, other times.

NEW YORK
Fort Drum, continued

☞ Sackets Harbor Battle Ground, site of war of 1812 battle. Nearby is the fascinating area called 1,000 Islands, rich in water recreation. Canada is 45 minutes away.

Locator 772-5869   **Medical 772-5236**   **Police 772-5156**

Fort Hamilton (NY02R1)
Fort Hamilton, NY 11252-5330

TELEPHONE NUMBER INFORMATION: Main installation numbers: C-718-630-4101, D-312-232-1110.

Location: From Belt Parkway, exit 2 (Fort Hamilton Parkway) to 100th St, right to Fort Hamilton Parkway, right to main gate. USM: L-2. NMC: New York, in the city.

Billeting Office: Building 109, Schum Ave, C-718-630-4052, 24 hours daily. Check in facility after 1400 hours daily. Check out 1000 hours daily. Government civilian employee billeting (on orders).

TML: Adams Guest House. Building 109. All ranks, leave or official duty. Bedroom, private bath (36). Kitchen, A/C, color TV in room & lounge, coin washer/dryer, ice vending. Older structure, renovated '91. Rates: $36 single, $42 two, maximum $45. Duty can make reservations, others Space-A.

TML: Transient quarters. Building 210. All ranks, leave or official duty. Bedrooms, shared bath (38). Above amenities. Rates $20 1 person, $25 two. TDY has priority, others Space-A.

TML: DV/VIP. Building 109, officers 06+, leave or official duty, C-EX-4324. Separate bedrooms, private bath (2). Refrigerator, color TV, coffee/bar set up, A/C, maid service. Rates: $40 single, $43 two or more, maximum $45. Duty and retirees can make reservations.

DV/VIP: Liaison & Protocol Office, building 302, room 13, C-EX-4324, 06+. Retirees Space-A.

TML Availability: Good, winter months. Difficult, summer months.

Locator 630-4958   **Medical 630-4615**   **Police 630-4456**

Griffiss Air Force Base (NY11R1)
Griffiss AFB, NY 13441-5000

TELEPHONE NUMBER INFORMATION: Main installation numbers: C-315-330-1110, D-312-587-1110.

Location: Off NY-49 in Rome. Entrance off NY-49 and from Chestnut St, Floyd St, and East Dominick St. USM: L-2. NMC: Utica, 17 miles southeast.

NEW YORK

Griffiss Air Force Base, continued

Billeting Office: Building 704, Wright Dr, C-**315-330-4391**, 24 hours daily. Check in facility, check out 1200 hours daily. Government civilian employee billeting.

TML: TLF. Buildings 490, 491, 492, all ranks, leave or official duty. Separate bedrooms, sleeps 5 persons, private bath (35). Kitchen, A/C, color TV, maid service, washer/dryer. Renovated. Rates: $21.50/22.50 per room, maximum charge. Maximum 5 persons per unit. Duty can make reservations, others Space-A.

TML: VAQ. Building 450, all ranks, leave or official duty. Bedroom, semi-private bath (44). Separate bedrooms (Chief suites), private bath (3). A/C, color TV, maid service, food/ice vending, washer/dryer. Rates: sponsor $9, $4.50 for second person; chief suites $13. Maximum charge $19.50. Maximum 2 persons suites. Duty can make reservations, others Space-A.

TML: VOQ. Building 704, officers, O1-O5, leave or official duty. Handicapped accessible. Bedroom, private bath (38). A/C, essentials, maid service, refrigerator, color TV in room & lounge, washer/dryer. Older structure, renovated. Rates: $9 per person, $4.50 for second person. Duty can make reservations, others Space-A.

TML: DV/VIP. Building 712, officers 06+, leave or official duty. Separate suites, private bath (9). A/C, color TV, maid service, washer/dryer. Older structure. Rates: $14/$7 second person, $13/$6.50 second person. Duty can make reservations, others Space-A.

DV/VIP: PAO, C-EX-7415, 06+.

TML Availability: Good. Best Dec-Mar. Difficult, other times.

☞ **Visit Fort Stanwix National Monument, a Revolutionary War stronghold. Lake Delta State Park is great for swimming, fishing, boating. Historic Erie Canal Village, west of Rome. Don't forget Niagara Falls, and beyond, Canada.**

Locator 330-2231   **Medical 330-4108**   **Police 330-2200**

New York Coast Guard Support Center (NY01R1)
Governors Island, NY 10004-5000

TELEPHONE NUMBER INFORMATION: Main installation numbers: C-212-668-7000, FTS-664-7000.

Location: Take free Governors Island Ferry from Battery Park area of Manhattan. USM: L-2. NMC: New York, 1 mile northwest.

Billeting Office: Building 293, opposite O'Club, C-**212-269-8878**, check in facility after 1300, check out 1100 hours daily. Reservations required. No government civilian employee billeting.

TML: Super 8 Motel. Building 293, all ranks, leave or official duty. Bedroom, 1 double bed, private bath (11); bedroom, 2 double beds, private bath (38); apartments, efficiency (PCS to Governor's Island) (8). Two handicapped accessible rooms. A/C, color TV, maid

NEW YORK
New York Coast Guard Support Center, continued

service, cribs, ice vending. Modern structure. Rates: single and double rooms $50 first person, $5 each additional person over 12; efficiency apartments PCS rates. Special weekend and holiday rates (higher). All major credit cards. All categories can make reservations at above number.

TML: BOQ. Officers all ranks (occasionally enlisted personnel may use if special circumstances warrant), leave or official duty. Rooms, private bath (80+), 10 rooms ground floor are efficiency. Single persons only. No families. Be prepared to share room. Rates: $7 per person on orders, $15 on leave. All categories may make reservations, C-212-668-3452.

DV/VIP: CO, C-EX-7251, 07+, building 12, suites, reservations required.

TML Availability: Good, Oct-May. Difficult, other times.

☞ **A favorite with New York city visitors who would rather spend their $ on theater, restaurants and shopping than on lodging. Comfortable, safe, and convenient. Ferry runs 24 hours, 7 days. Free on base parking.**

Locator 668-7000   **Medical 668-7167**   **Police 668-7474**

New York Naval Station (NY07R1)
Brooklyn, NY 11251-0001

TELEPHONE NUMBER INFORMATION: Main installation numbers: C-718-876-6283. D-none.

Location: I-95 N to Elizabeth, NJ, I-278 to Staten Island. Last exit before Verrrazano bridge, exit at Bay St, follow signs. USM: L-2, on Ft. Wadsworth. NMC: New York.

Billeting Office: None. Call **1-800-NAVY-INN**, D-312-624-1103, 24 hours daily for reservations. Check in between 1500 and 1800. Check out 1200. Notify Lodge of late check in, out. Eligibility: check Appendix D.

TML: Navy Lodge. All ranks. Bedrooms, 2 double beds, private bath, dining area (50). Handicapped accessible (2). Some rooms interconnecting. Kitchenette, (refrigerator, stove, microwave), utensils, A/C, CATV, room telephone, irons, boards, cribs, washer/dryer, housekeeping, food, ice vending, mini-mart, parking, play area for children, some rooms handicapped accessible. No pets (nearby kennel available). Rates: $46 ($90 interconnecting). All categories can make reservations. Rooms may be reserved for up to 30 days based on availability. Payment in advance (Diners Club, Visa, MasterCard) for stays shorter than four days, one week stays, every four days.

TML Availability: Good winter months, difficult summer.

☞ **The naval command moved here from Brooklyn, in '90. The station has two sites, Stapleton, and two miles south "Fort Wadsworth", (many "oldtimers" will recall staying there), where the new Navy Lodge, family housing, and support facilities are located. Staten Island itself belies the fact that you are still in New York City. Visit Tottenville, Victorian homes of Ward Hill, the US Navy Homeport waterfront, wildlife in wooded preserves, museums, golf, etc. etc. etc.**

New York Naval Station, continued

Locator 876-6426   Medical 911   Police 816-4833/1709

☺**Keep posted on new developments for New York City by reading Military Living's travel newsletter,** *R&R Space-A Report.*

Niagara Falls Air Reserve Base (NY12R1)
Niagara Falls International Airport
Niagara Falls, NY 14304-5000

TELEPHONE NUMBER INFORMATION: Main installation numbers: C-716-236-2000, D-312-489-3011.

Location: Take I-190 to Niagara Falls, exit Packard Rd and turn right - straight through to Lockport Road. Approximately 4 miles from the exit. From US62 West to Walmore Road, North to AFB. USM: L-3. NMC: City Niagara Falls 6 miles west of AFB.

Billeting Office: ATTN: SVH, building 312, Flint Ave. Reservations C-716-236-2014, D-312-489-2014, FAX D-312-489-6348, hours of operation 0700-2300. Checkout 1200. Government civilian employee billeting.

TML: VOQ. Building 312, officers all ranks, leave or official duty. Bedroom, private bath (43), telephone, refrigerator, AC, color TV and other essentials. Maid service, washer/dryers, ice vending, crib and cots. Older structure. Lounge with microwave. Rates: $6 per person. Duty can make reservations, others Space-A.

TML: VAQ/VIP. Building 312, officers O5 and above, GS/GM 13 and above, leave or duty. Living room, bedroom suites, private bath (6), A/C, telephone, color TV, refrigerator and other essentials. Maid service. Rates: $8 per person. Duty can make reservations, others Space-A.

TML: VAQ. Buildings 502 and 504, enlisted, all ranks, leave or official duty. Bedroom, 2 beds per room each building (34), TV, A/C refrigerator and other essentials. Common bath, 4 per building, maid service, washer/dryer and ice vending. Older structure renovated. Rates: $6 per person. Duty can make reservations, others Space-A.

TML: Senior NCO Quarters. Building 508, enlisted all ranks. Living/bedroom suites, private bath. TV, A/C refrigerator and other essentials. Rates: $8 per person.

TML: VOQ/VIP. DV Suites (5). Buildings 304E, 304W, 306E, 306W. Three bedrooms, queen bed w/private bath, shared living room and kitchenette. A/C, telephones, color TV, refrigerators, washer/dryers, maid service. Rates: $8 per person.

TML: VOQ/VIP. Building 308. Bedrooms, king bed, private bath (2). A/C, telephone, color TV, refrigerator. Shared living room, dining area and kitchenette. Washer/Dryer, maid service. Rates: $8 per person.

TML Availability: Good, Oct-Mar. Difficult, Apr-Sep.

☞ Niagara Falls, and the Niagara Power Vista, Old Fort Niagara, Our Lady of Fatima Shrine, and the Native American Center for the Living Arts, are all attractions in this area. Visit also the amusement park and scenic area nearby.

Locator 236-2002   Medical 236-2086/7   Police

NEW YORK

Plattsburgh Air Force Base (NY08R1)
Plattsburgh AFB, NY 12903-5000

TELEPHONE NUMBER INFORMATION: Main installation numbers: C-518-565-5000, D-312-689-5000.

Location: From I-87 take exit #36. Directions to AFB are clearly marked. USM: M-2. NMC: Plattsburgh, 4 miles northwest.

Billeting Office: Building 381, Club Rd, C-518-565-7614, 24 hours daily. Check in billeting, check out 1200 hours daily. Government civilian employee billeting VOQ.

TML: TLF. Building 164, all ranks, leave or official duty. Apartments, all private bath (15); bedroom, private bath (4); separate bedrooms, private bath (8); two bedroom, private bath (2); three bedroom, private bath (1). Kitchen (11 units), community kitchen, complete utensils, color TV in room & lounge, maid service, cribs/cots, washer/dryer, food/ice vending. Modern structure, renovated. Rates: $10 bedroom, $17 separate bedrooms, $23 two bedroom, $28 three bedroom. Duty can make reservations, others Space-A.

TML: VOQ. Building 381, officers all ranks, leave or official duty. Bedroom, semi-private bath (40); DV (06+) suites, private bath (4). Refrigerator, community kitchen, cribs/cots, essentials, color TV in room & lounge, maid service, washer/dryer, ice vending. Older structure, renovated. Rates: sponsor and adult $8 per person, maximum $16 per room. DV $14 per person, maximum $28. Maximum 2 per room. Children not authorized. Duty can make reservations, others Space-A.

TML: VAQ. Building 1944, enlisted all ranks, leave or official duty. Bedroom, semi-private bath (16). Refrigerator, cribs/cots, community kitchen, color TV in room & lounge, washer/dryer, food/ice vending. Older structure, renovated. Rates: sponsor and adult $8 per person. Maximum 2 per room, maximum charge $16. Children not authorized. Duty can make reservations, others Space-A.

DV/VIP: 380th AR & FW, Cmdr's Sec, C-EX-5171, 07+, retirees Space-A.

TML Availability: Very good. Best winter months. Difficult, other times.

☞ **On the edge of the Adirondack National Park and shores of Lake Champlain. Visit Montreal's art museums and the botanical garden. One hour to Lake Placid. There's shopping and restaurants in Plattsburgh too.**

Locator 565-5579   Medical 565-7223   Police 565-7111

•

Seneca Army Depot (NY03R1)
Romulus, NY 14541-5001

TELEPHONE NUMBER INFORMATION: Main installation numbers: C-607-869-1110, D-312-489-5110.

Location: On post. Twelve miles south of intersection of US-20/NY-96A near Geneva. Take New York State Thruway (I-90) to exit 42, and Hwy 96 south to main gate. USM: L-3. NMC: Rochester, NY, 55 miles SE.

NEW YORK

Seneca Army Depot, continued

Billeting Office: Housing Office, Recreation Division, building 116, C-**607-869-1211**, D-312-489-5314, open 0700-1630 M-F. Check in at facility, 1400 -1600 hours daily. Check out 0830 - 1030 hours. No government civilian employee billeting.

TML: Lake Shore Travel Camp. All ranks, PCS personnel. Mobile homes (19); three bedrooms private bath (9); two bedrooms (10), kitchenette, refrigerator, TV, utensils, washer/dryer available. Pets allowed. Rates: $30/day. Active duty, accompanied, unaccompanied dependents, all categories can make reservations. Active duty, reservists and national guard on orders taken space available. Write to: Seneca Army Depot, ATTN: SDSSE-HH (Travel Park), Romulus, NY 14541-5001, C-as above.

TML Availability: Good. Difficult, holidays.

☞ Located in the center of the Finger Lakes Region. Seneca Lake is the "lake trout capital of the world", the largest of the Finger Lakes. Good hunting, full range of support facilities on post.

Locator 869-1110   **Medical 869-1242**   **Police 869-0448**

Soldiers', Sailors' and Airmen's Club (NY17R1)
283 Lexington Avenue
New York, NY 10016-5000

TELEPHONE NUMBER INFORMATION: Main installation numbers: C-212-683-4353, D-None. In US toll free **1-800-678-TGIF**.

Location: In mid-town Manhattan on Lexington Avenue between 36th and 37th Sts. USM: L-2. NMC: New York, in the city.

Author's Note: The **Soldiers', Sailors' and Airmen's Club** is a tax exempt, not-for-profit organization founded in 1919 to serve the needs of service personnel while visiting New York. It is the only club of its kind in the city.

Office: Check in and out at the lobby desk, 24 hours daily. Check out 1230 hours.

TML: Hotel. Open to active duty enlisted ranks, service academy/ROTC students, all retirees and former service personnel and reservist, including officers with honorable discharge and allied member forces and their dependents 12 years and older. Note: unaccompanied spouses and widows with ID may use facilities on a Space-A basis. Bedrooms, most having 2 beds, hall baths (29). Facilities include lounges, library, TV rooms, pool room, and dining room. Older structure, renovations on-going. Rates: active, reservist enlisted and Academy, ROTC students $20 per night per person. All others $25 M-F, $30 weekends. Group special of $20 each (2 or more in a party). One night's credit at Su-Th rate for guests staying 7 nights or more. Dependents 12 years or older pay same rate as sponsor. Reservations for weekends suggested. Continental breakfast Sunday, no charge. Discount tickets to Broadway shows. Saturday free breakfast for active duty enlisted. Friday night, wine and cheese upon arrival (1900-2100).

☞ The SS&A has been in this location since 1926. Here's your chance to visit the Big Apple to shop and see the sights. There is controlled access, a helpful staff, and the building has a new fire alarm and communication systems. Definitely one of New York's best kept secrets!

NEW YORK

Stewart Army Sub-Post (NY09R1)
Newburgh, NY 12550-9999

TELEPHONE NUMBER INFORMATION: Main installation numbers: C-914-564-6309, D-312-247-3524.

Location: From I-87 take Newburgh exit to Union Ave, south to NY-207. Follow signs to Stewart Airport. USM: M-3. NMC: Newburgh, 4 miles northwest.
NEW YORK
Stewart Army Sub-Post, continued

Billeting Office: Five Star Inn. The West Point and STAS Guest House, building 2605, New Windsor, NY, C-**914-563-3311**, D-312-688-3009, 24 hrs. daily. Check out 1000 hours daily. Active duty and family, PCS, visiting relatives and guests of hospital patients, active, reservist and retired military personnel, civilians sponsored by military personnel; military and DOD civilians on TDY.

TML: Guest House. Building 2605, **Five Star Inn**, all ranks, leave or official duty. Bedroom, private bath (18); bedrooms, semi-private bath (34); apartments (8). A/C, vending, laundry, CATV, direct dial telephones, auto wake-up service, complimentary coffee, lounge, refrigerator, cribs, food and ice vending. Older structure, redecorated '92. Rates: $25, $4 second person. Maximum 3 per room. Children under 2 free. Reservations 30 days prior for Space-A, 60 days PCS. Reservations confirmed with credit card or advance deposit.

TML Availability: Fairly good, Oct-Mar. Difficult, other times.

☞ Visit the Crawford House in Newburgh, try antique shopping near Millbrook, tour a local winery, or try a balloon tour near Port Jervis. Visit Sugar Loaf Crafts Village - the Hudson River Valley is full of interesting things to do.

Locator 564-6309   **Medical 563-3430**   **Police 564-0580**

United States Military Academy, West Point (NY16R1)
West Point, NY 10996-5000

TELEPHONE NUMBER INFORMATION: Main installation numbers: C-914-938-4011, D-312-688-1110.

Location: Off I-87 or US-9 west. Clearly marked. USM: M-3. NMC: New York City, NY 36 miles south.

Billeting Office: Building 674, C-914-446-4731, 24 hours daily. Check in facility, check out 1200 hours daily. No government civilian employee billeting.

TML: Hotel Thayer. C-**914-446-4731**, or toll free **1-800-247-5047**, D-312-688-2632. Bedroom, private bath (200). A/C, color TV in room & lounge, maid service, cribs/cots $5 each, ice vending. Older structure, renovated. Rates: single room with shower $65-$85, double room with shower $70-$90, suites with kitchenette $105-$175. TDY rates available on request. Open to public. Reservations accepted 1 year in advance.

DV/VIP: Protocol Office, building 600, C-EX-4315/4316, 07/GS-16+. Retirees Space-A.

United States Military Academy, West Point, continued

TML Availability: Good, except during special holiday events at USMA.

☞ Part of the US Armed Forces Recreation System, the history of the Military Academy, sporting events, and special vacation packages are available at this castle-like hotel rising above the Hudson River.

Locator 938-4412   **Medical 938-3637**   **Police 938-3333**

North Carolina

Camp Lejeune Marine Corps Base (NC10R1)
Camp Lejeune MCB, NC 28542-5079

TELEPHONE NUMBER INFORMATION: Main installation numbers: C-919-451-1113, D-312-484-1113.

Location: Main gate is 6 miles east of junction of US-17 and NC-24. USM: M-5. NMC: Jacksonville, 3 miles northwest.

Billeting Office: Building 2617, **Seth-Williams**. C-919-451-2146/1385, 24 hours daily. Check in billeting, check out 1300 hours daily. Government civilian employee billeting.

TML: Hostess House. Building 896, off Holcomb Ave near MCBX. Check in after 1400 hours daily, 24 hour desk. All ranks. Leave or official duty. Bedroom, 2 double beds, semi-private bath, fold-out couch, sleeps 5 persons (90). Kitchen, utensils, A/C, color TV, maid service, cots ($1), coin washer/dryer, many extras. Modern structure, motel type. Rates: $24 per unit. Duty can make reservations, others Space-A.

TML: BOQ/BEQ. Building 2617 (BOQ), C-EX-2146/1385. Officer all ranks. Building HP-53 (BEQ), C-EX-5262. Enlisted E6-E9. Leave or official duty. Efficiencies, private bath, kitchenette (19); Suites, living room, bedroom, private bath, kitchenette, refrigerator w/ice maker (39); bedroom SNCO transient billeting (49). Utensils, AC, color TV in room & lounge, maid service, cribs/cots, washer/dryer, facilities for DAVs, coffee & coffee maker. Older structure, renovated. Rates: $6-$18. Duty can make reservations, others Space-A.

TML: DG/VIP. Building 2601: two bedroom suite, private bath, kitchen (1); bedroom suites, private bath, kitchen (2). Building 2607: separate bedroom suites, private bath, kitchenettes (6). All have A/C, maid service, washer/dryer, cribs. Rates: DV $11-$26 per unit. Building HP53, C-EX-5262: SNCO bedroom, private bath (2). All categories can make reservations.

DG/VIP: Protocol Office, C-EX-2523. 06+. Retirees and lower ranks Space-A.

TML Availability: Limited, year round.

☞ Nearby Onslow Beach offers swimming, surfing and picnicking, and local marinas offer boat rentals. Two 18 hole golf courses are also nearby.

Locator-451-3074   **Medical-451-4372**   **Police-451-2555**

NORTH CAROLINA

Cape Hatteras Coast Guard Recreational Quarters (NC09R1)
Group Cape Hatteras
Buxton, NC 27920-0604

TELEPHONE NUMBER INFORMATION: Main installation numbers: C-919-995-6435.

Location: From the North. Follow Route 12 from Nags Head about 50 miles to Buxton. In Buxton, turn left at Red Drum Texaco (Old Lighthouse Rd). Road leads to Group Office and Recreation Quarters. From the South. Follow Route 70 East from Moorehead City 45 miles to Cedar Island. Board Ocracoke Ferry (1.5 hr. ride w/toll charge). Follow Route 12 to Hatteras Island Ferry (no charge). On Hatteras proceed North Route 12 to Buxton. Turn right at Red Drum Texaco (Old Lighthouse Rd.) Road leads to Group Office and Recreation Quarters. USM: M-5. NMC: Elizabeth City, 110 miles northwest.

Billeting Office: None. Reservations required with advance payment 30-90 days by mail. Summer months C-**919-225-3551**. Address: Cape Hatteras Recreational Quarters, Group Cape Hatteras, P.O. Box 604, Buxton, NC 27920-0604.

TML: Rooms that sleep 4 (6), rollaway available. Private bath, portable refrigerator, TV. Rates: $24-$30. Room 2 sleeps 6, private bath, kitchen area, TV. Rate: $35-$50. Room 8 (VIP suite) 04+. Sleeps 6, private bath, kitchen area, TV. Rates: $55. All categories can make reservations.

TML Availability: Limited. Book early.

☞ Within walking distance of historic Cape Hatteras Lighthouse. Famous for fishing, a mecca for wind surfers - "the best surfing on the east coast". For those with less strenuous interest, peaceful, clean beaches, and solitude (off season).

Cherry Point Marine Corps Air Station (NC02R1)
Cherry Point MCAS, NC 28533-5079

TELEPHONE NUMBER INFORMATION: Main installation numbers: C-919-466-2811, D-312-582-1110.

Location: On NC-101 between New Bern and Morehead City, NC. US-70 south connects with NC-101 at Havelock, NC. USM: M-5. NMC: Morehead City, 18 miles southeast.

Billeting Office: Building 487 (Officer), building 3673 (enlisted ranks E1-E9). C-**919-466-3060**, 24 hours daily. Check in facility, check out 1100 hours daily. Government civilian employee billeting.

TML: Guest House (DGQ). 06+, leave or official duty. C-EX-2848. Four bedroom, private bath. Kitchen, complete utensils, A/C, color TV, maid service, washer/dryer. Rates: $25 (TDY).

TML: BOQ. Buildings 487, 496, officers all ranks. Leave or official duty. C-EX-5169. D-EX-5169. Check out 1200 hours. Bedroom, private bath (47); separate bedroom suites,

NORTH CAROLINA

Cherry Point MCAS, continued

private bath (29). Refrigerator, A/C, color TV, maid service, washer/dryer, ice vending. Older structure, renovated. Rates: single $10, suite $13. Duty, leave, retired can make reservations, others Space-A.

TML: DGQ. Officer 06+, leave or official duty. One bedroom suites. Kitchen, complete utensils, A/C, color TV, maid service. Older structure. Rates: $15 (TDY). All categories can make reservations.

TML Availability: Very good all year.

☞ New Bern museums, shopping and dining, area historical attractions, the sailing center at Oriental, where you can catch Neuse River blue crabs, the nearby Outer Banks, and Cape Lookout National Seashore - don't miss them!

Locator 466-2109   Medical 466-4410   Police 466-3615

Elizabeth City Coast Guard Support Center (NC03R1)
Elizabeth City CGSC, NC 27909-5006

TELEPHONE NUMBER INFORMATION: Main installation numbers: C-919-335-6397, FTS-919-335-6397.

Location: Take I-64 east to VA-104S to US-17 south to Elizabeth City, left on Halstead Blvd, 3 miles to main gate of Center. USM: M-5. NMC: Elizabeth City, in the city.

Billeting Office: Building 5, C-**919-335-6548**, 0800-1630 hours daily. Check in facility, check out 1200 hours daily. No government civilian employee billeting.

TML: Mobile homes. 16A-F, all ranks, leave or official duty. Two bedroom, private bath (3); three bedroom, private bath (3). Kitchen, limited utensils, A/C, black/white TV, coin washer/dryer. Modern structure. Rates: $20 per night, sleeps 6. Duty can make reservations, others Space-A.

TML Availability: Good, Oct-Apr. Difficult, other times.

☞ Visit Kitty Hawk and the Outer Banks. Read *Military RV, Camping & Rec Areas Around the World* for more information on this area.

Locator 335-6229   Medical 335-6460   Police 335-6398

Fort Bragg (NC05R1)
Fort Bragg, NC 28307-5000

TELEPHONE NUMBER INFORMATION: Main installation numbers: C-919-396-0011, D-312-236-0011.

NORTH CAROLINA
Fort Bragg, continued

Location: From I-95 exit to NC-24 west which runs through post as Bragg Blvd. From US-401 (Fayetteville Bypass) exit to All American Expressway, 5 miles to Fort. USM: L-5. NMC: Fayetteville, 15 miles southeast.

Billeting Office: Building D-3601 (**Moon Hall**), room 101, off Bastogne Dr, C-**919-396-5575**, 24 hours daily. Check in facility, check out 1100 hours daily. Government civilian employee billeting.

TML: Guest Houses. All ranks, leave or official duty. **Delmont House**, Bastogne Dr, building D-4215, C-**919-436-2211**, D-312-236-4496. **Normandy House**, Totten & Armistead St, building 1-4228, C-**919-436-2250**, D-312-236-1970. **Leal House**, Reilly Rd across from main PX, building 5-5047, C-**919-436-3033**, D-312-236-8770. Bedroom/private bath (111), separate bedroom suites, private bath (7). Kitchen (some), refrigerator, community kitchen, A/C, color TV in room & lounge, maid service, cribs/cots, washer/dryer, ice vending, facilities for DAVs (**Delmont House**). Modern structures. Rates: E1-E6 $20, E6+ $25. PCS can make reservations, others Space-A.

TML: VOQ/VEQ. Buildings D-3601, D-3705, M-1939. All ranks, leave or official duty. C-EX-7700. Bedroom, private bath (520); separate bedroom suites; private bath (27); Kitchen (suites), refrigerator, A/C, color TV, maid service, washer/dryer, ice vending, facilities for DAVs. Modern structures. Rates: $15 all ranks, $20 suites. Maximum 2 per unit. Duty can make reservations, others Space-A.

TML: DV/VIP. Building 1-4425. Officer 07+, leave or official duty. C-EX-2804. Three-bedroom suite, private bath (1). Kitchen, complete utensils, A/C, color TV, maid service, cribs/cots, washer/dryer. Modern structure. Rate: $17. All categories can make reservations.

DV/VIP: Protocol Office. C-EX-2804. 07+. Retirees Space-A.

TML Availability: Good, Sep-Apr. Difficult, other times.

☞ The 82nd Airborne Division War Memorial Museum has over 3,000 objects on view. The Historic Fayetteville Foundation gives walking tours of historical sites, and Sandhills area golf resorts are world famous.

Locator-396-1461   Medical 432-0301   Police-396-0391

Fort Fisher Air Force Recreation Area (NC13R1)
P.O. Box 380, Kure Beach, NC 28449-3321

TELEPHONE NUMBER INFORMATION: Main installation numbers: C-919-458-6549, D-312-488-8011, EX-458-6549.

Location: From interstate 95, traveling south from Virginia, or northern NC, take Hwy 117 exit. Follow south to Hwy 421 to Kure Beach. From I-95 traveling north from SC, take Hwy 74/76 into Wilmington, then south on Hwy 421 to Kure Beach. USM: L-5,6. NMC: Wilmington NC.

Fort Fisher AF Recreation Area, continued

Billeting Office: Building 118, Reception Center. **C-1-800-842-0659 or 1-919-458-6549, 0800 to 1800 daily.** Check in reception center, 1600 to 1800 daily. Check out 1100. Late checkouts call reservations. Rooms may not be ready before 1600, but use of resort facilities allowed until check in.

TML: The Air Force's only beachside resort. Operated by Seymour Johnson Air Force Base MWR Division, year round. All ranks. Total units - 136. Two lodges, bedrooms, common bath (52); suites, private bath (6) semi-private (7); beach cottages, four bedrooms, private and semi private baths, (4), three bedrooms (22); mobile homes (26). A/C in rooms/suites, some kitchenettes, refrigerators, handicapped accessible, maid service, CATV in most units and in lounge area. Complete utensils, linens, washer/dryer in cottages, washer/dryer, ice and food vending, essentials. Suites remodeled '91, rooms '92. Convenience store, gift and beach shop, restaurant, snack bar, recreation center, swimming pool, hot tub, sauna, exercise/weight room, racquetball, basketball and tennis courts, softball field, fishing pier and boat ramp. Access to beach, sailing, boating, fishing, swimming. Bicycle, power and sail boat rentals. Pets allowed in cottages only, with $25 extermination fee. All pets kept on leash.

Rates: winter (1 November-31 March) summer (1 April-31 October). Cottages (sleeps 6) $40-$60/day, $55-$75/weekend, $230-$380 standard week, $280-430 premium week. Executive Suite (sleeps 4, no children under 12) $25-$40/day, $35-$50/weekend, $150-$250 standard week, $175-$275 premium week. Executive room (sleeps 2, no children under 12), $20-$35/day, $30-$45/weekend, $125-$200 standard week, $150-$225 premium week. Lodge suite (sleeps 2) $10-$15/day, $15-$20 weekend, $75-$100 standard week, $100-$125 premium week. Additional persons in all units charged extra. Weekdays are Sun evening through Thurs evening. Weekends are Fri evening, Sat evening and evenings prior to a holiday. Standard weeks are Sat to Sat, Mon to Mon or Wed to Wed. Premium weeks are Fri to Fri or Sun to Sun. With free rollaway bed, linens and towels furnished ($5 per person).

Reservations: All categories. Active duty (Seymour Johnson AFB) 90 days ahead. All other duty 85 days ahead. Retirees 75 days ahead. All others, 60 days ahead. Confirmed with Visa, MasterCard, Diners Club, Seymour Johnson AFB Club Card, or advance payment. Limits to number of rooms reserved during Memorial Day to Labor Day. Cancellations 15 days prior, or one night fee.

TML Availability: Very good. Best, 1 November-31 March.

☞ Aside from all the recreational activities at this resort, the Fort Fisher State Historic Site, Civil War Museum, and USS NC Battleship Memorial, Orton and Poplar Grove Plantations are worth visiting.

New River Marine Corps Air Station (NC06R1)
Jacksonville, NC 28545-5079

TELEPHONE NUMBER INFORMATION: Main installation numbers: C-919-451-1113, D-312-484-1113.

Location: Off US-17, 2 miles south of Jacksonville. Clearly marked. USM: M-5. NMC: Jacksonville, 2 miles northeast.

NORTH CAROLINA
New River Marine Corps Air Station, continued

Billeting Office: Duty Office, building 705, Flounder Road. C-**919-451-6621/6903**, 24 hours. Check in at facility, check out 1200 hours daily. Government civilian employee billeting.

TML: BOQ. Building 705. Officers, all ranks; enlisted 6+, leave or official duty. Bedroom, private bath (44). Refrigerator, A/C, VCR, color TV in room & lounge, maid service, cribs/cots $2, essentials, washer/dryer, food/ice vending, coffee makers, microwave. Modern structure, remodeled. Rates leave status: $8 single room, $12 two room suite, $2 each additional person. Maximum 4 persons per unit. Duty can make reservations, others Space-A.

TML Availability: Good. Best Sep-Mar. Difficult other times.

☞ **Some area interests include Fort Macon, Hammocks Beach, Hanging Rock, Jones Lake, and Cape Hatteras National Seashore. North Carolina National forests and local festivals are all drawing cards for visitors.**

Locator-451-6568   **Medical-451-6532**   **Police-451-6111**

Pope Air Force Base (NC01R1)
Pope AFB, NC 28308-5225

TELEPHONE NUMBER INFORMATION: Main installation numbers: C-919-394-0001, D-312-486-1110

Location: Take I-95, exit to NC-87/24 W. Signs point the direction to AFB and Ft Bragg. USM: L-5. NMC: Fayetteville, 12 miles southeast.

Billeting Office: Building 235, Ethridge St, C-**919-394-0001**, 24 hours daily. Check in billeting, check out 1200 hours daily. Government civilian employee billeting with reservations.

TML: VOQ. Buildings 229-247, all ranks, leave or official duty. Bedroom, private bath (96); separate bedroom, private bath (12); eight bedroom units (8). Community kitchen, refrigerator, A/C, color TV, maid service, cribs, washer/dryer, ice vending. Older structure. Rates: $8. TDY can make reservations, others Space-A.

TML: VAQ. Building 287, enlisted all ranks, leave or official duty. Bedroom, shared bath (68); separate bedroom, private bath (4). Refrigerator, A/C, color TV, maid service, washer/dryer, ice vending. Older structure, renovated '91. Rates: $8. TDY can make reservations, others Space-A.

TML: DV/VIP. Building 219, officer 06+, leave or official duty. C-EX 4739. Bedroom, private bath (4). Kitchen, utensils, A/C, color TV, maid service, washer/dryer, ice vending. Older structure. Rates: $14 per person. All categories can make reservations.

TML: TLF. Building 229, all ranks, PCS in/out. Bedroom, private bath (8), kitchenette, utensils, A/C, color TV, maid service, washer/dryer. Rates: $16/day. PCS can make reservations, all others Space-A.

DV/VIP: Protocol Office. Building 309, C-EX-4739. 06+. Retirees Space-A.

NORTH CAROLINA

Pope Air Force Base, continued

TML Availability: Good, winter. Difficult, other times.

☞ Near Goldsboro, Cliffs of the Neuse River, picnicking, refreshments, fishing swimming and rental rowboats, museum. Also visit historic Fort Macon, the Cape Hatteras National Seashore, and Fayetteville.

Locator-394-4822   Medical-394-2232   Police-394-2800

Seymour Johnson Air Force Base (NC11R1)
Seymour Johnson AFB, NC 27531-5000

TELEPHONE NUMBER INFORMATION: Main installation numbers: C-919-736-5400, D-312-488-1110.

Location: From US-70 in Goldsboro take Seymour Johnson exit onto Berkeley Blvd to main gate. Clearly marked. USM: L-5. NMC: Raleigh, 50 miles northwest.

Billeting Office: Southern Pines Inn. ATTN: 4SG/SVH. Building 3804, Wright Ave. C-**919-778-6253**, 24 hours daily. Check in billeting, check out 1200 hours daily. Government civilian employee billeting VOQ.

TML: TLF. Building 3802. All ranks. Leave or official duty. Bedroom, private bath (3); separate bedrooms, private bath (22); two bedroom, private bath (2). Kitchen, limited utensils, A/C, color TV, maid service, washer/dryer, ice vending. Modern structure, renovated. Rates: $16 per unit. Maximum based on size of unit. Duty can make reservations, others Space-A.

TML: VOQ. Building 3804. Officers all ranks, leave or official duty. Bedroom, private and semi-private baths (38); separate bedrooms, private bath (6). Kitchen (1 unit), A/C, color TV in room & lounge, maid service, washer/dryer, ice vending. Modern structure, renovated. Rates: $8 per person. Maximum 2 persons. Duty can make reservations, others Space-A.

TML: VAQ. Building 3803. Enlisted all ranks. Leave or official duty. Bedroom, private and semi-private baths (21); separate bedrooms, private bath (3); bedroom, private bath (3). Color TV, maid service, washer/dryer, ice vending. Modern structure. Rates: $8 per person. Maximum 2 persons. Duty can make reservations, others Space-A.

TML: DV/VIP. Building 2820. Officer 06+. Leave or official duty. Separate bedrooms suites, private bath (2). Kitchen, color TV, maid service, washer/dryer. Older structure. Rates: $10 per person. Duty can make reservations, others Space-A at discretion of Wing Commander.

TML Availability: Good, Nov-Apr. Difficult, other times.

☞ Nearby Ashville is good for rafting, hiking and skiing, while Carowinds, in Charlotte, is a large family entertainment center. Ashboro's zoological park, and Raleigh, the state capital, are well worth visits.

Locator-736-5584   Medical-736-5577   Police-736-6413

North Dakota

Grand Forks Air Force Base (ND04R3)
Grand Forks AFB, ND 58205-0001

TELEPHONE NUMBER INFORMATION: Main installation numbers: C-701-747-3000, D-312-362-3000.

Location: From I-29 take US-2 west exit for 14 miles to Grand Forks, County Rd B-3 (Emerado/Air Base) 1 mile to AFB. USM: G,H-2. NMC: Grand Forks, 15 miles east.

Billeting Office: ATTN: 842CSG/SVH, building 117, Holzapple & 6th Ave, C-701-747-3069/70, 24 hours daily. Check in billeting, check out 1200 hours daily. Government civilian employee billeting.

TML: TLF. Across street from billeting, all ranks, leave or official duty. Efficiency apartments, private bath (40). Kitchen, limited utensils, A/C, color TV, maid service, washer/dryer, ice vending. Modern structure. Rates: $21 per unit. PCS in/out reservations required. Duty can make reservations, others Space-A.

TML: VOQ. Building 117, officers all ranks, leave or official duty. Two bedroom suites, private bath (9); bedroom, semi-private bath (8). Refrigerator, A/C, color TV, maid service, washer/dryer, ice vending. Rates: $9 per person. PCS in/out reservations required, duty can make reservations, others Space-A.

TML: VAQ. Building 117, enlisted all ranks, leave or official duty. Bedroom, semi-private bath (10); two bedroom suites, private bath (10). Refrigerator, color TV, maid service, washer/dryer, ice. Rates: $9 per person. PCS in/out reservations required. Duty can make reservations, others Space-A.

TML: DV/VIP. Building 132, officers 06+, leave or official duty. Four bedroom house, private bath, kitchen, living room, dining room, washer/dryer (1). Rates: $14 per person. For reservations contact Protocol (see below).

TML: DV/VIP. Building 117, enlisted E8-E9, leave or official duty. Two bedroom suites, private bath (2). Living room, refrigerator, color TV, A/C, maid service, washer/dryer, ice vending. Rates: $13 per person. For reservations contact Protocol.

DV/VIP: 42 AD Protocol Office, building 305, C-EX-4155, 06+. Retirees and lower ranks Space-A.

TML Availability: Good, winter. Difficult, spring and summer.

Locator 747-3344	Medical 747-5600	Police 747-5351

⊗**This facility did not respond to our inquiries, information may be outdated.**

Minot Air Force Base (ND02R3)
Minot AFB, ND 58705-5013

TELEPHONE NUMBER INFORMATION: Main installation numbers: C-701-723-1110, D-312-453-1110.

NORTH DAKOTA

Minot Air Force Base, continued

Location: On US-83, north of Minot. USM: G-2. NMC: Minot, 15 miles south.

Billeting Office: Sakajawea Inn. ATTN: 5 SVS/SVH, Billeting, building 173, Missile Ave and Summit Dr, C-**701-727-6161**, D-312-453-2184, 24 hours daily. Check in 1400, check out 1200 hours.

TML: TLF. Buildings 158-161, all ranks, leave or official duty, C-EX-2184. Separate bedroom apartments, private bath (39). Kitchen, complete utensils, A/C, color TV, housekeeping, washer/dryer, ice vending. Modern structure. Rates: $18-$19 per unit. Space-A reservations accepted; confirmation based on availability.

TML: VOQ. Buildings 169, 170, 175, 182, officers all ranks, leave or official duty, C-EX-2184. Bedrooms, private and semi-private bath (25). Refrigerator and/or complete kitchen, A/C, color TV, housekeeping, washer/dryer. Modern structure. Rates: $9-$14 per person. Space-A reservations accepted, confirmation based on availability.

TML: VAQ. Buildings 173, 183, 184, enlisted all ranks, leave or official duty, C-EX-2184. Bedroom, private and semi-private bath (25). Refrigerator and/or complete kitchen, A/C, color TV, housekeeping, washer/dryer, ice vending. Modern structure. Rates: $9-$14 per person. Space-A reservations accepted, confirmation based on availability.

TML: DVQ. Building 171, officers 06+, C-EX-2184. Suites, private bath (2). Kitchen, A/C, color TV, housekeeping, washer/dryer. Rates: $14 per person. Space-A reservations accepted, confirmation based on availability.

DV/VIP: Protocol Office, building 167, C-EX-3474.

TML Availability: Generally good. Difficult Jul and Oct.

☞ Gardens, swimming pools, tennis courts, city zoo are in Roosevelt Park. Visit **General Custer's command post at Fort Lincoln State Park, and the International Peace Garden on the Manitoba/North Dakota border.**

Locator 723-1841   **Medical 723-5474**   **Police 723-3096**

Rickenbacker Air National Guard Base (OH02R2)
Rickenbacker ANGB, OH 43217-5000

TELEPHONE NUMBER INFORMATION: Main installation numbers: C-614-492-8211, D-312-950-1110.

Location: From I-270 take Alum Creek exit south to ANGB. Also, accessible off US-23 onto OH-317. Clearly marked. USM: K-4. NMC: Columbus, 13 miles northwest.

Billeting Office: Building 92, C-**614-492-4545/46**, 24 hours daily. Check in facility, check out 1100 hours daily. Government civilian employee billeting.

OHIO
Rickenbacker Air National Guard Base, continued

TML: VOQ/VAQ. Building 92, all ranks, leave or official duty. Bedroom, semi-private bath (47). Refrigerator, A/C, color TV, maid service. Older structure. Rates: $6 per person. Duty can make reservations, others Space-A.

TML: DV/VIP. Building S-9, officers 06+, leave or official duty. Separate bedrooms, private bath (5). A/C, maid service. Older structure. Rates: $8 per person. Duty can make reservations, others Space-A.

DV/VIP: PAO, C-EX-8211/1110, 06+.

TML Availability: Good, Oct-May.

Locator 492-8211/1110   Medical 492-3165   Police 492-4727

⊗**This facility did not respond to our inquiries, information may be outdated. This facility is scheduled to close in '94.**

Wright-Patterson Air Force Base (OH01R2)
Wright-Patterson AFB, OH 45433-5000

TELEPHONE NUMBER INFORMATION: Main installation numbers: C-513-257-1110, D-312-787-1110.

Location: South of I-70, off I-675 at Fairborn. Also, access from OH-4, AFB clearly marked. USM: K-4. NMC: Dayton, 10 miles northwest.

Billeting Office: ATTN: 2750 ENSG/DESH, building 825, Schlatter Dr & Childlaw Rd, C-513-257-3451, 24 hours daily. Check in billeting, check out 1200 hours daily. Government civilian employee billeting.

TML: TLQ. Building 823, all ranks, leave or official duty, C-EX-3810. Bedroom, bath (40) Kitchen, complete utensils, microwaves, A/C, color TV, maid service, cribs, washer/dryer, ice vending. Modern structure, renovated. Rates: $16 per unit. Sleeps 5. Duty can make reservations, others Space-A.

TML: TAQ. Building 1217, all ranks, leave or official duty. Check out 1300 hours. Bedroom, 2 beds, semi-private bath (97); bedroom, private bath (11). Top three only. Refrigerator, microwave, A/C, color TV, maid service, washer/dryer, ice vending. Remodeled. Rates: sponsor $6. No families. Duty can make reservations, others Space-A.

TML: VOQ. Building 825, all ranks, leave or official duty. Bedroom, private bath (108); Bedroom, semi-private bath (492). Refrigerator, microwave, beverage, snacks, microwavable dinners, coffee maker, A/C, color TV, maid service, washer/dryer, ice vending. FAX service available at no charge for VOQ/VAQ quests. Rates: $8 per person. Maximum $16 per family. Maximum 3 per room. Duty can make reservations, others Space-A.

TML: DV/VIP. Building 826, call about eligibility, C-EX-3810. Leave or official duty. Two bedroom suites, private bath (22). Refrigerator, A/C, color TV, maid service, cribs/cots, washer/dryer, ice vending, microwaves, microwave dinners, beverage, snacks. Rates: $10 per person. Maximum 5 per suite. Duty can make reservations.

OHIO

Wright-Patterson Air Force Base, continued

TML: Hope Hotel and Conference Center, the Air Force's first private sector financed hotel. Building 825, all ranks, leave or official duty. DOD Civilian lodging. One and two bed rooms (doubles), private bath (260). A/C, CATV, ice vending, irons and boards available, handicapped accessible. Seven full service conference rooms available, catering available from on site restaurant. Rates: bedroom, double bed, private bath, $35.70 (2 persons). Bedroom, 2 double beds, private bath $38.85 (2 persons). Additional persons $5.25 each. Official duty reservations call billeting at C-**513-257-3810**, D-312-787-3810. Others, C-**513-257-1285**, D-213-787-1285.

DV/VIP: Protocol, 2750 ABW/CCP, building 10, C-EX-3118, 07/GS-16+. Retirees and lower ranks Space-A.

TML Availability: Good, late Nov, early Jan. Difficult other times.

☞ **The Air Force museum on base, and the city of Dayton with its art and natural history museums, local arts and the Nutter Sports Center all make this area an interesting place to visit.**

Locator 257-3231   Medical 257-2968   Police 257-6841

Altus Air Force Base (OK02R3)
Altus AFB, OK 73523-5000

TELEPHONE NUMBER INFORMATION: Main installation numbers: C-405-481/482-8100, D-312-866-1110.

Location: Off US-62 south of I-40 and west of I-44. From US-62 traveling west from Lawton, turn right at 1st traffic light in Altus and follow road to main gate northeast of Falcon Rd. USM: G-6. NMC: Lawton, 56 miles east.

Billeting Office: Building 82, C-**405-481-7356**, 24 hours daily. Check in billeting, check out 1400 hours daily, except TLF - 1200 hours daily. Government civilian employee billeting.

TML: VOQ. Buildings 81-85, officers all ranks. Bedroom, private bath (96); separate bedrooms, private bath (30). Kitchen, A/C, color TV, maid service, washer/dryer. Modern structure, hotel type lodging. Rates: $8 per person. Duty can make reservations, others Space-A.

TML: VAQ. Building 82, enlisted all ranks. Bedroom, common bath (198). A/C, color TV in room & lounge, maid service. Modern structure. Rates: $8 per person. Duty can make reservations, others Space-A.

TML: DV/VIP. Building 81, officer 04+, leave or official duty. Separate bedrooms private bath (6). Kitchen, A/C, color TV, maid service, washer/dryer. Modern structure, hotel type lodging. Rates: $14 per person. Duty can make reservations, others Space-A.

DV/VIP: Wing EXO, building 1, C-EX-7554, 06+. Retirees and lower ranks Space-A.

OKLAHOMA
Altus Air Force Base, continued

TML Availability: Good, Dec. Difficult, other times.

☞ Visit the Museum of the Western Prairie for the saga of the area's wild west roots. Quartz Mountain State Park hosts the county fairs, rodeos and roundups that are part of life here.

Locator 481-6392   Medical 481-5213   Police 481-7444

Fort Sill (OK01R3)
Fort Sill, OK 73503-5100

TELEPHONE NUMBER INFORMATION: Main installation numbers: C-405-351-8111, D-312-639-7090.

Location: From I-44 at Lawton take US-62/277, 4 miles northwest to post. Clearly marked. USM: G-6. NMC: Lawton, adjacent to city.

Billeting Office: ATTN: ATZR-EHB, building 5676, Fergusson Rd, C-**405-353-5007, 351-5000,** D-312-639-5000, 24 hours daily. Check in billeting, check out 1200 hours daily. Government civilian employee billeting DV/VOQ.

TML: Guest House. Office in building 5690, Geronimo Rd, C-405-351-3214, D-312-639-3214, 24 hours daily. Check in building 5690, all ranks, leave or official duty. Rooms (75). Refrigerator, microwave, kitchen, A/C, color TV in room & lounge, maid service, cribs/cots, washer/dryer, ice vending. Rates: E1-E4, $16 per room; E5, E6, W1, & 01, $17.50 per room; E7-E9, W2-W4, 02-03, $27 per room. 04-05, guests, $36 per room. PCS can make reservations, others Space-A.

TML: BOQ/BEQ. E7+. Official duty only, reservations not taken - waiting list maintained. Must be signed into unit to get on waiting list. Spaces in BOQ (137); spaces in BEQ (40). Modern structure, renovated. Rates: no charge for room; maid fee $2/$3 per day. Maximum 1 per room. Dependents not authorized.

TML: VOQ/VEQ. Both take overflow from Guest House. All ranks, official duty only. Spaces in VOQ (649); spaces in VEQ (246) and VIP suites (11). Modern structure, renovated. Rates: sponsor $14, adult $7 VOQ/VEQ, and $20.50-$25 VIP suites. No children. Billeting recommends that children stay in guest house with spouse. Duty can make reservations, others Space-A.

TML: DVQ. Building 460. Officer 06/GS-15+, leave or official duty, C-EX-5511. Kitchen, complete utensils. Modern structure, renovated. Rates: sponsor $25 at **Comanche House** (building 460); all other DVQs $20.50, additional adult $7. Duty can make reservations, others Space-A.

DV/VIP: Protocol Office, building 460, C-351-4825, 06/GS-15+. Retirees Space-A.

TML Availability: Fairly good, fall, winter, spring. Difficult, summer.

☞ Don't miss the original stone buildings constructed by the "Buffalo Soldiers" of the 10th Calvary, the Guardhouse where Geronimo was confined, the large museum on post, and the Museum of the Great Plains in Lawton.

Locator 351-6172   Medical 351-4878   Police 351-2102

OKLAHOMA

Tinker Air Force Base (OK04R3)
Tinker AFB, OK 73145-5000

TELEPHONE NUMBER INFORMATION: Main installation numbers: C-405-732-7321, D-312-884-1110.

Location: Southeast Oklahoma City, off I-40. Use gate 1 off Air Depot Blvd. Clearly marked. USM: G-6. NMC: Oklahoma City, 12 miles northwest.

Billeting Office: Indian Hills Inn. ATTN: 2854 SVS/SVH, building 5604, C-405-734-2822, 24 hours daily. Check in billeting, check out 1200 hours daily for DV, VOQ, VAQ, and TLQ. Government civilian employee billeting.

TML: TLF. Buildings 5824/26/28/30/32, all ranks, leave or official duty. Rooms (39). Refrigerator, A/C, color TV, maid service, washer/dryer. Rates: $20 per unit. Duty can make reservations, others Space-A.

TML: VOQ/VAQ. Buildings 5604/05/06, officers, all ranks, enlisted, all ranks, leave or official duty. Approximately 130 rooms, private and semi-private baths. Refrigerator, A/C, color TV, maid service, washer/dryer. Rates: $8 per person. Duty can make reservations, others Space-A.

TML: SNCO Quarters. Buildings 5915, 5908, enlisted E7-E9, leave or official duty. 21 rooms. Call about types of facilities available. Rates: $8 per room. Duty can make reservations, others Space-A.

DV/VIP: OC-ALC/CCP, building 3001, C-405-739-5511, 07/GS-16+. Retirees and lower ranks Space-A.

TML Availability: Good all year.

☞ In Oklahoma City visit the National Cowboy Hall of Fame and Western Heritage Center, the city Zoo, tour the mansions of Heritage Hills. Five municipal golf courses, four lakes, and many sports events are available.

Locator 734-2456   **Medical 734-8249**   **Police 734-2151**

Vance Air Force Base (OK05R3)
Vance AFB, OK 73705-5000

TELEPHONE NUMBER INFORMATION: Main installation numbers: C-405-237-2121, D-312-962-7110.

Location: Off US-81 south of Enid. Clearly marked. USM: G-5. NMC: Oklahoma City, 90 miles southeast.

Billeting Office: Building 714, Goad St, C-405-249-7358, D-312-962-7358, 24 hours daily. Check in billeting, check out 1200 hours daily. Government civilian employee billeting.

OKLAHOMA
Vance Air Force Base, continued

TML: TLF. Building 790, all ranks, leave or official duty. Separate bedrooms, private bath (10). Kitchen, utensils, A/C, color TV, maid service, cribs, washer/dryer, ice vending. Rates: E6-$14 per unit, E7+ $18 per unit. Duty can make reservations, others Space-A.

TML: VOQ/TAQ. Buildings 713, 714, all ranks, leave or official duty. Bedroom, private bath (28); separate bedroom suite, private bath (DV/VIP) (1); two bedroom suites, private bath (DV/VIP) (2). Kitchen, microwave, A/C, color TV in room & lounge, maid service, washer/dryer, ice vending, facilities for DAV's. Modern structure. Rates: $7 per person ($10 DV/VIP). Maximum $21 per family ($30 DV/VIP). Duty can make reservations, others Space-A.

DV/VIP: Retirees Space-A, duty reservations as above.

TML Availability: Difficult. Best, Dec, Jan.

☞ In Enid visit **Government Springs Park** where cowboys watered cattle 75 years ago - swimming pool, waterfall and lake for boating; and **Meadowlake Park** has an 18 hole golf course, amusement park, and a 14 acre lake.

Locator 249-7791   **Medical 249-7416**   **Police 249-7200**

Oregon

Kingsley Field (OR03R4)
Klamath Falls, OR 97603-0400

TELEPHONE NUMBER INFORMATION: Main installation numbers: C-503-885-6365, D-312-830-6365.

Location: On Highway 140. USM: B-3, NMC: Klamath Falls, 5 miles west.

Billeting Office: Building 208, Kingsley Street, C-**503-885-6365**, 0730-1530 hours M-F. After hours extra keys at Security Gate.

TML: VOQ. All ranks, leave or official duty. Suites, private bath (20); bedrooms, 2 beds, semi-private bath (40). Older structure, renovated. Rates: suites $8 per person, single rooms $6 per person. Students have priority in reservations, others Space-A.

TML Availability: Difficult, except for holidays.

☞ Experience top notch fishing, bald eagles that winter nearby, world class skiing, golf, horseback riding, camping, hunting. Then there's Crater Lake and Mt. Shasta within one hour's drive that makes this area a vacationer's paradise.

NOTE: Both VOQ and restaurant operated under contract to Commission for the Blind.

Pennsylvania

Carlisle Barracks (PA08R1)
Carlisle Barracks, PA 17013-5002

TELEPHONE NUMBER INFORMATION: Main installation numbers: C-717-245-3131, D-312-242-4141.

Location: From I-81 exit 16 to US-11, 2 miles southwest to Carlisle, signs clearly marked to Barracks and Army War College. USM: L-4. NMC: Harrisburg, 18 miles north.

Billeting Office: ATTN: ATZE-DI-GH, building 7, Ashburn St, C-717-245-4245, 0700-1800 hours weekdays, 0900-1600 hours weekends. Other hours building 400, pick up key at MP desk. Check in billeting, check out 1100 hours daily. Government civilian employee billeting. Note: only family members with valid ID card can stay at this facility.

TML: Guest House. Buildings 7, 37, all ranks, leave or official duty. Bedrooms, private bath (14); bedrooms, shared bath (4); bedrooms, community bath (6); VIP suites, private bath (1 night only) (4). Community kitchen, A/C, color TV in room & lounge, maid service, cribs/cots ($2), ice vending. Rates: $20 single, $25 double with private bath, $15-$20 with shared bath, $10-$15 with community bath, $25-$30 suites. PCS and guests of USAWC have priority. All categories can make reservations.

TML Availability: Good, Jan-May. Difficult, other times.

☞ An arsenal during the Revolutionary War; near the Gettysburg Battlefields; site of the Military History Institute (open to the public), Carlisle Barracks has an illustrious history worth tracing.

Locator 245-3131   **Medical 245-3915/3400**   **Police 245-4315**

Defense Distribution Region East (PA06R1)
New Cumberland, PA 17070-5001

TELEPHONE NUMBER INFORMATION: Main installation numbers: C-717-770-6011, D-312-977-6011, FTS-589-6011.

Location: From I-83 take exit 18 to PA 114. East for 1 mile to Old York Rd, left .75 mile to Ross Ave, right for 1 mile to main gate. USM: L-3,4. NMC: Harrisburg, 7 miles northeast.

Billeting Office: ATTN: WIH, building 268, J Ave, C-717-770-7035, 0700-1700 hours daily. Government civilian employee billeting in VOQ.

TML: VOQ/DV/VIP. Building 268, all ranks, leave or official duty. Bedroom, shared bath (18); separate bedroom, private bath (1); two bedroom, private bath (1). Refrigerator, community kitchen, A/C, color TV, maid service, cribs, cots, washer/dryer. Older structure, renovated. Rates: VOQ $12, DVQ $14. Duty with TDY orders can make reservations, others Space-A. Maximum 2 adults and 1 child per unit.

PENNSYLVANIA
Defense Distribution Region East, continued

DV/VIP: Protocol Office, building 81, C-EX-7192, 06/GS-15+, retirees and lower ranks Space-A.

TML Availability: Good, Oct-Dec and Feb-Mar. Difficult, other times.

☞ **Visit Hershey Park, famous Pennsylvania Dutch Country, Gettysburg National Military Park, and General Lee's Headquarters and Museum.**

Locator 770-6011   Medical 770-7281   Police 770-6222

Fort Indiantown Gap (PA04R1)
Annville, PA 17003-5011

TELEPHONE NUMBER INFORMATION: Main installation numbers: C-717-865-5444, EX-2512, D-312-277-2512.

Location: From I-81 take exit 29 west, north on PA-934 to facility. USM: L-3. NMC: Harrisburg, 20 miles southwest.

Billeting Office: ATTN: AFKA-ZQ-DE-H, building T-0-1, Fisher Ave at traffic light, C-717-865-2512, 0800-2330 hours daily. Check in billeting, check out 1100 hours daily.

TML: Reserve/National Guard post. VOQ/BEQ. Building T-0-1, officers all ranks, enlisted E7-E9, leave or official duty. Room, common bath (26); separate bedroom, private bath (5). A/C, color TV, maid service, washer/dryer, facilities for DAVs. Older structure, renovated. Rates: $7 and $9 per room. No dependents.

TML Availability: Difficult, most of the time. Best, Nov-Mar.

☞ **Guided tours at the local Tulpehocken Manor Inn and Plantation, Indian Echo Caverns, with a spectacular underground display, and local Pennsylvania German farm and village festivals and crafts demonstrations are "must sees."**

Locator 865-5444   Medical 865-2091   Police 865-2160

Letterkenny Army Depot (PA03R1)
Chambersburg, PA 17201-4150

TELEPHONE NUMBER INFORMATION: Main installation numbers: C-717-267-8111, D-312-570-1110.

Location: From I-81 exit 8 west on PA-997 to PA-233 on left and enter depot at Gate 6. USM: L-4. NMC: Harrisburg, 45 miles northeast.

Billeting Office: ATTN: SDSLE-EH, building 663, C-717-267-8890, 0730-1600 hours M-F. Other hours call security C-717-267-8800. Check in billeting, check out 1000 hours daily. Government civilian employee billeting.

PENNSYLVANIA

Letterkenny Army Depot

TML: Guest House. Building 539, all ranks, leave or official duty. One bedroom, private bath (1); one bedroom, private bath (1); half bedroom, private bath (1). Kitchen, limited utensils, A/C, color TV, maid service, cribs/cots, washer/dryer. Older structure, renovated. Rates: 1 bedroom $12, separate bedroom $14, 2 bedroom $17. Duty, DAVs, military widows can make reservations, others Space-A.

DV/VIP: ATTN: SDSLE-CA, building 500, C-EX-8659, DV/VIP determined by CO. Retirees Space-A.

TML Availability: Best, Sep-Mar.

☞ **Tour famous Gettysburg Battlefield, try local bass and trout fishing in Rocky Springs Reservoir, local hunting is very good, and state capitol, Harrisburg is of interest to visitors.**

Locator 264-1413   **Police 267-8800**

Philadelphia Naval Base/Station (PA09R1)
Philadelphia NB/S, PA 19112-5098

TELEPHONE NUMBER INFORMATION: Main installation numbers: C-215-897-5000, D-312-443-5000.

Location: Exit I-95 North at Broad St. Base gate is 200 yards south of exit. USM: N-4. NMC: Philadelphia, in the city.

Billeting Office: Building 1031, C-215-897-5317/8, 24 hours daily. Check in facility, check out 1100 hours daily. Government civilian employee billeting.

TML: Navy Lodge. Reservations call 1-800-NAVY INN. Lodge number is 465-9001. All ranks. Leave or official duty. Bedroom, 2 double beds, private bath (50). Kitchen, microwave, color TV, hairdryers, convenience store, vending machines, coin washer/dryer, ice vending. Rates: $36 per room. All categories can make reservations.

TML: BEQ. Building 1031, enlisted, all ranks, leave or official duty. C-215-897-5157/5160, FAX C-215-897-5159, D-312-443-5150. Bedroom, private bath (E1-E6)(72); bedroom, private bath (E7-E9)(54). Refrigerator, microwave, A/C, CATV, VCR rental, maid service, ice vending, in room phones, washer/dryer. Modern structure, renovated '91/'92. Rates: E1-E6 $6, E7-E9 $15 per night. Duty can make reservations, others Space-A.

TML: BOQ. Buildings 886, 887, officers, all ranks, C-215-897-5317/8, FAX-215-897-5316. Suites, (sitting room, bedroom, double bed (24); bedroom, shared bath (54); guesthouse (livingroom, kitchen, 3 bedrooms) (1). Refrigerator, microwave, coffee service, A/C, CATV, VCR rental, washer/dryer, in room phones, maid service, ice vending. Modern structure, renovated '91/'92. Rates: suites $15 per night; singles $8, guesthouse $20. Duty may make reservations, civilians on TAD orders, all others Space-A

DV/VIP: Quarters A. Historic building. Attn: Flag Lt, building 6, C-EX-7622, 06+. Suites, one bedroom (3); extra bedrooms for children. A/C, library, fireplace, sitting room, dining room, kitchen, meeting facilities, in room phones. Rates: $30, $3 children. Duty may make reservations, others Space-A.

PENNSYLVANIA
Philadelphia Naval Base/Station, continued

TML Availability: Good, winter months. Difficult other times.

☞ Visit the city of our nation's birth. The Liberty Bell, and many historic exhibits and museums, plus culture as only Philadelphia can do it. Billeting boasts this facility is going to be "another Hilton"!

Locator 897-5550   **Medical 897-6837**   **Police 897-4242**

Tobyhanna Army Depot (PA05R1)
Tobyhanna, PA 18466-5058

TELEPHONE NUMBER INFORMATION: Main installation numbers: C-717-894-7000, D-312-795-7110.

Location: I-80 East or West to I-380 North, exit 7 to depot. USM: L,M-3. NMC: Scranton, 24 miles northwest.

Billeting Office: ATTN: SDSTO-EH-F, building 1001, C-**717-894-7647**, 0800-1630 hours daily. Other hours Security, building 20, C-EX-7550. Check in billeting, check out 1000 hours daily.

TML: Guest House, building 1013, VOQ building 1005, all ranks, leave or official duty. Two bedroom, private bath (2); three bedroom, private bath (1). Kitchen, limited utensils, color TV, maid service, cribs, washer/dryer. One older structure, two newly renovated. Rates: sponsor $11, each additional person $3. Maximum $25 per family. Duty can make reservations, others Space-A.

DV/VIP: ATTN: Protocol Office, building 11-2, C-EX-6223, 06+. Retirees and lower ranks Space-A, no DV/VIP quarters.

TML Availability: Good, Apr-Nov. More difficult, other times.

☞ In the Pocono Mountains Resort Area. Hundreds of nearby lakes and streams provide fishing and water sports. State parks and forest picnic areas in the immediate area will lure visitors.

Locator 894-7000   **Medical 894-7121**   **Police 894-7550**

Willow Grove Naval Air Station (PA01R1)
Willow Grove NAS, PA 19090-5010

TELEPHONE NUMBER INFORMATION: Main installation numbers: C-215-443-1000, D-312-991-1000.

Location: Take PA Turnpike (I-276), exit 27 north on PA 611 5 miles to NAS. USM: N-4. NMC: Philadelphia, 21 miles south.

Billeting Office: Building 609, C-**215-443-6038/6041**, 24 hours daily. Check in facility, check out 1100 hours daily. Government civilian employee billeting at BOQ.

Willow Grove Naval Air Station, continued

TML: BOQ. Building 5, officers all ranks. Leave or official duty. Bedroom, common bath (20). A/C, refrigerator, microwave, color TV, maid service, washer/dryer. Older structure, renovated. Rates: $4 per person. PCS, TDY, active duty can make reservations, retirees, others Space-A.

TML: BEQ. Building 609, enlisted all ranks, leave or official duty. Bedroom, shared bath (40); two bedroom suites, private bath (6). A/C, maid service, refrigerator, microwave, color TV, washer/dryer. Rates: $3 per person. Maximum 5 per unit. Duty can make reservations, retirees, others Space-A.

TML: MWR Chalets, sleeps 6, two bedrooms + loft (2). C-215-443-6085 for information.

DV/VIP: PAO. Building 1 top deck, C-EX-1776/1777. DV/VIP determined by PAO. Retirees and lower ranks Space-A.

TML Availability: Fair except weekends when extremely limited due to Reserve Unit and individual training.

☞ See Philadelphia's Liberty Bell, Society Hill, New Market, summer open air concerts along the Parkway and at Robin Hood Dell. Visit the 9th Street Market in little Italy (Rocky Balboa made his famous run here).

Locator 443-1000   **Medical 443-1600**   **Police 443-6067**

Rhode Island

Newport Naval Education & Training Center (RI01R1)
Newport, RI 02841-0001

TELEPHONE NUMBER INFORMATION: Main installation numbers: C-401-841-2311, D-312-948-1110.

Location: From US-1 exit to RI-138 East over Jamestown/Newport bridge (toll) to Newport. Follow signs to naval base, gate 1. USM: M-3. NMC: Newport, 2 miles south.

Billeting Office: No central billeting office. Officers, building 684, **C-401-841-3156.** Enlisted, building 447, **C-401-841-4410,** both 24 hours daily. Check in facility 1300 hours. Check out 1100 hours daily. No government civilian employee billeting in BEQ.

TML: BOQ/BEQ. Bedroom, private/shared bath (575); separate bedrooms, private bath (4). Full facility. Rates: moderate, no families. Duty can make reservations, others space-A.

TML: Navy Lodge. Building 685, all ranks, leave or official duty. For reservations call **1-800-NAVY-INN.** Lodge number is 849-4500, 0700-2300 hours daily. Check out 1200 hours daily. Studio apartments, 2 double beds, 1 studio couch, sleeps 5, private bath (67). Kitchen, complete utensils, A/C, color TV in room & lounge, maid service, cribs, coin washer/dryer, ice vending. Modern structure. Rates: $34 per unit. All categories can make reservations.

RHODE ISLAND
Newport Naval E & T Center, continued

DV/VIP: Contact CO, C-EX-3715.

TML Availability: Good, winter months. Difficult, summer months.

☞ Stroll along cobblestone streets, or ocean front walks; admire turn-of-the-Century mansions; visit many national historic landmarks, and the Naval War College Museum. Admire the wonderful sailing vessels - this is Newport!

Locator 841-4001   **Medical 841-3111/2222**   **Police 841-3241**

South Carolina

Beaufort Marine Corps Air Station (SC01R1)
Beaufort MCAS, SC 29904-5000

TELEPHONE NUMBER INFORMATION: Main installation numbers: C-803-522-7100, D-312-832-7100.

Location: From I-95 exit at Pocataligo to SC-21, 4 miles to MCAS. Clearly marked. USM: L-6. NMC: Savannah, 40 miles south.

Billeting Office: BOQ, building 431, C-**803-522-7676**, front desk: C-803-522-7674, 24 hours daily. Check in facility, check out 1200 hours daily. Government civilian employee billeting.

TML: de Treville House, building 1108, C-**1-803-522-1633**. All ranks, leave or official duty. Bedroom, private bath (21); separate bedroom, private bath (21). Kitchen (in separate bedroom), A/C, cots ($5), cribs, ice vending. maid service, special facilities for DAVs, color TV, complete utensils, washer/dryer, playground, picnic area with grills. Handicapped accessible. Modern structure. Rates: $21 E1-E5; $26 for E6+; extra $10 for kitchen units. Maximum 5 per unit. All categories can make reservations. Non-military personnel visiting relatives stationed at Beaufort may stay on a Space-A basis.

TML: BOQ. Building 431, officers all ranks, enlisted E6-E9, leave or official duty. Bedrooms (officers)(39); suites, shared bath/private bath (officers)(5); bedroom, private/shared bath (enlisted) (17). Refrigerator, community kitchen, limited utensils, A/C, color TV room & lounge, maid service, cribs, washer/dryer, ice vending. Modern structure, renovated. Room and suite rates: duty $6 rooms, $10 suites; others $11 rooms, $17 suite, $2 each dependent, no children. Duty can make reservations, others Space-A.

DV/VIP: Contact CO, building 601, C-EX-7158. Retirees and lower ranks Space-A.

TML Availability: Very good, most of the year. Best, Sep-Apr.

Locator 522-7188   **Medical 522-7311**   **Police 522-7373**

SOUTH CAROLINA

Charleston Air Force Base (SC06R1)
Charleston AFB, SC 29404-5415

TELEPHONE NUMBER INFORMATION: Main installation numbers: C-803-566-2100, D-312-673-2100.

Location: From I-26 East exit to West Aviation Ave to traffic light, continue through light to 2nd light on right, follow Rd around end of runway to Gate 2 (River Gate). USM: L-6. NMC: Charleston, 5 miles southeast.

Billeting Office: Building 322, Davis Dr, C-803-552-9900, D-312-673-2100 EX-860. Toll free: **1-800-CHS-BEDS**, 24 hours daily. Reservations: M-F 0800-1700, C-**803-566-3806**, D-312-673-3806. Check in facility, check out 1200 hours daily. Government civilian employee billeting in contract quarters.

TML: VOQ/DV/VIP. Buildings 343, 346, 362, officers, all ranks, leave or official duty. Bedroom, shared bath (102); bedroom suites, private bath (06+) (7); room mini suites (4). Kitchen, refrigerator, A/C, maid service, cribs/cots, washer/dryer, ice vending. Modern structure. Rates: DV/VIP (suites) $14 per person, maximum $28; DV Mini-Suites & VOQ $8 per person, maximum $16. Maximum 5 per room. Duty can make reservations, others Space-A. No pets allowed.

TML: VAQ. Senior enlisted (E7+), building 344, leave or official duty. Bedroom, private bath (3); bedroom, shared bath (19). A/C, color TV, maid service, washer/dryer, ice vending. Rates: suites: $14 per person, maximum $28 per room; rooms: $8 per person, maximum $16 per room. Duty can make reservations, others space A. No pets.

TML: Junior enlisted (E1-E6), buildings 300, 302, 304, 344, leave or official duty. Bedroom, hall bath-males, shared bath-females (395). A/C, color TV, maid service, washer/dryer, ice vending. Rates: $8 per person. Duty can make reservations, others Space-A. No dependents, no pets.

TML: TLF. Building 330, all ranks. Bedroom suites, private bath, kitchen, sleeps 5 (18). A/C color TV, maid service, washer/dryer, ice vending. Rates: $20 per family. Duty can make reservations, others Space-A.

DV/VIP: Office of the Wing CP, building 103, room 1, C-EX-5644, 06+. Retirees Space-A. No pets allowed.

TML Availability: Good, Nov-Dec. Difficult, other times because of duty traffic.

☞ **Visit stately mansions along the Battery, and Boone Hall, where scenes from "Gone With the Wind" and "North and South" were filmed. Take a water tour, and visit historic Fort Sumter and Charleston Harbor.**

Locator 566-3282   Medical 566-2775   Police 566-3600

Charleston Naval Base/Station (SC04R1)
Charleston NB/S, SC 29408-5006

TELEPHONE NUMBER INFORMATION: Main installation numbers: C-803-743-4111, D-312-563-4111.

SOUTH CAROLINA
Charleston Naval Base/Station, continued

Location: From I-26 take Cosgrove Ave exit to Spruill Ave, right for 3 miles to main gate of base. USM: L-6. NMC: Charleston, 5 miles north.

Billeting Office: In BEQ, building 54, Osprey St, 24 hours daily. C-803-743-5268/5528. Check in billeting, check out 1200 hours daily. Government civilian employee billeting.

TML: Navy Lodge. Building 225, all ranks, leave or official duty. Reservations call 1-800-NAVY-INN. Lodge number is 747-7676, 24 hours daily. Bedroom, 2 double beds, private bath (45). Kitchenette, complete utensils, A/C, color TV, maid service, cribs, washer/dryer, ice vending. Modern structure. Rates: $32 subject to change. Maximum 5 per unit. All categories can make reservations.

TML: BOQ, **Sullivan Hall**, BEQ, building 54. Total 540 units. All ranks, official duty, leave Space-A, call above number. BOQ: buildings 4,5,6. Bedrooms, private bath (4); bedrooms, shared bath (some reserved for G.B.)(36), call below number. BEQ: 14 buildings, bedrooms, hall bath. Refrigerator, A/C, color TV in some rooms, maid service, washer/dryer. Rates: $5.50 per day. Duty on orders can make reservations, others Space-A.

TML: VOQ/DV/VIP. Building 28, officers all ranks, leave or official duty. C-803-743-5394/3939, 24 hours daily. Check out 1200 hours daily. VOQ: bedroom, private bath (179); separate bedroom, private bath (47); DV/VIP: bedroom, private bath (4); bedroom, queen bed, sitting room, pull out queen size couch (11). Refrigerator, A/C, color TV in room & lounge, maid service, cribs/cots, washer/dryer, ice vending. Modern structure. Rates: standard room $9.50, $8 additional person, no charge for children occupying one room. DV/VIP $10.50, $8 for additional person; double $16.50, $8 additional person. Duty can make reservations, 07+ one day in advance, others Space-A.

DV/VIP: CO's Office, C-EX-4111. E9, 07+.

TML Availability: Very good all year.

☞ **Visit the Patriots Point Maritime Museum, local Gardens, and the historic section of Charleston. Tourist information at the front desk gives local restaurants, shopping and activities for visitors.**

Locator 743-4111   **Medical 743-5130**   **Police 743-5555**

Fort Jackson (SC09R1)
Fort Jackson, SC 29207-5000

TELEPHONE NUMBER INFORMATION: Main installation number: C-803-751-7511, D-312-734-1110.

Location: Exit from I-20 north of the fort or from US-76/378 south of the fort or US-601 east of the fort. From I-20 take Ft Jackson or Two Notch Rd exit, left on Decker Blvd, right on Percival Rd to fort entrance. USM: L-6. NMC: Columbia, SC 12 miles southwest.

Billeting Office: Building 2785, corner Semmes Rd & Lee Rd, C-803-751-6223, D-312-734-6223. Toll free reservations for government official duty personnel (on post) and local hotels 1-800-221-3503, 24 hours daily. Check in billeting, check out 1000 hours daily. Government civilian employee billeting.

Fort Jackson, continued

SOUTH CAROLINA

TML: Guest House, **Palmetto Lodge**, building 6000, all ranks, leave or official duty, C-EX-4779. Bedroom, private bath, sleeps 6 persons (70). Kitchen, limited utensils, A/C, telephone, color TV in room & lounge, maid service, washer/dryer, ice vending. Rates: $24 per couple, PCS $16 per couple, $2 child over 12. No pets. Duty can make reservations, others Space-A.

TML: Kennedy Hall, building 2785, all ranks, leave or official duty. Bedroom, 1 bed, private bath (transient units) (92); BOQ units (30). Refrigerator, A/C, color TV, maid service, washer/dryer. Modern structure, remodeled. Rates: $22 per couple, PCS $12 per couple. Maximum 2 per unit. No children, no pets. Duty can make reservations, others Space-A.

TML: VEQ. Building 2464, enlisted all ranks, official duty. Bedroom, 1 bed, private bath (12). Refrigerator, color TV, maid service. Rates: sponsor $22 per couple, PCS $12 per couple. No children, no pets. Duty can make reservations, others Space-A.

TML: DV/VIP. Cottages, buildings 3640-3645, 4410, Legion Landing & Dozier House. Officers 05+, official duty. Check out 1100 hours. Bedroom, private bath (2), two bedroom, private bath (4), three bedroom, private bath suite (1). Kitchen, utensils, A/C, color TV, telephone, maid service. Remodeled. Rates: $22 per couple, $5 additional guests. No children, no pets. Duty can make reservations, others Space-A.

DV/VIP: Protocol Office, Hq Building, C-EX-6618, D-EX-5218, 06+.

TML Availability: Very good, Oct-May.

☞ **Riverbanks Zoological Park, Town Theater amateur productions, and a carriage ride along historic Broad Street compete with local golf courses, Lake Murray and numerous public recreation areas as local popular pastimes.**

Locator 751-7671   Medical 911   Police 751-3113

Myrtle Beach Air Force Base (SC07R1)
Myrtle Beach AFB, SC 29579-5001

TELEPHONE NUMBER INFORMATION: Main installation numbers: C-803-238-7211, D-312-748-7211.

Location: From I-95 exit east on US-501, right on US-17 (business) to AFB. Clearly marked. USM: L-6. NMC: Myrtle Beach, in city limits.

Billeting Office: ATTN: 354 CSG/SVH, building 126, A Ave & 4th St, C-**803-238-5101**, D-312-748-7691, 24 hours daily. Check in billeting, check out 1200 hours daily. Government civilian employee billeting. Tentative reservations accepted Space-A personnel 1 Sep - 31 Mar. Space-A can be bumped for priority one personnel (TDY, PCS, etc.).

TML: TLQ. Buildings 115, 127. All ranks, leave or official duty. Two bedroom, private bath (12); bedroom, private bath (2). Kitchen, complete utensils, A/C, color TV, maid service, cribs/cots, washer/dryer. Modern structure. Rates: $18 per family. PCS in/out can make reservations, others Space-A.

SOUTH CAROLINA
Myrtle Beach Air Force Base, continued

TML: VOQ. Building 126, all ranks, leave or official duty. Bedroom, shared bath (36); bedroom, private bath (2). Refrigerator, A/C, color TV, maid service, washer/dryer, ice vending. Modern structure, renovated. Rates: $9 per room per night. Maximum 1 per room. TDY can make reservations, others Space-A.

TML: VAQ. Building 249, all ranks, leave or official duty. Bedroom, 2 beds, shared bath (36); single bedroom Chief suite, private bath (1). Same amenities as VOQ. Modern structure, new carpeting, TVs. Rates: $7 per person. Chief Suite $10. Maximum 2 per room. TDY can make reservations, others Space-A.

TML: DV/VIP. Building 126, officer 06+, leave or official duty, C-EX-7673/5101. D-EX-7673/7691. Bedroom, private bath (2); two bedroom suite, private bath (1). Kitchen, complete utensils, A/C, color TV, maid service, cribs/cots, washer/dryer, ice vending. Modern structure, renovated. Rates: $10. Maximum charge $20 (1 bedroom), $40 (2 bedroom). Duty can make reservations, others Space-A.

DV/VIP: 354 TFW/CCE. Building 104, C-EX-7673, 06/GS-15+. Retirees Space-A.

TML Availability: Good, Nov-Feb. Difficult, other times.

☞ In one of the nation's outstanding seashore resorts, fishing, golfing, local state parks, and the historic area of Brookgreen Gardens are all local attractions.

⊗This base will close March 1993. How long billeting will remain open, or status of facilities upon closure is unknown at press time. Watch Military Living's *R&R Space-A Report* for the latest information.

Locator 238-7056   **Medical 238-7333**   **Police 238-7659**

Parris Island Marine Corps Recruit Depot (SC08R1)
Parris Island MCRD, SC 29905-5000

TELEPHONE NUMBER INFORMATION: Main installation numbers: C-803-525-2111, D-312-832-1110.

Location: From I-95 South exit at Beaufort to SC-170 or US-21, both east to SC-280 to SC-281 which leads to main gate of depot. USM: L-6. NMC: Savannah, 43 miles southwest.

Billeting Office: Billeting office, building 330, for information call C-EX-2731, Check in facility, check out 1100 hours. Government civilian employee billeting in Hostess House.

TML: Hostess House. Building 200, all ranks, leave or official duty C-803-525-2976/3460. Bedroom, 2 beds, sleep sofa, private bath (30). Kitchen, limited utensils, A/C, color TV in room & lounge, maid service, cribs, washer/dryer, ice vending, facilities for DAVs. Modern structure, renovated. Rates: officer/enlisted $25, $35 with kitchen. All categories can make reservations.

SOUTH CAROLINA

Parris Island Marine Corps Recruit Depot, continued

TML: TLQ. Building 254, officers all ranks, leave or official duty. Bedroom, private bath (6). Kitchen, complete utensils, A/C, color TV in room & lounge, maid service, cots, washer/dryer, ice vending. Older structure, renovated. Rates: $25-$35 per room. Maximum 4 persons. All categories can make reservations.

TML: BEQ. Building 331, enlisted E6-E9. Bedroom, private bath (71). Refrigerator, A/C, optional maid service, washer/dryer, ice vending. Modern structure. Rates: $4 per person. Maximum 1 per room.

TML: BOQ. Building 289, officers all ranks, leave or official duty, C-EX-2744/2731. Bedroom, private bath (19); bedrooms, common bath (4). A/C, color TV, washer/dryer, ice vending. Older structure. Rates: depends on status. Maximum 1 per room. Duty and retirees can make reservations.

DV/VIP: Building 254, officers O6, leave or official duty, C-EX-2976. Two bedroom suite, completely furnished, kitchen, private bath (1). Complete utensils, A/C, color TV, maid service, cribs, washer/dryer, ice vending. Rates: $40 per room. Maximum 4 per room. Duty, retired, DAVs, military widows, accompanied dependents of retirees can make reservations.

TML Availability: Good except graduation days.

Locator 525-3358   **Medical 525-3351**   **Police 525-3444**

Shaw Air Force Base (SC10R1)
Shaw AFB, SC 29152-5000

TELEPHONE NUMBER INFORMATION: Main installation numbers: C-803-668-8110, D-312-965-1110.

Location: Off US-76/378 8 mi west of Sumter, SC. Clearly marked. USM: L-6. NMC: Columbia, 35 miles west.

Billeting Office: Carolina Pines Inn, building 929, Myers St, C-803-668-3210, 24 hours daily. Check in facility, check out 1200 hours daily. Government civilian employee billeting.

TML: TLF. Buildings 931-934, all ranks, leave or official duty. Handicapped accessible. Separate bedrooms, sleeper sofa, private bath (40). Kitchenette, A/C, color TV (HBO & Disney), maid service, cribs/cots, washer/dryer. Modern structure. Rates: $20 per unit. Maximum 5 per apartment. Duty can make reservations, others Space-A.

TML: VAQ. Buildings 900, 929, enlisted all ranks, leave or official duty. Bedroom, 2 beds, shared bath (4 SNCO rooms have private bath)(64). A/C, color TV (HBO), maid service, cribs/cots, washer/dryer, ice vending. Modern structure. Rates: $7.50 per person, $10 room w/private bath. Maximum 2 per room. Duty can make reservations, others Space-A.

TML: VOQ. Buildings 911, 924, 927, officers all ranks, leave or official duty. Bedroom, private bath (68); separate bedroom suites, private bath (14). Kitchen, limited utensils, A/C, color TV (HBO), maid service, cribs/cots, washer/dryer, ice vending. Older structure. Rates: $8 per person. Maximum 2 per room. Duty can make reservations, others Space-A.

SOUTH CAROLINA
Shaw Air Force Base, continued

TML: DV/VIP. Building 924, officer 06+, leave or official duty. Separate bedroom suites, private bath (6). Kitchen, complete utensils, A/C, color TV (HBO), maid service, cribs/cots, washer/dryer, ice vending. Older structure, remodeled. Rates: $10 per person. Maximum $20 per room. Duty can make reservations, others Space-A.

DV/VIP: Protocol Office. C-EX-2156/2311, D-EX-2156/2311, 06+. Retirees Space-A.

TML Availability: Good. Best, Dec-Mar.

☞ An 18 hole golf course, 3 swimming pools, tennis courts and fitness center on base, and Columbia, the state capital, and Charleston, not to mention Myrtle Beach, the Blue Ridge and Smokey Mountains, are all within reach for visitors.

Locator 668-2166   **Medical 668-2571**   **Police 668-3628**

Short Stay Navy Recreation Area (SC02R1)
Moncks Corner, SC 29461-5000

TELEPHONE NUMBER INFORMATION: Main installation numbers: C-803-761-8353, D-312-563-5608

Location: Take I-26 to US 17-A toward Moncks Corner (15 miles). Left on US 52 for 3 miles. Follow signs to Navy Recreation Area. USM: L-6. NMC: Charleston, 35 miles South.

Billeting Office: Write to: Short Stay, Rt. 5, Box 320, Moncks Corner, SC 29461, C-**803-761-8353/743-5608,** D-312-563-5608, 24 hours daily. Check in at facility 1500 hours. Check out 1100 hours. Late checkout call C-803-761-8353. Government civilian employee billeting at NAVSTA. Security at front gate when office is closed.

TML: Six cabins, 38 villas. Cabins sleep 6, (2 full beds, 1 sleep sofa), private bath (6); two bedroom villa sleeps 4 (2 full beds), private bath (26); three bedroom villa sleeps 6 (3 full beds) (12). Three units handicapped equipped. Kitchenette, complete utensils, linens, washer/dryer ($.50), decks, picnic tables, grills, food and ice vending, color TV. New villas spring '91 (38), new, reservable recreation center, spring '92. Convenience store, snack bar, boat rental, bait & tackle, volleyball, swimming beach, game room, horseshoes, laundry, gas. Limits to capacity above. Rates: villas $25-$53 (low, mid, high seasons, military, civilian rates); cabins $28-$47. Write for brochure. All may reserve, first access to duty, second retirees, third DoD civilians in season. Off season more equal access). Cancellations 3 days prior to check-in date (later, $15 fee). One unit per I.D. per time period. Minimum age to reserve 18. Pets permitted in campground only. Restrictions apply.

DV/VIP: None.

TML Availability: Good. Best Sep-May, difficult June-Aug.

☞ Located on Lake Moultrie (60,000 acres), fishing, watersports, Charleston offers beaches, golf, historic sites. Read Military Living's *Military RV, Camping and Rec Areas Around the World* for more information.

Locator 761-8353   **Medical 743-5130**   **Police 743-5555**

South Dakota

Ellsworth Air Force Base (SD01R3)
Ellsworth AFB, SD 57706-5000

TELEPHONE NUMBER INFORMATION: Main installation numbers: C-605-385-1000, D-312-675-1000.

Location: Off I-90, 10 miles east of Rapid City. Clearly marked. USM: F-3. NMC: Rapid City, 10 miles west.

Billeting Office: Building 1103, 6th St, across from gym, C-605- 923-5861, D-312-675-2844, 24 hours daily. Check in facility, check out 1200 hours daily (TLF 1000 hours). No government civilian employee billeting.

TML: TLF. Building 4101, all ranks, leave or official duty, C-EX-1362. Bedroom, shared bath (4); double rooms, shared bath (21). Refrigerator, community kitchen, color TV, cribs, cots, maid service, washer/dryer, ice vending. Older structure. Rates: $15 per unit. Duty can make reservations, others Space-A.

TML: VOQ/VAQ. Building 1103, all ranks, leave or official duty. Two bedroom, private bath (VOQ) (51); bedroom, 1 bed each room, shared bath (VAQ) (70). Refrigerator, A/C, color TV in room & lounge, maid service, washer/dryer, ice vending. Older structure. Rates: $8 per person VOQ, $6 per person VAQ, maximum $16 per room. Maximum 3 per room. Duty can make reservations, others Space-A.

TML: DV/VIP. Building 4100, officers 06+, leave or official duty. Separate bedroom suites, private bath (6). Color TV, maid service. Older structure. Rates: $8 per person. Duty can make reservations, others Space-A.

DV/VIP: Protocol Office. Building 1103, C-923-5861, D-EX-2844, 06+. Retirees and lower ranks Space-A with approval of Protocol.

TML Availability: Good, Oct-Apr. More difficult, other times.

Locator 385-1379   **Medical 385-3430**   **Police 399-4001**

⊗**This facility did not respond to our inquiries, information may be outdated.**

Tennessee

Arnold Air Force Base (TN02R2)
Arnold AFB, TN 37389-5000

TELEPHONE NUMBER INFORMATION: Main installation numbers: C-615-454-3000, D-312-340-3000.

TENNESSEE
Arnold Air Force Base, continued

Location: From Tullahoma, take Air Engineering Development Center access highway. From I-24 take AEDC exit 117, 4 miles south of Manchester. Clearly marked. USM: J-5,6. NMC: Chattanooga, 65 miles southeast; Nashville, 65 miles northwest.

Billeting Office: The Forest Inn, building 3027, C-614-454-5498, M-F 0600-2200, Sa 1000-2000, Su 1200-2200. Other hours, SDO C-615-454-7752. Check in billeting, check out 1200 hours. No government civilian employee billeting.

TML: VOQ. Building 3027, all ranks, leave or official duty. Bedroom, shared bath (40); separate bedroom, shared bath (DV/VIP) (5). Refrigerator, community kitchen, limited utensils, A/C, color TV in room & lounge, maid service, cribs, washer/dryer, ice vending. Older structure. Rates: $8 per person, $14 DV/VIP. Duty can make reservations, others Space-A.

DV/VIP: Billeting Office. 06+, retirees, Space-A.

TML Availability: Good, all year.

☞ On this 44,000 acre installation, Woods Reservoir has a 75 miles shoreline. for fishing and all water sports. Visit the Grand Ole Opry, Music Row, the Parthenon, the Hermitage in Nashville. Civil War buffs: lots to see.

Locator 454-3000   **Medical 454-5351**   **Police 454-5222**

Memphis Naval Air Station (TN01R2)
Millington, TN 38054-2028

TELEPHONE NUMBER INFORMATION: Main installation numbers: C-901-873-5500, D-312-966-5500.

Location: From US-51 North at Millington, exit to Navy Rd, right to first gate on right, main gate. USM: I-6. NMC: Memphis, 20 miles southwest.

Billeting Office: Building S-61, C-901-873-5459/5384, 24 hours daily. Check in facility, check out 1200 hours daily. Government civilian employee billeting GS-9+.

TML: Navy Lodge. Buildings N-762, N-931, all ranks, leave or official duty. For reservations call 1-800-NAVY-INN, lodge number is 872-0121. Bedroom, private bath (48). Kitchen, complete utensils, A/C, color TV, maid service, coin washer/dryer. Modern structures, N-931 newer. Rates: N-931 $35 per unit, N-762 $31. All categories can make reservations. **Pets allowed in area adjacent to lodge.**

TML: BOQ/BEQ. All ranks, leave or official duty. Check in at facility. Officers: bedroom, private bath (82); enlisted: bedroom, private bath (some shared bath) (296). Refrigerator, A/C, color TV in room & lounge, maid service, washer/dryer, ice vending, special facilities for DAV's. Modern structure. Rates: BOQ $8-$20 per person, BEQ $6-$9 per person. Dependents must use Navy Lodge. Duty can make reservations, others Space-A.

DV/VIP: Cmdr, C-EX-5101/2, 06+. Retirees Space-A.

TML Availability: Good, Dec. Difficult, other times.

Memphis Naval Air Station, continued

TENNESSEE

 Shelby Forest State Park provides thousands of acres of native woodlands for walking, riding, picnicking and boating. The Memphis area is famous for bird and duck hunting.

Locator 873-5111   Medical 911   Police 873-5533

Texas

Air Force Village (TX28R3)
4917 Ravenswood Drive
San Antonio, TX 78227-4352

TELEPHONE NUMBER INFORMATION: Main installation numbers: C-512-673-2761, D-None.

Location: Off I-410 (Loop), take exit 4 (Lackland/Valley-Hi), near Lackland AFB, TX. USM: G-8. NMC: San Antonio, 6 miles northeast.

Billeting Office: Write or call for information to address and telephone number above.

TML: Guest Rooms. Officers all ranks, duty or retired. Rooms, private bath (8); Two bedroom apartment, private bath, kitchen, living room, furnished. For guests of residents, others Space-A.

TML Availability: Limited. Call in advance.

☞ See Air Force Village II listing.

Air Force Village II (TX43R3)
5100 John D. Ryan Boulevard
San Antonio, TX 78245

TELEPHONE NUMBER INFORMATION: Main installation numbers: C-512-677-8666. D-None.

Location: Eight miles west of San Antonio on US-90 West. USM: G-8. NMC: San Antonio, eight miles east.

Billeting Office: Check in at front desk of main building, 24 hours daily, C-512-677-8666. Air Force Village II is a retirement community with limited number of guestrooms and cottages. Check out 1300 hours. No government civilian employee billeting.

TML: Cottages and guestrooms. Officers all ranks, leave or official duty. Handicapped accessible. Bedroom, private bath (9); two bedroom cottages with kitchen, private bath (2). A/C, cribs/cots ($3), maid service, refrigerator, color TV, limited utensils in cottages. Modern structure. Rates: $39-$55 per night. Call for reservations information.

TEXAS
Air Force Village II, continued

TML Availability: Difficult all year.

☞ Nearby San Antonio, with its River Walk, historic monuments, and distinctly Mexican flavor, is a favorite destination for visitors. A wide variety of entertainment is available in this vibrant city.

Belton Lake Recreation Area (TX07R3)
Fort Hood, TX 76544-5000

TELEPHONE NUMBER INFORMATION: Main installation numbers: C-817-287/ 288-1110, D-312-737/738-1110.

Location: From I-35 take Killeen/Ft Hood exit; west on US-190, right on Hood Rd, right on North Ave, left on Martin Dr, to right on North Nolan Rd., area marked. USM: G-7. NMC: Austin, 60 miles south.

Billeting Office: Reservations Office, ATTN: AFZF-PA-CRD-OR-BLORA, Fort Hood, TX 76544-5056, C-817-287-2523, D-312-737-8303. Check in cottages after 1500 hours, check out 0730-1000 hours.

TML: Cottages. All ranks, leave or official duty. Bedroom, private bath, sleeps 4 persons (10). Kitchen, no utensils, A/C, color TV, fully equipped. Rates: 15 Apr-14 Oct $25-$30 daily; 15 Oct-14 Apr, $20-$25 daily, $15 deposit. All categories can make reservations. **No Pets.**

TML Availability: Good, winter months. Difficult, May-Sep.

☞ A full round of recreational opportunities is offered here: jet skiing, sailing, windsurfing, deck boats, fishing, paddle and ski boats can be rented; the Hideaway Inn Snack Bar, and Sierra Beach Swimming area are fun, fun, fun.

Bergstrom Air Force Base (TX27R3)
Bergstrom AFB, TX 78743-0001

TELEPHONE NUMBER INFORMATION: Main installation numbers: C-512-369-4100, D-312-685-1110.

Location: From US-183 or TX-71. Clearly marked. USM: G-7. NMC: Austin, 7 miles northwest.

Billeting Office: Building 3508, Sixth St. Reservations: C-512-369-2207, D-312-685-2207, 24 hours daily. Check in facilities, check out 1200 hours daily. Government civilian employee billeting.

TML: VOQ/VAQ. **Bergstrom Inn,** building 2104 (VAQ), buildings 3708-3709 (VOQ). All ranks, leave or official duty. VAQ: double bedrooms, shared bath (48); SNCO rooms, shared bath (6); suites, private bath (6). A/C, color TV, washer/dryer, lounge, maid

Bergstrom Air Force Base, continued

service. VOQ: single bedrooms, private bath (60); suites, private bath (30). Kitchen, A/C, color TV, maid service, washer/dryer, lounge. Older structure, remodeled. Rates: $6-$8 per person. Duty can make reservations.

TML: TLF. Buildings 3542-3548, all ranks, leave or official duty. Separate bedroom, private bath (40). A/C, cribs/cots, ice vending, kitchenette, complete utensils, washer/dryer, maid service. Handicapped accessible, modern structure. Rates: $20 per unit. Duty can make reservations, others Space-A.

TML: DV/VIP. Building 109, officer 06+, leave or official duty. Suites, private bath (6). Kitchen, living room, A/C, color TV, maid service, cots/cribs, washer/dryer. Rates: $10 per person. Duty can make reservations.

DV/VIP: PAO, C-EX-3710. 06+. Retirees and lower ranks Space-A.

TML Availability: Good, Jan, Feb, Mar.

☞ Old Pecan St/Sixth St is a seven block strip of renovated Victorian buildings, and a favorite place to shop and eat. Visit the Governor's Mansion, and Capitol - free tours Mon-Fri!

Locator 369-2214   **Medical 369-2333**   **Police 369-2604**

⊗This base will close in mid '93.

Brooks Air Force Base (TX26R3)
Brooks AFB, TX 78235-5000

TELEPHONE NUMBER INFORMATION: Main installation numbers: C-512-536-1110, D-312-240-1110.

Location: At intersection of I-37 and Loop 13 (Military Drive). USM: I-9. NMC: San Antonio, 5 miles northwest.

Billeting Office: Brooks Inn, building 214, 6th St, C-**512-536-1844**, 24 hours daily. Check in facility, check out 1200 hours daily. Government civilian employee billeting.

TML: TLF. Building 211, all ranks, leave or official duty. Handicapped accessible. Bedroom, private bath (8). Kitchen, living room, cribs, A/C, utensils, linen, maid service, washer/dryer. Rates: $16 (E1-E6), $20 (E7+). Duty can make reservations. PCS in 30 day limit. PCS out 7 day limit. PCS have priority, others Space-A.

TML: VAQ. Building 718, C-EX-3031, enlisted all ranks, leave or official duty. Separate bedrooms, private bath (2); two bedroom, shared bath (52). A/C, community kitchen, cribs/cots, ice vending, maid service, refrigerator, color TV, washer/dryer. Modern structure. Rates: $8-$12/person. Duty can make reservations, others Space-A.

TML: VOQ. Buildings 212, 214, 218, 220, C-EX-3031, officers all ranks, leave or official duty. Separate bedrooms, private bath (109); two bedroom, shared bath (50). A/C, cribs/cots, ice vending, maid service, refrigerator, color TV, washer/dryer. Modern structure. Rates: sponsor $8-$10. Maximum $20 per family. Duty can make reservations, others Space-A.

TEXAS
Brooks Air Force Base, continued

TML: DV/VIP. Officer 06+, leave or official duty, C-EX-3278. Separate bedrooms, living room, private bath (6). Maid service, washer/dryer. Rates: $14 per person. Duty can make reservations, others Space-A.

DV/VIP: PAO Office, C-EX-3238. 06+. Retirees Space-A.

TML Availability: Limited. Base has contract hotel/motel billeting. Contact Billeting Office, C-EX-1844.

☞ **Popular with Brooks' people are the recreation areas at Canyon Lake, on the Guadalupe River northwest of New Braunfels, which is itself an interesting place to visit as a center of Texas' German heritage.**

Locator 536-1841   **Medical 536-3278**

Carswell Air Force Base (TX21R3)
Carswell AFB, TX 76127-5000

TELEPHONE NUMBER INFORMATION: Main installation numbers: C-817-782-5000, D-312-739-1110.

Location: On TX-183. From Fort Worth, west on I-30, exit at Carswell AFB/Horne St. Follow signs to main gate. USM G-6. NMC: Fort Worth, 7 miles east.

Billeting Office: Carswell Inn, ATTN: 7th SVS/SVH, building 3140, corner 6th St & Meandering Rd, C-817-731-7003, 24 hours daily. Check in facility, check out 1200 hours daily. Government civilian employee billeting.

TML: TLF. Buildings 3112/13/14, all ranks, leave or official duty. Bedroom apartments, private bath (18). A/C, refrigerator, color TV, housekeeping service, cribs, washer/dryer. Modern structure. Rates: $18 per unit (E1-E4). $19 (E5 above). Maximum 5 per apartment. Duty can make reservations, others Space-A. **Kennel facility 2 miles from main gate.**

TML: VOQ. Buildings 3110/15, officers all ranks, leave or official duty. Bedroom, private bath (64); two room suites, living room, private bath (15). Refrigerator, microwave and limited utensils, A/C, color TV, housekeeping service, cribs, washer/dryer, ice. Modern structure. Rates: $11/$13, each additional person $5.50/$6.50. Maximum 2 per unit. TDY can make reservations, others Space-A.

TML: VAQ. Building 1565, enlisted all ranks, leave or official duty. Bedroom, shared bath (38); bedroom, 2 beds, shared bath (24); two room suites, private bath (4). Microwave, refrigerator, A/C, color TV, housekeeping service, washer/dryer, ice. Modern structure. Rates: $9/$13, single occupancy only. Duty can make reservations, others Space-A.

TML: DV0Q/VIP. Building 3140, officer 06+, leave or official duty. Two bedroom suites, shared bath (13). Refrigerator, microwave and limited utensils, A/C, color TV, housekeeping service, cribs, washer/dryer, ice. Modern structure. Rates: $13, each additional person, $6.50. Duty can make reservations, others Space-A.

DV/VIP: Protocol, C-EX-5377.

Carswell Air Force Base, continued

TML Availability: Good. Best, late Nov - mid Jan.

☞ Visit the historic Stockyard District, and then world renowned art museums. How about Southfork? Or the Water Gardens? Or Six Flags Over Texas, and the Opera? Fort Worth has come a long way since 1841!

Locator 782-7082   Medical 782-4000   Police 782-5200

⊗This base is scheduled to close Sep '93.

Chase Field Naval Air Station (TX23R3)
Chase Field NAS, TX 78103-5000

TELEPHONE NUMBER INFORMATION: Main installation numbers: C-519-354-5119, D-312-861-1110.

Location: Off US-181, 5 miles southeast of Beeville. Clearly marked. USM: G-8. NMC: Corpus Christi, 45 miles south/southeast.

Billeting Office: Building 2168, Constitution Street, C-**519-362-0884**, D-312-861-5480, 24 hours daily. Other hours Security Office, building 1011, C-519-362-5412. Check in facility, check out 1300 hours daily. Government civilian employee billeting.

TML: VOQ. Building 2135, all ranks, leave or official duty. Handicapped accessible. Bedroom, private bath (48). A/C, community kitchen, cribs, ice vending, maid service, refrigerator, color TV, washer/dryer. Family suites, 2 rooms w/private bath, kitchen (6). Rates: $6 per person officer, $4 per person enlisted. Duty can make reservations, others Space-A.

DV/VIP: Commanding Officer, C-EX-5213, 06+, retirees Space-A.

TML Availability: Good all year.

☞ Take a drive to Corpus Christi, and Port Aransas. Then loop down across Mustang and Padre Islands to enjoy a wide range of recreational opportunities including one of only eight national seashores.

Locator 354-5119   Medical 354-5292   Police 354-5412

⊗This base is scheduled to close in '93.

Corpus Christi Naval Air Station (TX10R3)
Corpus Christi, TX 78419-9999

TELEPHONE NUMBER INFORMATION: Main installation numbers: C-512-939-2811, D-312-624-1110.

Location: On TX-358, on southeast side of Corpus Christi. The south gate is on NAS Dr, USM: G-8. NMC: Corpus Christi, 10 miles northwest.

TEXAS
Corpus Christi Naval Air Station, continued

Billeting Office: Officer building 1281, Ocean Dr, C-**512-939-2388/89**, enlisted building 1739, Ave East, C-**512-939-2187**. BOQ/BEQ 24 hours, Navy Lodge 0800-1900 hours M-F, 0900-1700 hours Sa-Su, holidays. Other hours contact OD, building 2, C-512-939-2383. Check in facility, check out 1100 hours daily (1200 Navy Lodge). No government civilian employee billeting.

TML: Navy Lodge. Building 1281, all ranks, leave or official duty. Call **1-800-NAVY-INN**. Lodge number is 937-6361. Suites and 1 bedroom units, private bath (21); singles have double bed; suites have double bed, living room with sofa bed. Kitchen, complete utensils, A/C, color TV, maid service, coin washer/dryer, ice vending. Modern structure. Rates: $26 (singles), $32 (suites). All categories can make reservations.

TML: BOQ/BEQ. Officers building 1281, enlisted building 1732, all ranks, leave or official duty. Bedroom, private bath (81). Refrigerator, microwave, A/C, color TV in room & lounge, maid service, washer/dryer. Modern structure, renovated. Rates: $8 single, $10 studio, $15 mini suites. BEQ $4 single, $15 TV & suite. TDY, (leave), child, no charge. Maximum 3 persons. Duty can make reservations, others Space-A.

DV/VIP: Protocol Office. Building 1281, Admin Office, C-EX-2380/2389/3285. Commander's discretion. Retirees and lower ranks Space-A.

TML Availability: Very Good, Jan-Mar & Jun-Dec. Difficult, Apr-May.

☞ **The Padre Island National Seashore, the famous King Ranch, and the Confederate AF Flying Museum are all local sights worth seeing.**

Locator 939-2383   **Medical 939-3735/3839**   **Police 939-3460**

Dallas Naval Air Station (TX12R3)
Dallas, TX 75211-5000

TELEPHONE NUMBER INFORMATION: Main installation numbers: C-214-266-6111, D-312-874-6111.

Location: Exit from I-30 at loop 12 west of Dallas, go south on loop 12 to Jefferson Ave exit. NAS on left, south side, of ave. Near Grand Prairie. USM: H-7. NMC: Dallas, 15 miles northeast.

Billeting Office: Building 209, **Hutchins Hall**, Halsey Ave, C-**214-266-6155**, 24 hours daily. Check in facility, check out 1400 hours daily. Government civilian employee billeting.

TML: BOQ. Building 8, officers all ranks, leave or official duty, C-EX-6134/5. Bedroom, hall bath (80); suites (VIP); family room (1). Washer/dryer. Older structure. Rates: $6 per person (shared room); $8 per person (suites); $12 suites; $15 family room (Space-A). Duty can make reservations, others Space-A.

TML: BEQ. Buildings 209, 231, enlisted all ranks, leave or official duty. Beds, hall bath (564). Rates: $4 per day. Duty can make reservations, others Space-A.

DV/VIP: PAO, C-EX-6140. Commander's discretion.

Dallas Naval Air Station, continued

TML Availability: Difficult & unpredictable.

☞ Texas is "another country" and Dallas is big city Texas. Don't miss the museums, the shopping and especially Texas Barbecue!

Locator 266-6111   Medical-266-6283   Police 266-6105

Dyess Air Force Base (TX14R3)
Dyess AFB, TX 79607-5000

TELEPHONE NUMBER INFORMATION: Main installation numbers: C-915-696-3113, D-312-461-1110.

Location: Six miles southwest of Abilene. Main gate is 3 miles east of I-20. Accessible from I-20 & US-277. USM: G-7. NMC: Abilene, 6 miles northeast.

Billeting Office: Building 7409, Dyess Inn, Fifth St, C-915-696-8610, D-312-461-2681, 24 hours daily. Check in facility, check out 1200 hours daily. Government civilian employee billeting.

TML: TLF. Building 6240, all ranks, leave or official duty, handicapped accessible. Separate bedroom, private bath (sleeps 5)(40). Kitchen, complete utensils, A/C, color TV in room & lounge, cribs/cots, washer/dryer, ice vending. Modern structure. Rates: $19 per room. Duty can make reservations, others Space-A.

TML: VAQ. Building 7218, enlisted all ranks, leave or official duty. Double rooms, shared bath (70). Refrigerator, A/C, color TV, maid service, washer/dryer, ice vending. Rates: $9. Duty can make reservations, others Space-A.

TML: VOQ. Buildings 7403/07/09, 7420-22, officers all ranks, senior enlisted only. Handicapped accessible, leave or official duty. One bedroom, shared bath (174), separate bedroom DV/VIP suites (20), private bath. Kitchen (suites only), refrigerator, A/C, color TV, maid service, washer/dryer, ice vending. Older structure, remodeled. Rates: $9 - $14 per person. Maximum 2 per room. Duty can make reservations, others Space-A.

DV/VIP: 96/BMW. Protocol Office, C-EX-5610, 06+. Retirees and lower ranks Space-A.

TML Availability: Very good all year.

☞ Abilene has an award winning Zoo, and a collection of vintage aircraft on display at the base. Boating, fishing and sailing at Lake Fort Phantom Hill and Lake Abilene, and a visit to Buffalo Gap Historic Village a "must".

Locator 696-3098   Medical 696-2334   Police 696-2131

Flying K Recreation Ranch (TX11R3)
Kelly Air Force Base, TX 78241-5000

TELEPHONE NUMBER INFORMATION: Main installation numbers: C-512-925-1110, D-312-945-1110.

TEXAS
Flying K Recreation Ranch, continued

Location: Approximately 100 mi north of San Antonio on Lake Lyndon B Johnson. From US-281 in Marble Falls go west on TX FM-1431 for 3.3 miles, left on Wirtz Dam Rd, follow signs for 2.5 miles. USM: G-7. NMC: Austin, 60 miles SE.

Billeting Office: None. Reservations required with payment in full up to 28 days in advance (depending on status), beginning Th at 0800 in person, and 1400 by phone. Write to: Information Ticket and Tour, building 1662, Kelly AFB, TX 78241-5000, C-512-925-4585, D-312-945-4585/84, FAX-512-925-4586. Rec area address: Flying K Ranch, PO Box 155, Marble Falls, TX 78654.

TML: House trailers w/screened patio (21). A/C, CATV, kitchen w/utensils, linens provided, bring your own soap and towels. Boat and motor w/unit for additional fee. Rates: $26 per day Su - Th, $28 per day Fri - Sa, up to 4 persons, $3 each additional person.

TML Availability: Long term/monthly Dec - Mar. Day/weekly Apr - Nov. Best during Sep - Mar.

☞ **"One of the most beautiful recreation areas in the Air Force", in the Texas hill country, on Lake Lyndon B. Johnson. Don't miss the annual Black Bass Fishing Contest each year.**

Fort Bliss (TX06R3)
Fort Bliss, TX 79916-0058

TELEPHONE NUMBER INFORMATION: Main installation numbers: C-915-568-2121, D-312-978-0831.

Location: From I-10 take airport exit to Robert E Lee gate. From US-54 take Pershing Road to Ft Bliss. USM: E-7. NMC: El Paso, within city limits.

Billeting Office: Building 251, Club Rd, C-915-568-4888, 24 hours daily. Check in billeting, check out 1100 hours daily.

TML: Guest House. **The Inn at Fort Bliss,** C-915-565-7777, all ranks, leave or official duty. Deluxe kitchenette units with microwave and coffeemaker and additional standard units. CATV, A/C, cribs ($2), maid service, ice vending. Rates: For standard rooms, $31.75 single, $37.50 double, $5 each additional person; for deluxe rooms, $34.25 single, $41 double, $5 each additional person. Call for reservation information.

TML: Transient Facilities. Officer and senior enlisted, leave or official duty, C-EX 4888/2703. Building 251 for check-in. Shared bath, private bath, refrigerator, A/C, color TV, maid service. Also, 4 duplex brick cottages, 8 units each, separate units, private bath. Refrigerator, color TV, bedding. Rates: sponsor $18; cottages 627 & 631 $21, double occupancy. TDY to Fort Bliss can make reservations, others Space-A.

TML: Guest House (Wm Beaumont AMC, Ft Bliss control). Building 7008, E-4 and below. Official duty. C-EX 2381. Check in 1300-1600 hours, check out 1100 hours daily. After 1600 hours, check-in at Billeting Office, building 251. Bedroom, shared bath (8); two bedroom, shared bath (7); three bedroom, private bath (1). Refrigerator, A/C, color

TEXAS

Fort Bliss, continued

TV, maid service, cribs/cots, coin washer/dryer. Older structure. Rates: sponsor $10 shared bath, $3 each additional person; private bath $13, $3 each additional person. PCS can make reservations, others Space-A.

TML: Armed Services YMCA (Wm Beaumont AMC, Ft Bliss control). All ranks, leave or official duty, C-915-562-8461. Separate bedrooms with two double beds or a king size bed, private bath (52). Individual A/C heating, color TV, room telephones, modern kitchenette (most rooms), 24 hour laundromat, food/ice vending, playground, meeting rooms for parties/receptions. Rates: $22 without kitchen, $24 with kitchen. PCS, dependents, retirees, reservists/reservists' families, military widows/widowers, non ID-card holders visiting relatives and friends can make reservations. Reservations held until 1800 hours.

TML: DV/VIP. Three houses, 4 suites, officers 07+, leave or official duty, C-EX-5319. Completely furnished DV/VIP facility. Rates: $20-$25 daily. All categories can make reservations.

DV/VIP: Protocol Office, C-EX-5319/5225, 07+, retirees and lower ranks Space-A.

TML Availability: Good, Nov-Jan. Difficult, other times.

☞ **Don't miss the Aerial Tramway on McKinley Drive for spectacular views of New Mexico, Texas and Chihuahua, Mexico. Visit old Juarez and the Tiqua Indian Reservation. There are numerous military museums on post.**

Locator 568-1113   Medical 569-2331   Police 568-2115

Fort Hood (TX02R3)
Fort Hood, TX 76544-5000

TELEPHONE NUMBER INFORMATION: Main installation numbers: C-817-288-1110, 287-1110, D-312-738-1110.

Location: From I-35 North exit to US-190 West, 9 miles to Killeen. Main gate is clearly marked. USM: G-7. NMC: Killeen, at main entrance.

Billeting Office: Building 36006, Wratten Dr, C-817-288-2700, 24 hours daily. Check in facility, check out 1100 hours daily. Government civilian employee billeting.

TML: Poxon Guest House. Building 111, all ranks, leave or official duty, C-EX-3067. Bedroom, private bath (75). Refrigerator, community kitchen, A/C, color TV room & lounge, maid service, cribs/cots, washer/dryer, ice vending, handicapped accessible. Older structure, renovated. Rates: $14 single, $20 double, maximum $25 per large family (2 rooms). Duty can make reservations, others Space-A. **Kennels available.**

TML: VQ. Building 36006, all ranks, leave or official duty. Bedroom, private bath (225). Refrigerator, A/C, color TV, maid service, washer/dryer, ice vending. Older structure renovated. Rates: $15 TDY, $14 PCS, $6/2nd person. Duty can make reservations, others Space-A.

TML: VQ. Buildings 5786/88/90/92, all ranks, leave or official duty. Bedroom, shared bath (226). Refrigerator, community kitchen, A/C, color TV, maid service, washer/dryer,

TEXAS
Fort Hood, continued

ice vending. Older structure, renovated. Rates: $15 TDY, $14 PCS, $6/2nd person. Duty can make reservations, others Space-A.

TML: Junior Guest Quarters. Buildings 2305/06/07, enlisted E1-E4, leave or official duty, C-EX-3067. Bedroom, shared bath (48). Refrigerator, community kitchen, A/C, color TV in room & lounge, maid service, cribs/cots, washer/dryer. Older structure. Rates: $5 two persons; maximum $10 per family (2 rooms). Duty can make reservations, others Space-A.

TML: DV/VIP. Building 36006, officers 06+, leave or official duty, C-EX-5001. Two bedroom, private bath (10). Kitchen, utensils, A/C, color TV, maid service, cribs/cots, washer/dryer, ice vending. Older structure, remodeled. Rates: $22 1st TDY, $14 PCS, $6 2nd person. Duty can make reservations, others Space-A.

DV/VIP: Executive Service. Building 1, C-EX-5001, 06/GS-15+, retirees Space-A.

TML Availability: Good, winter months. Difficult, May-Sep.

☞ **Visitors should tour Lake Belton, and other lakes in the regions where boating, fishing, swimming and camping are main pursuits for residents.**

Locator 287-2137   **Medical 288-8133**   **Police 287-2176**

Fort Sam Houston (TX18R3)
Fort Sam Houston, TX 78234-5000

TELEPHONE NUMBER INFORMATION: Main installation numbers: C-512-221-1110/1211, D-312-471-1110/1211.

Location: Accessible from I-410 or I-35/US-81. USM: I-9. NMC: San Antonio, northeast section of city.

Billeting Office: Building 592, Dickman Rd, C-**512-221-6125/8946,** 24 hours daily. Check in facility, check out 1100 hours daily. Government civilian employee billeting.

TML: Guest House. Building 1002, Gorgas Circle, all ranks, leave or official duty, C-EX-2744. Rooms, private bath (134). Two room suites, community kitchen, refrigerator, A/C, color TV, maid service, cribs, coin washer/dryer, rollaway $1. Rates: $13-$17 rooms, $20 suites. Duty can make reservations, others Space-A.

TML: VOQ. Building 1384, officers all ranks, leave or official duty. Units, private bath (300). Kitchen, refrigerator, A/C, color TV, maid service, washer/dryer. Rates: sponsor $22.50, each additional person $11.25. Duty can make reservations, others Space-A.

TML: VOQ. Building 592, officers all ranks, TDY only. Rooms, private bath (150). Kitchen, refrigerator, A/C, color TV, maid service, washer/dryer. Rates: sponsor $22.50, each additional person $11.25.

TML: DV/VIP. Buildings 48 (Staff Post Rd), 107 (Artillery Post), officers 06+ and comparable grade DOD civilian, leave or official duty. Three bedroom suite, private bath (1); two bedroom suite, private bath (2), one bedroom suite, private bath (21). Breakfast

Fort Sam Houston, continued

served (M-F) both buildings. Refrigerator, A/C, color TV, honor bar, maid service. Recently renovated. Rates: $22.50 sponsor, $11.25 each additional person. All categories can make reservations. All except TDY subject to bump.

DV/VIP: PAO. C-EX-1211, 06+, retirees & lower ranks Space-A.

TML Availability: Good. Best Oct-Mar.

☞ Surrounded by San Antonio, this historic post has seen much colorful military history, from its namesake to the "Rough Riders" and Teddy Roosevelt, and key roles in WWI and WWII, to today's role as a medical training center.

Locator 221-2948   Medical 221-4104/6466   Police 221-6363

Goodfellow Air Force Base (TX24R3)
Goodfellow AFB, TX 76908-0001

TELEPHONE NUMBER INFORMATION: Main installation numbers: C-915-654-3231, D-312-477-3217.

Location: Off US-87 or US-277, clearly marked, USM: G-7, NMC: San Angelo, 2 miles northwest.

Billeting Office: building 3305, Kearney Blvd, C-915-654-3332, 24 hours daily. Check in facility, check out 1200 hours daily. Government civilian employee billeting.

TML: TLF. Buildings 910, 920, 922, 924, all ranks, leave or official duty. Handicapped accessible. Separate bedrooms, private bath (29). Kitchen, complete utensils, color TV, maid service, cribs, washer/dryer, ice vending. Modern structure. Rates: $14-E6, $18-E7+. PCS can make reservations, others Space-A.

TML: VAQ. Buildings 3307, 3311, enlisted all ranks, leave or official duty, handicapped accessible. Room with bed, shared bath (100); room with 2 beds, shared bath (270). Refrigerator, microwave, A/C, color TV, maid service, washer/dryer. Modern structure. Rates: $5 per person. Duty can make reservations, others Space-A.

TML: VOQ. Buildings 702, 711, officers all ranks, leave or official duty. Separate bedrooms, private bath (115). Kitchenette, microwave, A/C, color TV, maid service, washer/dryer, microwave. Modern structure. Rates: $6-$10 per person. TDY can make reservations, others Space-A.

TML: DV/EV. Building 910 (DV), building 3307 (EV), officers 06+, enlisted E9, leave or official duty. Separate bedrooms, private bath (10). Kitchen, complete utensils, A/C, color TV, maid service, washer/dryer, ice vending. Modern structure. Rates: $10 per person. Duty can make reservations, others Space-A.

TML Availability: Fairly good all year.

TEXAS
Goodfellow Air Force Base, continued

☞ Visit historic Fort Concho, a preserved Indian fort, and home of the "Buffalo Soldiers", the Concho River Walk and Plaza, and three lakes within 20 minutes of downtown feature camping, boating and fishing.

Locator 654-3231   Medical 654-3145   Police 654-3504

Kelly Air Force Base (TX03R3)
Kelly AFB, TX 78241-5000

TELEPHONE NUMBER INFORMATION: Main installation numbers: C-512-925-1110, D-312-945-1110.

Location: All of the following, I-10, I-35, I-37, I-410 intersect with US-90. From US-90 take either the Gen Hudnell or Gen McMullen exit and go south to Kelly AFB. USM: H-9. NMC: San Antonio, 7 miles northeast.

Billeting Office: Building 1650, Goodrich Rd, C-512-925-1844, 924-7201, D-312-945-1844, 24 hours daily. Check in billeting, check out 1200 hours daily. Government civilian employee billeting.

TML: VOQ. Building 1676, officers all ranks, leave or official duty. Bedroom, private bath (47). Kitchen (shared), microwave, A/C, CATV, maid service, washer/dryer, ice vending. Older structure. Rates: $8 per person. Maximum 2 persons. Duty can make reservations, others Space-A.

TML: VAQ. Building 1650, enlisted all ranks, leave or official duty. Bedroom, shared bath (E7-E8) (2); separate bedroom, private bath (E9) (2); bedroom, 2 beds, common bath (E1-E6) (22). Refrigerator, microwave, A/C, CATV, maid service, washer/dryer, ice vending. Older structure. Rates $8 per person. Maximum 2 persons. Duty can make reservations, others Space-A.

TML: DV/VIP. Building 1676, officers 07+, leave or official duty. Separate bedrooms, private bath (6). Kitchen, A/C, CATV, maid service, cribs/cots, washer/dryer, ice vending. Older structure. Rates: $10 per person. Maximum 4 persons. Duty can make reservations, others Space-A.

DV/VIP: Protocol Office, building 1680, C-EX-7678, 07/GS-16+. Retirees and lower ranks Space-A.

TML Availability: Fairly good all year.

☞ Your trip to San Antonio will be well remembered if you visit Sea World, the Alamo, historic mission sites, and cheer for the Spurs!

Locator 925-1841   Medical 925-4544   Police 925-6811

Kingsville Naval Air Station (TX22R3)
Kingsville NAS, TX 78363-5000

TELEPHONE NUMBER INFORMATION: Main installation numbers: C-512-595-6136, D-312-861-6136.

Location: Off US-77 South, exit to TX-425 Southeast to main gate. USM: G-8. NMC: Corpus Christi, 30 miles northeast.

Billeting Office: Building 2700, officers, C-**512-595-6321**, building 3730, enlisted, C-**512-595-6309**, 24 hours daily. Check in facility, check out 1200 hours daily. No government civilian employee billeting.

TML: BOQ/BEQ. Buildings 2700, 3729, 3730W, all ranks, handicapped accessible. Bedrooms, private bath, shared lounge (36); bedrooms, private bath, shared lounge (16). CATV, refrigerator, amenities, microwaves, A/C, laundry facilities, vending machines, maid service. Several upgraded rooms, new carpet, furniture. Rates: officer $8, accompanied $10; enlisted $4, accompanied $8 (rates going up); DOD civilian $24, accompanied $29. PCS-in, PCS-out personnel may make reservations, others Space-A.

DV/VIP: Protocol Office, building 700, C-EX-6481, 06+. VIP three room suites (3). Retirees Space-A.

TML Availability: Excellent Dec-Jan.

☞ **Home of the King Ranch, for Santa Gertrudis cattle, beautiful thoroughbred and quarter horses, the historic ranch house, and other interesting sites. Texas A&I University is located here. Corpus Christi, 40 miles Northeast.**

Locator 595-6136   Medical 595-6434   Police 595-6217

Lackland Air Force Base (TX25R3)
Lackland AFB, TX 78236-5000

TELEPHONE NUMBER INFORMATION: Main installation numbers: C-512-671-1110, D-312-473-1110.

Location: Off US-90 South. Loop 13 (Military Drive) bisects Lackland AFB. USM: H-9. NMC: San Antonio, 6 miles northeast.

Billeting Administrative Office: Building 10203, west side of base, C-**512-671-2523**, 0730-1630 M-F.

TML: TLQ/VAQ. All ranks, building 10203, west side of base, Feymoyer Street, 24 hours daily, C-EX-4270/4277. Check in facility, check out 1200 hours daily. Separate bedrooms, private bath (160); Two person rooms, semi-private baths (770) and 78 SNCO rooms, semi-private baths. A/C, color TV, maid service, cribs, washer/dryer, ice vending. Handicapped accessible. Modern structure. Rates: TLQ $16 - $22 per unit, VAQ $5 - $10 per unit. Duty can request reservations, all others Space-A.

TML: VOQ/DV/VIP: Building 2604, 24 hours daily, C-EX-3622, officers all ranks, leave or official duty. Separate bedrooms, shared bath (32); separate bedrooms, private bath

TEXAS
Lackland Air Force Base, continued

(96). Microwave, refrigerator, A/C, color TV, maid service, washer/dryer, ice/snack vending. Bedroom suites, private bath (DV/VIP) (16) Two bedroom suites, private bath (DV/VIP) (7). Refrigerator, 8 units have kitchen, A/C, color TV, maid service, washer/dryer, ice vending. Older structure, remodeled. Rates: $6-$10 per person. Duty can make reservations, others Space-A.

DV/VIP: Protocol Office, C-EX-2423. 06+. Retirees Space-A.

TML Availability: Good. Difficult, Jun-Aug.

☞ **San Antonio takes its name from Mission San Antonio de Valero or, the Alamo. Visiting the local Missions, and brushing up on the long history of this gracious city, is only one of a number of activities for visitors here.**

Locator 671-1110   Medical 670-7100   Police 671-2018

Laguna Shores Recreation Area (TX42R3)
Kelly Air Force Base, TX 78241-5000

TELEPHONE NUMBER INFORMATION: Main installation numbers: C-512-925-1110, D-312-945-1110.

Location: On Corpus Christi Naval Air Station. Take I-37 to exit 4A west of Corpus Christi, east on TX-358 approximately 17 miles to NAS. Enter at South Gate, follow Laguna Shores signs to office. USM: G-8. NMC: Corpus Christi, in city limits.

Billeting Office: None. Reservations required with payment in full (first month's payment for stays of 1 month or more). Write to Information Ticket and Tour, 2851 ABG/MWRT, building 1662, Kelly AFB, TX 78241-5000, C-**512-925-4585/84**, D-312-945-4585/84, FAX-512-925-4586. Laguna Shores office for information only call C-512-939-7783.

TML: Two bedroom homes, private bath (38). A/C, CATV, kitchen w/utensils, linens provided, bring your own soap and towels. Rates: $26 per day Su - Th, $28 per day Fri - Sa, up to 4 persons, $3 each additional person.

TML Availability: Long term/monthly Dec - Mar. Day/weekly Apr - Nov. Best during Sep - Mar.

☞ **Beaches, saltwater fishing, and exciting places to eat on the Texas coastline are favorites with visitors. The NAS offers a marina, golf course, bowling center, gym, rec center, picnic area, clubs, BX and commissary.**

Laughlin Air Force Base (TX05R3)
Laughlin AFB, TX 78843-5000

TELEPHONE NUMBER INFORMATION: Main installation numbers: C-512-298-3511, D-312-732-1110.

TEXAS

Laughlin Air Force Base, continued

Location: Take US-90 west from San Antonio, 150 miles or US-277 south from San Angelo, 150 miles to Del Rio area. The AFB is clearly marked off US-90. USM: G-8. NMC: Del Rio, 8 miles northwest.

Billeting Office: Building 470, 7th St, C-**512-298-5731**, 24 hours. Check in billeting, check out 1200 hours daily. No government civilian employee billeting.

TML: TLF. Buildings 460-463, all ranks, leave or official duty. Separate bedroom, private bath (20). Kitchen, utensils, A/C, color TV, maid service, cribs, washer/dryer (building 463), ice vending, special facilities for DAV's. Modern structure. Rates: E1-E6 $16 per unit, E7+ $20 per unit. Duty can make reservations, others Space-A.

TML: VOQ/VAQ. Building 470, all ranks, leave or official duty. Bedroom, shared bath (officers all ranks) (13); bedroom, shared bath (enlisted all ranks) (18). Refrigerator, A/C, color TV in room & lounge, maid service, cribs/cots, washer/dryer, ice vending. Older structure, renovated. Rates: $7 per person VOQ, $6 per person VAQ. Duty can make reservations, others Space-A.

TML: DV/VIP. Building 470, officers O6+, leave or official duty. Separate bedroom, private bath (2); three bedroom, private bath (4). Kitchen, utensils, color TV, maid service, cribs/cots, washer/dryer, ice vending. Older structure, renovated. Rates: $10 per person. Duty can make reservations, others Space-A.

DV/VIP: 47 TFW/CCP, building 338, room 1, C-EX-5041, O6+.

TML Availability: Good, Nov-Jan. Difficult, other times.

☞ Visit the historical district in Brown Plaza, particularly for Cinco de Mayo and Diez Y Seis de Septiembre celebrations. The Brinkley Mansion, Valverde Winery, and the visitor's center at Lake Amistad, are all worthwhile to visit.

Locator 298-5195   Medical 298-5225/3416   Police 298-5102

Randolph Air Force Base (TX19R3)
Randolph AFB, TX 78150-0001

TELEPHONE NUMBER INFORMATION: Main installation numbers: C-512-652-1110, D-312-487-1110.

Location: From I-35 take exit 172, Pat Booker Rd. From I-10 take exit 587, TX FM-1604. USM: I-8,9. NMC: San Antonio, 6 miles south.

Billeting Office: Building 118, C-**512-652-1844**, 24 hours daily. Check in billeting, check out 1200 hours daily. Government civilian employee billeting.

TML: TLF. Buildings 112, 152-155, all ranks, leave or official duty. Handicapped accessible (1). Bedroom, private bath (7); separate bedrooms, private bath (33). Kitchen (in 34 units), microwave, refrigerator (in 6 units), A/C, color TV, maid service, cribs/cots, washer/dryer, ice vending. Older structure, renovated. Rates $8-$20 per person, depending on unit and rank. Duty can make reservations, others Space-A.

TEXAS
Randolph Air Force Base, continued

TML: VOQ. Buildings 110, 111, 120, 121, 161, 162, 381, officers all ranks, leave or official duty. Bedroom, private bath (200); separate bedrooms, private bath (76); Two bedroom, private bath (2). A/C, cribs/cots, ice vending, maid service, refrigerator, color TV, limited utensils in some rooms, washer/dryer. Some modern, some older structures. Rates: $7-$10 per person. Duty can make reservations, others Space-A.

TML: VAQ. Buildings 861, 862, enlisted all ranks, leave or official duty. Bedroom, queen bed, private bath (22); bedroom, queen bed, shared bath (42); bedroom, queen bed, shared bath (2). A/C, cribs/cots, ice vending, maid service, refrigerator, color TV in rooms and lounge, washer/dryer, microwave (some). Modern structure. Rates: $7 per person, maximum $14 per room. TDY can make reservations, others Space-A.

DV/VIP: Protocol. Building 900, room 306, C-EX-4126, 07+/SES. Retirees and lower ranks Space-A.

TML Availability: Good, Nov-Feb. Difficult, other times.

☞ San Antonio is nestled between the Texas Hill Country and the coast, and there are a wealth of local things to do. Visit New Braunfels, to the north for a fascinating look at Texas' German past, and Sequin to the East.

Locator 652-1841   Medical 652-2734   Police 652-5700

Red River Army Depot (TX09R3)
Texarkana, TX 75507-0001

TELEPHONE NUMBER INFORMATION: Main installation numbers: C-903-334-2141, D-312-829-4110.

Location: From I-30 East or West, take Red River Army Depot exit #206 south 2 mi. Route clearly marked. USM: H-6,7. NMC: Texarkana, 20 miles east.

Billeting Office: ATTN: SDSRR-GH, building 34, Main Dr, 0700-1700 M-Th, C-903-334-3227. Other hours, contact SDO/NCO, building S-04, or Security Police C-EX-2911. Check in billeting, check out 1100 hours daily. No government civilian employee billeting.

TML: BOQ. Building #40, all ranks, leave or official duty. Bedroom, private bath (1), refrigerator/microwave, coffee service, private bath; separate livingroom/bedrooms, kitchenette/microwave, coffee service, private bath (5). A/C, CATV w/HBO & TV room, maid service, washer/dryer, roll-away beds. New building and furnishings. Rates: sponsor $10, additional adult, child, infant $4, maximum per family $18. Maximum five per room. Duty can make reservations. **Small pets if leashed outside OK.**

TML: DV/VIP. Building #40, officers 06+, leave or official duty. Report to Protocol Office, C-EX-2316. Separate rooms, one with refrigerator/microwave, coffee service, private bath; one with livingroom, bedroom, kitchenette/microwave, limited utensils, private bath (2). Rooms adjoin and may be used as a single, 2-bedroom unit. A/C, CATV w/HBO & TV room, maid service, washer/dryer, roll-away beds. New building and furnishings. Rates: same. Duty can make reservations, others Space-A.

TEXAS

Red River Army Depot, continued

DV/VIP: Protocol Office, ATTN: SDSRR-AP, building 15, C-EX-2316, 06+, GS-14+. Must be approved by commander. Retirees and lower ranks Space-A.

TML Availability: Extremely limited, best, Nov-Mar, worst, Apr-Oct.

☞ **Lake Texarkana, nine miles southwest of the city, offers all water sports. Many local golf courses, and September's Four States Fair and Rodeo are the pride of local residents.**

Locator 334-2141   Medical 334-2155   Police 334-2911

Reese Air Force Base (TX20R3)
Reese AFB, TX 79489-5000

TELEPHONE NUMBER INFORMATION: Main installation numbers: C-806-885-4511, D-312-838-1110.

Location: From west side of Loop 289 at Lubbock take 4th St West, 6 miles. Road terminates at AFB, main gate is one block north. USM: F-6. NMC: Lubbock, 12 miles east.

Billeting Office: The Reese Inn, building 1142, K St, C-**806-885-3155,** 24 hours daily. Check in billeting, check out 1200 hours daily. No government civilian employee billeting.

TML: TLF. Building 1150, all ranks, leave or official duty. Bedroom, private bath (25). Units 1 & 2 dedicated for DAVs. Kitchen, microwave, limited utensils, color TV, maid service, cribs/cots, washer/dryer, ice vending. Modern structure. Rates: E6- $15 per unit, E7+ $19 per unit. PCS can make reservations, others Space-A.

TML: VAQ. Building 1030, enlisted E1-E7, leave or official duty. Efficiency apartments, private bath (16). Kitchen, microwave, limited utensils, A/C, color TV, maid service, washer/dryer, ice vending. Modern structure. Rates: $6 per unit. TDY/PCS can make reservations, others Space-A.

TML: VAQ. Building 1030, E8-E9, leave or official duty. Bedroom SNCO suites, living room, private bath (4). Kitchen, microwave, limited utensils, A/C, color TV, maid service, cribs/cots, washer/dryer, ice vending. Modern structure. Rates: $10 per person. TDY/PCS can make reservations, others Space-A.

TML: VOQ. Building 1030, 01+. Efficiency rooms, private bath (14). Kitchen, microwave, limited utensils, A/C, color TV, maid service, washer/dryer, cots, ice vending. Modern structure. Rates $7 per person. TDY/PCS can make reservations, others Space-A.

TML: DV. Building 1030, O5+, leave or official duty. Bedroom/living room suites (2). Kitchen, microwave, limited utensils, A/C, color TV, VCR, maid service, cots, washer/dryer, ice vending. Modern structure. Rates: $10 per person. TDY/PCS can make reservations, others Space-A.

TEXAS
Reese Air Force Base, continued

TML: VIP. Building 1030, O5+, leave or official duty. Bedroom/living room suites (4). Kitchen, microwave, limited utensils, A/C, color TV, maid service, cribs/cots, washer/ dryer, ice vending. Modern structure. Rates: $7 per person. TDY/PCS can make reservations, others Space-A.

DV/VIP: Wing Protocol, building 800, C-EX-6187.

TML Availability: Good, winter months. Difficult, summer months.

☞ **Visit the Museum complex of Texas Tech, Moody Planetarium and Ranching Heritage Center. The Science Spectrum features "hands on" science exhibits. There's a Prairie Dog Town in Mackenzie State Park; local festivals are all fun.**

Locator 885-3276   **Medical 885-3285**   **Police 885-3333**

Sheppard Air Force Base (TX37R3)
Sheppard AFB, TX 76311-5000

TELEPHONE NUMBER INFORMATION: Main installation numbers: C-817-676-2511, D-312-736-1001.

Location: Take US-281 North from Wichita Falls, exit to TX-325 which leads to main gate, clearly marked. USM: G-6. NMC: Wichita Falls, 5 miles southwest.

Billeting Office: Sheppard Inn, ATTN: 3750 SVS/SVH, building 776, Ave H, C-817-855-7370, D-312-736-6359/4351, 24 hours daily. Check in billeting, check out 1200 hours daily. Government civilian employee billeting.

TML: TLF. Buildings 160-165, all ranks, leave or official duty, C-EX-2707. Separate bedrooms, private bath (50). Kitchen, utensils, A/C, color TV, maid service, cribs/cots, washer/dryer, ice vending. Modern structure. Rates: $14 E1-E6, $18 E7+. Maximum 4 per unit. Duty can make reservations, others Space-A.

TML: VAQ. Buildings 374, 776, enlisted all ranks, leave or official duty, C-EX-2707. D-EX-1844. Bedroom, two beds, private bath (437); separate bedrooms, private bath (7); bedroom, 1 bed, private bath (49); bedroom, two beds, shared bath (374); bedroom one bed, shared bath (48). A/C, ice vending, maid service, refrigerator, color TV, washer/dryer, microwaves in lounges. Modern structure. Rates: $5 per person standard room, $10 per person suites. Maximum 2 per room. Duty can make reservations, others Space-A.

TML: VOQ. Buildings 331, 332, 333, 370, Ave G, building 1511, Ream Ave, officer all ranks, leave or official duty, C-EX-2707, D-EX-1844. Bedroom, private bath (220); separate bedrooms, private bath (12); bedroom, shared bath (47). Refrigerator, A/C, color TV, washer/dryer. Rates: $6 per person standard room, $10 per person suite. Maximum 2 per room. Duty can make reservations, others Space-A.

TML: DV/VIP. Building 332, officer O6+, leave or official duty, C-EX-2123. D-EX-2123. Separate bedroom suites (6), private bath. A/C, kitchenette, maid service color TV, utensils, washer/dryer. Modern structure. Rates: $10 per person. Maximum 2 per room. Duty can make reservations, others Space-A.

Sheppard Air Force Base, continued

DV/VIP: ATTN: STTC/CCEX, Stop 1, building 400, C-EX-2123, D-EX-2123. 06+. Retirees and lower ranks Space-A.

TML Availability: Good during winter months, difficult Apr - Sep.

☞ Visit the Wichita Falls Museum and Art Center, Lucy Park, and the 3 1/2 mile walk to Wichita Falls' waterfall (the original washed away 100 years ago, and this one is man made!).

Locator 676-1841   Medical 676-2333   Police 676-6302

Dugway Proving Ground (UT04R4)
Dugway Proving Ground, UT 84022-1039

TELEPHONE NUMBER INFORMATION: Main installation numbers: C-801--831-2151, D-312-789-2151.

Location: Isolated but can be reached from I-80. Take Skull Valley Rd (exit 77) for 40 miles south. USM: D-3. NMC: Salt Lake City, 80 miles northeast.

Billeting Office: Building 5228, Valdez Circle, C-**801-831-2333/2334**, M-Th 0630-1845, F 0630-1445, closed weekends and holidays. After hours, Military Police Station, building 5438, C-EX-2933. Check in billeting, check out 1300 hours daily. Government civilian employee billeting.

TML: VOQ/DVQ. Buildings 5228, 5226, officer and enlisted, all ranks, leave or official duty. Bedroom, semi-private bath (54); separate bedrooms. Refrigerator, A/C (in building 5228), color TV in room & lounge, maid service, essentials, cribs/cots, washer/dryer, ice vending. Handicapped accessible. Older structures, remodeled. Rates: sponsor, $18 single room; suite $20, $5 each additional occupant. Duty can make reservations, others including contractors and social guests Space-A.

DV/VIP: STEDP-AG. Building 5450, C-EX-2020, 05/GS-14+. Retirees and lower ranks Space-A.

TML Availability: Good. Best, fall and winter.

☞ Pristine alpine mountains, vast deserts, the mysterious Great Salt Lake - this area offers a full round of outdoor activities without entry fees or hype, and is only minutes away from metropolitan Salt Lake City!

Locator 831-2151   Medical 831-2222   Police 831-2933

UTAH

Hill Air Force Base (UT02R4)
Hill AFB, UT 84056-5000

TELEPHONE NUMBER INFORMATION: Main installation numbers: C-801-777-7221, D-312-458-1110.

Location: Adjacent to I-15 between Ogden and Salt Lake City. Take exit 336, east on UT-193 to south gate. USM: D-4. NMC: Ogden, 8 miles north.

Billeting Office: ATTN: 2849 ABG/SVH, building 146, D St, C-801-777-2601, 24 hours daily. Check in billeting, check out 1200 hours daily. Government civilian employee billeting.

TML: TLF. Building 472, all ranks. Separate bedrooms, private bath (40). Kitchen, complete utensils, A/C, color TV, limited maid service, cribs, washer/dryer, ice vending, facilities for DAVs. Modern structure. Rates: $15. Maximum 5 per room. PCS/TDY can make reservations, others Space-A.

TML: VOQ. Buildings 141, 142, 150, 480, officers all ranks, leave or official duty. Bedroom, semi-private bath; 5/1-bedroom, private bath; 36 separate bedrooms, semi-private bath (52); separate bedrooms, private bath (6). Kitchen, A/C, color TV, maid service, cots, washer/dryer, ice vending. Older structures, renovated. Rates: $6 per person. No families. TDY can make reservations, others Space-A.

TML: VAQ. Building 521, enlisted all ranks, leave or official duty. Bedrooms, semi-private bath (64). Suites, semi-private bath (6). Refrigerator, A/C, color TV in room & lounge, maid service, cots, washer/dryer, ice vending. Handicapped accessible. Older structure, renovated. Rates: $5.50 per person. No families. Duty can make reservations, retirees Space-A.

TML: Hillhaus Lodge, Snowbasin Ski Resort. Outdoor Recreation/Thornton Community Center, building 460, C-801-777-3525, D-312-458-3525. All ranks, leave or official duty. Bedrooms, private bath (3); suites, private bath (4); loft, sleeps 7 (1). Lounge, sun deck, gas fireplace, snack bar, kitchen, dining area. A-frame, renovated. Sleep and Ski packages. Rates: suites $35, rooms $30, double occupancy, Th-Su, holidays; loft $10 ($40 entire loft). Entire lodge rental $225. Breakfast, lunch and dinner offered. **Note:** check Military RV, Camping & Rec Areas Around the World for more information.

TML: DV/VIP. Building 1118, officers 06+, Leave or official duty. Separate bedrooms, private bath (6). Kitchen, limited utensils, A/C, color TV, maid service, cots, washer/dryer, ice vending. Older structure, renovated. Rates: $6 per person. No families. Duty can make reservations, others Space-A.

DV/VIP: Protocol ALC/CCP, building 1102, C-EX-5565, 06+. Retirees Space-A.

TML Availability: Difficult.

Locator 777-1841   **Medical 911**   **Police 777-3056**

Tooele Army Depot (UT05R4)
Tooele, UT 84074-5008

TELEPHONE NUMBER INFORMATION: Main installation numbers: C-801-833-2124, D-312-790-2124.

Location: From west I-80, exit 99 to UT-36 south for 15 miles to main entrance. USM: D-4. NMC: Salt Lake City, 40 miles northeast.

Billeting Office: ATTN: SDSTE-IOH, building 1, Hq Loop, C-**801-833-2124**, 0630-1700 hours M-Th, closed on Friday. Other hours, SDO, building 1, C-801-833-2304. Check in billeting, check out 1200 hours daily. Government civilian employee billeting.

TML: VOQ/DVQ. Building 35, all ranks, leave or official duty. Two bedroom apartments, private bath (9). Kitchen, complete utensils, A/C, CATV, maid service, washer/dryer. Also bedroom apartments, private bath (2). Kitchen w/utensils, A/C, CATV, maid service, washer/dryer. Rates: sponsor $12, additional adults $6, no charge for children, maximum per family $18. Rates for TDY personnel: sponsor $20.25, additional adults $2.25, no charge for children, maximum charge $22.50. Reservations recommended. No pets.

Military Discount Lodging: Comfort Inn, 491 S Main, Tooele, C-**801-882-6100**. Best Western Inn, 365 N Main, Tooele, C-**801-882-5010**.

TML Availability: Good. Best, Dec-Mar.

☞ **Some special sights in Salt Lake City: the Mormon Temple and Temple Square, the Pioneer Memorial museum. There are several local ski resorts within reach of Tooele.**

Locator 833-2094   Medical 833-2572   Police 833-2314/2559

Vermont

NONE

Virginia

Cheatham Annex Naval Supply Center (VA02R1)
Williamsburg, VA 23187-8792

TELEPHONE NUMBER INFORMATION: Main installation numbers: C-804-887-4000, D-312-953-4000.

VIRGINIA
Cheatham Annex Naval Supply Center, continued

Location: From I-64 take exit 57-B on US-199 east to main gate of Cheatham Annex. USM: M-4. NMC: Williamsburg, 6 miles west.

Billeting Office: MWR, building 284, D St, C-804-887-7224/7101/7102, 0700-1530 hours week days, after duty hours, building 235, C-804-887-7453. No government civilian employee billeting.

TML: Recreation Cabins. Cabins 161, 163-165, 167-170, 261, 262, active duty and retirees only, handicapped accessible. Reservations required 90 days advance. Minimum 2 night stay in cabins. Eleven cottages, private bath, kitchen, complete utensils, refrigerator, cribs ($1), color TV, A/C, woodburning stove, boat, electric motor, battery charger, paddles, cushions. No woodburning stove in mobile homes. Rates: winter 1 Nov thru 31 Mar - cabins, $29-48 daily/$174-288 week. Summer 1 Apr thru 31 Oct - cabins, $35-51 daily/$192-306 week. First call first serve basis.

DV/VIP: Cabins 261, 170 reserved 06+. Commander's Office, C-EX-7108.

TML Availability: Good, Nov-Mar. Good Mon-Fri., Difficult, other months, Fri-Sun.

☞ Near Colonial Williamsburg/Jamestown, many museums. Busch Gardens. Great deer hunting, contact Special Services. Fitness Center, pool, racquetball, tennis courts, bowling alley, Snack Bar.

Locator 887-4000   **Medical 887-7222**   **Police 887-7222**

Dahlgren Naval Surface Warfare Center (VA06R1)
Dahlgren, VA 22448-5000

TELEPHONE NUMBER INFORMATION: Main installation numbers: C-703-663-8531, D-312-249-1110.

Location: From I-95 in Fredericksburg, VA, east on VA-3 to VA-206 (17 miles), left at Arnolds Corner, east to Dahlgren (11 miles). Also, US-301 south to VA-206, east to main gate of Center. USM: L-4. NMC: Washington, DC, 38 miles north.

Billeting Office: Building 960, C-703-663-7671/72, 24 hours daily. Check in billeting, check out 1200 hours daily. Government civilian employee billeting.

TML: BOQ. Buildings 217, 962, officers, all ranks, leave or official duty. Bedroom, private bath (12); separate bedrooms, private bath (20); two bedroom, private bath suite (DV/VIP) (1). Community kitchen, limited utensils, refrigerator, A/C, cribs/cots, essentials, ice vending, color TV in room & lounge, maid service, washer/dryer. Older structures, renovated. Rates: $10.(plus free market rate $5). Duty can make reservations, others Space-A.

TML: BEQ. Building 962 A wing, enlisted, E1-E4, leave or official duty. Bedroom, hall bath (53). A/C, essentials, ice vending, maid service, refrigerator, color TV in room & lounge, washer/dryer. Rates: $4 per room, per night. Duty can make reservations, others Space-A.

Dahlgren Naval Surface Warfare Center, continued

TML: TLQ. Building 962 D wing, all ranks, leave or official duty. Bedroom, private bath (10); two bedroom, private bath (4). A/C, community kitchen, cribs/cots, essentials, ice vending, maid service, refrigerator, color TV in room & lounge, washer/dryer. Older structure, renovated. Rates: same as BOQ. Duty can make reservations, others Space-A.

DV/VIP: Public Affairs Office, C-EX-8513, 06/SES equivalent +. Retirees Space-A.

TML Availability: Difficult. Best Nov-Feb.

☞ Take a walk through Dahlgren's Beaver Pond Nature Trail, and then savor the history of Washington's and Lee's birthplace, in historic Fredericksburg. The area is full of interesting historic sites.

Locator 663-8216/8701   Medical 911   Police 663-8500

Dam Neck Fleet Combat Training Center Atlantic (VA25R1)
Virginia Beach, VA 23461-5000

TELEPHONE NUMBER INFORMATION: Main installation numbers: C-804-433-2000, D-312-433-2000.

Location: On the oceanfront, "Dam Neck at the Dunes" is 2 miles southeast of Oceana NAS, off Dam Neck Road. USM:M-4,5. NMC: Virginia Beach, 2 miles northeast of the resort strip.

Billeting Office: "Dam Neck at the Dunes". Enlisted building 566C, C-**804-433-6691**. Check in facility 1400, check out 1000 hours daily. Officers building 241, C-**804-433-6366**. Check in/ check out same. Government civilian employee billeting.

TML: BOQ. Buildings 225, 241, officers all, leave or official duty. Bedroom, private bath (96); bedroom, living room, private bath (53); DV rooms, kitchenette, private bath (4); VIP suites, private bath, living room (13). Refrigerators, coffee makers, A/C, CATV and VCR, maid service, cots, washer/dryer, ice vending. Sun deck, hot tub and sauna. Modern structures. Rates: $10 per person standard room; $15 per person per suite; $25 per person DV rooms. Under five no charge. Duty on orders can make reservations, others Space-A.

TML: BEQ. Buildings 550, 532, 566, enlisted all ranks. Total 1,336 rooms including 56 Chief's rooms. Refrigerator, A/C, color TV and VCR, maid service, washer/dryer, pool tables. Modern structures. Others: Sun deck, BBQ, phone, CATV, washer/dryer and maid service. Rates: CPO $10; duty $5; others $5. Reservations accepted for official orders, others Space-A.

DV/VIP: Protocol Office, Taylor Hall, C-EX-6542. For 07/civilian equivalent+. Reservations: C-**804-433-7718**, D-312-433-7718, retirees space A.

TML Availability: Because this is a training command, availability is usually poor and only fair at best.

VIRGINIA
Dam Neck Fleet CTCA, continued

☞ Some rooms have ocean views. Building 241 and 225 are on the beach. Lake with boat rentals and fishing. Dam Neck is 1 mile from Ocean Breeze Water Park and the Marine Science Museum.

Locator 433-2000   **Medical 433-6327**   **Police 433-6302**

Fort A.P. Hill (VA17R1)
Bowling Green, VA 22427-5000

TELEPHONE NUMBER INFORMATION: Main installation numbers: C-804--633-5041, D-312-934-8710.

Location: From I-95, take Bowling Green/Fort A.P. Hill exit, US-17 (bypass) east to VA-2 south to Bowling Green, take VA-301 northeast to main gate. Also, exit I-95 to VA-207 north to VA-301 north and to main gate. USM: L-4. NMC: Fredericksburg, 14 miles northwest.

Billeting Office: Building TT-0114, 4th St, C-804-633-8335, 0800-1630 hours M-F, other hours, SDO, building TT-0101, C-804-633-8201. Check in billeting, check out 1200 hours. Government civilian employee billeting.

TML: Guest House. **Dolly's House.** All ranks, leave or official duty. Bedroom, private bath (2 rooms make a suite), (6); handicapped accessible (1). Same amenities as DV/VIP. New structure '90. Rates: $20 per unit. Reservations at above number.

TML: VOQ/VEQ. Buildings TT-0117-0119, TT-0125, TT-0146, officers all ranks, enlisted E7-E9, leave or official duty. Bedroom, semi-private bath (39). Community kitchen, limited utensils, A/C, color TV, maid service, ice vending. Older structures. Rates: $20 per person. TDY can make reservations, others Space-A.

TML: VOQ. Cottages, officers all ranks, enlisted E7-E9, leave or official duty. Bedroom, private bath (4); two bedroom, private bath (2); three bedroom, private bath (1); five bedroom, private bath (1). Kitchen, complete utensils, A/C, color TV, maid service, roll-aways ($10). Older structures. Rates: $20 per person. TDY can make reservations, others Space-A.

TML: DV/VIP. Buildings SS-0252-0254, PO-0290, officer 06+, C-EX-8205. Separate bedrooms, private bath (2); two bedroom, private bath (2); three bedroom, private bath (1). Kitchen, complete utensils, A/C, color TV, maid service, roll-aways ($10). Rates: $20 per person. TDY can make reservations, others Space-A.

TML: Recreation Lodge. Building SS-0251, all ranks, leave or official duty, C-**804-633-8219**. Nine bedroom, (sleeps 18) semi-private bath (1). Kitchen, complete utensils, freezer, ice maker, color TV, roll-aways ($10), 2 woodburning fireplaces, lounge chairs. Rates: $150 per day for groups of 6 or less, $25 each additional person. All categories can make reservations.

TML: Recreation Cabins. Buildings PO-0292/93/94, all ranks. Report to building TT-0106. Check out 1100 hours. Three bedroom, private bath (3). Kitchen, complete

Fort A. P. Hill, continued

utensils, A/C, color TV, washer/dryer. Modern structures. Rates: $10 per adult and $5 per child E1-E6, $20 per adult and $10 per child E7-E8, $13 E9+ and TDY. Maximum 6 persons per family. All categories can make reservations.

DV/VIP: Commander's Office, building TT-0101, C-EX-8205, 06+.

TML Availability: Good, Oct-Mar. Difficult, other times.

☞ This is a very rustic area, with good hunting and fishing in season. Dolly's House is named for Kitty "Dolly" Hill, wife of Gen. A.P. Hill, for whom the Fort is named. Support facilities: snack bar, exchange, bowling alley, and theater.

Locator 633-5041   Medical 833-8216   Police 633-8239

Fort Belvoir (VA12R1)
Fort Belvoir, VA 22060-5000

TELEPHONE NUMBER INFORMATION: Main installation numbers: C-703-545-6700, D-312-227-0101.

Location: From I-95 south or US-1 south take Fort Belvoir exits. Clearly marked, USM: M-7. NMC: Washington, DC, 10 miles northeast.

Billeting Office: Building 470, Gaillard Road, C-703-805-2333/2307, 24 hours daily. Billeting Manager, C-EX-2005. Check in billeting, check out 1200 hours daily. Government civilian employee billeting VOQ.

TML: VOQ/VEQ. Various buildings, officers all ranks, leave or official duty. Bedroom, private bath (VOQ) (319); bedroom, semi-private bath (VOQ)(92); separate bedroom, private bath (VOQ)(8); two bedroom, private bath (VEQ) (9); double rooms for E1-E6 shared bath (VEQ) (16); single rooms for E7-E9, private bath (VEQ) (8). Some kitchen/refrigerator, color TV, maid service, washer/dryer, cribs/rollaways. Modern structure. Rates: sponsor $25, spouse $5, child $3. Maximum $33 per family. TDY and PCS can make reservations. No pets.

TML: DV/VIP. Buildings 20 (O'Club), 470, officers 06+, leave or official duty. Separate bedroom suites, private bath (4); (470) bedroom, double bed, private bath (9). Kitchen, complete utensils, A/C, color TV, maid service, cribs/cots, ice vending. Modern structure, renovated '92. Rates: sponsor $30, spouse $5, child $3; maximum $38 per family. Duty can make reservations. No pets.

TML Availability: Good, Dec. Difficult, May-Sep.

☞ Exit Walker Gate to see George Washington's Mill, and visit nearby Woodlawn Plantation, Gunston Hall. See Capitol Hill in downtown Washington DC; northern Virginia is rich in colonial and Civil War history.

Locator 805-2043   Medical 805-0510   Police 805-3104

VIRGINIA

Fort Eustis (VA10R1)
Fort Eustis, VA 23604-5336

TELEPHONE NUMBER INFORMATION: Main installation numbers: C-804-878-1110, D-312-927-1110.

Location: From I-64, exit 60A to VA-105, west to fort. USM: N-5. NMC: Newport News, 13 miles southwest.

Billeting Office: ATTN: Billeting Office, ATZF-EHH, building 2110, Pershing Ave, C-804-888-0968, 804-878-5807/2337, D-312-927-2359, 24 hours daily. Check in billeting, check out 1000 hours daily. Government civilian employee billeting.

TML: VOQ/VEQ/DVQ/TLQ. Building 2110, all ranks, leave or official duty. Handicapped accessible. Suites (29) & 4 cottages for transient persons; VOQ: bedrooms (263); VEQ: bedrooms (449); DVQ suites (9). Refrigerator, community kitchen, kitchen (cottages and DVQ only), A/C, essentials, color TV in room & lounge, maid service, cribs/cots, washer/dryer, food/ice vending, handicapped accessible. Rates: VOQ, VEQ, TDY $16; non-duty, $22, $6 each additional non-duty person; PCS: $22; DVQ/cottages, $22, $6 each additional person. Priority for VOQ: officers attending Transportation Office Basic Course. Priority for VEQ: enlisted personnel attending Advanced Non-commissioned Officer Course and Basic Non-commissioned Officer Course. Duty can make reservations, others Space-A. Space-A check in 1800 hours. **Pets allowed $3/day.**

DV/VIP: Protocol Office. Building 210, Room 207, C-EX-6010/30. 06+. Retirees and lower ranks Space-A.

TML Availability: Good. Best Oct-May.

☞ Visit the Army Transportation Museum, tour historic Yorktown Battlefield, and Colonial Williamsburg for a crash course in United States' early history.

Locator 878-5215	Medical 878-4555	Police 878-4555

Fort Lee (VA15R1)
Fort Lee, VA 23801-5000

TELEPHONE NUMBER INFORMATION: Main installation numbers: C-804-734-1011, D-312-765-3000.

Location: From I-95 take Fort Lee/Hopewell exit, and follow VA-36 to main gate. USM: L-4. NMC: Petersburg, 3 miles west.

Billeting Office: Building P-8025, Mahone Ave, C-804-733-4100, D-312-687-6698/6694, 24 hours daily. Check in billeting, check out 1200 hours daily. Government civilian employee billeting VOQ.

TML: Guest House. Building 9056, all ranks, leave or official duty. Bedroom, 2 beds, sofa bed, living room, private bath (40). Refrigerator, A/C, color TV, maid service, cribs/cots, washer/dryer. Modern structure. Rates: sponsor $18-$24, 2nd person free, child no charge. Maximum $18-$24 per family. Duty can make reservations, others Space-A. Note: primarily for PCS in/out.

Fort Lee, continued

TML: VOQ. Buildings P-8025/26, P-9051-55, P-4229, officers all ranks, E7-E9, leave or official duty. Bedroom, private bath (482). Kitchen, A/C, color TV, maid service, washer/dryer, ice vending, handicapped accessible (2). Modern structures. Rates: sponsor $21, 2nd person $5. Maximum 2 per room. Duty can make reservations, others Space-A. Note: primarily for TDY personnel.

TML: DV/VIP. Davis House, building P-8042, officers 06+, enlisted E9. Official duty only. Two story, 4 bedroom house (1), livingroom, diningroom, kitchen, complete utensils, microwave, seating room, two private bathrooms, AC, color TV, maid service, handicapped accessible. Modern structure. Rates: sponsor $20, 2nd person $5. Maximum 2 per room. Duty can make reservations, others Space-A. Primarily for TDY personnel.

DV/VIP: Protocol Office, building P-5000, room 221, C-EX-3475, 06/GS-15+. Retirees and lower ranks Space-A.

TML Availability: Difficult. Best Dec, also on weekends and holidays.

☞ Visit the **Quartermaster Museum, and Battlefield Park, which is rich in Civil War history. Wonderful bass and crappie fishing is on the Chickahominy River. Virginia Beach swimming, fishing and boating is 85 miles east.**

Locator 734-2021   **Medical 734-3637**   **Police 734-2072**

Fort Monroe (VA13R1)
Fort Monroe, VA 23651-5000

TELEPHONE NUMBER INFORMATION: Main installation numbers: C-804-727-2111, D-312-680-2111.

Location: From I-64 exit Hampton and follow tour signs through Phoebus to Fort Monroe. USM: N-5. NMC: Hampton, 1 mile southeast.

Billeting Office: ATTN: ATZG-ISH, building T179, Pratt St, **C-804-727-2128,** D-312-680-2128, 0800-1645 hours M-F. Check in billeting. Check out 1000 hours. No government civilian employee billeting.

TML: VQ. Buildings 61, 80, 136, 137, all ranks, leave or official duty. Two bedroom suites, private bath (2); bedroom suites, private bath, kitchen w/utensils, A/C, color TV, maid service, cribs/cots, washer/dryer. Older Victorian, renovated. Rates: TDY sponsor $15, other sponsor $15, spouse $4/$5, child $1/$2. Duty can make reservations, others Space-A.

TML: DVQ. Building 80, officer 06+, leave or official duty, C-EX-4401. Check in Building 11, 0700-1645. Two bedroom suites, private bath (4). Kitchen, complete utensils, A/C, color TV, maid service, washer/dryer. Older Victorian, remodeled. Rates: TDY $22, others $22, spouse $10, child up to 16 $2, maximum $38 per family. Duty can make reservations, others Space-A. Check out 1100 hours daily.

DVQ: ATTN: Protocol Office, building 11, C-EX-4401, 06+.

TML Availability: Fairly good, Oct-Apr. More difficult, May-Sep.

VIRGINIA
Fort Monroe, continued

☞ A National Historic Landmark, touring Fort Monroe is a US history lesson. Historic Hampton is also nearby, as well as Williamsburg. This area is a treasure trove for history buffs.

Locator 727-2598   Medical 727-2840   Police 727-2238

Fort Myer (VA24R1)
Fort Myer, VA 22211-5050

TELEPHONE NUMBER INFORMATION: Main installation numbers: C-703-545-6700, D-312-227-0101.

Location: Adjacent to Arlington National Cemetery. Take Fort Myer exit from Washington Blvd, at 2nd St, or enter From US-50 (Arlington Blvd) first gate. Also, exit from Boundary Drive to 12th St north entrance near the Iwo Jima Memorial. USM: N-7. NMC: Washington, DC, 6 miles northeast.

Billeting Office: Building T-49, Jackson St, 24 hours daily, C-**703-696-3576/77**, D-312-696-3576/77. Check in billeting, check out 1200 hours daily. Government civilian employee billeting.

TML: VOQ/VEQ. Buildings T-49, T-52, all ranks, leave or official duty. VOQ: Bedroom, semi-private bath (16); separate bedrooms, private bath (4). VEQ: rooms, 2/3/4 beds in some rooms, semi-private bath (20). Refrigerator, A/C, color TV room & lounge, maid service, cribs/cots $3, washer/dryer, microwave in lobby. Rates: Sponsor $11, adult $11, spouse $3, child/infant up to 10 free. Duty can make reservations, others Space-A.

TML: DV/VIP. Building 50, officers O7+, leave or official duty. Bedroom suites, living room, private bath (18). Refrigerator, bar, A/C, color TV, telephone, maid service, cots, washer/dryer. Older structure. Rates: $30, spouse $5, child/infant up to 10 free. Duty can make reservations, others Space-A.

DV/VIP: Write to: DA Protocol, Pentagon, building 50, C-EX-7091, D-EX-7051, O7+. Retirees & lower ranks Space-A.

TML Availability: Good. Best, Nov-Dec.

☞ Tour Arlington National Cemetery for a fascinating look at military history and traditions. Don't miss the stables of ceremonial horses used in military funerals, the Old Guard Museum. Fort Myer is home to the US Army Band.

Locator 545-6700   Medical 696-3628   Police 696-3525

Fort Pickett (VA16R1)
Blackstone, VA 23824-5000

TELEPHONE NUMBER INFORMATION: Main installation numbers: C-804-292-8621, D-312-438-8621.

Fort Pickett, continued

Location: On US-460, 1 mile from Blackstone. Clearly marked. USM: L-4. NMC: Richmond, 60 miles northeast.

Billeting Office: ATTN: AFZA-FP-EH, building T-469, Military Rd, C-**804-292-8309/8320,** 0730-1600 duty days, other hours, PMO, building T-471, C-EX-8444. Check in billeting, check out 1000 hours daily. Government civilian employee billeting. Note: confirm all reservations by phone at least 24 hours in advance.

TML: VOQ. Cottages. Officers all ranks, E6-E9, leave or official duty. Bedroom, 2 beds private bath (13). Community kitchen, complete utensils, A/C, color TV lounge, maid service, cribs, cots $5 per adult. Older structures. Rates: $17-$20 per unit. Maximum 4 persons. Maximum 3 guests per sponsor. Duty can make reservations, others Space-A. **Pets allowed outside.**

TML: VOQ. Officers all ranks, leave or official duty. Bedroom, common bath (28); Bedroom suites, 2 beds, private bath (4). Community kitchen, complete utensils, A/C, color TV lounge, maid service, cribs, cots $5 per adult, washer/dryer. Older structures. Rates: $7-$11 per adult. Maximum 3 guests per sponsor. Duty can make reservations, others Space-A. **Pets allowed outside.**

TML: VEQ. Enlisted all ranks, leave or official duty. Bedroom, common bath (28); Bedroom suites, 2 beds, private bath (4). Community kitchen, complete utensils, A/C, color TV lounge, maid service, washer/dryer. Older structure. Rates: $7-$11 per adult. Maximum 3 guests per sponsor. Duty can make reservations, others Space-A. **Pets allowed outside.**

DV/VIP: PAO, building 472, C-EX-8303/2454, 05+. Retirees and lower ranks Space-A.

TML Availability: Good, Sep-Mar. Difficult, other times.

☞ **Some of the best hunting and fishing in the state of Virginia. Both Charlottesville and Richmond, the James River Plantations and Washington DC are within reach of this facility.**

Locator 292-2266/8525   Medical 292-2528   Police 292-8444

Fort Story (VA08R1)
Fort Story, VA 23459-5010

TELEPHONE NUMBER INFORMATION: Main installation numbers: C-804-422-7305, D-312-438-7305.

Location: From Interstate 64: take exit 79, Northamton Blvd (US-13) for 4.3 miles, take Shore Drive (Route 60) exit. (Sign = East-West Shore Drive, Beaches). Turn right to Shore Drive and after 5 miles turn left to West Gate, Fort Story (Route 305 North) just after the entrance to Seashore State Park). USM: N-5. NMC: Virginia Beach, 7 miles south.

Billeting Office: Building 582, Atlantic, C-**804-422-7321,** 0730-2330 hours daily. Check in billeting, check out 1000 hours daily. Government civilian employee billeting.

VIRGINIA
Fort Story, continued

TML: TLQ. Buildings 511, 526, 537, all ranks, leave or official duty. Bedroom, private bath (1); Two separate bedrooms, private bath. Kitchen, refrigerator, community kitchen, limited utensils, A/C, color TV room & lounge, maid service, essentials, cribs/cots, washer/dryer, accessible to handicapped (1). Older structures, redecorated. Rates: sponsor $22, each additional person $6. Duty can make reservations, others Space-A.

TML: DV/VIP. Cottages for 04, E9 and W4+, Memorial day-Labor day. Contact office of the Chief of Staff, ATTN: Cottage Reservations, USATCFE, Ft. Eustis, VA 23604-5000, C-804-878-4804, D-312-927-4804. Requests for reservations accepted first working day in January. 03 and below C-804-422-7106, D-312-438-7106, first working day for the next month, beginning 0730. Cottages are 2 bedroom (maximum 6 people). Cottages 709, 714 are 3 and 4 bedroom (both maximum 8 people). All have fully equipped kitchens, A/C/heat, CATV, on-post telephone, BBQ and picnic tables available. Cribs available on request. Maid service and towels on request. Sponsor or spouse must accompany group. Inventories taken. Off season (day after Labor Day to Thursday before Memorial Day Weekend) reservations for cottages except 714 (which remains under Ft. Eustis control): C-804-422-7106, D-312-438-7106, 0900-1100 hours. Reservations held to 2000. No shows (failure to cancel) counts against future reservations. One reservation per service member, summer season. One reservation per service member per month for winter season. Rates: summer - $22 per day, sponsor, $6 per person (12 and over), per day, $3 pet fee per day per pet. Off season rates: $22 per family per day, $3 per pet per day. Leave only, all categories can make reservations. Cottages on Chesapeake Bay/Atlantic Ocean. Swimming, Recreation Center, Gym, Bowling, Fishing/equipment available, golf.

DV/VIP: Handled by Fort Story/Ft Eustis as indicated above.

TML Availability: Good, Oct-Mar. Difficult, other times.

☞ **See the Old Cape Henry Lighthouse, Douglas MacArthur Memorial, Virginia Beach Science Museum, Williamsburg Pottery Factory. Busch Gardens, Ocean Breeze Park and Norfolk Naval Base nearby.**

Locator 422-7682   Medical 422-7802   Police 422-7141

Judge Advocate General's School (VA01R1)
Charlottesville, VA 22903-1781

TELEPHONE NUMBER INFORMATION: Main installation numbers: C-804-972-6300, D-312-274-7115.

Location: On the grounds of the University of Virginia at Charlottesville. Take the 250 bypass off I-64 to the Barracks Road exit, then turn right at light, then right onto Midmont, then right onto Arlington Blvd, then right at the top of the hill to the school. USM: L-4. NMC: Charlottesville, within city limits.

Billeting Office: ATTN: JAGS-SSL-H, basement of TJAGS, room 156B, C-804-972-6450, 0750-1650 daily. Other hours, SDO front desk. Check in facility, check out 1200 hours. Government civilian employee billeting only on orders to TJAGS.

Judge Advocate General's School, continued

TML: VEQ/VOQ. All ranks, leave or official duty. Handicapped accessible. Bedroom, one bed, private bath (77). A/C, community kitchen, cots ($2), ice vending, maid service, refrigerator, color TV, washer/dryer. Modern structure. Rates: TDY, sponsor $8, family member $5; active duty on leave and retirees $20, family members $5. Most space reserved for TJAGS students.

DV/VIP: ATTN: JAGS-SSJ-V, C-EX-6301, 06+. Retirees and leave Space-A. Sponsor $25, family member, $5.

TML Availability: Very limited, last two weeks in June. Difficult, other times.

☞ **Visit historic Monticello, Ash Lawn and the Michie Tavern. For outdoor activities, try Reynovia Lake, Montfair Camp Grounds, Lake Albemarle.**

Langley Air Force Base (VA07R1)
Langley AFB, VA 23665-5000

TELEPHONE NUMBER INFORMATION: Main installation numbers: C-804-764-9990, D-312-574-1110.

Location: From I-64 east in Hampton take Armistead Ave exit, go right to stop light; right onto La Salle Ave and enter AFB. USM: M-5. NMC: Hampton, 1 mile west.

Billeting Office: 1 SG/SVBB, building 75, Nealy Ave, C-**804-764-4051**, 24 hours daily. Check in billeting, check out 1200 hours daily. Government civilian employee billeting.

TML: TLQ. Buildings 78, 79, 94, 95, all ranks, leave or official duty. Separate bedrooms, private bath (39). Kitchen, complete utensils, A/C, color TV, maid service, cribs/cots, washer/dryer, ice vending. Modern structures, renovated. Rates: $18.50 per unit, sleeps 5. Duty can make reservations, others Space-A.

TML: TLQ. Buildings 1092-1098, all ranks, leave or official duty. Bedroom, private bath (39). Kitchen, complete utensils, A/C, color TV, maid service, cribs/cots, washer/dryer, ice vending. Modern structures. Rates: $18.50 per unit, sleeps 4. Duty can make reservations, others Space-A.

TML: VOQ. Buildings 67, 68, officers, leave or official duty. Bedroom, private bath (78). Kitchen, A/C, color TV, maid service, cots, washer/dryer, ice vending. Modern structures. Rates: $9 per person. Duty can make reservations, others Space-A.

TML: VAQ. Building 75, enlisted all ranks, leave or official duty. Bedroom, 2 beds, common bath (65); separate bedrooms, private bath for SNCOs (5). Refrigerator, A/C, color TV, maid service, washer/dryer, ice vending. Modern structure, renovated. Rates: $6 per person, maximum 2 per room. Duty can make reservations, others Space-A.

TML: DV/VIP. Buildings 472 (Lawson Hall), 448 (Dodd Hall), officers 06/GS-15+, leave or official duty, Lawson: C-EX-3467, Dodd: C-EX-5044. Lawson: separate bedroom suites, private bath (11). Dodd: separate bedroom suites, private bath (10). Kitchen, limited utensils, A/C, color TV, maid service, cribs/cots, washer/dryer, ice vending. Older structures, renovated. Rates: $10 per person. Maximum 2 per unit. Duty can make reservations, others Space-A.

VIRGINIA
Langley Air Force Base, continued,

DV/VIP: Protocol Office, building 703, C-EX-3467, 06+. Retirees and lower ranks Space-A.

TML Availability: Good, winter months. Difficult, summer months.

☞ **Historic Colonial Williamsburg, Busch Gardens, beautiful Virginia beach, and the Mariner's Museum are all closeby and worth a visit.**

Locator 764-5615   Medical 764-6833   Police 764-7771

Little Creek Naval Amphibious Base (VA19R1)
Norfolk, VA 23521-5001

TELEPHONE NUMBER INFORMATION: Main installation numbers: C-804--464-7000, D-312-680-7000.

Location: From I-64 south through Hampton Roads Bridge Tunnel take Northampton Blvd exit, 5 miles to base, exit VA-225. From Chesapeake Bay Bridge Tunnel proceed west on US-60 to base. USM: N-5. NMC: Norfolk, 11 miles southwest.

Billeting Office: ATTN: Code N73, officers in building 3408, A St, C-804-464-7522, enlisted in building 3601, 6th & 3rd Sts, C-804-464-7577. Check in facility, check out as indicated. Government civilian employee billeting.

TML: Navy Lodge. Building 3531, all ranks, leave or official duty. For reservations call **1-800-NAVY-INN**, lodge number is 464-6215. Check in prior to 1800 to avoid cancellation. Check out 1200 hours daily. Bedroom, 2 beds/studio couch, private bath (90). Kitchen, complete utensils, A/C, color TV, maid service, coin washer/dryer, ice vending. Modern structure. Rates: $34 per unit. All categories can make reservations. **No pets except birds in cages, fish in tanks.**

TML: BOQ. Building 3408, officers all ranks, leave or official duty, C-EX-7522. Check out 1330 hours daily. Bedroom, private bath (271); separate bedroom suites, private bath (18). Microwaves, A/C, CATV, maid service, washer/dryer, ice vending. Modern structure, renovated. Rates: $8 per person, suites $10. No accompanied members until Navy Lodge is full. Duty on orders can make reservations, others, 1 day basis, Space-A.

TML: BEQ. Building 3601, enlisted all ranks, leave or official duty, C-EX-7792, D-EX-7577. Check out 1100 hours daily. Bedroom, private bath (17); bedroom, 2 beds, private bath (20); bedroom, 3 beds, private bath (155); single rooms, private bath (E7-E9) (47); 3 man rooms, private bath (E5-E6) (186); 3 man rooms, private bath (E1-E4) (110). Refrigerator, A/C, CATV, maid service, washer/dryer, ice vending. Modern structure, renovated. Rates: E1-E6 $3 per person, E7+ $4. Dependents not authorized. Duty can make reservations 90 days advance, others Space-A.

TML: DV/VIP. Building 3186, officer 06+, leave or official duty, C-804-444-5901, D-312-564-5901. Check out 1200 hours daily. Separate bedroom suites, private

VIRGINIA
Little Creek Naval Amphibious Base, continued

bath (4). Queen beds, refrigerator, community kitchen, limited utensils, A/C, CATV, maid service, cots, ice vending. Older structure, remodeled. Rates: $15 per person active duty.

DV/VIP: SURFLANT-planetarium. Above number, 06+. Retirees Space-A.

TML Availability: Good, Oct-Dec. Difficult, Jun-Aug.

☞ History is all around Little Creek, with Jamestown and Williamsburg 1 hour north. Nearby beautiful Virginia beaches beckon, and a full range of shopping and entertainment is available in Norfolk.

Locator 464-7000   Medical 464-7879   Police 464-7621

Norfolk Naval Base (VA18R1)
Norfolk, VA 23511-5000

TELEPHONE NUMBER INFORMATION: Main installation numbers: C-804--444-0000, D-312-564-0000.

Location: From north take I-64 east, take naval base exit, follow signs. From south take I-64 exit to I-564 into Gate 2. USM: N-6. NMC: Norfolk, in city limits.

Billeting Office: BEQ: Billeting Code 06, building I-A, Pocahontas & Bacon Sts, C-804-444-2839, 0730-1600 hours daily, other hours, Central Assignments, building A-48, C-804-444-4425. BOQ: BOQ Billeting Fund, building A-128, Powhattan St off Maryland Ave, C-804-444-4151/3250, 24 hours daily. Check in facility, check out 1000 hours daily. Government civilian employee billeting.

TML: Navy Lodge. SDA-314, all ranks, leave or official duty. For reservations call 1-800-NAVY-INN, lodge number is 489-2656, 24 hours daily. Check out 1200 hours daily. Bedroom, 2 double beds, studio couch, private bath (290). Kitchen, complete utensils, A/C, color TV, HBO, maid service, cribs, coin washer/dryer, ice vending. Modern structure. Rates: $35 per unit. All categories can make reservations.

TML: BOQ. Buildings A-125, A-128, officers all ranks, leave or official duty. Bedroom, private bath (274); separate bedrooms, kitchen, private bath (3). Refrigerator, A/C, CATV room & lounge, maid service, cots ($2), washer/dryer, ice vending, sauna/exercise room, jacuzzi, sun deck. Modern structures. Rates: $9 per unit, $13 double. Duty can make reservations, others Space-A.

TML: BEQ. Buildings I-A (NAVSTA), U-16 (NAS), enlisted all ranks (no E7+ at NAS), leave or official duty. NAVSTA C-EX-4425, NAS C-EX-4983. Bedroom, hall bath (NAVSTA)(152); 5 buildings, hall bath (NAS). Check out NAVSTA 1300 hours daily, NAS 1000 hours daily. Both: Refrigerator, A/C, color TV room & lounge, maid service, washer/dryer, ice vending. Modern structures. Rates: $4 per person. Duty can make reservations, others Space-A.

DV/VIP: COMNAVBASE building KBB, C-EX-2788. CINCLANTFLT Camp Elmore, C-EX-6323, 07+, retirees Space-A. Suites used for 06+ with BOQ manager's permission (4). Rates: VIP suites $22, double $25.

VIRGINIA
Norfolk Naval Base, continued

TML Availability: Good, fall & winter. More difficult, other times.

☞ This is the largest naval base in the world. There is an interesting tour given daily. If you can see a ship launching, do so! Also, visit Hampton Roads Naval Museum, and the MacArthur Memorial. Nearby are Williamsburg, Yorktown and Jamestown.

Locator 444-0000   Medical 444-1531   Police 444-2361

Norfolk Naval Shipyard (VA26R1)
Norfolk, VA 23709-5000

TELEPHONE NUMBER INFORMATION: Main installation numbers: C-804-396-3000, D-none.

Location: Take I-64 to I-264 through the tunnel. First exit turn left into shipyard. USM: N-6. NMC: Virginia Beach, 15 miles northeast.

Billeting Office: Building 1504A, C-804-396-4449, D-312-961-4449, 24 hours daily. Check in at the facility, 24 hours daily, check out 1200 hours. Late checkout C-EX 4562. Government civilian employee billeting.

TML: BEQ. Building 1531, 1503 enlisted (E1-E9), 1504 (ships in overhaul, official duty only), all ranks, leave or official duty. Reservations accepted, 1503, 1531. Not for 1504. Check out 1200 hours daily. Rooms, semi-private bath (200); rooms, private bath (158); rooms for official ship overhaul duty only (building 1504)(242). Essentials, food vending, refrigerator in unit, no cooking allowed, maid service, color TV in room and in lounge, washer/dryer. Modern structure, remodeling '91, '92. Rates: sponsor $3. Family members not allowed to stay in facility, no guests of opposite sex in residents rooms. Active duty can make reservations, others Space-A. No pets.

TML: BOQ. Building 1530, officers all ranks, leave or official duty. Bedroom, private bath (78). Suites, VIP. Essentials, food vending, kitchenette, utensils, no stove, color TV room & lounge, maid service, cots, washer/dryer. Modern structures, new carpeting in VIP quarters, VCR's anticipated. Rates: sponsor $8, adult $4, VIP, $20. Maximum persons 4-5. No pets. All categories can make reservations, active duty, reserve and national guard on orders have priority, others Space-A.

TML: DV/VIP. Code 800, building 1500, Portsmouth Naval Shipyard, Portsmouth, VA 23709, C-EX-8605, D-EX-8605. Building 1530, 07+. Suites are retiree eligible.

TML Availability: Good. Best in Dec, difficult Sep.

☞ Virginia Beach's famed boardwalk and beaches will tempt summer visitors, shopping in downtown Norfolk, inspecting Williamsburg, or just relaxing in Red Wing Park will make a trip to this area worthwhile.

Locator 396-3000   Medical 396-3268   Police 396-5131

Oceana Naval Air Station (VA09R1)
Virginia Beach, VA 23460-5120

TELEPHONE NUMBER INFORMATION: Main installation numbers: C-804-433-2000, D-312-433-2000.

Location: From I-64 exit to Norfolk-Virginia Beach Expressway (VA-44 east), east on Virginia Beach Blvd. Bordered by Oceana Blvd (VA-615) and London Bridge Rd. Also, bordered by Potters and Harper Rds. USM: N-6. NMC: Virginia Beach, in city limits.

Billeting Office: Building 460, G St across from O'Club, C-804-433-3293, 24 hours daily. Check in billeting, check out 1100 hours daily. Government civilian employee billeting.

TML: BOQ. Building 460, officer all ranks, leave or official duty. Bedroom, private bath (102) (28 rooms with semi-private bath); bedroom suites (48), living room, private bath. A/C, community kitchen, cots ($4), essentials, ice/food vending, small kitchens (suites), maid service, refrigerator, color TV in room & lounge, washer/dryer. Older structure. Hotel type telephone systems. Rates: sponsor $7, (suite) $8, (VIP suite) $12, adult double sponsor rates, child over 2 years $4, infant no charge. No maximum charge. Maximum 4 in suites, 2 in rooms. Duty can make reservations. Reservations not taken for non-duty during summer months, others Space-A.

DV/VIP: Building 460, C-EX-3293, 06+, retirees and lower ranks Space-A.

TML Availability: Good, winter months. Difficult, summer months.

☛ **Great beaches at Virginia Beach. The Lighthouse Restaurant, south end of the beach on Atlantic Avenue has been recommended.**

Locator 491-4260   **Medical 433-2221/22**   **Police 433-9111**

☺**A new Navy Lodge is planned at this facility. Keep posted with details in Military Living's R&R Space-A Report.**

Quantico Marine Corps Combat Development Command (VA11R1)
Quantico, VA 22134-5001

TELEPHONE NUMBER INFORMATION: Main installation numbers: C-703-640-2121, D-312-278-2121.

Location: From I-95 north or south take Quantico/Triangle exit # 50A. US-1 north/south is adjacent to base. Clearly marked. USM: L-4. NMC: Washington, DC, 40 miles north.

Billeting Office: Building 2034, Little Hall, Barnett Ave, C-703-640-2681, 24 hours daily. Housing Office, 0800-1630 M-F. C-703-640-2711. Check in billeting, check out 1000 hours (1200 hours Hostess House). Government civilian employee billeting.

VIRGINIA
Quantico Marine Corps CDC, continued

TML: Hostess House. Building 3072, all ranks, leave or official duty. Deposit required first day for PCS prior to occupancy. Maximum stay 15 days, C-**703-640-2983/7959**. Bedroom, semi-private bath (73). A/C, color TV lounge, maid service, cribs ($.50), cots ($1), washer/dryer, vending machine. No pets. Older structure. Rates: $23 per person, $18 PCS with orders.

TML: SNCO Quarters. Building 3229, Shuck Hall, enlisted E6-E9, leave or official duty. C-**703-640-3148/3149**. Bedroom, private bath (TAD/TDY) (24); separate bedroom suite, private bath (1). Kitchen (suite only), refrigerator, A/C, color TV, maid service, cribs/cots, washer/dryer, ice vending. Older structure. Rates: $4 per room, $14 per suite. Maximum 1 per room, 4 per suite. Duty on orders or leave, retired, and dependents only.

TML: BOQ. Building 15, Liversedge Hall, officer all ranks, leave or official duty, C-**703-640-3148/3149**. Bedroom, semi-private bath (TAD/TDY)(72); separate bedrooms, private bath (TAD/TDY) (DV/VIP suites). Kitchen (6 units), refrigerator, community kitchen limited utensils, A/C, CATV, in room & lounge, maid service, cribs/cots, washer/dryer, ice vending, O'Club with bar at building 15. Older structure. Rates: $10, TAD/TDY $5; suites $25, $17 (TAD/TDY) without orders. All categories can make reservations. Call 30 days in advance.

TML: DV/VIP. Building 17, officer 07+, leave or official duty, C-**703-640-2786**. Bedroom suite, private bath; two bedroom suite, private bath (2). Refrigerator, community kitchen, A/C, color TV, maid service, cribs/cots, washer/dryer, ice vending, cash bar in suites. Older structure. Rates: $17 with orders, $25 without orders. Duty on orders or leave, retirees, and dependents only.

DV/VIP: Protocol, building 3250, C-EX-4477/2265, 07+. Retirees and lower ranks space-A.

TML Availability: Good, Oct-Apr. Difficult, summer months.

☞ Located on the Potomac River, near Washington DC. Woodbridge is the major shopping and recreation district closeby, but the battlefield of Manassas, Occoquan (craft shops and marinas) is also near.

Locator 640-2121   **Medical 640-2525**   **Police 640-2251**

Vint Hill Farms Station (VA03R1)
Warrenton, VA 22186-5013

TELEPHONE NUMBER INFORMATION: Main installation numbers: C-703-349-6000, D-312-229-6000.

Location: From Washington, DC area take I-66 west to Exit 10 A, 29/211 south, go about 8 miles south to VA 215 east (Vint Hill Rd), for about 2 miles, bear to the right on 652 east to main gate. USM: L-4. NMC: Washington DC, 45 miles northeast.

Billeting Office: Building 163, Helms St, C-**703-349-5139/ 6797/6796,** 0730-2300 hours M-F, 0800-1600 Sa, Su, holidays. After duty hours, building 162, C-703-349-5863. Check in after 1400 hours daily, check out 1100 hours. **No Pets.** Government civilian employee billeting.

VIRGINIA

Vint Hill Farms Station, continued

TML: Guest House. Building 168, all ranks, leave or official duty. Bedroom, private bath (14), 3 can be converted to a suite. Kitchenettes, kitchen amenities available for check out, essentials, CATV, washer/dryer, lounge, washer/dryer, ice machine, housekeeping. Modern structure. Rates: duty $25, additional person $1; Space-A $25 additional person $5. PCS, TDY have priority Space-A arrivals: M-F 1400-2300 hours, Sa-Su 1400-1600 hours check in.

TML: VOQ/VEQ. Building 163, all ranks, official duty. Bedroom, private bath (12); bedroom, semi-private bath (2). AC, refrigerator, microwaves, CATV, lounge, washer/dryer, ice machine. Modern structure. Rates: $10 per night, $5 each additional person. No families or children. Official duty may make reservations 30 days in advance.

TML: DVQ/VIP. Building 247, officer 06+, leave or official duty. Second floor O'Club. Separate bedroom suite, private bath (1). Refrigerator, A/C, CATV, housekeeping. Historical structure, remodeled. Rates: sponsor $30 per night, each additional person $5. Duty can make reservations, 30 days in advance.

TML Availability: Fairly good. Best Oct-May. Difficult, June-Sep.

☞ **Visit historic Bull Run Battlefield Park, the lovely Shenandoah Valley and Blue Ridge Mountains (Skyline Drive), fascinating Luray Caverns. Washington DC offers a full range of entertainment and shopping.**

Locator 349-6000   **Medical 349-6543**   **Police 349-6543**

Yorktown Naval Weapons Station (VA14R1)
Yorktown, VA 23691-5001

TELEPHONE NUMBER INFORMATION: Main installation numbers: C-804-887-4000, D-312-953-4000.

Location: From I-64 exit to US-143 west, .5 mile to US-238 left, .5 mile to gate 3, Skiffes Creek. USM: M-5. NMC: Newport News, 15 miles southeast.

Billeting Office: ATTN: BOQ/BEQ Officer, building 704, C-**804-887-7621**, 0800-1530 M-F. Check in facility, check out 1000 hours. Government civilian employee billeting if GS-7+ with advance reservations.

TML: BOQ. Building 704, officers all ranks, leave or official duty, C-EX-7621. After duty hours C-EX-7557. Bedroom, private bath, suite (DV/VIP) (1); separate bedroom suites, private bath (16). Community kitchen, A/C, color TV in room & lounge, maid service, cots, washer/dryer, ice vending, refrigerator. Modern structure. Rates: sponsor $8, maximum $16 per family. Duty can make reservations, others Space-A.

TML: BEQ. Buildings 706, 707, enlisted all ranks. Bedroom, semi-private bath (92). Lounge, recreational area. Rates: $4 per person.

DV/VIP: PAO, Building 31-A, C-EX-4141, 06/GS-15+.

TML Availability: Good, winter months. Limited, summer months.

VIRGINIA
Yorktown Naval Weapons Station, continued

☞ The Battlefield at Yorktown, restored Colonial Williamsburg, and the first permanent English settlement in America, are all within a 20 mile radius of the station. Check with Special Services on special tickets to events and parks.

Locator 887-4000   Medical 887-7404   Police 887-4677

Bangor Naval Submarine Base (WA08R4)
Bremerton, WA 98315-5000

TELEPHONE NUMBER INFORMATION: Main installation numbers: C-206-396-1110, D-312-744-1110.

Location: From Bremerton, on WA-3, follow signs "Hood Canal", bypassing Bremerton and Silverdale. Follow sub base signs to main gate. USM: A-1. NMC: Bremerton, 20 miles south.

Billeting Office: Family Housing, building 1101, room 119, C-**206-396-4410**, 0730-1600 hours daily. (BOQ & BEQ) **206-779-5514**, 24 hours daily. Check in facility, check out 1200 hours daily. Government civilian employee billeting.

TML: Navy Lodge. Building 2906, Trigger Rd, NSB Bangor, Silverdale, WA 98315. Reservations: **1-800-NAVY-INN**, lodge number is 779-9100. Check in at facility, check out 1100 hours. Late checkout call front desk. Bedroom, private bath, 2 queen size beds (45); bedroom, private bath, queen size bed and sofa sleeper (5). Two are handicapped accessible. Kitchenette, utensils, essentials, cribs, high chairs, food and ice vending, maid service, CATV, phones, coin washer/dryer. Rates: $39. Maximum 5 per room. Seeing eye dogs, fish, caged birds OK. Reservations all categories.

TML: BOQ. Building 2750, officers all ranks, leave or official duty. Bedroom, private bath,(66); suites, 2 with kitchen (VIP)(6). Microwave, color TV in room & lounge, essentials, cribs/cots, maid service, washer/dryer, food/ice vending, computer, jacuzzi. Modern structure. Rates: sponsor $8, adult, $4 child under 12. Suites $16, $4 each additional person. PCS are confirmed, duty, reservists can make reservations, others Space-A.

TML: BEQ. Building 2200, enlisted all ranks, leave or official duty. Bedroom, semi-private bath, 1-3 beds depending on rank (600); bedroom, private bath (Chiefs)(8). Refrigerator, color TV in lounge, maid service, cribs/cots, washer/dryer, food/ice vending, microwave. Modern structure. Rates: sponsor $4, adult, child $3 each. Duty can make reservations, others Space-A.

TML: VIP Cottage. Building 4189, officer 06+, leave or official duty. Bedroom cottage, private bath (1). Kitchen, complete utensils, maid service, cribs/cots, color TV. Renovated and remodeled. Rates: sponsor $16, adult, child $4 each. Maximum 4 persons. Duty can make reservations, others Space-A.

Bangor Naval Submarine Base, continued

DV/VIP: PAO, building 1100, room 213, C-EX-5514, 06+. Civilians determined by commander, retirees Space-A.

TML Availability: Fairly good. Best Oct-Apr, difficult May-Sep.

☞ Visit Poulsbo, known as "Little Norway", and stroll the boardwalk along Liberty Bay. Try Bremerton's Naval Shipyard Museum (Ferry Terminal on First St). For picnicking and boating visit Silverdale Waterfront Park.

Locator 396-6111   Medical 396-4222   Police 396-4444

Fairchild Air Force Base (WA02R4)
Fairchild AFB, WA 99011-5000

TELEPHONE NUMBER INFORMATION: Main installation numbers: C-509-247-1212, D-312-657-1110.

Location: Take US-2 exit from I-90 west of Spokane. Follow US-2 through Airway Heights, after 2 miles left to base main gate and Visitors' Control Center. USM: C-1. NMC: Spokane, 12 miles east.

Billeting Office: ATTN: 92CSG/SVH, building 2392, Short St, C-**509-247-5519**, 24 hours daily. Check in billeting, check out 1100 hours daily. Government civilian employee billeting official duty only.

TML: VOQ. Buildings 2392/93, all ranks, leave or official duty. Bedroom, private bath (27); separate bedrooms, private bath (8); two bedroom, private bath (11). Kitchen, color TV in room & lounge, maid service, cribs/cots, washer/dryer, ice vending, irons, ironing boards. Older structures. Rates: $9 per person, maximum $18 per family; DV/VIP $13 per person, $24 maximum per family. Duty can make reservations, others Space-A.

TML: VAQ. Building 2272, enlisted all ranks, leave or official duty. Bedroom, semi-private bath (29). Refrigerator, A/C, color TV, maid service, washer/dryer. Modern structure. Rates: $9 per room. Maximum 2 per room. TDY can make reservations, others Space-A.

TML: TLF. Building 2393, all ranks, leave or official duty. Two bedroom suites, private bath (8). Kitchen, complete utensils, color TV, maid service, cribs/cots, washer/dryer, ice vending. Older structure, renovated. Rates: $21.50-$22.50 per room. Maximum 2 per room.

DV/VIP: Building 2392, C-EX-2127. 06+. Retirees and lower ranks Space-A.

TML Availability: Good, Sep-Mar. More difficult, other times.

☞ Visit Manito Park and Botanical Gardens, while there look at the local pottery, the Cheney Cowles Museum and historic Campbell House. Try Factory Outlet shopping in Post Falls, Greyhound racing in Coeur D'Alene.

Locator 247-5875   Medical 247-5661   Police 247-5493

WASHINGTON

Fort Lewis (WA09R4)
Fort Lewis, WA 98433-0085

TELEPHONE NUMBER INFORMATION: Main installation numbers: C-206-967-1110, D-312-357-1110.

Location: On I-5, exit 120 in Puget Sound area, 14 miles north of Olympia, 12 miles south of Tacoma. Clearly marked. USM: A-2. NMC: Tacoma, 12 miles north.

Billeting Office: ATTN: AFZH-DEX, building 5228, between Utah and Pendleton Avenues, Main Post: C-**206-967-7862/2815**, D-312-357-2815/357-7862, 24 hours daily. For Madigan Army Medical Center C-**206-967-2664**, D-312-357-2664, 0730-1600 hours. Check in facility, check out 1000 hours. Government civilian employee billeting.

TML: Fort Lewis Lodge. Guest house, all ranks, leave or official duty. Bedroom, private bath (75); bedroom, private bath cottages, fully furnished for enlisted PCS families (8). Community kitchen each floor, CATV, maid service, recreation room, lounge, cribs/cots, coin washer/dryer, ice vending. Modern structure. Rates: based on rank of military member, $2 for each additional occupant. Maximum 5 per room. TDY can make reservations, others Space-A. **Twelve cage dog/cat boarding facility ($1.50 per space).**

TML: VOQ/VEQ. Main Post, two buildings all ranks, leave or official duty. (Clark House for PCS in/out families). Bedroom, private bath suites (16); bedroom private bath suites (27); single rooms (3). At Madigan Army Medical Center (MAMC) two buildings with suites (40), and single rooms (3). Some suites and singles share bath. Community kitchen on each floor, limited utensils, in-room fee beverage service, CATV, maid service, washer/dryer, cribs/cots available, no charge TDY. Older structures. Rates: $22, each additional person $2. TDY can make reservations, others Space-A.

TML: DVQ. Building 1020, **Bronson Hall**, officer 04+, leave or official duty. VIP suites, private bath (3); main post cabins (2); MAMC DVQ suites (5). Rates: $22 per night, $2 additional occupant. Cabins have kitchen. Refrigerator, in-room fee beverage service, CATV, maid service, washer/dryer. Older structure. Rates: sponsor $22, each additional person $2. Duty can make reservations, others Space-A.

TML: VOQ/VEQ. Building 9906, Lincoln St, officer, all ranks, leave or official duty. Single rooms, private bath (28). TV, refrigerator, community kitchen, maid service. Duty can make reservations, others Space-A.

TML: Klatawa Village, officer cabins. PCS in/out families. Main Post, family units (6). Small kitchen, limited utensils, color TV, maid service.

TML: Enlisted Cabins. PCS in/out families. Family units (11). Small kitchen, limited utensils, color TV, maid service.

DV/VIP: Protocol Office, building 2025, C-EX-5834, D-EX-5834, 07+.

TML Availability: Fair, Oct-Apr. Difficult, other times.

Fort Lewis, continued

☞ From majestic Mount Rainier, to the inland sea waters of Puget Sound, perfection for the outdoorsman. Tacoma, Olympia and Seattle are nearby.

Locator 967-6221   **Medical 967-6972**   **Police 967-3107**

Madigan Army Medical Center (WA15R4)
Tacoma, WA 98431-0001

TELEPHONE NUMBER INFORMATION: Main installation numbers: C-206-967-5151, D-312-357-5151.

Location: From I-5 north or south take the Madigan exit. Clearly marked. USM: B-1. NMC: Tacoma, 12 miles north.

Billeting Office: Building 9901, Lincoln St, C-**206-967-2664**, 0730-2300 hours daily. Other hours SDNCO, building 9901, information desk, C-206-967-7082. Check in billeting, check out 1000 hours daily. Government civilian employee billeting.

TML: Guest House. Building 9901, all ranks, leave or official duty. Bedroom, semi-private bath (4); separate bedrooms, semi-private bath (18). Community kitchen, refrigerator, limited utensils, maid service, cribs/cots, coin washer/dryer. Older structure. Rates: sponsor $6-$12, additional person $3. Maximum 3 per unit. MEDEVAC priority.

TML: VOQ/VEQ. Building 9906, all ranks, leave or official duty. Bedroom, semi-private bath (27). Community kitchen, refrigerator, limited utensils, maid service, washer/dryer. Older structure. Rates: $6-$12/person. TDY/med student reservations, others Space-A.

TML: DV/VIP. Building 9938, officers 03+, leave or official duty. Separate bedrooms, private bath (4); suite, private bath (06+ only) (1). Refrigerator, community kitchen, limited utensils, A/C, color TV, maid service, cribs/cots. Older structure. Rates: sponsor $8, additional person $3; suites: sponsor $15, each additional person $5. Maximum 3 per unit. TDY/MEDEVAC personnel can make reservations, others Space-A.

DV/VIP: CO's Office, building 9900, C-EX-6921, 03+. Retirees Space-A.

TML Availability: Fairly good. Best, Oct-May.

Locator 967-6221   **Medical 967-6972**   **Police 967-3107**

⊗**This facility did not respond to our inquiries, information may be outdated.**

McChord Air Force Base (WA05R4)
McChord AFB, WA 98438-0001

TELEPHONE NUMBER INFORMATION: Main installation numbers: C-206-984-1910, D-312-976-1110.

Location: From I-5 exit 125. Clearly marked. USM: A-2. NMC: Tacoma, 8 miles north.

WASHINGTON
McChord Air Force Base, continued

Billeting Office: Building 166, Main St, C-206-584-1471, 24 hours daily. Check in facility, check out 1200 hours daily. No government civilian employee billeting.

TML: VOQ/VAQ. Many buildings, all ranks, leave or official duty. Bedroom, private, semi-private, & common baths (172); separate bedrooms, private bath (18); two bedroom, private bath (19). Kitchen (VOQ), refrigerator (all), limited utensils, color TV, maid service, cribs/cots, washer/dryer, ice vending, facilities for DAVs. Older structures. Rates: $6 per person. Maximum 2 room suite $16, 1 room $8. Duty can make reservations, others Space-A.

TML: DV/VIP. Building 116, officer 06+, leave or official duty, **C-206-584-2621.** Bedroom suites, private bath (6); two bedroom suites, private bath (17); bedroom, private bath (48). Kitchen, complete utensils, color TV, maid service, cribs/cots, washer/dryer, ice vending. Older structure. Rates: $8 per person. Maximum $16 2 bedroom suite. Duty can make reservations, others Space-A.

DV/VIP: EXO 62/MAW/CCE, building 100, C-EX-2621, 06/GS-12+. Retirees and lower ranks Space-A.

TML Availability: Good, Nov-Feb. Difficult, Jun-Aug.

Locator 984-2474   **Medical 984-5601**   **Police 984-5624**

⊗**This facility did not respond to our inquiries, information may be outdated.**

Pacific Beach Ocean Getaway (WA16R4)
Puget Sound NS, WA 98115-5014

TELEPHONE NUMBER INFORMATION: Main installation numbers: C-206-526-3211, D-312-941-3211.

Location: Located on the coast in Pacific Beach, WA, 150 miles southwest of Seattle. Accessible from US-101 (Coastal Highway) and US-12 from Yakima. USM: B-1. NMC: Seattle, 150 miles northeast.

Billeting Office: On board Naval Station Seattle in building 193N, 1000-1600 hours M-F, 1000-1400 Sa, check out 1100 hours, C-1-800-626-4414 - reservations made over the phone are confirmed when payment are received. Send information requests to: OCEAN GETAWAY; Recreation Services, building 47/Code 60, Naval Station Puget Sound, Seattle, WA 98115-5014. Make checks payable to: Recreation Services. Cancellations must be in writing and received by Recreation Services 10 days prior to reservation date. Notices received less than 10 working days will be assessed one day's rental. Reservations not paid within 10 working days are subject to cancellation. Reservation Priority: (1 reservation per request) active duty-90 days, other military personnel 60 days, all other authorized personnel 30 days. Visa, MasterCard.

TML: Cabins and suites, all ranks, leave or official duty. Cabins, two, three and four bedrooms (28); suites, two bedroom, private bath (adults only) (4); studio, family units, sleeping units. Basic two bedroom cabin rate: E1-E5 $32, E6-E9 $45, officer $50, DOD $55; three bedroom cabin rate: E1-E5 $37, E6-E9 $50, officer $55, DOD $60; four bedroom cabin rate: E1-E5 $42, E6-E9 $55, officer $60, DOD $65; ocean side cabins add $5 per day, fireplace cabins add $8 per day; suite rate: E1-E5 $22, E6-E9 $25, officer $28,

Pacific Beach Ocean Getaway, continued

DOD $31; studio E1-E5 $17, E6-E9 $20, officer $23, DOD $26; family units have queen, double bed and set of bunk beds in one room, sleeping units have two sets of bunks, call for prices. Each cabin unit sleeps two people per bedroom. Cribs, high chairs, infant gates are available upon request ($5 per visit). Crib linens not provided. Lodging can be reserved from 2 nights up to 2 weeks. Extensions granted when space is available. Minimum of 2 nights required (F-Su), and 3 nights (Su-F). Holiday weekends minimum of 3 nights (F-M). All other requests on a Space-A basis. Note: sponsor must accompany guest during stay.

TML Availability: Fairly good. Best in winter months.

☞ **"May be the Navy's best kept vacation secret"! Social room with activities weekends off-season, and daily in spring, summer and fall. Ball field, horseshoe pits, picnicking, and whale watching platform, for what else? Watching whales!**

Puget Sound Naval Shipyard (WA11R4)
Bremerton, WA 98314-5000

TELEPHONE NUMBER INFORMATION: Main installation numbers: C-206-476-3711, D-312-439-3711.

Location: Take WA-16 West to end of freeway, Puget Sound NS clearly visible 3 miles north. USM: A-1. NMC: Seattle, 60 miles southeast.

Billeting Office: Building 865, C-206-476-7660, D-312-439-2637, 24 hours daily. Reservation desk 24 hours, C-**206-476-7627/7619**, D-312-439-7627, FAX-206-476-6895, check in facility, check out 1300 hours daily. Government civilian employee billeting.

TML: BEQ. Underwood Hall, Keppler Hall, Nibbe Hall, buildings 865, 885, 942. Enlisted all ranks, leave or official duty, C-**206-476-7619**, D-312-439-7627. Bedroom, shared bath (447); family rooms (6). Refrigerator in room, community kitchen 1st floor, color TV in room & lounge, housekeeping service, washer/dryer, ice, food vending, hot tub, mini gym, washer/dryer, microwave each floor, picnic facilities. Modern structure. Rates: $3 per person, family rooms $12. AD and retired can make reservations, others Space-A.

TML: BOQ. Building 847, officers all ranks & GS-7+, leave or official duty, C-**206-476-2840**, D-312-476-2840, FAX-206-476-0045. Bedroom, private bath (70); VIP/family suites, private bath (5). Refrigerators, cooking facility 1st floor, essentials, CATV in room & lounge, housekeeping service, washer/dryer, ice and food vending, complimentary coffee/doughnuts weekdays, telephones, sauna/spa, mini-gym, library and reading room, conference/meeting room, children's playground. Rates: $6 per person. Maximum 4 per room. Reservation services 24 hours.

DV/VIP: BOQ, Building 847, 06+, retirees Space-A, D-EX-2840.

TML Availability: Fairly good, Nov-Mar. More difficult, Jun-Sep.

WASHINGTON
Puget Sound Naval Shipyard, continued

☞ A beautiful Northwest location is supplemented by these lodging facilities, which won a navy FY 1991 Innkeeper award. These people take their job seriously!

Locator 476-3582   Medical 911   Police 476-3393

Naval Station Puget Sound (WA10R4)
Seattle, WA 98115-5000

TELEPHONE NUMBER INFORMATION: Main installation numbers: C-206-526-3211, D-312-941-3211.

Location: From I-5N take N 45th Street exit, continue E to WA-513 (Sandpoint Way) 2 miles. Station on the right clearly marked. USM: A-1. NMC: Seattle, 6 miles southwest.

Billeting Office: Building 224, B St, C-**206-526-3883/3884**, 24 hours daily. Check in billeting, check out 1200 hours daily.

TML: BEQ. Building 9, 224, active/reserve/enlisted, all ranks. Official duty/orders required. Leave status personnel on a Space-A basis only. Reservations required. Open Bay rooms (80) E1-E4 male; two man rooms (18) E1-E9 male; two man rooms (4) E1-E9 female; bath facilities for all rooms common-use.

TML: BOQ. Building 26. **At print time Officers Quarters unavailable due to 1990 fire. Tentative due date for new facilities mid to late 1992.**

TML Availability: Fluctuates due to large numbers reservists who have priority.

☞ Shuttle Express service available from Airport ($6 and $18). Metro Bus to downtown, waterfront, Pike Place Market, Seattle Center. Area offers freshwater and saltwater fishing, boating, sailing, skiing.

Locator 526-3211   Medical 526-3455   Police 526-3211

⊗Due to close in 1995. Retirees and Officers urged to seek lodging at other local commands.

Whidbey Island Naval Air Station (WA06R4)
Oak Harbor, WA 98278-5000

TELEPHONE NUMBER INFORMATION: Main installation numbers: C-206-257-2211, D-312-820-0111.

Location: Take WA-20 to Whidbey Island, 3 miles west of WA-20 on Ault Field Road. USM: B-1. NMC: Seattle, 90 miles southeast.

WASHINGTON

Whidbey Island Naval Air Station, continued

Billeting Office: Building 973, McCormick Center, C-206-257-2529, officer/CPO. Building 2701, 8th Street, C-209-257-5513, enlisted. Check in facility, check out 1200 hours daily. Government civilian employee billeting (on orders).

TML: BOQ. Building 973, officers, all ranks, leave or official duty. Bedroom, private bath (140). Refrigerator, maid service, essentials, food/ice vending, color TV in room & lounge, washer/dryer. Older structure. Rates: sponsor $8, adult/child over 12 $8, infant free. Maximum 2 persons per unit. Duty can make reservations, others Space-A.

TML: BEQ. Building 2701, all ranks, leave or official duty. Beds, 3 per room, shared bath (36). Refrigerator, color TV in room & lounge, maid service, ice/food vending, kitchen (suite), washer/dryer. Older structure. Rates: $4 per person. Duty can make reservations, others Space-A.

DV/VIP: CO Secretary, building 108, C-EX-2345, 06+.

TML Availability: Difficult on weekends due to Reserve Training. Best during winter.

☞ **Whidbey Island can also be reached by ferry from Mukiteo (north of Seattle) to Clinton, in South Whidbey. Visit the hamlet of Langley then take a two hour drive north to Oak Harbor through spectacular Puget Sound scenery.**

Locator 257-2211   **Medical 679-4400**   **Police 257-3122**

◉**Keep watching Military Living's *R&R Space-A Report* for news of a new Navy Lodge at this location.**

Wisconsin

Fort McCoy (WI02R2)
Sparta, WI 54656-5000

TELEPHONE NUMBER INFORMATION: Main installation numbers: C-608-388-2222, D-312-280-1110.

Location: From west on I-90 to north on WI-27 to northeast on WI-21 to fort. From east on I-90, to west on WI-21 to fort. USM: I-3. NMC: La Crosse, 35 miles southwest.

Billeting Office: ATTN: AFZR-DLH-B, building 2168, 8th St, C-608-388-2107, 24 hours daily. Check in billeting, check out 1100 hours daily. Government civilian employee billeting.

TML: TLQ. All ranks, leave or official duty. Bedroom, shared bath (230); bedroom, private bath (70); two bedroom (3) and four bedroom (2), private bath (4 units are trailers). Kitchen, complete utensils, A/C, color TV, cribs, cots ($3), essentials, washer/dryer. Older structure, new trailers. Rates: vary according to rank, status and quarters occupied, call for details. All categories can make reservations.

DV/VIP: Protocol Office, building 100, C-EX-3607, 06+, retirees and lower ranks Space-A.

WISCONSIN
Fort McCoy, continued

TML Availability: Fairly good, Jan-May and Sep-Dec. Difficult, other times.

☞ **Mid December through February the installation ski hill has good cross country and downhill skiing. For equipment rental, building 8061, C-EX-4498/3360.**

Locator 388-3116   Medical 338-2444   Police 115

Francis E. Warren Air Force Base (WY01R4)
Francis E. Warren AFB, WY 82005-5000

TELEPHONE NUMBER INFORMATION: Main installation numbers: C-307-775-1110, D-312-481-1110.

Location: Off I-25, 2 miles north of I-80, clearly marked. USM: F-4. NMC: Cheyenne, adjacent to the city.

Billeting Office: Building 216, Randall St, 24 hours daily, C-307-775-1844, check in facility, check out 1200 hours daily. Government civilian employee billeting.

TML: Guest Housing. Buildings 202, 238, 241, all ranks, leave or official duty. One, two and three bedroom apartments, private bath. Kitchen, living room, maid service, cribs and high chairs, washer/dryer, CATV, refrigerator in all units. Older structures, renovated. Rates: $22-$27 per night. All categories can make reservations.

TML: VOQ. Buildings 21, 74, 79, 129, 274, officers and civilians, leave or official duty. Two houses, one bedroom apartments, private bath, some with kitchen. Refrigerator, CATV, maid service, washer and dryer. Older structure, renovated. Rates $13 or $14 per person per night. All categories can make reservations.

TML: VAQ. Buildings 244, 275. DV/VIP units for E6 to E9. Single rooms, shared bath (3). Refrigerator, microwave, CATV, maid service, washer and dryer. Older structure, renovated. Rates: $9 or $14 per person per night.

DV/VIP: PAO. C-EX-2137/3052, E8+/06+. Retirees Space-A.

TML Availability: Good, except last week of July for Cheyenne Frontier Day Rodeo.

☞ **This base was once a frontier Army post, and many of its buildings are on the National Historic Register. Cowboy and Indian lore abound, and nearby Colorado skiing draws many visitors. Visit Fort Collins' Old Town nearer by.**

Locator 775-1841   Medical 775-3461   Police 775-3501

UNITED STATES POSSESSIONS

Guam

Agana Naval Air Station (GU03R8)
FPO AP 96539-5000

TELEPHONE NUMBER INFORMATION: Main installation numbers: C-011-671-351-1110, D-315-322-1100.

Location: Naval Air Station is in the middle of the island of Guam, on Marine Drive. Clearly marked. NMC: Agana, 3 miles southwest.

Billeting Office: BOQ/BEQ. C-011-671-344-5277, check in at facility, check out 1300 hours daily. No government civilian employee billeting.

TML: BOQ. Building 1300, officers all ranks, leave or official duty. Bedroom, shared bath (81); separate bedrooms, private bath (3). Refrigerator, A/C, color TV in lounge, maid service, washer/dryer, ice vending. Older structure. Rates: $4 per person, plus $10 fair market rental fee, family maximum $16, plus $8 fair market rental fee. Duty can make reservations, others Space-A.

TML: BEQ. Building 15, enlisted all ranks, leave or official duty. Beds, shared bath (850). A/C, color TV lounge, maid service, washer/dryer. Older structure. Rates: $4 per person. No dependents. Duty can make reservations, others Space-A.

DV/VIP: OD. 06/GS-15+, retirees Space-A.

TML Availability: Good, Apr-Dec. Difficult, other times.

Locator 344-6161   **Medical 344-8201/4140**   **Police 344-5160**

⊗**This facility did not respond to our inquiries, some data may be outdated.**

Andersen Air Force Base (GU01R8)
APO AP 96543-5000

TELEPHONE NUMBER INFORMATION: Main installation numbers: C-011-671-351-1110, D-315-322-1110.

Location: On the north end of the island, accessible from Marine Dr which extends entire length of the island of Guam. NMC: Agana, 15 miles south.

GUAM
Andersen Air Force Base, continued

Billeting Office: Building 27006, 4th & Caroline Ave, C-011-671-366-8201, D-315-366-8144, 24 hours daily. Check in billeting, check out 1200 hours daily. Government civilian employee billeting.

TML: VOQ. Buildings 25003, 27006, officers all ranks, leave or official duty. Bedroom, shared bath (100). Refrigerator, A/C, color TV, maid service, washer/dryer, ice vending. Older structure. Rates: $9 per person. Duty can make reservations, others Space-A.

TML: VAQ. Building 25003, enlisted all ranks, leave or official duty. Two bedrooms, shared bath (60). Refrigerator, A/C, color TV, washer/dryer. Older structure. Rates: $6.50 per person. Duty can make reservations, others Space-A.

TML: TLF. Building 1656, officer, enlisted, all ranks, PCS move or leave. Bedrooms, private bath, (18). Kitchenette, A/C, color TV, maid service, washer/dryer. Rates: $33 per unit. PCS can make reservations, others Space-A.

TML: DV/VIP. Building 27006, officer 06+, leave or official duty. Bedroom, private bath (7); separate bedroom, private bath suites (5). A/C, color TV, maid service, washer/dryer. Rates $10. Duty can make reservations, others Space-A.

DV/VIP: Protocol Office, 633 ABW, C-EX-4228, 07+, retirees Space-A.

TML Availability: Good, year round.

☞ **Lots of sunshine, beaches, coral reefs, exciting WWII shipwrecks to explore for scuba enthusiasts. Hikers enjoy tropical mountains and jungles.**

Locator 351-1110   Medical-363-297   Police 363-2913

Guam Naval Station (GU02R8)
FPO AP 96540-5000

TELEPHONE NUMBER INFORMATION: Main installation numbers: C-011-671-351-1110. D-315-322-1110.

Location: South on Marine Drive, through main gate, clearly marked. NMC: Agana, 10 miles north.

Billeting Office: Centralized, contact CBQ Barracks 18 lower, on Chapel Road off Marine Drive, C-011-671-339-5259, D-315-339-5139, FAX-011-671-339-5139, 24 hours daily. Check in facility, check out 1300 hours daily. TLA approved. Government civilian employee billeting.

TML: CBQ. Barracks 7, 22, officers, enlisted, government civilian employees (stateside hire), all ranks, leave or official duty. Bedroom, private bath (12); suites, private bath (52). Refrigerator, CATV and VCR, A/C, maid service, washer/dryer, ice, coffee maker. Rates: Barracks 7 $4 per person, Barracks 22 $10 per person. Duty can make reservations, others Space-A.

TML: BOQ. Buildings 2000, 179, officers and equivalent civilians, all ranks. Bedroom, private bath (58). Refrigerator, A/C, CATV and VCR, maid service, washer/dryer, ice and coffee maker. Rates: $7 per person, $7 per family member over 8 years old. Duty can make reservations, others Space-A.

Guam Naval Station, continued

DV/VIP: Flag Lt, C-EX-5202, 07+.

TML Availability: Fairly good. Best, December. Most difficult, Jul-Aug.

☞ **These quarters are within walking distance of all base support facilities. Scuba diving and other beach related activities are popular on pristine beaches. Sport fishing is good, as are visiting battleground monuments.**

Locator 351-1110   Medical 344-9369   Police 333-2989

☺**Watch for news of a new 100 room Navy Lodge at this location in mid '95. Keep updated with Military Living's R&R Space-A Report.**

Midway Island

Midway Island Naval Air Facility (MW01R8)
FPO AP 96516-1200

TELEPHONE NUMBER INFORMATION: Main installation numbers: Call Commander, Naval Base Pearl Harbor, below number, D-315-421-6000.

Location: On Midway Island in the Pacific Ocean, 1,300 air miles northwest of Honolulu, HI. NMC: Honolulu, 1,300 miles southeast.

Billeting Office: This station is in a Naval Defensive Sea Area and requires entry approval to visit, which is obtained thru the Commander, Naval Base Pearl Harbor C-808-471-7110. Entry is usually restricted to personnel visiting relatives on the island, and TDY personnel. No central billeting office. Contact BOQ, lower deck BOQ building "B". 0800-1630 hours duty days, C-EX-436. Other hours, OD, C-EX-777. Check in facility, check out 1000 hours daily. Government civilian employee billeting.

TML: BOQ. Building "B", C-EX-648, 24 hour desk at AMC Terminal. Officers all ranks, leave or official duty. Apartments, 1-& 2 bedroom, private bath (6); bedroom, shared bath (some). Kitchen, washer/dryer. Older structure. Rates: $37 per person. Enlisted check BEQ, C-EX-437.

TML Availability: Good, Feb-Aug.

☞ **For additional information call Hawaii information at 1-808-555-1212.**

Puerto Rico

Borinquen Coast Guard Air Station (PR03R1)
Aquadilla, PR 00604-5000

TELEPHONE NUMBER INFORMATION: Main installation numbers: C-809-882-3500, FTS-498-3500.

Location: At old Ramey AFB, north of Aquadilla. Take PR-2 from San Juan or north from Mayaguez to PR-110 North to CGAS. USM: J-5. NMC: San Juan, 65 miles east.

Billeting Office: La Plaza, room 26, C-809-882-3127/2581, 0800-1700 duty hours. Other hours, SDO, C-EX-3501. Check in billeting, check out 1200 hours daily. Government civilian employee billeting.

TML: Guest House. All ranks, leave or official duty. Bedroom, shared bath and private bath (5); three bedroom, private bath (4). Kitchen, complete utensils, A/C (2 units), color TV in room & lounge, maid service, cribs, washer/dryer. Older structure. Rates: (3 bedroom), $20 - 1 person, $26, - 2 persons, $32 - 3 persons; (1 bedroom) $11 - 1 person, $16 - 2 persons, $20 - 3 persons. Duty and retirees can make reservations, others Space-A. PCS have priority. Personnel on leave/anyone on vacation should apply at least 15 days in advance. **Pets OK.**

TML: Lighthouse, Borinquen Recreation Area, opened July '91. Two bedroom apartment suites, private bath (2); queen, 2 single beds, living, dining, kitchen, microwave, utensils, A/C, CATV, cribs, maid service, washer/dryer. No pets. Maximum capacity 4 persons. Rates: $34 active duty, $40 others. Duty may make reservations 45 days ahead, all others 30 days. Duty must make reservations (military widows make their own). Family members of legal age may use facilities unaccompanied, but duty who makes reservations assumes responsibility. Write to: Lighthouse Reservations, Aquadilla, Puerto Rico 00604, C-as above.

TML Availability: Very limited. Best, Sep-May.

☞ Recreation gear available for rent, and discount golf passes. Swimming pool on post, groceries 1 mile, picnic areas, Survival Beach belies its name - a lovely place to relax. Contact Special Services for all information 809-890-6236.

Locator 882-3500   **Medical 882-1500**   **Police 890-5201**

Fort Buchanan (PR01R1)
Fort Buchanan, PR 00934-5042

TELEPHONE NUMBER INFORMATION: Main installation numbers: C-809-783-2424, D-313-740-2424.

Location: From Munoz Rivera International Airport take highway 26 west toward Bayamon to highway 22 to the Fort Buchanan sign. NMC: San Juan, 6 miles southwest.

Fort Buchanan, continued   **PUERTO RICO**

Billeting Office: Building 119, C-809-792-7977, D-313-740-7221, 0700-1700 hours daily. Other hours SDO, building 390, C-EX-7123. Check in facility 1300, check out 1100 hours daily. No government civilian employee billeting.

TML: Su Casa Guest House, building 119, all ranks, leave or official duty. Handicapped accessible. Bedroom, private bath (each with double bed and sleeper sofa) (29). Refrigerator, community kitchen, A/C, CATV, maid service, cribs, cots, facilities for DAVs. Older structure, remodeled. Rates: $27 first person, $5 each additional person. PCS may make reservations with orders. Other active duty one week in advance, others Space-A.

DV/VIP: Headquarters Command, building 399, C-EX-7159, 06+. Reservations through Protocol Officer.

TML Availability: Good, Nov-Apr. Difficult, May-Nov.

☞ This is the capital of Puerto Rico. Visit El Morro Castle, Plaza las Americas Shopping Center, El Condado, local Bacardi Rum Distillers, and beautiful beaches. Post facilities include a gym swimming pool, PX and Commissary.

Locator 792-8296   Medical 792-8888   Police 792-7895

Roosevelt Roads Naval Station (PR02R1)
Box 3010, FPO AA 34051-5000

TELEPHONE NUMBER INFORMATION: Main installation numbers: C-809-865-2000, D-313-831-2000.

Location: From San Juan International Airport, turn left onto PR-26 for 20 minutes, turn left onto PR-3 (Carolina exit) for 30 minutes, then turn left after Puerto Del Rey Marina into NS. USM: K-9. NMC: San Juan, 50 miles northwest.

Billeting Office: Building 729 (officers), building 1708 (enlisted). C-809-865-2000-4334/3364 (officers), Ex-4145/4147 (enlisted), 24 hours daily. Check in billeting, check out 1100 hours daily. Government civilian employee billeting.

TML: CBQ. All ranks, leave or official duty. Handicapped accessible. Two bedroom apartments, private bath (8); three bedroom apartments, private bath (4). Kitchen, refrigerator, limited utensils, A/C, color TV, VCR, movies, phones, FAX, maid service, cots ($2), NEX mini mart. Modern structure. Rates: rooms (BEQ) $4, (VIP) $10; (BOQ) $8, (VIP) $15. Active duty on orders, PCS/TAD/TDY have priority for reservations, others Space-A.

TML: Guest House. Two bedroom houses (06+)(2). Kitchen, complete utensils, microwave, A/C, CATV, phone, maid service, washer/dryer. Rates: $20 per night. Duty can make reservations, others Space-A.

TML: Navy Lodge. All ranks, leave or official duty, C-1-800-NAVY-INN, lodge number is 865-8281/8282. Bedrooms, 2 double beds, private bath (72) (interconnecting units for large families, two handicapped accessible). Kitchenette, complete utensils, microwave,

PUERTO RICO
Roosevelt Roads Naval Station, continued

A/C, CATV, refrigerator, phone, maid service, coin washer/dryer, mini mart, children's playground. Rates: $40 per night. All categories can make reservations. Check in 1500 to 1800 hours. All major credit cards except American Express.

DV/VIP: C-EX-3364, 07+, retirees Space-A.

TML Availability: Good, Oct-Mar. Difficult, Apr-Sep.

☞ Don't miss El Yuunque (L-EE-UN-KEE) rain forest with its magnificent water falls, hiking trails, and restaurant. The new Navy Lodge is located on base directly across from the commissary and exchange. November 1990.

Locator 865-2000   **Medical 865-4133**   **Police 865-4123/4195**

-NOTES-

Big Bear Recreation Facility, Big Bear Lake, CA
(photo courtesy USMC)

US Navy Short Stay Recreation Area, Naval Station Charleston, SC *(photo courtesy US Navy)*

Fort Monmouth Billeting Office, NJ
(photo courtesy U.S. Army)

Fourth Cliff Recreation Area Cottage, MA
(photo courtesy USAF)

VIP Quarters, Andrews AFB, MD
(Military Living Photo by Michelle Rasberry)

Waianae Army Recreation Center, HI
(photo courtesy US Army)

Guest House, Oakland Army Base, CA
(photo courtesy US Army)

Fort Fisher Air Force Recreation Area, NC
(photo courtesy USAF)

Hale Koa AFRC, HI
(photo courtesy Hale Koa AFRC)

YMCA Hotel, Fort Bliss, TX
(photo courtesy YMCA)

Beach Cottages, Kaneohe Bay MCAS, HI
(photo courtesy USMC)

Fort Mason O'Club Billeting, CA
(photo courtesy US Army)

Navy Lodge Newport, RI
(photo courtesy US Navy)

Elliot Lake Recreation Area,
Red River Army Depot, TX
(US Army photo by Gary Sandlin)

Thayer Hotel, US Military Academy,
West Point, NY *(photo courtesy Thayer Hotel)*

Hillhaus Lodge (30 miles from Hill AFB) UT
(photo courtesy USAF)

Jean de Treville House, MCAS Beaufort, SC
(photo courtesy LCp. Joseph L. Claice)

Navy Lodge Staten Island, NY
(photo courtesy Navy Lodge Program)

FE Warren VIP Quarters, FE Warren AFB, WY
(photo courtesy Marilyn Depew)

Navy Lodge Norfolk, VA
(photo courtesy Navy Lodge Program)

Chiemsee Hotel AFRC, Chiemsee, Germany
(photo courtesy AFRC)

Navy Lodge Roosevelt Roads, Puerto Rico
(photo courtesy Navy Lodge Program)

Navy Lodge Rota, Spain
(photo courtesy Military Living subscriber)

Dragon Hill Hotel, Seoul, Korea
(photo courtesy Dragon Hill Hotel)

FOREIGN COUNTRIES

Antigua

Antigua Naval Facility (AN01R1)
St. Johns, West Indies
FPO AA 34054-5100

TELEPHONE NUMBER INFORMATION: Main installation numbers: C-1-809-462-3171, D-313-854-1110 (ask for Antigua EX-398).

Location: On the northeast side of the island of Antigua, 1 mile from Coolidge Airport. NMC: St Johns, 9 miles west.

Billeting Office: Quarterdeck, C-1-809-462-398, 24 hours daily. Check in facility, check out 1200 hours daily. Government civilian employee billeting.

TML: TLF. Buildings 1, 3, all ranks, official duty or leave. Building 3, BOQ: bedroom, private bath (2). Refrigerator, community kitchen, microwave, color TV/VCR, maid service, washer/dryer, ice vending. Building 1: bedroom, private bath (female enlisted) (1); bedroom, common bath (enlisted) (2). Refrigerator, maid service, washer/dryer. Rates: Moderate. Duty can make reservations, others Space-A.

DV/VIP: Adm Office, C-EX-386, 06+.

TML Availability: Very limited.

☞ Duty on leave are restricted to $20 per day in purchases except **snack bar and clubs. Retirees may use only club and medical facility due to SOFA.** Support Facilities: Special Service, Snack Bar, Medical, Gas Station, BX, All Hands Club, Theater. Great beaches, water sports.

Medical 462-3171

Australia

Harold E. Holt Naval Communications Station (AU01R8)
FPO AP 96550-5000

TELEPHONE NUMBER INFORMATION: Main installation numbers: C-61-099-49-3587/3239, D-315-371-1945/3587/3239.

Location: In Exmouth, a remote community on the Northwest Cape of Western Australia. The nearest city is Perth, AU about 800 miles south; the nearest town of any size is Carnarvon, 250 miles to the south. One road connects all of these, following the coast.

Billeting Office: BEQ 4, **C-61-099-49-3588/27**, 0700-1600 hours daily, other hours, Security Office, C-61-099-49-3332. Check in facility, check out 1200 hours daily. No government civilian employee billeting.

TML: BEQ. Enlisted all ranks. Duty only. Bedroom, latrine bath (2). Refrigerator, color TV in lounge, A/C, washer/dryer, ice vending. Rates: no charge. Maximum 1 per room.

Other: No BX or commissary privileges for personnel not assigned to station due to SOFA. Commonwealth Pass obtained from Civil Commissioner of Exmouth needed to enter the base. Local "no frills" type lodging available at Caravan Park on Lefroy St, C-EX-1331, Norcape Lodge at Town Beach Rd, C-EX-1334, and the Potshot Inn, C-EX-1200. You must have your own camper to use park-type facilities. No pets due to quarantine requirements. Very warm in summer, Oct-Apr. Very casual dress.

TML Availability: Limited for duty only.

☞ **This rugged and remote part of Australia offers fishing, beaches and spearfishing. Additional lodging available in Exmouth, where golf, tennis, Australian lawn bowls and other amenities are available.**

⊗**This station is being realigned. The process will be complete by the end of '93. How this will affect opportunities for visitors is not known at press time. Keep posted with *R&R Space-A Report*.**

Locator 3587   **Medical 3339**   **Police 3332**

Belgium

NATO/SHAPE Support Group (US) (BE01R7)
Hotel Raymond
APO AE 09708-5000

TELEPHONE NUMBER INFORMATION: Main installation numbers: C-(USA) 011-32-65-44-5111, ask operator to connect you; (BE) 065-31-1131/32.

Location: From Bruxelles Airport take E-10 direct to Paris, exit at Mons, Belgium and follow signs to "GARE" (train station). Hotel is across from GARE. HE: p-35, E/3. NMC: Brussels, 50 miles north.

Billeting Office: No central billeting office. Priority I, & II: AD, DOD civilian, PCS. Priority III: TDY, relative of hospital patient. Priority IV: TDY. Priority V: guest of AD/civilian at installation. Priority VI: leave, retirees. Note: Medal of Honor individual treated as Priority I. Check in 1300 hours, check out 1100 hours daily, C-(USA) **011-32-65-31-1131/32**, (BE) 065-31-1131/32. Government civilian employee billeting.

TML: Hotel Raymond, all ranks, leave or official duty. Handicapped accessible. Bedroom, private bath (68). Refrigerator, color TV, custodial service (except Sunday/holidays), cribs/cots, washer/dryer, cafeteria, buffet breakfast, nominal cost, food/ice vending. Rates: $36 primary occupant, $20 second occupant, $16 each additional occupant, free under 24 months. Family of 3 $72 - no charge for additional room. Family of 6 (3 rooms) $120. Space-A may check availability same day as arrival, above number.

TML Availability: Fairly good. Best Oct-Mid May.

 In Mons visit the Church of St Waudru. "The Belfry" is accessible by elevator. **Then visit the main square, town hall, and Van Gogh's house. To contact the Tourist Office, Grand-Place, 7000 Mons, call 065-33-55-80.**

Locator 44-5164   **Medical 423-3321**   **Police 065-22-3171**

Bermuda

Bermuda Naval Air Station (BM01R1)
FPO AE 09727-5000

TELEPHONE NUMBER INFORMATION: Main installation numbers: C-(USA) 1-809-293-5316, (BM) 0809-293-5316, D-312-938-5316.

Location: Bermuda is 600 miles east of Cape Hatteras, NC, in the Atlantic Ocean. NAS is on the north end of St David's Island near St George City. NMC: Hamilton, 6 miles southwest.

Billeting Office: Building 550, C-(USA) 1-809-293-6635, D-312-578-6635. Reservations: C-(USA) **1-809-293-5780**, (BM) 293-5780, 24 hours daily. Check in at facility 1600 hours, check out 1200 hours daily. Government civilian employee billeting.

BERMUDA
Bermuda Naval Air Station, continued

TML: BOQ/BEQ. Buildings 338, 344, 510, 550, all ranks, leave or official duty. BOQ (550/510) single and double rooms, hall bath; VIP suites, shared baths. BEQ (334/338) single rooms, hall bath; suites, shared bath. Refrigerator, A/C, CATV, maid service, washer/dryer, ice vending. Older structures, renovated. Rates: BOQ single $8, double $16, VIP $16; BEQ single $4, suites $10. Duty can make reservations, others Space-A.

DV/VIP: 06+, C-809-293-5530/6635.

TML Availability: Good, Nov-Dec. Limited due to downsizing.

☞ Don't miss the Front Street stores in Hamilton, Bermuda's capital. The best beaches are on the south shore; the most popular is Horseshoe Bay, a public strand that follows a sweeping arc around a blue-green bay. Enjoy!

Locator 293-5316   **Medical 293-6514**   **Police 293-6431**

Canada

Argentia Naval Facility (CN02R1)
FPO AE 09730-5000

TELEPHONE NUMBER INFORMATION: Main installation numbers: C-709--227-8555/8556, D-312-568-8662/8663/64.

Location: At the terminus of North Sydney (Nova Scotia) to Argentia (Newfoundland) Ferry Service. At Argentia there is access to the Trans-Canadian Highway, TCH-1, via CN-101, 25 miles northeast. The U.S. Naval Facility is in Argentia and is clearly marked. NMC: St John's, Newfoundland, 80 miles northeast.

Billeting Office: ATTN: CBQ Manager, Box 10, US Naval Facility, FPO AE 09730. Billeting coordinated at Strain Memorial Hall, building 848M, C-**709-227-8662/3/4**, D-312-568-8662/3/4, 24 hours daily. Check in facility, check out 1200 hours daily. Government civilian employee billeting.

TML: CBQ. Building 848M, **Strain Memorial Hall**. To reach it, turn right at intersection by railroad overpass, .5 mile to 10 story concrete building. Park in lower lot across the street from CBQ. All ranks. Leave or official duty. Handicapped accessible. Suites, private bath (36); bedrooms, shared bath (32). Refrigerator, community kitchen, color TV room & lounge, cribs/cots ($3), washer/dryer, ice vending, maid service, Quarters on 4th deck. and above. Meals available in galley on 2nd deck. Various clubs and vending machines on 1st deck. Older structure, renovated. Rates: $4 - $10 per person. Some DV/VIP lodging available in CBQ at rate of $8-$10 per person, fair market rental charge may apply. PCS, duty can make reservations, others Space-A.

TML: Northeast Arms Camp - 7 miles from facility. Recreation cabins (8), sleep up to 9 persons, 1 room with bath/shower, fireplace, cooking utensils, bunk beds, no bedding. Rates: $13 per day M-Th, $17 per day F-Su, $95 per week, $23 one night stay. Rentals: boats, canoes, motors. All categories can make reservations, priority assigned personnel, others Space-A. Contact MWR, building 846M, on the naval facility, Argentia **709-227-8709,** D-312-568-8709.

CANADA

Argentia Naval Facility, continued

DV/VIP: Executive Officer, building 848M, C-EX-5862. 06+.

TML Availability: Best, Oct through June. More difficult, July through Sept.

☞ This area is noted for its wonderful hunting and fishing. Note that retired personnel are not authorized use of exchange or commissary.

⊗This facility will close in '95.

Locator 227-8555   Medical 227-8444   Police 227-8777

Canadian Forces Base Trenton (CN04R1)
Astra, Ontario, CN KOK 1BO

TELEPHONE NUMBER INFORMATION: Main installation numbers: C-613-392-2811, D-312-827-7011.

Location: Take Highway 401 east 100 miles. May also be reached by crossing Canada/USA border at 1000 Islands, NY and proceeding west 70 miles on Highway 401. NMC: Toronto, 100 miles west.

Billeting Office: Building 76, C-**613-965-3793**, D-312-827-3793, 24 hours daily. Reservations not accepted for leave personnel and their family members. Write to: **Yukon Lodge**, CFB Trenton, Astra, Ontario KOK 1B0. Check in at the facility 24 hours, check out 1200 hours, late checkout not available. **Note: Canadian forces billeting.**

TML: Yukon Lodge, all ranks, leave or official duty. Bedrooms, 1-5 beds each, private and semi private baths. Cribs, food vending, color TV in room and lounge, washer/dryer, telephones. Older structure. Rates: adult $6, child $5.50, active duty $5, (Canadian). Verification of military/family member status required. No pets. Space-A lodging only.

DV/VIP: Base Protocol, CFB Trenton, Astra, Ontario, CN KOK 1BO. Building 22, 06+. Limited number of accommodations. C-613-965-3379, D-EX-3379.

TML Availability: Difficult. Best Oct-May, most difficult Jun-Sept.

☞ The Bay of Quinte Region is filled with wonderful fishing, camping, sailing and historical landmarks. Write to Central Ontario Travel Association, PO Box 1566, Peterborough, Ontario K9J 7H7, or call 1-800-461-1912 for more info.

Locator 392-2811   Medical 965-2111   Police 965-2253

Cuba

Guantanamo Bay Naval Station (CU01R1)
FPO AA 09593-5000

TELEPHONE NUMBER INFORMATION: Main installation numbers: C-011-53-99-XXXX, D-313-723-3690/564-4063.

Location: In the southeast corner of the Republic of Cuba. Guantanamo Bay Naval Station is accessible only by air. NMC: Miami, FL, 525 air miles northwest. Note: All personnel not assigned must have the permission of the Commander to visit Guantanamo Bay Naval Station.

Billeting Office: ATTN: BOQ Mgr, building 1670, Deer Point Rd, C-011-53-99-2402/3826/2238, D-313-564-4063, 24 hours daily. Check in facility, check out 1200 hours daily. Government civilian employee billeting.

TML: Navy Lodge. Naval Station, Box 38, FPO AA 09593-5000, all ranks, leave or official duty, reservations: **011-53-99-3103**, 0700-1800 daily. Check out 1200 hours daily. Bedroom, 2 double beds, studio couch, private bath (26). Kitchen, A/C, color TV, coin washer/dryer. Rates: $32 per unit. PCS only. Others must have sponsor.

TML: BOQ/BEQ. Buildings 1660, 1661, all ranks, leave or official duty. Bedroom, private bath (officer) (20); bedroom, hall bath (enlisted) (18). Refrigerator, community kitchen (officer, CPO), A/C, color TV in room & lounge, maid service, washer/dryer, ice vending. Modern structure. Rates: $2 per person. Duty can make reservations, others Space-A.

DV/VIP: BOQ. Building 1670, (C and D)-EX-2402/4063, 06+.

TML Availability: Good most of the year except holidays.

Locator 4453/4366   **Medical 4424/6395**   **Police 4105/3813/4145**

⊗**This facility did not respond to our inquiries, some information may be outdated. Navy Lodge information has been confirmed.**

Germany

Ansbach/Katterbach Community (GE60R7)
APO AE 09177-5000

TELEPHONE NUMBER INFORMATION: Main installation numbers: C-(USA) 011-49-981-83-XXX (Ansbach), 011-49-9802-832-XXX (Katterbach), (GE) 0981-83-XXX, 09802-832-XXX; ETS-468-7/8XXX (Ansbach), 467-2XXX (Katterbach); D-314-460-1110 Ask for ANS.

GERMANY

Ansbach/Katterbach Community, continued

Location: Exit from E-12 Autobahn east or west to GE-14 or 13 north 4 miles. Follow US Forces signs to Katterbach Kaserne. HE: p-40, E/2. NMC: Nürnberg, 26 miles northeast.

Billeting Office: Katterbach BOQ Office, C-(USA) **011-49-9802-832-812,** (GE) 09802-832-812, ETS-467-2812. Check in facility 0730-1630 M-W, 0730-1600 Th, 0730-1500 F. Other times, office of Deputy Cmdr, ETS-468-8437. Check out 1000 hours daily. Government civilian employee billeting.

TML: TLF, building 5908, all ranks, leave or official duty. Bedroom, private bath (28); separate bedroom, private bath (5). Cribs/cots available, shared kitchenette with microwave, maid service, color TV, VCR, utensils available, washer/dryer. Older structure. Leave status rates: $15 1st person, $10 2nd person, $5 each additional person; duty status rates: $21 1st person, $15 2nd person, $9 each additional person. PCS in/out can make reservations 30 days in advance, 2 weeks in advance for TDY, others Space-A.

DV/VIP: 235th BSB, ETS-468-1700, 06+, retirees Space-A.

TML Availability: Good. Best in Feb, Jun, Jul and Aug.

☞ Internationally famous for its yearly "Bach Week Ansbach", this Franconian capital also offers gourmet specialties, try "Schlotengeli", or "Pressack" with a cool Ansbach beer. Visit Orangerie Park at the "Hofgarten" afterwards!

Locator 468-8425   **Medical 09802-116**   **Police 114**

ⓈThis area has seen a drawdown of personnel, but has not closed. The O'club is closed for food services, but the basement "Little Italy" is open at press time. Keep posted by reading Military Living's R&R Space-A Report.

Augsburg Community (GE39R7)
APO AE 09178-5000

TELEPHONE NUMBER INFORMATION: Main installation numbers: C-(USA) 011-49-821-448-1700, (GE) 0821-448-1700, ETS-434-1700, D-314-434-1110.

Location: From Munich-Stuttgart, Autobahn E-8, exit at "Augsburg West" and follow "US Military Facilities Augsburg" signs to various Kasernes. HE: p-40, F/4-5. NMC: Augsburg, in the city.

Billeting Office: ATTN: AETS-AUG-EW, building 53, Reese Kaserne, Langemarck Str. C-(USA) 011-49-821-409001, (GE) 0821-409001, D-315-434-7270, 0730-1600 M-F. Check in facility, check out 1000 hours daily. Government civilian employee billeting.

TML: Guest House. Building 53, Reese Kaserne, Reinöl Str 74, Augsburg. All ranks, leave or official duty. Bedroom, 1 bed, hall bath (34); separate bedroom, private bath (20); suites with private bath (2). Refrigerator, color TV in room & lounge, maid service, cribs/cots ($6), washer/dryer, AAFES vending in building. Older structure, remodeled. Rates: sponsor $25-$33, child $6-$8. Duty can make reservations, others Space-A.

GERMANY
Augsburg Community, continued

TML: Guest House. Buildings 180, 181, 182, Sheridan Kaserne, all ranks, leave or official duty. Bedroom, hall bath (17); separate bedroom suites, private bath (3); building 181: suites, twin beds, private bath (16); building 182: bedrooms, shared bath (16); suites private bath (8). Refrigerator, color TV, maid service, washer/dryer. Older structure. Rates: sponsor $25 standard, $33 double occupancy, room w/shared bath, single $30, double $38. Room w/private bath, $35 single, $45 double. Regular suite $39 single, $55 double, additional occupants $6. Maximum 4 per room. Duty can make reservations, others Space-A.

DV/VIP: PAO. Determined by Commander. Retirees Space-A, suites are open to all ranks on a first come, first served basis. Rates: single $39, double $55, additional occupant $10.

TML Availability: Good, Jan-Apr. Difficult, Oct-Nov.

☞ **German history is mirrored in the 2,000 year story of Augsburg. Visit imperial Maximilianstrasse, and the romantic alleys of the Lech area. Towers, gates, churches and mansions continue to fascinate visitors.**

Locator 448-113   **Medical 449-4132**   **Police 448-114GERMANY**

Bad Aibling Station (GE91R7)
APO AE 09098-5000

TELEPHONE NUMBER INFORMATION: Main installation numbers: C-(USA) 011-49-8061-2405, (GE) 08061-2405, ETS-441-3893.

Location: From Autobahn A-8 (Munich-Salzburg) take Bad Aibling exit and follow signs through Bad Aibling to Munich on secondary road. Station is one mile out of town. HE p-40, G-5. NMC: Munich.

Billeting Office: Building 360, C-(USA) **011-49-8061-2405,** (GE) 08061-2405, D-314-441-3893. Check in 0700-2100, check out 1100 hours. Late checkout C-EX-5778/5779. Government civilian employee billeting.

TML: Visitors Quarters. Buildings 359, 361, all ranks, leave or official duty. Bedroom, living room, private bath (25); suites, living room, private bath (2); apartments, living room, private bath (2). Kitchenette (2 units), essentials, food and ice vending, color TV, maid service, cribs/cots, washer/dryer. Older structure, renovated '91. Rates: sponsor on leave or duty $30, family $35; VIP $45 per night, additional person $13. Maximum $43, $75, $84. Duty, reservists and national guard on orders can make reservations, others Space-A.

DV/VIP: Chief of Staff, building 302, 06, GS15+, others Space-A.

TML Availability: Very good. Best Dec-Jan, worst Feb-Nov.

Bad Aibling Sub-Community, continued

☞ Bad Aibling is a picturesque health resort near the Alpine mountains, excellent skiing opportunities are 20 minutes away in Austria. This location is only 50 miles from Salzburg on the crossroad to Italy.

Locator 441-3719   Medical 441-3781   Police 441-3822

☺This area will be greatly reduced in future. Keep posted on latest developments with Military Living's *R&R Space-A Report.*

Bad Kissingen Community (GE49R7)
APO AE 09265-5000

TELEPHONE NUMBER INFORMATION: Main installation numbers: C-(USA) 011-49-971-86-XXX, (GE) 0971-86-XXX, ETS-354-2XXX, D-314-350-1110 Ask for BKI.

Location: From the Kassel-Würzburg, E-70 Autobahn, exit Bad Kissingen/Hammelburg to GE-287 northwest for 9 miles. US Forces signs mark directions to installations. HE: p-36, G/6. NMC: Schweinfurt, 12 miles southeast.

Billeting Office: Housing Office, **Daley Barracks,** C-(USA) **011-49-971-86-721,** (GE) 0971-86-721, 0730-1600 hours daily. No government civilian employee billeting.

TML: Transient Billets, 11 Kurhausstrasse, C-EX-890. All ranks, leave or official duty. Color TV, refrigerator, private bath. Rates: $18 1st person single rooms, $6 each additional person, $25 1st person rooms with living room, $7 each additional person.

TML Availability: Limited.

Medical 354-2724   Police 354-2657

☺This facility did not respond to our inquiries, some data may be outdated.

Bad Kreuznach Community (GE01R7)
APO New York 09252-5000

TELEPHONE NUMBER INFORMATION: Main installation numbers: C-(USA) 011-49-671-609-XXXX, (GE) 0671-609-XXXX, ETS-490-XXXX, D-314-490-1110.

Location: Approximately 50 miles south from Frankfurt am Main, via Mainz to Bad Kreuznach Autobahn A-66 & A-60. Take B-41, at the east outskirt of the city, go south on Bosenheimer St, left on Alzyer St, to Nahe Club on the right, billeting next to club. HE: p-40, A/1. NMC: Bad Kreuznach, in city limits.

Billeting Office: ATTN: Family Housing Office, building 5649, Mannheimerstrasse, C-(USA) **011-49-671-609-77122,** (GE) 0671-609-77122, 0730-2100 hours daily, D-314-490-1700, ETS-490-1700. Check in facility, check out 1100 hours daily. Government civilian employee billeting.

GERMANY
Bad Kreuznach Community, continued

TML: Guest House/BOQ/BEQ/DV/VIP. Building 5649 (GH), 5648 (DV/VIP), all ranks, leave or official duty. Bedroom, shared bath (31); suites, private bath (DV/VIP) (3). Refrigerator, community kitchen, color TV, maid service, cribs ($2), cots ($4), washer/dryer. Older structure. Rates: sponsor $22, additional occupant $10. Duty can make reservations, others Space-A. **Pets OK for $5 per night.**

DV/VIP: Protocol Office, **Rose Barracks**, C-EX-6466, 06+. Retirees and lower ranks Space-A.

TML Availability: Good.

☞ **Visit the spa park on the slopes of the Hardt, the Oranienpark, Rose Island and the open air inhaling area with the Radon grading galleries for an interesting trip into German healthcare. Then take a sip of the local wine.**

Locator 490-6274   Medical 490-116   Police 490-114

Bamberg Community (GE34R7)
APO AE 09139-5000

TELEPHONE NUMBER INFORMATION: Main installation numbers: C-(USA) 011-49-951-300-XXXX, (GE) 0951-300-XXXX, ETS-469-XXXX, D-314-460-1110, ask for Bamburg.

Location: On GE 26/505. Warner Barracks, the main installation, is on the east side of the city between Zollner and Pödeldorter Strs. Follow signs. HE: p-40, E/1. NMC: Nürnberg, 30 miles southeast.

Billeting Office: Bamberg Inn. Guest House Office, building 7678, room 4, 1st floor, C-(USA) 011-49-951-300-1700, (GE) 0951-300-1700, 0800-1730 M-F, 1030-1430 hours Sa-Su. Other hours, Military Police, building 7108, ETS-469-7700. Check in facility 1400, check out 1100 hours daily. Government civilian employee billeting.

TML: Bamberg Inn. Guest Houses, building 7678, annex building 7070, 2nd floor, O'Club, Zollnerstrasse. All ranks, leave or official duty. Bedrooms, shared baths (4 family rooms)(43); suite, private bath (VIP)(1). Refrigerator, color TV, alarm clock/radios in all rooms, vending rooms (2 microwaves, snack coffee and coke machines), laundry room, housekeeping M-F, cribs, irons, ironing boards available, hall phones. Older structure, renovated. Rates: primary occupant $17, each additional occupant $5. TDY rates: primary $23, additional $11.50. PCS/TDY can make reservations, others Space-A. No pets.

DV/VIP: Deputy Community Cmdr. 05+. Retirees and lower ranks Space-A.

TML Availability: Limited.

☞ **With streets like a Gothic tapestry, Bamberg is unique. Wander among them and you will find St Michaels Church, the Old Town Hall, and a Baroque castle-the Concordia. Don't miss the Rose Garden, and "Little Venice".**

Locator 469-7738   Medical 469-8741/97   Police 469-7770

GERMANY

Bamberg Community, continued

⊗Warner Barracks will either reduce or close in future. Keep updated with Military Living's *R&R Space-A Report.*

Baumholder Community (GE03R7)
APO AE 09034-5000

TELEPHONE NUMBER INFORMATION: Main installation numbers: C-(USA) 011-49-6783-6-XXXX, (GE) 06783-6-XXXX, ETS-485-113 ask for BHR+EX, D-314-485-113 ask for BHR+EX.

Location: From Kaiserslautern, take Autobahn 62 toward Trier, exit north at Freisen and follow signs to Baumholder and Smith Barracks. HE: p-39, F/G1. NMC: Kaiserslautern, 35 miles southeast.

Billeting Office: Smith Barracks, Building 8076, C-(USA) **011-49-6783-6-5182** or (GE) 06783-5182, 0730-2400 M-F, C-EX-1700. Check in 1300-1700, check out 1100 hours daily. Government civilian employee billeting.

TML: Lagerhof Transient Billeting. Building 8076, all ranks, leave or official duty. Bedroom, private bath (10); two bedroom, private bath (19); four bedroom, private bath (1). Community kitchen, limited utensils, refrigerator, color TV lounge, maid service, cribs/cots, washer/dryer, color TVs. Older structure. Rates for PCS, TDY: 1st person $27, 2nd person $15, 3rd person $10; DVQ $22 each person. Duty can make reservations, others Space-A.

DV/VIP: Commander, C-EX-6300, 06/GS-12+.

TML Availability: Very good.

☞ Visit nearby Idar Oberstein for precious gems and stones, Trier's Roman ruins, the Mosel Valley's, castles and vineyards.

Locator 485-7551   Medical-485-6647   Police-485-7547

⊗This area will be greatly reduced in future. Keep posted on latest developments with Military Living's *R&R Space-A Report.*

Berlin Community (GE26R7)
APO AE 09235-5000

TELEPHONE NUMBER INFORMATION: Main installation numbers: C-(USA) 011-49-30-819-XXXX, (GE) 030-819-XXXX, ETS-332-XXXX, D-314-332-1110.

Location: Can be reached from the E-2, Helmstedt-Berlin Autobahn, by air to Tempelhof AB or via train from Frankfurt or Bremerhaven. HE: p-63, F/6. NMC: Berlin, in the city.

GERMANY
Berlin Community, continued

Billeting Office: Family Housing Branch, C-(USA) **011-49-30-819-6654,** (GE) 030-819-6654, 0815-1600 hours M-F. Other hours **Dahlem Guest House,** C-EX-6425. Check in facility, check out 1100 hours daily. Government civilian employee billeting.

TML: Guest House. **Dahlem Guest House,** 19 Ihnestrasse, all ranks, leave or official duty. Two bedrooms, private bath (4); four bedrooms, private bath (3); five bedrooms, private bath (6); six bed rooms, private bath (8); handicapped suite, private bath (1). Kitchen, maid service, washer/dryer, color TV. Modern structure. Rates: $35-$42 first person, $5 each additional person. Price includes continental breakfast. TDY/PCS can make reservations, others Space-A.

TML: Guest House. **Hotel Am Wannsee, Am Sandwerder,** all ranks, leave or official duty. Two bedroom, private bath (12); four bed suites, private bath (4). Color TV, maid service. Older structure. Rates: $50-$55 first person, $15-$20 each additional person. Price includes continental breakfast. TDY, PCS can make reservations, others 7 days in advance.

TML: Harnack House, 14-16 Ihnestrasse, all ranks, leave or official duty. Seven bedroom, private bath (1); five bedroom, private bath (1); four bedrooms, private bath (3); two bedroom, private bath (1); bedrooms, private bath (6). Color TV, maid service. Older structure. Rates: $35-$55 first person, $5-$7 each additional person. Price includes continental breakfast. PCS can make reservations, others Space-A. **Note: Although this facility was damaged by fire in '91, it has been refurbished and is scheduled to reopen Aug '92.**

DV/VIP: Protocol. Building 1, room 2024-2032, C-EX-6933, 06+. Retirees Space-A.

TML Availability: Good, Feb-May and Aug-Nov. Difficult, other times.

☞ **What can one say about Berlin? A truly great city that has everything for everyone. For tours call Special Services, EX-6523.**

Locator 332-92/7475   Medical 116   Police-332-3427

☺**At press time the closing of these facilities was scheduled for September '95. This will end a chapter of American presence in this famous city that many will mourn. Keep updated with Military Living's R&R Space-A Report.**

Bindlach/Bayreuth Sub-Community (GE50R7)
APO AE 09044-5000

TELEPHONE NUMBER INFORMATION: Main installation numbers: C-(USA) 011-49-9208-83-XXX, (GE) 09208-83-XXX, ETS-462-3XXX, D-314-460-1110 Ask for BDL.

Location: On GE-2, 60 miles north of Nürnberg, GE and north of Bayreuth, GE. Take the Bayreuth north exit from GE-2 for 2 miles. US Forces signs direct to Christensen Barracks. HE: p-40, F/1. NMC: Bayreuth, 2 miles southwest.

Billeting Office: Guest House, building 9350, C-**(USA) 011-49-9208-1549,** (GE) 09208-1549, ETS-462-3694 duty hours. Other hours SDO, ETS-462-3801. Check in facility, check out 1000 hours daily.

Bindlach/Bayreuth Sub-Community, continued

TML: TLF. All ranks, leave or official duty. Bedroom, private bath (10). TV, VCR, refrigerator, hair dryers, maid service, kitchen available, cots/cribs, washer/dryer. New structure. Rates: sponsor $19, each additional person $10. Rates will go up in future. Duty can make reservations, others Space-A.

DV/VIP: Sub-Community Commander, C-EX-836, 06+. Retirees Space-A.

TML Availability: Limited.

☞ **Bayreuth is home to the Richard Wagner Opera House, with its world famous festival held July and August. Margrave's Opera House and Eremitage are area highlights. Many crystal and porcelain factories; a great ski area.**

Locator 811   Medical 116   Police-114

Bitburg Air Base (GE04R7)
APO AE 09132-5000

TELEPHONE NUMBER INFORMATION: Main installation numbers: C-(USA) 011-49-6561-61-1110, (GE) 06561-61-1110, ETS-453-1110, D-314-453-1110.

Location: From Trier, take Hwy B-51 North to Bitburg or Prüm, turn right at the "Bitburg Flugplatz" sign. HE: p-39, F/1. NMC: Trier, 17 miles south.

Billeting Office: Baron Inn, building 101, C-(USA) **011-49-6561-62-1001**, (GE) 06561-62-1001, 24 hours daily. Check in facility, check out 1100 hours daily. Government civilian employee billeting.

TML: TLF. Baron Inn, buildings 102, 124, all ranks, leave or official duty. Bedroom, private bath (16); two bedroom, private bath (42). Kitchen, coffee, complete utensils, color TV in room & lounge, maid service, cribs/cots, playpens, highchairs, washer/dryer, ice vending, telephone. Modern structure, remodeled. Rates: $24 per unit. Maximum 5 per room. Duty can make reservations, others Space-A. **Note:** Innovations at this Inn, i.e. 24 hour convenience store, new reception area, interesting lobby library, put it in the running for the Air Force Innkeeper Award.

TML: VOQ. Buildings 101, 123, officers 01-05, leave or official duty. Bedroom, shared bath (2); bedroom, private bath (24). Kitchen, limited utensils, coffee, iron, color TV, telephone, maid service, cribs/cots, washer/dryer, ice vending. Modern structure. Rates: $9-$14 per person. Maximum 2 per room. Duty can make reservations, others Space-A.

TML: VAQ. Building 101, enlisted E1-E8, building 106, enlisted E1-E4, leave or official duty. Bedroom, shared bath (SNCO) (12); bedroom, 2 beds, shared bath (44); bedroom, 2 beds, common bath (46). Refrigerator, color TV, maid service, cribs/cots, washer/dryer, ice vending, coffee, iron, ironing boards, in room telephone, building 101, none in 106. Modern structures. Rates: $6.50 per person. Duty can make reservations, others Space-A.

TML: DVQ (DV/VIP). Building 101, officer 06+, E9, leave or official duty. Bedroom suites, private bath (8). Refrigerator, limited utensils, A/C, color TV, maid service, cribs/cots, washer/dryer, ice vending. Modern structure. Rates: $14 per person. Maximum 2 per room. Duty can make reservations, others Space-A.

GERMANY
Bitburg Air Base, continued

DV/VIP: Protocol Office, building 116, C-EX-7200, 06/GS-15+. Retirees and lower ranks Space-A.

TML Availability: Fairly good, Oct-Mar. Difficult, other times.

☞ There are wonderful volksmarch trails in the Eifel area. Don't miss a visit to nearby Trier, and it's magnificent Roman Black Gate, cathedral, beautiful "walkplatz" and shopping. A tour of the Mosel wine country is also "de rigueur".

Locator 453-7449   **Medical 116**   **Police 453-7400**

Bremerhaven Community (GE32R7)
APO AE 09069-5000

TELEPHONE NUMBER INFORMATION: Main installation numbers: C-(USA) 011-49-471-893-XXXX, (GE) 0471-893-XXXX, ETS-342-XXXX, D-314-342-1110.

Location: Exit from the A-27 Autobahn and follow signs to Harbor House Hotel. HE: p-33, D/4. NMC: Bremerhaven, in the city.

Billeting Office: Harbor House Hotel, buildings 602-604, 24 hours daily, C-(USA) 011-49-471-893-7604/7878/7657, (GE) 0471-893-7604/7878/7657, check in facility, check out 1100 hours daily. Government civilian employee billeting.

TML: Guest House. **Harbor House Hotel,** buildings 602-604. All ranks, leave or official duty. Bedroom, shared bath (68); bedroom, private bath (11); separate bedrooms, private bath (5). Refrigerator, community kitchen, color TV in room & lounge, maid service, cribs/cots ($5), washer/dryer. Older structure, renovated 1 building. Rates: $10 per person, $5 infant in crib/cot. Maximum 3 adults or 2 adults/2 children per room. Duty can make reservations, others Space-A. **Pets allowed on arrival or departure of PCS in/out.**

DV/VIP: Deputy Community Cmdr, C-EX-8094, 06+. Retirees and lower ranks Space-A.

TML Availability: Good.

Locator 342-8705   **Medical 116**   **Police 342-8252**

⊗**This facility did not respond to our inquiries, data may be outdated.**

Butzbach Sub-Community (GE51R7)
APO AE 09077-5000

TELEPHONE NUMBER INFORMATION: Main installation numbers: C-(USA) 011-49-6033-82-XXXX, (GE) 06033-82-XXXX, ETS-343-2XXX, D-314-320-1110 Ask for BUT.

Location: On GE-3, 12 miles south of Giessen, GE. May be reached from the Frankfurt-Giessen E-3 Autobahn. HE: p-36, E/5-6. NMC: Giessen, 12 miles north.

Butzbach Sub-Community, continued

Billeting Office: Transient Billeting Manager, C-(USA) **011-49-6033-83-727,** (GE) 06033-83-727. BOQ, #1 Ayers Kaserne, Kirchgöns. Check in facility, check out 1200 hours daily.

TML: BOQ. All ranks. Leave or official duty. Limited space for transients.

TML Availability: Very limited.

Locator 343-1110   **Medical 343-2824**   **Police 343-2829**

⊗**This facility did not respond to our inquiries, some data may be outdated.**

Chiemsee AFRC (GE08R7)
APO AE 09098-5000

TELEPHONE NUMBER INFORMATION: Main installation numbers: C-(USA) 011-49-8051-803172, (GE) 08051-803172, ETS-441-2355/396, FAX-011-49-8051-803-158.

Location: Located directly off Munich-Salzburg Autobahn A-8 southeast of Munich. Buses use Felden exit; automobiles continue for 800 meters and exit when you see the sign for AFRC Chiemsee. HE: p-94, B/3. NMC: Bad Aibling, 20 miles northwest.

Description of Area: The AFRC Chiemsee Recreation Area is situated along the shores of Germany's largest lake—Chiemsee. Enjoy water sports such as canoeing, paddleboats, sailing, windsurfing or swimming. Or take advantage of the nearby Chiemgauer Alps, which offer hiking, hang gliding and scenic panoramas of Chiemsee and the Alps. AFRC Chiemsee is near Austrian ski resorts such as Kitzbühel and Steinplatte. Ski programs for beginners to experts. Night life at AFRC Chiemsee includes a gourmet meal in the Lake Hotel Restaurant, dancing in the lake-front lounge, free movies, ice skating and swimming. Evening tours offered to Munich and Salzburg, where you can go disco-hopping, visit charming restaurants, beer cellars, wine parlors; these are beautiful cities after dark.

TML: Two hotels: the **Chiemsee Park Hotel** and **Chiemsee Lake Hotel** with accommodations for more than 300 guests.

Reservations: Accepted six months in advance with deposit within 30 days. Write to: AFRC Chiemsee Reservations, unit 24604, APO AE 09098, or US Rasthaus am Chiemsee, Felden 25, 8214 Bernau, C-(USA) **011-49-8051-803172,** (GE) 08051-803172, ETS-441-2355/396, Fax-(GE) 08051-803-158, 0800-1900, hours M-F, 0900-1700 Sa, closed Su and American holidays.

Eligibility: AD/Retired/DOD civilian assigned overseas. See Garmisch listing for details.

Facilities: Snackbar, laundromat, Lake Hotel restaurants & bars, check cashing, child care center, sports equipment rental, boat rental/launch, ESSO Station nearby, ice, recreation room.

Rates: E1-E5, deluxe double w/bath $39 (Park Hotel) $45 (Lake Hotel) (travelers not involved in group travel or conference $30), E6+ $45 (Park Hotel) $52 (Lake Hotel).

GERMANY
Chiemsee AFRC, continued

Single occupancy deduct $3 from double rate, more than two adult occupants, add $9 to double rate. Cribs $3/night, children under 16 free on available bed space - if cot or sofabed is needed, $6 per night will apply. Special group rates and prices of larger rooms available on request. **Free Group Travel:** Free round trip motorcoach transportation from your base to AFRC with a minimum of 25 participants (50% must be active duty military, including family members and DOD civilians), must stay minimum of 3 overnights. When 20 rooms are booked and confirmed, one free room is given the trip leader for the duration of the stay. Prices subject to change without notice.

Locator 440-355   **Medical 116**   **Police 114**

Darmstadt Community (GE37R7)
APO New York 09175-5000

TELEPHONE NUMBER INFORMATION: Main installation numbers: C-(USA) 011-49-6151-69-1700, (GE) 06151-69-1700, ETS-348-1700, D-none.

Location: Accessible from the E-5 and E-67 autobahns. One mile south of downtown Darmstadt. Follow signs to 32nd AADCOM (Cambrai Fritsch Kaserne). HE: p-40, B/1. NMC: Darmstadt, 1 mile north.

Billeting Office: Building 4090, Jefferson Village, C-(USA) 011-49-6151-68-111, (GE) 06151-68-111, D-348-1700, 0730-2100 M-F, Sa-Su 1200-2100. Check in 1300, check out 1100. Call before 1800 for late check-in. Government civilian employee billeting.

TML: Guest House. Building 4090, 4091, Jefferson Village, all ranks, leave or official duty. Single rooms, shared bath (20); suites, private bath (35). Refrigerator, community kitchen, utensils, color TV w/VCR, maid service, cribs/cots, washer/dryer, ice vending. Older structure, remodeled. Rates: shared bath $30, suites $40 per night, $10 additional person, children under 16 $5. Duty and DAVs can make reservations, others Space-A. **Note:** Building 4090 was opened Jun '91.

TML Availability: Good, Sep. More difficult, Oct-Jun.

☞ **Downtown Darmstadt has a great "walkplatz" for shopping, hike to the Odenwald from the railroad station, or tour the Mathildenhöhe, and the Kranichstein hunting palace on the city's outskirts.**

Locator 348-1700   **Medical 112**   **Police 348-7350**

Frankfurt Community (GE05R7)
APO AE 09228-5000

TELEPHONE NUMBER INFORMATION: Main installation numbers: C-(USA) 011-49-69-151-XXXX, (GE) 069-151-XXXX, ETS-320-XXXX, D-314-320-1110.

Location: The Ambassador Arms Hotel is on the corner of Miguel Allee and Hansa Allee within the General Creighton Abrams Complex in Frankfurt. HE: p-40, B/1. NMC: Frankfurt, 1.25 miles southeast.

GERMANY

Frankfurt Community, continued

Billeting Office: **Ambassador Arms Hotel**, building 2351, Sioli Str 2351, C-(USA) 011-49-69-151-7441, (GE) 069-151-7441, 0800-1700 M-F. AFRC reservation office: (USA) 011-49-69-151-568075/77/78, (GE) 069-151-568075/77/78. Check in facility, 1500 hours, check out 1100 hours daily. Government civilian employee billeting.

TML: Guest House DV/VIP. Buildings 2351/52/63/66/71, all ranks, leave or official duty, handicapped accessible, C-EX-5738 (on post) or C-069-550641 (off post). Rooms (139), bed spaces (339) (with 5 VIP suites, 9 kitchen suites, 1/2/3-bedroom apartments). Color TV, refrigerator, maid service, cribs/cots, coin washer/dryer, facilities for handicapped. Rates: TDY/PCS sponsor $35 (shared room and bath); $40 (private room and shared bath); $45 (private room and bath); sponsor $55 (DVQ suites); each additional person $20. Duty can make reservations, others Space-A.

NOTE: The **Ambassador Arms** offers all its guests a complimentary breakfast during the following hours: 0630-0830 M-F, 0800-1000 Sa-Su. Sunday brunch is offered at the Terrace Club between 1030-1330 hours at regular price.

DV/VIP: COFS, V Corps, Creighton Abrams Building, C-EX-7141, 07+. Retirees and lower ranks Space-A through Protocol only.

TML Availability: Good, winter. Difficult, summer.

☞ **Don't miss Goethe's birthplace! Take the Appel Wine Express to Sachsenhausen, across the river. Visit the Frankfurt Zoo. The whole southern part of the city is a forest with deer and hiking and biking paths. This is fun!**

Locator 320-1110   Medical 325-6111   Police 325-7637GERMANY

Fulda Community (GE35R7)
APO AE 09146-5000

TELEPHONE NUMBER INFORMATION: Main installation numbers: C-(USA) 011-49-661-86632, (GE) 0661-86632, D-314-661-86632.

Location: Take the Fulda Nord exit from E-70 Autobahn to GE-27 South, which will take you to Downs Barracks. HE: p-36, F/5. NMC: Frankfurt, 65 miles southwest.

Billeting Office: Buildings 7309, 7307, Housing Office, C-(USA) 011-49-661-86461, (GE) 0661-86461, D-314-661-86461, 0730-1600 hours M-F. Other hours SDO, building 7221, C-EX-86805/6. Check in at billeting, check out 1100 hours daily. Government civilian employee billeting.

TML: Fulda Blackhorse Inn. Guesthouse, VOQ, VEQ, DVQ, buildings 7307, 7309, all ranks, leave or official duty. Bedrooms and suites, private bath (VOQ/DV/VIP)(36); bedrooms, hall bath (VEQ) (8). Refrigerator in unit, essentials, food and ice vending, color TV, washer/dryer, maid service. Four community kitchens, limited utensils, range, microwave. Older structure, renovated '91. Rates: sponsor $23, adult $20, child/infant $15. Maximum capacity 4. No pets, local kennels available. PCS has priority, duty, DAVs, Reserve and National Guard on orders can make reservations, others Space-A.

DV/VIP: No DV/VIP office. Contact housing office, 06+.

TML Availability: Very good, anytime.

GERMANY
Fulda Community, continued

☞ Visitors will love this medieval town, and shouldn't miss the Benedictine Monastery and Castle, St Michael's Church, the Rathaus and beautiful half-timbered houses, to mention a few of the many attractions here.

Locator 86-827   Medical 86-116   Police 86-114

Garmisch AFRC (GE10R7)
APO AE 09053-5000

TELEPHONE NUMBER INFORMATION: Main installation numbers: C-(USA) 011-49-8821-750-575, (GE) 08821-750-575, ETS-440-2575.

Location: Take Autobahn E-6 south from Munich to Garmisch. From Austria take national roads numbered 2 or 187. HE: p-92, F/3. MNC: Munich, 60 miles north.

Description of Area: Garmisch has been Germany's leading winter recreation and sports area for over 50 years. Located 60 miles south of Munich, Garmisch sits at the foot of Germany's highest mountain, the Zugspitze. A $3 million renovation project was underway at press time at both the General Patton and General Von Steuben Hotels to increase room size and amenities, including new balconies, private baths, and entertainment systems. Kitchen, dining room, and lounge renovations will also upgrade guest services. Full range of ski programs, beginner to expert. Golf opportunities, indoor and outdoor tennis, kayaking, white-water rafting, windsurfing, mountaineering, arts and crafts. For 35 years AFRC Garmisch has provided the means for quality economy vacations.

TML: Two hotels: **General Patton, General Von Steuben and the Haus Flora.** Accommodations for about 540 guests per night.

Reservations: Accepted up to six months in advance. One year for groups of 25 or more. Deposits required within 30 days after booking. Write to: AFRC Garmisch Reservations Office, Unit 24501, APO AE 09053 or Osterfelderstr. 2, 8100 Garmisch-Partenkirchen. C-(USA) 011-49-8821-750575, (GE) 08821-750575, ETS-440-2575, FAX-(GE) 08821-3942. E-Mail: CFSC-HM-GCR-GE @MUNICH-EMHL. Office open 0800-2000 hours M-F, 0900-1700 Sa, closed Su.

TML Availability: Good except Jun-Aug and Christmas/New Year periods.

Season of Operation: Year round.

Eligibility: In general, all US Forces military and civilian personnel stationed in the USEUCOM area of responsibility, their family members, and visiting immediate family (when accompanied by the sponsor) may stay in AFRC hotels and camping areas. Also civilian US citizens employed by US government agencies and supporting institutions located in Germany, such as USO, Red Cross, and others. Also authorized are Canadian Armed Forces personnel and their family members (when accompanied by a sponsor stationed Germany), US military personnel stationed outside USEUCOM, retired US military and British Army of the Rhine personnel (stationed in Germany) and family members (when accompanied by the sponsor) on a Space-A basis. As of 1 July 1989, all restrictions governing use of AFRC facilities by retired US military personnel were lifted.

Garmisch AFRC, continued

Facilities: APO, AMEXCO Bank, beauty/barber shop, commissary, dispensary, chapel, Snack-O-Mat, library, sports shop, rec room, art shop, Bavarian Shop, class VI (Package Store), dental clinic, Foodland, PX, Stars & Stripes Bookstore, arts & crafts shop, child care center, hotel restaurants & bars, TV room and much more.

Rates: E1-E5, double w/bath $45. (individual travelers not involved in group travel or conference $30), E6+, double w/bath $49. Single occupancy deduct $3 from double rate, more than two adult occupants, add $9 to double rate. Cribs $3/night, children under 16 free on available bed space - if cot or sofabed is needed, $6 per night will apply. Special group rates and prices of larger rooms available on request. **Meal Plan:** half pension (breakfast buffet, dinner) $17. Full pension (breakfast buffet, lunch, dinner), $23. Sportweek pension (6 breakfast buffets, 4 dinners) $79. Children under 12 half price, purchased at front desk on arrival. No pets. Check on recreation prices in May. **Free Group Travel:** Free round trip motorcoach transportation from your base to AFRC with a minimum of 25 participants (50% must be active duty military, including family members and DOD civilians), must stay minimum of 3 overnights. When 20 rooms are booked and confirmed, one free room is given the trip leader for the duration of the stay. Prices are subject to change without notice.

Locator 343-1110   **Medical 440-2816**   **Police 440-2801**

Gelnhausen Sub-Community (GE89R7)
APO NY 09091-5000

TELEPHONE NUMBER INFORMATION: Main installation numbers: C-(USA) 011-49-6051-81-XXX, (GE) 06051-81-XXX, ETS-321-2XXX, D-314-320-1110 Ask for GLN.

Location: Take E-66 Autobahn northeast from Frankfurt for 25 miles, exit to GE-40 North and Gelnhausen. HE: p-38, F/6. NMC: Frankfurt, 25 miles southwest.

Billeting Office: O'Club, building 1617, C-(USA) **011-49-6051-81-708**, (GE) 06051-81-708, check in facility, check out 1100 hours daily.

TML: TLQ. O'Club, building 1617, officers all ranks, leave or official duty. Bedroom, private bath (6). Rates: $10 per person. Duty can make reservations, others Space-A. Also try BOQ, building 1804, ETS-321-2864.

TML Availability: Limited.

Locator 343-1110   **Medical 116**   **Police 114**

⊗**This facility did not respond to our inquiries, some data may be outdated.**

Giessen Community (GE23R7)
APO AE 09169-5000

TELEPHONE NUMBER INFORMATION: Main installation numbers: C-(USA) 011-49-641-402-XXXX, (GE) 0641-402-XXXX, ETS-343-XXXX, D-314-343-1110.

Location: Autobahn E-5 to Giessener Ring and take Grunberg exit. Follow signs to Giessen General Depot. HE: p-36, E/5. NMC: Giessen, in the city.

GERMANY
Giessen Community, continued

Billeting Office: ATTN: Guest House, building 32, C-(USA) **011-49-641-46215**, (GE) 0641-46215, ETS-343-6422, 0730-1600 hours daily. Other hours SDO, building 1, ETS-343-8434. Check in facility, check out 1200 hours daily. No government civilian employee billeting.

TML: Guest House. Building 63, Giessen General Depot, all ranks, leave or official duty. Bedroom, common bath (26); bedroom suites, private bath (DV/VIP) (3). Community kitchen, color TV, maid service, cribs/cots, washer/dryer. Older structure. Rates: $9.50 per person. Maximum 3 per unit. Duty can make reservations, others Space-A.

TML: Guest House. Building 4118, Butzbach, all ranks, leave or official duty. Bedroom, common bath (5). Community kitchen, color TV, maid service. Older structure. Rates: $9.50 per person. Maximum 3 persons. Duty can make reservations, others Space-A. **Pets allowed.**

DV/VIP: Cmdr. ETS-343-8434. Determined by Cmdr.

TML Availability: Good.

Locator 343-1110   **Medical 116**   **Police 343-6362**

⊗**This facility did not respond to our inquiries, some data may be outdated.**

Grafenwöhr Training Area (GE11R7)
APO AE 09114-5000

TELEPHONE NUMBER INFORMATION: Main installation numbers: C-(USA) 011-49-9641-83-XXXX, (GE) 09641-83-XXXX, ETS-475-XXXX, D-314-475-1110.

Location: From Autobahn E-6 exit at Pegnitz/Grafenwöhr, follow signs to training area. HE: p-40, G/1. NMC: Nürnberg, 56 miles southwest.

Billeting Office: Building 213, Opposite O'Club, C-(USA) **011-49-9641-83-6182/7100**, (GE) 09641-83-6182/7100, 0730-1900 hours daily. Other hours, Hq, building 621, C-EX-8306. Check in billeting, check out 1000 hours daily. No government civilian employee billeting.

TML: Guest House. Buildings 211, 215, all ranks, leave or official duty. Bedroom, hall bath (12); separate bedroom, private bath (10); two bedroom, hall bath (5); three bedroom, private bath (2). Kitchen, community kitchen, color TV, maid service, cribs, cots ($7), washer/dryer, ice vending. Older structure, renovated. Rates: private bath apartments $33, additional person $10; shared bath $19, additional person $5; room (single or double) $15, additional person $5. Duty can make reservations, others Space-A.

TML: VOQ, VEQ. Buildings 209, 213, officers all ranks, leave or official duty. Bedroom, private bath (3); separate bedroom, private bath (13); separate bedrooms, shared bath (10). Refrigerator, color TV, maid service, cribs, cots ($10), washer/dryer. Older structure, renovated. Rates: private bath $23.50, each additional dependent $10; shared bath $17, additional dependent $5. Maximum 2-3 persons per room. Duty can make reservations, others Space-A.

GERMANY

Grafenwöhr Training Area, continued

DV/VIP: Protocol Office, 7th Army Training Command, 06+, ETS-475-8316. DVQ suite available. Rates $40, additional person $10. Retirees and lower ranks Space-A.

TML Availability: Difficult. Best, Nov-Mar.

☞ **Interested in nutcrackers, stained glass crystal, and porcelain? Call Army Community Service for an exhaustive list of local castles, churches, clothing, restaurants and recreation.**

⊛**This training area will be returned to German control in future. Check the Amberg and Vilseck listings for additional local TML, and keep updated with Military Living's** *R&R Space-A Report.*

Locator 475-1110   Medical-116   Police 475-8319

Hahn Air Base (GE12R7)
APO AE 09109-5000

TELEPHONE NUMBER INFORMATION: Main installation numbers: C-(USA) 011-49-6543-51-7679, (GE) 06543-51-7679, ETS-450-1110, D-314-450-1110.

Location: On Hwy 327 between Morbach and Kastellaun, 2 kilometers from Sohren on B-50. HE: p-39, G/1. NMC: Frankfurt, 65 miles east.

Billeting Office: Building 407, Main St, C-(USA) **011-49-6543-51-7679**, (GE) 06543-51-7679, 24 hours daily. Check in billeting, check out 1200 hours daily. Government civilian employee billeting in contract hotels.

TML: TLF. Building 1380, all ranks, leave or official duty. Separate bedroom suites, private bath (19). Kitchen, limited utensils, color TV in room & lounge, maid service, essentials, cribs/cots, washer/dryer, ice vending. Older structure, renovated, remodeled. Rates: $30 per room. Maximum 5 persons. Duty can make reservations, others Space-A.

TML: VOQ. Building 407, all ranks, leave or official duty. Separate bedroom suites, private bath (VOQ VIP) (8); separate bedroom suites, private bath (VAQ VIP) (2); bedroom, shared bath (72). Kitchen, color TV in room & lounge, maid service, cribs/cots, washer/dryer, ice vending. Older structure. Rates: $7.50 (VAQ), $8 (VOQ), $14 (DV), under 2 years free. Maximum 2 per room. Duty can make reservations, others Space-A.

DV/VIP: Protocol Office, 50th TFW/CCE, building 401, C-EX-7221, 06+, retirees Space-A.

TML Availability: Limited, all year.

☞ **The cities of Trier (wonderful Roman ruins, shopping), Bernkastel (quite genuine castle, with a wonderful wine fest each year) and Idar-Oberstein (learn the mystery of the church and buy semi-precious gems) are within easy driving distance.**

Locator 450-7747   Medical 450-7430   Police-450-7795

GERMANY

Hanau Community (GE13R7)
APO AE 09165-5000

TELEPHONE NUMBER INFORMATION: Main installation numbers: C-(USA) 011-49-6181-88-1110, (GE) 06181-88-1110, ETS-322-1110, D-314-322-1110.

Location: From Autobahn 66 to Highway 8 or 40 to Hanau, New Argonner and Pioneer Housing Area south of Highway 8. Clearly marked. HE: p-36, E/6. NMC: Frankfurt, 15 miles west.

Billeting Office: ATTN: Billeting Office, building 318, Pioneer Housing, APO AE 09165, C-(USA) **011-49-6181-88-1110 (ask for billeting)**, (GE) 06181-88-1110 (ask for billeting), ETS-322-8947, 0730-1200/1230-1530 M,Tu,W,Th,F. Check in billeting, check out 0900 hours daily. Government civilian employee billeting.

TML: Guest House. Building 318, Pioneer Housing, all ranks, leave or official duty. Two bedroom, private bath (6); three bedroom, private bath (8); four bedroom, private bath (7). Cribs/cots, maid service, refrigerator, microwave, color TV, washer/dryer. Older structure. Rates: sponsor $31, second person $17, each additional $12. Maximum 2 per room. Duty can make reservations, others Space-A. **Pets OK with $25 non-refundable fee + $2 per pet per night.**

TML: Guest House. **New Argonner**, building 203, all ranks, leave or official duty. Bedroom, 2 beds, private bath (32). Cribs/cots, refrigerator, community microwaves, color TV, maid service, washer/dryer. Older structure, renovated. Rates: same as Guest House above. Maximum 2 per room. Duty can make reservations, others Space-A. **Pets OK with $25 non-refundable cleaning fee + $2 per pet per night.**

TML: VOQ. Building 204, 05+ and civilian equivalents. One bedroom suites, 2 beds, living room, private bath (2). Refrigerator, kitchenette with microwave, cribs/cots, color TV, VCR, maid service, washer/dryer. Older structure, renovated '91. Rates: same as Guest Houses. Maximum 2 per room. Duty can make reservations, others Space-A.

DV/VIP: PAO, building 1202, C-06181-13654, 06+, retirees and lower ranks Space-A.

TML Availability: Difficult.

☞ **Remember Hansel and Gretel, Snow White and Little Red Riding Hood? Visit the monument to native sons, the Grimm Brothers on the Marktplatz in the center of town. Many other attractions are located in Hanau.**

Locator 322-8351   Medical 116   Police 114

Heidelberg Community (GE33R7)
APO AE 09102-5000

TELEPHONE NUMBER INFORMATION: Main installation numbers: C-(USA) 011-49-6221-57-XXXX, (GE) 06221-57-XXXX, ETS-370-XXXX, D-314-370-XXXX.

Location: Access from the E-5 and E-656 autobahns. A spur off the E-656 autobahn terminates in Heidelberg. Follow signs to Mark Twain Village and Patrick Henry Village. From Frankfurt autobahn on A-5 toward Basel, exit at Schwetzingen (Patrick Henry

Heidelberg Community, continued

Village) turn left at stop light, right at 1st street to right, drive thru PHV, hotel sign in front of building 4527. From Karlsruhe autobahn or Basel on Autobahn A-5 toward Frankfurt, turn of at Schwetzingen (Patrick Henry Village), exit at stop light, turn left, then right at 1st street, then drive thru PHV Hotel sign, building 4527. HE: p-40, B/2. NMC: Heidelberg, in the city.

Billeting Office: Building 4527, North Lexington Ave, Patrick Henry Village, 24 hours. C-(USA) **011-49-6221-57-6941/8128,** (GE) 06221-57-6941/8128. To call from Heidelberg: 06221-79-5100. Check in facility, check out 1100 hours daily. Government civilian employee billeting. **Note: This community was named runnerup in the Worldwide Lodging Operation of the Year award for medium-size guesthouses in '92. In '91 it took first place.**

TML: Guest House. Building 4527, North Lexington Ave, Patrick Henry Village, all ranks, leave or official duty. **Reservations: 0730-1630 Mon-Fri.** Bedroom, shared bath (30); separate bedroom, private bath (120); two bedroom, private bath (6). Refrigerator, community kitchen, color TV, maid service, cribs/cots, washer/dryer. Older structure, renovated. Rates: varies widely according to status and type of room, call for information. PCS can make reservations, others Space-A. Payments can be made with VISA, MasterCard or Diners Club. **Pets allowed with one day room charge and $2 per day service charge.**

DV/VIP: SGS, HQ USAREUR, ETS-370-8707, 06/GS-15+. Retirees and lower ranks Space-A.

TML Availability: Difficult, all year.

☞ **Visit famous University of Heidelberg, and its Students' Inns - Roten Ochsen (Red Ox) and Zum Sepp'l are side by side on the Hauptstrasse. The Castle above the city, and bridge across the Neckar River also should not be missed.**

Locator 370-6832   **Medical 370-6978**   **Police 114**

Idar-Oberstein Sub-Community (GE53R7)
APO AE 09262-5000

TELEPHONE NUMBER INFORMATION: Main installation numbers: C-(USA) 011-49-6781-61-XXXX, (GE) 06781-61-XXXX, ETS-492-XXXX, D-314-485-1110 Ask for IDN.

Location: On GE-41 northeast of Birkenfeld; may be reached from the E-6, Mannheim-Saarbrucken Autobahn. HE: p-40, A/2. NMC: Kaiserslautern, 30 miles south.

Billeting Office: Building 9032, Strassburg Kaserne in the Algenrodt section of the city. C-(USA) **011-49-6781-61-6713,** (GE) 06781-61-6713, 24 hours. Check in facility, check out 1000 hours daily. Government civilian employee billeting.

TML: TLQ. Same as billeting office, all ranks, leave or official duty. Bedroom, shared bath (12). Refrigerator, community kitchen, limited utensils, maid service, cribs $1.50, washer/dryer. Older structure, renovated. Rates: sponsor $8, each additional person $4. Duty can make reservations, others Space-A.

GERMANY
Idar-Oberstein Sub-Community, continued

TML Availability: Good, winter months.

Locator 492-92   Medical 492-6886   Police 114

Ⓧ**This facility did not respond to our inquiries, some data may be outdated.**

Kaiserslautern Community (GE30R7)
APO AE 09054-5000

TELEPHONE NUMBER INFORMATION: Main installation numbers: C-(USA) 011-49-631-411-XXXX, (GE) 0631-411-XXXX, ETS-483-XXXX, D-314-489-1110.

Location: Off the E-6 Mannheim-Saarbrucken Autobahn. Take Kaiserslautern exit for Vogelweh Housing Area. Follow signs to housing area or Kapun Barracks (AS). HE: p-40, A/2. NMC: Kaiserslautern, 3 miles northeast.

Billeting Office: Building 1002, C-(USA) **011-49-631-411-7190/76491**, (GE) 0631-411-7190/7641, ETS-489-7190/7641 (Vogelweh Office), 24 hours daily. Under AF control at Ramstein AB, C-(USA) **011-49-6371-47-7864/7345**, (GE) 06371-47-7864/7345, ETS-480-5221 (Ramstein Office). Check in at Ramstein, check out 1000 hours daily. Government civilian employee billeting. **Note:** see Ramstein listing for more billeting.

TML: Guest House, building 1002, all ranks, leave or official duty. Bedrooms, suites shared bath, private bath (225); suites, livingroom, private bath (DV/VIP)(16). Community kitchen each floor, coin washer/dryer, color TV, radio. Older structure, renovated. Rates: $10 per person. Duty can make reservations, others Space-A.

DV/VIP: PAO. Ramstein AB, C-06371-47-6854, 06+, retirees Space-A.

TML Availability: Good.

☞ **The city hall (Rathaus), is the highest in Germany. There is an elegant restaurant in the penthouse. Visit the Pfalztheater for opera, operetta, plays and ballet. Harry's gift shop, known around the world by military families, is on 5-11 Manheimer Strasse (tel: 0631-67081).**

Locator 83-92   Medical 116   Police 114

Karlsruhe Community (GE14R7)
APO AE 09164-5000

TELEPHONE NUMBER INFORMATION: Main installation numbers: C-(USA) 011-49-721-759-XXXX, (GE) 0721-759-XXXX, ETS-376-XXXX, D-314-370-1110 Ask for KRE.

Location: Take the Karlsruhe exit off Autobahn E-4. Follow signs to Smiley Barracks. HE: p-40, B/3. NMC: Karlsruhe, in the city.

Billeting Office: Building 9942, Tennessee Ave, C-(USA) **011-49-721-759-1700**, (GE) 0721-759-1700, 24 hours daily. Check in facility, check out 1000 hours daily. Government civilian employee billeting.

GERMANY
Karlsruhe Community, continued

TML: Guest House. **Karlsruhe Lodge**, buildings 9941, 9942, all ranks, leave or official duty. Bedrooms, shared bath (58); suites, private bath (16). Kitchen (suites), refrigerator, community kitchen, limited utensils, color TV in room & lounge, maid service, cribs/cots, washer/dryer, ice vending, microwave. Older structure. Rates: sponsor $20, each additional person $8. Maximum 2 adults, 1 child. Duty can make reservations, others Space-A. **Pets OK ($2 per pet per day, $20 cleaning fee).**

TML Availability: Good, Sep-Mar. More difficult, other times.

☞ **Karlsruhe is known as a city of parks and gardens. The Baden State Theater's programs are renowned, check with MWR or ACS. Take a historical steam engine ride through the Alb valley, or a cruise on the MS Karlsruhe.**

Medical 376-6541   Police 376-6123

Landstuhl Army Medical Center (GE40R7)
APO AE 09094-5000

TELEPHONE NUMBER INFORMATION: Main installation numbers: C-(USA) 011-49-6371-86-XXXX, (GE) 06371-86-XXXX, ETS-486-XXXX, D-314-486-1110.

Location: Take the Landstuhl exit from the E-6 Mannheim-Saarbrücken Autobahn. Follow signs for "2nd General Hospital". HE: p-40, A/2. NMC: Kaiserslautern, 10 miles northeast.

Billeting Office: ATTN: 86 SVS/SVHG, APO AE 09094, C-(USA) **011-49-6371-486-8342**, (GE) 06371-486-8342, D-314-486-8342. Ramstein AB, 24 hours daily. Check in facility, check out 1000 hours daily. Government civilian employee billeting.

TML: VOQ/VAQ. Building 3752, all ranks, leave or official duty. Bedroom, shared bath (230). Community kitchen, refrigerator, color TV, maid service, washer/dryer. Older structure, remodeled. Rates: $12 per person, maximum $24 per room. Duty can make reservations, others Space-A. **Note:** Check Ramstein, Kaiserslautern listings for more billeting.

DV/VIP: Community Cmdr, C-EX-7183, 06+.

TML Availability: Good, Nov-Feb. Difficult, summer months.

☞ **Visit the Marktplatz in Kaiserslautern for a traditional German farmer's market. Also, ask at USO Kaiserslautern for directions to local fests and sights - they have a wealth of information to share!**

Locator 486-7183   Medical 486-8107   Police 486-7660

GERMANY

Mainz Community (GE41R7)
APO AE 09185-0029

TELEPHONE NUMBER INFORMATION: Main installation numbers: C-(USA) 011-49 6131-48-XXXX, (GE) 06131-48-XXXX, ETS-334-XXXX, D-314-320-1110 Ask for MNZ.

Location: Take the Mainz exit from the E-61 Autobahn to GE B-9. Follow the signs to Martin Luther King Village. HE: p-40, A/1. NMC: Mainz, in the city.

Billeting Office: Building 6706, Martin Luther King Village. C-(USA) **011-49-6131-48-38650,** (GE) 06131-48-38650, ETS-334-7396, 0600-2000 M-F, 0800-1600 Sa-Su. Check in facility, check out 1200 hours daily. Government civilian employee billeting.

TML: TLQ. Building 6706, all ranks, leave or official duty. Separate bedroom suites, private bath (16). Kitchen, color TV, maid service, cribs ($1), washer/dryer, ice vending. Older structure, renovated. Rates: sponsor $25, if sharing $17.50 each. Maximum $45 per room. Maximum 5 per room. Duty can make reservations, others Space-A. TDY/PCS have priority.

DV/VIP: Protocol Office, 05+. Retirees Space-A.

TML Availability: Good, all year.

Locator 48-38650   **Medical 116**   **Police 334-7111**

⊗**This facility did not respond to our inquiries, information may be outdated.**

Mannheim Community (GE43R7)
APO New York 09086-5000

TELEPHONE NUMBER INFORMATION: Main installation numbers: C-(USA) 011-49-621-730-XXXX, (GE) 0621-730-XXXX, ETS-380-XXXX, D-314-380-1110.

Location: Accessible from the E12/A6 Autobahns. Take the Viernheim exit, follow B38 to Benjamin Franklin Housing Area on Fürther Strasse. HE: p-40, B/2. NMC: Mannheim, 8 miles southwest.

Billeting Office: Building 312, Benjamin Franklin Housing Area (BFHA), Fürther Strasse, 0630-1800 daily. C-(USA) **011-49-621-730-8118/6547,** (GE) 0621-730-8118/ 6547, ETS-380-8118/6547.

TML: Guesthouse. **Franklin House,** building 312, Benjamin Franklin Housing Area, Fuertherstrasse, all ranks, leave or official duty, C-(USA) **011-49-621-730-1700/8118/ 6547,** (GE) 0621-730-1700/8118/6547. Two bedroom, private bath (39); suites, private bath (DV/VIP) (3). Maid service, cribs/cots, ice vending, kitchenette, CATV, washer/dryer, VIP suites have honor bars. Older structure, renovated. No pets. Rates: $25, dependents $11, $5 for additional persons over 2. Duty can make reservations, others Space-A.

DV/VIP: Call above number.

TML Availability: Good, Jul-Sep, Dec-Jun. Difficult, Sep-Nov.

Mannheim Community, continued

☞ Visit the National Theater, Observatory and Mannheim Castle. A good area for a Volksmarch, but for support facilities all you have to do is walk across the street!

Locator 730-1110   Medical 730-116   Police 730-1143

Neubrüecke Sub-Community (GE54R7)
APO AE 09260-4675

TELEPHONE NUMBER INFORMATION: Main installation numbers: C-(USA) 011-49-6782-13-XXX, (GE) 06782-13-XXX, ETS-493-7XXX, D-314-485-1110 Ask for NEU.

Location: On GE-41, about 20 miles SW from Rhein-Main Airport (Frankfurt), about 25 miles NW from Ramstein Air Base, near Baumholder. Follow signs to Neubrüecke Hospital. HE: p-39, G/1. NMC: Baumholder, 9 miles east.

Billeting Office: Building 9965, C-(USA) 011-49-6782-13-287/416, (GE) 06782-13-287/416, ETS-493-7287/7416, 0730-1700 M-F. After duty hours contact Security Police, building 9920, C-06782-13-415/309. Check in facility 1300-1700 hours, check out 1100 hours daily. Government civilian employee billeting.

TML: Guest House. Building 9961, all ranks, leave or official duty. Handicapped accessible. Two bedroom, shared bath (28); two bedroom, private bath (3). Refrigerator, community kitchen, limited utensils, color TV, maid service, cribs, washer/dryer. Older structure, remodeled. Rates for PCS/TDY on leave/vacation: sponsor $22, second person $15, additional person $10.

TML Availability: Best, Sep-Apr. Difficult, May-Aug.

☞ The Rheinland Pfalz is full of colorful villages that preserve many German traditional customs. If you are lucky, your visit may coincide with a local fest, particularly in spring and fall.

Medical 116   Police 114

Nürnberg Community (GE44R7)
APO AE 09696-5000

TELEPHONE NUMBER INFORMATION: Main installation numbers: C-(USA) 011-49-911-700-XXXX, (GE) 0911-700-XXXX, ETS-460-XXXX, D-314-460-1110.

Location: Access from Autobahns E-3 (east-west), E-6 (east-west), E-9 (north-south). Also from GE-2 & 4 (north-south) and GE-8 & 14 (east-west). The Bavarian American Hotel is located in the center of the city across from the main train station. HE: p-40, F/2. NMC: Nürnberg, in the city.

GERMANY
Nürnberg Community, continued

Billeting Office: Bavarian American Hotel, Bahnfof Strasse 3. C-(USA) **011-49-911-700-23440**, (GE) 0911-700-23440, ETS-460-6632, 24 hours. Also, W O Darby Kaserne, ETS-460-6888. Check in facility, check out 1200 hours daily. Government civilian employee billeting.

TML: Hotel. All ranks, leave or official duty. Single/double room, shared and private baths (130); separate bedroom suites, private bath (10). Color TV, lounge, maid service, cribs/cots, coin washer/dryer. No room service. Restaurant/bar in hotel, mini-shop, news stand, game rooms. Older structure. Rates: $22 per person, $40 for suites (PCS/TDY). All categories Space-A. Check the telephone numbers above for BOQ/BEQ space in the area.

DV/VIP: Deputy Community Commander, C-EX-6696, 06+. Retirees Space-A.

TML Availability: Good, Oct-Apr. Difficult, other times.

Locator 92   **Medical 460-5744**   **Police 460-6600**

⊗**This facility did not respond to our inquiries, some data may be outdated.**

Pirmasens Community (GE42R7)
APO AE 09189-5000

TELEPHONE NUMBER INFORMATION: Main installation numbers: C-(USA) 011-49-6331-86-XXXX, (GE) 06331-86-XXXX, ETS-495-XXXX, D-314-495-1110 Ask for PMS.

Location: On the triangle of GE-10 from Zweibrücken and GE-270 from Kaiserslautern. HE: p-39, G/2. NMC: Pirmasens, 1 mile southeast.

Billeting Office: ATTN: AERAS-AF-HU, building 4535, Bundestrasse 10, C-(USA) **011-49-6331-87050**, (GE) 06331-87050, ETS-495-1700, 0730-1800 M-F. Other hours SDO, building 4624, C-EX-6444, ETS-495-6444. Check in after 1300, check out 1000 hours daily. Government civilian employee billeting.

TML: Grenadier Guest House. Building 4535, all ranks, leave or official duty. Handicapped accessible. Bedroom, private bath (29); bedroom, shared bath (16); separate bedroom, private bath (2). Refrigerator, community kitchen, color TV, maid service, cribs/cots, washer/dryer. Older structure, renovated. Rates: sponsor $19, adult $4, child $4, infant $2. Maximum 3 per room. Duty can make reservations, others Space-A.

TML: DV/VIP. Building 4537, officers 06+. Separate bedroom suites, private bath (2). Kitchen, complete utensils, color TV, maid service, cribs/cots. Older structure, updated. Rates: call for rates. Maximum 3 per suite. Duty can make reservations, others Space-A.

DV/VIP: 59th Ordnance Brigade, SGS Office, building 4616, C-EX-7383, 06+. Retirees and lower ranks Space-A.

TML Availability: Good, Dec-Jan. Difficult, May-Aug.

Pirmasens Community, continued

☞ **Pirmasens is known for its international trade fair; a focal point for technical innovations in worldwide footwear manufacturing. It is also acknowledged as a tourist recreational center surrounded by mountains.**

Locator 495-7117   Medical 116   Police 114

Ramstein Air Base (GE24R7)
APO AE 09094-5000

TELEPHONE NUMBER INFORMATION: Main installation numbers: C-(USA) 011-49-6371-47-XXXX, (GE) 06371-47-XXXX, ETS-480-XXXX, D-314-480-1110.

Location: Two exits from Mannheim-Saarbrücken E-6 Autobahn, exit Landstuhl, turn left, follow signs to Ramstein. Also, west on B-40 to Landstuhl Str, turn right follow signs to Flugplatz Ramstein. HE: p-39, G/2. NMC: Kaiserslautern, 12 miles east.

Billeting Office: ATTN: Control Reservations for all facilities, building 305, Washington Ave, C-(USA) **011-49-6371-47-7864/7345**, (GE) 06371-47-7864/7345, 0730-1800 M-Th, 0730-1630 F. Check in facility, check out 1200 hours daily. Government civilian employee billeting. **Note:** see Kaiserslautern listing for more billeting.

TML: TLQ. Buildings 303, 1004, all ranks, leave or official duty. Bedroom, private bath (2); two bedroom, private bath (77). Kitchen, limited utensils, color TV in room & lounge, maid service, cribs/cots, washer/dryer, ice vending. Modern structure. Rates: $24 per unit. Maximum 4 per unit. Duty can make reservations, others Space-A.

TML: TAQ. Buildings 1003, 2408, 2409, 3752, 3756, enlisted all ranks, leave or official duty. Bedroom, 2 beds, shared bath (674); separate bedroom suites, private bath (2). Refrigerator, community kitchen (some), limited utensils, color TV in room & lounge, maid service, cribs/cots, washer/dryer, ice vending. Modern structure. Rates: $10 per person, maximum $20 per family. Duty can make reservations, others Space-A.

TML: VOQ. Buildings 304-306, 530, 540, 541, 1002, 3751, 3754. Officers all ranks. Bedroom, shared bath, private bath (533); separate bedrooms, private bath (27). Kitchen (some), refrigerator, limited utensils, color TV in room & lounge, maid service, cribs/cots, washer/dryer, ice vending. Modern structure. Rates: $10 per person, maximum $20 per family. Duty can make reservations, others Space-A.

TML: DV/VIP. Building 1018, officers 06+, leave or official duty. See numbers under Protocol below. Separate bedroom suites, private bath (11). Refrigerator, limited utensils, color TV, washer/dryer, ice vending. Modern structure, renovated. Rates: $22 per person. Duty can make reservations, others Space-A.

DV/VIP: Protocol, building 201. C-EX-4851. D-EX-7558, 06+. Retirees Space-A.

TML Availability: Very good all year. Best, winter months.

☞ **Small villages surround Ramstein, and it's fun to just drive through them, sometimes getting thoroughly lost - the people here are friendly and helpful, and many speak English. Kaiserslautern, and Landstuhl are nearby.**

Locator 480-6120/6989   Medical 486-82603   Police 480-5323

GERMANY

Rhein-Main Air Base (GE16R7)
APO AE 09057-5000

TELEPHONE NUMBER INFORMATION: Main installation numbers: C-USA: 011-49-69-699-1110, (GE) 069-699-1110, ETS-330-1110, D-314-330-1110.

Location: Adjacent to Frankfurt International Airport of E-5 Autobahn to Darmstadt. HE: p-40, B/1. NMC: Frankfurt, 10 miles north.

Billeting Office: Building 110, **Aerial Port Quarters**, C-(USA) 011-49-69-699-7682/83, (GE) 069-699-7682/83, 0730-1630 hours daily (an information recording is operational after hours). Other hours, Deputy Manager, C-EX-7266. Check in billeting, check out 1000 hours daily. Government civilian employee billeting on official duty.

TML: Aerial Port Quarters (Hotel), building 110, officer all ranks, leave or official duty. Bedroom, 2 beds, shared bath (250); separate bedroom, private bath (12); bedroom, private bath (4). Refrigerator, color TV, maid service, cribs, washer/dryer, ice vending. Older structure. Rates: $10 per person, maximum $20 per room. Maximum 2 per room. Duty can make reservations, others Space-A.

TML: VAQ. Building 345, enlisted all ranks, leave or official duty. Bedroom, private bath (5); separate bedrooms, hall bath (173). Refrigerator, color TV in room & lounge, maid service, washer/dryer. Older structure. Rates: $8 per person. Maximum 2 per room. Duty can make reservations, others Space-A.

DV/VIP: Protocol, 435 TAW/CCP, building 27, C-EX-6059, 06+/civilian equivalent. Retirees and lower ranks Space-A.

TML Availability: Good, Dec-Jan. Difficult, other times.

☞ Don't miss Frankfurt's famous Fairgrounds (Messa), for exhibits of all types, and the Frankfurt Zoo. The southern part of the city is a forest with deer, hiking and bicycling paths. Watch for special seasonal "fests".

Locator 7691/7348   Medical 7307   Police 114/7177

Schwäbisch Hall Sub-Community (GE17R7)
APO AE 09025-5000

TELEPHONE NUMBER INFORMATION: Main installation numbers: C-(USA) 011-49-791-45-XXX, (GE) 0791-45-XXX, ETS-426-4XXX, D-314-460-1110 Ask for SHL.

Location: Take B-14 or B-19 exit from Heilbronn/Nürnberg Autobahn. Go through Schwäbisch Hall, follow signs to Ellwagen/Dolan Barracks. HE: p-40, C/4. NMC: Stuttgart, 31 miles northeast.

Billeting Office: Schwäbisch Hall, Dolan Barracks, building 371, C-(USA) 011-49-791-45-530, (GE) 0791-45-530, 0730-1600 hours daily. Other hours CQ, building 306, EX-527. Check in facility, check out 1100 hours daily.

Schwäbisch Hall Sub-Community, continued

TML: Guest House. Building 371, all ranks, leave or official duty. Bedroom, private bath (3); separate bedrooms, hall bath (19); two room VIP suite, private bath (1). Refrigerator, community kitchen, color TV, maid service. Older structure. Rates: single occupant $20, double occupancy $25. Maximum 3 per room. All categories can make reservations.

DV/VIP: none. Call above number.

TML Availability: Good.

☞ **Dolan Barracks was a famous Luftwaffe base for the 3rd Reich, many original buildings still stand. Visit the "Rat-Haus", and St Michael's Church. The famous walled city of Rothenburg is 45 minutes away.**

Locator 426-4113   Medical 426-4566   Police 426-4807

Schweinfurt Community (GE48R7)
APO AE 09033-5000

TELEPHONE NUMBER INFORMATION: Main installation numbers: C-(USA) 011-49-9721-96-6245, (GE) 09721-96-6245, ETS-354-6245, D-314-350-1110, ask for Schweinfurt.

Location: 9 miles east of Kassel-Würzburg, E-70 autobahn. On GE-303, 2 miles past GE-B19. Follow US Forces signs. HE: p-40, D/1. NMC: Schweinfurt, in the city.

Billeting Office: Billeting Manager, building 89, 0730-1800 hours M-F, C-(USA) 011-49-9721-82931, (GE) 09721-82931, ETS-354-6245. After hours contact SDO, building 1, C-09721-96288, D-314-354-6288. Check in facility, check out 1000 hours daily. Government civilian employee billeting.

TML: Guest House. **Bradley Inn**, building 89, all ranks, leave or official duty. Bedroom, 2 beds, private bath (8); bedroom, 1 bed, private bath (6); separate bedrooms, private bath (34); two bedroom, private bath. Community kitchens, some utensils, color satellite TV, maid service, cribs/cots, washer/dryer, vending machine. Older structure, renovated. Rates: sponsor $29, each additional person $10, maximum $69 per family. Duty can make reservations, others Space-A.

DV/VIP: Chief, Community Operations, building 206, C-09721-803834, ETS-354-6715, 03/GS-12+. Retirees and lower ranks Space-A. VIP for **Bradley Inn**: C-09721-803834.

TML Availability: Good, all year.

☞ **Wednesday and Saturday morning, and Tuesday and Friday afternoon, the Schweinfurt Marktplatz hums with activity. Don't miss a colorful sight. Then stroll down to the Stadtpark and the Tiergehege near the Main River.**

⊗**This facility is due to close, keep updated with Military Living's R&R Space-A Report.**

Locator 354-6748   Medical 09721-82397   Police 09721-802160

GERMANY

Sembach Air Base (GE18R7)
APO AE 09136-5000

TELEPHONE NUMBER INFORMATION: Main installation numbers: C-(USA) 011-49-6302-67-XXXX, (GE) 06302-67-XXXX, ETS-496-XXXX, D-314-496-1110.

Location: From the E-12 Autobahn exit A-6 marked Enkenbach-Alsenborn and follow B-48 in the direction of Bad Kruznach. Immediately past town of Munchweiller right to Sembach AB. Also, accessible from B-40 North. HE: p-40, A/2. NMC: Kaiserslautern 9 miles west.

Billeting Office: ATTN: SVH/SUS, building 216, Radar Ave, (known as Dorm Row), C-(USA) **011-49-6302-67-7588/7149**, (GE) 06302-67-7588/7149, 24 hours daily. Check in billeting, check out 1000 hours daily. Government civilian employee billeting.

TML: VOQ/DV/VIP. Building 110, 1st, 2nd and 3rd floors, C-EX-6194. Officers all ranks, leave or official duty. Handicapped accessible. Bedroom, shared bath (42); separate bedroom suites, (DV/VIP) (9). Refrigerator, community kitchen, limited utensils, color TV, maid service, cribs/cots, washer/dryer, ice vending. Older structure. Rates: rooms $8 per person, suites $14 per person. Maximum 3 per unit. Duty can make reservations, others Space-A.

TML: VAQ. Buildings 210, 216, enlisted all ranks, leave or official duty. Building 210: bedroom, 2 beds, shared bath (220); separate bedroom suites, private bath (Chiefs) (3). Building 216: bedroom, 2 beds, hall bath (73). Maid service, color TV, cribs/cots, washer/dryer. Older structures, renovated. Rates: rooms $8 per person, suites $14. No families. Duty can make reservations, others Space-A.

DV/VIP: 66ECW/CCE, building 112, C-EX-7960, 06+, retirees Space-A.

TML Availability: Difficult. Best, Dec-Jan.

☞ **Located in the lovely Rheinland Pfalz region, the villages around Sembach can look like Walt Disney dreamscapes to visitors, particularly in spring. Here the people are friendly and outgoing, local sights include castles and local fests.**

Locator 496-7535   **Medical 116**   **Police 496-7171**

⊗**Sembach has been greatly reduced in size. The runway is closed and there is limited base support, but Kaiserslautern and Ramstein are within reach. Keep updated with Military Living's R&R Space-A Report.**

Spangdahlem Air Base (GE19R7)
APO AE 09126-5000

TELEPHONE NUMBER INFORMATION: Main installation numbers: C-(USA) 011-49-6545-61-1110, (GE) 06545-61-1110, ETS-452-1110, D-314-452-1110.

Location: From the Koblenz-Trier Autobahn E-1 exit at Wittlich, to B-50 west toward Bitburg. The AB is near Binsfeld 24 km west of Wittlich. Signs mark the AB entrance. HE: p-39, F/1. NMC: Trier, 21 miles southeast.

GERMANY

Spangdahlem Air Base, continued

Billeting Office: Eifel Arms, ATTN: 52nd SUS Sq, building 38, APO AE 09126-5000, C-(USA) 011-49-6545-61-6504, (GE) 06545-61-6504, 24 hours daily. Check in facility, check out 1100 hours daily. No government civilian employee billeting.

TML: VOQ/VAQ. Building 38, all ranks, leave or official duty. VOQ: bedrooms, shared bath (33); VAQ: bed spaces, shared bath (94). Refrigerator, color TV, maid service, washer/dryer, ice vending. Older structure, renovated. Rates: $8. Maximum 2 persons. Duty can make reservations, others Space-A.

TML: TLF. All ranks, leave or official duty. Separate bedrooms, private bath (56). Cribs, ice vending, kitchenette, maid service, color TV, complete utensils, washer/dryer. Modern structure. Rates $27 per unit. Duty can make reservations. TLF is for families and singles PCS in/out.

DV/VIP: Cmdr, 52 TFW/CC, C-EX-6434. Determined by Cmdr, 06+, retirees Space-A.

TML Availability: Limited all year. Best, Nov-Dec.

☞ Trier lies where the Saar and Mosel rivers meet, and is Germany's oldest city, dating from the 2nd century. Don't miss lunch in the shadow of the Porta Nigra, and a stroll past renaissance half-timbered houses in the Hauptmarkt.

Locator 452-6038   Medical 452-6588   Police 452-6666

Stuttgart Community (GE20R7)
APO AE 09154-5000

TELEPHONE NUMBER INFORMATION: Main installation numbers: C-(USA) 011-49-711-819-XXXX, (GE) 0711-819-XXXX, ETS-420-XXXX, D-420-1110.

Location: Can be reached from both E-11 and E-70 Autobahns. Look for signs to Robinson Barracks. HE: P-40, C/4. NMC: Stuttgart, within city limits.

Billeting Office: Hilltop Hotel, CMR 447, Box 2246, APO AE 09154, building 169, C-(USA) 011-49-711-859-523, (GE) 0711-859-523, ETS- 420-6209, 0730-1630 hours daily. Check in facility, check out 1100 hours daily. Government civilian employee billeting.

TML: Hilltop Hotel. Guest House, building 169/at Robinson Barracks, all ranks, leave or official duty. Check in 1400 hours daily. Bedroom, shared bath (60); separate bedroom suites, private bath (DV/VIP) (4). Refrigerator, color TV in room & lounge, maid service, cribs/cots, washer/dryer. Older structure, renovated. Rates: PCS/TDY, $45-$160/1-6 persons includes breakfast (add $20 full meals), each additional person $15. For leave and other Space-A, $35-$85 for 1-6 persons,(add $10 for meals). All Ranks Community Club, D-420-6169. Maximum 2 adults/2 children under 5 per room. Duty can make reservations, others Space-A.

DV/VIP: Cmdr, ETS-420-2038, 06/GS-15+. Retirees Space-A.

TML Availability: Very limited, all year.

GERMANY
Stuttgart Community, continued

☞ Starting the end of April the Stuttgarter Frülingsfest, with carnival attractions and beer tents is a must for visitors. Also don't miss the Cannstatter Volksfest, at Bad Cannstatt at the end of September.

Locator 819-6036   Medical 116   Police 420-8317

Tempelhof Central Airport (GE25R7)
APO AE 09187-5000

TELEPHONE NUMBER INFORMATION: Main installation numbers: C-(USA) 011-49-30-819-XXXX, (GE) 0819-XXXX, D-314-332-1110.

Location: At Platz der Luftbrücke, intersection of Columbia Damm and Tempelhofer Damm Streets. HE: p-63, F/5,6. NMC: Berlin, in the city.

Billeting Office: ATTN: 7350th ABG/SVH, building D2, C-(USA) **011-49-30-49819-5374**, (GE) 030-49819-5374, D-314-332-2178, FAX-C (USA) 011-49-30-49819-2271, D-314-332-2271, 0800-1600 M-F. VAQ, 24 hrs, D-314-332-5374. VOQ, Columbia House, O'Club, C-(USA) 011-49-30-49819-5591/5391, (GE) 030-49819-5591/5391, D-314-332-5591/5391, 0730-1600 hours M-F. Check in facility, check out 1300 hours daily. Government civilian employee billeting.

TML: Guest House/VOQ. Buildings C2, D2, all ranks, leave or official duty. Bedroom, hall bath (24); separate bedrooms, shared bath (13). VAQ and suites also available. Refrigerator, community kitchen, maid service, cribs/cots, washer/dryer, ice vending. Older structure, renovated. Rates: officers $10-$14 per person per night, enlisted $8, chief suites $14. Maximum 3-6 per unit. All categories can make reservations, others Space-A.

DV/VIP: Protocol Office, C-(USA) 011-49-30-49819-5151, (GE) 030-49819-5151, 06+.

TML Availability: Good.

☞ Berlin is full of art galleries, theaters and historical points. Festivals are held year round for all the family to enjoy, since unification the city has become even more interesting for visitors who now travel east to west freely.

Locator 332-5511   Medical 116   Police 332-5314

⊗Templehof Airport Billeting is scheduled to close June '93.

Vilseck Sub-Community (GE85R7)
APO AE 09112-5420

TELEPHONE NUMBER INFORMATION: Main installation numbers: C-(USA) 011-49-9662-1837, (GE) 09662-1837, D-none.

Vilseck Sub-Community, continued

Location: From Nürnberg take Hwy 14 east to Hahnbach, turn north to Vilseck. Also E9 Autobahn north of Nürnburg to E85 south, Vilseck is east 3-5 miles. HE: p-40, G/1,2. NMC: Nürnberg, 60 miles southwest.

Billeting Office: 7 ATC Rose Barracks, building 275, C-(USA) **011-49-9662-1837**, (GE) 09662-1837, ETS-476-2555, 24 hours daily. Check in at facility, check out 1100 hours. Government civilian employee billeting in VOQ. BEQ, BOQ, VIP, VOQ information incomplete.

TML: VEQ. Building 242, all ranks, leave or official duty. Rooms, private bath. Refrigerator, essentials, maid service, cribs/cots, washer/dryer. Modern structure, renovated. Rates: sponsor $23.50, additional adult $10, maximum charge per family $33.50, maximum 2 persons per unit. Pets allowed, fee $3 per day (spray fee $20). All categories may make reservations.

DV/VIP: Call above number, 06+, GS12+.

TML Availability: Very good. Best in winter, difficult Aug/Sep.

☞ **Vilseck is near Grafenwöer, and Amberg. Army Community Service (GM 8371, 7413) has a wonderful list of "points of interest" in the area put together by the Oberpfalz area women's clubs.**

Locator 476-113   Medical 476-116   Police 476-114

☉**This is a new listing, so if you stop here, please let us know any additional information. Military Living, PO Box 2347, Falls Church, VA 22042-0347.**

Wertheim Sub-Community (GE52R7)
APO AE 09047-5000

TELEPHONE NUMBER INFORMATION: Main installation numbers: C-(USA) 011-49-9342-75-XXX, (GE) 09342-75-XXX, ETS-355-5XXX, D-314-350-1110 Ask for WRT.

Location: Take the Marktheidenfeld-Wertheim exit from the Frankfurt-Nürnberg E-3 Autobahn. HE: p-40, D/1. NMC: Würzburg, 25 miles west.

Billeting Office: Building 6, O'Club, 0800-1700 hours daily, C-(USA) **011-49-9342-689**, (GE) 09342-689. Check in facility, check out 1100 hours daily. No government civilian employee billeting.

TML: TLQ. O'Club, building 6, all ranks, leave or official duty. Bedroom, 2 beds, hall bath (21); two bedroom, 2 beds each, hall bath (2); two bedroom suite, livingroom, private bath (1). Refrigerator, color TV lounge, maid service, cribs $1.50, washer/dryer, ice vending. Older structure, renovated. Rates: $6 first bed, $4 each additional bed, suites $25. Duty can make reservations, others Space-A.

DV/VIP: Deputy Community Commander, ETS-355-5724/5800, 06+. Retirees Space-A.

GERMANY
Wertheim Sub-Community, continued

TML Availability: Good, Feb-Apr.

Locator 355-92   **Medical 355-5695**   **Police 355-5818**

⊗**This facility did not respond to our inquiries, information may be outdated.**

Wiesbaden Community (GE27R7)
APO AE 09096-5000

TELEPHONE NUMBER INFORMATION: Main installation numbers: C-(USA) 011-49-611-82-XXXX, 705-XXXX, (GE) 0611-82-XXXX, ETS-337/339-XXXX, D-314-320-1110 Ask for WBN.

Location: Accessible from Autobahns E-3, E-5, E-61. Take exits marked Wiesbaden Air Base to Berlinerstrasse then Frankfurterstrasse to billeting office. HE: p-40, A/1. NMC: Wiesbaden, in the city.

Billeting Office: American Arms Hotel, 17 Frankfurterstrasse, 24 hours daily, C-(USA) **011-49-611-343035,** (GE) 0611-343035, ETS-339-3314. **Amelia Earhart Hotel,** Konrad Adenaur Ring 39, C-(USA) **011-49-611-816368,** (GE) 0611-816368, ETS-337-6200. Check in facility, check out 1100 hours daily. Government civilian employee billeting.

TML: Amelia Earhart Hotel, adjacent to USAF hospital. Enlisted all ranks, leave or official duty. Bedroom, private bath (385). Refrigerator, color TV in room and lounge, maid service, cribs/cots, washer/dryer, some units balconies. Some units DV/VIP suites with bar (E9). Modern structure, newly remodeled dining facility. TLA rates: $35 1st person, $15 each additional person. Duty can make reservations, others Space-A.

TML: American Arms Hotel, 17 Frankfurterstrasse, all ranks, leave or official duty. Bedroom, shared bath (96); separate bedroom, private bath (23); bedroom suites, private bath (23). Lounge, maid service, cribs/cots, washer/dryer, ice vending. Modern structure, renovated. Restaurant, bar, weinstube. Rates: Same as above. Duty can make reservations, others Space-A.

TML: On Wiesbaden Air Base there are 92 Transient Officer billets, and 172 Enlisted billets, call ETS-339-6525 for information and accommodations.

DV/VIP: Contact hotel manager at either hotel listed above, 06+. Retirees and lower ranks Space-A.

TML Availability: Good.

☞ Hainerberg Shopping Center is 3 blocks away from lodging and is "shop til you drop" country! In the center of Wiesbaden, you are also within walking distance of wonderful architectural and cultural treasures (Wiesbaden had little damage during WWII).

Locator WBNC-705055   Medical 885-441   Police 114

Wildflecken Community (GE86R7)
APO AE 09026-5000

TELEPHONE NUMBER INFORMATION: Main installation numbers: C-(USA) 011-9745-1239, (GE) 09745-1239, D-314-326-3553/3964.

Location: Take the Autobahn toward Kassel and Fulda (A-66). Exit at Fulda and follow signs to Coburg. After coming over the Schwedenschanze, follow signs to Wildflecken. Then follow signs to the US Army Post. HE: p-36,F-G/6. NMC: Fulda, 25 miles north.

Billeting Office: Building 32, 16th St, C-(USA) 011-9745-1239, (GE) 09745-1239, D-D-314-326-3824, 0730-1600 M-F, closed US and German holidays. Extra keys available with Staff Duty NCO, building 1. Check in billeting, check out 1100 hours. Government civilian employee billeting.

TML: Guesthouse. Building 2, all ranks. Bedroom, private and hall bath (9); separate bedroom, private bath (1); two bedroom, hall bath (3). Other accommodations available. Refrigerator, community kitchens, baths, laundry facilities, color TV. Rates: $19, additional occupant $5. All categories can make reservations. Duty personnel have priority. **Pets OK for $3.50 per night.**

TML: VOQ/VEQ. Buildings 25, 26, all ranks. Bedroom, hall bath (29). Bedroom, hall bath (27). Other accommodations available. Refrigerator, TV, common use kitchens, baths, laundry facilities. Rates: $17, additional person $5. All categories can make reservations. Duty personnel have priority.

TML: DVQ. Building 50, officers 06+, enlisted E-9. Separate bedroom suites, private bath (4). Kitchenette, complete utensils, color TV. Rates: $40, additional person $10. All categories can make reservations. Duty personnel have priority.

TML Availability: Best, Nov thru Feb. Difficult Jun thru Oct.

☞ **Excellent downhill and cross country skiing, volksmarching country. In warm, friendly villages where fresh trout is a specialty. Close to the former East zone, where guard towers still standing are a wallchipper's delight.**

Locator 326-3471	Medical 326-3662	Police 326-898

Worms/Northpoint/Weierhof Community (GE31R7)
APO AE 09058-3879

TELEPHONE NUMBER INFORMATION: Main installation numbers: C-(USA) 001-49-6241-48-XXXX, (GE) 06241-48-XXXX, ETS-383-XXXX, D-314-383-1110.

Location: Take the Worms exit from the Mannheim-Saarbrücken E-6 Autobahn. Follow the signs to Thomas Jefferson Village. HE: p-40, B/2. NMC: Worms, in the city.

Billeting Office: Weierhof Inn, building 5032, Liebenauer Strasse, C-(USA) 001-49-6241-48-7374/7763, (GE) 06241-48-7374/7763, 0730-1830 M-F. Other hours, OD, building 5814, C-EX-7234. Check in facility, check out 1200 hours daily. Government civilian employee billeting.

GERMANY
Worms/Northpoint/Weierhof Community, continued

TML: TLF. All ranks, leave or official duty. Bedroom, shared bath (15); VIP suites (5), family suites, separate bedroom, living room, private bath, bar (4). Refrigerator, color TV, VCR on request, cribs/cots ($2). Older structure. Rates: sponsor $21, each additional person $4.50 (rooms); sponsor $32, each additional person $4.50 (VIP suites). TDY can make reservations, others Space-A.

TML Availability: Good, Nov-Apr. Difficult, other times.

☞ Astonishing antiquity is everyday reality in Worms Cathedral, completed in 1184. Just outside the city visit Liebfrauen kirche, from where the famous Liebfraunmilch wine was born. Don't miss any local "fests" - they're great fun.

Locator 383-92	Medical 116	Police 114

⊗The official reply states that "The Weierhof Inn is earmarked to be returned to the Rheinland Pfalz". Keep tuned to R&R Space-A Report for further developments.

Würzburg Community (GE21R7)
APO New York 09244-5000

TELEPHONE NUMBER INFORMATION: Main installation numbers: C-(USA) 011-49-931-899-XXXX; (GE) 0931-899-XXXX, ETS-350-XXXX, D-314-350-1110.

Location: From west on Autobahn E-3 take Heidingsfield exit to Rottendorfer Str north to Leighton Barracks. Take first right after Hq, building 6, proceed to building 2. HE: p-40, D/1. NMC: Würzburg, 1 miles south.

Billeting Office: ATTN: Guest House, CZN-161. Building 2, Leighton Barracks, C-(USA) 011-49-931-700201, (GE) 0931-700201, D-314-350-1700, 0730-1600 hours. Other hours SDO, building 6, C-EX-6223. Check in facility, check out 1000 hours daily. Government civilian employee billeting.

TML: American Guest House, building 2, all ranks, leave or official duty. Bedrooms, common bath (48); separate bedroom suite (VIP) (2). Kitchen (suites), refrigerator, color TV, maid service, cribs ($2), washer/dryer. Older structure. Rates: singles $20, $6 each additional person; suites $28, $7 each additional person. Duty can make reservations, others Space-A. **Note: when this facility is filled, guests are referred to the following officers' clubs, which have limited billeting, however, reservations may be made with them as well.**

TML: Top of the Marne Officer's Club, Leighton Barracks (across from American Guest House), C-0931-709097/8. Bedrooms, doubles and singles, basin, hall shower (6); separate bedroom suite (VIP) (1). Color TV, maid service, cribs ($5), washer/dryer. Older structure. Rates: bedrooms $38; suites $45 per day. Duty can make reservations, others Space-A.

TML: Kitzengen Officer's Club, Kitzengen, Harvey Barracks, C-09321-31836. Bedrooms, hall bath (10); separate bedroom suite, private bath (VIP) (1), two bedroom suite, private bath (VIP) (1). Refrigerator, maid service, color TV, cribs ($5) washer/dryer. Duty can make reservations, others Space-A.

GERMANY

Würzburg Community, continued

DV/VIP: SGS, Protocol, building 6, C-EX-8308/8306, 06/GS-15+. Retirees Space-A.

TML Availability: Good, Oct-Mar. Difficult, other times.

☞ **The Annual Mozart Festival in summer, famous Franken wine in the light of a thousand candles at the Würzburg Castle, the old walled city of Rothenburg on the Talber, and the Marienberg Castle will put you in a mood to stay in Franconia.**

Locator 350-98   **Medical 116**   **Police-114**

Iraklion Air Station (GR02R9)
APO New York 09291-5000

TELEPHONE NUMBER INFORMATION: Main installation numbers: C-(USA) 011-30-81-761-281/2/3, (GR) 761-281/2/3, D-314-668-1110.

Location: On the Greek Island of Crete. From Iraklion Airport, right at main entrance past the Greek Military base, next left. Straight for 20 minute drive to Gournes, AS on the left. HE: p-85, B/3. NMC: Iraklion, 8 miles west.

Billeting Office: ATTN: 7276th ABG/SVH, building 208, North St, C-(USA) 011-30-81-761-3942/3842, (GR) 761-3942/2842, 0730-2330 hours duty days. Other hours, Security Police C-EX-3426. Check in billeting, check out 1000 hours daily.

TML: TLF. Daedalian, leave or official duty. Apartments, private bath (18). Kitchen, complete utensils, color TV, maid service, cribs/cots, ice vending. Modern structure. Rates: $24 per room per night. Duty can make reservations, others Space-A.

TML: VAQ. Building 308, enlisted E1-E6, leave or official duty. Bedrooms (double occupancy) (8). Refrigerator, color TV in room & lounge, maid service. Modern structure. Rates: $7.50 per person. Maximum 2 per room. Duty can make reservations, others Space-A.

TML: VOQ. Building 208, officers all ranks, E7-E9, leave or official duty. bedroom, shared bath (16); separate bedroom, private bath (DV/VIP) (4). A/C, color TV in room & lounge, maid service, cots, washer/dryer, ice vending. Modern structure. Rates: $8 per person; DV/VIP $14 per person. Duty can make reservations, others Space-A.

DV/VIP: Building 208, Section 1, C-EX-3556, 06+. Retirees and lower ranks Space-A.

TML Availability: Good, winter and early spring. Difficult, summer months.

☞ **Iraklion has miles of historic streets, made for wandering. Visitors should not miss seeing Knossos Palace, the archeological museum in Iraklion, Saint Titus' Church and the Minoan Palace of Phaistos. Many beautiful local beaches.**

Locator 3859/3426   **Medical 3525**   **Police 3426**

Hong Kong

China Fleet Club (HK01R8)
Fleet House, 6 Arsenal Street
Wanchai, Hong Kong

TELEPHONE NUMBER INFORMATION: Main installation number: C-(USA) 011-852-529-6001, (HK) 0852-529-6001, D-none.

Location: Located at 6 Arsenal Street, Wanchai, Hong Kong. NMC: Hong Kong, in the city.

Billeting Office: None. Check in at front desk. C-(USA) **011-852-529-6001, EX-522,** (HK) 0852-529-6001, EX 522, FAX-011-852-865-6380.

TML: British Royal Navy Club, all ranks, leave or official duty. The China Fleet Club is a non government service club which provides hotel accommodation for active duty and retired British, American and other Nato service personnel. The Club has 38 twin bedrooms, all of which have full en suite facilities, color TV, and mini bar. Other facilities include a restaurant, meeting room, lounges, auditorium, bowling alley, squash courts and snooker room. One of the club's featured attractions is a two floor shopping mall, which is administered by the US Navy Contracting Department. The shopping mall also has a "pack and wrap" facility and a US Navy Post Office. Accommodation rates: twin bed-room, officers - HK$650.- per night, enlisted personnel - HK$550.00 per night. Rates include all taxes. Reservations can be secured with a check for one night's room charge per week booked.

TML Availability: Unknown.

☞ **Teeming Hong Kong can be enjoyed simply by walking around, or you can take a ferry, to the outlying islands of Lantau, Lamma, Cheung Chau, and Peng Chau. Go on weekdays and enjoy seeing rural China.**

Iceland

Keflavik Naval Station (IC01R7)
FPO AE 09728-0334

TELEPHONE NUMBER INFORMATION: Main installation numbers: C-(USA) 011-354-25-0111 (IC 25-0111), D-(USA) 312-450-0111 (Europe) D-314-228-0111.

Location: IAP shares landing facilities with Naval Station. From Reykjavik seaport take Hwy S follow signs to Keflavik. Well marked. Naval Station is 2.5 miles before town of Keflavik. HE: p-1, A/2. NMC: Reykjavik, 35 miles north.

Billeting Office: ATTN: COQ, building 761, C-(USA) **011-354-25-4333,** (IC) 25-4333, 24 hours daily. Check in at billeting, check out 1200 hours daily. No government civilian employee billeting.

ICELAND

Keflavik Naval Station, continued

TML: Navy Lodge. Naval Station, Box 10, building 786. All ranks, leave or official duty. C-(USA) **354-25-2000-EX-7594/2210**, (IC) 25-2000-EX-7594/2210. One and two bedroom units, private bath (31). Kitchen (11 units), community kitchen, color TV in room & lounge, maid service, cribs/cots, coin washer/dryer, ice vending. Older structure. Rates: $27-$35 per unit. Maximum 6 persons. All categories can make reservations.

TML: CBQ. Buildings 761, 763, all ranks, leave or official duty. Bedroom, private bath (51); bedrooms, shared bath (32). Color TV in room & lounge, maid service, washer/dryer. Older structure. Rates: enlisted $8, officer and equivalent $10 per person. Sponsors for duty personnel can make reservations, others Space-A.

DV/VIP: Commander Iceland Defense Force, Box 1, FPO NY 09571-5000, C-EX-4414. 05+, retirees Space-A. **Note:** All numbers are C- or D- extensions.
TML Availability: Lodge, good in winter months; billeting, fair. Lodge, difficult, Apr-Aug; billeting, poor.

☞ Into summer skiing? Visit the Kerlingarfjoll area. Fishing? July and August are best for brown trout, char and salmon. For sightseeing, bird watching and camping info write Iceland National Tour Office, 75 Rockefeller Plaza, NY 10019.

Locator 2100   **Medical 3301**   **Police 2211**

Admiral Carney Park (IT03R7)
Naples, IT
FPO AE 09619-5000

TELEPHONE NUMBER INFORMATION: Main installation numbers: C-(USA) 011-39-81-526-1579, (IT) 081-526-1579, D-314-625-4834.

Location: On the west coast of Italy in Admiral Carney Park, 7 miles from Naples and 5 miles from US Naval Support Activity, Naples. HE: p-51, E/6. NMC: Naples, 7 miles south.

Billeting Office: Admiral Carney Park, Naples, Italy, ATTN: MWR, PSC 810, Box 13, FPO AE 09619, C-(USA) **011-39-81-526-3396/1579**, (IT) 081-526-3396/1579, D-314-625-4834, FAX-011-39-81-570-4581. Reservations required. Check in facility 1300, check out 1030 hours daily. No pets. Operates year round.

TML: The 54 acre recreational and sports complex is contained within the walls of a crater. All ranks. Handicapped accessible. Bedroom cabins (13); two bedroom cabins (13). Bath house and laundromat separate, kitchenette, refrigerator, no utensils, grill and picnic area, linens, blankets, no towels. Rates: $25-$35 per night per cabin, weekly rates available. Maximum 4 per cabin. All categories can make reservations up to 3 months in advance.

TML Availability: Good, winter months. Difficult, summer months.

ITALY
Admiral Carney Park, continued

☞ Visit historic Pompeii, Herculanum, the popular beaches on Capri, and Ischia. In Naples the National Museum, the Art Gallery of Capodimonte are nearby. This is a full rec park - for more details see Military RV, Camping & Rec Areas Around The World.

Aviano Air Base (IT04R7)
APO AE 09601-5000

TELEPHONE NUMBER INFORMATION: Main installation numbers: C-(USA) 011-39-434-65-7520, (IT) 0434-65-7520, D-314-632-7520.

Location: Adjacent to town of Aviano in Pordenone province. Thirty miles east of Udine, IT and 50 miles northeast of Venice. From A-28 North exit Pordenone to IT-159 for 8 miles to Aviano AB. HE: p-93, C/4. NMC: Pordenone, 8 miles north.

Billeting Office: Building 256, Pedemante St, C-(USA) **011-39-434-65-2306,** (IT) 0434-65-2306, D-314-632-7262, FAX-011-39-434-660598, 24 hours daily. Check in facility, check out 1200 hours daily. Government civilian employee billeting.

TML: VOQ/VAQ/TAQ. Buildings 232, 255, 256, 273, 274. All ranks, leave or official duty. Double rooms, private bath (17); bedroom, private bath, suites (DV/VIP) (2). Dependents OK. Rates: moderate.

DV/VIP: PAO, Building T-8, room 204, C-04493-7-331, 06+.

TML Availability: Good, Dec-Jan. More difficult, other times.

☞ Don't miss the Castello di Aviano, Aviano's castle ruins. Pordenone (eight miles south) for shopping, strolling and cappuccino. Many other sights are nearby, but don't miss Margraten American War Cemetery.

Locator 2734   **Medical 116**   **Police 7200**

Camp Darby (IT10R7)
APO AE 09613-5000

TELEPHONE NUMBER INFORMATION: Main installation numbers: C-(USA) 011-39-50-54-7111, (IT) 050-54-7111, ETS-633-7225.

Location: Located midway between Livorno & Pisa. From Autostrada A-1 take Pisa Sud exit. Turn left and continue to end of road, left onto Via Aurelia (SS 1), right to S. Piero A'Grado & follow Camp Darby signs. HE: p-50, A/3. NMC: Pisa, 6 miles north.

Billeting Office: Building 202, C-EX-7225, 0800-1800 M-F, 0900-1400 Sa, Su, after duty hours, w/prior reservations, building 731, MP Desk. Check in billeting, check out 1000 hours daily. Rec area open year round.

ITALY

Camp Darby, continued

TML: Sea Pines Lodge, building 836. C-(USA) **011-39-50-54-7225,** (IT) 050-54-7225, 0700-2200 hours daily. All ranks, leave or official duty. Bedroom, private bath (24). Sleeps up to 4 persons, 1 double or 2 twin beds, 2 bunk beds. Refrigerator, community kitchen, limited utensils, color TV in room & lounge, maid service, cribs ($3), cots ($5), washer/dryer. Modern structure. Rates: 1 person $25, 2 persons $35, 3 persons $40, 4 persons $45. **Pets allowed, $3.50 per night + $50 damage deposit.** Government civilian employee billeting (official duty). All categories may make reservations.

TML: Casa Toscana, CMR 426, APO AE 09613. Reservations: C-(USA) **011-39-50-54-7448/7580,** (IT) 050-54-7448/7580. Check in Billeting, above building, hours. Rooms, suites and apartments. Bedroom, shared bath (2); separate bedroom, private bath (23); suite (1). Kitchenette, utensils (apartments only), refrigerator, essentials, cribs, maid service (M-F), DAVs (ground floor), color TV. New A/C, carpeting, TV's, renovation '91. Rates: rooms $30, additional person $10; apartments $50 (1-2 persons), additional person $10, DVQ (1-2 persons) $60, additional person $10. **Pets allowed at undetermined charge.** Government civilian employee billeting (official duty. All categories may make reservations.

DV/VIP: Commander, 8th TASG, APO AE 09613, building 302, C-EX-7505, 06/GS-13+, retirees Space-A.

TML Availability: Difficult, best Oct-Nov, worst Jul-Aug.

☞ **Located in the choice Tuscany region of Italy, one hour from Florence. Camp Darby even has its own stretch of Mediterranean beach at the resort town of Tirrenia. The famous Leaning Tower of Pisa 6 is miles away.**

Locator 112   **Medical 116**   **Police 114**

La Maddalena Navy Support Office (IT13R7)
FPO AE 09612-5000

TELEPHONE NUMBER INFORMATION: Main installation numbers: C-(USA) 011-39-789-790270, (IT) 0789-790270, D-314-726-2701.

Location: Located off the northern tip of the island of Sardinia. Take the main road (IT-125) north from Olbia to Palau, then take a 15 minute ferry ride to La Maddalena and follow signs to the installation. HE: p-54, C/1. NMC: Olbia, 28 miles southeast.

Billeting Office: Calabro Hall, C-EX-790297, D-726-2971, 0800-1700 daily. C-(USA) **011-39-789-722-287,** (IT) 0789-790-297, D-314-726-2971. After hours contact NSO at C-EX-790-244. Check in facility, check out anytime.

TML: Building 300, all ranks, PCS personnel only. Bedroom, 1 bed, shared bath (17); bedroom, 2 beds, shared bath (36); separate bedrooms, private bath (12). Handicapped accessible. A/C, ice vending, maid service, refrigerator, color TV, washer/dryer. Modern structure. Rates: no charge. Maximum 2 per room. **Note: A new berthing faciity will be operational within a year at that time temporary lodging may be available.**

DV/VIP: Protocol Office, building 300, Apt 9, C-EX-722318, D-EX-2141, 06+ Lower ranks may use if BOQ is full.

ITALY
La Maddalena Navy Support Activity, continued

TML Availability: Best after Sep. Difficult during summer months.

Locator 789-722318   Medical 275   Police 244

Naples Naval Support Activity (IT05R7)
FPO AE 09619-1000

TELEPHONE NUMBER INFORMATION: Main installation numbers: C-(USA) 011-39-81-724-1110, (IT) 081-724-1110, D-314-625-1110.

Location: In Naples, a large port city south of Rome on the N-S Autostrada (toll road) and IT-1. HE: p-51, E/6. NMC: Naples, in the city.

Billeting Office: BEQ. Building 71, C-(USA) **011-39-81-724-4842,** (IT) 081-724-4842. Check in facility, check out 1200 hours daily. Government civilian employee billeting.

TML: BEQ. Building 71, enlisted all ranks, leave or official duty. Single rooms, hall and common bath. Refrigerator, color TV lounge, essentials, maid service, washer/dryer, food/ice vending, microwaves in lounges. Older structure. Upgrades in '89. New quarters complex anticipated '92. Rates: $6 per person. Dependents not authorized. Duty can make reservations, others Space-A.

TML: Navy Lodge. **Hotel Costa Bleu,** Pinetamare. All ranks, leave or official duty, C-(USA) **011-39-81-509-7120/21/22/23,** (IT) 081-509-7120/21/22/23. Apartments: bedroom/sitting room, private bath (14); two bedroom, 2 bath (75); three bedroom, 2 bath (8); four bedroom, 3 bath (4). Full kitchen, utensils, Italian espresso maker, color TV w/military channel, washer/drying rack, bar/restaurant, weekend theater, game room, summer pool park for children, in housing area w/medical support, mini mart 1 mile, Naval Support Activity, 19 miles. No pets, kennel available $3.50. Rates: Based on number of occupants/fluctuating per diem. April 92 costs: 1 person, $67.04, 2 persons $103.14, 3 persons $128.92, 4 persons $154.71, 5 persons $180.49. PCS have priority, others may make reservations at above number. Availability: May-Sept difficult, other times good.

DV/VIP: Building 71, C-EX-4567, NSA Protocol Office.

TML Availability: Extremely limited. Best, winter.

☞ **From the Navy Lodge, visit Caserta, which has a palace and gardens reminiscent of Versailles, and Pozzouli for its volcanic activity and Roman ruins. Naples itself has wonderful possibilities. Contact MWR for tours.**

Locator 4556   Medical 300/301   Police 4686

San Vito dei Normanni Air Station (IT07R7)
APO AE 09605-5000

TELEPHONE NUMBER INFORMATION: Main installation numbers: C-(USA) 011-39-831-42-1110, (IT) 0831-42-1110, D-314-622-1110 .

San Vito dei Normanni Air Station, continued

Location: On the heel of Italy's boot midway between the port cities of Brindisi and the town of San Vito dei Normanni. The AS is on SS-379 serving the area. Four miles from the Adriatic shore. Follow the signs to "U S Base". HE: p-52, G/2. NMC: Brindisi, 5 miles south.

Billeting Office: Building 455, Jefferson Ave, C-(USA) **011-39-831-42-3850**, (IT) 0831-42-3850, 0700-2200 daily. Check in facility, check out 1100 hours daily. Government civilian employee billeting.

TML: TLF/VOQ/VAQ/DVQ. Buildings 601-603, 435. All ranks, leave or official duty. VOQ: bedroom, private bath, shared kitchen (10). VAQ: double rooms, 2 beds, hall bath (no females)(10); single room, private bath (2). TLF: bedroom, living room w/sofabed, chair bed, kitchenette, (maximum 5 persons, 2 rooms can be assigned) (30). DVQ: suites, livingroom, private bath (3); two bedroom livingroom, private bath (1). Kitchen, complete utensils, A/C, color TV in room & lounge, maid service, cribs/cots, washer/dryer, ice vending. Modern structure, renovated. Rates: VOQ/VAQ $6, per person, maximum $12; TLF $26 per person; DVQ $14 per person, maximum $28. Duty can make reservations, others Space-A.

DV/VIP: Protocol Office. D-EX-3482, 06/GS-15+. Retirees & lower ranks Space-A.

TML Availability: Best, Nov-Apr. More difficult, other times.

☞ **From Brindisi 10 boats a day to Greece draw many tourists. The beaches are also popular here. Visit Lecce, 1/2 hour away for interesting churches, museums and shopping. Taranto, 1 hour away is larger and has excellent shopping.**

Locator 3408   **Medical 3511**   **Police 114**

Sigonella Naval Air Station (IT01R7)
FPO AE 09627-5000

TELEPHONE NUMBER INFORMATION: Main installation numbers: C-(USA) 011-39-95-56-1110 (NAS I), 86-1110 (NAS II) (IT) 095-56-1110, D-314-624-1110.

Location: On the east coast of the Island of Sicily. Accessible from A-19 or IT-417. HE: p-53, E/4. NMC: Catania, IT, 10 miles northeast.

Billeting Office: ATTN: PAO, Air Term, C-(USA) **011-39-95-56-5575**, (IT) 095-56-5575, 24 hours daily. Check in facility, check out 1200 hours daily. Government civilian employee billeting.

TML: BOQ/BEQ. All ranks, leave or official duty, C-EX-2300/1. Bedroom, private bath (42); separate bedroom suites, private bath (DV/VIP) (11). A/C, color TV, maid service, washer/dryer, ice vending. Older structure. Rates: $8 per person. Maximum $25 per family. Maximum 3 per unit. Duty can make reservations, others Space-A.

DV/VIP: PAO, building 545, C-EX-5251/5252, 06+. Retirees Space-A. No dependents under age 15.

ITALY
Sigonella Naval Air Station, continued

TML Availability: Good, Dec-Jan. Difficult, other times.

Locator 0   Medical 4333 (NAS I)   Police 4201/2

⊗**This facility did not respond to our inquiries, some data may be outdated.**

Vicenza Community (IT06R7)
Caserma Carlo Ederle
APO AE 09630-5000

TELEPHONE NUMBER INFORMATION: Main installation numbers: C-(USA) 011-39-444-51-5190, (IT) 0444-51-5190, D-314-634-7301.

Location: Take the Vicenza east exit from the Number 4 Autostrada which runs from Trieste to Milano. Follow signs to Caserma Carlo Ederle or SETAF Hq's. HE: p-91, H/6. NMC: Vicenza, in the city.

Billeting Office: Building 136, 8th St, C-(USA) **011-39-444-51-5190,** (IT) 0444-51-5190, D-314-634-7301, 0600-2200 hours daily. Other hours, SDO in building 109, D-EX-7711. Check in 1500 hours, check out 1200 hours daily. Government civilian employee billeting.

TML: Guest House/DVQ. Building 136, all ranks, leave or official duty. Handicapped accessible. Three bedroom suites, private bath (25); DVQ suites, private bath (4). Kitchen, complete utensils, A/C (DVQ only), color TV, maid service, cots/cribs, VCRs. Modern structure, remodeled. Rates: sponsor $28, each additional person $10, TDY $42 (Guest House); sponsor $38, each additional person $10, TDY $52, (DVQ). Maximum 6 per room. Reservations required. **Pets allowed at a nominal fee.**

DV/VIP: Vicenza Billeting Activity, Hq 80th BSB, DEH, building 136, room 601, D-314-EX-7712, 05/GS-15+. Retirees Space-A.

TML Availability: Good, Oct-Nov. Difficult, May-Sep.

☞ Verona, the city of Romeo and Juliet, is rich in monuments of every period and a modern and hospitable city. Don't miss the Roman Arena, which is still an active entertainment site. Venice, Florence, Pisa, and many others are close.

Locator 634-1110   Medical 97 or 113   Police 7626

Atsugi Naval Air Facility (JA14R8)
FPO AP 96306-5000

TELEPHONE NUMBER INFORMATION: Main installation numbers: C-(USA) 011-81-462-51-1520-EX, (JA) 0462-51-1520, D-dial C-number then ask for EX-6880/1/2/3.

JAPAN

Atsugi Naval Air Facility, continued

Location: In central Japan off Tokyo Bay. Yokohama is 15 miles east and Tokyo is 28 miles northeast. Camp Zama is 5 miles north. NMC: Tokyo, 28 miles northeast.

Billeting Office/Navy Lodge: Building 987, Navy Lodge, Box 10, FPO AP 96306. All ranks, leave or official duty. Handicapped accessible. C-(USA) 011-81-462-51-1520, (JA) 0462-51-1520, D-315-228-6880, 0700-2300 hours daily. Check out 1100 hours. Bedroom, 2 double beds, private bath (30). Kitchen, cribs, essentials, ice vending, maid service, refrigerator, special facilities for DAVs, color TV lounge, washer/dryer. Modern structure. Rates: $34 per unit. Maximum 4 persons per unit. All categories can make reservations. **TML Availability:** Extremely limited. Best Jan-May.

☞ **Book a one day tour of Tokyo through MWR at Atsugi, or just ask the friendly Navy Lodge people to provide you with maps, directions and info, but don't miss seeing as much as you can of this marvelous city!**

Camp S. D. Butler Marine Corps Base (JA07R8)
FPO AP 96379-0935

TELEPHONE NUMBER INFORMATION: Main installation numbers: C-(USA) 011-81-98892-5111, (JA) 098892-5111, D-315-635-2191/3749.

Location: Four miles south of Okinawa City on Hwy 330 at Camp Foster 2 miles north of Futenma. NMC: Naha, 7 miles south.

Billeting Office: ATTN: FACS, Billeting/Housing Coordinator, building 11, C-(USA) 011-81-98892-2191/3749, (JA) 098892-2191/3749, D-315-635-2191/3749, 0730-2400 daily. Other hours, building 1, OD, D-315-635-7218/2644. Check in facility, check out 1200 hours daily. Government civilian employee billeting.

TML: TLF. Courtney Lodge, building 2540, Camp Courtney, all ranks, leave or official duty, C-EX-9578, D-315-622-9578. Suites, private bath (16). Refrigerator, A/C, CATV in room & lounge, maid service, cribs/cots, coin washer/dryer. Modern structure. Rates: $25 per unit. Maximum 3 per unit.

TML: TLF. Hansen Lodge, building 2540, Camp Hansen, all ranks, leave or official duty. C-EX 4511, D-623-4511. Same as Courtney except bedroom, shared bath (18). Older structure. Rates: $8 per room. Maximum 2 per room. Reservations accepted.

TML: Kuwae Lodge, building 400, Camp Lester, all ranks, leave or official duty. C-EX 0214, D-634-0214. Rooms with kitchen (165). Washer/dryer, playroom, rec rooms. Rates: $22-$26 single, $44-$46 double adjoining rooms, $66-$70 3 room suite. Reservations accepted 30 days in advance.

TML: WesPac Inn. Camp Foster, (TQ) all ranks, leave or official duty. Futenma, (VOQ) officers, all ranks, leave or official duty, C-EX-2191/3749, D-315-635-2191/3749. Separate bedroom, living room, private bath (20); (Futenma) bedroom, private bath (12); separate bedroom, private bath (4); suites, private bath (2). Maximum 2 per suite, 1 per room. Kitchen, A/C, color TV, maid service, washer/dryer, video cassette reception in room. Older structure, renovated. Rates: $10, $15, $20 according to rank and status. Duty can make reservations, others Space-A.

JAPAN
Camp S. D. Butler Marine Corps Base, continued

TML: DV/VIP. **Day House, Okinawa House, Awase House,** buildings 4205, 4222, 4515. Same as above. Rates: $30.

DV/VIP: Protocol Office, building 1, SD Bulter MCB, C-EX 7274, D-315-635-7274. Protocol Office, building 4225, III MEF, Camp Courtney, C-EX 7749, D-315-635-7749. Protocol Office, Building 1, 1st MAW, SC Butler MCB, C-EX 2901, D-315-635-2901.

TML Availability: Good. Best, Aug-Mar. More difficult, other times.

☞ **Don't miss seeing Nakagusuku Castle, left over from Okinawa's feudal period, and the Nakamura House, which displays Okinawan lifestyle of yesteryear. Check with the USO for locations and possible tours.**

Locator 635-7456   Medical 634-1756   Police 635-7441

Camp Zama (JA06R8)
APO AP 96343-0069

TELEPHONE NUMBER INFORMATION: Main installation numbers: C-(USA) 011-81-4062-51-1520, (JA) 04062-51-1520, D-315-233-3830/4474.

Location: 25 miles south of Tokyo or north of Yokohama. Excellent rail service. NMC: Tokyo, 25 miles north.

Billeting Office: ATTN: APAJ-GH-EH-HB, building 563, Sand St, C-(USA) **011-81-4062-51-1520 (ask for 233-3830/4474)**, (JA) 04062-51-1520 (ask for 233-3830/4474), D-315-233-4474/3830, 24 hours daily. Check in facility, check out 1200 hours daily. Government civilian employee billeting.

TML: VOQ/VEQ. Building 742, all ranks, official duty, or leave. Handicapped accessible 1st floor. Bedroom, private bath (38). Refrigerator, microwave, stocked bar, community kitchen, A/C, color TV and VCR, maid service, washer/dryer, ice and food vending. Modern structure. Rates: sponsor $16, $3 each additional person. Duty can make reservations, others Space-A. **Pets boarded at clinic for $4 per day.**

TML: Guest House. Building 552, all ranks, PCS in and out, or official duty. Handicapped accessible 1st floor. Separate bedroom, private bath (56). Kitchenettes, complete utensils, maid service, color TV and VCR, A/C, ice vending, washer/dryer. New structure, furnishings '92. Rates: sponsor $25, $4 each additional person. Duty can make reservations, others Space-A.

TML: Guest House. Building 780, all ranks, PCS in/out. Handicapped accessible 1st floor. Bedroom, hall bath (5); two bedroom, hall bath (14); three bedroom, private bath (2). A/C, refrigerator, microwave, complete utensils, community kitchen, color TV and VCR, maid service, washer/dryer, ice vending. Older structure, refurbished '91. Rates: sponsor $14-$22, $4 each additional person. Duty can make reservations, others Space-A.

TML: DVQ. Building 550, officer 06+, official duty or leave. Handicapped accessible 1st floor. Separate bedroom, private bath (12). A/C, community kitchen, cots/cribs ($5), maid service, refrigerator, stocked bar, microwaves, TV and VCR, ice vending, washer/dryer. Modern structure, refurbished '91. Rates: sponsor: $20, $5 each additional person. Duty can make reservations, others Space-A. **Pets boarded at clinic for $4 per day.**

Camp Zama, continued

DV/VIP: USARJ Protocol Office, building 101. C-233-4019, 07+, retirees Space-A.

TML Availability: Guest House: good, DVQ: good, Jan-Feb difficult. VOQ/VEQ: good, Jan-Feb difficult.

☞ **Check with the ITT office on base for local tours. A round trip shuttle bus to Tokyo (the New Sanno Hotel) is available, as are trips to Disneyland, Kamakura, Hakone, Mount Fuji, Kyoto, Nikko and Seto.**

Locator 04062-51-1520   Medical 233-4127   Police 233-3473

Iwakuni Marine Corps Air Station (JA12R8)
FPO AP 96310-5410

TELEPHONE NUMBER INFORMATION: Main installation numbers: C-(USA) 011-81-827-21-4171, (JA) 0827-21-4171, D-315-253-5409.

Location: Facing the Inland Sea on the south portion of the island of Honshu, 450 miles southwest of Tokyo, .5 miles off JA-188 on JA-189. NMC: Hiroshima, 25 miles north.

Billeting Office: Building 603, C-(USA) **011-81-827-21-4171-EX-3181**, (JA) 0827-21-4171-EX-3181, D-315-253-5409, 24 hours daily. Check in building 603, check out 1200 hours daily. Government civilian employee billeting.

TML: Transient Billeting. Buildings 203, 420, 603, 611, 1189, all ranks, leave or official duty, C-EX-3221. Some facilities handicapped accessible. Bedroom, common bath (enlisted) (19); separate bedroom, private bath (SNCOs and officers) (51); two bedroom, private bath (DV-Shogun House) (1); bedroom, two beds, common bath (enlisted) (17). Kitchenette (building 603), refrigerator, limited utensils, A/C, color TV, maid service, cribs/cots, ice vending. Modern structure. Rates: sponsor and adults $5 officers, SNCOs $4, E-5 and below $3, 12 and under $2. Duty can make reservations, others Space-A.

DV/VIP: DGR, building 511, D-315-236-4211.

TML Availability: Good. Difficult, Feb. and Mar.

☞ **See the famous Kintai Bridge, and view the Iwakuni Castle Ropeway. Hiroshima is 50 minutes by train, and visitors should see the Peace Memorial Park, Atomic Bomb Memorial Dome, and reconstructed Hiroshima Castle.**

Locator 3114/4211   Medical 5571   Police 3222

Kadena Air Base (JA08R8)
APO AE 96239-5000

TELEPHONE NUMBER INFORMATION: Main installation numbers: C-(USA) 011-81-61-172-41100, (JA) 061-172-41100, D-315-630-1110.

Location: Take Hwy 58 North from Naha to Kadena's Gate 1 on the right immediately north of USMC Air Station Futenma. NMC: Naha, 12 miles south.

JAPAN
Kadena Air Base, continued

Billeting Office: ATTN: 18 CSPTS/CTSB, building 332, Beeson Ave, C-(USA) **011-81-61172-43817**, (JA) 061172-43817, D-315-634-1100, 24 hours daily. Check in at billeting, check out 1200 hours daily. Government civilian employee billeting.

TML: TLF. Family Quarters. Building 437, 507, all ranks, leave or official duty. Handicapped accessible. Apartments (98). A/C, refrigerator, kitchen, complete utensils, color TV, maid service, cribs, rollaway, washer/dryer. Modern structure. Rates: $35 per unit. Maximum 6 persons per unit. Duty can make reservations, others Space-A.

TML: VAQ. Buildings 317, 322, 504, 506, 509, 510, enlisted all ranks. Bedroom, private bath (58); separate bedrooms, semi-private bath (120); two bedroom, private bath (30). A/C, maid service, refrigerator, color TV, washer/dryer. Rates: $5.50 per person per night. Maximum 2 persons. Duty can make reservations, others Space-A.

TML: VOQ. Buildings 304, 306, 311, 314, 315, 316, 318, 502, 508, 512, officers all ranks. Bedroom, private bath (157); separate bedroom, semi-private bath (40). A/C, maid service, refrigerator, color TV, washer/dryer. Rates: $8.50 per person. Maximum 2 persons. Duty can make reservations, others Space-A.

TML: DV/VIP. Buildings 78, 315, 2024, officers 06+, leave or official duty. Bedroom, private bath (20); three bedroom, private bath (2). A/C, essentials, kitchen, complete utensils, maid service, color TV lounge, washer/dryer. Rates: $8.50 per person. Duty can make reservations, others Space-A.

DV/VIP: Protocol Office, building 10, D-315-634-3548, 06+.

TML Availability: Good, Dec-Jan. Difficult, spring & summer.

☞ **This is the cross roads of the Pacific, and a great Space-A departure point, but don't miss seeing the Children's Park Zoo in Okinawa City, the Ryukyuan Village and Takoyama Habu Center. Near Nenoko see the Shell house, visited by shell collectors.**

Locator 634-1110　　　　**Medical 634-3333**　　　　**Police 634-2475**

Misawa Air Base (JA03R8)
APO JA 96319-5000

TELEPHONE NUMBER INFORMATION: Main installation numbers: C-(USA) 011-81-176-53-5181, (JA) 0176-53-5181, D-315-226-3526/4294.

Location: On the northeast portion of the Island of Honshu, 400 miles north of Tokyo. NMC: Hachinohe City, 17 miles southeast.

Billeting Office: Misawa Inn, 432 CSPTS/CTSB, Unit 5019, APO AP 96319, building 674, C-(USA) **011-81-176-53-5181-EX-3526**, (JA) 0176-53-5181-EX-3526, 24 hours daily. Check in billeting, check out 1200 hours daily.

TML: TLF. Buildings 696-699, all ranks, leave or official duty. Two bedroom apartments, shared bath (16). Kitchen, refrigerator, utensils, color TV, VCR, maid service, cribs/cots, washer/dryer. Older structure. Rates: $28 per unit. Duty can make reservations, others Space-A.

JAPAN

Misawa Air Base, continued

TML: VOQ. Buildings 662, 664, officers 01-06, leave or official duty. Bedroom, private bath (56). Kitchen, utensils, refrigerator, color TV, VCR, maid service, washer/dryer, ice vending. Older structure, renovated. Rates: $8 per person. Duty can make reservations, others Space-A.

TML: VAQ. Building 669, enlisted all ranks, leave or official duty. Bedroom, common bath (32); two separate bedroom, private bath, (E9). Prime Knight Aircrew Quarters, (10); suites, private bath (E9) (2). Refrigerator, color TV, VCR, maid service, washer/dryer, ice vending. Rates: $8 per person. Duty and civilians on official duty can make reservations, others Space-A.

TML: DV/VIP. Building 17, officer 06+ (M&F), leave or official duty. Bedroom, private bath, suites (4). Kitchen, utensils, refrigerator, A/C, color TV, VCR, maid service. Modern structure, renovated. Rates: $8 per person. Duty can make reservations, others Space-A.

DV/VIP: 432 TFW/CCE. C-EX-4804, 06+. Retirees Space-A.

TML Availability: Good, Dec-Feb. Difficult, other times.

☞ **Enjoy the excellent eating establishments in downtown Misawa, and try a hot bath at Komakis. Explore the Komaki Onsen, Komaki Grand and the Second Grand Hotels. Get hints from MWR (building 407) for trips farther afield.**

Locator 0176-53-5181   **Medical 226-2985**   **Police 226-4358**

The New Sanno US Forces Center (JA01R8)
APO AP 96337-0110

TELEPHONE NUMBER INFORMATION: Main installation numbers: C-(USA) 011-81-3-3440-7871, (JA) 03-3440-7871.

Location: At 4-12-20 Minami Azabu, Minato-ku, Tokyo 106, a five minute walk from nearest subway station, Hiroo (Hibiya line). NMI: Tokyo Administrative Facility/Hardy Barracks, 10 miles. NMC: Tokyo, in city limits.

Description: Located in a quiet residential area not far from downtown Tokyo, only a five-minute walk from the nearest subway station, Hiroo. Offers guests commercial hotel quality accommodations and food service at affordable prices. Each of 149 guest rooms features private bath or shower, and central heating and air conditioning. Rental VCRs and videos are available. Two traditional Japanese-style suites for guests to enjoy the full flavor of the Orient.
   A family dining room, Japanese-style restaurant, Continental-style restaurant, lounge and 24 hour snack bar are available to guests of the New Sanno. Entertainment and special events are scheduled on a regular basis in The New Sanno's main ballroom which can seat up to 350 guests, and banquet and conference facilities are available.
   There is a rooftop pool (seasonal), an exercise room and video game room, first and second floor arcades with a Navy Exchange, Stars & Stripes bookstore, convenience store and concessionaires. An APO, military banking facility, pack & wrap service, barber shop, beauty salon, flower shop and laundry and dry cleaning, plus public restrooms (handicapped accessible) on the lobby level, and other American-style conveniences make the New Sanno a meeting place for military personnel and their families touring Tokyo.

JAPAN
The New Sanno US Forces Center, continued

Tours, theater, concert and sporting event tickets are available through the Information and Tours Desk. They can also book airline and steamship reservations, C-03-3440-7871 EX 720011. If you are arriving at Narita International Airport, an economical airport express bus is available to the New Sanno's front door. Daily buses run to and from Yokota Air Base (schedule available at AMC terminal).

The New Sanno is a Joint Services, all ranks facility managed by the US Navy as Executive Agent.

Season of Operation: Year round.

Eligibility: Active/Retired/US Embassy Tokyo/UN Command(Rear), Active Reserves, DoD and other Federal Civilian Employees on official orders to or through Japan.

Reservations: Recommended 45 days in advance with one nights deposit for each room reserved. Deposits by check, money order, American Express, Diners' Club, MasterCard, VISA. Address: The New Sanno Hotel, APO AP 96337-0110, Attn: Reservations. C-(USA) **011-81-3-3440-7871-EX-7121**, (JA) 03-3440-7871-EX-7121, D-315-229-7121, TELEX: 2427 125 SANTEL J; FAX-C-011-81-03-440-7824, D-315-229-7102.

Room Rates for the New Sanno U S Forces Center

Room Type	No.	I*	II*	III*	IV*
Single (Queen bed)	43	$25	$32	$38	$52
Double (Queen + single bed)	78	$35	$41	$48	$65
King Suite (King + sofa)	17	$50	$54	$58	$76
Twin Suite (2 twins + sofa)	3	$50	$54	$58	$76
Family Suite (sgl room + bunk)	2	$50	$61	$72	$90
Family Room (twin suite, 2 twins, 2 bunks + sleeper sofa)	1	$50	$61	$72	$90
Japanese Suite	2	$63	$68	$74	$94

*I: E1-E5; II: E6-03, WO1-WO4; III:04-010; IV: retired/non-DoD. I, II & III include comparable DoD Civilian grades. II includes DAVs, Unremarried Widows and Orphans (all with DD1173).

ALL RATES SUBJECT TO CHANGE.

Restrictions: No pets.

Sasebo Naval Base (JA15R8)
FPO AP 96322-1100

TELEPHONE NUMBER INFORMATION: Main installation numbers: C-(USA) 011-81-956-24-6111, (JA) 0956-24-6111, D-(USA) 315-252-1110, (JA) 315-237-1110.

Location: From either Nagasaki or Fukuoka on the Nishi-Kyushu Expressway to SASEBO exit (both in Japanese and English). Follow Route 35 to downtown SASEBO, ask directions to naval base. Far southwestern Japan, on the Korean Strait, NMC: Fukuoka, 50 miles northeast.

Sasebo Naval Base, continued

Billeting Office: ATTN: BOQ/BEQ Manager, Fleet Activities, Sasebo, PSC 476, Box 1, FPO AP 97622-1100. Building 63, C-(USA) **011-81-956-24-6111, EX(BOQ) 3794, EX(BEQ) 3413,** (JA) 0956-24-6111, above extensions, 24 hours daily. Check in port operations, check out 1200 hours daily. Government Civilian Employee billeting.

TML: BOQ, BEQ. Buildings 1455, 63, 46, all ranks, leave or official duty. Bedrooms (163). Kitchenette, utensils, refrigerator, microwave, essentials, color TV in room and lounge, VCR, maid service, food and ice vending, cribs, washer/dryer. Modern structure. New BOQ/BEQ expected in future. Rates: $4 per unit, per person. No charge for children under 8, $16 maximum for family. Maximum 4 per unit. Duty may make reservations, retirees, widows, DAVs Space-A. No pets.

TML: Navy Lodge, ATTN: Navy Fleet Activities Sasebo, PSC 476, Box 30, FPO AP 96322-0003. Reservations: **at press time this number was not available, call 1-800-NAVY INN for number,** 0630-2230 hours daily. All ranks, leave or official duty. Bedroom, 2 double beds, private bath (26). A/C, color TV, maid service, coin washer/dryer, ice vending. Modern structure, opened May '92. Rates: $34. All categories can make reservations.

TML: DV/VIP. Building 80, C-above number, EX 3401, leave or official duty. Duty can make reservations, others Space-A.

DV/VIP: Commander, Fleet Activities Sasebo, Attn: Protocol Officer, PSC 476, Box 1, FPO AP 96322-1100, BOQ 06+, BEQ E9+.

TML Availability: Fairly good, Apr-Aug. Difficult, Sep-Dec.

☞ **Mount Yumihari has an excellent view. Take a 99 Islands boat cruise, from nearby Kashimae Pier (15 minutes from base by car). Hachiman Shrine is a 20 minute walk from base. Nagasaki and Fukuoka are one hour drives.**

Locator 3311   Medical 3826   Police 3447

Okuma Recreation Center (JA09R8)
Kadena AFB, APO AP 96368-5000

TELEPHONE NUMBER INFORMATION: Main installation numbers: C-(USA) 011-81-61172-41100, (JA) 061172-41100, D-315-630-1110.

Location: On Hwy 58, 50 miles north of Kadena AB, Okinawa. Left off Hwy 58 before Hentona. NMC: Naha, JA 62 miles south.

Billeting Office: ATTN: Leisure Resources Center, Schilling Rec Center, 18th CSW/SSRR, APO AP 96368-5000. Duty, retired, DOD civilians assigned overseas. Reservation required up to 30 days in advance, C-(USA) **011-81-61172-41100,** (JA) 061172-41100, D-315-634-4601, 0700-2200 hours daily (summer), W-M (winter), building 116, check in 1500 hours at facility, check out 1100 hours daily. Operates year round.

JAPAN
Okuma Recreation Center, continued

TML: Rec Cabana's. All ranks, leave or official duty. Bedroom, 2 double beds, shared bath, (30); bedroom, 2 double beds, private bath (10); bedrooms, 1 double, 1 single bed, private bath, (12); separate bedroom suites, 4 double beds, private bath (9); VIP suite (1). Refrigerator, A/C, color TV (some), maid service, cribs/cots ($3), washer/dryer, ice vending (small fee), fully furnished. Concrete block construction. Rates: shared bath $22.50/daily; private bath $30/daily; suites, VIP $37.50/daily;. All categories can make reservations.

DV/VIP: Protocol, building 10, 313 Air Division, Kadena AB, Okinawa, C-EX-0106, 06+. Retirees and lower ranks Space-A.

TML Availability: Good, Nov-Dec. Difficult, other times.

☞ **Great beach rec area. For full details and camping opportunities, see Military Living's *Military RV, Camping & Rec Areas Around The World*.**

⊗**This facility did not respond to our inquiries, some data may be outdated.**

Tama Hills Recreation Center (JA10R8)
Yokota Air Base
APO AP 96328-5000

TELEPHONE NUMBER INFORMATION: Main installation numbers: C-(USA) 011-81-423-77-7009, (JA) 0423-77-7009, D-315-224-3421/3422.

Location: Fifteen miles southeast of Yokota AB. NMC: Tokyo, 45 mile train ride.

Billeting Office: 475 ABW/MWRL, Yokota AB, APO AE 96328-5000, C-(USA) **001-81-423-77-7009,** (JA) 0423-77-7009, D-315-224-3421/3422, 24 hours daily. Check in at facility 1400, check out 1100 hours daily. Operates year round. Reservations required with first days rent.

TML: Rec Lodge and cabins. All ranks, leave or official duty. Reservations required. Suites, private bath (6); double rooms, private bath (14); executive and single cabins, private bath (18). Refrigerator, A/C, color TV, maid service, washer/dryer, ice vending. Rates: $20 to $30. All categories can make reservations. **Pets allowed in cabins.**

TML Availability: Good, Oct-Mar. Difficult, other times.

☞ **This is a 500 acre retreat west of Tokyo, reopened after extensive renovations in 1983. Its a quiet getaway offering many facilities. See Military Living;s *Military RV, Camping & Rec Areas Around The World* for more details.**

Locator 0423-77-7009   Police 224-3421-EX-40

Tokyo Administration Facility (JA02R8)
APO AP 96337-0007

TELEPHONE NUMBER INFORMATION: Main installation numbers: C-(USA) 011-81-03-440-7881, (JA) 003-440-7881, D-315-229-3270/3345.

Location: At #7-23-17 Roppongi, Minato-ku, Tokyo. Near Imperial Palace and 10 miles by taxi from New Sanno Hotel. NMC: Tokyo, in the city.

Billeting Office: Hardy Barracks, building 1, Room 413-A, C-(USA) 011-1-03-440-3270/3345, (JA) 003-440-3270/3345, 24 hours daily. Check in at facility 1600, check out 1200 hours daily. Government civilian employee billeting.

TML: VOQ/VEQ. All ranks, leave or official duty. Bedroom, shared bath (19); separate bedroom suites, private bath (2). Refrigerator, community kitchen, A/C, color TV, VCR, micro-fridge, coffee, maid service, cribs, washer/dryer. Older structure. Remodeled March '90. Rates: sponsor $15-$20, each additional person $2-$5. Maximum per family $30. Reservation info not provided. Pets not allowed.

DV/VIP: Call Camp Zama, building 101, room W-223, D-315-233-4019, for assistance.

TML Availability: Good. Best months Jan-May.

☞ **Check with the New Sanno Hotel for guided tours, or just pick up some city maps. Then visit the Ginza, Kabuki theater, Asakusa (the entertainment district), and its Kannon Temple, Ueno Park, Zoo, and shopping are musts.**

Yokosuka Fleet Activities (JA05R8)
Box 40, Code 450
FPO AP 96349-1110

TELEPHONE NUMBER INFORMATION: Main installation numbers: C-(USA) 011-81-468-26-1911, (JA) 0468-26-1911, D-315-234-1110.

Location: About 20 miles south of Tokyo and 25 miles north of Yokohama. NMC: Tokyo, 20 miles north. Excellent train service.

Billeting Office: Building G-27, Clements St, C-(USA) 011-81-0468-26-1911-EX 7777, (JA) 0468-26-1911-EX-7777, D-315-234-7777, FAX-011-81-468-76-1911-EX-5088, FAX D-315-234-5088 (BEQ); C-0468-26-1911-EX-7317, D-315-234-7317 (BOQ), 24 hours daily. Navy Lodge: Fleet Activities, Code 700, FPO Seattle 98762-5000. Check in facility, check out before 1200 hours daily. Government civilian employee billeting.

TML: Navy Lodge. Building J-197-J-200 (main building), all ranks, leave or official duty, Reservations: **above number, no ex.** Bedroom, private bath (81); two bedroom, private bath (27); bedroom, hall bath (19). Kitchen (12 rooms), refrigerator (all), utensils, A/C, color TV in room & lounge, maid service, cribs/cots, coin washer/dryer, ice vending. Modern structure. Rates: $28 average. Maximum 6 persons each unit. No dependent children without sponsor. Reservations accepted.

JAPAN
Yokosuka Fleet Activities, continued

TML: BEQ. Building 1492, enlisted, all ranks, leave or official duty. Bedroom, 3 beds, private bath (232). Refrigerator, A/C, color TV room & lounge, maid service, washer/dryer. Modern structure. Rates: $4 per person. Maximum 3 per room. Duty can make reservations, others Space-A.

TML: BOQ. Buildings 1556, 1723, officer all ranks, leave or official duty. Bedroom, private bath (95). Kitchen, A/C, color TV room and lounge, maid service, washer/dryer, barber shop. Modern structure. Rates: $5 per person. Duty can make reservations, others Space-A. Note: most rooms have only 1 single bed.

TML: CPOQ. Building 1475, enlisted E7-E9, leave or official duty. Bedroom, private bath (62). Refrigerator, community kitchen, A/C, color TV room & lounge, maid service, washer/dryer, ice vending. Modern structure. Rates: $2 per person. Duty can make reservations, others Space-A. Note: all beds are singles with limited room for cots.

TML: Other. **NASU Lodge.** 100 miles north of Tokyo. Rec Service Office. C-EX-5613/7306. Two-story wood-frame building accommodates up to 26 persons. Japanese style floor and bath. Kitchen and lodging requirements. Near many rec areas for skiing, fishing, hiking, horseback riding. Reservations taken 1 month in advance. Call for rates. Group rates available. All ranks.

DV/VIP: Protocol Office, C-0468-26-1911-EX-5685, D-315-234-7317, 07+. Retirees Space-A.

TML Availability: Good. Somewhat difficult, Jun-Sep.

☞ **Located close to Tokyo, near many historic Japanese shrines, beautiful beaches, a 10 minute walk to a shopping mall, and 2 hours from Disneyland Tokyo, Yokosuka boasts "the best MWR facility in the Pacific."**

Locator 213   **Police 5347**

◐**A new 164 unit replacement Navy Lodge will open in late '92 at this installation. Keep updated with Military Living's R&R Space-A Report.**

Yokota Air Base (JA04R8)
APO AP 96328-5000

TELEPHONE NUMBER INFORMATION: Main installation numbers: C-(USA) 011-81-425-52-2511, (JA) 0425-52-2511, D-315-248-1101.

Location: Take JA-16 South from Tokyo. AB is 1 mile west of Fussa JA. Clearly marked. NMC: Tokyo, 35 miles northeast.

Billeting Office: ATTN: SVH Billeting, building 10, Bobzien Ave & 1st St, C-(USA) **011-81-425-52-2511-EX-5-7712**, (JA) 0425-52-2511-EX-5-7712, D-315-225-9270, 24 hours daily. Check in billeting, check out 1200 hours daily. Government civilian employee billeting.

Yokota Air Base, continued

TML: TLF. Building 10, all ranks, leave or official duty, C-EX-9270. Four bedroom, shared bath (31). Kitchen, utensils, A/C, color TV in room & lounge, maid service, cribs, washer/dryer, handicapped accessible. Modern structure. Rates: $32 per room. Duty can make reservations, others Space-A. **Limited pet care available on base.**

TML: VOQ. Buildings 14, 120, 131-134, officers all ranks, leave or official duty, C-EX-9270. Bedroom, private bath (136); suites, separate bedroom, private bath, (15). Refrigerator, A/C, color TV, maid service, washer/dryer. Older structure. Rates: $8 per person. Duty can make reservations, others Space-A.

TML: BOQ. Buildings 116, 117, 220, 413, officers all ranks, leave or official duty. C-EX-9355. Separate bedroom, private bath (232). Kitchen, A/C (Building 220, 413), washer/dryer. Modern structure. Rates: not provided. **Caged birds & fish only.**

TML: VAQ. Building 16, enlisted all ranks, leave or official duty, C-EX-9270. Bedroom, common bath (80); two bedroom (22). Refrigerator, A/C, color TV, maid service, washer/dryer. Older structure. Rates: $6 per person. Maximum 4 per unit. Duty can make reservations, others Space-A.

TML: DV/VIP. SNCO, building 32, enlisted E7-E9, leave or official duty, C-EX-9270. Suites, bedroom, private bath, (3). Refrigerator, A/C, TV, maid service, washer/dryer. Modern structure. Rates: $10 per person. Duty can make reservations, others Space-A.

TML: DV/VIP. Buildings 13, 17, 32, officers 06+ (M&F), leave or official duty, C-EX-9270. Separate bedroom, private bath, suites (9); two bedroom, private bath, suites (4). Kitchen, utensils, A/C, color TV, maid service, cribs, washer/dryer. Older structure. Rates: $10 per person. Duty can make reservations, others Space-A.

DV/VIP: 5th AF/CSP, C-EX-5-4141, 06+. Retirees and lower ranks Space-A.

TML Availability: Good, Oct-Mar. Difficult, other times.

Locator 225-8390   **Medical 225-9111**   **Police 116**

Chinhae Naval Facility (RK06R8)
FPO AP 96269-5000

TELEPHONE NUMBER INFORMATION: Main installation numbers: C-(USA) 011-82-2-791-3110, ask for Chinhae, (RK) 2-791-3110, D-315-762-5771.

Location: On the east coast of Korea, south of Pusan. Take the Seoul-Pusan expressway to Pusan, exit and continue along the coast for 25 miles south.

Billeting Office: Billeting Office, duty hours. C-(USA) **011-82-2-791-3110, ask for Chinhae, then EX-5336,** D-315-762-5771. Check in facility, check out 1200 hours daily.

KOREA
Chinhae Naval Facility, continued

TML: Officers' Club. Officers, all ranks, leave or official duty. Bedroom, 4 double beds, private bath (4). A/C, telephone, maid service. Older structure, renovated. Rates: moderate. Duty can make reservations, others Space-A.

TML Availability: Good.

☞ **If you are lucky enough to be in Chinhae in April (1-15) you will see the city covered in cherry blossoms, folk dances, and visit fascinating street markets, plus many other activities. This is a very interesting port city.**

Medical 417

Dragon Hill Lodge (RK09R8)
HC East
APO AP 96205-0427

TELEPHONE NUMBER INFORMATION: Main installation number: C-(USA) 011-82-2-790-0016, (RK) 2-790-0016.

Location: Located on South Post, Yongsan, in Seoul. From Kimpo International Airport, enter the Olympics Stadium Expressway 88 for approximately 15 miles, then take the Panpo Bridge exit and cross the bridge. Look for the Capital Hotel on the right side as you come off the bridge. Stay on the right side of the road and do not go under ground where the road splits. Go to the major intersection and turn left (one mile from bridge), enter the 2nd gate on the left side (gate 10) and proceed to the Lodge. NMC: Seoul, in the city.

Billeting Office: None. Check in at front desk. C-(USA) **011-82-2-7918-2222**, (RK) 2-7918-2222, D-315-738-2222, FAX-011-822-792-0036 (FAX Korea 2-792-0036).

TML: New Lodge in '90, all ranks, leave or official duty, handicapped accessible. Bedroom, private bath (267); two bedroom, private bath (10). A/C, kitchenette, refrigerator, microwave, complete utensils, cots ($10), cribs, ice vending, maid service, handicapped accessible facilities, color TV, VCRs, washer/dryer, recreation facilities, shopping at The Gallery, The Square, Cookies &Cream snack shop, Stars and Stripes Bookstore, Coffee Kiosk. Modern structure, remodeled. Rates: $35-$55 per room for personnel on leave/vacation status; $75 per room for active duty personnel on TDY, PCS/TLA $65. Maximum 4 persons. All categories can make reservations. **Pets can be boarded at vet clinic near Gate 17, South Post.**

TML Availability: Good. Best, Oct-May.

☞ **See Myong-Dong (Seoul's Ginza), Korea House, Duksoo Palace. The National Museum and Folk Museum on Kyongbok Palace grounds acquaint visitors with Korean culture. Don't miss Walker Hill tourist complex twenty minutes away.**

Locator 724-6830   **Medical 737-3545**   **Police-724 6363/4300**

Kunsan Air Base (RK05R8)
APO AP 96264-5000

TELEPHONE NUMBER INFORMATION: Main installation numbers: C-(USA) 011-82-42-782-4110, (RK) 1-011-82-782-4110, D-315-782-4110.

Location: On the west central coast of RK. Exit from Seoul-Pusan expressway, directions to AB clearly marked. NMC: Kunsan City, 7 miles north.

Billeting Office: ATTN: 8CSG/SVH, building 392, West 9th St, C-(USA) 011-82-42-782-4604, (RK) 1-011-82-42-782-4110, D-315-782-4604 hours daily. Check in billeting. Check out 1100 hours daily. Government civilian employee billeting.

TML: VOQ. Building 392, officers all ranks, leave or official duty, C-EX-4604. Bedroom, common bath (20). Refrigerator, A/C, color TV, maid service, washer/dryer. Older structure. Rates: moderate. Duty can make reservations, others Space-A.

TML Availability: Limited.

☞ **Kunsan is a deep water port on the Yellow Sea, and a major fishing port. The mountainous areas of Korea are dotted with temples and shrines of both Japanese and Korean influence and are set in magnificent natural scenery.**

Locator 782-4351   Medical 782-4333   Police 782-4944

Osan Air Base (RK04R8)
APO AP 96266-5000

TELEPHONE NUMBER INFORMATION: Main installation numbers: C-(USA) 011-82-332-284-4110, (RK) 1-011-82-284-4110, D-315-284-4110.

Location: Off the Seoul-Pusan expressway 38 miles south of Seoul. Directions to AB clearly marked. Adjacent to Song Tan City. NMC: Seoul, 38 miles north.

Billeting Office: ATTN: 51 CSG/SVH (PACAF), building 771, (RK) 1-011-82-284-4672/6768 24 hours daily. Check in billeting, check out 1200 hours daily. Government civilian employee billeting.

TML: TLF. Building 1007, all ranks, leave or official duty. Separate bedroom, sleeps 5, private bath (17). Kitchen, fully equipped, A/C, color TV, maid service, cribs, washer/dryer. Modern structure. Rates: $24 per unit. Maximum 5 per unit. Duty can make reservations, others Space-A.

TML: VOQ. Buildings 1001, 1003, officers, all ranks, leave or official duty. Bedroom, private bath (65). Kitchen, limited utensils, A/C, color TV, maid service, cribs, washer/dryer. Modern structure. Rates: $9 per person, maximum $24 per unit. Maximum 3 persons. Duty can make reservations, others Space-A.

TML: VOQ/VAQ. Officers, building 485, all ranks, leave or official duty. Bedroom with 2 beds, common bath (258). Refrigerator, community kitchen, limited utensils, A/C, color TV, maid service, washer/dryer. Modern structure. Rates: $6 per person, maximum $8 per family. Duty can make reservations, others Space-A.

KOREA
Osan Air Base, continued

TML: DV/VIP. On Hill 180. Officer 06+, leave or official duty. Bedroom, private and semi-private baths (11); One separate bedroom suite, private bath. Refrigerator, A/C, color TV, maid service, cribs/cots, washer/dryer. Modern structure. Rates: $10 per person. Maximum 2 persons. Duty can make reservations, others Space-A.

DV/VIP: Protocol Officer, 314th AD, C-EX-4-6700, 06+. Retirees and lower ranks Space-A.

TML Availability: Best, Nov-Feb. Difficult, other times.

☞ **Don't miss seeing Duksoo Palace (home of the National Museum), Kyonbok and Changduk Palaces, and the Secret Garden and Puyong Pavilion in Seoul. Onyang (a hotspring resort), and Walker Hill resort shouldn't be missed.**

Locator-8144   **Medical-118**   **Police-116**

Yongsan Army Garrison (RK07R8)
APO AP 96205-5000

TELEPHONE NUMBER INFORMATION: Main installation numbers: C-(USA) 011-82-2-7914-8205/8184, (RK) 2-7914-8205/8184, D-315-724-8205/8184.

Location: In the Yongsan district of Seoul. NMC: Seoul, in the city.

Billeting Office: Billeting Office, building 1112, C-(USA) **011-82-2-7914-8205/8184** (RK) 2-7914-8205/8184, 24 hours daily. Check in facility, check out 1200 hours daily. No government civilian employee billeting.

TML: VOQ. Buildings 8102, 8103, 8104, officers all ranks, enlisted E7-E9. Official duty only. Separate bedroom suites, private bath (3); two bedroom, shared bath (1). Refrigerator, A/C, cribs, color TV, maid service, washer/dryer. Modern structure. Rates: $15 per person, maximum $20 per family. Duty can make reservations, others Space-A.

TML: VEQ. Buildings 4110, enlisted E1-E6, leave or official duty. Separate bedroom, common bath (29). Refrigerator, community kitchen, A/C, color TV, maid service, washer/dryer. Modern structure. Rates: $4 per room. Duty can make reservations, others Space-A.

TML: DVQ. Buildings 3723, 4436, 4464, 4468, officer 07+ or civilian equivalent, leave or official duty. C-EX-7913-3315. Separate bedroom, private bath. Community kitchen, kitchenette, complete utensils, cribs, color TV, A/C, maid service. Modern structure. Rates: sponsor $25, adults $12.50, children $5. Duty can make reservations, others Space-A.

DV/VIP: Sec Joint Stall, Protocol Branch, SJS-P, HHC, EUSA, building 2472. C-EX-7913-3315, D-315-723-3315, 07+ or civilian equivalent. Lower ranks Space-A.

TML Availability: Good, but reserve early.

Locator 2-7912-8205   **Medical 293-4581**

⊗**This facility did not respond to our inquiries, some data may be outdated.**

Netherlands

Schinnen Community (NT02R7)
APO AE 09703-5000

TELEPHONE NUMBER INFORMATION: Main installation numbers: C-(USA) 011-31-45-26-2230, (NT) 045-26-2230, D-None.

Location: Take Autobahn A-2, A-76 or E-9. Also NE-39, exit at Schinnen, cross railroad tracks, turn left to base, Emma Mine. HE: p-35, G/2. NMC: Maastricht, NT, 15 miles southwest.

Billeting Office: Officers' Club, or US Protocol Office, building H105. C-(USA) 011-31-45-26-2230, (NT) 045-26-2230, 0800-2230 hours duty days. Call C-045-26-3188 after hours. Check in facility, check out 1200 hours daily. Government civilian employee billeting in local hotels.

TML: Officers' Club, officers all ranks, leave or official duty. Double rooms, private bath (20); bedroom, private bath suites (DV/VIP) (2). Dependents OK. Rates: reasonable.

DV/VIP: PAO, building T-8, room 204, C-04493-7-331, 06+.

TML Availability: Limited.

Locator 04493-7-199   **Medical-04526-3-177**   **Police 04493-7-323**

Sösterberg Air Base (NT01R7)
APO AE 09719-5000

TELEPHONE NUMBER INFORMATION: Main installation numbers: C-(USA) 011-31-3463-5-8499, (NT) 03463-5-8499, D-314-363-8499.

Location: On Utrechtsweg between Utrecht and Amersfoort in Huis ter Heide. Take the turn to Den Dolder. HE: p-34, D-E/4. NMC: Utrecht, NT, 8 miles southwest.

Billeting Office: ATTN: 32 TFS/SVH, building 31, W S Camp, 24 hours daily. C-(USA) 011-31-3463-5-8499, (NT) 03463-5-8499. Check in billeting, check out 1200 hours daily.

TML: TAQ. Building 31, enlisted all ranks, leave or official duty. Bedroom, private bath (4); two bedrooms, shared bath (14). Color TV, maid service, cribs, refrigerator. Modern structure. Rates: Not specified, call. Duty can make reservations, others Space-A.

TML: VOQ. Building A-27, officers all ranks, leave or official duty. Bedroom, shared bath (5). Refrigerator, color TV, maid service, cribs/cots. Older structure. Rates: $6.50 per person. Maximum $13 per family. Duty can make reservations, others Space-A.

NETHERLANDS
Sösterberg Air Base, continued

DV/VIP: Protocol, Building 101, C-EX-8132, 06+. Retirees and lower ranks Space-A.

TML Availability: Good, Oct-Feb. Difficult, other times.
Locator 363-8599   Medical 363-8540   Police 363-3012

⊗**This facility did not respond to our inquiries, some data may be outdated.**

Fort Clayton (PN02R3)
APO AA 34004-5000

TELEPHONE NUMBER INFORMATION: Main installation numbers: C-(USA) 011-507-285-6666, (PN) 285-6666, D-313-285-6666.

Location: Near the Pacific Ocean entrance to the Panama Canal. Take Gaillard Hwy toward the Miraflores Locks. NMC: Panama City, 8 miles southwest.

Billeting Office: Building 518, Hospital Rd, Fort Clayton, C-(USA) 011-507-85-4451/3251, (PN) 287-4451-3251, 0700-1530 M-F. Check in billeting, check out 1100 hours daily.

TML: Clayton Guest House. Building 518, all ranks, leave or official duty. Bedroom, private bath (34); separate bedroom, private bath (5). Refrigerator, A/C, color TV, recreation room & lounge, maid service, cribs/folding beds, washer/dryer, ice vending, dining hall. Older structure. Rates: regular $22 per person, $27 maximum; large room $26 per person, $31 maximum for family. Official duty and hospital visits can make reservations, others Space-A.

TML: Atlantic Guest House. Building 402, Ft Espinar, all ranks, leave or official duty, C-(USA) 011-507-298-4081/4828, (PN) 298-4081/4828. Bedroom, private bath (19); separate bedroom, private bath (2). A/C, lounge (Tropical Den), breakfast available, community kitchen, cribs, ice vending, maid service, refrigerator, color TV, washer/dryer. Rates: regular $22 per person, $27 maximum; large room $26 per person, $31 maximum. Duty can make reservations, others Space-A.

TML: Gold Coast Inns, Ft Sherman. All ranks, C-(USA) 011-507-289-4081/4828, (PN) 289-4081/4828. Check ins from the Atlantic Guest house in building 402, Ft Espinar. Houses fully furnished with two separate bedrooms and private bath (2). Kitchenette, cooking utensils, A/C, refrigerator, color TV, maid service, washer/dryer, outdoor picnic tables with grills.

TML: Quarry Heights VOQ, in Panama City, building 119, enlisted E7+/officers, all ranks, leave or official duty. C-(USA) 011-507-282-4899, (PN) 282-4899, 0730-1600 M-F. After hours call 287-4451/3251 at **Clayton Guest House** for check ins and reservations. Separate bedroom, private bath (13). Refrigerator, A/C, color TV, maid service, vending machine. Older structure. Rates: $22 per person, $27 maximum per family. Duty can make reservations, others Space-A.

PANAMA

Fort Clayton, continued

TML: DV/VIP. **Casa Caribe**, building 77, Ft Amador, enlisted E9/officer 06+, leave or official duty. Protocol: C-(USA) **011-507-87-5057/5059**, (PN) 87-5057/5059. Bedroom, private bath (4); separate bedroom with private bath (2). Refrigerator, A/C, color TV, maid service, washer/dryer. Central kitchen, breakfast served M-F, 0630-0900. Rates: regular $28, $33 maximum per family; suite $32, $37 maximum. Duty can make reservations, others Space-A.

DV/VIP: Protocol Office, building 95, room 171. C-287-5057/8, E9/06+, retirees and lower ranks Space-A.

TML Availability: Good, Nov-Jan. Difficult, other times.

☞ **Panama City is a shoppers paradise - see the Via España - and if you have time don't miss San Blas for a pre-Columbian vision, and the forts of Portobelo. A railroad runs along the Canal itself all the way to Colon at the Pacific Ocean.**

Locator 287-4053   **Medical 282-5222**   **Police 110**

Howard Air Force Base (PN01R3)
APO AA 34001-5000

TELEPHONE NUMBER INFORMATION: Main installation numbers: C-(USA) 507-84-3010, (PN) 284-84-3010, D-313-284-3010.

Location: Adjacent to Thatcher Hwy (K-2) on Pacific side of Panama. NMC: Panama City, 10 miles west.

Billeting Office: Building 708, C-(USA) **507-84-4914/5306**, (PN) 284-84-4914/5305, FAX-507-84-4985, 24 hours daily. Check in billeting, check out 1200 hours daily. No government civilian employee billeting.

TML: TLQ. Building 1511, all ranks, leave or official duty. C-EX-4914/4556. Two bedroom apartments (6). Kitchen, complete utensils, A/C, color TV, maid service, cribs/cots, washer/dryer. Older structure, refurbished. Rates: $24 per room per night. Maximum 6 per room. Duty can make reservations, others Space-A.

TML: TAQ. Buildings 186, 710, enlisted E1-E6, leave or official duty. Rooms, shared/common bath (52). Refrigerator, A/C, color TV, maid service, washer/dryer, ice vending. Older structure. Rates: $5.50 per person, maximum 2 persons. Duty reservations, others Space-A.

TML: BEQ. Building 519, enlisted E7-E9, official duty only. Separate bedroom, private bath (22). Kitchen, A/C, washer/dryer. Older structure. Rates: No charge. Permanent party only. No dependents.

TML: BOQ. Buildings 19, 21, officers all ranks, official duty only. Separate bedroom, private bath (48). Kitchen, A/C, washer/dryer. Rates: No charge. Permanent party only. No dependents.

TML: VOQ. Buildings 13, 14, 117, 119, 174, officers all ranks, leave or official duty. Bedroom, private bath (2); separate bedroom, private bath (32). Refrigerator, A/C, color

PANAMA
Howard Air Force Base, continued

TV, maid service, washer/dryer, ice vending. Older structure, remodeled. Rates: $8.50 per person, maximum $17 per family. Maximum 2 per room. Duty can make reservations, others Space-A.

TML: DV/VIP. Buildings 16, 119, 519, officers 06+, leave or official duty. Separate bedroom suite, private bedroom (1); two bedroom suite, private bath (1); three bedroom suite, private bedroom (1). Kitchen, utensils, A/C, color TV, maid service, washer/dryer, ice vending. Rates: $8.50 per person. Maximum 2 per room. Duty can make reservations, others Space-A.

DV/VIP: USAFSO/CCP, Howard, C-EX-84-4601, 06+, retirees and lower ranks Space-A.

TML Availability: Difficult at all times.

☞ **In Panama City visit the Avenida de los Martires and Avenida Central for shopping. Don't miss the church on Santa Ana Plaza, and San Jose church in Old Panama. Casco Viejo is quaint with Spanish and French architecture.**

Locator 84-3010   **Medical 84-4100**

Rodman Naval Station(PN09R3)
APO AA 34061-1000

TELEPHONE NUMBER INFORMATION: Main installation numbers: C-(USA) 011-507-83-XXXX, (PN) 283-XXXX, D-313-221-3859.

Location: On the west bank of the Panama Canal, one mile left of Tatcher Ferry Bridge (Bridge of the Americas). Panama City, 18 miles northwest.

Billeting Office: US NAVSTA PAN Canal, unit 6262, FPO AA 34061-1000. Building 77, C-(USA) **011-507-83-4440/4619**, (PN) 283-4440/4619, 0600-2400 daily. Check in billeting, check out 1100 hours daily. After hours CDO, Quarter Deck, building 51, C-EX-83-4166. Government Civilian Employee billeting.

TML: Guest House, BOQ, BEQ. All ranks, official duty. Bedroom, private bath; suites, private bath; apartments, private bath; rooms, 2 beds, kitchenette, shared bath (enlisted); bedroom, shared bath (enlisted) (30). Kitchenette, complete utensils, color TV, maid service, washer/dryer, ice vending. No pets. Modern structure. Rates: officers, $8, enlisted $4, VIP $15. Duty can make reservations, others Space-A.

DV/VIP: Combined Bachelor Quarters, US NAVSTA Rodman, unit 6262, FPO AA 34061, C-above numbers, 05+, reservations, Space-A.

TML Availability: Difficult. Best Dec-Feb, difficult Jul-Sep.

☞ **Duty free shopping at the International Airport, and Colon Free Zone, and Folklore nights at local hotels featuring Panamanian Cuisine are favorite pastimes here. Fishing, both lake and ocean, the canal itself and historic sites are also popular.**

Medical 284-3014   **Police 283-5611/12**

Portugal

Lajes Field, Azores (PO01R7)
APO AE 09720-5000

TELEPHONE NUMBER INFORMATION: Main installation numbers: C-(USA) 011-351-95-52101, EX-5178/6176, (PO) 95-52101, D-314-723-1410 (CONUS direct). Contact: 65th SVS/SVH, APO AE 09720.

Location: On Terceira Island (Azores PO) 20 miles long & 12 miles wide. Lajes Field is 2 miles west of Praia da Vitoria, PO, on Mason Hwy. NMC: Lisbon, 850 miles east.

Billeting Office: Mid-Atlantic Lodge, building T-166, C-(USA) **011-351-95-5178/7283,** (PO)95-5178/7283, 24 hours daily for check in at facility, check out 1200 hours. Government civilian employee billeting.

TML: TLF. Building T-306, all ranks, leave or official duty. Handicapped accessible. Bedroom apartments, living room, private bath (30). Kitchenette, color TV, cribs/cots, washer/dryer. Modern structure. Rate: $20-$32 per room. Maximum 5 per room. Active duty PCS out with family can make reservations, others Space-A. VOQ, VAQ: $8 per night, reservations TDY, PCS only, others Space-A. **Kennel available on base for a small fee.**

DV/VIP: Contact billeting office, 06+. Retirees and lower ranks Space-A, $14 per night.

TML Availability: Best, Nov-Apr. Difficult, May-Oct.

☞ **Each island is unique, visit them all, if you can. Attend a formal bullfight, or a street bullfight (the bull is not killed here!), or listen to one of many village bands perform during a colorful religious holiday procession.**

Locator 6130/4237   **Medical 232617**   **Police 23222**

Spain

Moron Air Base (SP01R7)
APO AE 09643-5000

TELEPHONE NUMBER INFORMATION: Main installation numbers: C-(USA) 011-34-55-848111, (SP) 95-58-48111, D-314-722-1110, FAX-011-34-54840123.

Location: Sevilla, Spain to Alcala, Spain on N-334, pass Alcala to SE-333. At intersection of SE-342 and B-333 proceed on SE-342 to Moron AB. Base well marked. NMC: Sevilla, 40 miles northwest.

Billeting Office: Hotel Frontera. ATTN: 7120 ABF/SVH, building P-303, 1st St, C-(USA) **011-34-55-848089,** (SP) 95-55-848089, 24 hours daily. Check in facility, check out 1200 hours daily. Government civilian employee billeting. **ATTENTION: AD not assigned in Spain, retired personnel, widow(ers), government civilian**

SPAIN
Moron Air Base, continued

employees not assigned in Spain, dependents of all groups, are not permitted to purchase any articles free of Spanish taxes on any military installation, i.e. Foodland. Military ID card holder visitors to Spain are permitted to make purchases in open messes, Stars & Stripes, and billeting. Also, personnel arriving by military air at Torrejon AB and Rota NAS are advised to contact security or passenger service for immigration clearance. This notice applies to other Spanish listings.

TML: VOQ/VAQ/DV/VIP. Hotel Frontera, building P-303, all ranks, leave or official duty. Separate bedroom, shared bath (55). Some DV suites, private bath. Refrigerator, community kitchen, A/C, color TV lounge, maid service, washer/dryer. Modern structure. Rates: $9 per person VOQ, $8 per person VAQ, $14 DV/VIP. Maximum 2 plus one crib per unit. Duty can make reservations, others Space-A.

DV/VIP: Billeting, C-and D-EX-2798. Determined by Commander, retirees Space-A.

TML Availability: Good Nov-Mar, fairly good Apr-Oct (difficult in '92 due to World's Fair). **Note:** All numbers are C- or D- extensions.

☞ Soak up the light and landscape of Sevilla along the Guadalquivir (Great River), and then visit the Cathedral (third largest in the world) and the Giralda Tower. Don't miss the gardens of the Alcázar and the many others in the city.

Locator 1110   **Medical 8069**   **Police 8132**

Rota Naval Air Station (SP02R7)
Box 2, FPO AE 09645-5000

TELEPHONE NUMBER INFORMATION: Main installation numbers: C-(USA) 011-34-56-862-780, (From Spain but outside the province of Cadiz dial 956-862-780), D-314-727-0111.

Location: On Spain's South Atlantic Coast. Accessible from E-25 South and SP-342 West. HE: p-61, C-5. NMC: Cadiz, 22 miles south.

Billeting Office: Building 1610, Flor St, C-(USA) **011-34-56-862-780**, (SP) 821-750, (outside province of Cadiz) 956-86-2780, 0830-1700 hours daily. Check in 24 hours daily at facility, check out 1200. Government civilian employee billeting.

TML: Navy Lodge. Naval Station, Box 17, building 1674, all ranks, leave or official duty. C-(USA) **011-34-56-862-780, EX-2037**, (SP)956-862-780 EX-2037. Bedroom, private bath (22). Kitchen, utensils, A/C, color TV in room & lounge, maid service, cribs/cots, coin washer/dryer. Modern structure. Rates: $42 per unit. Maximum 5 persons. All categories can make reservations.

TML: BOQ. Building 39, officers all ranks, leave or official duty, C-EX-1750/53. Bedroom, shared bath (168); separate bedroom, private bath (43); suites, (VIP) (21). Refrigerator, A/C, color TV in lounge, maid service, cribs, washer/dryer, 2 rec rooms, conference room. Modern structure. Rates: $8 per person, $18 per person (DV/VIP). Duty can make reservations, others Space-A.

SPAIN

Rota Naval Air Station, continued

TML: BEQ. Buildings 36-39, enlisted all ranks, leave or official duty, C-EX-2460/2680. Bedroom, common bath (298); bedroom, hall bath (E7+) (54). Refrigerator (22/1-bedroom only), color TV in lounge, maid service, washer/dryer. Modern structure, remodeled. Rates: $4 per person, maximum 1-4 persons per unit. Duty can make reservations, others Space-A.

DV/VIP: Protocol Office. Building 1, 2nd floor, C-EX-2744. 06+. Retirees Space-A.

TML Availability: Good, winter months. Difficult, Jun-Sep.

☞ **Gate security is tight. Commissary and NEX unavailable to retirees. Inquire at Navy Family Services about tours of Cadiz, a shopper's delight. Inquire at Osborne and Terry Bodegas for a tour of sherry facilities.**

Medical 2225   Police 2000

☺A new 26 room Navy Lodge is being planned for early '94. Keep posted on developments with Military Living's R&R Space-A Report.

Ankara Air Station (TU01R9)
APO AE 09822-5000

TELEPHONE NUMBER INFORMATION: Main installation numbers: C-(USA) 011-90-4-125-9943, (TU) 4-125-9943, D-314-672-5000.

Location: From Esenboga Airport take bus or taxi to Balgat. NMC: Ankara, in the city.

Billeting Office: ATTN: 7217th ABG/SVH. Building 135, Karyagdi Sokak 13, Cankaya, Ankara. C-(USA) **011-90-4-138-9453**, (TU) 4-138-9453, D-314-672-3128/3183, 24 hours daily. Check in billeting, check out 1300 hours daily.

TML: VOQ, VAQ, building 135, all ranks, leave or official duty. VOQ: bed spaces in 4 apts, shared bath, downtown Ankara (7). Kitchen, utensils, color TV, maid service, washer/dryer. VAQ: bed spaces in three bedroom apts, shared bath, in downtown Ankara (45 spaces 11 units). Kitchen (7 units, microwave in others), refrigerator, utensils, color TV, maid service, washer/dryer. Modern structure. Rates: $8-$14 per person. Duty can make reservations, others Space-A. No pets. There is a 20-unit TLF facility and Airmen's BEQ on Ankara AS. $32 per unit for TLF.

DV/VIP: Hq TUSLOG, Building 2001, C-EX-3198, E9/06+. Retirees and lower ranks Space-A.

TML Availability: Good, Oct-May. Difficult, other times.

TURKEY
Ankara Air Station, continued

☞ This is a modern and medieval city. Tour the Citadel, and see the spectacular view of the Anatolian countryside. Check with MWR for touring opportunities to such sites as Ani, on the Russian border.

Locator 4116   Medical PTT-125-2329   Police 2241

Incirlik Air Base (TU03R9)
APO AE 09824-5000

TELEPHONE NUMBER INFORMATION: Main installation numbers: C-(USA) 011-90-71-119062/111285, (TU) 71-119062/111285, D-314-676-1110.

Location: From Adana, east on E-5 for 3 miles, left at sign for Incirlik. Base is clearly marked. NMC: Adana, 3 miles west.

Billeting Office: ATTN: 39 CSS/SVH, building 952, 6th St, 24 hours daily. Check in facility, check out 1100-1200 hours daily. C-(USA) **011-90-71-116709/86**, (TU) 71-116709/86, FAX-011-90-71-6766709. Government civilian employee billeting.

TML: TLF. Building 1066, **Hodja.** All ranks, leave or official duty. Separate bedroom, living room, dining room, private bath (49). Kitchen, complete utensils, microwave, A/C, color TV in room & lounge, maid service, cribs/cots, washer/dryer, ice vending, facilities for DAVs, irons, clock-radios. Modern structure. Rates: $32 per unit; $50 double. TDY/PCS can make reservations, others Space-A.

TML: VOQ. Buildings 934/36/38/40/52, 1010/12, officers, all ranks. Leave or official duty. Bedroom, shared bath (24); bedroom, private bath (64); bedroom, 2 beds, private bath (may be reserved for air crews) (12). Refrigerator, A/C, color TV in room & lounge, maid service, washer/dryer. Older structure, renovated. Rates: $14 per person. Duty can make reservations, others Space-A.

TML: VAQ. Buildings 1004/42/44/46/48/50/52, 902/04/06/08/18/20, enlisted, all ranks, leave or official duty. Bedroom, 2 beds, private bath (may be reserved for air crews) (36); bedroom, 2/3 beds, common bath (E1-E6)(no females or children due to common bath) (156); separate bedroom suites, private bath (E7-E9) (7 day limit) (2). Refrigerator, A/C, color TV, maid service, washer/dryer. Older structure, renovated. Rates: $8 per person. Duty can make reservations, others Space-A.

TML: DV/VIP. Building 1072, officer 06+, leave or official duty. Separate bedroom suites, private bath (6); bedroom, private bath, contract quarters for TDY, funded travel orders only (95). Kitchen, limited utensils, A/C, color TV, maid service, washer/dryer, ice vending, alcoholic beverages and soft drinks stocked in room on "Honor System." Older structure. Rates: $14 per person. Duty can make reservations, others Space-A.

DV/VIP: Protocol Office, 39 TACG/CCE, C-EX-6347, E9, 06/GS-15+. Retirees and lower ranks Space-A.

TML Availability: Good all year.

Incirlik Air Base, continued

☞ Historic sites near Adana include Misis (Roman), Yilanlikale (Castle of Snakes), Karatepe (Hittite) and Payas (16th Century and Alexander the Great). There's much more to see and do. A tour here is "no turkey"!

Locator 6289   Medical 6666   Police-3200

Izmir Air Station (TU04R9)
APO AE 09821-5000

TELEPHONE NUMBER INFORMATION: Main installation numbers: C-(USA) 011-90-51-215560, (TU) 51-215560, D-314-675-1110 EX-3379, FAX-011-90-51-215564

Location: In the center of Izmir on the central west coast of Turkey. HE: p-82, G/6. NMC: Izmir, in the city.

Billeting Office: Kordon Hotel. D-314-675-1110-EX-3490, 0730-1700 daily. Check in facility, check out 1200 hours daily. Government civilian employee billeting.

TML: TLQ. **Kordon Hotel,** all ranks, leave or official duty, handicapped accessible. Bedroom, private bath (82); two bedroom, private bath (6); DV suites, private bath (6). Refrigerator, A/C, color TV in room & lounge, maid service, cribs/cots, washer/dryer, ice vending. Part modern and part older, renovated structure. Rates: $28-$44 per room. Maximum 3 per unit. Duty can make reservations. TDY/PCS have priority, others Space-A.

DV/VIP: Protocol Office, 7241 ABG/CCE, facility #48, room 603. D-314-675-1110-EX-3341, 06+/E9. Retirees and lower ranks Space-A.

TML Availability: Good, except May-Oct.

☞ Visit the tours desk, MWR for one day, overnight and multi-day excursions to Ephesus, Pergamon, Pamukkale, Aphrodisias, Istanbul, and the Greek Islands. East and west meet here, don't miss the fascinating consequences!

Medical 3357   Police 3222

Sinop Army Field Station (TU02R9)
APO AE 09820-5000

TELEPHONE NUMBER INFORMATION: Main installation numbers: C-(USA) 011-90-3761-5431/5432, (TU) 3761-5431/5432, D-314-672-1110 Ask for Sinop.

Location: Take the coastal highway west from Samsun until you reach Sinop. There are no major highways that connect Sinop to the rest of Turkey. There is daily bus service to Samsun (3 hour trip), and Istanbul (12 hour trip). There is a community airport in Samsun. NMC: Samsun 100 miles east.

TURKEY
Sinop Army Field Station, continued

Billeting Office: Building S-512, **Barbaros Cadisi,** 0730-1630 hours M-F, C-(USA) 011-90-3761-5431, **EX-213,** (TU) 3761-5431 EX-213, other hours, DEH C-EX-345, or SDO/MP C-EX-222/256. Check in facility, check out 1200 hours daily. Government civilian employee billeting.

TML: Hotel Melia Kasim, Hotel 117-Sinop, Karakum Hotel. All ranks, leave or official duty. Bedroom, private bath (120). Color TV, maid service, washer/dryer. Modern structure. Rates: $35 per room. Maximum 2 per room. All categories can make reservations, others Space-A. Note: limited DVQ facilities. Call for information.

DV/VIP: PAO, ATTN: IAEN-DPCA, C-EX-209/334, 06/GS-16+. Retirees and lower ranks Space-A.

TML Availability: Fairly good. Best, Sep-May. Access to the installation requires prior approval of commander.

Locator-0   **Medical 331**   **Police 222**

⊗**This facility did not respond to our inquiries, some data may be outdated.**

United Kingdom

RAF Alconbury (UK01R7)
APO AE 09470-5000

TELEPHONE NUMBER INFORMATION: Main installation numbers: C-(USA) 011-44-480-82-3000, (UK) 0480-82-3000, D-314-223-3000.

Location: From London, take A-1 North to A-604, exit marked RAF Alconbury, follow signs. Approximately 65 miles north of London. HE: p-13, D/3. NMC: Huntingdon, 4 miles east.

Billeting Office: ATTN: 10th SVS/SVH, building 639, Texas St, C-(USA) 011-44-480-6000, (UK) 0480-82-6000, FAX-011-44-480-454127, 24 hours daily. Check in facility, check out 1000 hours daily. Government civilian employee billeting.

TML: VOQ. Buildings 639, 640, officers all ranks, leave or official duty. Bedroom, 2 beds, shared bath (40); suites, private bath (DV/VIP) (6). Refrigerator, color TV in room & lounge, maid service, cribs/cots, washer/dryer, telephone, facilities for DAVs. Modern structure. Rates: room $8 per person, suite $14 per person. Maximum 2 per suite. Duty can make reservations, others Space-A.

TML: VAQ. Building 652, 692, enlisted all ranks. Two bedroom, shared bath (38); bedroom suites, shared bath (4); separate bedroom suites, private bath (3). Building 692: two bedrooms, central bathroom (46). Refrigerator, color TV, maid service, washer/dryer. Modern structure. Rates: $8 per person rooms; $10-$14 per person suites. Duty can make reservations, others Space-A.

TML: All ranks TLF also available. Suites, private bath (20). Rates: $28 per unit.

RAF Alconbury, continued

DV/VIP: Hq 10th TRW, C-EX-2111/2112, 06+. Retirees and lower ranks Space-A.

TML Availability: Good, Aug-Mar. Difficult, other times.

☞ East Anglia, Essex, Suffolk and Norfolk is full of historical sights. Start with the village of Little Stukeley (interesting church with carvings), and pass on to Huntingdon, where Romans first settled, and there's a bridge dating from 1332.

Locator 2565   **Medical 116**   **Police 114**

RAF Bentwaters/Woodbridge (UK12R7)
APO AE 09497-5000

TELEPHONE NUMBER INFORMATION: Main installation numbers: C-(USA) 011-44-394-43-3000, (UK) 0394-43-3000, D-314-223-3000.

Location: Take A-12 from Ipswich to exit signs east on B1069 to Melton, for twin bases of RAF Bentwaters/Woodbridge. HE: p-13, F/1. NMC: Ipswich, 15 miles southeast.

Billeting Office: ATTN: 81 SVS/SVH, building 629, behind the NCO Club, C-(USA) 011-44-394-1844/2281, (UK) 0394-43-1844/2281, 24 hours daily. Check in facility, check out 1200 hours daily. Government civilian employee billeting.

TML: TLF. Buildings 166-168, 174,175 all ranks, leave or official duty. Separate bedrooms, private bath (40). Kitchen, complete utensils, color TV, maid service, cribs/cots, washer/dryer, ice vending. Modern structure. Rates: $25 per unit, maximum 5 per unit. Duty can make reservations, others Space-A.

TML: VAQ. Building 759, enlisted all ranks, leave or official duty. Bedroom, semi private bath (60). Modern structure. Rates: $7.50 per person, maximum $15 per room. Duty can make reservations, others Space-A.

TML: BOQ. Building 629, officers, all ranks, leave or official duty. Bedroom, semi-private bath (4 with private bath) (23). Refrigerator, CATV in room and lounge, maid service, cribs, washer/dryer. Older structure, renovated. Rates $8.50 per person, maximum $17 per room. Duty can make reservations, others Space-A.

DV/VIP: PAO, 81st TFW/CCP, C-EX-2101/02/05, 06+. Retirees and lower ranks Space-A.

TML Availability: Seasonal. Fairly good over-all, best Dec-Mar.

☞ In Woodbridge visit Shire Hall, built in 1570, and the Kings' Head Inn, and the Bell and Steelyard, two interesting pubs. The history of East Anglia's changing coast can be seen at the Dunwich Museum.

Locator 1841   **Medical 2574**   **Police 2204**

⊗Billeting at this facility is scheduled to close Jun '93, and the base in Sep as of press time. Keep updated with Military Living' *R&R Space-A Report* for more recent information.

UNITED KINGDOM

Brawdy Wales Naval Facility (UK02R7)
FPO AE 09420-5000

TELEPHONE NUMBER INFORMATION: Main installation numbers: C-(USA) 011-44-437-760654, (From UK Haverfordwest) 437-5452, D-314-391-4356.

Location: From London, take M-4 to Swansea, A-40 to Haverfordwest, A-487 to Brawdy. HE: p-12, C/2. NMC: Haverfordwest, Wales, UK 10 miles south.

Billeting Office: Naval Facility, C-(USA) **011-44-437-5452/4356/4236**, (UK) 0437-5452/4356/4236, 0800-1600 hours daily. Check in facility, check out as arranged. No government civilian employee billeting.

TML: RAF Berthing Facilities. All ranks, leave or official duty. Arrange by telephone C-EX-5452 with Naval Facility Brawdy. Rooms in the Officers' or Enlisted Mess. Color TV lounge, washer/dryer. Older structure. Rates: moderate. All categories can make reservations. Following support facilities are available: Exchange, Package Store, Commissary, Gas Station, Clubs/Messes.

TML Availability: Depends on berthing requirements at the time.

RAF Chicksands (UK04R7)
APO AE 09193-5000

TELEPHONE NUMBER INFORMATION: Main installation numbers: C-(USA) 011-44-462-812571-EX-400, (From UK Hitchin 0462-812571), D-314-234-1110.

Location: From London, take M-1 North to Luton, A-6 North to A-507 or A-600 to Shefford. Both A-507 and A-600 pass one of the Chicksands RAF gates. HE: p-13, D/1. NMC: Bedford, 10 miles northwest.

Billeting Office: Building 403, Wellington Dr, C-(USA) **011-44-462-816868**, (UK) 0462-816868, D-314-234-2400, 24 hours daily. Check in facility, check out 1100 hours daily. No government civilian employee billeting.

TML: VAQ. Building 403/4, enlisted E1-E6, leave or official duty. Bedroom, common bath (67); separate bedroom, private bath (6). Refrigerator, color TV in room & lounge, maid service, cribs/cots, washer/dryer, ice vending. Older structure. Rates: $8 per person. Maximum $16 per family. Duty can make reservations, others Space-A.

TML Availability: Good, winter. Difficult, summer.

Locator 2382   **Medical 2387**   **Police 2213**

⊗**This facility did not respond to our inquiries, some data may be outdated.**

UNITED KINGDOM

Edzell Naval Security Group Activity
(UK06R7)
FPO AE 09419-5000

TELEPHONE NUMBER INFORMATION: Main installation numbers: C-(USA) 011-44-356-4431, (From UK Edzell 03564-431), D-314-229-1110.

Location: From Aberdeen take A-92 to A-94 South, follow Perth/Dundee signs. Last town before Edzell is Lawrencekirk, look for RAF Edzell signs to base. HE: p-6, G/6. NMC: Aberdeen, 40 miles north.

Billeting Office: Campbell Hall, C-(USA) **011-44-356-2218,** (UK) 03562-218, 24 hours daily. Check in facility, check out 1000 hours daily. No government civilian employee billeting.

TML: Navy Lodge. All ranks, leave or official duty, C-(USA) **011-44-356-2269,** (UK) 03562-269, 1000-1700 M-F, 1000-1330 Sa. Two bedroom mobile homes, private bath (8). Kitchen, complete utensils, color TV, maid service, cribs, coin washer/dryer, snack machine. Older structure. Rates: $34 per unit, sleeps 4-6 persons. Duty can make reservations, PCS priority, others Space-A.

TML: BOQ. Officers' Open Mess. Officers all ranks, leave or official duty, C-(USA) **011-44-356-2218,** (UK) 03562-2218, D-314-229-4218. Separate bedroom, private bath (3). Kitchen, limited utensils, maid service, washer/dryer. Modern structure. Rates: Moderate. Maximum 2-3 persons per unit. Duty can make reservations, others Space-A.

TML: BEQ. Building 333, enlisted all ranks, leave or official duty. Extensions same as BOQ. One to four person rooms with shower/bathroom (4). Refrigerator, color TV lounge, maid service, washer/dryer. Modern structure. Rates: Moderate. Duty can make reservations, others Space-A.

DV/VIP: PAO, Building 22, C-(USA) 010-03564-431, Ext. 2237, D-314-229-43337, 07+.

TML Availability: Good, Nov-Feb. Difficult, other times. **Note: All numbers are C- or D- extensions.**

☞ **Edzell has become a resort, with golf course, tennis and bowling green. Beautiful walks in every direction, and castle ruins are nearby. Aberdeen and Dundee, both large cities, are within an hour's drive.**

Locator 2351   **Medical 2264/5**   **Police 2880/2882**

☺**This location has begun construction on a new Navy Lodge scheduled for opening in Feb '93. Keep updated by reading Military Living's** *R&R Space-A Report.*

RAF Greenham Common/Welford (UK05R7)
APO AE 09462-5000

TELEPHONE NUMBER INFORMATION: Main installation numbers: C-011-44-635-51-2000, (UK) 0635-51-2000, D-314-266-1110.

UNITED KINGDOM
RAF Greenham Common/Welford, continued

Location: Take M-4 from Heathrow Airport, exit 13, Newbury, A-34 South for 1 mile to Newbury and GC/W RAF. HE: p-13, BC/3. NMC: Newbury, Berks, 4 miles north.

Billeting Office: Building 228, C-(USA) **011-44-635-51-2761**, (UK) 0635-51-2761, 24 hours daily. Check in facility, check out 1200 hours daily. Government civilian employee billeting in VOQ.

TML: TLF. Building 221. All ranks, leave or official duty. Two bedroom cottage, private bath (1). Kitchen, complete utensils, color TV, maid service, washer/dryer. Older structure, renovated. Rates: $24 per night. Duty and retired can make reservations, others Space-A.

TML: VAQ. Building 148, enlisted all ranks, leave or official duty. Bedroom, common bath (10); separate bedroom, private bath (2). Refrigerator, TV, washer/dryer. Rates: $7.50 per person. Maximum $22.50. Maximum 3 persons double, 1 single. Duty can make reservations, others Space-A.

TML: Greenham Lodge. Building 228, officers all ranks, leave or official duty. Two bedroom, private bath (15); separate bedroom suites, private bath (5). Kitchen (3 units), refrigerator, community kitchen, TV, maid service, washer/dryer, ice vending. Older structure. Rates: $12 per person. Maximum $24 per family, maximum 6 per unit. Duty can make reservations, others Space-A.

DV/VIP: Protocol Office, C-EX-2500, 06+. Retirees Space-A. **Note: All numbers are C- or D-extensions.**

TML Availability: Limited. Best, Dec.

☞ **Newbury, Reading and Oxford are within a 35 mile radius. Visit Hiclere Castle, Stonehenge, Bath, and Littlecote Manor "the Land that's Trapped in Time". Fifteen miles west lies Portsmouth Naval Harbor.**

Locator 2222   **Medical 2116**   **Police 2200**

⊗**Some facilities will begin to close in Sep '92.**

RAF Lakenheath (UK07R7)
APO AE 09464-5000

TELEPHONE NUMBER INFORMATION: Main installation numbers: C-(USA) 011-44-638-52-1110, (UK) 0638-52-1110, D-314-226-1110.

Location: From London, go north on the M-11 to the 45 east, to the A-11 to A-1065. HE: p-13, E/1. NMC: Cambridge, 30 miles south.

Billeting Office: Liberty Lodge, building 956, C-(USA) **011-44-638-52-1844/2172,** (UK) 0638-52-1844/2177, FAX-011-44-638-532606, 24 hours daily. Check in facility, check out 1000 hours daily. Government civilian employee billeting.

TML: TLF. Various buildings, all ranks, leave or official duty. Bedrooms, private bath (31). Kitchen, complete utensils, color TV, maid service, cribs/cots, washer/dryer. Modern structure. Rates: $24 per unit. Duty can make reservations, others Space-A.

RAF Lakenheath, continued

TML: VAQ. Building 980, all ranks. Shared bedroom (E1-E6), shared bath (32); SNCO bedrooms (E7-E8) with kitchen (2). Shared kitchen, color TV, maid service, washer/dryer. Older structure. Rates: $8 per person shared rooms, $10 per person SNCO rooms. Maximum 2 persons. Duty can make reservations, others Space-A.

TML: VOQ. Building 978, all ranks, leave or official duty. Separate bedrooms, private bath (28). Shared kitchen, maid service, color TV, washer/dryer. Rates: $8 per person. Maximum $16 per unit. Maximum 2 per unit. Duty can make reservations, others Space-A.

TML: DV/VIP. Various buildings, officers 06+, enlisted E9, leave or official duty. C-0638-52-3500, D-314-226-3500. Separate bedroom, private bath (8); suites (DV 06+). Kitchenette, cribs, color TV, maid service, washer/dryer. Older structure. Rates: $14 per person. Maximum $28 per suite. Duty can make reservations, others Space-A.

DV/VIP: 48 TFW/CCP, building 1156. C-EX-3500, 06+ & E9. Retirees and lower ranks Space-A. **Note: all numbers are C- or D- extensions.**

TML Availability: Limited.

☞ **Don't miss seeing Cambridge College, which attracts thousands of tourists each year. Visit the ITT Travel office for information on the many attractions of London. Lakenheath is the largest US Air Force operated facility in England.**

Locator 1841   **Medical 2226**   **Police 3631**

London Service Clubs (UK13R7)

Union Jack Club
Sandell Street, Waterloo
London, SE1 8UJ, United Kingdom

TELEPHONE NUMBER INFORMATION: C-(USA) 011-44-71-928-6401, (UK) 071-928-6401, D-None.

Location: Opposite Waterloo Station (train), central London. HE: p-13, D/3. NMC: London, in the city.

Billeting Office: Address as above. Advance booking office C-(USA) **011-44-71-928-4814,** (UK) 071-928-4814, FAX-011-(0)71-620-0565, the club embodies the original Women's Services and Families Club. Allied Forces are welcomed and granted Temporary Honorary Membership, 24 hours. Check in 1300 hours, check out 1000 hours daily.

TML: Club/Hotel. All ranks, leave only. Reservations accepted above number. All charges include VAT. Check accepted when supported by cheque card. Meals paid for when taken, 10% discount for 7 days booking or more, deposit of one night when booking, refundable if canceled 48 hours in advance of arrival.

UNITED KINGDOM
London Service Clubs, continued

Other: Rooms, single (170); rooms, twin-bed (63). Wash basins, H/C water, with baths, showers, and bath (WC) centrally located on each floor; rooms, private shower, WC (75); twin-bed rooms, private bath (23); family suites, twin beds, double bunk-bed, private bath and WC (10). Bring own soap and towels. Bar, color TV, launderette, reading and writing rooms, conference and banqueting areas. Rates: Call above number. Excellent public transportation service, limited car parking facilities. Club will provide rates and other info upon request. An Officers' Annex recently opened consists of a bar/anteroom, a dining room, and bedroom accommodations for individuals and families. All serving and retired officers are eligible.

Note: this is a private club and is not government/military billeting.

TML Availability: Good, but book early.

☞ Ten minutes walk will take you to the West End and theaterland. With buses and underground trains right on the doorstep, all of London is easily accessible. Don't miss a trip to Harrod's for shopping, Kensington Gardens for a stroll, and all the history of London!

Victory Services Club
63/79 Seymour Street, London W2 2HF

TELEPHONE NUMBER INFORMATION: C-(USA) **011-44-71-723-4474**, (UK) 071-723-4474, D-none, FAX-011-(0)71-724-1134.

Location: Two blocks from the Marble Arch station, easy walking distance to the American Embassy, Navy Annex, Mayfair and Oxford Streets. HE: p-13, D/3. NMC: London, in the city.

Billeting Office: Address as above, reservations as above. This is a members only club. The following are eligible to join. A) serving and ex-service personnel of all ranks of the Armed Forces of the Crown, including those of the Commonwealth and members of NATO Forces stationed in the UK; B) spouses of members of the club; C) widows and widowers of ex-service personnel. The membership year is from 1 April and 31 March. Membership Fees: £7.50 annually, £150.00 pounds lifetime. Write to the club for an application and further details.

TML: Club/hotel. All ranks. Bedroom accommodations for 30 members with 75 double bedrooms for married members. Checks accepted when supported by a cheque card. Club facilities include a modern restaurant/grill room, bars, lounges, ballroom, game room, television rooms and library. Rates: twin rooms £39; single rooms £19.50. No rooms with private shower/bath. All categories can make reservations.

TML Availability: Good, but book early.

☞ Founded in 1907, the present magnificent site was opened in 1948. In WWII it was the site of the American Red Cross Columbia Club - the largest in Great

London Service Clubs, continued

Britain. The Club is a two minute walk from Marble Arch in the busy West End. Speakers Corner is just across the street. London's main rail terminal are all close by.

Note: other non-government TML in England is available at the **Portsmouth Royal Sailors Home Club**, Queen Street, Portsmouth, PO1, 3HS, telephone 0705-824231; and the **Royal Fleet Club**, 9-12 Morice Square, Davenport, Plymouth PL1 4PQ, telephone 0752-52723.

RAF Mildenhall (UK08R7)
APO AE 09459-5000

TELEPHONE NUMBER INFORMATION: Main installation numbers: C-(USA) 011-44-638-51-2655/2407/2203/1844, (UK) 0638-51-2655/2407/2203/1844, D-314-238-2407/2203/2989/1844.

Location: From London or Cambridge follow A-11(M) to Newmarket and Barton Mills. Take A-1101 for 2.5 miles through Mildenhall Town to Beck Row Village and the AB. HE: p-13, E/1. NMC: Cambridge, 30 miles southwest.

Billeting Office: 513 SVS/SVH, Billeting Manager, building 459, C-(USA) **011-44-638-51-3044**, (UK) 0638-51-3044, D-314-238-3044, 24 hours daily. Check in facility, 1700 check out 1100 hours daily. Government civilian employee billeting.

TML: TLF. Building 104, all ranks. Two bedroom apartments, private bath (40). Kitchen, microwave, complete utensils, color TV, VCR, complimentary video rental, maid service, cribs, washer/dryer. Modern structure. Rates: $24 per unit. Maximum 4 per room. Duty can make reservations, others Space-A.

TML: VAQ. 100 and 400 area, enlisted all ranks, leave or official duty. Shared rooms with open bay restrooms. Rates: $8 per person. Duty can make reservations, other Space-A.

TML: VOQ. 200 and 400 area. Officers all ranks, leave or official duty. Bedroom, shared bath (8). Color TV, maid service, washer/dryer. Rates: $7.50 per person. Duty can make reservations, others Space-A.

TML: DV/VIP. Officer 06+, leave or official duty. Bedroom suites, private bath (1). Rates: Moderate. Duty can make reservations, others Space-A.

DV/VIP: Protocol Office, 3rd AF, building 239. C-EX-2777, 07+. Retirees and lower ranks (06) Space-A.

TML Availability: Extremely limited. Best, Nov-Dec. **Note: All numbers C- or D-extensions.**

☞ Shopping and antique hunting is popular in the area. Discover the story of Mildenhall Treasure in the Mildenhall Museum on High Street. Most active Space-A airport in the UK. Daily Bus to Lakenheath RAF and AMC Terminal.

Locator 2669   Medical 2657   Police 2667

UNITED KINGDOM

RAF Upper Heyford/Croughton (UK09R7)
APO AE 09466-5000

TELEPHONE NUMBER INFORMATION: Main installation numbers: C-(USA) 011-44-869-23-4975, (UK) 0869-23-4975, D-314-263-1110.

Location: From London take M-40 to Oxford, then either A-423 (Oxford-Banbury) or A-43 (Oxford-Northamton), signs to base. HE: p-13, C/2. NMC: Oxford, 12 miles south.

Billeting Office: ATTN: 20th SVS/SVH, building 73, Castle St, back of O'Club, 24 hours daily. C-(USA) 011-44-869-23-4905/4557, (UK) 0869-23-4905/4557, D-314-263-4905/4557. Check in facility, check out 1000 hours daily. Government civilian employee billeting.

TML: TLF. Building 41, all ranks, leave or official duty. Separate bedroom, private bath, kitchen, limited utensils, pull out twin, sofa (30). Refrigerator, color TV in room and lounge, maid service, cribs/cots, washer/dryer, ice machine. Modern structure. Rates: $24 per night. Maximum 5 persons. TDY/PCS/in can make reservations, others Space-A.

TML: VAQ. Building 78, enlisted all ranks. Bedroom, 2 single beds, private bath (E1-E6 share) (31); bedroom suites, private bath (E7+)(8). Refrigerator/microwave, no utensils (check out of Family Services), cribs/cots, washer/dryer, maid service. Modern structure. Rates: $8 per person rooms, maximum $16; suites $10 per person suites, maximum $20. Families can be placed here. TDY/PCS/in can make reservations, others Space-A.

TML: VOQ. Buildings 74, 77, all ranks, leave or official duty. Bedroom, private bath (building 77) (35); bedroom, shared bath (26). Kitchenette, no utensils (check out of Family Services), color TV in room and lounge, cribs/cots, washer/dryer. Rates: $8 per person per night, maximum $16. Families can be placed here. TDY/PCS/in can make reservations, others Space-A.

DV/VIP: Hq 10th TRW, C-EX-4848 (06+); C-EX-4135 (E7+). Retirees and lower ranks Space-A.

TML Availability: Good, Aug-Mar. Difficult, other times.

☞ **East Anglia, Essex, Suffolk and Norfolk is full of historical sights. See Blenheim Palace and the extensive Churchill collection, and don't miss Oxford and it's history, shopping and quaintness.**

Locator 4975/4433   **Medical 116**   **Police 4337**

⊗Upper Heyford is due to draw down by September '93, at press time it is unknown how this will affect billeting.

APPENDIX A

Country and State Abbreviations Used in this Book

COUNTRY

AN-Antigua
AU-Austraila
BE-Belgium
CN-Canada
CU-Cuba
GE-Germany
GR-Greece
GU-Guam*
HK-Hong Kong
IC-Iceland
IT-Italy
JA-Japan

MW-Midway*
NT-Netherlands
PN-Panama
PO-Portugal (Azores)
PR-Puerto Rico*
RP-Republic of Korea
TU-Turkey
UK-United Kingdom
US-United States

_____

*US Possession or Territory

STATE

AK-Alaska
AL-Alabama
AR-Arkansas
AZ-Arizona
CA-California
CO-Colorado
CT-Connecticut
DC-District of Columbia
DE-Delaware
FL-Florida
GA-Georgia
HI-Hawaii
IA-Iowa
ID-Idaho
IL-Illinois
IN-Indiana
KS-Kansas
KY-Kentucky
LA-Louisiana
MA-Massachusetts
MD-Maryland
ME-Maine
MI-Michigan
MN-Minnesota
MO-Missouri
MS-Mississippi

MT-Montana
NE-Nebraska
NC-North Carolina
ND-North Dakota
NH-New Hampshire
NJ-New Jersey
NM-New Mexico
NY New York
NV-Nevada
OH-Ohio
OK-Oklahoma
OR-Oregon
PA-Pennsylvania
RI-Rhode Island
SC-South Carolina
SD-South Dakota
TN-Tennessee
TX-Texas
UT-Utah
VA-Virgina
VT-Vermont
WA-Washington
WI-Wisconsin
WV-West Virginia
WY-Wyoming

APPENDIX B

General Abbreviations Used in this Book

This appendix contains general abbreviations used in this book. Commonly understood abbreviations and standard abbreviations found in addresses have not been included in order to save space.

A

AAF-Army Airfield
AAFES-Army/Air Force Exchange System
AB-Air Base
A/C-Air Conditioning
AD-Active Duty
AF-Air Force
AFB-Air Force Base
AFRC-Air Force Reserve Center
AFRC-Armed Forces Recreation Center
AAF-Air Force Auxilary Field
ACS-Army Community Services
AFRES-Air Force Reserve
AFS-Air Force Station
AMC-Army Medical Center
ANGB-Air National Guard Base
APG-Army Proving Ground
APO-Army Post Office
AS-Air Station

B

BAQ-Bachelor Airmens' Quarters
BEQ-Bachelor Enlisted Quarters
BOQ-Bachelor Officers' Quarters
BW-Black & White Television

C

CATV-color cable television
CG-Coast Guard
CGAS-Coast Guard Air Station
CMDR-Commander
CO-Commanding Officer
C-Commercial Telephone System
CPO-Chief Petty Officer
CSM-Command Sergeant Major
CQ-Charge of Quarters

D

D-Defense Switched Network
DAVs-Disabled American Veterans
DO-Duty Officer

DoD-Department of Defense
DV-Distinguished Visitor
DVQ-Distinguished Visitor Quarters
DVOQ-Distinguished Visitor Officer's Quarters
DGQ-Distinguished Guest Quarters

E

ETS-Estimated Time of Separation
ETS-European Telephone System
EX-Telephone Extension

F

FPO-Fleet Post Office
FTS-Federal Telephone System
FCFS-First Come, First Served

G

GH-Guest House

H

HE-Hallwag Europe (atlas)
Hq-Headquarters

I

IAP-International Airport
ITT-Information, Tickets & Tours
ITR-Information, Ticketing and Registration

K

Km-Kilometer

M

MC-Marine Corps
MCAS-Marine Corps Air Station
MCB-Marine Corps Base
MCBX-Marine Corps Exchange
MCRC-Marine Corps Recruiting Station
MWR-Morale, Welfare and Recreation

N
NAB-Naval Amphibious Base
NAF-Non-appropriated Funds
NAS-Naval Air Station
NB-Naval Base
NCO-Noncommissioned Officer
NG-National Guard
NMC-Nearest Major City
NMI-Nearest Military Installation
NS-Naval Station
NSB-Navy Submarine Base
NSO-Navy Security Office
NSWC-Naval Surface Weapon Center
NTC-Naval Training Center
NWC-Naval Weapons Center

O
O'Club-Officers' Club
OD-Officer of the Day
OIC-Officer in Charge

P
PAO-Public Affairs Officer
PCS-Permanent Change of Station
PERS-person
PMO-Provost Marshall's Office

R
RAF-Royal Air Force
Rec-Recreation

S
SDO-Staff Duty Officer
SDNCO-Senior Duty Non-Commissioned Officer
SEBQ-Sailors' Enlisted Bachelors Quarters
SNCO-Senior Non-Commissioned Officer
Space-A-space available

T
TAD-Temporary Attached Duty
TAQ-Temporary Airmens' Quarters
TDY-Temporary Duty
TFL-Temporary Family Lodging
TEQ-Temporary Enlisted Quarters
TLA-Temporary Lodging Allowance
TLF-Transient Lodging Facility
TLQ-Temporary Living Quarters
TML-Temporary Military Lodging
TOQ-Transient Officers' Quarters

TV-Television
TVEQ-Temporary Visiting Enlisted Quarters
TVOQ-Temporary Visiting Officers' Quarters
TQ-Temporary Quarters

U
US-United States
USA-United States Army
USAF-United States Air Force
USCG-United States Coast Guard
USEUCOM-U.S. European Command
USM-U.S. Military Installation Road Map
USMA-U.S. Military Academy
USMC-United States Marine Corps
USNCOQ-Unacommpanied Senior Non-Commissioned Officers' Quarters
USN-United States Navy

V
VAQ-Visiting Airmens' Quarters
VEQ-Visiting Enlisted Quarters
VIP-Very Important Person
VHA-Variable Housing Allowance
VOQ-Visiting Officer Quarters
VQ-Visiting Quarters, all ranks

W
WSMR-White Sands Missle Range

APPENDIX C

Temporary Military Lodging Questions and Answers

Answers below are based on information available to us at press time. Due to the fact that policies differ from installation to installation, these general answers must be accepted only as guides...not rules. Specific questions should be directed to each individual installation at the time of your visit. Policies often change.

1.) What types of lodging are available on military installations? There are numerous types of lodging. They range from very modern, modular-constructed, complete housekeeping units which will sleep a family of five with all the amenities found in a good motel (plus a furnished kitchenette) such as found in Navy Lodges, to the old faithful guest houses...relics of World War II, which are often barracks-type buildings. Some may have been improved while others are definitely sub-standard. Some are the modern hotel type such as the Hale Koa (Hawaii), the New Sanno (Japan) and Dragon Hill (Yongson, Korea). There is also the modern motel type lodging such as the Super 8's at Governor's Island, and another lodging chain at Fort Bliss. Somewhere in between, you will find the VOQ type accommodations that usually consist of private rooms with a shared bath between rooms. If you are the "picky" type, we suggest you take a look before signing in, if possible.

2.) Were the units mentioned above constructed with tax dollars? According to information given TML, the answer on most of the lodging is an emphatic "NO." The newer construction was built from non-appropriated funds or grants from welfare funds, generated from profits from Exchanges, etc. The exception to this is in cases where old unused family housing initially built with appropriated funds has been converted into temporary lodging faclities. Also, TML is frequently available in bachelor officers, NCO and enlisted grade quarters which have been constructed with appropriated funds.

3.) What does space-available (Space-A) mean?
The purpose of having lodging on military installations is to accommodate duty personnel and those arriving or departing an installation on permanent change of station (PCS) orders. Those on orders generally have first priority on all lodging. After these needs have been met, if there is any space left over, leave personnel may utilize the facilities on a Space-A basis. During the summer months, Space-A lodging may be more difficult to obtain than during the spring, fall, and winter.

4.) How about advance reservations? While many installations will accept reservations from those on duty, leave travelers will generally find that they cannot make reservations in advance but are accepted on a Space-A basis on arrival at the billeting office. Navy Lodges do accept reservations from all categories. As we are listing the lodging of five different services in this book, the rules may vary greatly from place to place. Please call in advance to check on specific policies on making reservations at the time of your trip. You may be surprised and find that the place you want to visit will accept your reservation.

5.) Can retirees use military lodging? Definitely...usually on the same Space-A basis as active duty on leave. Retirees will also find that they are welcome to use the lodging on many installations overseas, even though they may be restricted from using the commissary or exchange in most overseas areas due to the Status of Forces Agreement.

6.) Are Reservists eligible for TML? Many favorable changes have occurred for reservists as a result of the war in Southwest Asia. Reservists and accompanying dependents may now use Navy Lodges and most recreational lodging such as that listed in our book, **Military RV, Camping and Rec Areas Around the World**. This includes the popular Hale Koa Hotel in Hawaii. We have not seen any new information on the use of TML at other services' lodging facilities, however, for Space-A lodging. If we receive new information on the subject, we will include it in our all ranks travel newsletter, **Military Living's R&R Space-A Report.**
Other rules have changed. Reservists now have full time use of the Exchanges, and commissary use has been extended, so they may use commissary facilities 12 days during the year, rather than only during their active duty training. Reservists on active duty training and their families are eligible to use all lodging at that time. Readers of our publications who are in the Reserves have reported to us that they have occasionally been allowed to use TML. Since rules can differ from place to place, we recommend that you inquire at each location if interested.

7.) Your book often refers to Defense Switched Network (DSN, or D-) phone numbers. What are they? Defense Switched Network numbers are military phone numbers which are to be used only by those on **official business**. Such numbers can normally be dialed only from a military installation and are monitored to assure their use is not violated. As many of our readers use military lodging and facilities while traveling on duty, and many government offices use our book as a reference guide, we publish the Autovon numbers, when available, as a service to them.

8.) What is DV/VIP lodging? It is lodging for distinguished official visitors. Some installations will have a few rooms or a small guest house available for them. If these facilities are not being used by official visitors, many installations will often extend the courtesy of their use to qualified active duty personnel on leave status or retirees on a day-to-day Space-A basis. Most military installations we surveyed referred to DV/VIP as grades 06 and above. Just a few included lower officer grades and senior NCOs in this category. The Marine Corps calls their distinguished visitors lodging Distinguished Guest Quarters (DGQ's). Since 1977, we have noted that many more Air Force bases are providing DV/VIP lodging for their senior NCOs. Those in the DV/VIP category should check our listings in this book for more complete information and inquire at each installation upon arrival. Distinguished visitors will usually find that it is best to make advance reservations through the Protocol Office or Visitor's Bureau of the installation concerned. In some cases, the billeting office has authority to place personnel in the quarters and coordinates the visit for the traveler.

9.) My husband is enlisted. What chance do we have at staying in military lodging? Better than ever. In the past few years, concentrated efforts have been made to provide more temporary lodging for enlisted members. Please notice in our listing the numerous references to quarters for all ranks. In the newer Air Force Transient Living Quarters, Navy Lodges, and Army Guest Houses, rank has absolutely no privileges. All ranks are accommodated on an equal basis. Policies may vary on other types of lodging. At some places, enlisted have priority.

10.) May 100% DAVs use TML? Most military lodging units accept 100% DAVs (Disabled American Veterans) on a Space-A basis if it is possible. In fact, the Hale Koa R&R hotel specifically mentions 100% DAVs in their brochure as being eligible. One problem that 100% DAVs have encountered has been caused by the color of their ID card. It is the same color (buff or butterscotch) as carried by family members. Many times 100% DAVs are turned away from facilities which require family members to be accompanied by their sponsor. The "ID card-checking authority" assumes this military member is not a military member but a "dependent" or family member. Watch for more info on this subject in Military Living's R&R report.

11.) How about Navy - Bachelor Quarters (BQ)? We are told that a few Bachelor Enlisted Quarter (BEQ) locations have unsuitable facilities for family members - central baths (latrines), etc. However, most BEQs have suitable facilities. Also, Bachelor Officer Quarters (BOQs) are almost always suitable. They will generally accept family members accompanying their sponsor. Rules can vary from installation to installation. If a Navy Lodge is not available, always ask about the possible use of the BOQ.

12.) What about widows, widowers, and unaccompanied dependents? The news gets better each time we report in our new TML book. Dependents of active duty personnel who are involved in a PCS move may now use TML and may make reservations at the installation they are leaving and at the new one to which they are assigned. They may also use TML en route on a Space-A basis. This includes TML in TLFs and in VOQs or VAQs.

Unaccompanied dependents of military members on leave and also widows/ers of deceased members may use TML on a space-available basis in VAQs or VOQs if this policy has been approved by the base commander. (Therefore, this may NOT be in effect at all Air Force installations.) This does not include the use of TLFs.

Other services generally have always allowed unaccompanied military family members to use TML on a Space-A basis. This, of course, has and will continue to differ from installation to installation. Navy Lodges, however, welcome dependent children, and non-ID card holders when accompanied by a parent or guardian authorized to utilize Navy Lodges.

APPENDIX D

Billeting Regulations and Navy Lodge Information
Army Billeting Operations Regulations

The following has been extracted from Army Regulation 210-11, effective 15 July 1983.

Army regulation 210-11 prescribes policies, procedures, and instructions relating to the billeting function, which encompasses the management and operation of unaccompanied personnel housing (UPH) to include permanent party and temporary duty (TDY)) and guest house (GH) accommodations under the jurisdiction of the Department of the Army (DA).

Objectives. The objectives of the UPH and GH program are to provide: a.) Adequate housing for eligible military and DOD civilian personnel, permanently assigned or in a TDY status. b.) Short-term accommodations for military personnel and families (arriving or departing incident to permanent change of station (PCS)) and authorized visitors.

Transient Quarters Operations. Quarters will be identified by use as follows. a.) Visiting Officer Quarters (VOQ) and Visiting Enlisted quarters (VEQ). VOQ and VEQ support TDY military and civilian personnel to include distinguished visitors who normally use DVQ. b.) Guest Houses (GH). GHs provide short-term accommodations for accompanied and unaccompanied military personnel and eligible DOD civilians arriving or departing installations incident to PCS. Also included are active military personnel on leave, active or retired military personnel in military hospitals, and guests of service members. Retired military personnel and families may occupy GHs if space is available. The different services sometimes refer to these categories of housing in different terms. Refer to the above abreviations list for information on any terms you find mysterious.

Each category of transient quarters (e.g. VOQ, VEQ, DVQ, or GH) will be a separate operation. Twenty-four hour check-in and check-out service should be provided. When twenty-four hour service is not appropriate, another installation activity may assist visitors arriving during non-duty hours.

Services and Supplies. As a minimum, the following services will be provided. a.) In-room maid service. b.) Bathroom facilities with two towels and one washcloth per occupant daily, cloth bathmat, soap, and toilet paper. c.) One clean drinking glass or cup per occupant. d.) Minimum of one trash receptacle or one wastebasket per room. e.) Information on service charges, telephone service, post transportation, taxis, other local transportation, religious services, dining facilities, post exchange, post recreational activities, commercial laundry, washers and dryers, commissary, and emergency and medical facilities. f.) Vending machines to provide soft drinks, candy, cigarettes, and if washing machines are available, small packaged laundry soap. g.) When kitchen facilities are not available in GH, provisions for warming baby formula and bottles. h.) Alarm clock or radio or wakeup service.

Guest House Operations. GHs may be established as hotel- or motel-like furnished rooms, furnished apartments or houses, or other facilities. The use of GHs is a privilege afforded military personnel, with or without families, and eligible DOD civilians primarily to assist in moves incident to PCS. GHs will be voluntarily occupied except as otherwise prescribed, and occupants will pay a service charge established by the installation commander. The occupants will be advised of the rates and method of payment prior to occupancy.

Personnel having priority I status for occupancy of GHs are: active duty military of all grades (and eligible DOD civilians in foreign areas), accompanied or unaccompanied, departing or arriving incident to PCS; visiting relatives and guests of patients in military hospitals or military patients in local hospitals; active and retired military personnel and other personnel undergoing outpatient medical treatment who must stay overnight near a military medical facility. Note: installation commanders may establish priorities within priority I to meet special needs.

Personnel having priority II status for occupancy of GHs are: friends and relatives visiting service personnel stationed at the installation.

Unless prohibited by international agreement, the following personnel may occupy GHs on a space-available basis: military personnel in a leave, pass, or transient status; retired military personnel in a transient status; other personnel in a transient status who are entitled to dependency benefits.

Reservations. Only personnel in priority I may reserve GHs. Reservations will be on a first-come basis without regard to rank. Reservations should not be accepted more than 60 days in advance. Requests must include expected arrival time and date. Members on PCS will provide a copy of PCS orders or the special order number, date, and issuing headquarters with the reservation request.

Personnel visiting hospital patients must give the patient's name with the reservation request. Reservations are conditional pending confirmation of patient status.

Navy Lodges

Navy Lodge Mission. The Navy Lodge mission is to provide U.S. military personnel accompanied by dependents under Permanent Change of Station (PCS) orders with temporary lodging accommodation, and to provide lodging for all other authorized guests.

Accompanied PCS personnel may make reservations at any time in advance. Active duty personnel may make reservations up to 60 days in advance and all other personnel (retirees, DOD on orders, reservists, and DOD with exchange priviledges) may make their reservations up to 30 days in advance. Naval Hospital Lodge mission is to provide authorized guests with temporary accommodations with the following priorities.

Priority I: Members of the immediate family of in-patients who are seriously or critically ill and sponsors of children who are undergoing or convalescing from serious surgery.
Priority II: Members of the immediate family of all other in-patients.

Reservations: Reservations will be held only to 1800 (6:00 pm) hours unless guaranteed with a credit card or an advanced deposit. Check-in time is normally 1500 (3:00 pm), earlier arrivals will be accomodated if possible. Reserved accomodations have priority over guests who wish to extend the length of their stay. Navy Lodges accept MasterCard, Visa, Diners Club and Discover for payment and also guarantee a reservations if arrivals will be after 6:00 pm. Reservations can be made by dialing the toll-free reservation number **1-800-NAVY-INN** for CONUS lodges. Overseas reservations currently must be made by contacting the individual lodge. **OCONUS Navy Lodge numbers are in the individual listings, or you may call the toll free number for these overseas numbers.** Current plans call for overseas lodges to be included on the 1-800-NAVY-INN by 1993/1994 time frame. New locations for Navy Lodges in 1992 are at Sasebo, Japan (26 units), and Bangor (Silverdale) Washington (50 units).

New Jersey residents may dial 1-201-323-11-3 or DSN 624-1103. Note: *the New Jersey number is subject to change.* **The DSN number for reservations if dialing from overseas is 565-2027.**

With regard to Navy permament party housing operations, **Unaccompanied Officer Personnel Housing (UOPH) and Unaccompanied Enlisted Personnel Housing (UEPH) facilities have been re-designated as Bachelor Officer Quarters (BOQ) and Bachelor Enlisted Quarters (BEQ). BOQ and BEQ facilities both admit retirees and other transients on a space-available basis.** Lodging facilities exist at approximately 175 Naval installations around the world. While retirees and family members are authorized use of these facilities, specific rules vary around the world and are at the discretion of the local commander.

Marine Corps Billeting Operations Regulations

The following has been extracted from the Real Property Facilities Manual, Volume XI, Marine Corps Bachelor Housing Management dated 28 October 1985 and updated thru 10 November 1988.

Transient Quarters Operation. Transient quarters are operated primarily to provide a service to duty transient personnel and TAD students. Adequate quarters shall be set aside to accommodate TAD transient personnel. When designated transient quarters are fully occupied, transients may voluntarily occupy permanent party quarters.

The following personnel are entitled to designated TAD transient quarters on a confirmed reservation basis: a.) Military personnel and DOD civilians on TAD orders. b.) U.S. and foreign civilians traveling as guests of the Armed Forces. c.) Reserve personnel in TAD status, unit training status, and annual trainees on individual orders. d.) TAD foreign nationals or foreign military trainees engaged in or sponsored by military assistance or similar training programs unless prohibited by the Status of Forces Agreement (SOFA). e.) Family members on medical TAD orders. f.) Military personnel with or without family members, arriving or departing for overseas installations on PCS when TLF or permanent housing is not immediately available. g). Families of members overseas.

The following personnel may occupy designated transient quarters on a space-available basis: a.) Retirees, military personnel on leave, family members, or guests of military personnel assigned to the activity if TLF space is not available. b.) DOD civilian employees and their families arriving or departing incident to PCS when TLFs are not available. c.) Guests of the activity commander. Non-duty transients shall be advised at the time of registration that occupancy is strictly on a day-to-day, space-available basis and that they must vacate not later than the following day if the quarters are required for duty transients.

Distinguished Guest Quarters (DGQ's) are also available to accommodate the frequent travel of high ranking officials, both civilian and military. DGQ's are under the control of the installation commander.

Services and Supplies. As a minimum, transient quarters should provide the same facilities, services, and supplies which would ordinarily be provided a permanent BOQ/BEQ resident of the same grade. Transient units should be considered adequate only when meal facilities (commercial or government) are available during reasonable hours for three meals a day, within a reasonable walking distance or with transportation provided.

The following services and supplies are required in all units used for transient personnel: a.) Twenty-four hour check-in or check-out service, 24-hour wake-up service, or issue of an alarm clock. b.) Custodial service in all common-use areas. c.) Daily maid service. d.) Change of bed linens when guests depart, or once a week minimum for long-term guests. e.) At least one towel, bar of soap, and drinking glass per guest. f.) Lock and key for doors to all separate units, and inside and outside locks or latches on all bathroom facilities between rooms.

Coast Guard Temporary Guest Housing Facility Policies

The following has been extracted from Coast Guard Commandant Publication P1710.14 dated 18 January 1989.

Most large Coast Guard installations have developed guest housing in response to the need for temporary lodging for Coast Guard members and their families. These facilities are operated and managed by the Coast Guard Nonappropriated Fund Activity (NAFA). Since each installation manages its own GH, each has its own rules and regulations regarding usage.

Guest housing was developed mainly for use by active duty Coast Guard members and their families traveling under PCS orders; however, Coast Guard personnel in other than PCS status and members of the other uniformed services are allowed to use some Coast Guard guest housing facilities. It is always advisable to call the facility you intend to visit to determine your eligibility.

Air Force Billeting Operations Regulations

The following has been extracted from Air Force Regulation 90-9 dated 31 October 1984 and updated thru 27 March 1989.

Transient Quarters Operation. Transient Quarters are operated to provide a service to duty transient personnel and TDY students. The operation of transient quarters is based on the need of the services and the availability of quarters at an installation.

Personnel Eligible for Transient Quarters: The following personnel are eligible to occupy Visiting Officer Quarters (VOQ) and Visiting Enlisted Quarters (VEQ) commensurate with their grade on a space-confirmed basis. The order in which the following are listed does not indicate a priority: a.) TDY personnel, including crew members. b.) TDY U.S. civilian employees, and civilians traveling under competent authority. c.) Members of the Air National Guard and Air Force Reserve on annual tours, school tours, special tours of active duty, or active duty for training. d.) Members of the Air National Guard and Air Force Reserve on inactive duty training. e.) TDY or TDY student, foreign military, or civilian personnel sponsored through security assistance, allied exchange, or foreign liaison programs. f.) USAFA and AFROTC cadets traveling on official orders. g.) Aircraft passengers on official orders or emergency leave at aerial ports of embarkation, if aerial port quarters are not available. h.) Dependents on medical TDY orders. i.) Military and civilian personnel using military aircraft in TDY or PCS status who, for reasons beyond their control, remain overnight (RON) at locations other than their TDY or PCS location. j.) Contract engineering and technical services personnel (CETSP). k.) Guests of the armed forces as determined by the installation commander. l.) Applicants for an Air force commission. m.) Active duty personnel on emergency leave. n.) Unaccompanied personnel, including civilians, entitled to permanent quarters who are temporarily without permanent housing due to PCS travel orders. o.) Military and civilian personnel and their families arriving or departing an overseas location incident to PCS, if no other government temporary lodging is available. p.) Military and civilian personnel in a TDY status to nearby locations who desire government quarters in lieu of commerical quarters. q.) Personnel on permissive TDY orders.

The following personnel are eligible to occupy VOQ/VEQ on a space-available basis. Maximum stay is 30 days during any one visit. Extensions must be approved by the installation commander. The order in which the following are listed does not indicate a priority: a.) Dependents accompanying official TDY personnel. b.) Married military and civilian personnel with their families in CONUS who are temporarily without permanent housing due to PCS orders, only when TLFs (see below) are not available. c.) Unaccompanied personnel entitled to permanent quarters who arrive or depart incident to PCS and are temporarily without permanent housing. d.) Dependents of members who are patients in Air

Force hospitals, only if TLF not available. e.) Retirees and retirement eligible Reservists in a nonduty status (who have DD Form 2 AF Res with a copy of ARPC certificate of retirement eligibility) and their dependents. f.) Active duty members and their dependents on ordinary leave, environmental and morale leave (EML), or travel status. g.) U.S. civilians and their dependents on EML orders from overseas duty assignments, only if TLF is not available. h.) Active status and/or in training Air National Guard and Air Force Reserve members and their dependents. i.) Space-available passengers aboard military aircraft interrupted short of destination, or passengers arriving at ports for space-available travel on departing military flights. j.) AFROTC cadets, organizations, and youth groups when approved by the installation commander. k.) Civilian Air Patrol (CAP) members on official visits. Note: transient dependents of deceased military members and dependents unaccompanied by their active or retired military sponsor, or U.S. civilian sponsor in overseas areas, may occupy transient quarters when approved by the installation commander.

Temporary Lodging Facility Operations. Temporary Lodging Facilities (TLFs) are operated to provide temporary housing to authorized personnel at the lowest possible cost consistent with giving good service.

Eligibility For and Assignment to TLFs. Personnel listed below are eligible to occupy TLFs. Assignments are made without regard to rank and on a first-come-first-served basis. Following personnel have priority 1 status: a.) Active duty military members accompanied by their dependents or their dependents alone, incident to PCS, separation, or retirement. b.) Civilian and military friends and relatives of patients in Air Force hospitals. c.) Hospital outpatients. d.) Personnel who are accompanied by dependents and in permissive TDY, ordinary leave, or terminal leave status, and traveling for the purpose of house hunting in conjunction with PCS, retirement, or separation.

Following personnel have priority 2 status: a.) Military members and dependents on leave or delay en route. b.) Military and civilian personnel, whether or not accompanied by dependents, on TDY when VOQ or VAQ facilities are fully occupied. c.) Retired military members and dependents. d.) Unaccompanied married personnel and unmarried members being joined by or acquiring dependents. e.) Unaccompanied married personnel and unmarried members incident to PCS, if neither transient nor permanent party government quarters are available. f.) Civilians accompanied by their dependents incident to PCS, active status Air National Guard and Air Force Reserve not in a duty status and their dependents.

Following personnel have priority 3 status: a.) Friends and relatives of assigned military personnel. Note: Personnel in priorities 2 and 3 are accommodated on a space-available basis and are required to vacate quarters no later than the next day after quarters are required by personnel in priority 1.

Reservations. Only personnel in priority 1 may request advance reservations. Reservation request should include expected arrival time and date. Reservations will not be held beyond 1700 hours unless the billeting office is notified in advance of personal needs for a later arrival time. Normal check out time is 1200 hours.

Services and Supplies. Maid service is normally supplied on a daily basis, to include light dusting and vacuuming as required, clean towels and glasses, cleaning of bathroom, emptying of trash containers, and bedmaking with weekly changing of linen unless there is a change in occupant(s).

-NOTES-

APPENDIX E

Installations That Did Not Respond To Our Request for Information

The installations listed below may have temporary military lodging facilities. These installations, however, did not respond to our request for information, so we cannot positively confirm or deny the existence of TML facilities at the following locations.

UNITED STATES

Alaska
Galena Airport (AK20R5)

California
San Diego Naval Training Center (CA54R4)

Connecticut
Long Island Sound Coast Guard Group (CT04R1)

Hawaii
Pearl Harbor Naval Base (HI19R6)

Missouri
Whiteman Air Force Base (MO04R2)

New Mexico
Holloman Air Force Base (NM05R3)

North Dakota
Grand Forks Air Force Base (ND04R3)

Ohio
Rickenbacker Air National Guard Base (OH02R2)

South Dakota
Ellsworth Air Force Base (SD01R3)

Washington
Madigan Army Medical Center (WA15R4)
McChord Air Force Base (WA05R4)

FOREIGN COUNTRIES

*Guam
Agana Naval Air Station (GU03R8)

Cuba
Guantanamo Bay Naval Station (CU01R1)

Germany
Bremerhaven Community (GE32R7)
Gelnhausen Sub-Community (GE89R7)
Giessen Community (GE23R7)
Idar Oberstein Sub-Community (GE53R7)
Mainz Community (GE41R7)

Italy
Sigonella Naval Air Station (IT01R7)

United Kingdom
RAF Chicksands (UK04R7)

*United States Possession

APPENDIX F

Temporary Military Lodging Has or Will Close.

Arizona
Williams Air Force Base (1993)

Arkansas
Eaker AFB (1992)

California
Fort Ord (1996)
George Air Force Base (1992)
Long Beach Naval Station (1996)
Moffett Field Naval Air Station
(1997)
Treasure Island Naval Base (1997)
Tustin Marine Corps Air Station
(1997)

Colorado
Lowry Air Force Base (1994)

Illinois
Chanute Air Force Base (1993)

Indiana
Fort Benjamin Harrison (1997)
Grissom Air Force Base (1994)

Louisiana
England Air Force Base (1992)

Maine
Loring Air Force Base (1994)

Massachusetts
Fort Devens (1995)

Michigan
Wurtsmith Air Force Base (1993)

Missouri
Richards-Gebaur Air Force Base
(1994)

Ohio
Rickenbacker Air National Guard
Base (1994)

Pennsylvania
Philadelphia Naval Base/Station
(1996)

South Carolina
Myrtle Beach Air Force Base
(1993)

Texas
Bergstrom Air Force Base (1993)
Carswell Air Force Base (1993)
Chase Field Naval Air Station
(1993)

Washington
Puget Sound Naval Station (1995)

Germany
Amberg Sub Community (1992)
Bad Tölz Military Community
(1992)
Hessich Oldendorf Air Base (1992)
Neu Ulm Military Community
(1992)
Templehof Airport (1993)
Zweibrücken Air Base (1992)

Greece
Hellenikon Air Base (1992)

Italy
Comiso Air Base (1992)

Korea
Kwang Ju Air Base (1992)
Suwon Air Base (1992)
Taegu Air Base (1992)

Spain
Torrejon Air Base (1992)
Zaragoza Air Base (1992)

United Kingdom
RAF Fairford (1992)
RAF Wethersfield (1992)
RAF Bentwaters/Woodbridge
(1992)

HOTEL/MOTEL DIRECTORY

Military families enjoy using military lodging because they feel at home there. Unfortunately, many times, particularly during peak season, military lodging can be fully occupied.

In view of this, we surveyed a number of hotels/motels throughout the U.S., asking if they wanted to offer special military rates to military I.D. card holders. By offering military rates, they are expressing a desire to attract you to their lodging facilities. While the exact price may change, you should be able to obtain their current military rate.

Should you have difficulty obtaining a military rate at the hotels/motels listed, ask to speak with a management representative and show them their listing, which they previously authorized. If this is not satisfactory, you may choose to try elsewhere. In any case, always show your military I.D. and establish the price to be paid before signing in. Also, please mention their listing in Military Living's *Temporary Military Lodging Around The World*.

ENLARGED SAMPLE LISTING

HOTEL NAME

HOTEL ADDRESS

HOTEL TELEPHONE

CRAWFORD INN FALLS CHURCH
137 N. Washington Street
Falls Church, VA 22046-0347
(703) 237-0203 / 800-555-1212
M $49-51 C $52-54 R $55-57 1, 2, 3, 4, 5, 6, 7

Lodging INDEX

M = Single Military Rate
C = Single Corporate Rate
R = Single Regular Rate
1 = Rates May Vary,
    please call to verify
2 = Restaurant Nearby
    or on Premises
3 = Swimming Pool
4 = Free Parking
5 = Courtesy Car Available
6 = Rooms for Handicapped
7 = Complimentary Breakfast

ALABAMA

Ramada Airport
5216 Airport Highway
Birmingham, Alabama 32512
(205) 591-7900 / (800) 764-2426
M $41 C $55 R $57 1, 2, 3, 4, 5, 6

CALIFORNIA

Sheraton Anaheim Hotel
1015 W. Ball Road
Anaheim, California 92802
(714) 778-1700 / (800) 325-3535
M $62.50 C $85 R $125 1, 2, 3, 4, 6

Residence Inn by Marriott
10 Morgan
Irvine, California 92718
(714) 380-3000 / (800) 331-3131
M $92 C $92 R $102 2, 3, 4, 6, 7

Ramada LAX Airport South
5250 W. El Segundo Boulevard
Los Angeles, California 90250
(310) 536-9800 / (800) 547-2329
M $79 C $85 R $98 2, 3, 4, 5, 6, 7

Executive Inn (Suites)
16505 Condit Road
Morgan Hill, California 95037
(408) 778-0404 / (800) 626-4224
M $55 C $55 R $65 1, 2, 3, 4, 6, 7

Radisson Inn-National City
700 National City Boulevard
National City, California 91950
(619) 336-1100 / (800) 333-3333
M $44 C $55 R $59 2, 3, 4, 5, 6

Radisson Suites-National City
801 National City Boulevard
National City, California 91950
(619) 336-1100 / (800) 333-3333
M $59 C $69 R $74 2, 4, 6, 7
Complimentary hordoeuvres, beer, wine

Newport Classic Inn
2300 West Coast Highway
Newport, California 92663
(714) 722-2999 / (800) 633-3199
M $55 C $55-65 R $76-96 1, 2, 3, 4, 5, 6, 7

Marine's Memorial Club
609 Sutter Street
San Francisco, California 94102
(415) 673-6672 / (800) 5-MARINE
M $60 R $85 1, 2, 3, 6

CALIFORNIA

The Lombard Hotel
1015 Geary Street
San Francisco, California 94109
(415) 673-5232 / (800) 227-3608
M $58 C $65 R $80 2, 5

Comfort Inn
1215 South First Street
San Jose, California 95110
(408) 280-5300 / (800) 221-2222
M $50 C $50 R $55 1, 2, 4, 6, 7

Comfort Inn Airport
1310 North First Street
San Jose, California 95112
(408) 453-1100 / (800) 221-2222
M $52 C $52 R $58 1, 2, 3, 4, 5, 6, 7

Executive Inn (Suites)
3930 Monterey Road
San Jose, California 95111
(408) 281-8700 / (800) 453-7755
M $55 C $55 R $60 1, 2, 4, 6, 7

Executive Inn (Suites)
1300 Camden Avenue
San Jose-Campbell, California 95008
(408) 559-3600 / (800) 888-3611
M $62 C $72 R $80 1, 2, 4, 6, 7

Woolley's Petite Suites
2721 Hotel Terrace Road
Santa Ana, California 92705
(714) 540-1111 / (800) 762-2597
M $56 C $59 R $62 1, 2, 3, 4, 5, 6, 7

CONNECTICUT

Windsor Court Hotel
383 South Center Street
Windsor Locks, Connecticut 06096
(203) 623-9811
M $46.43 C $48 R $68 2, 4, 5, 6

FLORIDA

Crestview Holiday Inn
I-10 & St. 85
Crestview, Florida 32536
(904) 682-6111
M $36 C $40-43 R $43-46 1, 2, 3, 4, 6, 7

International Inn On The Beach
313 South Atlantic Avenue
Daytona Beach, Florida 32118
(904) 255-7491 / (800) 556-8855
M $32 C $37 R $45 1, 2, 3, 4, 7

Sunglow Resort
3647 South Atlantic Avenue
Daytona Beach Shores, Florida 32127
(904) 756-4005 / (800) 225-3396
M $63 C $63 R $70 2, 3, 4

Holiday Inn-Fort Walton Beach
U.S. 98 & Santa Rosa Boulevard
Fort Walton Beach, Florida 32548
(904) 243-9181 / (800) HOLIDAY
M $62 C $75-115 R $75-115 1, 2, 3, 4, 6

Holiday Inn Orlando Winter Park
626 Lee Road
Orlando, Florida 32810
(407) 645-5600 / (800) HOLIDAY
M $50 C $61 R $70 2, 3, 4, 6

Ramada Bayview
7601 Scenic Highway
Pensacola, Florida 32504
(904) 477-7155 / (800) 282-1212
M $36 C $42 R $50 2, 3, 4, 5, 6

HAWAII

**Hawaii Bed & Breakfast, retired
military hosts, quiet beach near
Honolulu. $45 per day per room.
Hayward Hale, Box 344, Waimanalo,
HI 96795, 1-(800) 259-8646**

ILLINOIS

The Naperville Inn
1801 N. Naper Boulevard
Naperville, Illinois 60563
(708) 505-4900 / (800) 325-3535
M $50-72 C $79 R $89 1, 2, 3, 4, 5, 6

NEW YORK

New York Vista Hotel
3 World Trade Center
New York, New York 10048
(212) 938-9100 / (800) 258-2505
M $123 C $207 R $215 1, 2, 3, 6

LOUISIANA

Travelodge - New Orleans West
2200 Westbank Expressway
Harvey, Louisiana 70058
(504) 366-5311 / (800) 255-3050
M $34 C $35 R $39 2, 3, 4, 6

SOUTH CAROLINA

Ramada Inn
226 North Washington Street
Sumter, South Carolina 29150
(803) 775-2323 / (800) 457-6884
M $34.90 C $37.90 R $39.90 1, 2, 3, 4, 6

MARYLAND

Econo Lodge Baltimore West
Exit 15A off 695, Baltimore National Pike
Catonsville, Maryland 21228
(410) 744-5000 / (800) 237-2218
M $35 C $35 R $39 2, 3, 4, 5, 6
Efficiencies weekly/monthly call for rate

NEW JERSEY

Ramada Renaissance Hotel
Three Tower Center Boulevard
East Brunswick, New Jersey 08816
(908) 828-2000 / (800) 228-9898
M $63 C $99 R $130 1, 2, 3, 4, 6

VIRGINIA

Forte Cherry Blossom
3030 Columbia Pike
Arlington, Virginia 22204
(703) 521-5570 / (800) 255-3050
M $56 C $58 R $64 1, 2, 4, 6, 7

Ramada Renaissance Hotel
Ballston Metro Center
950 N. Stafford Street
Arlington, Virginia 22203
(703) 528-6000 / (800) 228-9898
M $100.23 C $120 R $140 1, 2, 3, 4, 6, 7

Econo Lodge Springfield
6868 Springfield Boulevard
Springfield, Virginia 22150
(703) 644-5311 / (800) 4-CHOICE
M $ 41 C $ 43 R $48 2, 4, 6

Days Inn Tysons Corner
1587 Spring Hill Road
Vienna, Virginia 22182
(703) 448-8020 / (800) 325-2525
Daily $66, Seven days $49,
Eight or more $39
1, 2, 3, 4, 5, 6, 7

MILITARY *Living's*

Military RV, Camping & Rec Areas Around The World

Crawford & Crawford
ISBN 0-914862-37-5

MILITARY *Living's*

Military RV, Camping & Rec Areas

Armed Forces Recreation Center (AFRC) Campground,
Garmisch, Germany

*Officer or Enlisted, Active or Retired, Guard
and Reserve, Plus Eligible Family Members -
You can save $$$ and Have a Lot of Fun
With This Book!*

ANOTHER SOURCE FOR LODGING

Have you ever considered staying at a military recreation area? To show where they are, Military Living has published its all new *Military RV, Camping & Rec Areas Around The World* guidebook. This complete revision is even bigger and better than ever. It has 240 pages giving the latest information on 237 locations.

There is also a photo insert included for the first time which shows some of the areas listed in the new book. In spite of closures at some installations, we actually had a gain in our number of listings. Many new facilities have opened.

Army, Navy and Air Force Times published a full-of-fun travel supplement which was included with its 4 May 1992 issue. Did you see it? It featured a lot of RV, camping and rec area news. We were pleased that our new book was featured, too.

One thing to remember about this book, you do not have to sleep in a pup tent to enjoy the facilities listed. Now, if you really want to sleep in one, go right ahead, but we also list the recreation areas which often have attractive permanent lodging available.

This is a book for anyone who loves the outdoors, whether it is tent camping, using a "pop-up", your own RV or using the permanent lodging facilities available at so many locations.

You can save a bundle by buying your book at your favorite military exchange. Look for the cover shown on the previous page which features the Armed Forces Recreation Center campsite in Garmisch, Germany.

If the book is not available and you want one quick, either call or write us at **Military Living, PO Box 2347, Falls Church, VA 22042-0347**; phone **(703) 237-0203**; FAX (703) 237-2233. Phone orders are accepted with Visa, MasterCard, AmExpress or Diners. The mail order price is $11.95 plus 4.5% sales tax if mailed to a Virginia address. (Add $1 for 1st class mail.)

WE GET LETTERS!

Ann & Roy, your books have saved me countless dollars, francs, pounds and D-marks! - Walter Klepeis, Jamaica, NY.

Just as I get that "back home feeling" at each military installation I visit, I also feel among friends when I read your newsy R&R Space-A Report. Thank you for your great publications! The work involved must be horrendous, and the price is a real bargain. - LTC & Mrs. Raymond C. Hershey, Ret., Santa Rosa, CA.

Our travel dreams came true...thanks to Military Living's Space-A air publications. By Space-A, we visited our two military sons stationed a world apart, one in Osan, Korea, and one in Alice Springs, Australia. As a bonus, we also visited Alaska and Hawaii. - T/Sgt (USAF Ret) and Mrs. James R. Stover, Hettinger, ND.

My wife, Margy and I recently went on our first Space-A flight and enjoyed it very much. We are the owners of four of your publications and we always recommend them to anyone who is qualified to fly or stay at military bases. Your books are great, and we would never travel anywhere without them. I am a retired Navy Chief Petty Officer of twenty years, and I retired in 1971. It took a long time before I took advantage of the many benefits available to me such as Space-A air travel. But the next trip will not take nearly so long. - Jim & Margy Young, Shillington, PA.

Thanks for the memories as we recall past "adventures" when we read in R&R of some areas we have had the pleasure of visiting in the past. We have truly enjoyed each and every one of the R&R Space-A Reports. Since 1983, we have traveled to Europe four times, each trip better than the last. Please enroll us for five more wonderful years. - LTC and Mrs. Harry Bargdill, USA, Ret, Delaware, OH.

Please see Military Living's Special Offer on the next page. Thank you.

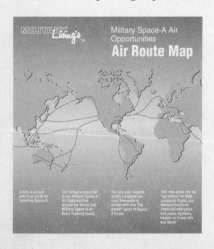

HOPS!
This is the basic book you need to learn the rules and customs of flying Space-A on U.S. Military Aircraft. It can save you thousands of dollars!

EVER FLOWN SPACE-A BEFORE?

Almost a million military personnel, active and retired, along with families on overseas flights, fly Space-A on U.S. military aircraft every year. They're the ones seeing the world on a shoe-string, thanks to this marvelous fringe benefit.

Sad to say, even with this number flying, there are *still* vacant seats available on many flights. **Are you missing out on all the fun?** Don't know how to go about it? Military Living Publications has the answer for you!

We have four different Space-A air publications to help you. But if you are a newcomer, we recommend that you get started with two which will help you understand how this system works.

First, there is the new book, *Space-A Air Basic Training*. This is the basic guide you need to learn the rules and customs of flying Space-A on U.S. military aircraft. It was written especially for those who have never flown Space-A or those who have not flown in recent years are not acquainted with the many new rules. It is also superb for Reserve and Guard members, active, "gray area," and retired who are unsure about how to go about taking advantage of this military fringe benefit that can save them thousands of dollars.

Secondly, our first-time ever published *Military Space-A Air Opportunities Air Route Map* gives you the big picture of scheduled military air missions. It shows you the "hubs" and where their scheduled flights go.

Designed with a Mercator World Projection centered on North and South America. Side #1 displays scheduled flights for worldwide air routes in their own distinctive colors for East and West Coast CONUS departure and arrival stations. It has blow ups of important overseas areas also showing point-to-point flights in the overseas area and CONUS and Overseas MEDEVAC flights. **In addition, the latest addresses and phone numbers are included for military air terminals shown on the front side of the map**.

This can be your "hip-pocket" guide to carry along with you on your trips. It is big, but it folds down to 8" wide by 9 " high and can be folded one more time if desired. The back side gives you information on International Civil Aviation Organization Location Identifiers (ICAO) to Federal Aviation Administration (FAA). Locations Identifiers (LI) conversion tables, Julian Date calendars, time zone conversion charts and Military 24 Hour Clock included. This map will pay for itself over and over again. In fact, it is worth more than its weight in gold!

As a valued purchaser of this book, *Temporary Military Lodging Around The World*, we have a special offer for you to get started on Space-A Air Travel. Normally, these two publications sell for **$21.00** if both are purchased by mail order from us. By mentioning that you have purchased the book, *Temporary Military Lodging Around The World*, we will make these two publications available to you by mail order for $16.00, a savings of $5! This is over 20% off of our published mail-order prices. Just ask for the Space-A Dollar $aver and mention that you purchased TML. In addition, we will send you a free sample copy of our six-time yearly all ranks military travel newsletter, (worth about $2.50 just by itself!). *Actually, our subscribers tell us this newsletter has saved them thousands of travel dollars.*

Please send a $16 check or money order or give us your Visa, MasterCard, AmExpress or Diners Club number and expiration date. Or, you may call in or FAX your order to us with your credit card. Here are the phone numbers: Phone (703) 237-0203; FAX (703) 237-2233. Our address is: Military Living, PO Box 2347, Falls Church, VA 22042-0347.

Please note that this special offer is only available from the publisher and may not be combined with any other discount. Thank you.

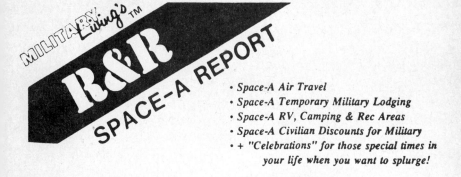

- *Space-A Air Travel*
- *Space-A Temporary Military Lodging*
- *Space-A RV, Camping & Rec Areas*
- *Space-A Civilian Discounts for Military*
- *+ "Celebrations" for those special times in your life when you want to splurge!*

Did you know that Military Living publishes a separate travel newsletter? It is completely different from our local Washington, D.C., area magazine. Published six times yearly, the *R&R Space-A Report* keeps subscribers informed of important news regarding military recreation. The main topics covered are military space-available air travel, temporary military lodging and military RV, camping and rec areas around the world. Our readers learn FIRST about changes which may affect their travels.

News about military discounts in civilian hotels, motels and attractions are also included. Our readers use the *R&R Space-A Report* as a central clearing house of information. Sometimes, just one tip from one of their letters can save you a lot of hassles and/or money. For subscription info, call Military Living at (703) 237-0203, or see the handy coupon in the back of this book. Major credit cards are accepted. Thanks!

To order, see Central Order Coupons in back of book.

Space-A Travel Newsletter

(Space-A Air . . . Space-A RV & Camping . . . Space-A Temporary Military Lodging)

FREE COPIES FOR PURCHASERS of THIS BOOK

"TRAVEL ON LESS PER DAY.... THE MILITARY WAY"

We'd like to acquaint you with our travel newsletter, Military Living's R&R Space-A Report. It gives late breaking info on Space-A air travel, new info on military camping and rec areas, and temporary military lodging plus informative and helpful reader trip reports.

We'll send you two back issues (a $4.65 value) if you will send $2.50 to cover cost of processing, postage and handling.

To get your copies, send your name and address and $2.50 to:

Military Living R&R (Dept. SA)
Box 2347
Falls Church, Virginia 22042-0347

Note: We regret that this must be a one-time offer and may not be used to extend a current R&R Space-A Report subscription or combined with any other discount.

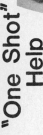

This unique map will help you locate military RV, camping and rec areas which are located both on and off U.S. military installations. To order see Central Order Coupon on following page.

CENTRAL ORDER COUPON
Military Living Publications
P.O. Box 2347, Falls Church VA 22042-0347, TEL: 703-237-0203·FAX: 703-237-2233

Item No.	Publications	Qty.	Item No.	Publications	Qty.
#14	U.S. Military Installation Road Map. Lists over 550 military installations and rec areas (folded) $5.95		#8	U.S. Forces Travel & Transfer Guide, USA and Caribbean Areas. This book should be in every car $11.95	
#17	(2 wall maps unfolded in a hard tube) $15.00				
#19	Military Space-A Air Opportunities Air Route Map. An essential map for Space-A air travelers. (folded) $10.00		#9	U.S. Forces Travel & Transfer Guide, Europe and Near East Areas. The complete military guide to Europe. $16.95	
#20	(2 unfolded wall maps in a hard tube) $25.00				
#6	Assignment Washington II Military Atlas. Maps & Charts of Washington Area Military Installations $8.95		#10 #11	U.S. Military Museums, Historic Sites & Exhibits. (soft cover) $16.95 (hard cover) $26.95	
#15	Desert Shield Commemorative Maps. A fantastic keepsake of the war! (folded) $7.00		#18	Military Space-A Air Basic Training. Brand new! This is a basic book you need to learn the rules and customs of flying Space-A. $11.00	
#16	(2 unfolded wall maps in a hard tube) $16.00				
#13	Military RV, Camping & Rec Areas Around the World. You can have fun with this book. $11.95		#200	Military Living Magazine, Camaraderie Washington. Local Washington area magazine mailed First Class Mail. 1 year (12 issues) $10.00	
#1	Military Space-A Air Opportunities Around the World. The one everyone is talking about. $15.95		#300	R&R Space-A Report. The worldwide travel newsletter. 5 yrs.-$47. 2 yrs.-$22. 3 yrs.-$30. 1 yr.-$14. (6 issues per year)	
#12	Temporary Military Lodging Around the World. Our all-time best seller. $13.95				

If you are an R&R Space-A Report subscriber, you may deduct   **Total: $**_____
$1.00 per book. (No discount on R&R Report itself   VA addressees add 4.5% sales tax: **$**_____
or on the maps or atlas.) For 1st Class Mail,   (Books & Maps only)
add $1.00 per book or map. Mail Order Prices are for U.S., APO & FPO addresses. Please consult publisher for International Mail Price. Sorry, no billing. GREAT FUND RAISERS! Please write for wholesale rates.

We're as close as your telephone...by using our Telephone Ordering Service. We honor American Express, MasterCard, VISA, Diner's Club, and Carte Blanche. Call us at **703-237-0203** or FAX 703-237-2233 and order today! Sorry, no collect calls. Or...fill out and mail the order coupon below.

Name:_____
Street:_____
City/State/Zip:_____
Phone:_____
Signature:_____
Rank:_____ or Rank of Sponsor_____
Branch of Service:_____
Active Duty:___ Retired:___ Widower:___ 100% Disabled Veteran:___ Guard: ___ Reservist:___
Other:_____
Card No.:_____ Card Expiration Date:_____
Mail check/money order to: Military Living Publications, P.O. Box 2347, Fall Church, VA 22042-0347.
Telephone: 703-237-0203, or FAX 703-237-2233.
These prices were in effect as of 1 Dec 1991. Should you be using this order form at a much later date, prices could have changed a little. If so, please check here if we may ship your order and include a bill for the difference.
☐
YES

The Only Military Museum Book!

Military Living's

U.S. Military Museums Historic Sites & Exhibits

by

Bryce D. Thompson

A guide to Army, Navy, Air Force, Marine Corps, Coast Guard and N.O.A.A. museums in the U.S. and overseas. Also includes other military museums, relevant aviation and maritime museums, sites associated with the history of all military powers in the U.S. and its territories and historic warships and submarines. Hundreds of places for the family to explore our nation's military history.

Look for this book at your U.S. military exchanges and Stars & Stripes newsstands overseas. If not available, you may order by mail at P. O. Box 2347, Falls Church, Virginia 22042-0347, or by phone (703) 237-0203 with VISA/MasterCard/American Express/Carte Blanche/Diners. See the central order coupons at the back of this book.

Military Living Publications
P. O. Box 2347
Falls Church, Virginia 22042-0347
(703) 237-0203
FAX (703) 237-2233

CENTRAL ORDER COUPON
Military Living Publications

P.O. Box 2347, Falls Church VA 22042-0347, TEL: 703-237-0203•FAX: 703-237-2233

Item No.	Publications	Qty.	Item No.	Publications	Qty.
#14 #17	U.S. Military Installation Road Map. Lists over 550 military installations and rec areas (folded) $5.95 (2 wall maps unfolded in a hard tube) $15.00		#8	U.S. Forces Travel & Transfer Guide, USA and Caribbean Areas. This book should be in every car $11.95	
#19 #20	Military Space-A Air Opportunities Air Route Map. An essential map for Space-A air travelers. (folded) $10.00 (2 unfolded wall maps in a hard tube) $25.00		#9	U.S. Forces Travel & Transfer Guide, Europe and Near East Areas. The complete military guide to Europe. $16.95	
#6	Assignment Washington II Military Atlas. Maps & Charts of Washington Area Military Installations $8.95		#10 #11	U.S. Military Museums, Historic Sites & Exhibits. (soft cover) $16.95 (hard cover) $26.95	
#15 #16	Desert Shield Commemorative Maps. A fantastic keepsake of the war! (folded) $7.00 (2 unfolded wall maps in a hard tube) $16.00		#18	Military Space-A Air Basic Training. Brand new! This is a basic book you need to learn the rules and customs of flying Space-A. $11.00	
#13	Military RV, Camping & Rec Areas Around the World. You can have fun with this book. $11.95		#200	Military Living Magazine, Camaraderie Washington. Local Washington area magazine mailed First Class Mail. 1 year (12 issues) $10.00	
#1	Military Space-A Air Opportunities Around the World. The one everyone is talking about. $15.95		#300	R&R Space-A Report. The worldwide travel newsletter. 5 yrs.-$47. 2 yrs.-$22. 3 yrs.-$30. 1 yr.-$14. (6 issues per year)	
#12	Temporary Military Lodging Around the World. Our all-time best seller. $13.95				

If you are an R&R Space-A Report subscriber, you may deduct $1.00 per book. (No discount on R&R Report itself or on the maps or atlas.) **For 1st Class Mail, add $1.00 per book or map.** Mail Order Prices are for U.S., APO & FPO addresses. Please consult publisher for International Mail Price. Sorry, no billing. GREAT FUND RAISERS! Please write for wholesale rates.

Total: $ _____

VA addressees add 4.5% sales tax: $ _____
(Books & Maps only)

We're as close as your telephone...by using our Telephone Ordering Service. We honor American Express, MasterCard, VISA, Diner's Club, and Carte Blanche. Call us at **703-237-0203** or FAX 703-237-2233 and order today! Sorry, no collect calls. Or...fill out and mail the order coupon below.

Name: _____

Street: _____

City/State/Zip: _____

Phone: _____

Signature: _____

Rank: _____ or Rank of Sponsor _____

Branch of Service: _____

Active Duty:__ Retired:__ Widower:__ 100% Disabled Veteran:__ Guard: __ Reservist:__

Other: _____

Card No.: _____ Card Expiration Date: _____

Mail check/money order to: Military Living Publications, P.O. Box 2347, Fall Church, VA 22042-0347. Telephone: **703-237-0203**, or FAX 703-237-2233.

These prices were in effect as of 1 Dec 1991. Should you be using this order form at a much later date, prices could have changed a little. If so, please check here if we may ship your order and include a bill for the difference.

☐
YES

MILITARY Living's™

Temporary Military Lodging
Around the World

Armed Forces Recreation Center (AFRC)
Hale Koa Hotel, Honolulu, Hawaii

*--Travel on less per day
--the military way!
--Officer or enlisted,
active or retired...you
can save $$$ with this
book!*

Do you sometimes get tired of RVing or camping in the rough? This book shows you where you can settle down in a military hotel room, stretch out in the shower and relax. This all-time best seller has saved thousands of military families money. And, thousands of rooms are available for all Services. It gives more lodging information than any other book.

To order, see Central Order Coupons in back of book.

This is our most advanced Space-A air travel book. It has 400 pages and is an all-new revision in 1992 in our famous chart format. The book has 348 worldwide listings of installations in the U.S. and overseas that offer Space-A air opportunities for all Services: Air Force, Navy, Marine Corps, Army and Coast Guard. Also includes Guard and Reserve flights. This is "the book everyone is talking about"!

To order, see Central Order Coupons in back of book.

UPDATES

This book is completely revised about every two years. This is because of the massive amounts of correspondence required to get completely updated information from over 400 military lodging facilities all over the world.

Between editions of this book, and all of our other popular travel books, we publish news about temporary military lodging, military RV, camping and rec areas, military Space-A air travel, and discounts in the civilian travel sector for military personnel and their families.

WHERE?

MILITARY Living's ™ R&R SPACE-A REPORT

- *Space-A Air Travel*
- *Space-A Temporary Military Lodging*
- *Space-A RV, Camping & Rec Areas*
- *Space-A Civilian Discounts for Military*
- *+ "Celebrations" for those special times in your life when you want to splurge!*

You'll find all new information and updates in Military Living's six time yearly military travel newsletter, *Military Living's R&R Space-A Report*. This "over the back fence" type newsletter serves as a reader clearinghouse of information. With hundreds of our subscribers trekking around the globe at any given time, Military Living happily receives their letters and "handouts" collected which affect military travel, whether it is leave or duty.

By sharing their information through R&R Headquarters, other subscribers are encouraged to share with them. In addition, Ann & Roy Crawford, and members of their staff, travel to many military installations, off-site military recreation areas, and civilian attractions reporting their findings in the newsletter, too. What a network we have! Readers especially like the long reports on military rec areas which include photos, along with first hand reports.

Subscription information is included in the coupons in the back of this book. If you would like to see two sample back issues of *Military Living's R&R Space-A Report,* please send $2.50 to Military Living, PO Box 2347, Falls Church, VA 22042-0347.

MILITARY LIVING PUBLICATIONS
TEL: 703-237-0203
FAX: 703-237-2233